SOCIOLOGY
READINGS

TITLES OF RELATED INTEREST FROM PINE FORGE PRESS

Sixth Edition

SOCIOLOGY
Exploring the Architecture of Everyday Life
READINGS

DAVID M. NEWMAN
DePauw University

JODI A. O'BRIEN
Seattle University

EDITORS

SAGE Publications
Thousand Oaks ■ London ■ New Delhi

For information:

Pine Forge Press
An imprint of Sage Publications, Inc.
2455 Teller Road
Thousand Oaks, California 91320
E-mail: order@sagepub.com

Sage Publications Ltd.
6 Bonhill Street
London EC2A 4PU
United Kingdom

Sage Publications India Pvt. Ltd.
B-42, Panchsheel Enclave
Post Box 4109
New Delhi 110 017 India

Printed in the United States of America

Library of Congress Cataloging-in-Publication Data

Sociology : exploring the architecture of everyday life : readings / edited by David M. Newman, Jodi O'Brien.—6th ed.
    p. cm.
Includes bibliographical references.
ISBN 1-4129-2813-3 (pbk.)
1. Sociology. I. Newman, David M., 1958- II. O'Brien, Jodi.
HM586.S64 2006
301—dc22

                          2005028067

This book is printed on acid-free paper.

06   07   08   09   10   10 9 8 7 6 5 4 3 2 1

Acquiring Editor:	Benjamin Penner
Associate Editor:	Margo Beth Crouppen
Editorial Assistant:	Annie Louden
Production Editor:	Astrid Virding
Typesetter:	C&M Digitals (P) Ltd.
Cover Designer:	Michelle Lee Kenny

Contents

PART II
THE CONSTRUCTION OF SELF AND SOCIETY   43

Preface

One of the greatest challenges we face as teachers of sociology is getting our students to see the relevance of the course material to their own lives and to fully appreciate its connection to the larger society. We teach our students to see that sociology is all around us. It's in our families, our careers, our media, our jobs, our classrooms, our goals, our interests, our desires, even our minds. Sociology can be found at the neighborhood pub, the maintenance bay at the local gas station, and the highest offices of government. It's with us when we're alone and when we're in a mob of people. Sociology can answer questions of global as well as private significance—from how some countries create and maintain dominance over others to why we find some people attractive and not others; from why poverty, discrimination, crime, and homelessness exist to why many Americans eat scrambled eggs rather than rice for breakfast.

With these ideas in mind we set out to compile this collection of short articles, chapters, and excerpts designed to help introduce you to sociology. Instructors and students alike responded quite positively to the readings in the first five editions of this book. It would have been easy simply to include those same readings in this sixth edition. But we very much wanted the book to stay fresh and contemporary. And we especially wanted to emphasize the importance of race, social class, and gender in people's everyday lives. Of the 36 selections in this edition, 14 are new. Four others are articles that appeared in earlier editions, were taken out, but are now back "by popular demand." We have also moved several readings to chapters different from the ones in which they appeared in previously because they fit better in their new locations.

As in the first five editions, these selections are intended to be vivid, provocative, and eye-opening examples of the practice of sociology. Many of the readings are drawn from carefully conducted social research. They provide important illustrations of how sociologists support their theories, insights, and ideas with empirical evidence. Others are personal narratives that put human faces on matters of sociological relevance. Some were written quite recently; others are sociological "classics." In addition to accurately representing the sociological perspective and providing rigorous coverage of the discipline, we hope the selections are thought-provoking, generate lots of discussion, and are enjoyable to read.

The readings represent a variety of styles. Some use common, everyday experiences and phenomena (such as drug use, disability, employment, athletic performance, religious devotion, the experience of time, the balance of work and family) to illustrate the relationship between the individual and society. Others focus on important social issues or problems (imprisonment, race relations, poverty, educational inequalities, sexuality, immigration, global economics, environmental degradation, political extremism) or on specific historical events (massacres during war, drug scares, anti-smoking legislation, early movements for women's rights). You needn't be a trained sociologist to see the world sociologically. So this book includes articles written by psychologists, anthropologists, social commentators, and journalists as well as by sociologists.

To help you get the most out of these selections, we've written brief introductions to each chapter that provide the sociological context for the readings and include some reflections points for comparing and contrasting the readings in each section and across sections. For those of you who are also reading the accompanying textbook, these introductions will furnish a quick intellectual link between the readings and information in the textbook. We have also included in these introductions, brief instructions on what to look for when you read the selections in a given chapter. After each reading you will find a set of discussion questions to ponder. Many of these questions ask you to apply a specific author's conclusions to some contemporary issue in society or to your own life experiences. It is our hope that these questions will generate a lot of classroom debate and help you see the sociological merit of the readings.

A Web site established for this sixth edition includes do-it-yourself reviews and tests for students, Web-based activities designed to enhance learning, and a chat room where students and teachers can post messages and debate matters of sociological significance. The site can be accessed via the Pine Forge Web site at www.pineforge.com.

Books like these are enormous projects. We would like to thank Jerry Westby, Ben Penner, Diana Axelsen, Annie Louden, Astrid Virding, Margo Crouppen, and the rest of the staff at Pine Forge Press for their useful advice and assistance in putting this reader together. We are especially grateful to the following people for their helpful suggestions regarding the various readings that are new to this edition: Lise Nelson, Val Jenness, Rebecca Bordt.

Enjoy!

David M. Newman
Department of Sociology/Anthropology
DePauw University
Greencastle, IN 46135
E-Mail: DNEWMAN@DEPAUW.EDU

Jodi O'Brien
Department of Sociology
Seattle University
Seattle, WA 98122
E-mail: JOBRIEN@SEATTLEU.EDU

Acknowledgments

We appreciate the many helpful comments offered by the reviewers of all the editions of this book:

Sharon Abbott, Fairfield University

Deborah Abowitz, Bucknell University

Stephen Adair, Central Connecticut State University

Rebecca Adams, University of North Carolina, Greensboro

Ron Aminzade, University of Minnesota

Afroza Anwary, Carleton College

George Arquitt, Oklahoma State University

Carol Auster, Franklin and Marshall College

Ellen C. Baird, Arizona State University

David Bogen, Emerson College

Frances A. Boudreau, Connecticut College

Todd Campbell, Loyola University, Chicago

Wanda Clark, South Plains College

Thomas Conroy, St. Peter's College

Norman Conti, Duquesne University

Doug Currivan, University of Massachusetts, Boston

Jeff Davidson, University of Delaware

Kimberly Davies, Augusta State University

Tricia Davis, North Carolina State University

James J. Dowd, University of Georgia

Charlotte A. Dunham, Texas Tech University

Charles Edgley, Oklahoma State University

Rachel Einwohner, Purdue University

Shalom Endleman, Quinnipiac College

Rebecca Erickson, University of Akron

Kimberly Faust, Winthrop University

Catherine Fobes, Alma College

Lara Foley, University of Tulsa

Patrick Fontane, St. Louis College of Pharmacy

Michael J. Fraleigh, Bryant University

Barry Goetz, University of Dayton

Lorie Schabo Grabowski, University of Minnesota

Valerie Gunter, University of New Orleans

Roger Guy, Texas Lutheran University

Charles Harper, Creighton University

Douglas Harper, Duquesne University

Peter Hennen, University of Minnesota

Max Herman, Rutgers University

Susan Hoerbelt, Hillsborough Community College

Gary Hytreck, Georgia Southern University

Valerie Jenness, University of California, Irvine

Kathryn Johnson, Barat College

Richard Jones, Marquette University

Tom Kando, California State University, Sacramento

Steve Keto, Kent State University

Peter Kivisto, Augustana College

Marc LaFountain, State University of West Georgia

Sharon Melissa Latimer, West Virginia University

Joseph Lengermann, University of Maryland, College Park

Lynda A. Litteral, Grossmont Community College

Fred Maher, Temple University

Kristen Marcussen, University of Iowa

Benjamin Mariante, Stonehill College

Joseph Marolla, Virginia Commonwealth University

Michallene McDaniel, University of Georgia

James R. McIntosh, Lehigh University

Jerome McKibben, Fitchburg State University

Ted P. McNeilsmith, Adams State College

Melinda J. Milligan, Sonoma State Univeristy

Susannne Monahan, Montana State University

Kelly Murphy, University of Pittsburgh

Daniel Myers, University of Notre Dame

Elizabeth Ehrhardt Mustaine, University of Central Florida

Riad Nasser, Farleigh Dickinson University

Anne Nurse, College of Wooster

Marjukka Ollilainen, Weber State University

Toska Olson, Evergreen State College

Robert Pankin, Providence College

Paul Paolucci, Eastern Kentucky University

Larry Perkins, Oklahoma State University, Stillwater

Bernice Pescosolido, Indiana University, Bloomington

Mike Plummer, Boston College

Edward Ponczek, William Rainey Harper College

Tanya Poteet, Capital University

Sharon E. Preves, Grand Valley State University

Judith Richlin-Klonsky, University of California, Los Angeles

Robert Robinson, Indiana University, Bloomington

Mary Rogers, University of West Florida

Sally S. Rogers, Montgomery College

Michael Ryan, University of Louisiana, Lafayette

Douglas Schrock, Florida State University

Mark Shibley, Southern Oregon University

Thomas Shriver, Oklahoma State University

Kathleen Slevin, College of William and Mary

Lisa White Smith, Christopher Newport University

Eldon Snyder, Bowling Green State University

Nicholas Sofios, Providence College

Kandi Stinson, Xavier University

Richard Tardanico, Florida International University

Robert Tellander, Sonoma State University

Kathleen Tiemann, University of North Dakota

Steven Vallas, George Mason University

Tom Vander Ven, Indiana University, South Bend

John Walsh, University of Illinois, Chicago

Gregory Weiss, Roanoke College

Marty Wenglinsky, Quinnipiac College

Stephan Werba, Catonsville Community College

Cheryl E. Whitley, Marist College

Norma Williams, University of North Texas

Janelle Wilson, University of Minnesota, Duluth

Mark Winton, University of Central Florida

Cynthia A. Woolever, Hartford Seminary

Matt Wray, University of Nevada, Las Vegas

Ashraf Zahedi, Stanford University

Stephen Zehr, University of Southern Indiana

About the Editors

David M. Newman (Ph.D., University of Washington) is Professor of Sociology at DePauw University. In addition to the introductory course, he teaches courses in research methods, family, social psychology, and deviance. He has won teaching awards at both the University of Washington and DePauw University. His other written work includes *Identities and Inequalities: Exploring the Intersections of Race, Class, Gender, and Sexuality* (McGraw-Hill).

Jodi O'Brien (Ph.D., University of Washington) is Professor of Sociology at Seattle University. She teaches courses in social psychology, sexuality, inequality, and classical and contemporary theory. She writes and lectures on the cultural politics of transgressive identities and communities. Her other books include *Everyday Inequalities* (Basil Blackwell), *Social Prisms: Reflections on Everyday Myths and Paradoxes* (Pine Forge Press), and *The Production of Reality: Essays and Readings on Social Interaction, Fourth Edition* (Pine Forge Press).

PART I

The Individual and Society

Taking a New Look at a Familiar World

The primary theme of sociology is that our everyday thoughts and actions are the product of a complex interplay between massive social forces and personal characteristics. We can't understand the relationship between individuals and their societies without understanding the connection between both. As C. Wright Mills discusses in the introductory article, the "sociological imagination" is the ability to see the impact of social forces on our private lives. When we develop a sociological imagination, we gain an awareness that our lives unfold at the intersection of personal biography and social history. The sociological imagination encourages us to move beyond individualistic explanations of human experiences to an understanding of the mutual influence that individuals and society have on one another. So, rather than study what goes on within people, sociologists study what goes on between and among people, as individuals, groups, organizations, or entire societies. Sociology teaches us to look beyond individual personalities and focus instead on the influence of social phenomena in shaping our ideas of who we are and what we think we can do.

When we examine the social influences on our behavior, things that were once familiar and taken for granted suddenly become unfamiliar and curious. During the course of our lives we are rarely forced to examine *why* we do the common things we do; we just do them. But if we take a step back and examine our common customs and behaviors, they begin to look as strange as the "mystical" rituals of some far off, exotic land. It is for this reason that Horace Miner's article, "Body Ritual Among the Nacirema," has become a classic in sociology and anthropology. As you read these two well-known articles, consider the process of using the sociological imagination to understand your own life and the lives of others. When you think about other cultures, how can you be sure that your perceptions, as an outsider, are not as bizarre as Miner's perspective on the Nacirema? When done well, sociological research helps us to understand different points of view and different cultural contexts from the perspective of insiders. As you read the selections in this book, consider what kind of insight and training you need in order to develop not only a sociological imagination, but a sociological eye, or point of view.

The Sociological Imagination

C. Wright Mills

(1959)

"The individual can . . . know his own chances in life only by becoming aware of those of all individuals in his circumstances."

Nowadays men often feel that their private lives are a series of traps. They sense that within their everyday worlds, they cannot overcome their troubles, and in this feeling, they are often quite correct: What ordinary men are directly aware of and what they try to do are bounded by the private orbits in which they live; their visions and their powers are limited to the close-up scenes of job, family, neighborhood; in other milieux, they move vicariously and remain spectators. And the more aware they become, however vaguely, of ambitions and of threats which transcend their immediate locales, the more trapped they seem to feel.

Underlying this sense of being trapped are seemingly impersonal changes in the very structure of continent-wide societies. The facts of contemporary history are also facts about the success and the failure of individual men and women. When a society is industrialized, a peasant becomes a worker; a feudal lord is liquidated or becomes a businessman. When classes rise or fall, a man is employed or unemployed; when the rate of investment goes up or down, a man takes new heart or goes broke. When wars happen, an insurance salesman becomes a rocket launcher; a store clerk, a radar man; a wife lives alone; a child grows up without a father. Neither the life of an individual nor the history of a society can be understood without understanding both.

Yet men do not usually define the troubles they endure in terms of historical change and institutional contradiction. The well-being they enjoy, they do not usually impute to the big ups and downs of the societies in which they live. Seldom aware of the intricate connection between the patterns of their own lives and the course of world history, ordinary men do not usually know what this connection means for the kinds of men they are becoming and for the kinds of history-making in which they might take part. They do not possess the quality of mind essential to grasp the interplay of man and society, of biography and history, of self and world. They cannot cope with their personal troubles in such ways as to control the structural transformations that usually lie behind them.

Surely it is no wonder. In what period have so many men been so totally exposed at so fast a pace to such earthquakes of change? That Americans have not known such catastrophic changes as have the men and women of other societies is due to historical facts that are now quickly becoming "merely history." The history that now affects every man is world history. Within this scene and this period, in the course of a single generation, one-sixth of mankind is transformed from all that is feudal and backward into all that is modern, advanced, and fearful. Political colonies are freed, new and less visible forms of imperialism installed. Revolutions occur; men feel the intimate grip of new kinds of authority. Totalitarian societies rise, and are smashed to bits—or succeed fabulously. After two centuries of ascendancy, capitalism is shown up as only one way to make society into an industrial apparatus. After two centuries of hope, even formal democracy is restricted to a quite small portion of mankind. Everywhere in the underdeveloped world, ancient ways of life are broken up and vague expectations become urgent demands. Everywhere in the overdeveloped world, the means of authority and of violence become total in scope and bureaucratic in form. Humanity itself now lies before us, the supernation at either pole concentrating its most coordinated and massive efforts upon the preparation of World War Three.

The very shaping of history now outpaces the ability of men to orient themselves in accordance with cherished values. And which values? Even when they do not panic, men often sense that older ways of feeling and thinking have collapsed and that newer beginnings are ambiguous to the point of moral stasis. Is it any wonder that ordinary men feel they cannot cope with the larger worlds with which they are so suddenly confronted? That they cannot understand the meaning of their epoch for their own lives? That—in defense of selfhood—they become morally insensible, trying to remain altogether private men? Is it any wonder that they come to be possessed by a sense of the trap?

It is not only information that they need—in this Age of Fact, information often dominates their attention and overwhelms their capacities to assimilate it. It is not only the skills of reason that they need—although their struggles to acquire these often exhaust their limited moral energy.

What they need, and what they feel they need, is a quality of mind that will help them to use information and to develop reason in order to achieve lucid summations of what is going on in the world and of what may be happening within themselves. It is this quality, I am going to contend, that journalists and scholars, artists and publics, scientists and editors are coming to expect of what may be called the sociological imagination.

The sociological imagination enables its possessor to understand the larger historical scene in terms of its meaning for the inner life and the external career of a variety of individuals. It enables him to take into account how individuals, in the welter of their daily experience, often become falsely conscious of their social positions. Within that welter, the framework of modern society is sought, and within that framework the psychologies of a variety of men and women are formulated. By such means the personal uneasiness of individuals is focused upon explicit troubles and the indifference of publics is transformed into involvement with public issues.

The first fruit of this imagination—and the first lesson of the social science that embodies it—is the idea that the individual can understand his own experience and gauge his own fate only by locating himself within his period, that he can know his own chances in life only by becoming aware of those of all individuals in his circumstances. In many ways it is a terrible lesson; in many ways a magnificent one. We do not know the limits of man's capacities for supreme effort or willing degradation, for agony or glee, for pleasurable brutality or the sweetness of reason. But in our time we have come to know that the limits of "human nature" are frighteningly broad. We have come to know that every individual lives, from one generation to the next, in some society; that he lives out a biography, and that he lives it out within some historical sequence. By the fact of his living he contributes, however minutely, to the shaping of this society and to the course of its history, even as he is made by society and by its historical push and shove.

The sociological imagination enables us to grasp history and biography and the relations between the two within society. That is its task and its promise. To recognize this task and this promise is the mark of the classic social analyst. It is characteristic of Herbert Spencer—turgid, polysyllabic, comprehensive; of E. A. Ross—graceful, muckraking, upright; of Auguste Comte and Emile Durkheim; of the intricate and subtle Karl Mannheim. It is the quality of all that is intellectually excellent in Karl Marx; it is the clue to Thorstein Veblen's brilliant and ironic insight, to Joseph Schumpeter's many-sided constructions of reality; it is the basis of the psychological sweep of W. E. H. Lecky no less than of the profundity and clarity of Max Weber. And it is the signal of what is best in contemporary studies of man and society.

No social study that does not come back to the problems of biography, of history, and of their intersections within a society has completed its intellectual journey. Whatever the specific problems of the classic social analysts, however limited or however broad the features of social reality they have examined, those who have been imaginatively aware of the promise of their work have consistently asked three sorts of questions:

1. What is the structure of this particular society as a whole? What are its essential components, and how are they related to one another? How does it differ from other varieties of social order? Within it, what is the meaning of any particular feature for its continuance and for its change?

2. Where does this society stand in human history? What are the mechanics by which it is changing? What is its place within and its meaning for the development of humanity as a whole? How does any particular feature we are examining affect, and how is it affected by, the historical period in which it moves? And this period—what are its essential features? How does it differ from other periods? What are its characteristic ways of history making?

3. What varieties of men and women now prevail in this society and in this period? And what varieties are coming to prevail? In what ways are they selected and formed, liberated and repressed, made sensitive and blunted? What kinds of "human nature" are revealed in the conduct and character we observe in this society in this period? And what is the meaning for "human nature" of each and every feature of the society we are examining?

Whether the point of interest is a great power state or a minor literary mood, a family, a prison, a creed—these are the kinds of questions the best social analysts have asked. They are the intellectual pivots of classic studies of man in society—and they are the questions inevitably raised by any mind possessing the sociological imagination. For that imagination is the capacity to shift from one perspective to another—from the political to the psychological; from examination of a single family to comparative assessment of the national budgets of the world; from the theological school to the military establishment; from considerations of an oil industry to studies of contemporary poetry. It is the capacity to range from the most impersonal and remote transformations to the most intimate features of the human self—and to see the relations between the two. Back of its use there is always the urge to know the social and historical meaning of the individual in the society and in the period in which he has his quality and his being.

That, in brief, is why it is by means of the sociological imagination that men now hope to grasp what is going on in the world, and to understand what is happening in themselves as minute points of the intersections of biography and history within society. In large part, contemporary man's self-conscious view of himself as at least an outsider, if not a permanent stranger, rests upon an absorbed realization of social relativity and of the transformative power of history. The sociological imagination is the most fruitful form of this self-consciousness. By its use men whose mentalities have swept only a series of limited orbits often come to feel as if suddenly awakened in a house with which they had only supposed themselves to be familiar. Correctly or incorrectly, they often come to feel that they can now provide themselves with adequate summations, cohesive assessments, comprehensive orientations. Older decisions that once appeared sound now seem to them products of a mind unaccountably dense. Their capacity for astonishment is made lively again. They acquire a new way of thinking, they experience a transvaluation of values: in a word, by their reflection and by their sensibility, they realize the cultural meaning of the social sciences.

Perhaps the most fruitful distinction with which the sociological imagination works is between "the personal troubles of milieu" and "the public issues of social structure." This distinction is an essential tool of the sociological imagination and a feature of all classic work in social science.

Troubles occur within the character of the individual and within the range of his immediate relations with others; they have to do with his self and with those limited areas of social life of which he is directly and personally aware. Accordingly, the statement and the resolution of troubles properly lie within the individual as a biographical entity and within the scope of his immediate milieu—the social setting that is directly open to his personal experience and to some extent his willful activity. A trouble is a private matter: values cherished by an individual are felt by him to be threatened.

Issues have to do with matters that transcend these local environments of the individual and the range of his inner life. They have to do with the organization of many such milieux into the institutions of an historical society as a whole, with the ways in which various milieux overlap and interpenetrate to form the larger structure of social and historical life. An issue is a public matter: some value cherished by publics is felt to be threatened. Often there is a debate about what that value really is and about what it is that really threatens it. This debate is often without focus if only because it is the very nature of an issue, unlike even widespread trouble, that it cannot very well be defined in terms of the immediate and everyday environments of ordinary men. An issue, in fact, often involves a crisis in institutional arrangements, and often too it involves what Marxists call "contradictions" or "antagonisms."

In these terms, consider unemployment. When, in a city of 100,000, only one man is unemployed, that is his personal trouble, and for its relief we properly look to the character of the man, his skills, and his immediate opportunities. But when in a nation of 50 million employees, 15 million men are unemployed, that is an issue, and we may not hope to find its solution within the range of opportunities open to any one individual. The very structure of opportunities has collapsed. Both the correct statement of the problem and the range of possible solutions require us to consider the economic and political institutions of the society, and not merely the personal situation and character of a scatter of individuals.

Consider war. The personal problem of war, when it occurs, may be how to survive it or how to die in it with honor; how to make money out of it; how to climb into the higher safety of the military apparatus; or how to contribute to the war's termination. In short, according to one's values, to find a set of milieux and within it to survive the war or make one's death in it meaningful. But the structural issues of war have to do with its causes; with what types of men it throws up into command; with its effects upon economic and political, family, and religious institutions, with the unorganized irresponsibility of a world of nation-states.

Consider marriage. Inside a marriage a man and a woman may experience personal troubles, but when the divorce rate during the first four years of marriage is 250 out of every 1,000 attempts, this is an indication of a structural issue having to do with the institutions of marriage and the family and other institutions that bear upon them.

Or consider the metropolis—the horrible, beautiful, ugly, magnificent sprawl of the great city. For many upper-class people, the personal solution to "the problem of the city" is to have an apartment with private garage under it in the heart of the city, and forty miles out, a house by Henry Hill, garden by Garrett Eckbo, on a hundred acres of private land. In these two controlled environments—with a small staff at each end and a private helicopter connection—most people could solve many of the problems of personal milieux caused by the facts of the city. But all this, however splendid, does not solve the public issues that the structural fact of the city poses. What should be done with this wonderful monstrosity? Break it all up into scattered units, combining residence and work? Refurbish it as it stands? Or, after evacuation, dynamite it and build new cities according to new plans in new places? What should those plans be? And who is to decide and to accomplish whatever choice is made? These are structural issues; to confront them and to solve them requires us to consider political and economic issues that affect innumerable milieux.

Insofar as an economy is so arranged that slumps occur, the problem of unemployment becomes incapable of personal solution. Insofar as war is inherent in the nation-state system and in the uneven industrialization of the world, the ordinary individual in his restricted milieu will be powerless—with or without psychiatric aid—to solve the troubles this system or lack of system imposes upon him. Insofar as the family as an institution turns women into darling little slaves and men into their chief providers and unweaned dependents, the problem of a satisfactory marriage remains incapable of purely private solution. Insofar as the overdeveloped megalopolis and the overdeveloped automobile are built-in features of the overdeveloped society, the issues of urban living will not be solved by personal ingenuity and private wealth.

What we experience in various and specific milieux, I have noted, is often caused by structural changes. Accordingly, to understand the changes of many personal milieux we are required to look beyond them. And the number and variety of such structural changes increase as the institutions within which we live become more embracing and more intricately connected with one another. To be aware of the idea of social structure and to use it with sensibility is to be capable of tracing such linkages among a great variety of milieux. To be able to do that is to possess the sociological imagination. . . .

THINKING ABOUT THE READING

Consider the political, economic, familial, and cultural circumstances into which you were born. Make a list of some of these circumstances and also some of the major historical events that have occurred in your lifetime. How do you think these historical and social circumstances may have affected your personal "biography"? Can you think of ways in which your actions have influenced the course of other people's lives? Identify some famous people and consider how the intersection of "history and biography" led them to their particular position. How might the outcome have differed if some of the circumstances in their lives were different?

Body Ritual Among the Nacirema

Horace Miner

(1956)

The anthropologist has become so familiar with the diversity of ways in which different peoples behave in similar situations that he is not apt to be surprised by even the most exotic customs. In fact, if all of the logically possible combinations of behavior have not been found somewhere in the world, he is apt to suspect that they must be present in some yet undescribed tribe. This point has, in fact, been expressed with respect to clan organization by Murdock (1949, p. 71). In this light, the magical beliefs and practices of the Nacirema present such unusual aspects that it seems desirable to describe them as an example of the extremes to which human behavior can go.

Professor Linton first brought the ritual of the Nacirema to the attention of anthropologists twenty years ago (1936, p. 326), but the culture of this people is still very poorly understood. They are a North American group living in the territory between the Canadian Cree, the Yaqui and Tarahumara of Mexico, and the Carib and Arawak of the Antilles. Little is known of their origin, although tradition states that they came from the east. According to Nacirema mythology, their nation was originated by a culture hero, Notgnihsaw, who is otherwise known for two great feats of strength—the throwing of a piece of wampum across the river Pa-To-Mac and the chopping down of a cherry tree in which the Spirit of Truth resided.

Nacirema culture is characterized by a highly developed market economy which has evolved in a rich natural habitat. While much of the people's time is devoted to economic pursuits, a large part of the fruits of these labors and a considerable portion of the day are spent in ritual activity. The focus of this activity is the human body, the appearance and health of which loom as a dominant concern in the ethos of the people. While such a concern is certainly not unusual, its ceremonial aspects and associated philosophy are unique.

The fundamental belief underlying the whole system appears to be that the human body is ugly and that its natural tendency is to debility and disease. Incarcerated in such a body, man's only hope is to avert these characteristics through the use of the powerful influences of ritual and ceremony. Every household has one or more shrines devoted to this purpose. The more powerful individuals in this society have several shrines in their houses and, in fact, the opulence of a house is often referred to in terms of the number of such ritual centers it possesses. Most houses are of wattle and daub construction, but the shrine rooms of the more wealthy are walled with stone. Poorer families imitate the rich by applying pottery plaques to their shrine walls.

While each family has at least one such shrine, the rituals associated with it are not family ceremonies but are private and secret. The rites are normally only discussed with children, and then only during the period when they are being initiated into these mysteries. I was able, however, to establish sufficient rapport with the natives to examine these shrines and to have the rituals described to me.

The focal point of the shrine is a box or chest which is built into the wall. In this chest are kept the many charms and magical potions without which no native believes he could live. These preparations are secured from a variety of specialized practitioners. The most powerful of these are the medicine men, whose assistance must be rewarded with substantial gifts. However, the medicine men do not provide the curative potions for their clients, but decide what the ingredients should be and then write them down in an ancient and secret language. This writing is understood only by the medicine men and by the herbalists who, for another gift, provide the required charm.

The charm is not disposed of after it has served its purpose, but is placed in the charm-box of the household shrine. As these magical materials are specific for certain ills, and the real or imagined maladies of the people are many, the charm-box is usually full to overflowing. The magical packets are so numerous that people forget what their purposes were and fear to use them again. While the natives are very vague on this point, we can only assume that the idea in retaining all the old magical materials is that their presence in the charm-box, before which the body rituals are conducted, will in some way protect the worshipper.

Beneath the charm-box is a small font. Each day every member of the family, in succession, enters the shrine room, bows his head before the charm-box, mingles different sorts of holy water in the font, and proceeds with a brief rite of ablution. The holy waters are secured from the Water Temple of the community, where the priests conduct elaborate ceremonies to make the liquid ritually pure.

In the hierarchy of magical practitioners, and below the medicine men in prestige, are specialists whose designation is best translated "holy-mouth-men." The Nacirema have an almost pathological horror of and fascination with the mouth, the condition of which is believed to have a supernatural influence on all social relationships. Were it not for the rituals of the mouth, they believe that their teeth would fall out, their gums bleed, their jaws shrink, their friends desert them, and their lovers reject them. They also believe that a strong relationship exists between oral and moral characteristics. For example, there is a ritual ablution of the mouth for children which is supposed to improve their moral fiber.

The daily body ritual performed by everyone includes a mouth-rite. Despite the fact that these people are so punctilious about care of the mouth, this rite involves a practice which strikes the uninitiated stranger as revolting. It was reported to me that the ritual consists of inserting a small bundle of hog hairs into the mouth, along with certain magical powders, and then moving the bundle in a highly formalized series of gestures.

In addition to the private mouth-rite, the people seek out a holy-mouth-man once or twice a year. These practitioners have an impressive set of paraphernalia, consisting of a variety of augers, awls, probes, and prods. The use of these objects in the exorcism of the evils of the mouth involves almost unbelievable ritual torture of the client. The holy-mouth-man opens the client's mouth and, using the above-mentioned tools, enlarges any holes which decay may have created in the teeth. Magical materials are put into these holes. If there are no naturally occurring holes in the teeth, large sections of one or more teeth are gouged out so that the supernatural substance can be applied. In the client's view, the purpose of these ministrations is to arrest decay and to draw friends. The extremely sacred and traditional character of the rite is evident in the fact that the natives return to the holy-mouth-man year after year, despite the fact that their teeth continue to decay.

It is to be hoped that, when a thorough study of the Nacirema is made, there will be careful inquiry into the personality structure of these people. One has but to watch the gleam in the eye of a holy-mouth-man, as he jabs an awl into an exposed nerve, to suspect that a certain amount of sadism is involved. If this can be established, a very interesting pattern emerges, for most of the population shows definite masochistic tendencies. It was to these that Professor Linton referred in discussing a distinctive part of the daily body ritual which is performed only by men. This part of the rite involves scraping and lacerating the surface of the face with a sharp instrument. Special women's rites are performed only four times during each lunar month, but what they lack in frequency is made up in barbarity. As part of this ceremony, women bake their heads in small ovens for about an hour. The theoretically interesting point is that what seems to be a preponderantly masochistic people have developed sadistic specialists.

The medicine men have an imposing temple, or *latipso*, in every community of any size. The more elaborate ceremonies required to treat very sick patients can only be performed at this temple. These ceremonies involve not only the thaumaturge but a permanent group of vestal maidens who move sedately about the temple chambers in distinctive costume and headdress.

The *latipso* ceremonies are so harsh that it is phenomenal that a fair proportion of the really sick natives who enter the temple ever recover. Small children whose indoctrination is still incomplete have been known to resist attempts to take them to the temple because "that is where you go to die." Despite this fact, sick adults are not only willing but eager to undergo the protracted ritual purification, if they can afford to do so. No matter how ill the supplicant or how grave the emergency, the guardians of many temples will not admit a client if he cannot give a rich gift to the custodian. Even after one has

gained admission and survived the ceremonies, the guardians will not permit the neophyte to leave until he makes still another gift.

The supplicant entering the temple is first stripped of all his or her clothes. In everyday life the Nacirema avoids exposure of his body and its natural functions. Bathing and excretory acts are performed only in the secrecy of the household shrine, where they are ritualized as part of the body-rites. Psychological shock results from the fact that body secrecy is suddenly lost upon entry into the *latipso*. A man, whose own wife has never seen him in an excretory act, suddenly finds himself naked and assisted by a vestal maiden while he performs his natural functions into a sacred vessel. This sort of ceremonial treatment is necessitated by the fact that the excreta are used by a diviner to ascertain the course and nature of the client's sickness. Female clients, on the other hand, find their naked bodies are subjected to the scrutiny, manipulation, and prodding of the medicine men.

Few supplicants in the temple are well enough to do anything but lie on their hard beds. The daily ceremonies, like the rites of the holy-mouth-men, involve discomfort and torture. With ritual precision, the vestals awaken their miserable charges each dawn and roll them about on their beds of pain while performing ablutions, in the formal movements of which the maidens are highly trained. At other times they insert magic wands in the supplicant's mouth or force him to eat substances which are supposed to be healing. From time to time the medicine men come to their clients and jab magically treated needles into their flesh. The fact that these temple ceremonies may not cure, and may even kill the neophyte, in no way decreases the people's faith in the medicine men.

There remains one other kind of practitioner, known as a "listener." This witch-doctor has the power to exorcise the devils that lodge in the heads of people who have been bewitched. The Nacirema believe that parents bewitch their own children. Mothers are particularly suspected of putting a curse on children while teaching them the secret body rituals. The counter-magic of the witch-doctor is unusual in its lack of ritual. The patient simply tells the "listener" all his troubles and fears, beginning with the earliest difficulties he can remember. The memory displayed by the Nacirema in these exorcism sessions is truly remarkable. It is not uncommon for the patient to bemoan the rejection he felt upon being weaned as a babe, and a few individuals even see their troubles going back to the traumatic effects of their own birth.

In conclusion, mention must be made of certain practices which have their base in native esthetics but which depend upon the pervasive aversion to the natural body and its functions. There are ritual fasts to make fat people thin and ceremonial feasts to make thin people fat. Still other rites are used to make women's breasts larger if they are small, and smaller if they are large. General dissatisfaction with breast shape is symbolized in the fact that the ideal form is virtually outside the range of human variation. A few women afflicted with almost inhuman hypermammary development are so idolized that they make a handsome living by simply going from village to village and permitting the natives to stare at them for a fee.

Reference has already been made to the fact that excretory functions are ritualized, routinized, and relegated to secrecy. Natural reproductive functions are similarly distorted. Intercourse is taboo as a topic and scheduled as an act. Efforts are made to avoid pregnancy by the use of magical materials or by limiting intercourse to certain phases of the moon. Conception is actually very infrequent. When pregnant, women dress so as to hide their condition. Parturition takes place in secret, without friends or relatives to assist, and the majority of women do not nurse their infants.

Our review of the ritual life of the Nacirema has certainly shown them to be a magic-ridden people. It is hard to understand how they have managed to exist so long under the burdens which they have imposed upon themselves. But even such exotic customs as these take on real meaning when they are viewed with the insight provided by Malinowski when he wrote (1948, p. 70):

> Looking from far and above, from our high places of safety in the developed civilization, it is easy to see all the crudity and irrelevance of magic. But without its power and guidance early man could not have mastered his practical difficulties as he has done, nor could man have advanced to the higher stages of civilization.

REFERENCES

Linton, R. (1936). *The study of man.* New York: Appleton-Century.

Malinowski, B. (1948). *Magic, science, and religion.* Glencoe, IL: Free Press.

Murdock, G. P. (1949). *Social structure.* New York: Macmillan.

THINKING ABOUT THE READING

What do you think of this culture? Do their ways seem very foreign or are there some things that seem familiar? This article was written more than 40 years ago and, of course, much has changed since then. How might you update this description of the

"Nacirema" to account for current values and rituals? Imagine you are an anthropologist from a culture completely unfamiliar with Western traditions. Using your own life as a starting point, think of common patterns of work, leisure, learning, intimacy, eating, sleeping, and so forth. Are there some customs that distinguish your group (religious, racial, ethnic, friendship, and so on) from others? See if you can find the reasons why these customs exist. Which customs serve an obvious purpose (for example, health)? Which might seem arbitrary and silly to an outside observer?

2 Seeing and Thinking Sociologically

Where is society located? This question is intriguing: society shapes our behavior and beliefs through social institutions such as religion, law, education, economics, and family. At the same time, we shape society through our interactions with one another and our participation in social institutions. In this way, we can say that society exists as an objective entity that transcends us. But it is also a construction that is created, reaffirmed, and altered through everyday interactions and behavior. Humans are social beings. We constantly look to others to help define and interpret the situations in which we find ourselves. Other people can influence what we see, feel, think, and do. But it's not just other people who influence us. We also live in a *society*, which consists of socially recognizable combinations of individuals—relationships, groups, and organizations—as well as the products of human action—statuses, roles, culture, and institutions. When we behave, we do so in a social context that consists of a combination of institutional arrangements and interpersonal expectations. Thus, our behavior in any given situation is our own, but the reasons we do what we do are rooted in these more complex social factors.

The influence of social structure on our personal actions is often felt most forcefully when we are compelled to obey the commands of someone who is in a position of authority. In "The My Lai Massacre: A Military Crime of Obedience," Herbert Kelman and Lee Hamilton describe a specific example of a crime in which the individuals involved attempted to deny responsibility for their actions by claiming that they were following the orders of a military officer who had the legitimate right to command them. This incident occurred in the midst of the Vietnam War. Arguably, people do things under such trying conditions that they wouldn't ordinarily do, even—as in this case—kill defenseless people. Kelman and Hamilton make a key sociological point by showing that these soldiers were not necessarily psychological misfits who were especially mean or violent. Instead, the researchers argue, they were ordinary people caught up in tense circumstances that made obeying the brutal commands of an authority seem like the normal and morally acceptable thing to do.

The impact of society in our everyday lives is often obscured by the tendency to see people's accomplishments in individualistic, sometimes biological terms. This tendency toward "individualistic" explanations is particularly pronounced in U.S. society. Consider athletic performance. I'm sure you've seen televised coverage of the Olympics. Most people are in awe of these remarkable athletes—the elite of their respective sports—competing at a level far beyond the reach of "normal" people. As we watch them perform, it's easy to conclude that these athletes are a different breed, that they have some inborn, personal quality—call it "talent"—that propels them to world-class achievements. But Daniel Chambliss, in "The Mundanity of Excellence," argues that, as much as we'd like to believe otherwise, these world-class athletes are not that different from the rest of us. Their excellence comes from fundamentally ordinary activities that take place within identifiable social worlds that have their own unique values, attitudes, and behavior patterns. By explaining athletic excellence in such a way, Chambliss illustrates the sociological perspective on understanding social life: Behavior commonly attributed to innate qualities can be better understood by examining the broader social context within which it takes place.

Something to Consider as You Read:

As you read and compare these selections, consider the effects of social context on both soldiers and athletes. How might a particular context, especially the presence of particular commanders or coaches, lead you to behave in ways you might not think possible?

The My Lai Massacre

A Military Crime of Obedience

Herbert Kelman and V. Lee Hamilton

(1989)

March 16, 1968, was a busy day in U.S. history. Stateside, Robert F. Kennedy announced his presidential candidacy, challenging a sitting president from his own party—in part out of opposition to an undeclared and disastrous war. In Vietnam, the war continued. In many ways, March 16 may have been a typical day in that war. We will probably never know. But we do know that on that day a typical company went on a mission—which may or may not have been typical—to a village called Son (or Song) My. Most of what is remembered from that mission occurred in the subhamlet known to Americans as My Lai 4.

The My Lai massacre was investigated and charges were brought in 1969 and 1970. Trials and disciplinary actions lasted into 1971. Entire books have been written about the army's year-long cover-up of the massacre (for example, Hersh, 1972), and the cover-up was a major focus of the army's own investigation of the incident. Our central concern here is the massacre itself—a crime of obedience—and public reactions to such crimes, rather than the lengths to which many went to deny the event. Therefore this account concentrates on one day: March 16, 1968.

Many verbal testimonials to the horrors that occurred at My Lai were available. More unusual was the fact that an army photographer, Ronald Haeberle, was assigned the task of documenting the anticipated military engagement at My Lai—and documented a massacre instead. Later, as the story of the massacre

emerged, his photographs were widely distributed and seared the public conscience. What might have been dismissed as unreal or exaggerated was depicted in photographs of demonstrable authenticity. The dominant image appeared on the cover of *Life*: piles of bodies jumbled together in a ditch along a trail—the dead all apparently unarmed. All were Oriental, and all appeared to be children, women, or old men. Clearly there had been a mass execution, one whose image would not quickly fade.

So many bodies (over twenty in the cover photo alone) are hard to imagine as the handiwork of one killer. These were not. They were the product of what we call a crime of obedience. Crimes of obedience begin with orders. But orders are often vague and rarely survive with any clarity the transition from one authority down a chain of subordinates to the ultimate actors. The operation at Son My was no exception.

"Charlie" Company, Company C, under Lt. Col. Frank Barker's command, arrived in Vietnam in December 1967. As the army's investigative unit, directed by Lt. Gen. William R. Peers, characterized the personnel, they "contained no significant deviation from the average" for the time. Seymour S. Hersh (1970) described the "average" more explicitly: "Most of the men in Charlie Company had volunteered for the draft; only a few had gone to college for even one year. Nearly half were black, with a few Mexican-Americans. Most were eighteen to twenty-two years old. The favorite reading matter of Charlie Company, like that of other line infantry units in Vietnam, was comic books" (p. 18). The action at My Lai, like that throughout Vietnam, was fought by a cross-section of those Americans who either believed in the war or lacked the social resources to avoid participating in it. Charlie Company was indeed average for that time, that place, and that war.

Two key figures in Charlie Company were more unusual. The company's commander, Capt. Ernest Medina, was an upwardly mobile Mexican-American who wanted to make the army his career, although he feared that he might never advance beyond captain because of his lack of formal education. His eagerness had earned him a nickname among his men: "Mad Dog Medina." One of his admirers was the platoon leader Second Lt. William L. Calley, Jr., an undistinguished, five-foot-three-inch junior-college dropout who had failed four of the seven courses in which he had enrolled his first year. Many viewed him as one of those "instant officers" made possible only by the army's then-desperate need for man-power. Whatever the cause, he was an insecure leader whose frequent claim was "I'm the boss." His nickname among some of the troops was "Surfside 5½," a reference to the swash-buckling heroes of a popular television show, "Surfside 6."

The Son My operation was planned by Lieutenant Colonel Barker and his staff as a search-and-destroy mission with the objective of rooting out the Forty-eighth Viet Cong Battalion from their base area of Son My village. Apparently no written orders were ever issued. Barker's superior, Col. Oran Henderson, arrived at the staging point the day before. Among the issues he reviewed with the assembled officers were some of the weaknesses of prior operations by their units, including their failure to be appropriately aggressive in pursuit of the enemy. Later briefings by Lieutenant

Colonel Barker and his staff asserted that no one except Viet Cong was expected to be in the village after 7 A.M. on the following day. The "innocent" would all be at the market. Those present at the briefings gave conflicting accounts of Barker's exact orders, but he conveyed at least a strong suggestion that the Son My area was to be obliterated. As the army's inquiry reported: "While there is some conflict in the testimony as to whether LTC Barker ordered the destruction of houses, dwellings, livestock, and other foodstuffs in the Song My area, the preponderance of the evidence indicates that such destruction was implied, if not specifically directed, by his orders of 15 March" (Peers Report, in Goldstein et al., 1976, p. 94).

Evidence that Barker ordered the killing of civilians is even more murky. What does seem clear, however, is that—having asserted that civilians would be away at the market—he did not specify what was to be done with any who might nevertheless be found on the scene. The Peers Report therefore considered it "reasonable to conclude that LTC Barker's minimal or nonexistent instructions concerning the handling of noncombatants created the potential for grave misunderstandings as to his intentions and for interpretation of his orders as authority to fire, without restriction, on all persons found in target area" (Goldstein et al., 1976, p. 95). Since Barker was killed in action in June 1968, his own formal version of the truth was never available.

Charlie Company's Captain Medina was briefed for the operation by Barker and his staff. He then transmitted the already vague orders to his own men. Charlie Company was spoiling for a fight, having been totally frustrated during its months in Vietnam—first by waiting for battles that never came, then by incompetent forays led by inexperienced commanders, and finally by mines and booby traps. In fact, the emotion-laden funeral of a sergeant killed by a booby trap was held on March 15, the day before My Lai. Captain

Medina gave the orders for the next day's action at the close of that funeral. Many were in a mood for revenge.

It is again unclear what was ordered. Although all participants were alive by the time of the trials for the massacre, they were either on trial or probably felt under threat of trial. Memories are often flawed and self-serving at such times. It is apparent that Medina relayed to the men at least some of Barker's general message—to expect Viet Cong resistance, to burn, and to kill livestock. It is not clear that he ordered the slaughter of the inhabitants, but some of the men who heard him thought he had. One of those who claimed to have heard such orders was Lt. William Calley.

As March 16 dawned, much was expected of the operation by those who had set it into motion. Therefore a full complement of "brass" was present in helicopters overhead, including Barker, Colonel Henderson, and their superior, Major General Koster (who went on to become commandant of West Point before the story of My Lai broke). On the ground, the troops were to carry with them one reporter and one photographer to immortalize the anticipated battle.

The action for Company C began at 7:30 as their first wave of helicopters touched down near the subhamlet of My Lai 4. By 7:47 all of Company C was present and set to fight. But instead of the Viet Cong Forty-eighth Battalion, My Lai was filled with the old men, women, and children who were supposed to have gone to market. By this time, in their version of the war, and with whatever orders they thought they had heard, the men from Company C were nevertheless ready to find Viet Cong everywhere. By nightfall, the official tally was 128 VC killed and three weapons captured, although later, unofficial body counts ran as high as 500. The operation at Son My was over. And by nightfall, as Hersh reported: "the Viet Cong were back in My Lai 4, helping the survivors bury the dead. It

took five days. Most of the funeral speeches were made by the Communist guerrillas. Nguyen Bat was not a Communist at the time of the massacre, but the incident changed his mind. 'After the shooting,' he said, 'all the villagers became Communists'" (1970, p. 74). To this day, the memory of the massacre is kept alive by markers and plaques designating the spots where groups of villagers were killed, by a large statue, and by the My Lai Museum, established in 1975 (Williams, 1985).

But what could have happened to leave American troops reporting a victory over Viet Cong when in fact they had killed hundreds of noncombatants? It is not hard to explain the report of victory; that is the essence of a cover-up. It is harder to understand how the killings came to be committed in the first place, making a cover-up necessary.

Mass Executions and the Defense of Superior Orders

Some of the atrocities on March 16, 1968, were evidently unofficial, spontaneous acts: rapes, tortures, killings. For example, Hersh (1970) describes Charlie Company's Second Platoon as entering "My Lai 4 with guns blazing" (p. 50); more graphically, Lieutenant "Brooks and his men in the second platoon to the north had begun to systematically ransack the hamlet and slaughter the people, kill the livestock, and destroy the crops. Men poured rifle and machine-gun fire into huts without knowing—or seemingly caring—who was inside" (pp. 49–50).

Some atrocities toward the end of the action were part of an almost casual "mopping-up," much of which was the responsibility of Lieutenant LaCross's Third Platoon of Charlie Company. The Peers Report states: "The entire 3rd Platoon then began moving into the western edge of My Lai (4), for the mop-up operation. . . . The squad . . . began to burn the houses in the southwestern portion of the hamlet" (Goldstein et al., 1976, p. 133). They became mingled with other platoons during a series of rapes and killings of survivors for which it was impossible to fix responsibility. Certainly to a Vietnamese all GIs would by this point look alike: "Nineteen-year-old Nguyen Thi Ngoc Tuyet watched a baby trying to open her slain mother's blouse to nurse. A soldier shot the infant while it was struggling with the blouse, and then slashed it with his bayonet." Tuyet also said she saw another baby hacked to death by GIs wielding their bayonets. "Le Tong, a twenty-eight-year-old rice farmer, reported seeing one woman raped after GIs killed her children. Nguyen Khoa, a thirty-seven-year-old peasant, told of a thirteen-year-old girl who was raped before being killed. GIs then attacked Khoa's wife, tearing off her clothes. Before they could rape her, however, Khoa said, their six-year-old son, riddled with bullets, fell and saturated her with blood. The GIs left her alone" (Hersh, 1970, p. 72). All of Company C was implicated in a pattern of death and destruction throughout the hamlet, much of which seemingly lacked rhyme or reason.

But a substantial amount of the killing was organized and traceable to one authority: the First Platoon's Lt. William Calley. Calley was originally charged with 109 killings, almost all of them mass executions at the trail and other locations. He stood trial for 102 of these killings, was convicted of 22 in 1971, and at first received a life sentence. Though others—both superior and subordinate to Calley—were brought to trial, he was the only one convicted for the My Lai crimes. Thus, the only actions of My Lai for which anyone was ever convicted were mass executions, ordered and committed. We suspect that there are commonsense reasons why this one type of killing was singled out. In the midst of rapidly moving events with people running about, an execution of stationary targets is literally a still life that stands out and whose participants are clearly visible. It can be proven that specific people committed specific deeds. An execution, in contrast to the shooting of someone on the run, is also more likely to meet the legal definition of an act resulting from intent—with malice aforethought. Moreover, American military law specifically forbids the killing of unarmed civilians or military prisoners, as does the Geneva Convention between nations. Thus common sense, legal standards, and explicit doctrine all made such actions the likeliest target for prosecution.

When Lieutenant Calley was charged under military law it was for violation of the Uniform Code of Military Justice (UCMJ) Article 118 (murder). This article is similar to civilian codes in that it provides for conviction if an accused:

> without justification or excuse, unlawfully kills a human being, when he—
>
> 1. has a premeditated design to kill;
> 2. intends to kill or inflict great bodily harm;
> 3. is engaged in an act which is inherently dangerous to others and evinces a wanton disregard of human life; or
> 4. is engaged in the perpetration or attempted perpetration of burglary, sodomy, rape, robbery, or aggravated arson. (Goldstein et al., 1976, p. 507)

For a soldier, one legal justification for killing is warfare; but warfare is subject to many legal limits and restrictions, including, of course, the inadmissibility of killing unarmed noncombatants or prisoners whom one has disarmed. The pictures of the trail victims at My Lai certainly portrayed one or the other of these. Such an action would be illegal under military law; ordering another to commit such an action would be illegal; and following such an order would be illegal.

But following an order may provide a second and pivotal justification for an act that would be murder when committed by a civilian.

American military law assumes that the subordinate is inclined to follow orders, as that is the normal obligation of the role. Hence, legally, obedient subordinates are protected from unreasonable expectations regarding their capacity to evaluate those orders:

> An order requiring the performance of a military duty may be inferred to be legal. An act performed manifestly beyond the scope of authority, or pursuant to an order that a man of ordinary sense and understanding would know to be illegal, or in a wanton manner in the discharge of a lawful duty, is not excusable. (Par. 216, Subpar. *d*, Manual for Courts Martial, United States, 1969 Rev.)

Thus what *may* be excusable is the good-faith carrying out of an order, as long as that order appears to the ordinary soldier to be a legal one. In military law, invoking superior orders moves the question from one of the action's consequences—the body count—to one of evaluating the actor's motives and good sense.

In sum, if anyone is to be brought to justice for a massacre, common sense and legal codes decree that the most appropriate targets are those who make themselves executioners. This is the kind of target the government selected in prosecuting Lieutenant Calley with the greatest fervor. And in a military context, the most promising way in which one can redefine one's undeniable deeds into acceptability is to invoke superior orders. This is what Calley did in attempting to avoid conviction. Since the core legal issues involved points of mass execution—the ditches and trail where America's image of My Lai was formed—we review these events in greater detail.

The day's quiet beginning has already been noted. Troops landed and swept unopposed into the village. The three weapons eventually reported as the haul from the operation were picked up from three apparent Viet Cong who fled the village when the troops arrived and were pursued and killed by helicopter gunships. Obviously the Viet Cong did frequent the area. But it appears that by about 8:00 A.M. no one who met the troops was aggressive, and no one was armed. By the laws of war Charlie Company had no argument with such people.

As they moved into the village, the soldiers began to gather its inhabitants together. Shortly after 8:00 A.M. Lieutenant Calley told Pfc. Paul Meadlo that "you know what to do with" a group of villagers Meadlo was guarding. Estimates of the numbers in the group ranged as high as eighty women, children, and old men, and Meadlo's own estimate under oath was thirty to fifty people. As Meadlo later testified, Calley returned after ten or fifteen minutes: "He [Calley] said, 'How come they're not dead?' I said, 'I didn't know we were supposed to kill them.' He said, 'I want them dead.' He backed off twenty or thirty feet and started shooting into the people—the Viet Cong— shooting automatic. He was beside me. He burned four or five magazines. I burned off a few, about three. I helped shoot 'em" (Hammer, 1971, p. 155). Meadlo himself and others testified that Meadlo cried as he fired; others reported him later to be sobbing and "all broke up." It would appear that to Lieutenant Calley's subordinates something was unusual, and stressful, in these orders.

At the trial, the first specification in the murder charge against Calley was for this incident; he was accused of premeditated murder of "an unknown number, not less than 30, Oriental human beings, males and females of various ages, whose names are unknown, occupants of the village of My Lai 4, by means of shooting them with a rifle" (Goldstein et al., 1976, p. 497).

Among the helicopters flying reconnaissance above Son My was that of CWO Hugh Thompson. By 9:00 or soon after, Thompson had noticed some horrifying events from his perch. As he spotted wounded civilians, he sent down smoke markers so that soldiers on the ground could treat them. They killed them instead. He reported to headquarters, trying to persuade someone to stop what was going on. Barker, hearing the message, called down to Captain Medina. Medina, in turn, later claimed to have told Calley that it was "enough for today." But it was not yet enough.

At Calley's orders, his men began gathering the remaining villagers—roughly seventy-five individuals, mostly women and children—and herding them toward a drainage ditch. Accompanied by three or four enlisted men, Lieutenant Calley executed several batches of civilians who had been gathered into ditches. Some of the details of the process were entered into testimony in such accounts as Pfc. Dennis Conti's: "A lot of them, the people, were trying to get up and mostly they was just screaming and pretty bad shot up. . . . I seen a woman tried to get up. I seen Lieutenant Calley fire. He hit the side of her head and blew it off" (Hammer, 1971, p. 125).

Testimony by other soldiers presented the shooting's aftermath. Specialist Four Charles Hall, asked by Prosecutor Aubrey Daniel how he knew the people in the ditch were dead, said: "There was blood coming from them. They were just scattered all over the ground in the ditch, some in piles and some scattered out 20, 25 meters perhaps up the ditch. . . . They were very old people, very young children, and mothers. . . . There was blood all over them" (Goldstein et al., 1976, pp. 501–502). And Pfc. Gregory Olsen corroborated the general picture of the victims: "They were—the majority were women and children, some babies. I distinctly remember one middle-aged Vietnamese male dressed in white right at my feet as I crossed. None of the bodies were mangled in any way. There was blood. Some appeared to be dead, others followed me with their eyes as I walked across the ditch" (Goldstein et al., 1976, p. 502).

The second specification in the murder charge stated that Calley did "with premeditation, murder an unknown number of Oriental human beings, not less than seventy, males and females of various ages, whose names are unknown, occupants of the village of My Lai 4, by means of shooting them with a rifle" (Goldstein et al., 1976, p. 497). Calley was also charged with and tried for shootings of individuals (an old man and a child); these charges were clearly supplemental to the main issue at trial—the mass killings and how they came about.

It is noteworthy that during these executions more than one enlisted man avoided carrying out Calley's orders, and more than one, by sworn oath, directly refused to obey them. For example, Pfc. James Joseph Dursi testified, when asked if he fired when Lieutenant Calley ordered him to: "No I just stood there. Meadlo turned to me after a couple of minutes and said 'Shoot! Why don't you shoot! Why don't you fire!' He was crying and yelling. I said, 'I can't! I won't!' And the people were screaming and crying and yelling. They kept firing for a couple of minutes, mostly automatic and semi-automatic" (Hammer, 1971, p. 143). . . .

Disobedience of Lieutenant Calley's own orders to kill represented a serious legal and moral threat to a defense *based* on superior orders, such as Calley was attempting. This defense had to assert that the orders seemed reasonable enough to carry out; that they appeared to be legal orders. Even if the orders in question were not legal, the defense had to assert that an ordinary individual could not and should not be expected to see the distinction. In short, if what happened was "business as usual," even though it might be bad business, then the defendant stood a chance of acquittal. But under direct command from "Surfside 5½," some ordinary enlisted men managed to refuse, to avoid, or at least to stop doing what they were ordered to do. As "reasonable men" of "ordinary sense and understanding," they had apparently found something awry that morning; and it would have been hard for an officer to plead successfully that he was more ordinary than his men in his capacity to evaluate the reasonableness of orders.

Even those who obeyed Calley's orders showed great stress. For example, Meadlo eventually began to argue and cry directly in front of Calley. Pfc. Herbert Carter shot himself in the foot, possibly because he could no longer take what he was doing. We were not destined to hear a sworn version of the incident, since neither side at the Calley trial called him to testify.

The most unusual instance of resistance to authority came from the skies. CWO Hugh Thompson, who had protested the apparent carnage of civilians, was Calley's inferior in rank but was not in his line of command. He was also watching the ditch from his helicopter and noticed some people moving after the first round of slaughter—chiefly children who had been shielded by their mothers' bodies. Landing to rescue the wounded, he also found some villagers hiding in a nearby bunker. Protecting the Vietnamese with his own body, Thompson ordered his men to train their guns on the Americans and to open fire if the Americans fired on the Vietnamese. He then radioed for additional rescue helicopters and stood between the Vietnamese and the Americans under Calley's command until the Vietnamese could be evacuated. He later returned to the ditch to unearth a child buried, unharmed, beneath layers of bodies. In October 1969, Thompson was awarded the Distinguished Flying Cross for heroism at My Lai, specifically (albeit inaccurately) for the rescue of children hiding in a bunker "between Viet Cong forces and advancing friendly forces" and for the rescue of a wounded child "caught in the intense crossfire" (Hersh, 1970, p. 119). Four months earlier, at the Pentagon, Thompson had identified Calley as having been at the ditch.

By about 10:00 A.M., the massacre was winding down. The remaining actions consisted largely of isolated rapes and killings, "clean-up" shootings of the wounded, and the destruction of the village by fire. We have already seen some

examples of these more indiscriminate and possibly less premeditated acts. By the 11:00 A.M. lunch break, when the exhausted men of Company C were relaxing, two young girls wandered back from a hiding place only to be invited to share lunch. This surrealist touch illustrates the extent to which the soldiers' action had become dissociated from its meaning. An hour earlier, some of these men were making sure that not even a child would escape the executioner's bullet. But now the job was done and it was time for lunch—and in this new context it seemed only natural to ask the children who had managed to escape execution to join them. The massacre had ended. It remained only for the Viet Cong to reap the political rewards among the survivors in hiding.

The army command in the area knew that something had gone wrong. Direct commanders, including Lieutenant Colonel Barker, had firsthand reports, such as Thompson's complaints. Others had such odd bits of evidence as the claim of 128 Viet Cong dead with a booty of only three weapons. But the cover-up of My Lai began at once. The operation was reported as a victory over a stronghold of the Viet Cong Forty-eighth. . . .

William Calley was not the only man tried for the event at My Lai. The actions of over thirty soldiers and civilians were scrutinized by investigators; over half of these had to face charges or disciplinary action of some sort. Targets of investigation included Captain Medina, who was tried, and various higher-ups, including General Koster. But Lieutenant Calley was the only person convicted, the only person to serve time.

The core of Lieutenant Calley's defense was superior orders. What this meant to him—in contrast to what it meant to the judge and jury—can be gleaned from his responses to a series of questions from his defense attorney, George Latimer, in which Calley sketched out his understanding of the laws of war and the actions that constitute doing one's duty within those laws:

Latimer: Did you receive any training which had to do with the obedience to orders?

Calley: Yes, sir.

Latimer: . . . what were you informed [were] the principles involved in that field?

Calley: That all orders were to be assumed legal, that the soldier's job was to carry out any order given him to the best of his ability.

Latimer: . . . what might occur if you disobeyed an order by a senior officer?

Calley: You could be court-martialed for refusing an order and refusing an order in the face of the enemy, you could be sent to death, sir.

Latimer: [I am asking] whether you were required in any way, shape or form to make a determination of the legality or illegality of an order?

Calley: No, sir. I was never told that I had the choice, sir.

Latimer: If you had a doubt about the order, what were you supposed to do?

Calley: . . . I was supposed to carry the order out and then come back and make my complaint. (Hammer, 1971, pp. 240–241)

Lieutenant Calley steadfastly maintained that his actions within My Lai had constituted, in his mind, carrying out orders from Captain Medina. Both his own actions and the orders he gave to others (such as the instruction to Meadlo to "waste 'em") were entirely in response to superior orders. He denied any intent to kill individuals and any but the most passing awareness of distinctions among the individuals: "I was ordered to go in there and destroy the enemy. That was my job on that day. That was the mission I was given. I did not sit down and think in terms of men, women, and children. They were all classified the same, and that was the classification that we dealt with, just as enemy soldiers." When Latimer

asked if in his own opinion Calley had acted "rightly and according to your understanding of your directions and orders," Calley replied, "I felt then and I still do that I acted as I was directed, and I carried out the orders that I was given, and I do not feel wrong in doing so, sir" (Hammer, 1971, p. 257).

His court-martial did not accept Calley's defense of superior orders and clearly did not share his interpretation of his duty. The jury evidently reasoned that, even if there had been orders to destroy everything in sight and to "waste the Vietnamese," any reasonable person would have realized that such orders were illegal and should have refused to carry them out. The defense of superior orders under such conditions is inadmissible under international and military law. The U.S. Army's *Law of Land Warfare* (Dept. of the Army, 1956), for example, states that "the fact that the law of war has been violated pursuant to an order of a superior authority, whether military or civil, does not deprive the act in question of its character of a war crime, nor does it constitute a defense in the trial of an accused individual, unless he did not know and could not reasonably have been expected to know that the act was unlawful" and that "members of the armed forces are bound to obey only lawful orders" (in Falk et al., 1971, pp. 71–72).

The disagreement between Calley and the court-martial seems to have revolved around the definition of the responsibilities of a subordinate to obey, on the one hand, and to evaluate, on the other. This tension . . . can best be captured via the charge to the jury in the Calley court-martial, made by the trial judge, Col. Reid Kennedy. The forty-one pages of charge include the following:

> Both combatants captured by and noncombatants detained by the opposing force . . . have the right to be treated as prisoners. . . . Summary execution of detainees or prisoners is forbidden by law. . . . I therefore instruct you

. . . that if unresisting human beings were killed at My Lai (4) while within the effective custody and control of our military forces, their deaths cannot be considered justified. . . . Thus if you find that Lieutenant Calley received an order directing him to kill unresisting Vietnamese within his control or within the control of his troops, *that order would be an illegal order.*

A determination that an order is illegal does not, of itself, assign criminal responsibility to the person following the order for acts done in compliance with it. Soldiers are taught to follow orders, and special attention is given to obedience of orders on the battlefield. Military effectiveness depends on obedience to orders. On the other hand, the obedience of a soldier is not the obedience of an automaton. A soldier is a reasoning agent, obliged to respond, not as a machine, but as a person. The law takes these factors into account in assessing criminal responsibility for acts done in compliance with illegal orders.

> The acts of a subordinate done in compliance with an unlawful order given him by his superior are excused and impose no criminal liability upon him unless the superior's order is one which a man of *ordinary sense and understanding* would, under the circumstances, know to be unlawful, or if the order in question is actually known to the accused to be unlawful. (Goldstein et al., 1976, pp. 525–526; emphasis added)

By this definition, subordinates take part in a balancing act, one tipped toward obedience but tempered by "ordinary sense and understanding."

A jury of combat veterans proceeded to convict William Calley of the premeditated murder of no less than twenty-two human beings. (The army, realizing some unfortunate connotations in referring to the victims as "Oriental human beings," eventually referred to them as "human beings.") Regarding the first specification in the murder charge, the bodies on the trail, [Calley] was convicted of premeditated murder of not less than one person. (Medical testimony had been able to pinpoint only one person whose wounds as revealed in Haeberle's photos were sure to be immediately fatal.) Regarding the second specification, the bodies in the ditch, Calley was convicted of the premeditated murder of not less than twenty human beings. Regarding additional specifications that he had killed an old man and a child, Calley was convicted of premeditated murder in the first case and of assault with intent to commit murder in the second.

Lieutenant Calley was initially sentenced to life imprisonment. That sentence was reduced: first to twenty years, eventually to ten (the latter by Secretary of Defense Callaway in 1974). Calley served three years before being released on bond. The time was spent under house arrest in his apartment, where he was able to receive visits from his girlfriend. He was granted parole on September 10, 1975.

Sanctioned Massacres

The slaughter at My Lai is an instance of a class of violent acts that can be described as sanctioned massacres (Kelman, 1973): acts of indiscriminate, ruthless, and often systematic mass violence, carried out by military or paramilitary personnel while engaged in officially sanctioned campaigns, the victims of which are defenseless and unresisting civilians, including old men, women, and children. Sanctioned massacres have occurred throughout history. Within American history, My Lai had its precursors in the Philippine war around the turn of the century (Schirmer, 1971) and in the massacres of American Indians. Elsewhere in the world, one recalls the Nazis' "final solution" for European Jews, the massacres and deportations of Armenians by Turks, the liquidation of the kulaks and the great purges in the Soviet Union, and more recently the massacres in Indonesia and Bangladesh, in Biafra and Burundi, in South Africa and Mozambique, in Cambodia and Afghanistan, in Syria and Lebanon. . . .

The occurrence of sanctioned massacres cannot be adequately explained by the existence of psychological forces—whether these be characterological dispositions to engage in murderous violence or profound hostility against the target—so powerful that they must find expression in violent acts unhampered by moral restraints. Instead, the major instigators for this class of violence derive from the policy process. The question that really calls for psychological analysis is why so many people are willing to formulate, participate in, and condone policies that call for the mass killings of defenseless civilians. Thus it is more instructive to look not at the motives for violence but at the conditions under which the usual moral inhibitions against violence become weakened. Three social processes that tend to create such conditions can be identified: authorization, routinization, and dehumanization. Through authorization, the situation becomes so defined that the individual is absolved of the responsibility to make personal moral choices. Through routinization, the action becomes so organized that there is no opportunity for raising moral questions. Through dehumanization, the actors' attitudes toward the target and toward themselves become so structured that it is neither necessary nor possible for them to view the relationship in moral terms.

Authorization

Sanctioned massacres by definition occur in the context of an authority situation, a situation in which, at least for many of the participants, the moral principles that generally govern human relationships do not apply. Thus, when acts of violence are explicitly ordered, implicitly encouraged, tacitly approved, or at least permitted by legitimate authorities, people's readiness to

commit or condone them is enhanced. That such acts are authorized seems to carry automatic justification for them. Behaviorally, authorization obviates the necessity of making judgments or choices. Not only do normal moral principles become inoperative, but—particularly when the actions are explicitly ordered—a different kind of morality, linked to the duty to obey superior orders, tends to take over.

In an authority situation, individuals characteristically feel obligated to obey the orders of the authorities, whether or not these correspond with their personal preferences. They see themselves as having no choice as long as they accept the legitimacy of the orders and of the authorities who give them. Individuals differ considerably in the degree to which—and the conditions under which—they are prepared to challenge the legitimacy of an order on the grounds that the order itself is illegal, or that those giving it have overstepped their authority, or that it stems from a policy that violates fundamental societal values. Regardless of such individual differences, however, the basic structure of a situation of legitimate authority requires subordinates to respond in terms of their role obligations rather than their personal preferences; they can openly disobey only by challenging the legitimacy of the authority. Often people obey without question even though the behavior they engage in may entail great personal sacrifice or great harm to others.

An important corollary of the basic structure of the authority situation is that actors often do not see themselves as personally responsible for the consequences of their actions. Again, there are individual differences, depending on actors' capacity and readiness to evaluate the legitimacy of orders received. Insofar as they see themselves as having had no choice in their actions, however, they do not feel personally responsible for them. They were not personal agents, but merely extensions of the authority. Thus, when their actions cause harm to others, they can feel relatively free of guilt. A similar mechanism operates when a person engages in antisocial behavior that was not ordered by the authorities but was tacitly encouraged and approved by them—even if only by making it clear that such behavior will not be punished. In this situation, behavior that was formerly illegitimate is legitimized by the authorities' acquiescence.

In the My Lai massacre, it is likely that the structure of the authority situation contributed to the massive violence in both ways—that is, by conveying the message that acts of violence against Vietnamese villagers were *required*, as well as the message that such acts, even if not ordered, were *permitted* by the authorities in charge. The actions at My Lai represented, at least in some respects, responses to explicit or implicit orders. Lieutenant Calley indicated, by orders and by example, that he wanted large numbers of villagers killed. Whether Calley himself had been ordered by his superiors to "waste" the whole area, as he claimed, remains a matter of controversy. Even if we assume, however, that he was not explicitly ordered to wipe out the village, he had reason to believe that such actions were expected by his superior officers. Indeed, the very nature of the war conveyed this expectation. The principal measure of military success was the "body count"—the number of enemy soldiers killed—and any Vietnamese killed by the U.S. military was commonly defined as a "Viet Cong." Thus, it was not totally bizarre for Calley to believe that what he was doing at My Lai was to increase his body count, as any good officer was expected to do.

Even to the extent that the actions at My Lai occurred spontaneously, without reference to superior orders, those committing them had reason to assume that such actions might be tacitly approved of by the military authorities. Not only had they failed to punish such acts in most cases, but the very strategies and tactics that the authorities consistently devised were based on the proposition that the civilian population of South Vietnam—whether "hostile"

or "friendly"—was expendable. Such policies as search-and-destroy missions, the establishment of free-shooting zones, the use of antipersonnel weapons, the bombing of entire villages if they were suspected of harboring guerrillas, the forced migration of masses of the rural population, and the defoliation of vast forest areas helped legitimize acts of massive violence of the kind occurring at My Lai.

Some of the actions at My Lai suggest an orientation to authority based on unquestioning obedience to superior orders, no matter how destructive the actions these orders call for. Such obedience is specifically fostered in the course of military training and reinforced by the structure of the military authority situation. It also reflects, however, an ideological orientation that may be more widespread in the general population. . . .

Routinization

Authorization processes create a situation in which people become involved in an action without considering its implications and without really making a decision. Once they have taken the initial step, they are in a new psychological and social situation in which the pressures to continue are powerful. As Lewin (1947) has pointed out, many forces that might originally have kept people out of a situation reverse direction once they have made a commitment (once they have gone through the "gate region") and now serve to keep them in the situation. For example, concern about the criminal nature of an action, which might originally have inhibited a person from becoming involved, may now lead to deeper involvement in efforts to justify the action and to avoid negative consequences.

Despite these forces, however, given the nature of the actions involved in sanctioned massacres, one might still expect moral scruples to intervene; but the likelihood of moral resistance is greatly reduced by transforming the action into routine, mechanical, highly programmed operations. Routinization fulfills two functions. First, it reduces the necessity of making decisions, thus minimizing the occasions in which moral questions may arise. Second, it makes it easier to avoid the implications of the action, since the actor focuses on the details of the job rather than on its meaning. The latter effect is more readily achieved among those who participate in sanctioned massacres from a distance—from their desks or even from the cockpits of their bombers.

Routinization operates both at the level of the individual actor and at the organizational level. Individual job performance is broken down into a series of discrete steps, most of them carried out in automatic, regularized fashion. It becomes easy to forget the nature of the product that emerges from this process. When Lieutenant Calley said of My Lai that it was "no great deal," he probably implied that it was all in a day's work. Organizationally, the task is divided among different offices, each of which has responsibility for a small portion of it. This arrangement diffuses responsibility and limits the amount and scope of decision making that is necessary. There is no expectation that the moral implications will be considered at any of these points, nor is there any opportunity to do so. The organizational processes also help further legitimize the actions of each participant. By proceeding in routine fashion—processing papers, exchanging memos, diligently carrying out their assigned tasks—the different units mutually reinforce each other in the view that what is going on must be perfectly normal, correct, and legitimate. The shared illusion that they are engaged in a legitimate enterprise helps the participants assimilate their activities to other purposes, such as the efficiency of their performance, the productivity of their unit, or the cohesiveness of their group (see Janis, 1972).

Normalization of atrocities is more difficult to the extent that there are constant reminders of the true meaning of the enterprise. Bureaucratic inventiveness in the use of language helps to cover up such meaning. For example, the SS had a set of *Sprachregelungen,* or "language rules," to govern descriptions of their extermination program. As Arendt (1964) points out, the term *language rule* in itself was "a code name; it meant what in ordinary language would be called a lie" (p. 85). The code names for killing and liquidation were "final solution," "evacuation," and "special treatment." The war in Indochina produced its own set of euphemisms, such as "protective reaction," "pacification," and "forced-draft urbanization and modernization." The use of euphemisms allows participants in sanctioned massacres to differentiate their actions from ordinary killing and destruction and thus to avoid confronting their true meaning.

Dehumanization

Authorization processes override standard moral considerations; routinization processes reduce the likelihood that such considerations will arise. Still, the inhibitions against murdering one's fellow human beings are generally so strong that the victims must also be stripped of their human status if they are to be subjected to systematic killing. Insofar as they are dehumanized, the usual principles of morality no longer apply to them.

Sanctioned massacres become possible to the extent that the victims are deprived in the perpetrators' eyes of the two qualities essential to being perceived as fully human and included in the moral compact that governs human relationships: *identity*—standing as independent, distinctive individuals, capable of making choices and entitled to live their own lives—and *community*—fellow membership in an interconnected network of individuals who care for each other and respect each other's individuality and rights (Kelman, 1973; see also Bakan, 1966, for a related distinction between "agency" and "communion"). Thus, when a group of people is defined entirely in terms of a category to which they belong, and when this category is excluded from the human family, moral restraints against killing them are more readily overcome.

Dehumanization of the enemy is a common phenomenon in any war situation. Sanctioned massacres, however, presuppose a more extreme degree of dehumanization, insofar as the killing is not in direct response to the target's threats or provocations. It is not what they have done that marks such victims for death but who they are—the category to which they happen to belong. They are the victims of policies that regard their systematic destruction as a desirable end or an acceptable means. Such extreme dehumanization becomes possible when the target group can readily be identified as a separate category of people who have historically been stigmatized and excluded by the victimizers; often the victims belong to a distinct racial, religious, ethnic, or political group regarded as inferior or sinister. The traditions, the habits, the images, and the vocabularies for dehumanizing such groups are already well established and can be drawn upon when the groups are selected for massacre. Labels help deprive the victims of identity and community, as in the epithet "gooks" that was commonly used to refer to Vietnamese and other Indochinese peoples.

The dynamics of the massacre process itself further increase the participants' tendency to dehumanize their victims. Those who participate as part of the bureaucratic apparatus increasingly come to see their victims as bodies to be counted and entered into their reports, as faceless figures that will determine their productivity rates and promotions. Those who participate in the massacre directly—in the field, as it were—are reinforced in their perception of the victims as less than human by observing their very victimization. The only way they can justify what is being done to these people—both by others and by themselves—and the only way they can extract some degree of meaning out of the absurd events in which they find themselves participating (see Lifton, 1971, 1973) is by coming to believe that the victims are subhuman and deserve to be rooted out. And thus the process of dehumanization feeds on itself.

REFERENCES

Arendt, H. (1964). *Eichmann in Jerusalem: A report on the banality of evil.* New York: Viking Press.

Bakan, D. (1966). *The duality of human existence.* Chicago: Rand McNally.

Department of the Army. (1956). *The law of land warfare* (Field Manual, No. 27–10). Washington, DC: U.S. Government Printing Office.

Falk, R. A.; Kolko, G.; & Lifton, R. J. (Eds.). (1971). *Crimes of war.* New York: Vintage Books.

French, P. (Ed.). (1972). *Individual and collective responsibility: The massacre at My Lai.* Cambridge, MA: Schenkman.

Goldstein, J.; Marshall, B.; & Schwartz, J. (Eds.). (1976). *The My Lai massacre and its cover-up: Beyond the reach of law?* (The Peers Report with a supplement and introductory essay on the limits of law). New York: Free Press.

Hammer, R. (1971). *The court-martial of Lt. Calley.* New York: Coward, McCann, & Geoghegan.

Hersh, S. (1970). *My Lai 4: A report on the massacre and its aftermath.* New York: Vintage Books.

_____. (1972). *Cover-up.* New York: Random House.

Janis, I. L. (1972). *Victims of groupthink: A psychological study of foreign-policy decisions and fiascoes.* Boston: Houghton Mifflin.

Kelman, H. C. (1973). Violence without moral restraint: Reflections on the dehumanization of victims and victimizers. *Journal of Social Issues, 29*(4), 25–61.

Lewin, K. (1947). Group decision and social change. In T. M. Newcomb & E. L. Hartley

(Eds.), *Readings in social psychology.* New York: Holt.

Lifton, R. J. (1971). Existential evil. In N. Sanford, C. Comstock, & Associates, *Sanctions for evil: Sources of social destructiveness.* San Francisco: Jossey-Bass.

_____. (1973). *Home from the war—Vietnam veterans: Neither victims nor executioners.* New York: Simon & Schuster.

Manual for courts martial, United States (rev. ed.). (1969). Washington, DC: U.S. Government Printing Office.

Schirmer, D. B. (1971, April 24). My Lai was not the first time. *New Republic,* pp. 18–21.

Williams, B. (1985, April 14–15). "I will never forgive," says My Lai survivor. *Jordan Times* (Amman), p. 4.

THINKING ABOUT THE READING

According to Kelman and Hamilton, social processes can create conditions under which usual restraints against violence are weakened. What social processes were in evidence during the My Lai massacre? The incident they describe provides us with an uncomfortable picture of human nature. Do you think most people would have reacted the way the soldiers at My Lai did? Are we all potential massacrers? Does the phenomenon of obedience to authority go beyond the tightly structured environment of the military? Can you think of incidents in your own life when you've done something—perhaps harmed or humiliated another person—because of the powerful influence of others? How might Kelman and Hamilton explain the actions of the individuals who carried out the hijackings and attacks of September 11, 2001, or of the American soldiers who abused Iraqi prisoners in their custody?

The Mundanity of Excellence
An Ethnographic Report on Stratification and Olympic Swimmers

Daniel F. Chambliss

(1989)

Olympic sports and competitive swimming in particular provide an unusually clear opportunity for studying the nature of excellence. In other fields, it may be less clear who are the outstanding performers: the best painter or pianist, the best businessperson, the finest waitress or the best father. But in sport (and this is one of its attractions) success is defined more exactly, by success in competition. There are medals and ribbons and plaques for first place, second, and third; competitions are arranged for the head-to-head meeting of the best competitors in the world; in swimming and track, times are electronically recorded to the hundredth of a second; there are statistics published and rankings announced, every month or every week. By the end of the Olympic Games every four years, it is completely clear who won and who lost, who made the finals, who participated in the Games, and who never participated in the sport at all.

Within competitive swimming in particular, clear stratification exists not only between individuals but also between defined levels of the sport as well. At the lowest level, we see the country club teams, operating in the summertime as a loosely run, mildly competitive league, with volunteer, part-time coaches. Above that there are teams that represent entire cities and compete with other teams from other cities around the state or region; then a "Junior Nationals" level of competition, featuring the best younger (under 18 years old) athletes; then the Senior Nationals level (any

age, the best in the nation); and finally, we could speak of world- or Olympic-class competitors. At each such level, we find, predictably, certain people competing: one athlete swims in a summer league, never seeing swimmers from another town; one swimmer may consistently qualify for the Junior Nationals, but not for Seniors; a third may swim at the Olympics and never return to Junior Nationals. The levels of the sport are remarkably distinct from one another.

. . . Because success in swimming is so definable, . . . we can clearly see, by comparing levels and studying individuals as they move between and within levels, what exactly produces excellence. In addition, careers in swimming are relatively short; one can achieve tremendous success in a brief period of time. Rowdy Gaines, beginning in the sport when 17 years old, jumped from a country club league to a world record in the 100 meter freestyle event in only three years. This allows the researcher to conduct true longitudinal research in a few short years. . . .

. . . This report draws on extended experience with swimmers at every level of ability, over some half a dozen years. Observation has covered the span of careers, and I have had the chance to compare not just athletes within a certain level (the view that most coaches have), but between the most discrepant levels as well. Thus these findings avoid the usual . . . problem of an observer's being familiar mainly with athletes at one level. . . .

The Nature of Excellence

By "excellence" I mean "consistent superiority of performance." The excellent athlete regularly, even routinely, performs better than his or her competitors. Consistency of superior performances tells us that one athlete is indeed better than another, and that the difference between them is not merely the product of chance. This definition can apply at any level of the sport, differentiating athletes. The superiority discussed here may be that of one swimmer over another, or of all athletes at one level (say, the Olympic class) over another. By this definition, we need not judge performance against an absolute criterion, but only against other performances. There are acknowledged leaders on every team, as well as teams widely recognized as dominant.

To introduce what are sources of excellence for Olympic athletes, I should first suggest saving the demonstration for later—what *does not* produce excellence.

(1) Excellence is not, I find, the product of socially deviant personalities. These swimmers don't appear to be "oddballs," nor are they loners ("kids who have given up the normal teenage life").[1] If their achievements result from a personality characteristic, that characteristic is not obvious. Perhaps it is true, as the mythology of sports has it, that the best athletes are more self-confident (although that is debatable); but such confidence could be an effect of achievement, not the cause of it.[2]

(2) Excellence does *not* result from quantitative changes in behavior. Increased training time, *per se*, does not make one swim fast; nor does increased "psyching up," nor does moving the arms faster. Simply doing more of the same will not lead to moving up a level in the sport.

(3) Excellence does *not* result from some special inner quality of the athlete. "Talent" is one common name for this quality; sometimes we talk of a "gift," or of "natural ability." These terms are generally used to mystify the essentially mundane processes of achievement in sports, keeping us away from a realistic analysis of the actual factors creating superlative performances, and protecting us from a sense of responsibility for our own outcomes.

So where does excellence—consistent superiority of performance—come from?

I. Excellence Requires Qualitative Differentiation

Excellence in competitive swimming is achieved through qualitative differentiation from other swimmers, not through quantitative increases in activity. . . .

. . . I should clarify what is meant here by "quantitative" and "qualitative." By quantity, we mean the number or amount of something. Quantitative improvement entails an increase in the number of some one thing one does. An athlete who practices 2 hours a day and increases that activity to 4 hours a day has made a quantitative change in behavior. Or, one who swims 5 miles and changes to 7 miles has made a quantitative change. She does more of the same thing; there is an increase in quantity. Or again, a freestyle swimmer who, while maintaining the same stroke technique, moves his arms at an increased number of strokes per minute has made a quantitative change in behavior. Quantitative improvements, then, involve doing *more of the same thing*.

By quality, though, we mean the character or nature of the thing itself. A qualitative change involves modifying what is actually being done, not simply doing more of it. For a swimmer doing the breaststroke, a qualitative change might be a change from pulling straight back with the arms to sculling them outwards, to the sides; or from lifting oneself up out of the water at the turn to staying low near the water. Other qualitative changes might include competing in a regional meet instead of local meets; eating vegetables and complex carbohydrates rather than fats and sugars; entering one's weaker events instead of only one's stronger events; learning to do a flip turn with freestyle, instead of merely turning around and pushing off; or training at near-competition levels of intensity, rather than casually. Each of these involves doing things differently than before, not necessarily doing more. Qualitative improvements involve doing *different kinds of things*.

Now we can consider how qualitative differentiation is manifested:

Different levels of the sport are qualitatively distinct. Olympic champions don't just do much more of the same things that summer-league country club swimmers do. They don't just swim more hours, or move their arms faster, or attend more workouts. What makes them faster cannot be quantitatively compared with lower-level swimmers, because while there may be quantitative differences—and certainly there are, for instance in the number of hours spent in workouts—these are not, I think, the decisive factors at all.[3]

Instead, they do things differently. Their strokes are different, their attitudes are different, their groups of friends are different, their parents treat the sport differently, the swimmers prepare differently for their races, and they enter different kinds of meets and events. There are numerous discontinuities of this sort between, say, the swimmer who competes in a local City League meet and one who enters the Olympic Trials. Consider three dimensions of difference:

(1) Technique: The styles of strokes, dives and turns are dramatically different at different levels. A "C" (the lowest rank in United States Swimming's ranking system) breast-stroke swimmer tends to pull her arms far back beneath her, kick the legs out very wide without bringing them together at the finish, lift herself high out of the water on the turn, fail to take a long pull underwater after the turn, and touch at the finish with one hand, on her side. By comparison, an "AAAA" (the highest rank) swimmer, sculls the arms out to the side and sweeps back in (never actually pulling backwards), kicks narrowly with the feet finishing together, stays low on the turns, takes a long underwater pull after the turn, and touches at the finish with both hands. Not only are the strokes different, they are so different that the "C" swimmer may be amazed to see how the "AAAA" swimmer looks when swimming. The appearance alone is dramatically different, as is the speed with which they swim. . . .

(2) Discipline: The best swimmers are more likely to be strict with their training, coming to workouts on time, carefully doing the competitive strokes legally (i.e., without violating the technical rules of the sport),[4] watch what they eat, sleep regular hours, do proper warmups before a meet, and the like. Their energy is carefully channeled. Diver Greg Louganis, who won two Olympic gold medals in 1984, practices only three hours each day—not a long time—divided into two or three sessions. But during each session, he tries to do every dive perfectly. Louganis is never sloppy in practice, and so is never sloppy in meets.[5]

(3) Attitude: At the higher levels of competitive swimming, something like an inversion of attitude takes place. The very features of the sport that the "C" swimmer finds unpleasant, the toplevel swimmer enjoys. What others see as boring—swimming back and forth over a black line for two hours, say—they find peaceful, even meditative,[6] often challenging, or therapeutic. They enjoy hard practices, look forward to difficult competitions, try to set difficult goals. Coming into the 5:30 A.M. practices at Mission Viejo, many of the swimmers were lively, laughing, talking, enjoying themselves, perhaps appreciating the fact that most people would positively hate doing it. It is incorrect to believe that top athletes suffer great sacrifices to

achieve their goals. Often, they don't see what they do as sacrificial at all. They like it.

These qualitative differences are what distinguish levels of the sport. They are very noticeable, while the quantitative differences between levels, both in training and in competition, may be surprisingly small indeed. . . . Yet very small quantitative differences in performance may be coupled with huge qualitative differences: In the finals of the men's 100-meter freestyle swimming event at the 1984 Olympics, Rowdy Gaines, the gold medalist, finished ahead of second-place Mark Stockwell by .44 seconds, a gap of only 8/10 of 1%. Between Gaines and the 8th place finisher (a virtual unknown named Dirk Korthals, from West Germany), there was only a 2.2% difference in time. Indeed, between Rowdy Gaines, the fastest swimmer in the world that year, and a respectable 10-year-old, the quantitative difference in speed would only be about 30%.

Yet here, as in many cases, a rather small *quantitative* difference produces an enormous *qualitative difference:* Gaines was consistently a winner in major international meets, holder of the world record, and the Olympic Gold Medalist in three events.

Stratification in the sport is discrete, not continuous. There are significant, qualitative breaks—discontinuities—between levels of the sport. These include differences in attitude, discipline, and technique which in turn lead to small but consistent quantitative differences in speed. Entire teams show such differences in attitude, discipline, and technique, and consequently certain teams are easily seen to be "stuck" at certain levels.[7] Some teams always do well at the National Championships, others do well at the Regionals, others at the County Meet. And certainly swimmers typically remain within a certain level for most of their careers, maintaining throughout their careers the habits with which they began. Within levels, competitive improvements for such swimmers are typically marginal, reflecting only differential growth rates (early onset of puberty, for instance) or the jockeying for position within the relatively limited sphere of their own level. . . .

. . . Athletes move up to the top ranks through *qualitative jumps:* noticeable changes in their techniques, discipline, and attitude, accomplished usually through a change in settings (e.g., joining a new team with a new coach, new friends, etc.) who work at a higher level. Without such qualitative jumps, no major improvements (movements through levels) will take place. . . .

This is really several worlds, each with its own patterns of conduct. . . . If, as I have suggested, there really are qualitative breaks between levels of the sport, and if people really don't "work their way up" in any simple additive sense, perhaps our very conception of a single swimming world is inaccurate. I have spoken of the "top" of the sport, and of "levels" within the sport. But these words suggest that all swimmers are, so to speak, climbing a single ladder, aiming towards the same goals, sharing the same values, swimming the same strokes, all looking upwards towards an Olympic gold medal. But they aren't.[8] Some want gold medals, some want to make the team, some want to exercise, or have fun with friends, or be out in the sunshine and water. Some are trying to escape their parents. The images of the "top" and the "levels" of swimming which I have used until now may simply reflect the dominance of a certain faction of swimmers and coaches in the sport: top is what *they* regard as the top, and their definitions of success have the broadest political currency in United States Swimming. Fast swimmers take as given that faster is better—instead of, say, that more beautiful is better; or that parental involvement is better; or that "wellrounded" children (whatever that may mean) are better. . . .

So we should envision not a swimming world, but multiple worlds[9] (and changing worlds is a major step toward excellence), a horizontal rather than vertical differentiation of the sport. What I have called "levels" are better described as "worlds" or "spheres." In one such world, parents are loosely in charge, coaches are teenagers employed as lifeguards, practices are held a few times a week, competitions are scheduled perhaps a week in advance, the season lasts for a few weeks in the summertime, and athletes who are much faster than the others may be discouraged by social pressure even from competing, for they take the fun out of it.[10] The big event of the season is the City Championship, when children from the metropolitan area will spend two days racing each other in many events, and the rest of the time sitting under huge tents playing cards, reading, listening to music, and gossiping. In another world, coaches are very powerful, parents seen only occasionally (and never on the pool deck), swimmers travel thousands of miles to attend meets, they swim 6 days a week for years at a time, and the fastest among them are objects of respect and praise. The big event of the season may be the National Championships, where the athletes may spend much time—sitting under huge tents, playing cards, reading, listening to music and gossiping.[11]

Each such world has its own distinctive types of powerful people and dominant athletes, and being prominent in one world is no guarantee of being prominent in another.[12] At lower levels, the parents of swimmers are in charge; at the higher levels, the coaches; perhaps in the Masters teams which are made up only of swimmers over 25 years old, the swimmers themselves. Each world, too, has its distinctive goals: going to the Olympics, doing well at the National Junior Olympics, winning the City Meet, having a good time for a few weeks. In each world the techniques are at least somewhat distinct (as with the breaststroke, discussed above), and certain demands are made on family and friends. In all of these ways, and many more, each so-called "level" of competitive swimming is qualitatively different

than others. The differences are not simply quantifiable steps along a one-dimensional path leading to the Olympic Games. Goals are varied, participants have competing commitments, and techniques are jumbled.

II. Why "Talent" Does Not Lead to Excellence

. . . "Talent" is perhaps the most pervasive lay explanation we have for athletic success. Great athletes, we seem to believe, are born with a special gift, almost a "thing" inside of them, denied to the rest of us—perhaps physical, genetic, psychological, or physiological. Some have "it," and some don't. Some are "natural athletes," and some aren't. While an athlete, we acknowledge, may require many years of training and dedication to develop and use that talent, it is always "in there," only waiting for an opportunity to come out. When children perform well, they are said to "have" talent; if performance declines, they may be said to have "wasted their talent." We believe it is that talent, conceived as a substance behind the surface reality of performance, which finally distinguishes the best among our athletes.

But talent fails as an explanation for athletic success, on conceptual grounds. It mystifies excellence, subsuming a complex set of discrete actions behind a single undifferentiated concept. To understand these actions and the excellence which they constitute, then, we should first debunk this concept of talent and see where it fails. On at least three points, I believe, "talent" is inadequate.

Factors other than talent explain athletic success more precisely. We can, with a little effort, see what these factors are in swimming: geographical location, particularly living in southern California where the sun shines year round and everybody swims; fairly high family income, which allows for the travel to meets and payments of the fees entailed in the sport, not to mention sheer access to swimming pools when one is young; one's height, weight, and proportions; the luck or choice of having a good coach, who can teach the skills required; inherited muscle structure—it certainly helps to be both strong and flexible; parents who are interested in sports. Some swimmers, too, enjoy more the physical pleasures of swimming; some have better coordination; some even have a higher percentage of fast-twitch muscle fiber. Such factors are clearly definable, and their effects can be clearly demonstrated. To subsume all of them, willynilly, under the rubric of "talent" obscures rather than illuminates the sources of athletic excellence.

It's easy to do this, especially if one's only exposure to top athletes comes once every four years while watching the Olympics on television, or if one only sees them in performances rather than in day-to-day training. Say, for instance, that one day I turn on the television set and there witness a magnificent figure skating performance by Scott Hamilton. What I see is grace and power and skill all flowing together, seemingly without effort; a single moving picture, rapid and sure, far beyond what I could myself do. . . . "His skating," I may say, referring to his actions as a single thing, "is spectacular." With that quick shorthand, I have captured (I believe) at a stroke the wealth of tiny details that Hamilton, over years and years, has fitted together into a performance so smoothly that they become invisible to the untrained eye.[13] Perhaps, with concentration, Hamilton himself can feel the details in his movements; certainly a great coach can see them, and pick out the single fault or mistake in an otherwise flawless routine. But to me, the performance is a thing entire.

Afterwards, my friends and I sit and talk about Hamilton's life as a "career of excellence," or as showing "incredible dedication," "tremendous motivation"—again, as if his excellence, his dedication, his motivation somehow exist all-at-once. His excellence becomes a thing inside of him which he periodically reveals to

us, which comes out now and then; his life and habits become reified. "Talent" is merely the word we use to label this reification.

But that is no explanation of success.

Talent is indistinguishable from its effects. One cannot see that talent exists until after its effects become obvious. Kalinowski's research on Olympic swimmers demonstrates this clearly.

> One of the more startling discoveries of our study has been that it takes a while to recognize swimming talent. Indeed, it usually takes being successful at a regional level, and more often, at a national level (in AAU swimming) before the child is identified as talented. (p. 173)

> "They didn't say I had talent until I started to get really good [and made Senior Nationals at sixteen]; then they started to say I had talent . . ." (p. 174)

> . . . despite the physical capabilities he was born with, it took Peter several years (six by our estimate) to appear gifted. This is the predominant, though not exclusive, pattern found in our data on swimmers. Most of them are said to be "natural" or "gifted" after they had already devoted a great deal of time and hard work to the field. (p. 194)

> . . . whatever superior qualities were attributed to him as he grew older and more successful, they were not apparent then [before he was thirteen]. (p. 200)

The above quotations suggest that talent is *discovered* later in one's career, the implication being that while the athlete's ability *existed* all along, we were unaware of it until late. Kalinowski, like many of us, holds to the belief that there must be this thing inside the athlete which precedes and determines success, only later to be discovered. But the recurring evidence he finds suggests a different interpretation: perhaps there is no such thing as "talent," there is only the outstanding performance itself. He sees success and immediately infers behind it a cause, a cause *for which he has no evidence other than the success itself.* Here, as elsewhere, talent (our name for this cause) cannot be measured, or seen, or felt in any form other than the success to which it supposedly gives rise. . . .

The "amount" of talent needed for athletic success seems to be strikingly low. It seems initially plausible that one must have a certain level of natural ability in order to succeed in sports (or music or academics). But upon empirical examination, it becomes very difficult to say exactly what that physical minimum is. Indeed, much of the mythology of sport is built around people who lack natural ability who went on to succeed fabulously. An entire genre of inspirational literature is built on the theme of the person whose even normal natural abilities have been destroyed: Wilma Rudolph had polio as a child, then came back to win the Olympic 100-Meter Dash. Glenn Cunningham had his legs badly burned in a fire, then broke the world record in the mile. Such stories are grist for the sportswriter's mill.

More than merely common, these stories are almost routine. Most Olympic champions, when their history is studied, seem to have overcome sharp adversity in their pursuit of success. Automobile accidents, shin splints, twisted ankles, shoulder surgery are common in such tales. In fact, they are common in life generally. While some necessary minimum of physical strength, heart/lung capacity, or nerve density may well be required for athletic achievement (again, I am *not* denying differential advantages), that minimum seems both difficult to define and markedly low, at least in many cases. Perhaps the crucial factor is not natural ability at all, but the willingness to overcome natural or unnatural disabilities of the sort that most of us face, ranging from minor inconveniences in getting up and going to work, to accidents and injuries, to gross physical impairments.

And if the basic level of talent needed, then, seems so low as to be nearly universally available, perhaps the very concept of talent itself—no longer differentiating among performers—is better discarded altogether. It simply doesn't explain the differences in outcomes. Rather than talk about talent and ability, we do better to look at what people actually do that creates outstanding performance.

The concept of talent hinders a clear understanding of excellence. By providing a quick . . . "explanation" of athletic success, it satisfies our casual curiosity while requiring neither an empirical analysis nor a critical questioning of our tacit assumptions about top athletes. At best, it is an easy way of admitting that we don't know the answer. . . . But the attempt at explanation fails. . . . Through the notion of talent, we transform particular actions that a human being does into an object possessed, held in trust for the day when it will be revealed for all to see.

This line of thought leads to one more step. Since talent can be viewed only indirectly in the effects that it supposedly produces, its very existence is a matter of faith. The basic dogma of "talent" says that what people do in this world has a cause lying behind them, that there is a kind of backstage reality where the real things happen, and what we—you and I—see here in our lives (say, the winning of a gold medal) is really a reflection of that true reality back there. Those of us who are not admitted to the company of the elect—the talented—can never see what that other world of fabulous success is really like, and can never share those experiences. And accepting this faith in talent, I suggest, we relinquish our chance of accurately understanding excellence. . . .

III. The Mundanity of Excellence

"People don't know how ordinary success is," said Mary T. Meagher, winner of 3 gold medals in the Los Angeles Olympics, when asked what the public least understands about her sport.

She then spoke of starting her career in a summer league country club team, of working her way to AAU meets, to faster and faster competitions, of learning new techniques, practicing new habits, meeting new challenges.[14] What Meagher said—that success is ordinary—in some sense applies, I believe, to other fields of endeavor as well: to business, to politics, to professions of all kinds, including academics. In what follows I will try to elaborate on this point, drawing some examples from the swimming research, and some from other fields, to indicate the scope of this conception.

Excellence is mundane. Superlative performance is really a confluence of dozens of small skills or activities, each one learned or stumbled upon, which have been carefully drilled into habit and then are fitted together in a synthesized whole. There is nothing extraordinary or superhuman in any one of those actions; only the fact that they are done consistently and correctly, and all together, produce excellence. When a swimmer learns a proper flip turn in the freestyle races, she will swim the race a bit faster; then a streamlined push off from the wall, with the arms squeezed together over the head, and a little faster; then how to place the hands in the water so no air is cupped in them; then how to lift them over the water; then how to lift weights to properly build strength, and how to eat the right foods, and to wear the best suits for racing, and on and on.[15] Each of those tasks seems small in itself, but each allows the athlete to swim a bit faster. And having learned and consistently practiced all of them together, and many more besides, the swimmer may compete in the Olympic Games. The winning of a gold medal is nothing more than the synthesis of a countless number of such little things—even if some of them are done unwittingly or by others, and thus called "luck."

So the "little things" really do count. We have already seen how a very small (in quantitative terms) difference can produce a noticeable success. Even apparent flukes can lead to gold medal performances:

In the 100-Meter Freestyle event in Los Angeles, Rowdy Gaines, knowing that the starter for the race tended to fire the gun fast, anticipated the start; while not actually jumping the gun, it seems from video replays of the race that Gaines knew exactly when to go, and others were left on the blocks as he took off. But the starter turned his back, and the protests filed afterwards by competitors were ignored. Gaines had spent years watching starters, and had talked with his coach (Richard Quick) before the race about this starter in particular. (Field notes; see Chambliss, 1988, for full description)

Gaines was not noticeably faster than several of the other swimmers in the race, but with this one extra tactic, he gained enough of an advantage to win the race. And he seemed in almost all of his races to find such an advantage; hence the gold medal. Looking at such subtleties, we can say that not only are the little things important; in some ways, the little things are the only things. . . .

In swimming, or elsewhere, these practices might at first glance seem very minimal indeed:

When Mary T. Meagher was 13 years old and had qualified for the National Championships, she decided to try to break the world record in the 200-Meter Butterfly race. She made two immediate qualitative changes in her routine: first, she began coming on time to all practices. She recalls now, years later, being picked up at school by her mother and driving (rather quickly) through the streets of Louisville, Kentucky, trying desperately to make it to the pool on time. That habit, that discipline, she now says, gave her the sense that every minute of practice time counted. And second, she began doing all of her turns, during those practices, correctly, in strict accordance with the competitive rules. Most swimmers don't do this; they turn rather casually, and tend to touch with one hand instead of two (in the butterfly, Meagher's stroke). This, she says, accustomed her to doing things one step better than those around her—always. Those are the two major changes she made in her training, as she remembers it.[16]

Meagher made two quite mundane changes in her habits, either one of which anyone could do, if he or she wanted. Within a year Meagher had broken the world record in the butterfly. . . .

Motivation is mundane, too. Swimmers go to practice to see their friends, to exercise, to feel strong afterwards, to impress the coach, to work towards bettering a time they swam in the last meet. Sometimes, the older ones, with a longer view of the future, will aim towards a meet that is still several months away. But even given the longer-term goals, the daily satisfactions need to be there. The mundane social rewards really are crucial (see Chambliss, 1988, Chapter 6). By comparison, the big, dramatic motivations— winning an Olympic gold medal, setting a world record—seem to be ineffective unless translated into shorter-term tasks. Viewing "Rocky" or "Chariots of Fire" may inspire one for several days, but the excitement stirred by a film wears off rather quickly when confronted with the day-to-day reality of climbing out of bed to go and jump in cold water. If, on the other hand, that day-to-day reality is itself fun, rewarding, challenging; if the water is nice and friends are supportive, the longer-term goals may well be achieved almost in spite of themselves. Again, Mary T. Meagher:

> I never looked beyond the next year, and I never looked beyond the next level. I never thought about the Olympics when I was ten; at that time I was thinking about the State Championships. When I made cuts for Regionals [the next higher level of competition], I started thinking about Regionals; when I made cuts for National Junior Olympics, I started thinking about National Junior Olympics . . . I can't even think about the [1988] Olympics right now. . . . Things can overwhelm you if you think too far ahead. (Interview notes)

This statement was echoed by many of the swimmers I interviewed. While many of them were working towards the Olympic Games, they divided the work along the way into achievable steps, no one of which was too big. They found their challenges in small things: working on a better start this week, polishing up their backstroke technique next week, focusing on better sleep habits, planning how to pace their swim. . . .

. . . Many top swimmers are accustomed to winning races in practice, day after day. Steve Lundquist, who won two gold medals in Los Angeles, sees his success as resulting from an early decision that he wanted to win every swim, every day, in every practice. That was the immediate goal he faced at workouts; just try to win every swim, every lap, in every stroke, no matter what. Lundquist gained a reputation in swimming for being a ferocious workout swimmer, one who competed all the time, even in the warmup. He became so accustomed to winning that he entered meets knowing that he could beat these people—he had developed the habit, every day, of never losing. The short-term goal of winning this swim, in this work-out, translated into his ability to win bigger and bigger races. Competition, when the day arrived for a meet, was not a shock to him, nothing at all out of the ordinary.[17]

This leads to a third and final point.

In the pursuit of excellence, maintaining mundanity is the key psychological challenge. In common parlance, winners don't choke. Faced with what seems to be a tremendous challenge or a strikingly unusual event, such as the Olympic Games, the better athletes take it as a normal, manageable situation[18] ("It's just another swim meet," is a phrase sometimes used by top swimmers at a major event such as the Games) and do what is necessary to deal with it. Standard rituals (such as the warmup, the psych, the visualization of the race, the taking off of sweats, and the like) are ways of importing one's daily habits into the novel situation, to make it as normal an event as possible.

Swimmers like Lundquist, who train at competition-level intensity, therefore have an advantage: arriving at a meet, they are already accustomed to doing turns correctly, taking legal starts, doing a proper warmup, and being aggressive from the outset of the competition. If each day of the season is approached with a seriousness of purpose, then the big meet will not come as a shock. The athlete will believe "I belong here, this is my world"—and not be paralyzed by fear or self-consciousness. The task then is to have training closely approximate competition conditions. . . .

The mundanity of excellence is typically unrecognized. I think the reason is fairly simple. Usually we see great athletes only after they have become great—after the years of learning the new methods, gaining the habits of competitiveness and consistency, after becoming comfortable in their world. They have long since perfected the myriad of techniques that together constitute excellence. Ignorant of all of the specific steps that have led to the performance and to the confidence, we think that somehow excellence sprang full grown from this person, and we say he or she "has talent" or "is gifted." Even when seen close up, the mundanity of excellence is often not believed:

> Every week at the Mission Viejo training pool, where the National Champion Nadadores team practiced, coaches from around the world would be on the deck visiting, watching as the team did their workouts, swimming back and forth for hours. The visiting coaches would be excited at first, just to be here; then soon—within an hour or so usually—they grew bored, walking back and forth looking at the deck, glancing around at the hills around the town, reading the bulletin boards, glancing down at their watches, wondering, after the long flight out to California, when something dramatic was going to happen. "They all have to come to Mecca, and see what we do," coach Mark Schubert said. "They think we have some big secret." (Field notes)

But of course there is no secret; there is only the doing of all those little things, each one done correctly, time and again, until excellence in every detail becomes a firmly ingrained habit, an ordinary part of one's everyday life.

Conclusions

The foregoing analysis suggests that we have overlooked a fundamental fact about Olympic class athletes; and the argument may apply far more widely than swimming, or sports. I suggest that it applies to success in business, politics, and academics, in dentistry, bookkeeping, food service, speechmaking, electrical engineering, selling insurance (when the clients are upset, you climb in the car and go out there to talk with them), and perhaps even in the arts.[19] Consider again the major points:

(1) *Excellence is a qualitative phenomenon.* Doing more does not equal doing better. High performers focus on qualitative, not quantitative, improvements; it is qualitative improvements which produce significant changes in level of achievement; different levels of achievement really are distinct, and in fact reflect vastly different habits, values, and goals.

(2) *Talent is a useless concept.* Varying conceptions of natural ability ("talent," e.g.) tend to mystify excellence, treating it as the inherent possession of a few; they mask the concrete actions that create outstanding performance; they avoid the work of empirical analysis and logical explanations (clear definitions, separable independent and dependent variables, and at least an attempt at establishing the temporal priority of the cause); and finally, such conceptions perpetuate the sense of innate psychological differences between high performers and other people.

(3) *Excellence is mundane.* Excellence is accomplished through the doing of actions, ordinary in themselves, performed consistently and carefully, habitualized, compounded

together, added up over time. While these actions are "qualitatively different" from those of performers at other levels, these differences are neither unmanageable nor, taken one step at a time, terribly difficult. Mary T. Meagher came to practice on time; some writers always work for three hours each morning, before beginning anything else; a businessperson may go ahead and make that tough phone call; a job applicant writes one more letter; a runner decides, against the odds, to enter the race; a county commissioner submits a petition to run for Congress; a teenager asks for a date; an actor attends one more audition. Every time a decision comes up, the qualitatively "correct" choice will be made. The action, in itself, is nothing special; the care and consistency with which it is made is.

Howard Becker has presented a similar argument about the ordinariness of apparently unusual people in his book *Outsiders* (1961). But where he speaks of deviance, I would speak of excellence. Becker says, and I concur:

> We ought not to view it as something special, as depraved or in some magical way better than other kinds of behavior. We ought to see it simply as a kind of behavior some disapprove of and others value, studying the processes by which either or both perspectives are built up and maintained. Perhaps the best surety against either extreme is close contact with the people we study. (Becker, p. 176)

After three years of field work with world-class swimmers, having the kind of close contact that Becker recommends, I wrote a draft of some book chapters, full of stories about swimmers, and I showed it to a friend. "You need to jazz it up," he said. "You need to make these people more interesting. The analysis is nice, but except for the fact that these are good swimmers, there isn't much else exciting to say about them as individuals." He was right, of course. What these athletes do was rather interesting, but the people themselves were

only fast swimmers, who did the particular things one does to swim fast. It is all very mundane. When my friend said that they weren't exciting, my best answer could only be, simply put: *That's the point.*

NOTES

The author wishes to thank Randall Collins and Gary Alan Fine for their comments on an earlier draft of this paper.

1. In fact, if anything they are more socially bonded and adept than their peers. The process by which this happens fits well with Durkheim's (1965) description of the sources of social cohesion.

2. These issues are addressed at length in "The Social World of Olympic Swimmers." Daniel F. Chambliss, in preparation.

3. True, the top teams work long hours, and swim very long distances, but (1) such workouts often begin after a swimmer achieves national status, not before, and (2) the positive impact of increased yardage seems to come with huge increases, e.g., the doubling of workout distances—in which case one could argue that a *qualitative* jump has been made. The whole question of "how much yardage to swim" is widely discussed within the sport itself.

Compare the (specious, I think) notion that a longer school day/term/year will produce educational improvements.

4. One day at Mission Viejo, with some sixty swimmers going back and forth the length of a 50-meter pool, coach Mark Schubert took one boy out of the water and had him do twenty pushups before continuing the workout. The boy had touched the wall with one hand at the end of a breaststroke swim. The rules require a two-handed touch.

One hundred and twenty hands should have touched, one hundred and nineteen *did* touch, and this made Schubert angry. He pays attention to details.

5. From an interview with his coach, Ron O'Brien.

6. Distance swimmers frequently compare swimming to meditation.

7. For example: several well-known teams consistently do well at the National Junior Olympics ("Junior Nationals," as it is called informally), and

yet never place high in the team standings at the National Championships ("Senior Nationals"), the next higher meet.

These teams actually prevent their swimmers from going to the better meet, holding them in store for the easier meet so that the team will do better at that lesser event. In this way, and in many others, teams choose their own level of success.

8. March and Olsen make a similar point with regard to educational institutions and organizations in general: organizations include a variety of constituents with differing goals, plans, motivations, and values. Unity of purpose, even with organizations, cannot simply be assumed. Coherence, not diversity, is what needs explaining. March and Olsen, 1976.

9. See Shibutani in Rose, 1962, on "social worlds." Blumer, 1969.

10. These fast swimmers who come to slow meets are called hot dogs, showoffs, or even jerks. (Personal observations.)

11. Again, personal observations from a large number of cases. While there are significant differences between swimmers of the Olympic class and a country club league, the basic sociability of their worlds is not one of them.

12. "Indeed, prestige ladders in the various worlds are so different that a man who reaches the pinnacle of success in one may be completely unknown elsewhere." Shibutani in Rose, 1962.

Similarly in academia: one may be a successful professor at the national level and yet find it difficult to gain employment at a minor regional university. Professors at the regional school may suspect his/her motives, be jealous, feel that he/she "wouldn't fit in," "won't stay anyway," etc. Many top-school graduate students discover upon entering the markets that noname colleges have no interest in them; indeed, by attending a Chicago or Harvard Ph.D. program one may limit oneself to the top ranks of employment opportunities.

13. "Now, no one can see in an artist's work how it evolved: that is its advantage, for wherever we can see the evolution, we grow somewhat cooler. The complete art of representation wards off all thought of its solution; it tyrannizes as present perfection" (Nietzsche, 1984, p. 111).

14. Meagher's entire career is described in detail in Chambliss, 1988.

15. Such techniques are thoroughly explained in Maglischo (1982) and Troup and Reese (1983).

16. Interview notes.

17. Interview notes.

18. An interesting parallel: some of the most successful generals have no trouble sleeping before and after major battles. For details on Ulysses Grant and the Duke of Wellington, see Keegan, p. 207. 19. Professor Margaret Bates, an opera enthusiast, tells me that this "mundanity of excellence" argument applies nicely to Enrico Caruso, the great singer, who carefully perfected each ordinary detail of his performance in an effort to overcome a recognized lack of "natural ability."

REFERENCES

Blumer, Herbert. 1969. *Symbolic Interactionism.* Englewood Cliffs: Prentice Hall.

Chambliss, Daniel F. 1988. *Champions: The Making of Olympic Swimmers.* New York: Morrow.

Durkheim, Emile. 1965. *The Elementary Forms of the Religious Life.* New York: Free Press.

Kalinowsky, Anthony G. "The Development of Olympic Swimmers," and "One Olympic Swimmer," in Bloom (1985), pp. 139–210.

Keegan, John. 1987. *The Mask of Command.* New York: Viking.

Maglischo, Ernest W. 1982. *Swimming Faster.* Palo Alto: Mayfield.

March, James G. and Olsen, Johan P. 1976. *Ambiguity and Choice in Organizations.* Bergen, Norway: Universitetsforlaget.

Nietzsche, Friedrich. 1984. *Human, All Too Human.* Lincoln.: University of Nebraska Press.

Shibutani, T. "Reference Groups and Social Control," in Rose, Arnold M. 1962. *Human Behavior and Social Process.* Boston: Houghton Mifflin, pp. 128–147.

Troup, John and Reese, Randy. 1983. *A Scientific Approach to the Sport of Swimming.* Gainesville, FL: Scientific Sports.

THINKING ABOUT THE READING

Why does Chambliss feel that "talent" is a useless concept in explaining success among world-class swimmers? Where, instead, does he think that athletic excellence comes from? Why do you suppose we have such a strong tendency to focus on "talent" or "natural ability" in explaining superior performances? If it's true, as Chambliss suggests, that factors such as geographical location, high family income and interest, and the luck of having a good coach can all play an important role in creating world-class swimmers, then there are probably many potentially successful athletes who don't have the opportunity to excel in certain sports because of their social circumstances. Relatively few inner-city kids grow up to succeed in "wealthy" sports like swimming, tennis, and golf. On the other hand, the inner city produces many of the world's best basketball, football, and track stars. What sorts of social circumstances encourage success in these sports? Can you identify other areas of life (other than sports, that is) where achievement might similarly be affected by the kinds of social circumstances described in this article?

PART II

The Construction of
Self and Society

Building Reality

The Social Construction of Knowledge

ociologists often talk about reality as a *social construction*. What they mean is that truth and knowledge are discovered, communicated, reinforced, and changed by members of society. Truth doesn't just fall from the sky and hit us on the head. What is considered truth or knowledge is specific to a given culture. All cultures have certain rules for determining what counts as good and right and true. As social beings, we respond to our interpretations and definitions of situations, not to the situations themselves. We learn what sorts of interpretations are expected and reasonable from our cultural environment. Thus, we make sense of situations and events in our lives by applying culturally shared definitions and interpretations. In this way, we distinguish fact from fantasy, truth from fiction, myth from reality. This process of interpretation or "meaning making" is tied to interpersonal interaction, group membership, culture, history, power, economics, religion, and politics.

Cultures also have rules for who the "keepers of truth" are. Not all of us possess the same ability to define reality. Individuals and groups in positions of power have the ability to control information, define values, create myths, manipulate events, and ultimately influence what others take for granted. In contemporary society the mass media are especially influential in shaping perceptions of reality.

In "The Crack Attack," Craig Reinarman and Harry Levine show us how the news media function to *create* a reality that the public takes for granted. They focus, in particular, on the emergence of "the crack problem" in American society. In the late 1980s, crack, a cocaine derivative, came to be seen as one of the most evil scourges on the social landscape. Even today we hear it described with terms like *plague* and *epidemic*. We hear horror stories about crack babies—children born addicted to the drug—whose lives are marked by emotional, intellectual, and behavioral suffering. But Reinarman and Levine point out that the terrified public concern over crack—the reality of the crack problem—is as much a function of media publicity, political opportunism, and the class, race, and ethnicity of crack users as it is a consequence of the actual chemical power and physical danger of the substance itself. In this sense, media representations don't merely reflect some "objective" reality, they actually help to create it.

Discovering truth and determining useful knowledge are the goals of any academic discipline. The purpose of an academic field such as sociology is to provide the public with useful and relevant information about how society works. This task is typically accomplished through systematic social research—experiments, field research, unobtrusive research, and surveys. But gathering trustworthy data can be difficult.

People sometimes lie or have difficulty recalling past events in their lives. Sometimes the simple fact of observing people's behavior changes that behavior. And sometimes the information needed to answer questions about important, controversial issues is hard to obtain without raising ethical issues.

Moreover, sometimes the very characteristics and phenomena we're interested in understanding are difficult to observe and measure. Unlike other disciplines in, say, the natural sciences, sociologists deal with concepts that can't be seen and touched. In "Concepts, Indicators, and Reality," Earl Babbie give us a brief introduction to some of the problems researchers face when they try to transform important, but abstract, concepts into *indicators* (things that researchers can systematically quantify so they can generate statistical information). In so doing, he shows us that although sociologists provide us with useful empirical findings about the world in which we live, an understanding of the measurement difficulties they face will provide us with the critical eye of an informed consumer as we go about digesting research information.

Something to Consider as You Read:

Babbie's comments also remind us that even scientists must make decisions about how to interpret and define information. Thus, scientists, working within academic communities, define truth and knowledge. This knowledge is often significant and useful. But we need to remember that knowledge is the construction of a group of people following particular rules, not something that is just "out there." When reading the two selections in this section, consider the kind of rules scientists use in deciding if something is worth studying. What rules do media journalists use in deciding whether a story is interesting? What role might politics play in decisions of both science and the media about what topics to focus on? In your assessment, what makes one more or less truthful than the other?

The Crack Attack

Politics and Media in the Crack Scare

Craig Reinarman and Harry G. Levine

(1997)

America discovered crack and overdosed on oratory.

—*New York Times* (Editorial, October 4, 1988)

This *New York Times* editorial had a certain unintended irony, for "America's paper of record" itself had long been one of the leading orators, supplying a steady stream of the stuff on which the nation had, as they put it, "overdosed." Irony aside, the editorial hit the mark. The use of powder cocaine by affluent people in music, film, sports, and business had been common since the 1970s. According to surveys by the National Institute on Drug Abuse (NIDA), by 1985, more than twenty-two million Americans in all social classes and occupations had reported at least trying cocaine. Cocaine smoking originated with "freebasing," which began increasing by the late 1970s (see Inciardi, 1987; Siegel, 1982). Then (as now) most cocaine users bought cocaine hydrochloride (powder) for intranasal use (snorting). But by the end of the 1970s, some users had begun to "cook" powder cocaine down to crystalline or "base" form for smoking. All phases of freebasing, from selling to smoking, took place most often in the privacy of homes and offices of middle-class or well-to-do users. They typically purchased cocaine in units of a gram or more costing $80 to $100 a gram. These relatively affluent "basers" had been discovering the intense rush of smoking cocaine, as well as the risks, for a number of years before the term

"crack" was coined. But most such users had a stake in conventional life. Therefore, when they felt their cocaine use was too heavy or out of control, they had the incentives and resources to cut down, quit, or get private treatment.

There was no orgy of media and political attention in the late 1970s when the prevalence of cocaine use jumped sharply, or even after middle-class and upper-class users began to use heavily, especially when freebasing. Like the crack users who followed them, basers had found that this mode of ingesting cocaine produced a much more intense and far shorter "high" because it delivered more pure cocaine into the brain far more directly and rapidly than by snorting. Many basers had found that crack's intense, brutally brief rush, combined with the painful "low" or "down" that immediately followed, produced a powerful desire immediately to repeat use—to binge (Waldorf et al., 1991).

Crack's pharmacological power alone does not explain the attention it received. In 1986, politicians and the media focused on crack—and the drug scare began—when cocaine smoking became visible among a "dangerous" group. Crack attracted the attention of politicians and the media because of its downward mobility to and increased visibility in ghettos and barrios. The new users were a different social class, race, and status (Duster, 1970; Washton and Gold, 1987). Crack was sold in smaller, cheaper, precooked units, on ghetto streets, to poorer, younger buyers who were already seen as a threat (*e.g., New York Times,* August 30, 1987; *Newsweek,* November 23, 1987; *Boston Globe,* May 18, 1988). Crack spread cocaine smoking into poor populations already beset with a cornucopia of troubles (Wilson, 1987). These people tended to have fewer bonds to conventional society, less to lose, and far fewer resources to cope with or shield themselves from drug-related problems.

The earliest mass media reference to the new form of cocaine may have been a *Los Angeles Times* article in late 1984 (November 25, p. cc1) on the use of cocaine "rocks" in ghettos and barrios in Los Angeles. By late 1985, the *New York Times* made the national media's first specific reference to "crack" in a story about three teenagers seeking treatment for cocaine abuse (November 17, p. B12). At the start of 1986, crack was known only in a few impoverished neighborhoods in Los Angeles, New York, Miami, and perhaps a few other large cities. . . .

The Frenzy: Cocaine and Crack in the Public Eye

When two celebrity athletes died in what news stories called "crack-related deaths" in the spring of 1986, the media seemed to sense a potential bonanza. Coverage skyrocketed and crack became widely known. "Dramatic footage" of black and Latino men being carted off in chains, or of police breaking down crack house doors, became a near nightly news event. In July 1986 alone, the three major TV networks offered seventy-four evening news segments on drugs, half of these about crack (Diamond et al., 1987; Reeves and Campbell, 1994). In the months leading up to the November elections, a handful of national newspapers and magazines produced roughly a thousand stories discussing crack (Inciardi,

1987, p. 481; Trebach, 1987, pp. 6–16). Like the TV networks, leading news magazines such as *Time* and *Newsweek* seemed determined not to be outdone; each devoted five cover stories to crack and the "drug crisis" in 1986 alone.

In the fall of 1986, the CBS news show *48 Hours* aired a heavily promoted documentary called "48 Hours on Crack Street," which Dan Rather previewed on his evening news show: "Tonight, CBS News takes you to the streets, to the war zone, for an unusual two hours of hands-on horror." Among many shots from hidden cameras was one of New York Senator Alphonse D'Amato and then-U.S. Attorney Rudolf Guiliani, *in cognito,* purchasing crack to dramatize the brazenness of street corner sales in the ghetto. All this was good business for CBS: the program earned the highest Nielsen rating of any similar news show in the previous five years—fifteen million viewers (Diamond et al., 1987, p. 10). Three years later, after poor ratings nearly killed *48 Hours,* the show kicked off its season with a three-hour special, "Return to Crack Street."

The intense media competition for audience shares and advertising dollars spawned many similar shows. Three days after "48 Hours on Crack Street," NBC ran its own prime-time special, "Cocaine Country," which suggested that cocaine and crack use had become pandemic. This was one of dozens of separate stories on crack and cocaine produced by NBC alone—an unprecedented fifteen hours of air time—in the seven months leading up to the 1986 elections (Diamond et al., 1987; Hoffman, 1987). By mid-1986, *Newsweek* claimed that crack was the biggest story since Vietnam and Watergate (June 15, p. 15), and *Time* soon followed by calling crack "the Issue of the Year" (September 22, 1986, p. 25). The words "plague," "epidemic," and "crisis" had become routine. The *New York Times,* for example, did a three-part, front-page series called "The Crack Plague" (June 24, 1988, p. A1).

The crack scare began in 1986, but it waned somewhat in 1987 (a nonelection year).

In 1988, drugs returned to the national stage as stories about the "crack epidemic" again appeared regularly on front pages and TV screens (Reeves and Campbell, 1994). One politician after another reenlisted in the War on Drugs. In that election year, as in 1986, overwhelming majorities of both houses of Congress voted for new antidrug laws with long mandatory prison terms, death sentences, and large increases in funding for police and prisons. The annual federal budget for antidrug efforts surged from less than $2 billion in 1981 to more than $12 billion in 1993. The budget for the Drug Enforcement Administration (DEA) quadrupled between 1981 and 1992 (Massing, 1993). The Bush administration alone spent $45 billion—more than all other presidents since Nixon combined—mostly for law enforcement (Horgan, 1993; Office of National Drug Control Policy, 1992). . . .

An April 1988 ABC News special report termed crack "a plague" that was "eating away at the fabric of America." According to this documentary, Americans spend "$20 billion a year on cocaine," American businesses lose "$60 billion" a year in productivity because their workers use drugs, "the educational system is being undermined" by student drug use, and "the family" is "disintegrating" in the face of this "epidemic." This program did not give its millions of viewers any evidence to support such dramatic claims, but it did give them a powerful *vocabulary of attribution:* "drugs," especially crack, threatened all the central institutions in American life—families, communities, schools, businesses, law enforcement, even national sovereignty.

This media frenzy continued into 1989. Between October 1988 and October 1989, for example, the *Washington Post* alone ran 1565 stories—28,476 column inches—about the drug crisis. Even Richard Harwood (1989), the *Post*'s own ombudsman, editorialized against what he called the loss of "a proper sense of perspective" due to such a "hyperbole epidemic." He said that "politicians are doing a number on people's heads." In the fall of 1989, another major new federal antidrug bill to further increase drug war funding (S-1233) began winding its way through Congress. In September, President Bush's "drug czar," William Bennett, unveiled his comprehensive battle plan, the *National Drug Control Strategy.* His introduction asks, "What . . . accounts for the intensifying drug-related chaos that we see every day in our newspapers and on television? One word explains much of it. That word is *crack.* . . . Crack is responsible for the fact that vast patches of the American urban landscape are rapidly deteriorating" (The White House, 1989, p. 3, original emphasis). . . .

On September 5, 1989, President Bush, speaking from the presidential desk in the Oval Office, announced his plan for achieving "victory over drugs" in his first major prime-time address to the nation, broadcast on all three national television networks. We want to focus on this incident as an example of the way politicians and the media systematically misinformed and deceived the public in order to promote the War on Drugs. During the address, Bush held up to the cameras a clear plastic bag of crack labeled "EVIDENCE." He announced that it was "seized a few days ago in a park across the street from the White House" (*Washington Post,* September 22, 1989, p. A1). Its contents, Bush said, were "turning our cities into battle zones and murdering our children." The president proclaimed that, because of crack and other drugs, he would "more than double" federal assistance to state and local law enforcement (*New York Times,* September 6, 1989, p. A11). The next morning the picture of the president holding a bag of crack was on the front pages of newspapers across America.

About two weeks later, the *Washington Post,* and then National Public Radio and other newspapers, discovered how the president of the United States had obtained his bag of crack. According to White House and DEA officials, "the idea of the President holding up crack was [first] included in some drafts" of his speech.

Bush enthusiastically approved. A White House aide told the *Post* that the president "liked the prop. . . . It drove the point home." Bush and his advisors also decided that the crack should be seized in Lafayette Park across from the White House so the president could say that crack had become so pervasive that it was being sold "in front of the White House" (Isikoff, 1989).

This decision set up a complex chain of events. White House Communications Director David Demarst asked Cabinet Affairs Secretary David Bates to instruct the Justice Department "to find some crack that fit the description in the speech." Bates called Richard Weatherbee, special assistant to Attorney General Dick Thornburgh, who then called James Milford, executive assistant to the DEA chief. Finally, Milford phoned William McMullen, special agent in charge of the DEA's Washington office, and told him to arrange an undercover crack buy near the White House because "evidently, the President wants to show it could be bought anywhere" (Isikoff, 1989).

Despite their best efforts, the top federal drug agents were not able to find anyone selling crack (or any other drug) in Lafayette Park, or anywhere else in the vicinity of the White House. Therefore, in order to carry out their assignment, DEA agents had to entice someone to come to the park to make the sale. Apparently, the only person the DEA could convince was Keith Jackson, an eighteen-year-old African-American high school senior. McMullan reported that it was difficult because Jackson "did not even know where the White House was." The DEA's secret tape recording of the conversation revealed that the teenager seemed baffled by the request: "Where the [expletive deleted] is the White House?" he asked. Therefore, McMullan told the *Post,* "we had to manipulate him to get him down there. It wasn't easy" (Isikoff, 1989).

The undesirability of selling crack in Lafayette Park was confirmed by men from Washington, D.C., imprisoned for drug selling, and interviewed by National Public Radio. All

agreed that nobody would sell crack there because, among other reasons, there would be no customers. The crack-using population was in Washington's poor African-American neighborhoods some distance from the White House. The *Washington Post* and other papers also reported that the undercover DEA agents had not, after all, actually seized the crack, as Bush had claimed in his speech. Rather, the DEA agents purchased it from Jackson for $2,400 and then let him go.

This incident illustrates how a drug scare distorts and perverts public knowledge and policy. The claim that crack was threatening every neighborhood in America was not based on evidence; after three years of the scare, crack remained predominantly in the inner cities where it began. Instead, this claim appears to have been based on the symbolic political value seen by Bush's speech writers. When they sought, after the fact, to purchase their own crack to prove this point, they found that reality did not match their script. Instead of changing the script to reflect reality, a series of high-level officials instructed federal drug agents to *create* a reality that would fit the script. Finally, the president of the United States displayed the procured prop on national television. Yet, when all this was revealed, neither politicians nor the media were led to question the president's policies or his claims about crack's pervasiveness.

As a result of Bush's performance and all the other antidrug publicity and propaganda, in 1988 and 1989, the drug war commanded more public attention than any other issue. The media and politicians' antidrug crusade succeeded in making many Americans even more fearful of crack and other illicit drugs. A *New York Times/CBS News* poll has periodically asked Americans to identify "the most important problem facing this country today." In January 1985, 23% answered war or nuclear war; less than 1% believed the most important problem was drugs. In September 1989, shortly after the president's speech and the blizzard of drug stories that followed, 64% of those polled believed that drugs were now the most important problem, and only 1% thought that war or nuclear war was most important. Even the *New York Times* declared in a lead editorial that this reversal was "incredible" and then gently suggested that problems like war, "homelessness and the need to give poor children a chance in life" should perhaps be given more attention (September 28, 1989, p. A26).

A year later, during a lull in antidrug speeches and coverage, the percentage citing "drugs" as the nation's top problem had dropped to 10%. Noting this "precipitous fall from a remarkable height," the *Times* observed that an "alliance of Presidents and news directors" shaped public opinion about drugs. Indeed, once the White House let it be known that the president would be giving a prime-time address on the subject, all three networks tripled their coverage of drugs in the two weeks prior to his speech and quadrupled it for a week afterward (*New York Times*, September 6, 1990, p. A11; see also Reeves and Campbell, 1994). All this occurred while nearly every index of drug use was dropping.

The crack scare continued in 1990 and 1991, although with somewhat less media and political attention. By the beginning of 1992— the last year of the Bush administration—the War on Drugs in general, and the crack scare in particular, had begun to decline significantly in prominence and importance. However, even as the drug war was receiving less notice from politicians and the media, it remained institutionalized, bureaucratically powerful, and extremely well funded (especially police, military, and education/propaganda activities).

From the opening shots in 1986 to President Bush's national address in 1989, and through all the stories about "crack babies" in 1990 and 1991, politicians and the media depicted crack as supremely evil—*the* most important cause of America's problems. As recently as February of 1994, a prominent *New York Times* journalist repeated the claim

that "An entire generation is being sacrificed to [crack]" (Staples, 1994). As in all drug scares since the nineteenth-century crusade against alcohol, a core feature of drug war discourse is the *routinization of caricature*—worst cases framed as typical cases, the episodic rhetorically recrafted into the epidemic.

Official Government Evidence

On those rare occasions when politicians and journalists cited statistical evidence to support their claims about the prevalence of crack and other drug use, they usually relied on two basic sources, both funded by the National Institute on Drug Abuse. One was the Drug Abuse Warning Network (DAWN), a monitoring project set up to survey a sample of hospitals, crisis and treatment centers, and coroners across the country about drug-related emergencies and deaths. The other was the National Household Survey on Drug Abuse among general population households and among young people. Other data sources existed, but these usually were either anecdotal, specific to a particular location, or based on a skewed sample. Therefore, we review what these two NIDA data sources had to say about crack because they were the only national data and because they are still considered by experts and claims makers to be the most reliable form of evidence available.

The Drug Abuse Warning Network

DAWN collects data on a whole series of drugs—from amphetamine to aspirin—that might be present in emergencies or fatalities. These data take the form of "mentions." A drug mention is produced when a patient, or someone with a patient, tells attending medical personnel that the patient recently used the drug, or occasionally, if a blood test shows the presence of the drug. These data provided perhaps the only piece of statistical support for the crack scare. They indicated that cocaine was "mentioned" in an increasing number of emergency room episodes in the 1980s. During 1986, as the scare moved into full swing, there were an estimated 51,600 emergency room episodes in which cocaine was mentioned (NIDA, 1993a). In subsequent years, the estimated number of such mentions continued to rise, providing clear cause for concern. By 1989, for example, the estimated number of emergency room episodes in which cocaine was mentioned had more than doubled to 110,000. Although the estimate dropped sharply in 1990 to 80,400, by 1992, it had risen again to 119,800 (NIDA, 1993a).

Unfortunately, the meaning of a mention is ambiguous. In many of these cases, cocaine was probably incidental to the emergency room visit. Such episodes included routine cases in which people went to emergency rooms, for example, after being injured as passengers in auto accidents and in home accidents. Moreover, in most cases, cocaine was only one of the drugs in the person's system; most people had also been drinking alcohol. Finally, the DAWN data do not include information about preexisting medical or mental health conditions that make any drug use, legal or illegal, more risky. For all these reasons, one cannot properly infer direct cause from the estimates of emergency room mentions. Cocaine did play a causal role in many of these emergency cases, but no one knows how many or what proportion of the total they were.

The DAWN data on deaths in which cocaine was mentioned by medical examiners also must be closely examined. When the crack scare got under way in 1986, coroners coded 1092 deaths as "cocaine related" (NIDA, 1986a), and as crack spread, this number, too, increased substantially. In 1989, the secretary of health and human services reported a 20% decline in both deaths and emergency room episodes in which cocaine was mentioned, but both indices rose again in 1991 and 1992. The 1992 DAWN figures showed 3020 deaths in which cocaine was mentioned (NIDA, 1992).

But cocaine *alone* was mentioned in only a fraction of these deaths; in 1986, for example, in less than one in five (NIDA, 1986a). In most of these cases, cocaine had been used with other drugs, again, most often alcohol. Although any death is tragic, cocaine's role in such fatalities remains ambiguous. "Cocaine related" is not the same as "cocaine caused," and "cocaine-related deaths" does not mean "deaths *due to* cocaine." There is little doubt that cocaine contributes to some significant (but unknown) percentage of such deaths. But journalists, politicians, and most of the experts on whom they relied never acknowledged the ambiguities in the data. Nor did they commonly provide any comparative perspective. For example, for every *one* cocaine-related death in the U.S., there have been approximately two hundred tobacco-related deaths and at least fifty alcohol-related deaths. Seen in this light, cocaine's role in mortality and morbidity was substantially less than media accounts and political rhetoric implied.

More serious interpretive and empirical difficulties appeared when the DAWN data were used to support claims about crack. Despite all the attention paid to the crack "plague" in 1986, when crack was allegedly "killing a whole generation," the DAWN data contained *no specific information on crack* as distinct from cocaine. In fact, the DAWN data show that in the vast majority of both emergencies and deaths in which cocaine received a mention, the mode of ingestion of cocaine was *not* "smoking" and therefore could not have been caused by crack. Thus, although it is likely that crack played a role in some of the emergencies and deaths in which cocaine was "mentioned," the data necessary to attribute them accurately to crack did not exist.

NIDA Surveys

The NIDA-sponsored surveys of drug use produce the data that are the statistical basis of all estimates of the prevalence of cocaine and other drug use. One of the core claims in the crack scare was that drug use among teenagers and young adults was already high and that it was growing at an alarming rate. Although politicians and the media often referred to teen drug use as an "epidemic" or "plague," the best official evidence available at the time did not support such claims. The National Household Survey on Drug Abuse surveys over eight thousand randomly selected households each year. These surveys show that the number of Americans who had used any illegal drug in the previous month began to decline in 1979, and in the early years of the crack scare, use of drugs, including cocaine, continued to decline (*New York Times,* September 24, 1989, p. A1; *Newsweek,* February 19, 1990, p. 74). Lifetime prevalence of cocaine use among young people (the percentage of those twelve through twenty-five years old who had "ever" tried it) peaked in 1982, *four years before the scare began,* and continued to decline after that (NIDA, 1991, p. 14). The sharpest rise in lifetime prevalence among young adults had taken place between 1972 and 1979; it produced no claims of an epidemic or plague by politicians and journalists (Johnston et al., 1988; NIDA, 1986b).

In February 1987, NIDA released the results of its 1986 annual survey of high school seniors. The *New York Times* handling of the story shows how even the most respectable media institutions sometimes skew facts about drug use to fit a story line. In the article's "lead," the *Times* announced a rise in the percentage of high school seniors reporting "daily" use of cocaine. Only later did one learn that this had risen very slightly and, more important for evaluating claims of a "plague," that daily use among seniors had now reached 0.4%. Daily crack use, even by this fraction of 1% of high school seniors, is surely troubling, but it hardly constituted a new drug epidemic or plague. Still later in the story, the *Times* presented a table showing other declines in cocaine use by young adults and high school

seniors. Indeed, as the *Times* noted toward the end of its piece, virtually all forms of teenage drug use (including marijuana, LSD, and heroin) had declined—as they had in previous years (*New York Times,* February 24, 1987, p. A21; cf. Johnston et al., 1988; NIDA, 1991).

Two leading NIDA scholars, reporting in 1986 on the results of the household survey in *Science* magazine, wrote that "both annual prevalence and current prevalence [of all drug use] among college students and the total sample up to four years after high school has been relatively stable between 1980 and 1985" (Kozel and Adams, 1986, p. 973). The director of NIDA's high school surveys, Dr. Lloyd Johnston, made a similar point in 1987: "To some degree the fad quality of drugs has worn off" (*New York Times,* February 24, 1987, p. A21). When the findings of the high school senior survey for 1987 were released, the survey's director reported that "the most important" finding was that cocaine had again "showed a significant drop in use." He even reported a decline in the use of crack (Johnston et al., 1988).

These reported declines were in keeping with the general downward trend in drug use. In the early 1980s, according to the NIDA surveys, about one in six young Americans had tried cocaine powder. But between 1986 and 1987, the proportion of both high school seniors and young adults who had used cocaine in any form in the previous year dropped by 20% (Johnston et al., 1988). Further, two-thirds of those who had ever tried cocaine had not used it in the previous month. Although a significant minority of young people had tried cocaine powder at some point, the great majority of them did not continue to use it.

There had been a few signs of increasing cocaine use. The proportion of youngsters who reported using cocaine at least once in the previous month had increased slightly over the years, although it never exceeded 2% of all teens in the seven national household surveys between 1972 and 1985. The 1988 NIDA household survey found an increase in the number of adult daily users of cocaine, presumably the group that included crack addicts. But this group constituted only about 1.3% of those adults who had ever used cocaine. NIDA also estimated that about 0.5% of the total U.S. adult population had used cocaine in the week prior to the survey (NIDA, 1988).

But aside from these few slight increases, almost all other measures showed that the trends in official drug use statistics had been down even before the scare began. . . . The figures for cocaine use in particular were dropping just as crisis claims were reaching a crescendo, and had dropped still further precisely when the Bush/Bennett battle plan was being announced with such fanfare in 1989. Indeed, as White House officials anonymously admitted a few weeks after the president's "bag of crack" speech, the new plan's "true goals" were far more modest than its rhetoric: the Bush plan was "simply to move the nation 'a little bit' beyond where current trends would put it anyway" *(New York Times,* September 24, 1989, p. A1).

National Survey Data on Crack

Tom Brokaw reported on *NBC Nightly News* in 1986 (May 23) that crack was "flooding America" and that it had become "America's drug of choice." His colleagues at the other networks and in the print media had made similar claims. An ordinarily competent news consumer might well have gathered the impression that crack could be found in the lockers of most high school students. Yet, at the time of these press reports, *there were no prevalence statistics at all on crack* and no evidence of any sort showing that smoking crack had become the preferred mode even of cocaine use, much less of drug use.

When NIDA released the first official data on crack a few months later, they still did not support claims about widespread crack use. On

the contrary, the NIDA survey found that most cocaine use could not have been crack because the preferred mode of use for 90% of cocaine users was "sniffing" rather than smoking (NIDA, 1986a; see also Inciardi, 1987). An all-but-ignored Drug Enforcement Administration press release issued in August 1986, during the first hysterical summer of the crack scare, sought to correct the misperception that crack use was now the major drug problem in America. The DEA said, "Crack is currently the subject of considerable media attention. . . . The result has been a distortion of the public perception of the extent of crack use as compared to the use of other drugs. . . . [Crack] presently appears to be a secondary rather than primary problem in most areas" (Drug Enforcement Administration, cited in Diamond et al., 1987, p. 10; Inciardi, 1987, p. 482).

The first official measures of the prevalence of teenage crack use began with NIDA's 1986 high school survey. It found that 4.1% of high school seniors reported having *tried* crack (at least once) in the previous year. This figure dropped to 3.9% in 1987 and to 3.1% in 1988, a 25% decline (Johnston et al., 1988; *National Report on Substance Abuse,* 1994, p. 3). This means that at the peak of crack use, 96% of America's high school seniors had never tried crack, much less gone on to more regular use, abuse, or addiction. Any drug use among the young is certainly worrisome, particularly when in such an intense form as crack. However, at the start of the crusade to save "a whole generation" of children from death by crack in the spring of 1986, the latest official data showed a national total of eight "cocaine-related" deaths of young people age eighteen and under for the preceding year (Trebach, 1987, p. 11). There was no way to determine whether any of these deaths involved crack use or even if cocaine was in fact the direct cause.

In general, the government's national surveys indicate that a substantial minority of teenagers and young adults experiment with illicit drugs. But as with other forms of youthful deviance, most tend to abandon such behavior as they assume adult roles. Politicians, the media, and antidrug advertisements often claimed that cocaine is inevitably addicting but that crack is still worse because it is "instantaneously addicting." However, according to the official national surveys, two-thirds of Americans of all ages who had ever tried cocaine had not used it in the month prior to the surveys. It is clear that the vast majority of the more than twenty-two million Americans who have tried cocaine do not use it in crack form, do not escalate to regular use, and do not end up addicted. . . .

In sum, the official evidence on cocaine and crack available during the crack scare gave a rather different picture than Americans received from the media and politicians. The sharp rise in mentions of cocaine in emergency room episodes and coroners' reports did offer cause for concern. But the best official evidence of drug use never supported the claims about an "epidemic" or "plague" throughout America or about "instantaneous addiction." Moreover, as media attention to crack was burgeoning, the actual extent of crack use was virtually unknown, and most other official measures of cocaine use were actually decreasing. Once crack use was actually measured, its prevalence turned out to be low to start with and to have declined throughout the scare (*National Report on Substance Abuse*, 1994, p. 3).

Crack as an Epidemic and Plague

The empirical evidence on crack use suggests that politicians and journalists have routinely used the words "epidemic" and "plague" imprecisely and rhetorically as words of warning, alarm, and danger. Therefore, on the basis of press reports, it is difficult to determine if there was any legitimacy at all in the description of crack use as an epidemic or plague. Like most other drug researchers and epidemiologists, we have concluded that crack addiction has never been anything but relatively rare across the great middle strata of the U.S. population. If the word "epidemic" is used to mean a disease or diseaselike condition that is "widespread" or "prevalent," then there has never been an epidemic of crack addiction (or even crack use) among the vast majority of Americans. Among the urban poor, however, especially African-American and Latino youth, heavy crack use has been more common. An "epidemic of crack *use*" might be a description of what happened among a distinct minority of teenagers and young adults from impoverished urban neighborhoods in the mid to late 1980s. However, many more people use tobacco and alcohol heavily than use cocaine in any form. Alcohol drinking and tobacco smoking each kills far more people than all forms of cocaine and heroin use combined. Therefore, "epidemic" would be more appropriate to describe tobacco and alcohol use. But politicians and the media have not talked about tobacco and alcohol use as epidemics or plagues. The word "epidemic" also can mean a rapidly spreading disease. In this precise sense as well, in inner-city neighborhoods, crack use may have been epidemic (spreading rapidly) for a few years among impoverished young African-Americans and Latinos. However, crack use was never spreading fast or far enough among the general population to be termed an epidemic there.

"Plague" is even a stronger word than epidemic. Plague can mean a "deadly contagious disease," an epidemic "with great mortality," or it can refer to a "pestilence," an "infestation of a pest, [*e.g.,*] a plague of caterpillars." Crack is a central nervous system stimulant. Continuous and frequent use of crack often burns people out and does them substantial psychological and physical harm. But even very heavy use does not usually directly kill users. In this sense, crack use is not a plague. One could say that drug dealers were "infesting" some blocks of some poor neighborhoods in some cities, that there were pockets of plague in some specific areas; but that was not how "crack plague" was used.

When evaluating whether the extent and dangers of crack use match the claims of politicians and the media, it is instructive to compare how other drug use patterns are discussed. For example, an unusually balanced *New York Times* story (October 7, 1989, p. 26) compared crack and alcohol use among suburban teenagers and focused on the middle class. The *Times* reported that, except for a few "urban pockets" in suburban counties, "crack and other narcotics are rarely seen in the suburbs, whether modest or wealthy." . . .

The *Times* also reported that high school seniors were outdrinking the general adult population. Compared to the 64% of teenagers, only 55% of adults had consumed alcohol in the last month. Furthermore, teenagers have been drinking more than adults since at least 1972, when the surveys began. Even more significant is the *kind* of drinking teenagers do—what the *Times* called "excessive 'binge' drinking": "More than a third of the high school seniors had said that in the last two weeks they had had five or more drinks in a row." Drinking is, of course, the most widespread form of illicit drug use among high school students. As the *Times* explained, on the weekend, "practically every town has at least one underage party, indoors or out" and that "fake identification cards, older siblings, friends, and even parents all help teenagers obtain" alcohol.

The point we wish to emphasize is that even though illicit alcohol use was far more prevalent than cocaine or crack use, and even though it held substantial risk for alcohol dependence, addiction, drinking-driving deaths, and other alcohol-related problems, the media and politicians have not campaigned against teen drunkenness. Used as a descriptive term meaning "prevalent," the word "epidemic" fits teenage drinking far better than it does teenage crack use. Although many organizations have campaigned against drinking and driving by teenagers, the politicians and media have not used terms like "epidemic" or "plague" to call attention to illicit teenage drinking and drunkenness. Unlike the *Times* articles on crack, often on the front page, this article on teen drunkenness was placed in the second section on a Saturday.

It is also worth noting the unintentionally ironic mixing of metaphors, or of diagnoses and remedies, when advocates for the War on Drugs described crack use as an epidemic or plague. Although such disease terminology was used to call attention to the consequences of crack use, most of the federal government's domestic responses have centered on using police to arrest users. Treatment and prevention have always received a far smaller proportion of total federal antidrug funding than police and prisons do as a means of handling the "epidemic." If crack use is primarily a crime problem, then terms like "wave" (as in crime wave) would be more fitting. But if this truly is an "epidemic"—a widespread disease—then police and prisons are the wrong remedy, and the victims of the epidemic should be offered treatment, public health programs, and social services. . . .

The Political Context of the "Crack Crisis"

If the many claims about an "epidemic" or "plague" endangering "a whole generation" of youth were at odds with the best official data, then what else was animating the new War on Drugs? In fact, even if all the exaggerated claims about crack had been true, it would not explain all the attention crack received. Poverty, homelessness, auto accidents, handgun deaths, and environmental hazards are also widespread, costly, even deadly, but most politicians and journalists never speak of them in terms of crisis or plague. Indeed, far more people were (and still are) injured and killed every year by domestic violence than by illicit drugs, but one would never know this from media reports or political speeches. The existence of government studies suggesting that crack contributed to the deaths of a small proportion of its users, that an unknown but somewhat larger minority of users became addicted to it, that its use was related to some forms of crime, and so on were neither necessary nor sufficient conditions for all the attention crack received (Spector and Kitsuse, 1977).

Like other sociologists, historians, and students of drug law and public policy, we suggest that understanding antidrug campaigns requires more than evidence of drug abuse and drug-related problems, which can be found in almost any period. It requires analyzing these crusades and scares as phenomena in their own right and understanding the broader social, political, and economic circumstances under which they occur (see, *e.g.,* Bakalar and Grinspoon, 1984; Brecher, 1972; Duster, 1970; Gusfield, 1963, 1981; Lindesmith, 1965; Morgan, 1978; Musto, 1973; Rumbarger, 1989). The crack scare also must be understood in terms of its political context and its appeal to important groups within American society. The mass media and politicians, however, did not talk about drugs this way. Rather, they decontextualized the drama, making it appear as if the story had no authors aside from dealers and addicts. Their writing of the crack drama kept abusers, dealers, crimes, and casualties under spotlights while hiding other important factors in the shadows. We suggest that over and above the very real problems some users suffered with crack, the rise of the New Right and the competition between political parties in a conservative context contributed significantly to the making of the crack scare.

The New Right and Its Moral Ideology

During the post-Watergate rebuilding of the Republican Party, far right wing political organizations and fundamentalist Christian groups set about to impose what they called "traditional family values" on public policy. This self-proclaimed "New Right" felt increasingly threatened by the diffusion of modernist values, behaviors, and cultural practices—particularly by what they saw as the interconnected forms of 1960s hedonism involved in sex outside (heterosexual) marriage and consciousness alteration with (illicit) drugs. The New Right formed a core constituency for Ronald Reagan, an extreme conservative who had come to prominence as governor of California in part by taking a hard line against the new political movements and cultural practices of the 1960s.

Once he became president in 1981, Reagan and his appointees attempted to restructure public policy according to a radically conservative ideology. Through the lens of this ideology, most social problems appeared to be simply the consequences of *individual moral choices* (Ryan, 1976). Programs and research that had for many years been directed at the social and structural sources of social problems were systematically defunded in budgets and delegitimated in discourse. Unemployment, poverty, urban decay, school crises, crime, and all their attendant forms of human troubles were spoken of and acted upon as if they were the result of *individual* deviance, immorality, or weakness. The most basic premise of social science— that individual choices are influenced by social circumstances—was rejected as left-wing ideology. Reagan and the New Right constricted the aperture of attribution for America's ills so that only the lone deviant came into focus. They conceptualized people *in* trouble as people who *make* trouble (Gusfield, 1985); they made social control rather than social welfare the organizing axis of public policy (Reinarman, 1988).

With regard to drug problems, this conservative ideology is a form of *sociological denial.* For the New Right, people did not so much abuse drugs because they were jobless, homeless, poor, depressed, or alienated; they were jobless, homeless, poor, depressed, or alienated because they were weak, immoral, or foolish enough to use illicit drugs. For the right wing, American business productivity was not lagging because investors spent their capital on mergers and stock speculation instead of on new plants and equipment, or for any number of other economic reasons routinely mentioned in the *Wall Street Journal* or *Business Week*. Rather, conservatives claimed that businesses had difficulty competing partly because many workers were using drugs. In this view, U.S. education was in trouble not because it had suffered demoralizing budget cuts, but because a "generation" of students was "on drugs" and their teachers did not "get tough" with them. The new drug warriors did not see crime plaguing the ghettos and barrios for all the reasons it always has, but because of the influence of a new chemical bogeyman. Crack was a godsend to the Right. They used it and the drug issue as an ideological fig leaf to place over the unsightly urban ills that had increased markedly under Reagan administration social and economic policies. "The drug problem" served conservative politicians as an all-purpose scapegoat. They could blame an array of problems on the deviant individuals and then expand the nets of social control to imprison those people for causing the problems.

The crack crisis had other, more specific political uses. Nancy Reagan was a highly visible anti-drug crusader, crisscrossing the nation to urge schoolchildren to "Just Say No" to drugs. Mrs. Reagan's crusade began in 1983 (before crack came into existence) when her "p.r.-conscious operatives," as *Time* magazine called them, convinced her that "serious-minded displays" of "social consciousness" would "make her appear more caring and less frivolous." Such a public relations strategy was important to Mrs. Reagan. The press had often criticized her for spending hundreds of thousands of dollars on new china for the White House, lavish galas for wealthy friends, and high-fashion evening gowns at a time when her husband's economic policies had induced

a sharp recession, raised joblessness to near Depression-era levels, and cut funding for virtually all programs for the poor. *Time* explained that "the timing and destinations of her antidrug excursions last year were coordinated with the Reagan-Bush campaign officials to satisfy their particular political needs" (*Time*, January 14, 1985, p. 30). . . .

Political Party Competition

The primary political task facing liberals in the 1980s was to recapture some of the electorate that had gone over to the Right. Reagan's shrewdness in symbolically colonizing "middle American" fears put Democrats on the defensive. Most Democrats responded by moving to the right and pouncing upon the drug issue. Part of the early energy for the drug scare in the spring and summer of 1986 came from Democratic candidates trading charges with their Republican opponents about being "soft on drugs." Many candidates challenged each other to take urine tests as a symbol of their commitment to a "drug-free America." One Southern politician even proposed that candidates' spouses be tested. A California senatorial candidate charged his opponent with being "a noncombatant in the war on drugs" (*San Francisco Chronicle*, August 12, 1986, p. 9). By the fall of 1986, increasingly strident calls for a drug war became so much a part of candidates' standard stump speeches that even conservative columnist William Safire complained of antidrug "hysteria" and "narcomania" (*New York Times*, September 11, 1986, p. A27). Politicians demanded everything from death penalties in North America to bombing raids in South America.

Crack could not have appeared at a more opportune political moment. After years of dull debates on budget balancing, a "hot" issue had arrived just in time for a crucial election. In an age of fiscal constraint, when most problems were seen as intractable and most solutions costly, the crack crisis was the one "safe" issue on which all politicians could take "tough stands" without losing a single vote or campaign contribution. The legislative results of the competition to "get tough" included a $2 billion law in 1986, the so-called "Drug-Free America Act," which whizzed through the House (392 to 16) just in time for members of Congress to go home and tell their constituents about it. In the heat of the preelection, antidrug hysteria, the symbolic value of such spending seemed to dwarf the deficit worries that had hamstrung other legislation. According to *Newsweek,* what occurred was "a can-you-top-this competition" among "election-bound members of both parties" seeking tough antidrug amendments. The 1986 drug bill, as Representative David McCurdy (D-Okla) put it, was "out of control," adding through a wry smile, "but of course I'm for it" (September 22, 1986, p. 39).

The prominence of the drug issue dropped sharply in both political speeches and media coverage after the 1986 election, but returned during the 1988 primaries. Once again the crack issue had political utility. One common observation about the 1988 presidential election campaigns was that there were no domestic or foreign policy crises looming on which the two parties could differentiate themselves. As a *New York Times* headline put it: "Drugs as 1988 Issue: Filling a Vacuum" (May 24, 1988, p. A14). In the 1988 primary season, candidates of both parties moved to fill this vacuum in part by drug-baiting their opponents and attacking them as "soft on drugs." In the fall, both Democrats Dukakis and Bentsen and Republicans Bush and Quayle claimed that their opponents were soft on drugs while asserting that their side would wage a "*real* War on Drugs." And, just as they did before the 1986 election, members of Congress from both parties overwhelmingly passed a new, even more strict and costly antidrug bill.

The antidrug speeches favoring such expenditures became increasingly transparent as posturing, even to many of the speakers. For example, Senator Christopher Dodd (D-Conn) called the flurry of antidrug amendments a "feeding frenzy" (*New York Times,* May 22, 1988, p. E4). An aide to another senator admitted that "everybody was scrambling to get a piece of the action" (*New York Times,* May 24, 1988, p. A14). Even President Reagan's spokesperson, Marlin Fitzwater, told the White House press corps that "everybody wants to out-drug each other in terms of political rhetoric" (*Boston Globe,* May 18, 1988, p. 4). But however transparent, such election-year posturing—magnified by a media hungry for the readers and ratings that dramatic drug stories bring—enhanced the viability of claims about the menace of crack far more than any available empirical evidence could. In the fall of 1989, Congress finalized yet another major antidrug bill costing more than the other two combined. According to research by the Government Accounting Office, the federal government spent more than $23 billion on the drug war during the Reagan era, three-fourths of it for law enforcement (*Alcoholism and Drug Abuse Week,* 1989, p. 3). . . .

Politicians and the media were *forging,* not following, public opinion. The speeches and stories *led* the oft-cited poll results, not the other way around. In 1987, between elections—when drug problems persisted in the ghettos and barrios but when the drug scare was not so enflamed by election rhetoric and media coverage—only 3 to 5% of those surveyed picked drugs as our most important problem (*New York Times,* May 24, 1988, p. A14). But then again in 1989, immediately following President Bush's speech escalating the drug war, nearly two-thirds of the people polled identified drugs as America's most important problem. When the media and politicians invoked "public opinion" as the driving force behind their actions against crack, they inverted the actual causal sequence (Edelman, 1964, p. 172).

We argued in the previous section that the New Right and other conservatives found ideological utility in the crack scare. In this section, we have suggested that conservatives were not the only political group in America to help foment the scare and to benefit from it. Liberals and Democrats, too, found in crack and drugs a means of recapturing Democratic defectors by appearing more conservative. And they too found drugs to be a convenient scapegoat for the worsening conditions in the inner cities. All this happened at a historical moment when the Right successfully stigmatized the liberals' traditional solutions to the problems of the poor as ineffective and costly. Thus, in addition to the political capital to be gained by waging the war, the new chemical bogeyman afforded politicians across the ideological spectrum both an explanation for pressing public problems and an excuse for not proposing the unpopular taxing, spending, or redistributing needed to do something about them.

The End of the Crack Scare

In the 1980s, the conservative drive to reduce social spending exacerbated the enduring problems of impoverished African-American and Latino city residents. Partly in response, a minority of the young urban poor turned either to crack sales as their best shot at the American Dream and/or to the crack high as their best shot at a fleeting moment of pleasure. Inner-city churches, community organizations, and parent groups then tried to defend their children and neighborhoods from drug dealing and use on the one hand and to lobby for services and jobs on the other hand. But the crack scare did not inspire politicians of either party to address the worsening conditions and growing needs of the inner-city poor and working class or to launch a "Marshall Plan for cities." In the meantime, the white middle-class majority viewed with

alarm the growing numbers, visibility, and desperation of the urban poor. And for years many Americans believed the central fiction of the crack scare: that drug use was not a symptom of urban decay but one of its most important causes.

All this gave federal and local authorities justificaton for widening the nets of social control. Of course, the new drug squads did not reduce the dangerousness of impoverished urban neighborhoods. But the crack scare did increase criminal justice system supervision of the underclass. By 1992, one in four young African-American males was in jail or prison or on probation or parole—more than were in higher education. . . . During the crack scare, the prison population more than doubled, largely because of the arrests of drug users and small dealers. This gave the U.S. the highest incarceration rate in the world (Currie, 1985; Irwin and Austin, 1994).

By the end of 1992, however, the crack scare seemed spent. There are a number of overlapping reasons for this. Most important was the failure of the War on Drugs itself. Democrats as well as Republicans supported the War on Drugs, but the Reagan and Bush administrations initiated and led it, and the drug war required support from the White House. George Bush appointed William Bennett to be a "tough" and extremely high profile "drug czar" to lead the campaign against drugs. But Bennett, criticized for his bombastic style, quit after only eighteen months (some press accounts referred to it as the "czar's abdication"). After that, the Bush administration downplayed the drug war, and it hardly figured at all in the presidential primaries or campaign in 1992. Bill Clinton said during the campaign that there were no easy solutions to drug problems and that programs that work only on reducing supply were doomed to fail. The Clinton administration eschewed the phrase "War on Drugs," and Lee Brown, Clinton's first top drug official, explicitly rejected the title of drug czar (Reinarman, 1994). After billions of tax dollars had been spent and millions of young Americans had been imprisoned, hard-core drug problems remained. With so little to show for years of drug war, politicians seemed to discover the limits of the drug issue as a political weapon. Moreover, with both parties firmly in favor of the "get tough" approach, there was no longer any partisan political advantage to be had.

The news media probably would have written dramatic stories about the appearance of smokeable cocaine in poor neighborhoods at any time. Television producers have found that drug stories, especially timely, well-advertised, dramatic ones, often receive high ratings. But the context of the Reagan-led drug war encouraged the media to write such pieces. Conservatives had long complained that the media had a liberal bias; in the mid-1980s, drug coverage allowed the media to rebut such criticism and to establish conservative credentials (Reeves and Campbell, 1994). As we have suggested, news coverage of drugs rose and fell with political initiatives, especially those coming from the president. Therefore, as the White House withdrew from the drug issue, so did the press.

After about 1989, it became increasingly difficult to sustain the exaggerated claims of the beginning of the crack scare. The mainstream media began to publish stories critical of earlier news coverage (though usually not their own). . . . *Newsweek* finally admitted in 1990 what it called the "dirty little secret" about crack that it had concealed in all of its earlier scare stories: "A lot of people use it without getting addicted," and that the anonymous "media" had "hyped instant and total addiction" (February 19, 1990, pp. 74–75). As early as 1988, it was clear that crack was not "destroying a whole generation"; it was not even spreading beyond the same poverty context that had long given rise to hard-core heroin addiction. Moreover, because of the obvious destructive effects of heavy use, people

in ghettos and barrios had come to view "crack heads" as even lower in status than winos or junkies. Even crack dealers preferred powder cocaine and routinely disparaged crack heads (Williams, 1989). All of this meant that drugs in general, and crack in particular, declined in newsworthiness. Media competition had fueled the crack scare in its early years, and the same scramble for dramatic stories guaranteed that the media would move on to other stories. By 1992, the crack scare had faded beyond the media's horizon of hot new issues.

Finally, the crack scare could recede into the background partly because it had been *institutionalized.* Between 1986 and 1992, Congress passed and two presidents signed a series of increasingly harsh antidrug laws. Federal antidrug funding increased for seven successive years, and an array of prison and police programs was established or expanded. All levels of government, from schools to cities, counties, and states, established agencies to warn about crack and other drug problems. And multimillion-dollar, corporate-sponsored, private organizations such as the Partnership for a Drug-Free America had been established to continue the crusade.

Conclusion

Smoking crack *is* a risky way to use an already potent drug. Despite all the exaggerations, heavy use of it *has* made life more difficult for many people—most of them from impoverished urban neighborhoods. If we agree that too many families have been touched by drug-related tragedies, why have we bothered criticizing the crack scare and the War on Drugs? If even a few people are saved from crack addiction, why should anyone care if this latest drug scare was in some measure concocted by the press, politicians, and moral entrepreneurs to serve their other agendas? Given the damage that drug abuse can do, what's the harm in a little hysteria? . . .

First, we suspect that drug scares do not work very well to reduce drug problems and that they may well promote the behavior they claim to be preventing. For all the repression successive drug wars have wrought (primarily upon the poor and the powerless), they have yet to make a measurable dent in our drug *problems*. For example, prompted by the crack crisis and inspired by the success of patriotic propaganda in World War II, the Partnership for a Drug-Free America ran a massive advertising campaign to "unsell drugs." From 1987 to 1993, the Partnership placed over $1 billion worth of advertising donated by corporations and the advertising industry. The Partnership claims to have had a "measurable impact" by "accelerating intolerance" to drugs and drug users. The Partnership claims it "can legitimately take some of the credit for the 25% decline in illicit drug usage since our program was launched" (Hedrick, 1990). However, the association between the Partnership's antidrug advertising and the declines in drug use appears to be spurious. Drug use was declining well before the Partnership's founding; taking credit for what was already happening is a bit like jumping in front of a parade and then claiming to have been leading it all along. More important, drug *use* increased in the mid 1990s among precisely those age groups that had been targeted by Partnership ads, while drug *problems* continued throughout their campaign. Furthermore, Partnership ads scrupulously avoided any mention of the two forms of drug use most prevalent among youth: smoking and drinking. This may have something to do with the fact that the Partnership for a Drug-Free America is a partnership between the media and advertising industries, which make millions from alcohol and tobacco advertising each year, and with the fact that alcohol and tobacco companies contribute financially to the Partnership's campaign against illicit drugs. Surely public health education is important, but there is no evidence that selective antidrug propaganda and scare tactics have significantly reduced drug problems.

Indeed, hysterical and exaggerated antidrug campaigns may have increased drug-related harm in the U.S. There is the risk that all of the exaggerated claims made to mobilize the population for war actually arouse interest in drug use. In 1986, the *New England Journal of Medicine* reported that the frequency of teenage suicides increases after lurid news reports and TV shows about them (Gould and Shaffer, 1986; Phillips and Carstensen, 1986). Reports about drugs, especially of new and exotic drugs like crack, may work the same way. In his classic chapter, "How to Launch a Nation Wide Drug Menace," Brecher (1972) shows how exaggerated newspaper reports of dramatic police raids in 1960 functioned as advertising for glue sniffing. The arrests of a handful of sniffers led to anti–glue sniffing hysteria that actually spread this hitherto unknown practice across the U.S. In 1986, the media's desire for dramatic drug stories interacted with politicians' desire for partisan advantage and safe election-year issues, so news about crack spread to every nook and cranny of the nation far faster than dealers could have spread word on the street. When the media and politicians claimed that crack is "the most addictive substance known to man," there was some commonsense obligation to explain why. Therefore, alongside all the statements about "instant addiction," the media also reported some very intriguing things about crack: "whole body orgasm," "better than sex," and "cheaper than cocaine." For TV-raised young people in the inner city, faced with a dismal social environment and little economic opportunity, news about such a substance in their neighborhoods may have functioned as a massive advertising campaign for crack.

Further, advocates of the crack scare and the War on Drugs explicitly rejected public health approaches to drug problems that conflicted with their ideology. The most striking and devastating example of this was the total rejection of syringe distribution programs by the Reagan and Bush administrations and by drug warriors such as Congressman Charles Rangel. People can and do recover from drug addiction, but no one recovers from AIDS. By the end of the 1980s, the fastest growing AIDS population was intravenous drug users. Because syringes were hard to get, or their possession criminalized, injectors shared their syringes and infected each other and their sexual partners with AIDS. In the early 1980s, activists in a number of other Western countries had developed syringe distribution and exchange programs to prevent AIDS, and there is by now an enormous body of evidence that such programs are effective. But the U.S. government has consistently rejected such "harm reduction" programs on the grounds that they conflict with the policy of "zero tolerance" for drug use or "send the wrong message." As a result, cities such as Amsterdam, Liverpool, and Sydney, which have needle exchange programs, have very low or almost no transmission of AIDS by intravenous drug users. In New York City, however, roughly half the hundreds of thousands of injection drug users are HIV positive or already have AIDS. In short, the crack scare and the drug war policies it fueled will ultimately contribute to the deaths of tens of thousands of Americans, including the families, children, and sexual partners of the infected drug users.

Another important harm resulting from American drug scares is they have routinely blamed individual immorality and personal behavior for endemic social and structural problems. In so doing, they diverted attention and resources away from the underlying sources of drug abuse and the array of other social ills of which they are part. One necessary condition for the emergence of the crack scare (as in previous drug scares) was the linking of drug use with the problems faced by racial minorities, the poor, and youth. In the logic

of the scare, whatever economic and social troubles these people have suffered were due largely to their drug use. Obscured or forgotten during the crack scare were all the social and economic problems that underlie crack abuse—and that are much more widespread—especially poverty, unemployment, racism, and the prospects of life in the permanent underclass.

Democrats denounced the Reagan and Bush administrations' hypocrisy in proclaiming "War on Drugs" while cutting the budgets for drug treatment, prevention, and research. However, the Democrats often neglected to mention an equally important but more politically popular development: the "Just Say No To Drugs" administrations had, with the help of many Democrats in Congress, also "just said no" to virtually every social program aimed at creating alternatives for and improving the lawful life chances of inner-city youth. These black and Latino young people were and are the group with the highest rate of crack abuse. Although most inner-city youth have always steered clear of drug abuse, they could not "just say no" to poverty and unemployment. Dealing drugs, after all, was (and still is) accurately perceived by many poor city kids as the highest-paying job—straight or criminal—that they are likely to get.

The crack scare, like previous drug scares and antidrug campaigns, promoted misunderstandings of drug use and abuse, blinded people to the social sources of many social problems (including drug problems), and constrained the social policies that might reduce those problems. It routinely used inflated, misleading rhetoric and falsehoods such as Bush's televised account of how he came into possession of a bag of crack. At best, the crack scare was not good for public health. At worst, by manipulating and misinforming citizens about drug use and effects, it perverted social policy and political democracy.

REFERENCES

Alcoholism and Drug Abuse Week, "$23 Billion Spent on Federal Drug Effort Since 1981." July 5, 1989, pp. 3–4.

Anderson, Jack, and Michael Binstein, "Drug Informants Beating the System." *Washington Post,* September 10, 1992, p. D23.

Bakalar, James B., and Lester Grinspoon, *Drug Control in a Free Society.* Cambridge: Cambridge University Press, 1984.

Belenko, Steven, and Jeffrey Fagan, "Crack and the Criminal Justice System." New York: New York City Criminal Justice Agency, 1987.

Brecher, Edward M., *Licit and Illicit Drugs.* Boston: Little, Brown, 1972.

Chin K.-L, "Special Event Codes for Crack Arrests." Internal memorandum, New York City Criminal Justice Agency, 1988.

Currie, Elliott, *Confronting Crime.* New York: Pantheon, 1985.

Diamond, Edwin, Frank Accosta, and Leslie-Jean Thornton, "Is TV News Hyping America's Cocaine Problem?" *TV Guide,* February 7, 1987, pp. 4–10.

Drug Enforcement Administration, "Special Report: The Crack Situation in the U.S." Unpublished, Strategic Intelligence Section. Washington, DC: DEA, August 22, 1986.

Duster, Troy, *The Legislation of Morality.* New York: Free Press, 1970.

Edelman, Murray, *The Symbolic Uses of Politics.* Urbana: University of Illinois Press, 1964.

Gould, Madelyn S., and David Shaffer, "The Impact of Suicide in Television Movies: Evidence of Imitation." *New England Journal of Medicine* 315:690–694 (1986).

Grinspoon, Lester, and James B. Bakalar, *Cocaine: A Drug and Its Social Evolution.* New York: Basic Books, 1976.

Gusfield, Joseph R., *Symbolic Crusade.* Urbana: University of Illinois Press, 1963.

———, *The Culture of Public Problems.* Chicago: University of Chicago Press, 1981.

———, "Alcohol Problems—An Interactionist View," in J. P. von Wartburg et al., eds., *Currents in Alcohol Research and the Prevention of Alcohol Problems.* Berne, Switzerland: Hans Huber, 1985.

Harwood, Richard, "Hyperbole Epidemic." *Washington Post,* October 1, 1989, p. D6.

Hedrick, Thomas A., Jr., "Pro Bono Anti-Drug Ad Campaign Is Working." *Advertising Age,* June 25, 1990, p. 22.

Himmelstein, Jerome, *The Strange Career of Marijuana.* Westport, CT: Greenwood Press, 1983.

Hoffman, Abbie, *Steal This Urine Test: Fighting Drug Hysteria in America.* New York: Penguin Books, 1987.

Horgan, John, "A Kinder War." *Scientific American,* July 25, 1993, p. 6.

Inciardi, James, "Beyond Cocaine: Basuco, Crack, and Other Coca Products." *Contemporary Drug Problems* 14:461–492 (1987).

Irwin, John, and James Austin, *It's About Time: America's Imprisonment Binge.* Belmont, CA: Wadsworth, 1994.

Isikoff, Michael, "Drug Buy Set Up for Bush Speech: DEA Lured Seller to Lafayette Park." *Washington Post,* September 22, 1989, p. A1.

Johnson, Bruce D., et al., *Taking Care of Business: The Economics of Crime by Heroin Abusers.* Lexington, MA: Lexington Books, 1985.

Johnston, Lloyd D., Patrick M. O'Malley, and Jerald G. Bachman, *Illicit Drug Use, Smoking, and Drinking by America's High School Students, College Students, and Young Adults, 1975–1987.* Washington, DC: National Institute on Drug Abuse, 1988.

Kitsuse, John I., and Aaron V. Cicourel, "A Note on the Use of Official Statistics." *Social Problems* 11:131–139 (1963).

Kozel, Nicholas, and Edgar Adams, "Epidemiology of Drug Abuse: An Overview." *Science* 234:970–974 (1986).

Lindesmith, Alfred R., *The Addict and the Law.* Bloomington: Indiana University Press, 1965.

Massing, Michael, Review essay on "Swordfish," *New York Review of Books,* July 15, 1993, pp. 30–32.

Morgan, Patricia, "The Legislation of Drug Law: Economic Crisis and Social Control," *Journal of Drug Issues* 8:53–62 (1978).

Musto, David, *The American Disease: Origins of Narcotic Control.* New Haven, CT: Yale University Press, 1973.

National Institute on Drug Abuse, *Data from the Drug Abuse Warning Network: Annual Data 1985*. Statistical Series 1, #5. Washington, DC: National Institute on Drug Abuse, 1986a.

———, *National Household Survey on Drug Abuse, 1985*. Washington, DC: Division of Epidemiology and Statistical Analysis, National Institute on Drug Abuse, 1986b.

———, *National Household Survey on Drug Abuse: 1988 Population Estimates*. Washington, DC: Division of Epidemiology and Prevention Research, National Institute on Drug Abuse, 1988.

———, *National Household Survey on Drug Abuse: Main Findings 1990*. Washington, DC: Epidemiology and Prevention Research, National Institute on Drug Abuse, 1990.

———, *Annual Medical Examiner Data, 1991: Data from the Drug Abuse Warning Network*. Washington, DC: Division of Epidemiology and Prevention Research, National Institute on Drug Abuse, 1992.

———, *Estimates from the Drug Abuse Warning Network: 1992 Estimates of Drug-Related Emergency Room Episodes*. Washington, DC: Substance Abuse and Mental Health Services Administration, U.S. Dept. of Health and Human Services, 1993a.

———, *National Household Survey on Drug Abuse: Population Estimates 1992*. Washington, DC: Substance Abuse and Mental Health Services Administration, U.S. Dept. of Health and Human Services, 1993b.

National Report on Substance Abuse, "Federal Officials Express Alarm at Youth's Rising Illicit Drug Use." February 11, 1994, p. 2.

New York Times, "No Change in Basics: Bush Rejects Any Fundamental Shift, Instead Vowing Unprecedented Vigor." September 6, 1989, p. A11.

Office of National Drug Control Policy, *National Drug Control Strategy: Budget Summary*. Washington, DC: U.S. Government Printing Office, 1992.

Phillips, David P., and Lundie L. Carstensen, "Clustering of Teenage Suicides After Television News Stories About Suicide." *New England Journal of Medicine* 315:685–689 (1986).

Reeves, Jimmie L., and Richard Campbell, *Cracked Coverage: Television News, the Anti-Cocaine Crusade, and the Reagan Legacy*. Durham, NC: Duke University Press, 1994.

Reinarman, Craig, "The Social Construction of an Alcohol Problem: The Case of Mothers Against Drunk Drivers and Social Control in the 1980s." *Theory and Society* 17:91–119 (1988).

———, "Glasnost in U.S. Drug Policy?: Clinton Constrained." *International Journal of Drug Policy* 5:42–49 (1994).

Rogin, Michael Paul, *Ronald Reagan, the Movie: and Other Episodes in Political Demonology*. Berkeley: University of California Press, 1987.

Rumbarger, John, *Profits, Power, and Prohibition*, Albany: State University of New York Press, 1989.

Ryan, William, *Blaming the Victim*. New York: Vintage, 1976.

Schneider, Joseph, and John I. Kitsuse, eds., *Studies in the Sociology of Social Problems*. Norwood, NJ: Ablex, 1984.

Siegel, Ronald, "Cocaine Smoking." *Journal of Psychoactive Drugs* 14:271–359 (1982).

Spector, Malcolm, and John Kitsuse, *Constructing Social Problems*. Menlo Park, CA: Cummings, 1977.

Staples, Brent, "Coke Wars." *New York Times Book Review,* February 6, 1994, p. 11.

Trebach, Arnold, *The Great Drug War*. New York: Macmillan, 1987.

University of Michigan, "Drug Use Rises Among American Teen-Agers." News and Information Services, January 27, 1994.

Waldorf, Dan, Craig Reinarman, and Sheigla Murphy, *Cocaine Changes*. Philadelphia: Temple University Press, 1991.

Washton, Arnold, and Mark Gold, "Recent Trends in Cocaine Abuse," *Advances in Alcohol and Substance Abuse* 6:31–47 (1987).

The White House, *National Drug Control Strategy*. Washington, DC: U.S. Government Printing Office, 1989.

Williams, Terry, *The Cocaine Kids*. Reading, MA: Addison-Wesley, 1989.

Wilson, William Julius, *The Truly Disadvantaged*. Chicago: University of Chicago Press, 1987.

Zinberg, Norman E., *Drug, Set, and Setting: The Basis for Controlled Drug Use*. New Haven, CT: Yale University Press, 1984.

THINKING ABOUT THE READING

How does Reinarman and Levine's article support the contention that reality is a social construction? Consider the broader implications of their argument: The use of certain substances becomes a serious social problem *not* because it is an objectively dangerous activity but because it receives sufficient media and political attention. What does this contention suggest about the way social problems and public fears are created and maintained in society? What does it tell us about our collective need to identify a scapegoat for our social problems? Why are there such vastly different public attitudes and legal responses to crack cocaine versus powder cocaine? Can you think of other situations in which heightened media coverage and political attention have created widespread public concern and moral outrage where none was warranted? How has this article affected your views about the "War on Drugs" and the decriminalization of illegal drugs?

Concepts, Indicators, and Reality

Earl Babbie

(1986)

Measurement is one of the fundamental aspects of social research. When we describe science as logical/empirical, we mean that scientific conclusions should (1) make sense and (2) correspond to what we can observe. It is the second of these characteristics I want to explore in this essay.

Suppose we are interested in learning whether education really reduces prejudice. To do that, we must be able to measure both prejudice and education. Once we've distinguished prejudiced people from unprejudiced people and educated people from uneducated people, we'll be in a position to find out whether the two variables are related.

Social scientific measurement operates in accordance with the following implicit model:

- Prejudice exists as a *variable*: some people are more prejudiced than others.
- There are numerous *indicators* of prejudice.
- None of the indicators provides a perfect reflection of prejudice as it "really" is, but they can point to it at least approximately.
- We should try to find better and better indicators of prejudice—indicators that come ever closer to the "real thing."

This model applies to all of the variables social scientists study. Take a minute to look through the following list of variables commonly examined in social research.

Arms race	Tolerance
Religiosity	Fascism
Urbanism	Parochialism
TV watching	Maturity
Susceptibility	Solidarity
Stereotyping	Instability
Anti-Semitism	Education
Voting	Liberalism
Dissonance	Authoritarianism
Pessimism	Race
Anxiety	Happiness
Revolution	Powerlessness
Alienation	Mobility
Social class	Consistency
Age	Delinquency
Self-esteem	Compassion
Idealism	Democracy
Prestige	Influence

Even if you've never taken a course in social science, many of these terms are at least somewhat familiar to you. Social scientists study things that are of general interest to everyone. The nuclear arms race affects us all, for example, and it is a special concern for many of us. Differences in *religiosity* (some of us are more religious than others) are also of special interest to some people. As our country has evolved from small towns to large cities, we've all thought and talked more about *urbanism*—the good and bad associated with city life. Similar interests can be identified for all of the other terms.

My point is that you've probably thought about many of the variables mentioned in the list. Those you are familiar with undoubtedly have the quality of reality for you: that is, you know they exist. Religiosity, for example, is real. Regardless of whether you're in favor of it, opposed to it, or don't care much one way or the other, you at least know that religiosity exists. Or does it?

This is a particularly interesting question for me, since my first book, *To Comfort and to Challenge* (with Charles Glock and Benjamin Ringer), was about this subject. In particular, we wanted to know why some people were more religious than others (the sources of religiosity) and what impact differences in religiosity had on other aspects of life (the consequences of religiosity). Looking for the sources and consequences of a particular variable is a conventional social scientific undertaking; the first step is to develop a measure of that variable. We had to develop methods for distinguishing religious people, nonreligious people, and those somewhere in between.

The question we faced was, if religiosity is real, how do we know that? How do we distinguish religious people from nonreligious people? For most contemporary Americans, a number of answers come readily to mind. Religious people go to church, for example. They believe in the tenets of their faith. They

pray. They read religious materials, such as the Bible, and they participate in religious organizations.

Not all religious people do all of these things, of course, and a great deal depends on their particular religious affiliation, if any. Christians believe in the divinity of Jesus; Jews do not. Moslems believe Mohammed's teachings are sacred; Jews and Christians do not. Some signs of religiosity are to be found in seemingly secular realms. Orthodox Jews, for example, refrain from eating pork; Seventh-Day Adventists don't drink alcohol.

In our study, we were interested in religiosity among a very specific group: Episcopal churchmembers in America. To simplify our present discussion, let's look at that much narrower question: How can you distinguish religious from nonreligious Episcopalians in America?

As I've indicated above, we are likely to say that religious people attend church, whereas nonreligious people do not. Thus, if we know someone who attends church every week, we're likely to think of that person as religious; indeed, religious people joke about church-members who only attend services on Easter and at Christmas. The latter are presumed to be less religious.

Of course, we are speaking rather casually here, so let's see whether church attendance would be an adequate measure of religiosity for Episcopalians and other mainstream American Christians. Would you be welling to equate religiosity with church attendance? That is, would you be willing to call religious everyone who attended church every week, let's say, and call nonreligious everyone who did not?

I suspect that you would not consider equating church attendance with religiosity a wise policy. For example, consider a political figure who attends church every Sunday, sits in the front pew, puts a large contribution in the collection plate with a flourish, and by all other evidence seems only interested in being known as a religious person for the political advantage that may entail. Let's add that the politician in question regularly lies and cheats, exhibits no Christian compassion toward others, and ridicules religion in private. You'd probably consider it inappropriate to classify that person as religious.

Now imagine someone confined to a hospital bed, who spends every waking minute reading in the Bible, leading other patients in prayer, raising money for missionary work abroad—but never going to church. Probably this would fit your image of a religious person.

These deviant cases illustrate that, while church attendance is somehow related to religiosity, it is not a sufficient indicator in and of itself. So how can we distinguish religious from nonreligious people?

Prayer is a possibility. Presumably, people who pray a lot are more religious than those who don't. But wouldn't it matter what they prayed for? Suppose they were only praying for money. How about the Moslem extremist praying daily for the extermination of the Jews? How about the athlete praying for an opponent to be hit by a truck? Like church attendance, prayer seems to have something to do with religiosity, but we can't simply equate the two.

We might consider religious beliefs. Among Christians, for example, it would seem to make sense that a person who believes in God is more religious than one who does not. However, this would require that we consider the person who says, "I'll believe anything they say just as long as I don't rot in Hell" more religious than, say, a concerned theologian who completes a lifetime of concentrated and devoted study of humbly concluding that who or what God is cannot be known with certainty. We'd probably decide that this was a misclassification.

Without attempting to exhaust all the possible indicators of religiosity, I hope it's clear that we would never find a single measure that will satisfy us as tapping the real essence of religiosity. In recognition of this, social researchers use a combination of indicators to create a *composite measure*—an index or a scale—of variables such as religiosity. Such a measure might include all of the indicators discussed so far: church attendance, prayer, and beliefs.

While composite measures are usually a good idea, they do not really solve the dilemma I've laid out. With a little thought, we could certainly imagine circumstances in which a "truly" religious person nonetheless didn't attend church, pray, or believe, and we could likewise imagine a nonreligious person who did all of those things. In either event, we would have demonstrated the imperfection of the composite measure.

Recognition of this often leads people to conclude that variables like religiosity are simply beyond empirical measurement. This conclusion is true and false and even worse.

The conclusion is false in that we can make any measurement we want. For example, we can ask people if they attend church regularly and call that a measure of religiosity just as easily as Yankee Doodle called the feather in his hat macaroni. In our case, moreover, most people would say that what we've measured is by no means irrelevant to religiosity.

The conclusion is true in that no empirical measurement—single or composite—will satisfy all of us as having captured the essence of religiousness. Since that can never happen, we can never satisfactorily measure religiosity.

The situation is worse than either of these comments suggests in that the reason we can't measure religiosity is that it doesn't exist! Religiosity isn't real. Neither is prejudice, love, alienation, or any of those other variables. Let's see why.

There's a very old puzzle I'm sure you're familiar with: when a tree falls in the forest, does it make a sound if no one is there to hear it? High school and college students have struggled with that one for centuries. There's no doubt that the unobserved falling tree will still crash through the branches of its neighbors, snap its own limbs into pieces, and slam against the ground. But would it make a sound?

If you've given this any thought before, you've probably come to the conclusion that the puzzle rests on the ambiguity of the word *sound*. Where does sound occur? In this example, does it occur in the falling tree, in the air, or in the ear of the beholder? We can be reasonably certain that the falling tree generates turbulent waves in the air; if those waves in the air strike your ear, you will experience something we call *hearing*. We say you've heard a sound. But do the waves in the air per se qualify as sound?

The answer to this central question is necessarily arbitrary. We can have it be whichever way we want. The truth is that (1) a tree fell; (2) it created waves in the air; and (3) if the waves reached someone's ear, they would cause an experience for that person. Humans created the idea of *sound* in the context of that whole process. Whenever waves in the air cause an experience by way of our ears, we use the term *sound* to identify that experience. We're usually not too precise about where the sound happens: in the tree, in the air, or in our ears.

Our imprecise use of the term *sound* produces the apparent dilemma. So what's the truth? What's really the case? Does it make a sound or not? The truth is that (1) a tree fell; (2) it created waves in the air; and (3) if the waves reached someone's ear, they would cause an experience for that person. That's it. That's the final and ultimate truth of the matter.

I've belabored this point, because it sets the stage for understanding a critical issue in social research—one that often confuses students. To move in the direction of that issue, let's shift from sound to sight for a moment. Here's a new puzzle for you: are the tree's leaves green if no one is there to see them? Take a minute to think about that, and then continue reading.

Here's how I'd answer the question. The tree's leaves have a certain physical and chemical composition that affects the reflection of light rays off of them; specifically, they only reflect the green portion of the light spectrum. When rays from that portion of the light spectrum hit our eyes, they create an experience we call the color green.

"But are the leaves green if no one sees them?" you may ask. The answer to that is whatever we want it to be, since we haven't specified where the color green exists: in the physical/chemical composition of the leaf, in the light rays reflected from the leaf, or in our eyes.

While we are free to specify what we mean by the color green in this sense, nothing we do can change the ultimate truth, the ultimate reality of the matter. The truth is that (1) the leaves have a certain physical and chemical composition; (2) they reflect only a portion of the light spectrum; and (3) that portion of the light spectrum causes an experience if it hits our eyes. That's the ultimate truth of the universe in this matter.

By the same token, the truth about religiosity is that (1) some people to go church more than others; (2) some pray more than others; (3) some believe more than others; and so forth. This is observably the case.

At some point, our ancestors noticed that the things we're discussing were not completely independent of one another. People who went to church seemed to pray more, on the whole, than people who didn't go to church. Moreover, those who went to church and prayed seemed to believe more of the church's teachings than did those who neither went to church nor prayed. The observation of relationships such as these led them to conclude literally that "there is more here than meets the eye." The term *religiosity* was created to represent the *concept* that all the concrete observables seemed to have in common. People gradually came to believe that the concepts were real and the "indicators" only pale reflections.

We can never find a "true" measure of religiosity, prejudice, alienation, love, compassion, or any other such concepts, since none of them exists except in our minds. Concepts are "figments of our imaginations." I do not mean to suggest that concepts are useless or should be dispensed with. Life as we know it depends on the creation and use of concepts, and science would be impossible without them. Still, we should recognize that they are fictitious, then we can trade them in for more useful ones whenever appropriate.

THINKING ABOUT THE READING

Define the following terms: "poverty," "happiness," "academic effort," "love." Now consider what indicators you would use to determine people's levels of each of these concepts. The indicator must be something that will allow you to clearly determine whether or not someone is in a particular state (such as, poor or not poor; happy or not happy; in love or not in love). For example, you might decide that "blushing" in the presence of someone is one indicator of being "in love" or that the number of hours a person spends studying for a test is an indicator of "academic effort." What's wrong with simply asking people if they're poor, if they're in love, if they're happy, or if they work hard? Consider the connection between how a concept is defined and how it can be measured. Is it possible that sociology sometimes uses concepts that seem meaningless because they are easier to "see" and measure?

4 Building Order
Culture and History

Culture provides members of a society with a common bond and a set of shared rules and beliefs for making sense of the world in similar ways. This shared cultural knowledge makes it possible for people to live together in a society. Sociologists refer to shared cultural expectations as social norms. Norms are the rules and standards that govern all social encounters and the mechanisms that provide order in our day-to-day lives. Shared norms make it possible to know what to expect from others and what others can expect from us. When norms are violated, we are reminded of the boundaries of social behavior: the culturally shared rules for what is defined as right and wrong.

Norms are culturally specific. Indeed, the more ethnically and culturally diverse a society is, the greater the likelihood of normative clashes between groups. We can see clear evidence of the power of cultural norms when we examine how members of a different society handle some taken-for-granted aspect of everyday life. Take, for instance, the experience of time. If you've ever traveled abroad you know that people perceive the importance of time differently. In some places everyday life is incredibly fast-paced; in others it seems frustratingly slow and lethargic. In the industrialized world, events are often meticulously timed and scheduled. But in less developed parts of the world, time is much less restrictive and events occur more spontaneously. In "A Geography of Time," anthropologist Robert Levine uses his own travel experiences and observations to examine the impact of culture on the perception and use of time. He shows us how conflicts can result from clashes between people operating on different conceptions of time (what he calls *clock time* and *event time*). His comparison of the way time is experienced in other cultures versus our own reminds us that the time norms we consider to be normal and superior are in the end arbitrary and not shared worldwide. This is a humbling but important lesson for people who assume that their cultural way of life is natural and normal.

We don't have to travel to a foreign country to see the clash of different cultural beliefs and expectations. Such clashes can be quite confusing and painful for newly arrived immigrants from countries with vastly different cultural traditions. In the article "The Melting Pot," Anne Fadiman examines the experiences of Hmong refugees in the United States. Hundreds of thousands of Hmong people have fled Laos since that country fell to communist forces in 1975. Most have settled in the United States. Virtually every element of Hmong culture and tradition stands in stark contrast to the highly modernized cultural of U.S. society. The Hmong have been described in the

U.S. media as simplistic, primitive, and throwbacks to the Stone Age. This article vividly portrays the everyday conflicts immigrants face as they straddle two vastly different cultures.

Something to Consider as You Read:

How do cultural practices provide social order? Where is this order located? In our minds? In our interactions with others? Think about what happens to your own sense of order when you become immersed in a different culture. For instance, does your perception of time or use of language change? What are some of the challenges you might face in trying to maintain your own cultural beliefs and practices while living in a completely different culture? As you read and compare these two selections, think about why some cultures consider their ways to be better and more "real" than others. Do you think this tendency is a hallmark of all cultures, or just some?

A Geography of Time

Robert Levine

(1997)

Living on Event Time

Anyone who has traveled abroad—or waited in a doctor's office, for that matter—knows that the clock, or even the calendar, is sometimes no more than an ornament. The event at hand, on these occasions, often begins and ends with complete disregard for the technicalities of a timepiece. We in the industrialized world expect punctuality. But life on clock time is clearly out of line with virtually all of recorded history. And it is not only from a historical perspective that these temporal customs are so deviant. Still today, the idea of living by the clock remains absolutely foreign to much of the world.

One of the most significant differences in the pace of life is whether people use the hour on the clock to schedule the beginning and ending of activities, or whether the activities are allowed to transpire according to their own spontaneous schedule. These two approaches are known, respectively, as living by clock time and living by event time. The difference between clock and event time is more than a difference in speed, although life certainly does tend to be faster for people on clock time. Let me again turn to a personal example.

A few years after my stay in Brazil I became eligible for a sabbatical leave from my university. I decided to invest my term of "rest and renewal" in a study of international differences in the pace of life. I also chose to use the opportunity to live out a childhood dream—to travel around the world.

Precisely where I would go wasn't altogether clear. The phrase "travel around the orld" had a lovely ring to it, but I must admit that I wasn't certain just what it entailed. Never having done very well in geography, I had very little grasp of how the nations of the world are arranged and even less notion of their innards. Not knowing what I'd encounter, it was impossible to plan exactly where to visit or how long I would stay in each country. I decided, instead, to let the trip evolve its own form. Fortunately, the research I had designed allowed me the flexibility to decide where and when to collect data along the way.

I bought a map of the world and marked the locations of the four most exotic sights I could invoke: The Great Wall of China, Mount Everest, the Taj Mahal and the Great Pyramids of Egypt. I drew a line connecting the marks. Although I was uncertain how many of these wonders I'd actually see, they gave my trip a rough outline. I decided to fly to the edge of Western Asia and then make my way by land, moving in a rough westerly direction, around the globe. Searching the map for Asia's outside edge, my finger landed on Indonesia.

I purchased a one-way plane ticket to Jakarta, with stops along the way in Japan, Taiwan, and Hong Kong. Beyond that, I had no tickets. From Indonesia I would travel up the Malaysian peninsula toward Thailand, and then west across Asia toward home. My only rules would be to travel no better than second class and to stay on the ground as much as possible. I gave up my house lease, loaned out my car, put my possessions in storage, and told everyone who needed to know I'd be gone for the semester. (Professors don't think in terms of months. Our unit of time is the semester.)

The semester stretched into two semesters (one year, tossing in a summer vacation).

The trip began with a flight from San Francisco to Tokyo. Settling in for the long ride, I tried to focus on what I was beginning. My first thought was that I had no keys in my pocket. Next, that in place of an appointment calendar, I was carrying, for the first time in my life, a journal. Then came the realization that I had no commitments. There was nothing, other than carrying out my very flexible research plans, that needed to be done. I didn't have to be any place at any specific time for six whole months. There were no plans or schedules to interfere with whatever might come along. I could let my opportunities come forth on their own and I would choose those I wished to follow. I was free, free, free!

My joy lasted nearly half a minute. Then the terror: What in the world would I do for a whole semester without a schedule or plans? I looked ahead and saw layers and layers of nothing. How would I fill my time? I have never in my life so yearned for an appointment—with anyone for anything. It really was pitiful. Here I was freer and more mobile than most people in the world could ever dream of being. I was Marlon Brando on his motorcycle—with a passport, a Ph.D., and a steady paycheck. And I responded with an anxiety attack.

When I dozed off a little later on the flight, I dreamed about a passage from William Faulkner's *Light in August*. It is when the character named Christmas, hungry and fleeing from the sheriff, becomes obsessed with time. I later looked up the actual quotation:

... *I have not eaten since I have not eaten since* trying to remember how many days it had been since Friday in Jefferson, in the restaurant where he had eaten his supper, until after a while, in the lying still with waiting until the men should have eaten and gone to the field, the name of the day of the week seemed more important than the food. Because when the men were gone at last and he descended,

emerged, into the level, jonquil-colored sun and went to the kitchen door, he didn't ask for food at all . . . he heard his mouth saying "Can you tell me what day this is? I just want to know what day this is."

"What day it is?" Her face was gaunt as his, her body as gaunt and as tireless and as driven. She said: "You get away from here! It's Tuesday! You get away from here! I'll call my man!"

He said, "Thank you," as the door banged.

After finally arriving in Tokyo, I checked into a hotel room an ex-student had reserved for me. This was the only room reservation I had for the next six months (twelve months, actually but, mercifully, I didn't know that then). After unpacking, I put on the robe and slippers provided by the hotel. The bottom of the robe showed considerably more thigh than its maker had intended and the slippers only fit over three of my toes. But I liked the image and, coupled with a dip in the hot tub and a very large bottle of Sapporo beer, I went to sleep with some iota of hope for my immediate future.

The next morning I awoke to a view of green tiled roofs, banyan trees, and an enormous reclining Buddha. At the sight of my little robe and slippers my anticipation returned. I was ready to let events take their own course. What to do first? I loved my hot tub the night before, so decided to start my day with another long dip. Then I found a tea shop next door. The waiter spoke a little English, the food was good, and there was even a *Herald Tribune* to keep me company. After breakfast I explored my neighborhood reclining Buddha, who turned out to be resting in a large temple surrounded by a lovely park. I took out a book to read, stretched my legs and watched life in Tokyo parade by.

Next? A friend had given me a list of gardens he thought I'd enjoy seeing. Why not? I randomly chose one, and thoroughly enjoyed the visit. That evening I had a nice dinner at a restaurant near my hotel. I ended my day with a hot tub, my robe and slippers, and a Sapporo.

The following morning I shot out of bed with an adrenalin charge. What might this new day have in store? How to begin? A hot bath first, of course. Then, recalling the pleasant morning before, I returned to my tea shop for breakfast. After that I could think of no place on earth I would rather be than sitting beside my local Buddha. That afternoon I tried another garden. In the evening I returned to the same restaurant. And, of course, I took a hot bath and nursed my Sapporo before turning in. Another lovely day.

Day three went something like: hot tub/breakfast at the tea shop/Buddha/gardens/dinner/hot tub/Sapporo. The next day was the same. As was the next. And the next.

Looking back at that first week, I see you could have set a clock by my activities. What time is it, you ask? "He's reading his book in the park, so it must be 10 o'clock." "Now he's leaving the hot tub, so that must mean a little after eight." Without intending it, I'd created the structure I so craved on my plane trip. Ironically, one of the very reasons I chose a career in academia in the first place was because it, more than other professions, allowed me to arrange my own time. But when confronted with no limits, I had bounced to the other extreme. To my surprise as well as humbling disappointment, I had built a tighter schedule than the one I lived at work.

Drowning in Event Time

My behavior, I now recognize, was a textbook struggle between the forces of clock time, on the one hand, and event time on the other. Under clock time, the hour on the timepiece governs the beginning and ending of activities. When event time predominates, scheduling is determined by activities. Events begin and end when, by mutual consensus, participants "feel" the time is right. The distinction between clock and event time is profound. The sociologist Robert Lauer conducted in his book *Temporal Man* an intensive review of the literature concerning the meaning of time throughout history. The most fundamental difference, he found, has been between people operating by the clock versus those who measure time by social events.[1]

Many countries extoll event time as a philosophy of life. In Mexico, for example, there is a popular adage to "Give time to time" (*Darle tiempo al tiempo*). Across the globe in Africa, it is said that "Even the time takes its time." Psychologist Kris Eysell, while a Peace Corps volunteer in Liberia, was confronted by a variation on this African expression. She describes how every day, as she made her eight-mile walk from home to work, complete strangers would call out to her along the way: "Take time, Missy."

My experiences in Japan were those of a clock time addict floundering in situations where programming by the clock had lost its effectiveness. I was, I have since come to learn, drowning in good company. The social psychologist James Jones had even more complicated temporal challenges during his stay in Trinidad. Jones, an African-American, is quite familiar with the casualness of what used to be called "colored people's time" (CPT). But he was unprepared for the quagmire of life on event time. Jones first confronted the popular motto "Anytime is Trinidad time" soon after arriving, and said he spent the rest of his stay trying to understand just what it meant:

CPT simply implied that coming late to things was the norm and contrasted with the Anglo-European penchant for punctuality and timeliness. Over the course of my year in Trinidad, though, I came to understand that Trinidadians had personal control over time. They more or less came and went as they wanted or felt. "I didn't feel to go to work today," was a standard way of expressing that choice. Time was reckoned more by behavior than the clock. Things started when people arrived and ended when they left, not when the clock struck 8:00 or 1:00.[2]

To visitors from the world of clocks, life conducted on event time often appears, in James Jones's words, to be "chronometric anarchy."

Where Are the Cows? Measuring Time in Burundi

When event time people do listen to the clock, it is often nature's clock they hear. Salvatore Niyonzima, one of my former graduate students, describes his home country of Burundi as a classic example of this.

As in most of Central Africa, Niyonzima says, life in Burundi is guided by the seasons. More than 80 percent of the population of Burundi are farmers. As a result, "people still rely on the phases of nature," he explains. "When the dry season begins it is time for harvesting. And when the rainy season comes back—then, of course, it's time to return to the fields and plant and grow things, because this is the cycle."

Appointment times in Burundi are also often regulated by natural cycles. "Appointments are not necessarily in terms of a precise hour of the day. People who grew up in rural areas, and who haven't had very much education, might make an early appointment by saying, 'Okay, I'll see you tomorrow morning when the cows are going out for grazing.'" If they want to meet in the middle of the day, "they set their appointment for the time 'when the cows are going to drink in the stream,' which is where they are led at midday." In order to prevent the youngest cows from drinking too much, Niyonzima explains, farmers typically spend two or three hours with them back in a sheltered place, while their elders are still drinking from the stream. "Then in the afternoon, let's say somewhere around three o'clock, it's time again to get the young cows outside for the evening graze. So if we want to make a late appointment we might say 'I'll see you when the young cows go out.'"

Being any more precise—to say, for example, "I'll meet you in the latter part of the time when the cows are out drinking"—would

be, Niyonzima says, "just too much. If you arrange to come to my place when the cows are going to drink water, then it means it's around the middle of the day. If it's an hour earlier or an hour later, it doesn't matter. He knows that he made an appointment and that he'll be there." Precision is difficult and mostly irrelevant because it is hard to know exactly at what time people will be leading the cows out in the first place. "I might decide to lead them to the river one hour later because I either got them out of the home later or it didn't look like they really had that much to eat because the place where they were grazing didn't have very much pasture."

People in Burundi use similarly tangible images to mark the nighttime. "We refer to a very dark night as a 'Who are you?' night," Niyonzima explains. "This means that it was so dark that you couldn't recognize anybody without hearing their voice. You know that somebody is there but can't see them because it is so dark, so you say 'Who are you?' as a greeting. They speak and I hear their voice and now I recognize who they are. 'Who are you?'–time is one way to describe when it gets dark. We might refer back to an occasion as having occurred on a 'Who are you?' night."

Specifying precise nighttime appointments, Niyonzima says, "gets difficult. 'Who are you?' simply refers to the physical condition of darkness. I certainly wouldn't give a time like 8 P.M. or 9 P.M. When people want to name a particular time of the night, they might use references to aspects of sleep. They may, for example, say something occurred at a time 'When nobody was awake' or, if they wanted to be a little more specific, at the time 'When people were beginning the first period of their sleep.' Later in the night might be called 'Almost the morning light' or the time 'When the rooster sings'; or, to get really specific, 'When the rooster sings for the first time' or the second time, and so on. And then we're ready for the cows again."

Contrast the natural clocks of Burundi to the clock time scheduling that prevails in the dominant Anglo culture of the United States. Our watches dictate when it is time to work and when to play; when each encounter must begin and end.

Even biological events are typically scheduled by the clock. It is normal to talk about it being "too early to go to sleep" or "not yet dinner time," or too late to take a nap or eat a snack. The hour on the clock, rather than the signal from our bodies, usually dictates when it is time to begin and stop. We learn these habits at a very early age. A newborn is fully capable of recognizing when he or she is hungry or sleepy. But it is not long before parents either adjust their baby's routine to fit their own or, in response to whatever may be the prevailing cultural standards (often defined by popular Dr. Spock–type advice manuals), train the child to eat and sleep to more "healthy" rhythms. The baby then learns when to be hungry and when to be sleepy.

As adults, some people are particularly susceptible to the control of the clock. Several years ago, in a series of classic studies, social psychologist Stanley Schachter and his colleagues observed the eating behaviors of obese and normalweight people. Schachter theorized that a major factor in obesity is a tendency for eating to be governed by external cues from the surrounding environment. People of normal weight, he believed, are more responsive to their internal hunger pangs. One powerful external cue, Schachter hypothesized, is the clock.

To test his theory, Columbia University dormitory students were brought into a room in which the experimenters had doctored the clocks so that some subjects thought it was earlier than their usual dinner time and others thought it was later than their usual dinner time. Participants were told to help themselves to a bowl of crackers in front of them. As Schachter predicted, the obese people ate more crackers when they thought it was after their dinner time than when they were made to believe that it was not yet time for dinner. The time on the clock had no bearing on how many

crackers the normal-weight subjects ate. They ate when they were hungry. The overweight people ate when the time on the clock said it was appropriate.[3] As my over-threehundred-pound uncle replied when I once asked him if he was hungry, "I haven't been hungry in 45 years."

Is Time Money?

When the clock predominates, time becomes a valuable commodity. Clock time cultures take for granted the reality of time as fixed, linear, and measurable. As Ben Franklin once advised, "Remember that time is money." But to event time cultures, for whom time is considerably more flexible and ambiguous, time and money are very separate entities.

The clash between these attitudes can be jarring. When, on my sabbatical trip, I moved out of my hot tub/breakfast/Buddha routine and made a trip to the Taj Mahal, for example, the most frequent comments I heard spoken by firstworld visitors referred to the amount of work that went into the building—variations on the question, "How long must that have taken?" Perhaps the second most frequent comment I heard from tourists in India went something like: "That embroidery must have taken forever. Can you imagine how much that would cost back home?" Finding bargains on foreigners' time is, in fact, a favorite vacation activity of many Westerners. But these comments wouldn't mean much to the Indian artist who spent months embroidering a fabric or to their ancestors who'd built the Taj Mahal. When event time predominates, the economic model of clock time makes little sense. Time and money are independent entities. You need to give time to time, as they say in Mexico.

In my travels in South America and Asia I have repeatedly been confused, and sometimes even harassed, by comments such as: "Unlike you Americans, time is not money for us." My usual response is something like: "But our time is all we have. It's our most valuable, our only really valuable, possession. How can you waste it like that?" Their typical retort—usually in a less frantic tone than my own—begins with unqualified agreement that time is, indeed, our most valuable commodity. But it is for exactly this reason, event timers argue, that time shouldn't be wasted by carving it into inorganic monetary units.

Burundi again provides a case in point. "Central Africans," Salvatore Niyonzima says, "generally disregard the fact that time is always money. When I want the time to wait for me, it does. And when I don't want to do something today—for any reason, whatever reason—I can just decide to do it tomorrow and it will be as good as today. If I lose some time I'm not losing something very important because, after all, I have so much of it."

Jean Traore, an exchange student from Burkina Faso in Eastern Africa, finds the concept of "wasting time" confusing. "There's no such thing as wasting time where I live," he observes. "How can you waste time? If you're not doing one thing, you're doing something else. Even if you're just talking to a friend, or sitting around, that's what you're doing." A responsible Burkina Faso citizen is expected to understand and accept this view of time, and to recognize that what is truly wasteful—sinful, to some—is to not make sufficient time available for the people in your life.

Mexico is another example. Frustrated U.S. business people often complain that Mexicans are *plagued* by a lack of attachment to time. But as writer Jorge Castaneda points out, "they are simply different . . . Letting and watching time go by, being late (an hour, a day, a week), are not grievous offenses. They simply indicate a lower rung on the ladder of priorities. It is more important to see a friend of the family than to keep an appointment or to make it to work, especially when work consists of hawking wares on street corners." There is also an economic explanation: "There is a severe lack of incentives for being on time, delivering on time, or working overtime. Since most people

are paid little for what they do, the prize for punctuality and formality can be meaningless: time is often not money in Mexico."

Event time and clock time are not totally unrelated. But event time encompasses considerably more than the clock. It is a product of the larger gestalt; a result of social, economic, and environmental cues, and, of course, of cultural values. Consequently, clock time and event time often constitute worlds of their own. As Jorge Castaneda observes about Mexico and the United States, "time divides our two countries as much as any other single factor."[4]

Other Event Time Cultures

Life in industrialized society is so enmeshed with the clock that its inhabitants are often oblivious to how eccentric their temporal beliefs can appear to others. But many people in the world aren't as "civilized" as us. (Psychologist Julian Jaynes defines civilization as "the art of living in towns of such size that everyone does not know everyone else.") Even today, organic clocks like Burundi's time of the cows are often the only standard that insiders are willing to accept. For many, if not most, people in the world, living by mechanical clocks would feel as abnormal and confusing as living without a concrete schedule would to a Type A Westerner.

Anthropologists have chronicled many examples of contemporary event time cultures. Philip Bock, for example, analyzed the temporal sequence of a wake conducted by the Micmac Indians of Eastern Canada. He found that the wake can be clearly divided into gathering time, prayer time, singing time, intermission, and mealtime. But it turns out that none of these times are directly related to clock time. The mourners simply move from one time to another by mutual consensus. When do they begin and end each episode? When the time is ripe and no sooner.[5]

Robert Lauer tells of the Nuers from the Sudan, whose calendars are based on the seasonal changes in their environment. They construct their fishing dams and cattle camps, for example, in the month of *kur*. How do they know when it is *kur*? It's *kur* when they're building their dams and camps. They break camp and return to their villages in the months of *dwat*. When is it *dwat*? When people are on the move.[6] There's an old joke about an American on a whirlwind tour of Europe who is asked where he is. "If it's Tuesday," he responds, "this must be Belgium." If Nuers were asked the same question they might answer: "If it's Belgium, this must be Tuesday."

Many people use their social activities to mark time rather than the other way around. In parts of Madagascar, for example, questions about how long something takes might receive an answer like "the time of a rice-cooking" (about half an hour) or "the frying of a locust" (a quick moment). Similarly, natives of the Cross River in Nigeria have been quoted as saying "the man died in less than the time in which maize is not yet completely roasted" (less than fifteen minutes). Closer to home, not too many years ago the *New English Dictionary* included a listing for the term "pissing while"—not a particularly exact measurement, perhaps, but one with a certain crosscultural translatability.

Most societies have some type of week, but it turns out it's not always seven days long. The Incas had a ten-day week. Their neighbors, the Muysca of Bogota, had a three-day week. Some weeks are as long as sixteen days. Often the length of the week reflects cycles of activities, rather than the other way around. For many people, their markets are the main activity requiring group coordination. The Khasis of Assam, Pitirim Sorokin reports, hold their market every eighth day. Being practical people, they've made their week eight days long and named the days of the week after the places where the main markets occur.[7]

Natives of the Andaman jungle in India are another people with little need to buy calendars. The Andamanese have constructed a complex annual calendar built around the sequence of dominant smells of trees and flowers in their environment. When they want to check the time of year, the Andamanese simply smell the odors outside their door.[8]

The monks in Burma have developed a foolproof alarm clock. They know it is time to rise at daybreak "when there is light enough to see the veins in their hand."[9]

There are groups who, even though they have wristwatches, prefer to measure time imprecisely. The anthropologist Douglas Raybeck, for example, has studied the Kelantese peasants of the Malay Peninsula, a group he refers to as the "coconut-clock" people. The Kelantese approach to time is typified by their coconut clocks—an invention they use as a timer for sporting competitions. This clock consists of a half coconut shell with a small hole in its center that sits in a pail of water. Intervals are measured by the time it takes the shell to fill with water and then sink—usually about three to five minutes. The Kelantese recognize that the clock is inexact, but they choose it over the wristwatches they own.[10]

Some people don't even have a single-word equivalent of "time." E. R. Leach has studied the Kachin people of North Burma. The Kachin use the word *ahkying* to refer to the time of the clock. The word *na* refers to a long time, and *tawng* to a short time. The word *ta* refers to springtime and *asak* to the time of a person's life. A Kachin wouldn't regard any of these words as synonymous with another. Whereas time for most Westerners is treated as an objective entity—it is a noun in the English language—the Kachin words for time are treated more like adverbs. Time has no tangible reality for the Kachin.[11]

Many North American Indian cultures also treat time only indirectly in their language. The Sioux, for example, have no single word in their language for "time," "late," or "waiting." The Hopi, observes Edward Hall, have no verb tenses for past, present, and future. Like the Kachin people, the Hopi treat temporal concepts more like adverbs than nouns. When discussing the seasons, for example, "the Hopi cannot talk about summer being hot, because summer is the quality hot, just as an apple has the quality red," Hall reports. "Summer and hot are the same! Summer is a *condition:* hot." It is difficult for the Kachin and the Hopi to conceive of time as a quantity. Certainly, it is not equated with money and the clock. Time only exists in the eternal present.

Many Mediterranean Arab cultures define only three sets of time: no time at all, now (which is of varying duration), and forever (too long). As a result, American businessmen have often encountered frustrating communication breakdowns when trying to get Arabs to distinguish between different waiting periods—between, say, a long time and a very long time.[12]

I ran into similar dictionary problems once when trying to translate a time survey into Spanish for a Mexican sample. Three of my original English questions asked people when they would "expect" a person to arrive for a certain appointment, what time they "hoped" that person would arrive, and how long they would "wait" for them to arrive. It turns out that the three English verbs "to expect," "to hope," and "to wait" all translate into the single Spanish verb "*esperar.*" (The same verb is used in Portuguese.) I eventually had to use roundabout terms to get the distinctions across.

There is an old Yiddish proverb that says, "It's good to hope, it's the waiting that spoils it." Compare this to a culture whose language does not routinely distinguish between expecting, hoping, and waiting, and you have a pretty clear picture of how the latter feels about the clock. At first, I was frustrated by the inability to translate my questionnaires. Later, though, I came to see that my translation failures were telling me as much about Latin American concepts of time as were their responses to my formal questions. The silent and verbal languages of time feed upon each other.

Keeping Everything From Happening at Once

The primary function of clock time, it may be argued, is to prevent simultaneously occurring events from running into one another. "Time is nature's way of keeping everything from happening at once," observes a contemporary item of graffiti. The more complex our network of activities, the greater the need to formalize scheduling. A shared commitment to abide by clock time serves to coordinate traffic. The Khasis and Nuers are able to avoid governance by the clock because the demands on their time are relatively distinct and uncomplicated.

But we don't have to cross continents to see groups still operating on event time. Even in clock-time-dominated cultures, there are people whose temporal demands more closely resemble the sparsity of Asian villagers than that of the surrounding clock-coordinated society. In these subcultures, life takes on the cadence of event time.

Alex Gonzalez, a fellow social psychologist raised in a Mexican-American barrio in Los Angeles, has described the attitude toward time among his childhood friends who remain in his old neighborhood. Many of these people are unemployed, have little prospect of employment, and, he observes, almost no future time perspective. His old neighborhood, Gonzalez says, is filled with people who congregate loosely each day and wait for something to capture their interest. Their problem is not so much finding time for their activities as it is to find activities to fill their time. They stay with the event until, by mutual consent, it feels like time to move on. Time is flat. Watches are mostly ornaments and symbols of status. They're rarely for telling time.[13]

How would these people react if you gave them a Day Runner? Probably like Jonathan Swifts's Lilliputians did to Gulliver, who looked at his watch before doing anything. He called it his oracle. The Lilliputians he met in his travels decided that Gulliver's watch must be his God. In other words, they thought he was crazy.

The Advantage of Temporal Flexibility

Clock time cultures tend to be less flexible in how they schedule activities. They are more likely to be what anthropologist Edward Hall calls monochronic or M-time schedulers: people who like to focus on one activity at a time. Event time people, on the other hand, tend to prefer polychronic or P-time scheduling: doing several things at once.[14] M-time people like to work from start to finish in linear sequence: the first task is begun and completed before turning to another, which is then begun and completed. In polychronic time, however, one project goes on until there is an inclination or inspiration to turn to another, which may lead to an idea for another, then back to the first, with intermittent and unpredictable pauses and resumptions of one task or another. Progress on P-time occurs a little at a time on each task.

P-time cultures are characterized by a strong involvement with people. They emphasize the completion of human transactions rather than keeping to schedules. Two Burundians deep in conversation, for example, will typically choose to arrive late for their next appointment rather than cut into the flow of their discussion. Both would be insulted, in fact, if their partner were to abruptly terminate the conversation before it came to a spontaneous conclusion. "If you value people," Hall explains about the sensibility of P-time cultures, "you must hear them out and cannot cut them off simply because of a schedule."

P-time and M-time don't mix well. Allen Bluedorn, a professor of management at the University of Missouri, and his colleagues have found that M-time individuals are happier and more productive in M-time organizations while polychronic people do better in polychromic ones. These findings are applicable not only to foreign cultures, but also to different organizational cultures in the United States.[15]

Both M-time and clock time thinking tend to be concentrated in achievement-oriented, industrialized societies like the United States. P-time and event time are more common in third-world economies. In general, people who live on P-time are less productive—by Western economic standards, at least—than are M-time people. But there are occasions when polychronicity is not only more people-oriented, but also more productive. Rigid adherence to schedules can cut things short just when they are beginning to move forward. And as the invention of the word processor has taught even the most rigid of M-time people, working in nonlinear progression, spontaneously shifting attention from one section of a project to another, making connections from back to front as well as vice versa, can be both liberating and productive.

The most fruitful approach of all, however, is one that moves flexibly between the worlds of P-time and M-time, event time and clock time, as suits the situation. Some of the newer entrants into the economics of industrialization have managed monetary success without wholesale sacrifice of their traditional commitment to social obligations. Once again, the Japanese, with their blend of traditional Eastern and modern Western cultures, provide a noteworthy example.

A few years ago, I received a letter from Kiyoshi Yoneda, a businessman from Tokyo who has spent more than five years living in the West. My research on cross-national differences in the pace of life, which found that the Japanese had the fastest pace of life in the world, had just been reported in the international press. Mr. Yoneda wrote because he was concerned (with good reason, I might add) about the superficiality of my understanding of Japanese attitudes toward time. He wanted me to understand that the Japanese may be fast, but that doesn't mean that they treat the clock with the same reverence as people in the West.

Meetings in Japan, he pointed out, start less punctually and end much more "sluggishly" than they do in the United States. "In the Japanese company I work for," he wrote, "meetings go all the way until some agreement is made, or until everybody is tired; and the end is not sharply predefined by a scheduled time. The agreement is often not clearly stated. Perhaps in order to compensate [for] the unpredictability of the closing time of a meeting, you are not blamed if you [go] away before the meeting is over. Also, it's quite all right to sleep during the meeting. For instance, if you are an engineer and not interested in the money-counting aspects of a project, nobody expects you to stay wide awake paying attention to discussions concerning details of accounting. You may fall asleep, do your reading or writing, or stand up to get some coffee or tea."

Monochronic and polychronic organizations each have their weaknesses. Monochronic systems are prone to undervaluing the humanity of their members. Polychronic ones tend toward unproductive chaos. It would seem that the most healthy approach to P-time and M-time is to hone skills for both, and to execute mixtures of each to suit the situation. The Japanese blend offers one provocative example of how people take control of their time, rather than the other way around.

More Time Wars

Because cultural norms are so widely shared by the surrounding society, people often forget that their own rules are arbitrary. It is easy to confuse cultural normalcy with ethnocentric superiority. When people of different cultures interact, the potential for misunderstanding exists on many levels. For example, members of Arab and Latin cultures usually stand much

closer when they're speaking to people than we do in the United States, a fact we frequently misinterpret as aggression or disrespect. Similarly, we often misconstrue the intentions of people with temporal customs different from our own. Such are the difficulties of communicating the silent languages of culture.

Nearly every traveler has experienced these blunders, in the forms of their own misunderstanding of the motives of the surrounding culture as well as others' misinterpretations of theirs. A particularly frequent source of mishaps involves clashes between clock time and event time. Fortunately, most of our stumblings are limited to unpleasant miscommunications. When misunderstandings occur at a higher level, however, they can be serious business.

An example of this occurred in 1985, when a group of Shiite Muslim terrorists hijacked a TWA jetliner and held 40 Americans hostage, demanding that Israel release 764 Lebanese Shiite prisoners being held in prison. Shortly after, the terrorists handed the American hostages over to Shiite Muslim leaders, who assured everybody that nothing would happen if the Israelis met their demands.

At one point during the delicate negotiations Ghassan Sablini, the number-three man in the Shiite militia Amal (who had assumed the role of militant authorities), announced that the hostages would be handed back to the hijackers in two days if no action was taken on their demand that Israel release its Shiite prisoners. This created a very dangerous situation. The U.S. negotiators knew that neither they nor the Israelis could submit to these terrorist demands without working out a face-saving compromise. But by setting a limit of "two days" the Shiite leaders made a compromise unlikely and had elevated the crisis to a very dangerous level. People held their breath. At the last minute, however, Sablini was made to understand how his statement was being interpreted. To everyone's relief, he explained: "We said a couple of days but we were not necessarily specifying 48 hours."[16]

Forty deaths and a possible war were nearly caused by a miscommunication over the meaning of the word "day." To the U.S. negotiators, the word referred to a technical aspect of time: 24 hours. For the Muslim leader, a day was merely a figure of speech meaning "a while." The U.S. negotiators were thinking on clock time. Sablini was on event time.

NOTES

1. Lauer, R. (1981). *Temporal Man: The Meaning and Uses of Social Time*. New York: Praeger.

2. Jones, J. (1993). An exploration of temporality in human behavior. In Schank, R., and Langer, E. (eds.), *Beliefs, Reasoning, and Decision-Making: Psycho-Logic in Honor of Bob Abelson*. Hillsdale, NJ: Lawrence Erlbaum.

3. Schachter, S., and Gross, L. (1968). Manipulated time and eating behavior. *Journal of Personality and Social Psychology* 10, 93–106.

4. Castaneda, J. (1995, July). Ferocious differences. *The Atlantic Monthly*, 68–76, 73, 74.

5. Bock, P. (1964). Social structure and language structure. *Southwestern Journal of Anthropology* 20, 393–403.

6. Lauer, R. H. (1981). *Temporal Man: The Meaning and Uses of Social Time*. New York: Praeger.

7. Sorokin, P. (1964). *Sociocultural Causality, Space, Time*. New York: Russel and Russel.

8. Rifkin, J. (1987, September/October). Time wars: A new dimension shaping our future. *Utne Reader*, 46–57.

9. Thompson, E. P. (1967). Time, work-discipline, and industrial capitalism. *Past and Present* 38, 56–97.

10. Raybeck, D. (1992). The coconut-shell clock: Time and cultural identity. *Time and Society* 1 (3), 323–40.

11. Leach, E. R. (1961). *Rethinking Anthropology*. London: Athlone Press.

12. Hall, E. (1983). *The Dance of Life*. Garden City, NY: Doubleday.

13. Gonzalez has also done important research on the subject of time. See Gonzalez, A., and Zimbardo, P. (1985, March). Time in perspective. *Psychology Today*, 20–26.

14. Hall, E. (1983). *The Dance of Life*. Garden City, NY: Doubleday.

15. Bluedorn, A., Kaufman, C., and Lane, P. (1992). How many things do you like to do at once? An introduction to monochronic and polychronic time. *Academy of Management Executive* 6, 17–26.

16. UPI (1985, June 23). Ships with 1,800 Marines off Lebanon. Reprinted in *The Fresno Bee*, A1.

THINKING ABOUT THE READING

What is the difference between clock time and event time? How are these different types of time related to the level of development of a particular culture? Levine seems to be arguing that event time is a less stressful and healthier way for people to live their lives than clock time, even though clock time is a characteristic of more "advanced" societies. Do you think an achievement-oriented, technologically complex society like the United States could ever exist on event time? What kind of time interval do you use to plan your day? Minutes, half hours, hours? What effect do you think digital technology has had on your internal clock and on the organization of your daily life? How do you think culture influences expectations of "busy-ness"? Consider some of the differences in the work cycles of farmers who organize labor in terms of seasons and daylight, and the work cycles of assembly-line employees who have to punch a time clock when they arrive and leave work. Go to a busy public space and "do nothing" for ten minutes. Watch your thoughts and body. What does this exercise tell you about the time rhythms of this culture?

The Melting Pot

Anne Fadiman

(1997)

The Lee family—Nao Kao, Foua, Chong, Zoua, Cheng, May, Yer, and True—arrived in the United States on December 18, 1980. Their luggage consisted of a few clothes, a blue blanket, and a wooden mortar and pestle that Foua had chiseled from a block of wood in Houaysouy. They flew from Bangkok to Honolulu, and then to Portland, Oregon, where they were to spend two years before moving to Merced. Other refugees told me that their airplane flights—a mode of travel that strained the limits of the familiar Hmong concept of migration—had been fraught with anxiety and shame: they got airsick, they didn't know how to use the bathroom but were afraid to soil themselves, they thought they had to pay for their food but had no money, they tried to eat the Wash'n Dris. The Lees, though perplexed, took the novelties of the trip in stride. Nao Kao remembers the airplane as being "just like a big house."

Their first week in Portland, however, was miserably disorienting. Before being placed by a local refugee agency in a small rented house, they spent a week with relatives, sleeping on the floor. "We didn't know anything so our relatives had to show us everything," Foua said. "They knew because they had lived in America for three or four months already. Our relatives told us about electricity and said the children shouldn't touch those plugs in the wall because they could get hurt. They told us that the refrigerator is a cold box where you put meat. They showed us how to open the TV so we could see it. We had never seen a toilet before and we thought maybe the water in it was to drink or cook with. Then our relatives told us what it was, but we didn't know whether we should sit or whether we should stand on it. Our relatives took us to the store but we didn't know that the cans and packages had food in them. We could tell what the meat was, but the chickens and cows and pigs were all cut up in little pieces and had plastic on them. Our relatives told us the stove is for cooking the food, but I was afraid to use it because it might explode. Our relatives said in America the food you don't eat you just throw away. In Laos we always fed it to the animals and it was strange to waste it like that. In this country there were a lot of strange things and even now I don't know a lot of things and my children have to help me, and it still seems like a strange country."

Seventeen years later, Foua and Nao Kao use American appliances, but they still speak only Hmong, celebrate only Hmong holidays, practice only the Hmong religion, cook only Hmong dishes, sing only Hmong songs, play only Hmong musical instruments, tell only Hmong stories, and know far more about current political events in Laos and Thailand than about those in the United States. When I first met them, during their eighth year in this country, only one American adult, Jeanine Hilt, had ever been invited to their home as a guest. It would be hard to imagine anything further from the vaunted American ideal of assimilation, in which immigrants are expected to submerge their cultural differences in order to embrace a shared national identity. *E pluribus unum:* from many, one.

During the late 1910s and early 1920s, immigrant workers at the Ford automotive plant in Dearborn, Michigan, were given free, compulsory "Americanization" classes. In addition to English lessons, there were lectures on work habits, personal hygiene, and table manners. The first sentence they memorized was "I am a good American." During their graduation ceremony they gathered next to a gigantic wooden pot, which their teachers stirred with ten-foot ladles. The students walked through a door into the pot, wearing traditional costumes from their countries of origin and singing songs in their native languages. A few minutes later, the door in the pot opened, and the students walked out again, wearing suits and ties, waving American flags, and singing "The Star-Spangled Banner."

The European immigrants who emerged from the Ford Motor Company melting pot came to the United States because they hoped to assimilate into mainstream American society. The Hmong came to the United States for the same reason they had left China in the nineteenth century: because they were trying to *resist* assimilation. As the anthropologist Jacques Lemoine has observed, "they did not come to our countries only to save their lives, they rather came to save their selves, that is, their Hmong ethnicity." If their Hmong ethnicity had been safe in Laos, they would have preferred to remain there, just as their ancestors—for whom migration had always been a problem-solving strategy, not a footloose impulse—would have preferred to remain in China. Unlike the Ford workers who enthusiastically, or at least uncomplainingly, belted out the "The Star-Spangled Banner" (of which Foua and Nao Kao know not a single word), the Hmong are what sociologists call "involuntary migrants." It is well known that involuntary migrants, no matter what pot they are thrown into, tend not to melt.

What the Hmong wanted here was to be left alone to be Hmong: clustered in all-Hmong enclaves, protected from government interference, self-sufficient, and agrarian. Some brought hoes in their luggage. General Vang Pao has said, "For many years, right from the start, I tell the American government that we need a little bit of land where we can grow vegetables and build homes like in Laos. . . . I tell them it does not have to be the best land, just a little land where we can live." This proposal was never seriously considered. "It was just out of the question," said a spokesman for the State Department's refugee program. "It would cost too much, it would be impractical, but most of all it would set off wild protests from [other Americans] and from other refugees who weren't getting land for themselves." . . .

Just as newly arrived immigrants in earlier eras had been called "FOBs"—Fresh Off the Boat—some social workers nicknamed the incoming Hmong, along with the other Southeast Asian refugees who entered the United States after the Vietnamese War, "JOJs": Just Off the Jet. Unlike the first waves of Vietnamese and Cambodian refugees, most of whom received several months of vocational and language training at regional "reception centers," the Hmong JOJs, who arrived after the centers had closed, were all sent directly to their new homes. (Later on, some were given "cultural orientation" training in Thailand before flying to the United States. Their classes covered such topics as how to distinguish a one-dollar bill from a ten-dollar bill and how to use a peephole.) The logistical details of their resettlement were contracted by the federal government to private nonprofit groups known as VOLAGs, or national voluntary resettlement agencies, which found local sponsors. Within their first few weeks in this country, newly arrived families were likely to deal with VOLAG officials, immigration officials, public health officials, social service officials, employment officials, and public assistance officials. The Hmong are not known for holding bureaucrats in high esteem. As one proverb puts it, "To see a tiger is to die; to see an official is to become destitute." In a study of adaptation problems among Indochinese refugees, Hmong respondents rated "Difficulty with American Agencies" as a more serious problem than either "War Memories" or "Separation from Family." Because many of the VOLAGs had religious affiliations, the JOJs also often found themselves dealing with Christian ministers, who, not surprisingly, took a dim view of shamanistic animism. A sponsoring pastor in Minnesota told a local newspaper, "It would be wicked to just bring them over and feed and clothe them and let them go to hell. The God who made us wants them to be converted. If anyone thinks that a gospel-preaching church would bring them over and not tell them about the Lord, they're out of their mind." The proselytizing backfired. According to a study of Hmong mental health problems, refugees sponsored by this pastor's religious organization were significantly more likely, when compared to other refugees, to require psychiatric treatment.

The Hmong were accustomed to living in the mountains, and most of them had never seen snow. Almost all their resettlement sites had flat topography and freezing winters. The majority were sent to cities, including Minneapolis, Chicago, Milwaukee, Detroit, Hartford, and Providence, because that was where refugee services—health care, language classes, job training, public housing—were concentrated. To encourage assimilation, and to avoid burdening any one community with more than its "fair share" of refugees, the Immigration and Naturalization Service adopted a policy of dispersal rather than clustering. Newly arrived Hmong were assigned to fifty-three cities in twenty-five different states: stirred into the melting pot in tiny, manageable portions, or, as John Finck, who worked with Hmong at the Rhode Island Office of Refugee Resettlement, put it, "spread like a thin layer of butter throughout the country so

they'd disappear." In some places, clans were broken up. In others, members of only one clan were resettled, making it impossible for young people, who were forbidden by cultural taboo from marrying within their own clan, to find local marriage partners. Group solidarity, the cornerstone of Hmong social organization for more than two thousand years, was completely ignored.

Although most Hmong were resettled in cities, some nuclear families, unaccompanied by any of their extended relations, were placed in isolated rural areas. Disconnected from traditional supports, these families exhibited unusually high levels of anxiety, depression, and paranoia. In one such case, the distraught and delusional father of the Yang family—the only Hmong family sponsored by the First Baptist Church of Fairfield, Iowa—attempted to hang himself in the basement of his wooden bungalow along with his wife and four children. His wife changed her mind at the last minute and cut the family down, but she acted too late to save their only son. An Iowa grand jury declined to indict either parent, on the grounds that the father was suffering from Post-Traumatic Stress Disorder, and the mother, cut off from all sources of information except her husband, had no way to develop an independent version of reality.

Reviewing the initial resettlement of the Hmong with a decade's hindsight, Lionel Rosenblatt, the former United States Refugee Coordinator in Thailand, conceded that it had been catastrophically mishandled. "We knew at the start their situation was different, but we just couldn't make any special provisions for them," he said. "I still feel it was no mistake to bring the Hmong here, but you look back now and say, 'How could we have done it so shoddily?'" Eugene Douglas, President Reagan's ambassador-at-large for refugee affairs, stated flatly, "It was a kind of hell they landed into. Really, it couldn't have been done much worse."

The Hmong who sought asylum in the United States were, of course, not a homogeneous lump. A small percentage, mostly the high-ranking military officers who were admitted first, were multilingual and cosmopolitan, and a larger percentage had been exposed in a desultory fashion to some aspects of American culture and technology during the war or while living in Thai refugee camps. But the experience of tens of thousands of Hmong was much like the Lees'. It is possible to get some idea of how monumental the task of adjustment was likely to be by glancing at some of the pamphlets, audiotapes, and videos that refugee agencies produced for Southeast Asian JOJs. For example, "Your New Life in the United States," a handbook published by the Language and Orientation Resource Center in Washington, D.C., included the following tips:

Learn the meaning of "WALK"–"DON'T WALK" signs when crossing the street.

To send mail, you must use stamps.

To use the phone:

1) Pick up the receiver
2) Listen for dial tone
3) Dial each number separately
4) Wait for person to answer after it rings
5) Speak.

The door of the refrigerator must be shut.

Never put your hand in the garbage disposal.

Do not stand or squat on the toilet since it may break.

Never put rocks or other hard objects in the tub or sink since this will damage them.

Always ask before picking your neighbor's flowers, fruit, or vegetables.

In colder areas you must wear shoes, socks, and appropriate outerwear. Otherwise, you may become ill.

Always use a handkerchief or a kleenex to blow your nose in public places or inside a public building.

Never urinate in the street. This creates a smell that is offensive to Americans. They also believe that it causes disease.

Spitting in public is considered impolite and unhealthy. Use a kleenex or handkerchief.

Picking your nose or your ears in public is frowned upon in the United States.

The customs they were expected to follow seemed so peculiar, the rules and regulations so numerous, the language so hard to learn, and the emphasis on literacy and the decoding of other unfamiliar symbols so strong, that many Hmong were overwhelmed. Jonas Vangay told me, "In America, we are blind because even though we have eyes, we cannot see. We are deaf because even though we have ears, we cannot hear." Some newcomers wore pajamas as street clothes; poured water on electric stoves to extinguish them; lit charcoal fires in their living rooms; stored blankets in their refrigerators; washed rice in their toilets; washed their clothes in swimming pools; washed their hair with Lestoil; cooked with motor oil and furniture polish; drank Clorox; ate cat food; planted crops in public parks; shot and ate skunks, porcupines, woodpeckers, robins, egrets, sparrows, and a bald eagle; and hunted pigeons with crossbows in the streets of Philadelphia.

If the United States seemed incomprehensible to the Hmong, the Hmong seemed equally incomprehensible to the United States. Journalists seized excitedly on a label that is still trotted out at regular intervals: "the most primitive refugee group in America." (In an angry letter to the *New York Times,* in which that phrase had appeared in a 1990 news article, a Hmong computer specialist observed, "Evidently, we were not too primitive to fight as proxies for United States troops in the war in Laos.") Typical phrases from newspaper and magazine stories in the late seventies and eighties included "low-caste hill tribe," "Stone Age," "emerging from the mists of time," "like Alice falling down a rabbit hole." Inaccuracies were in no short supply. A 1981 article in the *Christian Science Monitor* called the Hmong language "extremely simplistic"; declared that the Hmong, who have been sewing *paj ntaub* [embroidered cloth] with organic motifs for centuries, make "no connection between a picture of a tree and a real tree"; and noted that "the Hmong have no oral tradition of literature. . . . Apparently no folk tales exist." Some journalists seemed to shed all inhibition, and much of their good sense as well, when they were loosed on the Hmong. My favorite passage is a 1981 *New York Times* editorial about the large number of Hmong men who had died unexpectedly in their sleep, killed—or so it was widely believed at the time—by their own nightmares.[1] After explaining that the Hmong "attributed conscious life to natural objects," the writer asked,

> What were these nightmares? Did a palm tree's fronds turn into threatening fingers? Did a forest move and march with the implacability of the tide? Did a rose stretch on its stalk and throttle the sleeper?
>
> Or did a gasoline hose curl and crush like a python? Was one of the dreamers pinned by a perambulating postbox? Or stabbed by scissors run amok?

("Or did the editorial writer drop acid?" I wrote in the newspaper margin when I first read this.)

Timothy Dunnigan, a linguistic anthropologist who has taught a seminar at the University of Minnesota on the media presentation of Hmong and Native Americans, once remarked to me, "The kinds of metaphorical language that we use to describe the Hmong say far more about us, and our attachment to our own frame of reference, than they do about

the Hmong." So much for the Perambulating Postbox Theory. Dunnigan's comment resonates with Dwight Conquergood's observation about the uneasiness Westerners feel when confronted with the Other—for who could be more Other than the Hmong? Not only did they squat on toilets and eat skunks, not only did they bang gongs and sacrifice cows, but they also displayed what struck many people as an offensively selective interest in adopting the customs of the majority culture. For example, many Hmong quickly learned how to use telephones and drive cars, because those skills fit their own agenda of communicating with other Hmong, but failed to learn English. In 1987, when Senator Alan Simpson, then the ranking minority member of the Senate Subcommittee on Immigration and Refugee Affairs, called the Hmong "the most indigestible group in society," he sounded much like the authorities in China long ago, who were grievously insulted when the Hmong refused to speak Chinese or eat with chopsticks.

It could not be denied that the Hmong were genuinely mysterious—far more so, for instance, than the Vietnamese and Cambodians who were streaming into the United States at the same time. Hardly anyone knew how to pronounce the word "Hmong." Hardly anyone—except the anthropology graduate students who suddenly realized they could write dissertations on patrilineal exogamous clan structures without leaving their hometowns—knew what role the Hmong had played during the war, or even what war it had been, since our government had succeeded all too well in keeping the Quiet War quiet. Hardly anyone knew they had a rich history, a complex culture, an efficient social system, and enviable family values. They were therefore an ideal blank surface on which to project xenophobic fantasies.

The most expedient mode of projection has always been the rumor, and the Hmong attracted more than their share. This was to be expected. After all, the Hmong of China had

had wings under their armpits and small tails. In prevalence and nastiness, American rumors about the Hmong are at least an even match for the Hmong rumors about America that circulated in the refugee camps of Thailand. Some samples: The Hmong run a white slave trade. The Hmong are given cars by the government. The Hmong force their children to run in front of cars in order to get big insurance settlements. The Hmong sell their daughters and buy their wives. Hmong women think speed bumps are washboards for scrubbing clothes, and they get run over by eighteen-wheelers. The Hmong eat dogs.[2] (That one comes complete with its own set of racist jokes. "What's the name of the Hmong cookbook? *101 Ways to Wok Your Dog.*") The dog-eating rumor has joined the national pantheon of deathless urban legends, right up there with alligators in the sewers and worms in the Big Macs. . . .

Not everyone who wanted to make the Hmong feel unwelcome stopped at slander. In the words of the president of a youth center in Minneapolis, his Hmong neighbors in the mid-eighties were "prime meat for predators." In Laos, Hmong houses had no locks. Sometimes they had no doors. Cultural taboos against theft and intra-community violence were poor preparation for life in the high-crime, inner-city neighborhoods in which most Hmong were placed. Some of the violence directed against them had nothing to do with their ethnicity; they were simply easy marks. But a good deal of it was motivated by resentment, particularly in urban areas, for what was perceived as preferential welfare treatment.[3]

In Minneapolis, tires were slashed and windows smashed. A high school student getting off a bus was hit in the face and told to "go back to China." A woman was kicked in the thighs, face, and kidneys, and her purse, which contained the family's entire savings of $400, was stolen; afterwards, she forbade her children

to play outdoors, and her husband, who had once commanded a fifty-man unit in the Armée Clandestine, stayed home to guard the family's belongings. In Providence, children were beaten walking home from school. In Missoula, teenagers were stoned. In Milwaukee, garden plots were vandalized and a car was set on fire. In Eureka, California, two burning crosses were placed on a family's front lawn. In a random act of violence near Springfield, Illinois, a twelve-year-old boy was shot and killed by three men who forced his family's car off Interstate 55 and demanded money. His father told a reporter, "In a war, you know who your enemies are. Here, you don't know if the person walking up to you will hurt you."

In Philadelphia, anti-Hmong muggings, robberies, beatings, stonings, and vandalism were so commonplace during the early eighties that the city's Commission on Human Relations held public hearings to investigate the violence. One source of discord seemed to be a $100,000 federal grant for Hmong employment assistance that had incensed local residents, who were mostly unemployed themselves and believed the money should have been allocated to American citizens, not resident aliens. In one of the most grievous incidents, Seng Vang, a Hmong resident of Quebec who was visiting his mother, brothers, and sisters in west Philadelphia, was beaten with steel rods and a large rock, and left on the street with two broken legs and a brain injury. Later that day, a rifle shot was fired into his mother's apartment, breaking a window near the spot where she stood washing dishes. When Vang was treated at the University of Pennsylvania hospital, he was given a blood transfusion that was probably tainted. He was gravely ill for months with a rare form of hepatitis, and, seized by justifiable paranoia, became convinced that his doctors, too, had tried to kill him.

One thing stands out in all these accounts: the Hmong didn't fight back. I pondered that fact one day as I was thumbing through the index of Charles Johnson's *Dab Neeg Hmoob: Myths, Legends and Folk Tales from the Hmong of Laos,* which contained the following entries:

Fighting

Enemies fighting . . . 29–46, 52–58, 198, 227, 470–471

Revenge

Murdered man reincarnated to revenge his death . . . 308–309

Cruel 9-tongued eagle has tongues cut out . . . 330

Ngao Njua boils king who sent away her husband . . . 362

Family kills tiger murderer of daughter, husband & children . . . 403

. . .

Vengeance

Punishment of evil-doers by lightning . . . 11, 20

Wildcat tortured & killed to avenge murder of woman . . . 436–437

To quote from the last folktale cited: "Quickly, the rooster came down, seized the cat, threw him into the mortar of the rice mill, and started in immediately pounding him with the heavy pestle: DA DUH NDUH! DA DUH NDUH! He kept pounding until all the wildcat's bones were completely broken. And that's how the wildcat died, and that's how the story ends." It was clear that the Hmong were hardly the docile, passive, mild-mannered Asians of popular stereotype. Why hadn't the Americans who tormented the Hmong ended up like that wildcat?

Charles Johnson's background notes to another tale in *Dab Neeg Hmoob* provide a partial explanation:

Our interviews indicate that the Hmong do not fight very much. When they do, it is with fists and feet. (In contrast with some neighboring peoples [in Laos] who tend to fight a lot, seem to take it lightly, and can be friends later, if two Hmong fight once, they are likely to take it very seriously, as a big issue which they do not forget, and may remain enemies forever.)

. . . The Hmong do have an ideal of patience and stoical self-control, alluded to in the idiomatic expression often used by the Hmong to admonish someone who is acting impatiently or impulsively, or by parents in teaching good behavior to their children: "Ua siab ntev" (literally, Make, do, or act with a long liver, that is, a spirit or attitude of long-suffering, patient endurance of wrongs or difficulties).

Although on the battlefield the Hmong were known more for their fierceness than for their long livers, in the United States many were too proud to lower themselves to the level of the petty criminals they encountered, or even to admit they had been victims. An anthropologist named George M. Scott, Jr., once asked a group of Hmong in San Diego, all victims of property damage or assault, why they had not defended themselves or taken revenge. Scott wrote, "several Hmong victims of such abuse, both young and old, answered that to have done so, besides inviting further, retaliatory, abuse, would have made them feel 'embarrassed' or ashamed. . . . In addition, the current president of Lao Family [a Hmong mutual assistance organization], when asked why his people did not 'fight back' when attacked here as they did in Laos, replied simply, 'because nothing here is worth defending to us.'"

There were exceptions, of course. If he was threatened with what he perceived as unbearable *poob ntsej muag* (loss of face), a Hmong sometimes decided that his shame and embarrassment would be even greater if he didn't fight back than if he did. Several Hmong in Fresno, hearing rumors that their welfare grants might be terminated because they owned cars, sent death threats ("You take away my grant and I'm going to blow your head off") to the county Social Services Department. As visual aids, they enclosed bullets and pictures of swords in their envelopes. (The grants were not terminated, and the bullets and swords were never used.) In Chicago, an elderly Hmong man and his son, insulted because an American driver had honked at them loudly and persistently, hit the American over the head with a steering-wheel locking device. The injury required thirteen stitches. When the men, Ching and Bravo Xiong, were brought to trial for aggravated battery, they asked the judge to allow each party to tell his side of the story and then drink a mixture of water and the blood of a sacrificed rooster. According to Hmong tradition, anyone who drinks rooster blood after telling a lie is destined to die within a year, so if a man partakes willingly, he is recognized as a truthteller. The judge denied this request. Instead, he sentenced the younger Xiong to two weekends in jail and six hundred hours of community service. He also ordered both men to learn English and study American culture.

Such incidents were rare. Most Hmong kept an apprehensive distance from the American penal system, which was radically different from their own. There were no prisons in their villages in Laos. The Hmong sense of justice was pragmatic and personal: how would incarceration benefit the victim? Corporal punishment was also unknown. Instead, various forms of public humiliation—a powerful deterrent in a society where loss of face was considered a worse fate than death—were employed. For example, a thief who had stolen four bars of silver might be forced to repay five bars to the victim and then be hauled off to the village chief with his hands tied, while the entire community jeered. The victim ended up enriched, the criminal suffered the shame he deserved, the criminal's innocent family kept its primary provider in the household, and any would-be thieves in the village were discouraged from potential crimes by witnessing the disgraceful spectacle. The Hmong who came to this country had heard that if they hurt someone, for whatever the reason, they would be sent to an American prison, and most of them were willing to do almost anything to avoid such an unimaginable calamity. Chao Wang Vang, a Fresno resident who had been charged with misdemeanor manslaughter after a fatal traffic accident, hanged himself in the county jail before his case came to court, not knowing he had the right to a trial and believing he would be imprisoned for the rest of his life.

In any case, Hmong who were persecuted by their neighbors could exercise a time-honored alternative to violence: flight. . . . Between 1982 and 1984, three quarters of the Hmong population of Philadelphia simply left town and joined relatives in other cities. During approximately the same period, one third of all the Hmong in the United States moved from one city to another. When they decided to relocate, Hmong families often lit off without notifying their sponsors, who were invariably offended. If they couldn't fit one of their possessions, such as a television set, in a car or bus or U-Haul, they left it behind, seemingly without so much as a backward glance. Some families traveled alone, but more often they moved in groups. When there was an exodus from Portland, Oregon, a long caravan of overloaded cars motored together down Interstate 5, bound for the Central Valley of California. With this "secondary migration," as sociologists termed it, the government's attempt to stir the Hmong evenly into the melting pot was definitively sabotaged.

Although local violence was often the triggering factor, there were also other reasons for migrating. In 1982, when all refugees who had lived in the United States for more than eighteen months stopped receiving Refugee Cash Assistance—the period of eligibility had previously been three years—many Hmong who had no jobs and no prospects moved to states that provided welfare benefits to two-parent families. Their original host states were often glad to get rid of them. For a time, the Oregon Human Resources Department, strapped by a tight state budget, sent refugees letters that pointedly detailed the levels of welfare benefits available in several other states. California's were among the highest. Thousands of Hmong also moved to California because they had heard it was an agricultural state where they might be able to farm. But by far the most important reason for relocating was reunification with other members of one's clan. Hmong clans are sometimes at odds with each other, but within a clan, whose thousands of members are regarded as siblings, one can always count on support and sympathy. A Hmong who tries to gain acceptance to a kin group other than his own is called a *puav*, or bat. He is rejected by the birds because he has fur and by the mice because he has wings. Only when a Hmong lives among his own subspecies can he stop flitting restlessly from group to group, haunted by the shame of not belonging.

The Hmong may have been following their venerable proverb, "There's always another mountain," but in the past, each new mountain had yielded a living. Unfortunately, the most popular areas of secondary resettlement all had high unemployment rates, and they got higher. For example, in the Central Valley—which had no Hmong in 1980 and more than 20,000 three years later—the economic recession of 1982 shut down dozens of factories and other businesses, driving up local unemployment and forcing the Hmong to compete with out-of-work Americans for even the most unskilled jobs. The dream of farming quickly fizzled for all but a few hundred. Hmong farmers knew a great deal about torching fields for slash-and-burn agriculture, planting mountain rice with dibble sticks, and tapping opium pods, but they had much to learn (to quote from the course plan for a not-very-successful Hmong training program) about

crop varieties, soil preparation, machinery and equipment, timing and succession of planting, seeds and transplants, fertilizer, pest and weed management, disease control, irrigation, erosion control, record-keeping, harvesting, washing and handling, grading and size selection, packing, conditioning, market selection, product planning, pricing strategies, shipping and receiving, advertising, merchandising, verbal and non-verbal communication skills for dealing with consumers, etc.

By 1985, at least eighty percent of the Hmong in Merced, Fresno, and San Joaquin counties were on welfare.

That didn't halt the migration. Family reunification tends to have a snowball effect. The more Thaos or Xiongs there were in one place, the more mutual assistance they could provide, the more cultural traditions they could practice together, and the more stable their community would be. Americans, however, tended to view secondary migration as an indication of instability and dependence. . . .

Seeing that the Hmong were redistributing themselves as they saw fit, and that they were becoming an economic burden on the places to which they chose to move, the federal Office of Refugee Resettlement tried to slow the migratory tide. The 1983 Highland Lao Initiative, a three-million-dollar "emergency effort" to bolster employment and community stability in Hmong communities outside California, offered vocational training, English classes, and other enticements for the Hmong to stay put. Though the initiative claimed a handful of modest local successes, the California migration was essentially unstoppable. By this time, most Hmong JOJs were being sponsored by relatives in America rather than by voluntary organizations, so the government no longer had geographic control over their placements. The influx therefore came—and, in smaller increments, is still coming—from Thailand as well as from other parts of America. Therefore, in addition to trying to prevent the Hmong from moving to high-welfare states, the Office of Refugee Resettlement started trying to encourage the ones who were already there to leave. Spending an average of $7,000 per family on moving expenses, job placement, and a month or two of rent and food subsidies, the Planned Secondary Resettlement Program, which was phased out in 1994, relocated about 800 unemployed Hmong families from what it called "congested areas" to communities with "favorable employment opportunities"—i.e., unskilled jobs with wages too low to attract a full complement of local American workers.

Within the economic limitations of blue-collar labor, those 800 families have fared well. Ninety-five percent have become self-sufficient. They work in manufacturing plants in Dallas, on electronics assembly lines in Atlanta, in furniture and textile factories in Morganton, North Carolina. More than a quarter of them have saved enough money to buy their own houses, as have three quarters of the Hmong families who live in Lancaster County, Pennsylvania, where the men farm or work in food-processing plants, and the women work for the Amish, sewing quilts that are truthfully advertised as "locally made." Elsewhere, Hmong are employed as grocers, carpenters, poultry processors, machinists, welders, auto mechanics, tool and die makers, teachers, nurses, interpreters, and community liaisons. In a survey of Minnesota employers, the respondents were asked "What do you think of the Hmong as workers?" Eighty-six percent rated them "very good." . . .

Some younger Hmong have become lawyers, doctors, dentists, engineers, computer programmers, accountants, and public administrators. Hmong National Development, an association that promotes Hmong self-sufficiency, encourages this small corps of professionals to serve as mentors and sponsors for other Hmong who might thereby be induced to follow suit. The cultural legacy of mutual assistance has been remarkably adaptive. Hundreds

of Hmong students converse electronically, trading gossip and information—opinions on the relevance of traditional customs, advice on college admissions, personal ads—via the Hmong Channel on the Internet Relay Chat system. . . . There is also a Hmong Homepage on the World Wide Web (http://www.stolaf .edu/people/cdr/hmong/) and several burgeoning Hmong electronic mailing lists, including Hmongnet, Hmongforum, and Hmong Language Users Group.[4]

The M.D.s and J.D.s and digital sophisticates constitute a small, though growing, minority. Although younger, English-speaking Hmong who have been educated in the United States have better employment records than their elders, they still lag behind most other Asian-Americans. As for Hmong workers over thirty-five, the majority are immovably wedged at or near entry level. They can't get jobs that require better English, and they can't learn English on their current jobs. The federal *Hmong Resettlement Study* cited, as an example, a Hmong worker in Dallas who after three years on the job was unable to name the machine he operated. He stated that he never expected a promotion or a pay raise other than cost-of-living increases. Other Hmong have been thwarted by placing a higher value on group solidarity than on individual initiative. In San Diego, the manager of an electronics plant was so enthusiastic about one Hmong assembly worker that he tried to promote him to supervisor. The man quit, ashamed to accept a job that would place him above his Hmong coworkers.

For the many Hmong who live in high-unemployment areas, questions of advancement are often moot. They have no jobs at all. This is the reason the Hmong are routinely called this country's "least successful refugees." It is worth noting that the standard American tests of success that they have flunked are almost exclusively economic. If one applied social indices instead—such as rates of crime, child abuse, illegitimacy, and divorce—the Hmong would probably score better than most refugee groups (and also better than most Americans), but those are not the forms of success to which our culture assigns its highest priority. Instead, we have trained the spotlight on our best-loved index of failure, the welfare rolls. In California, Minnesota, and Wisconsin, where, not coincidentally, benefits tend to be relatively generous and eligibility requirements relatively loose, the percentages of Hmong on welfare are approximately forty-five, forty, and thirty-five (an improvement over five years ago, when they were approximately sixty-five, seventy, and sixty). The cycle of dependence that began with rice drops in Laos and reinforced with daily handouts at Thai refugee camps has been completed here in the United States. The conflicting structures of the Hmong culture and the American welfare system make it almost impossible for the average family to become independent. In California, for example, a man with seven children—a typical Hmong family size—would have to make $10.60 an hour, working forty hours a week, to equal his welfare stipend and food stamp allowance. But with few marketable skills and little English, he would probably be ineligible for most jobs that paid more than minimum wage, at which, even at the newly elevated rate of $5.15 an hour, he would have to work an improbable eighty-two hours a week in order to equal his welfare allotment. In addition, until the mid-nineties in most states, if he worked more than one hundred hours a month—as a part-time worker trying to acquire job skills, for example, or a farmer in the start-up phase—his family would lose their entire welfare grant, all their food stamps, and their health insurance.[5]

The 1996 welfare reform bill, which in its present form promises to deny benefits to legal immigrants, has stirred up monumental waves of anxiety among the Hmong. Faced with the possibility of having their assistance cut off, some have applied for citizenship, although many middle-aged Hmong find the English language requirement an insuperable obstacle. (The hurdles are lower for older Hmong who came to the United States shortly after the end of the war in Laos. The language rule is waived for "lawful permanent residents" age fifty or older who have been in this country for at least twenty years, and for those age fifty-five or older who have been here at least fifteen years. The Lees, who are considering applying for citizenship, would qualify for this waiver.) Some Hmong have moved, or are planning to move, to states with better job markets. Some will become dependent on their relatives. Because a few states will probably elect to use their own funds to assist legal immigrants, some will simply continue to depend on welfare in altered, reduced, and more precarious forms.

Few things gall the Hmong more than to be criticized for accepting public assistance. For one thing, they feel they deserve the money. Every Hmong has a different version of what is commonly called "The Promise": a written or verbal contract, made by CIA personnel in Laos, that if they fought for the Americans, the Americans would aid them if the Pathet Lao won the war. After risking their lives to rescue downed American pilots, seeing their villages flattened by incidental American bombs, and being forced to flee their country because they had supported the "American War," the Hmong expected a hero's welcome here. According to many of them, the first betrayal came when the American airlifts rescued only the officers from Long Tieng, leaving nearly everyone else behind. The second betrayal came in the Thai camps, when the Hmong who wanted to come to the United States were not all automatically admitted. The third betrayal came when they arrived here and found they were ineligible for veterans' benefits. The fourth betrayal came when Americans condemned them for what the Hmong call "eating welfare." The fifth betrayal came when the Americans announced that the welfare would stop.

Aside from some older people who consider welfare a retirement benefit, most Hmong would prefer almost any other option—if other options existed. What right-thinking Hmong would choose to be yoked to one of the most bureaucratic institutions in America? (A tip from "Your New Life in the United States," on applying for cash assistance: "You should have as many of the following documents available as possible: I-94—take the original, if you can; rent bill or lease; Social Security card; any pay stubs; bank account statement or savings passbook; utility bills; medical bills or proof of medical disability; employment registration card.") What Hmong would choose to become addicted to a way of life that some clan leaders have likened to opium? And what Hmong would choose the disgrace of being *dev mus nuam yaj,* a dog waiting for scraps? Dang Moua, the Merced businessman who had kept his family alive en route to Thailand by shooting birds with a homemade crossbow, once told me, "One time when I am first in America, a Korean man tell me that if someone is lazy and doesn't work, the government still pay them. I say, you crazy! That doesn't ring my bell at all! I am not afraid of working! My parents raised me as a man! I work till the last day I leave this earth!" And indeed, Dang held three concurrent nearly full-time jobs, as a grocer, an interpreter, and a pig farmer. He was once a clerk-typist in the American Embassy in Vientiane and speaks five languages, so his success is not one most Hmong could reasonably be expected to emulate. More typical are two middle-aged men who were interviewed in San Diego for a survey on refugee adaptation. The first said:

> I used to be a real man like any other man, but not now any longer. . . . We only live day by day, just like the baby birds who are only staying in the nest opening their mouths and waiting for the mother bird to bring the worms.

The second said:

> We are not born to earth to have somebody give us feed; we are so ashamed to depend on somebody like this. When we were in our country, we never ask anybody for help like this. . . . I've been trying very hard to learn English and at the same time looking for a job. No matter what kind of job, even the job to clean people's toilets; but still people don't even trust you or offer you such work. I'm looking at me that I'm not even worth as much as a dog's stool. Talking about this, I want to die right here so I won't see my future.

These men were both suffering from a global despair to which their economic dependence was only one of many contributing factors. In the survey for which they were interviewed, part of a longitudinal study of Hmong, Cambodians, Vietnamese, and Chinese-Vietnamese refugees, the Hmong respondents scored lowest in "happiness" and "life satisfaction." In a study of Indochinese refugees in Illinois, the Hmong exhibited the highest degree of "alienation from their environment." According to a Minnesota study, Hmong refugees who had lived in the United States for a year and a half had "very high levels of depression, anxiety, hostility, phobia, paranoid ideation, obsessive compulsiveness and feelings of inadequacy." (Over the next decade, some of these symptoms moderated, but the refugees' levels of anxiety, hostility, and paranoia showed little or no improvement.) The study that I found most disheartening was the 1987 California Southeast Asian Mental Health Needs Assessment, a statewide epidemiological survey funded by the Office of Refugee Resettlement and the National Institute of Mental Health. It was shocking to look at the bar graphs comparing the Hmong with the Vietnamese, the Chinese-Vietnamese, the Cambodians, and the Lao—all of whom, particularly the Cambodians, fared poorly compared to the general population—and see how the Hmong stacked up: Most depressed. Most psychosocially dysfunctional.

Most likely to be severely in need of mental health treatment. Least educated. Least literate. Smallest percentage in labor force. Most likely to cite "fear" as a reason for immigration and least likely to cite "a better life."

The same bleak ground was covered from the Hmong point of view by Bruce Thowpaou Bliatout, a public health administrator in Portland, Oregon. Dr. Bliatout, who is Hmong, explained in an article on mental health concepts that such issues as job adjustment and family happiness are regarded by the Hmong as problems of the liver. If patience, as Charles Johnson noted in *Dab Neeg Hmoob,* is attributed to a long—that is, a robust and healthy—liver, what Americans would call mental illness is attributed to a liver that has become diseased or damaged through soul loss. According to Bliatout, who provided case histories for each one, some illnesses common among Hmong in the United States are:

Nyuab Siab

> Translation: Difficult liver.
> Causes: Loss of family, status, home, country, or any important item that has a high emotional value.
> Symptoms: Excessive worry; crying; confusion; disjointed speech; loss of sleep and appetite; delusions.

Tu Siab

> Translation: Broken liver.
> Causes: Loss of family member; quarrel between family members; break of family unity.
> Symptoms: Grief; worry; loneliness; guilt; feeling of loss; insecurity.

Lwj Siab

> Translation: Rotten liver.
> Causes: Stressful family relations; constant unfulfillment of goals.
> Symptoms: Loss of memory; short temper; delusions.

Before I came to Merced, Bill Selvidge described to me the first Hmong patient he had ever seen. Bruce Thowpaou Bliatout would have diagnosed this patient as having a difficult liver; Bill thought of it, not so differently, as a broken heart. "Mr. Thao was a man in his fifties," said Bill. "He told me through an interpreter that he had a bad back, but after I listened for a while I realized that he'd really come in because of depression. It turned out he was an agoraphobe. He was afraid to leave his house because he thought if he walked more than a couple of blocks he'd get lost and never find his way home again. What a metaphor! He'd seen his entire immediate family die in Laos, he'd seen his country collapse, and he never *was* going to find his way home again. All I could do was prescribe antidepressants."

Mr. Thao turned out to be the first of a long procession of depressed Hmong patients whom Bill was to treat over the next three years. Bill cut to the nub of the matter when he described the man's profound loss of "home." For the Hmong in America—where not only the social mores but also the sound of every birdsong, the shape of every tree and flower, the smell of the air, and the very texture of the earth are unfamiliar—the ache of homesickness can be incapacitating. . . .

The home to which the older Hmong dream of returning—which they call *peb lub tebchaws,* "our fields and our lands"—is prewar Laos. Their memories of wartime Laos are almost unrelievedly traumatic: a "bereavement overload" that critically magnifies all their other stresses. Richard Mollica, a psychiatrist who helped found the IndoChinese Psychiatry Clinic in Boston, found that during the war and its aftermath, Hmong refugees had experienced an average of fifteen "major trauma events," such as witnessing killings and torture. Mollica has observed of his patients, "Their psychological reality is both full and empty.

They are 'full' of the past; they are 'empty' of new ideas and life experiences."

"Full" of both past trauma and past longing, the Hmong have found it especially hard to deal with present threats to their old identities. I once went to a conference on Southeast Asian mental health at which a psychologist named Evelyn Lee, who was born in Macao, invited six members of the audience to come to the front of the auditorium for a role-playing exercise. She cast them as a grandfather, a father, a mother, an eighteen-year-old son, a sixteen-year-old daughter, and a twelve-year-old daughter. "Okay," she told them, "line up according to your status in your old country." Ranking themselves by traditional notions of age and gender, they queued up in the order I've just mentioned, with the grandfather standing proudly at the head of the line. "Now they come to America," said Dr. Lee. "Grandfather has no job. Father can only chop vegetables. Mother didn't work in the old country, but here she gets a job in a garment factory. Oldest daughter works there too. Son drops out of high school because he can't learn English. Youngest daughter learns the best English in the family and ends up at U.C. Berkeley. Now you line up again." As the family reshuffled, I realized that its power structure had turned completely upside down, with the twelve-year-old girl now occupying the head of the line and the grandfather standing forlornly at the tail.

Dr. Lee's exercise was an eloquent demonstration of what sociologists call "role loss." Of all the stresses in the Hmong community, role loss . . . may be the most corrosive to the ego. Every Hmong can tell stories about colonels who became janitors, military communications specialists who became chicken processors, flight crewmen who found no work at all. Dang Moua's cousin Moua Kee, a former judge, worked first in a box factory and then on the night shift in a machine shop. "When you have no country, no land, no house, no power, everyone is the same," he said with a shrug. Major Wang Seng Khang, a former battalion commander who served as leader for 10,000 Hmong in his refugee camp, took five years to find a job as a part-time church liaison. Even then, he depended on his wife's wages from a jewelry factory to pay the rent and on his children to translate for him. Of himself and his fellow leaders, he said, "We have become children in this country."

And in this country the real children have assumed some of the power that used to belong to their elders. The status conferred by speaking English and understanding American conventions is a phenomenon familiar to most immigrant groups, but the Hmong, whose identity has always hinged on tradition, have taken it particularly hard. "Animals are responsible to their masters, and children to their parents," advised a Hmong proverb that survived unquestioned for countless generations. In prewar Laos, where families worked in the fields all day and shared a single room at night, it was not uncommon for children and their parents to be together around the clock. Remoteness and altitude insulated their villages from the majority culture. Hmong children here spend six hours in school and often several more at large in their communities, soaking up America. "My sisters don't feel they're Hmong at all," my interpreter, May Ying Xiong, once told me. "One of them has spiked hair. The youngest one speaks mostly English. I don't see the respect I gave elders at that age." Lia's sister May said, "I know how to do *paj ntaub,* but I hate sewing. My mom says, why aren't you doing *paj ntaub*? I say, Mom, this is America."

Although Americanization may bring certain benefits—more job opportunities, more money, less cultural dislocation—Hmong parents are likely to view any earmarks of assimilation as an insult and a threat. "In our families, the kids eat hamburger and bread," said Dang Moua sadly, "whereas the parents prefer hot soup with vegetables, rice, and meat like tripes or liver or kidney that the young ones don't want. The old ones may have no driver's licenses and they ask the young ones to take them some place. Sometimes the kid say I'm too busy. That is a serious situation when the kid will not obey us. The old ones are really upset." Rebellious young Hmong sometimes go beyond refusing to chauffeur their parents, and tangle with drugs or violence. In 1994, Xou Yang, a nineteen-year-old high-school dropout from Banning, California, robbed and murdered a German tourist. His father, a veteran of the war in Laos, told a reporter, "We have lost all control. Our children do not respect us. One of the hardest things for me is when I tell my children things and they say, 'I already know that.' When my wife and I try to tell my son about Hmong culture, he tells me people here are different, and he will not listen to me."

Sukey Waller, Merced's maverick psychologist, once recalled a Hmong community meeting she had attended. "An old man of seventy or eighty stood up in the front row," she said, "and he asked one of the most poignant questions I have ever heard: 'Why, when what we did worked so well for two hundred years, is everything breaking down?'" When Sukey told me this, I understood why the man had asked the question, but I thought he was wrong. Much has broken down, but not everything. Jacques Lemoine's analysis of the postwar hegira—that the Hmong came to the West to save not only their lives but their ethnicity—has been at least partially confirmed in the United States. I can think of no other group of immigrants whose culture, in its most essential aspects, has been so little eroded by assimilation. Virtually all Hmong still marry other Hmong, marry young, obey the taboo against marrying within their own clans, pay brideprices, and have large families. Clan and lineage structures are intact, as is the ethic of group solidarity and mutual assistance. On most weekends in Merced, it is

possible to hear a death drum beating at a Hmong funeral or a *txiv neeb's* gong and rattle sounding at a healing ceremony. Babies wear strings on their wrists to protect their souls from abduction by *dabs*. People divine their fortunes by interpreting their dreams. (If you dream of opium, you will have bad luck; if you dream you are covered with excrement, you will have good luck; if you dream you have a snake on your lap, you will become pregnant.) Animal sacrifices are common, even among Christian converts, a fact I first learned when May Ying Xiong told me that she would be unavailable to interpret one weekend because her family was sacrificing a cow to safeguard her niece during an upcoming open-heart operation. When I said, "I didn't know your family was so religious," she replied, "Oh yes, we're Mormon."

Even more crucially, the essential Hmong temperament—independent, insular, antiauthoritarian, suspicious, stubborn, proud, choleric, energetic, vehement, loquacious, humorous, hospitable, generous—has so far been ineradicable. Indeed, as George M. Scott, Jr., has observed, the Hmong have responded to the hardships of life in the United States "by becoming *more* Hmong, rather than less so." Summing up his impressions of the Hmong in 1924, François Marie Savina, the French missionary, attributed their ethnic durability to six factors: religion; love of liberty; traditional customs; refusal to marry outside their race; life in cold, dry, mountainous areas; and the toughening effects of war. Even though their experience here has been suffused with despair and loss, the 180,000 Hmong who live in the United States are doing passably or better on the first four counts.[6]

I was able to see the whole cycle of adjustment to American life start all over again during one of my visits to Merced. When I arrived at the Lees' apartment, I was surprised to find it crammed with people I'd never met before. These turned out to be a cousin of Nao Kao's named Joua Chai Lee, his wife, Yeng Lor, and their nine children, who ranged in age from eight months to twenty-five years. They had arrived from Thailand two weeks earlier, carrying one piece of luggage for all eleven of them. In it were packed some clothes, a bag of rice, and, because Joua is a *txiv neeb's* assistant, a set of rattles, a drum, and a pair of divinatory water-buffalo horns. The cousins were staying with Foua and Nao Kao until they found a place of their own. The two families had not seen each other in more than a decade, and there was a festive atmosphere in the little apartment, with small children dashing around in their new American sneakers and the four barefooted adults frequently throwing back their heads and laughing. Joua said to me, via May Ying's translation, "Even though there are a lot of us, you can spend the night here too." May Ying explained to me later that Joua didn't really expect me to lie down on the floor with twenty of his relatives. It was simply his way, even though he was in a strange country where he owned almost nothing, of extending a face-saving bit of Hmong hospitality.

I asked Joua what he thought of America. "It is really nice but it is different," he said, "It is very flat. You cannot tell one place from another. There are many things I have not seen before, like that"—a light switch—"and that"— a telephone—"and that"—an air conditioner. "Yesterday our relatives took us somewhere in a car and I saw a lady and I thought she was real but she was fake." This turned out to have been a mannequin at the Merced Mall. "I couldn't stop laughing all the way home," he said. And remembering how funny his mistake had been, he started to laugh again.

Then I asked Joua what he hoped for his family's future here. "I will work if I can," he said, "but I think I probably cannot. As old as I am, I think I will not be able to learn one word of English. If my children put a heart to it, they will be able to learn English and get really smart. But as for myself, I have no hope."

NOTES

1. Sudden Unexpected Death Syndrome, which until the early 1980s was the leading cause of death among young Hmong males in the United States, is triggered by cardiac failure, often during or after a bad dream. No one has been able to explain what produces the cardiac irregularity, although theories over the years have included potassium deficiency, thiamine deficiency, sleep apnea, depression, culture shock, and survivor guilt. Many Hmong have attributed the deaths to attacks by an incubuslike *dab* [spirit] who sits on the victim's chest and presses the breath out of him.

2. Like most false rumors, these all grew from germs of truth. The white-slavery rumor originated in press accounts of Vietnamese crimes in California, most of which were themselves probably unfounded. The car rumor originated in the Hmong custom of pooling the savings of several families to buy cars and other items too expensive for one family to afford. The insurance rumor originated in the $78,000 that a Hmong family in Wisconsin was awarded after their fourteen-year-old son was killed after being hit by a car. The daughter-selling rumor originated in the Hmong custom of brideprice, or "nurturing charge," as it is now sometimes called in the United States in order to avoid just such misinterpretations. The speed-bump rumor originated in the many nonlethal domestic faux pas the Hmong have actually committed. The dog-eating rumor, which, as I've mentioned elsewhere, is current in Merced, originated in Hmong ritual sacrifices.

3. Like all low-income refugees, newly arrived Hmong were automatically eligible for Refugee Cash Assistance. The RCA program enabled Hmong who would otherwise have been ineligible for welfare in some states—for instance, because an able-bodied male was present in the home—to receive benefits. But it did not enable Hmong families to receive more money than American families. In a given state, Refugee Cash Assistance payments were always identical to benefits from AFDC (Aid to Families with Dependent Children, the form of public assistance most people mean by the word "welfare").

4. The Hmong Channel is accessed almost exclusively by Hmong users. The Hmong Homepage and the electronic mailing lists also have an

audience of Americans with an academic or professional interest in Hmong culture, as well as a number of Mormon elders who have been assigned missionary work in Hmong communities.

5. At the request of local public assistance agencies, the infamous "100-Hour Rule," which prevented so many Hmong from becoming economically self-sufficient, was waived in the majority of states, starting with California, between 1994 and 1996. "Basically, it required people not to work,"

explained John Cullen, who directed Merced's Human Services Agency during the last years of the rule's sway. The 100-Hour Rule was replaced by a formula of gradually decreasing benefits based on earnings.

6. About 150,000 Hmong—some of whom resettled in countries other than the United States, and some of whom are still in Thailand—fled Laos. The Hmong now living in the United States exceed that number because of their high birthrate.

THINKING ABOUT THE READING

Why has it been so difficult for Hmong refugees to adjust to life in the United States? How do the experiences of younger Hmong compare to those of their elders? Why are the Hmong such a popular target of anti-immigrant violence and persecution? Why is the U.S. government so unwilling to grant the Hmong their wish to be "left alone"? In other words, why is there such a strong desire to assimilate them into American culture? On a more general level, why is there such distaste in this society when certain ethnic groups desire to retain their traditional way of life? Consider the differences that might emerge between different generations within immigrant families? What aspects of culture are the most difficult to maintain through the generations?

5 Building Identity

Socialization

Sociology teaches us that humans don't develop in a social vacuum. Other people, cultural practices, historical events, and social institutions shape what we do and say, what we value, and who we become. Our self-concept, identity, and sense of self-worth are derived from our interactions with other people. We are especially tuned into the reactions, real or imagined, of others.

Socialization is the process by which individuals learn their culture and learn to live according to the norms of their society. Through socialization we learn how to perceive our world, gain a sense of our own identity, and discover how to interact appropriately with others. This learning process occurs within the context of several social institutions—schools, religious institutions, the media, and the family—and it extends beyond childhood. Adults must be resocialized into a new galaxy of norms, values, and expectations each time they leave or abandon old roles and enter new ones.

The conditions into which we are born shape our initial socialization in profound ways. Characteristics such as race and social class are particularly significant factors in socialization processes. In "Life as the Maid's Daughter," sociologist Mary Romero describes a research interview with a young Chicana regarding her recollections of growing up as the daughter of a live-in maid for a white, upper-class family living in Los Angeles. Romero describes the many ways in which this girl learns to move between different social settings, adapt to different expectations, and occupy different social roles. This girl must constantly negotiate the boundaries of inclusion and exclusion, as she struggles between the socializing influence of her own ethnic group and that of the white, upper-class employers she and her mother live with. Through this juggling, she illustrates the ways in which we manage the different, often contradictory, identities that we take on in different situations.

Negotiating the boundaries between inclusion and exclusion is also the theme of "Boyhood, Organized Sports, and the Construction of Masculinities." Michael Messner uses the world of organized sports to describe some of the ways boys learn to be boys. He shows that many of the behaviors and traits commonly associated with masculinity are not inborn but are learned, especially through organized competitive sports. Participation (and success) in sports is one very significant place where boys learn the meaning and expression of masculinity and what it takes to be accepted by their peers.

Because our self concepts incorporate so many different social positions, our identities sometimes conflict. Take religion and sexuality, for example. Conservative religions, such as evangelical Christianity, have strong, sometimes hostile prohibitions against certain forms of sexual expression, especially homosexuality. When most people think of gay men and lesbians who belong to conservative churches, they conjure up images of people who either have to hide their sexuality or leave the church altogether. However, in "The Gospel Hour," Edward Gray and Scott Thumma examine the experiences of people who are openly gay and openly Christian. They focus, in particular, on the identity strategies used by a group of gay evangelicals who frequent an Atlanta gay bar where drag performers sing classic and contemporary gospel hymns. Within these ritual performances, participants craft new identities for themselves where the combination of homosexuality and Christianity is neither odd nor blasphemous; it's simply normal.

Something to Consider as You Read:

According to sociologists, we are shaped by our cultural environment and by the influences of significant people and groups in our lives. Consider some of the people or groups whose opinions matter to you. Can you imagine them as a kind of audience in your head observing and reacting to your behavior? Think about the desire to feel included. To what extent has this desire shaped your participation in a group that has had an impact on your self image? How important are "role models" in the socialization process? If someone is managing conflicting identities and has no role models or others in similar situations, how might this conflict affect their sense of self and their relationships with others? What do these readings suggest about the importance of being the "right person in the right place" even if that's not all you feel yourself to be. How do you think power and authority affect people's sense of self and their right to be whomever they want to be in any situation?

Life as the Maid's Daughter

An Exploration of the Everyday Boundaries of Race, Class, and Gender

Mary Romero

(1995)

Introduction

. . . My current research attempts to expand the sociological understanding of the dynamics of race, class, and gender in the everyday routines of family life and reproductive labor. . . . I am lured to the unique setting presented by domestic service . . . and I turn to the realities experienced by the children of private household workers. This focus is not entirely voluntary. While presenting my research on Chicana private household workers, I was approached repeatedly by Latina/os and African Americans who wanted to share their knowledge about domestic service—knowledge they obtained as the daughters and sons of household workers. Listening to their accounts about their mothers' employment presents another reality to understanding paid and unpaid reproductive labor and the way in which persons of color are socialized into a class-based, gendered, racist social structure. The following discussion explores issues of stratification in everyday life by analyzing the life story of a maid's daughter. This life story illustrates the potential of the standpoint of the maid's daughter for generating knowledge about race, class, and gender. . . .

Social Boundaries Presented in the Life Story

The first interview with Teresa,[1] the daughter of a live-in maid, eventually led to a life history

project. I am intrigued by Teresa's experiences with her mother's white, upper-middle-class employers while maintaining close ties to her relatives in Juarez, Mexico, and Mexican friends in Los Angeles. While some may view Teresa's life as a freak accident, living a life of "rags to riches," and certainly not a common Chicana/o experience, her story represents a microcosm of power relationships in the larger society. Life as the maid's daughter in an upper-middle-class neighborhood exemplifies many aspects of the Chicano/Mexicano experience as "racial ethnics" in the United States, whereby the boundaries of inclusion and exclusion are constantly changing as we move from one social setting and one social role to another.

Teresa's narrative contains descriptive accounts of negotiating boundaries in the employers' homes and in their community. As the maid's daughter, the old adage "Just like one of the family" is a reality, and Teresa has to learn when she must act like the employer's child and when she must assume the appropriate behavior as the maid's daughter. She has to recognize all the social cues and interpret social settings correctly—when to expect the same rights and privileges as the employer's children and when to fulfill the expectations and obligations as the maid's daughter. Unlike the employers' families, Teresa and her mother rely on different ways of obtaining knowledge. The taken-for-granted reality of the employers' families do not contain conscious experiences of negotiating race and class status, particularly not in the intimate setting of the home. Teresa's status is constantly changing in response to the wide range of social settings she encounters—from employers' dinner parties with movie stars and corporate executives to Sunday dinners with Mexican garment workers in Los Angeles and factory workers in El Paso. Since Teresa remains bilingual and bicultural throughout her life, her story reflects the constant struggle and resistance to maintain her Mexican identity, claiming a reality that is neither rewarded nor acknowledged as valid.

Teresa's account of her life as the maid's daughter is symbolic of the way that racial ethnics participate in the United States; sometimes we are included and other times excluded or ignored. Teresa's story captures the reality of social stratification in the United States, that is, a racist, sexist, and class-structured society upheld by an ideology of equality. I will analyze the experiences of the maid's daughter in an upper-middle-class neighborhood in Los Angeles to investigate the ways that boundaries of race, class, and gender are maintained or diffused in everyday life. I have selected various excerpts from the transcripts that illustrate how knowledge about a class-based and gendered, racist social order is learned, the type of information that is conveyed, and how the boundaries between systems of domination impact everyday life. I begin with a brief history of Teresa and her mother, Carmen.

Learning Social Boundaries: Background

Teresa's mother was born in Piedras Negras, a small town in Aguas Calientes in Mexico. After her father was seriously injured in a railroad accident, the family moved to a small town outside Ciudad Juarez. Teresa's mother soon became involved in a variety of activities to earn money. She sold food and trinkets at the railroad station and during train stops boarded the trains seeking customers. By the time she was fifteen she moved to Juarez and took a job as a domestic, making about eight dollars a week. She soon crossed the border and began working for Anglo families in the country club area in El Paso. Like other domestics in El Paso, Teresa's mother returned to Mexico on weekends and helped support her mother and sisters. In her late twenties she joined several of her friends in their search for better-paying jobs in Los Angeles. The women immediately found jobs in the garment industry. Yet, after six months in the sweatshops, Teresa's mother went to an agency in search of domestic work. She was placed in a very exclusive Los Angeles neighborhood. Several years later Teresa was born. Her friends took care of the baby while Carmen continued working; childcare became a burden, however, and she eventually returned to Mexico. At the age of thirty-six Teresa's mother returned to Mexico with her newborn baby. Leaving Teresa with her grandmother and aunts, her mother sought work in the country club area. Three years later Teresa and her mother returned to Los Angeles.

Over the next fifteen years Teresa lived with her mother in the employer's (Smith) home, usually the two sharing the maid's room located off the kitchen. From the age of three until Teresa started school, she accompanied her mother to work. She continued to live in the Smiths' home until she left for college. All of Teresa's live-in years were spent in one employer's household. The Smiths were unable to afford a full-time maid, however, so Teresa's mother began doing day work throughout the neighborhood. After school Teresa went to whatever house her mother was cleaning and waited until her mother finished working, around 4 or 6 P.M., and then returned to the Smiths' home with her mother. Many prominent families in the neighborhood knew Teresa as the maid's daughter and treated her accordingly. While Teresa wanted the relationship with the employers to cease when she went to college and left the neighborhood, her mother continued to work as a live-in maid with no residence other than the room in the employer's home; consequently, Teresa's social status as the maid's daughter continued.

Entrance Into the Employers' World

Having spent her first three years in a female-dominated and monolingual, Spanish-speaking household in Juarez and in a Mexican immigrant community in Los Angeles, Teresa had a great deal to learn about the foreign environment presented by her mother's working conditions as a live-in maid. As a pre-schooler, Teresa began to learn that her social status reflected her mother's social position. In Mexico her mother was the primary wage earner for her grandmother and aunts. In this Mexican household dominated by women, Teresa received special attention and privileges as Carmen's daughter. Teresa recalled very vivid memories about entering the employers' world and being forced to learn an entirely new set of rules and beliefs of a Euro-American social order that consisted of a white, monolingual, male-dominated, and upper-middle-class family life. Teresa's account of her early years in the employers' homes is clearly from the perspective of the maid's daughter. She was an outsider and had to learn the appropriate behavior for each setting.

Rules were a major theme in Teresa's recollections of growing up in the employers' homes. She was very much aware of different rules operating in each home and of the need to act accordingly. In one of her mother's work sites, she was expected to play with the employer's children, in another she was allowed to play with their toys in specific areas of the house, and in other workplaces she sat quietly and was not allowed to touch the things around her. From the beginning she was socialized by

the employers and their children, who emphasized conformity and change to their culture. The employers did not make any attempt to create a bicultural or multicultural environment in their homes or community. Teresa was expected to conform to their linguistic norms and acquiesce to becoming "the other"—the little Spanish-speaking Mexican girl among the English-speaking white children.

In the following excerpt Teresa describes her first encounter with the boundaries she confronted in the employers' homes. The excerpt is typical of her observances and recollections about her daily life, in which she is constantly assessing the practices and routines and reading signs in order to determine her position in each social setting and, thus, select the appropriate behavior. While the demands to conform and change were repeated throughout her experiences, Teresa did not embrace the opportunity to assimilate. Her resistance and struggle against assimilation is evident throughout her account, as indicated by her attempt to leave the employer's home and her refusal to speak English:

> I started to realize that every day I went to somebody else's house. Everybody's house had different rules. . . . My mother says that she constantly had to watch me, because she tried to get me to sit still and I'd be really depressed and I cried or I wanted to go see things, and my mother was afraid I was going to break something and she told me not to touch anything. The kids wanted to play with me. To them, I was a novelty and they wanted to play with the little Mexican girl. . . .
>
> I think I just had an attitude problem as I describe it now. I didn't want to play with them, they were different. My mother would tell me to go play with them, and in a little while later I'd come back and say: "Mama no me quieren aguntar"—obviously it was the communication problem. We couldn't communicate. I got really mad one day at these girls, because "no me quieran aguntar," and they did not understand what I was trying to say. They couldn't, we couldn't play, so I

decided that I was going to go home, and that I didn't like this anymore. So I just opened the door and I walked out. I went around the block and I was going to walk home, to the apartment where we lived. I went out of the house, and walked around and went the opposite direction around the block. The little girls came to my mom and said: "Carmen your little daughter she left!" So my mom dropped everything and was hysterical and one of the older daughters drove my mom around and she found me on the corner. My mom was crying and crying, upset, and she asked me where I was going and I said: "Well, I was going to go home, porque no me quieran aguntar," and I didn't want to be there anymore, and I was gonna walk home. So my mother had to really keep an eye on me.

I would go to the Jones' [employers], and they had kids, and I would just mostly sit and play with their toys, but I wouldn't try to interact with them. Then they tried to teach me English. I really resented that. They had an aquarium and fishes and they would say: "Teresa, can you say Fiishh?" and I would just glare at them, just really upset. Then I would say "Fish, no, es pescado." You know, like trying to change me, and I did not want to speak their language, or play with their kids, or do anything with them. At the Smiths they tried to teach me English. There were different rules there. I couldn't touch anything. The first things I learned were "No touch, no touch," and "Don't do this, don't do that."

At different houses, I started picking up different things. I remember that my mother used to also work for a Jewish family, when I was about five, the Altman's. We had to walk to their house. Things were different at the Altman's. At the Altman's they were really nice to me. They had this little metal stove that they let me play with. I would play with that. That was like the one thing I could play with, in the house. I immediately—I'd get there and sit down in my designated area that I could be in, and I'd play there. Sometimes, Ms. Altman would take me to the park and I'd play there. She would try to talk to me. Sometimes I would talk and sometimes I would just sit there.

Teresa's account of going to work with her mother as a toddler was not a story of a child running freely and exploring the world around her; instead, her story was shaped by the need to learn the rules set by white, monolingual, English-speaking adults and children. The emphasis in her socialization within employers' homes was quite different than that given to the employers' male children; rather than advocating independence, individuality, and adventure, Teresa was socialized to conform to female sex roles, restricting her movement and playing with gendered toys. Learning the restrictions that limit her behavior—"No touch. Don't do this"—served to educate Teresa about her social status in the employers' homes. She was clearly different from the other children, "a novelty," and was bound by rules regulating her use of social space and linguistic behavior. Teresa's resistance against changing her language points to the strong self-esteem and pride in her culture and Mexican identity that she obtained from her experience in a Mexican household. Teresa's early memories were dominated by pressure to assimilate and to restrain her movement and activity to fit into a white, male-dominated, upper-middle-class household.

The context in which Teresa learned English was very significant in acquiring knowledge about the social order. English was introduced into her life as a means of control and to restrict her movement within employers' homes. The employers' children were involved in teaching Teresa English, and they exerted pressure that she conform to the linguistic norms governing their households. Teresa was not praised or rewarded for ability to speak Spanish, and her racial and cultural differences were only perceived positively when they served a function for the employer's family, such as a curiosity, entertainment, or a cross-cultural experience. While her mother continued to talk to Teresa in Spanish when they were alone, Carmen was not able to defend her daughter's right to decide which language to speak in the presence of the employers' families. Furthermore, Teresa observed her mother serving and waiting on the employers' families, taking orders, and being treated in a familiar manner. While Teresa referred to the employers formally, by their last names, the employers' children called Teresa's mother by her first name. The circumstances created an environment whereby all monolingual, Spanish-speaking women, including her mother, were in powerless positions. The experiences provided Teresa with knowledge about social stratification—that is, the negative value placed on the Spanish language and Mexican culture—as well as about the social status of Spanish-speaking Mexican immigrant women.

One of the Family

As Teresa got older, the boundaries between insider and outsider became more complicated, as employers referred to her and Carmen as "one of the family." Entering into an employer's world as the maid's daughter, Teresa was not only subjected to the rules of an outsider but also had to recognize when the rules changed, making her momentarily an insider. While the boundaries dictating Carmen's work became blurred between the obligations of an employee and that of a friend or family member, Teresa was forced into situations in which she was expected to be just like one of the employer's children, and yet she remained the maid's daughter. . . .

Living under conditions established by the employers made Teresa and her mother's efforts to maintain a distinction between their family life and an employer's family very difficult. Analyzing incidents in which the boundaries between the worker's family and employer's family were blurred highlights the issues that complicate the mother-daughter relationship. Teresa's account of her mother's hospitalization was the first of numerous conflicts between the two that stemmed from the live-in situation and their relationships with

the employer's family. The following excerpt demonstrates the difficulty in interacting as a family unit and the degree of influence and power employers exerted over their daily lives:

When I was about ten my mother got real sick. That summer, instead of sleeping downstairs in my mother's room when my mother wasn't there, one of the kids was gone away to college, so it was just Rosalyn, David and myself that were home. The other two were gone, so I was gonna sleep upstairs in one of the rooms. I was around eight or nine, ten I guess. I lived in the back room. It was a really neat room because Rosalyn was allowed to paint it. She got her friend who was real good, painted a big tree and clouds and all this stuff on the walls. So I really loved it and I had my own room. I was with the Smiths all the time, as my parents, for about two months. My mother was in the hospital for about a month. Then when she came home, she really couldn't do anything. We would all have dinner, the Smiths were really, really supportive. I went to summer school and I took math and English and stuff like that. I was in this drama class and I did drama and I got to do the leading role. Everybody really liked me and Ms. Smith would come and see my play. So things started to change when I got a lot closer to them and I was with them alone. I would go see my mother everyday, and my cousin was there. I think that my cousin kind of resented all the time that the Smiths spent with me. I think my mother was really afraid that now that she wasn't there that they were going to steal me from her. I went to see her, but I could only stay a couple of hours and it was really weird. I didn't like seeing my mother in pain and she was in a lot of pain. I remember before she came home the Smiths said that they thought it would be a really good idea if I stayed upstairs and I had my own room now that my mother was going to be sick and I couldn't sleep in the same bed 'cause I might hurt her. It was important for my mother to be alone. And how did I feel about that? I was really excited about that [having her own room]—you know. They said, "Your mom she is probably not going to like it and she might get upset about it, but I think that we can convince her that it is ok." When my mom came home, she understood that she couldn't be touched and that she had to be really careful, but she wanted it [having her own room] to be temporary. Then my mother was really upset. She got into it with them and said, "No, I don't want it that way." She would tell me, "No, I want you to be down here. ¿Qué crees que eres hija de ellos? You're gonna be with me all the time, you can't do that." So I would tell Ms. Smith. She would ask me when we would go to the market together, "How does your mom seem, what does she feel, what does she say?" She would get me to relay that. I would say, " I think my mom is really upset about me moving upstairs. She doesn't like it and she just says no." I wouldn't tell her everything. They would talk to her and finally they convinced her, but my mom really, really resented it and was really angry about it. She was just generally afraid. All these times that my mother wasn't there, things happened and they would take me places with them, go out to dinner with them and their friends. So that was a real big change, in that I slept upstairs and had different rules. Everything changed. I was more independent. I did my own homework; they would open the back door and yell that dinner was ready—you know. Things were just real different.

The account illustrates how assuming the role of insider was an illusion because neither the worker's daughter nor the worker ever became a member of the white, middle-class family. Teresa was only allowed to move out of the maid's quarter, where she shared a bed with her mother, when two of the employer's children were leaving home, vacating two bedrooms. This was not the first time that "space" determined whether Teresa was included in the employer's family activities. Her description of Thanksgiving dinner illustrates that she did not decide when to be included but, rather, the decision was based on the available space at the table:

I never wanted to eat with them, I wanted to eat with my mom. Like Thanksgiving, it was always an awkward situation, because I never knew, up until dinnertime, where I was going to sit, every single time. It depended on how many guests they had, and how much room there was at the table. Sometimes, when they invited all their friends, the Carters and the Richmans, who had kids, the adults would all eat dinner in one room and then the kids would have dinner in another room. Then I could go eat dinner with the kids or sometimes I'd eat with my mom in the kitchen. It really depended.

Since Teresa preferred to eat with her mother, the inclusion was burdensome and unwanted. In the case of moving upstairs, however, Teresa wanted to have her "own" bedroom. The conflict arising from Teresa's move upstairs points to the way in which the employer's actions threatened the bonds between mother and daughter.

Teresa and Carmen did not experience the boundaries of insider and outsider in the same way. Teresa was in a position to assume a more active family role when employers made certain requests. Unlike her mother, she was not an employee and was not expected to clean and serve the employer. Carmen's responsibility for the housework never ceased, however, regardless of the emotional ties existing between employee and employers. She and her employers understood that, whatever family activity she might be participating in, if the situation called for someone to clean, pick up, or serve, that was Carmen's job. When the Smiths requested Teresa to sit at the dinner table with the family, they placed Teresa in a different class position than her mother, who was now expected to serve her daughter alongside her employer. Moving Teresa upstairs in a bedroom alongside the employer and their children was bound to drive a wedge between Teresa and Carmen. There is a long history of spatial deference in domestic service, including separate entrances, staircases, and eating and sleeping arrangements. Carmen's room reflected her position in the household. As the maid's quarter, the room was separated from the rest of the bedrooms and was located near the maid's central work area, the kitchen. The room was obviously not large enough for two beds because Carmen and Teresa shared a bed. Once Teresa was moved upstairs, she no longer shared the same social space in the employer's home as her mother. Weakening the bonds between the maid and her daughter permitted the employers to broaden their range of relationships and interaction with Teresa.

Carmen's feelings of betrayal and loss underline how threatening the employers' actions were. She understood that the employers were in a position to buy her child's love. They had already attempted to socialize Teresa into Euro-American ideals by planning Teresa's education and deciding what courses she would take. Guided by the importance they place on European culture, the employers defined the Mexican Spanish spoken by Teresa and her mother as inadequate and classified Castillan Spanish as "proper" Spanish. As a Mexican immigrant woman working as a live-in maid, Carmen was able to experience certain middle-class privileges, but her only access to these privileges was through her relationship with employers. Therefore, without the employers' assistance, she did not have the necessary connections to enroll Teresa in private schools or provide her with upper-middle-class experiences to help her develop the skills needed to survive in elite schools. Carmen only gained these privileges for her daughter at a price; she relinquished many of her parental rights to her employers. To a large degree the Smiths determined Carmen's role as a parent, and the other employers restricted the time she had to attend school functions and the amount of energy left at the end of the day to mother her own child.

Carmen pointed to the myth of "being like one of the family" in her comment, "¿Qué crees

que eres hija de ellos? You're gonna be with me all the time, you can't do that." The statement underlines the fact that the bond between mother and daughter is for life, whereas the pseudofamily relationship with employers is temporary and conditional. Carmen wanted her daughter to understand that taking on the role of being one of the employer's family did not relinquish her from the responsibility of fulfilling her "real" family obligations. The resentment Teresa felt from her cousin who was keeping vigil at his aunt's hospital bed indicated that she had not been a dutiful daughter. The outside pressure from an employer did not remove her own family obligations and responsibilities. Teresa's relatives expected a daughter to be at her mother's side providing any assistance possible as a caretaker, even if it was limited to companionship. The employer determined Teresa's activity, however, and shaped her behavior into that of a middle-class child; consequently, she was kept away from the hospital and protected from the realities of her mother's illness. Furthermore, she was submerged into the employer's world, dining at the country club and interacting with their friends.

Her mother's accusation that Teresa wanted to be the Smiths' daughter signifies the feelings of betrayal or loss and the degree to which Carmen was threatened by the employer's power and authority. Yet Teresa also felt betrayal and loss and viewed herself in competition with the employers for her mother's time, attention, and love. In this excerpt Teresa accuses her mother of wanting to be part of employers' families and community:

> I couldn't understand it—you know—until I was about eighteen and then I said, "It is your fault. If I treat the Smiths differently, it is your fault. you chose to have me live in this situation. It was your decision to let me have two parents, and for me to balance things off, so you can't tell me that I said this. You are the one who wanted this." When I was about eighteen we got into a huge fight on Christmas. I hated

the holidays because I hated spending them with the Smiths. My mother always worked. She worked on every holiday. She loved to work on the holidays! She would look forward to working. My mother just worked all the time! I think that part of it was that she wanted to have power and control over this community, and she wanted the network, and she wanted to go to different people's houses.

As employers, Mr. and Mrs. Smith were able to exert an enormous amount of power over the relationship between Teresa and her mother. Carmen was employed in an occupation in which the way to improve working conditions, pay, and benefits was through the manipulation of personal relationships with employers. Carmen obviously tried to take advantage of her relationship with the Smiths in order to provide the best for her daughter. The more intimate and interpersonal the relationship, the more likely employers were to give gifts, do favors, and provide financial assistance. Although speaking in anger and filled with hurt, Teresa accused her mother of choosing to be with employers and their families rather than with her own daughter. Underneath Teresa's accusation was the understanding that the only influence and status her mother had as a domestic was gained through her personal relationships with employers. Although her mother had limited power in rejecting the Smiths' demands, Teresa held her responsible for giving them too much control. Teresa argued that the positive relationship with the Smiths was done out of obedience to her mother and denied any familial feelings toward the employers. The web between employee and employers' families affected both mother and daughter, who were unable to separate the boundaries of work and family.

Maintaining Cultural Identity

A major theme in Teresa's narrative was her struggle to retain her Mexican culture and her political commitment to social justice. Rather than internalizing meaning attached to Euro-American practices and redefining Mexican culture and bilingualism as negative social traits, Teresa learned to be a competent social actor in both white, upper-middle-class environments and in working- and middle-class Chicano and Mexicano environments. To survive as a stranger in so many social settings, Teresa developed an acute skill for assessing the rules governing a particular social setting and acting accordingly. Her ability to be competent in diverse social settings was only possible, however, because of her life with the employers' children. Teresa and her mother maintained another life—one that was guarded and protected against any employer intrusion. Their other life was Mexican, not white, was Spanish speaking, not English speaking, was female dominated rather than male dominated, and was poor and working-class, not upper-middle-class. During the week Teresa and her mother visited the other Mexican maids in the neighborhoods, on weekends they occasionally took a bus into the Mexican barrio in Los Angeles to have dinner with friends, and every summer they spent a month in Ciudad Juarez with their family. . . .

Teresa's description of evening activity with the Mexican maids in the neighborhood provides insight into her daily socialization and explains how she learned to live in the employer's home without internalizing all their negative attitudes toward Mexican and working-class culture. Within the white, upper-class neighborhood in which they worked, the Mexican maids got together on a regular basis and cooked Mexican food, listened to Mexican music, and gossiped in Spanish about their employers. Treated as invisible or as confidants, the maids were frequently exposed to the intimate details of their employers' marriages and family life. The Mexican maids voiced their disapproval of the lenient child-rearing practices and parental decisions, particularly surrounding drug usage and the importance of material possessions:

> Raquel was the only one [maid] in the neighborhood who had her own room and own tv set. So everybody would go over to Raquel's. . . . This was my mother's support system. After hours, they would go to different people's [maid's] rooms depending on what their rooms had. Some of them had kitchens and they would go and cook all together, or do things like play cards and talk all the time. I remember that in those situations they would sit, and my mother would talk about the Smiths, what they were like. When they were going to negotiate for raises, when they didn't like certain things, I would listen and hear all the different discussions about what was going on in different houses. And they would talk, also, about the family relationships. The way they interacted, the kids did this and that. At the time some of the kids were smoking pot and they would talk about who was smoking marijuana. How weird it was that the parents didn't care. They would talk about what they saw as being wrong. The marriage relationship, or how weird it was they would go off to the beauty shop and spend all this money, go shopping and do all these weird things and the effect that it had on the kids.

The interaction among the maids points to the existence of another culture operating invisibly within a Euro-American and male-dominated community. The workers' support system did not include employers and addressed their concerns as mothers, immigrants, workers, and women. They created a Mexican-dominated domain for themselves. Here they ate Mexican food, spoke Spanish, listened to the Spanish radio station, and watched novellas on TV. Here Teresa was not a cultural artifact but, instead, a member of the Mexican community.

In exchanging gossip and voicing their opinions about the employers' lifestyles, the maids rejected many of the employers' priorities in life. Sharing stories about the employers'

families allowed the Mexican immigrant women to be critical of white, upper-middle-class families and to affirm and enhance their own cultural practices and beliefs. The regular evening sessions with other working-class Mexican immigrant women were essential in preserving Teresa and her mother's cultural values and were an important agency of socialization for Teresa. For instance, the maids had a much higher regard for their duties and responsibilities as mothers than as wives or lovers. In comparison to their mistresses, they were not financially dependent on men, nor did they engage in the expensive and time-consuming activity of being an ideal wife, such as dieting, exercising, and maintaining a certain standard of beauty in their dress, makeup, and hairdos. Unlike the employers' daughters, who attended cotillions and were socialized to acquire success through marriage, Teresa was constantly pushed to succeed academically in order to pursue a career. The gender identity cultivated among the maids did not include dependence on men or the learned helplessness that was enforced in the employers' homes but, rather, promoted self-sufficiency. However, both white women employers and Mexican women employees were expected to be nurturing and caring. These traits were further reinforced when employers asked Teresa to babysit for their children or to provide them with companionship during their husbands' absences.

So, while Teresa observed her mother adapting to the employers' standards in her interaction with their children, she learned that her mother did not approve of their lifestyle and understood that she had another set of expectations to adhere to. Teresa attended the same schools as employers' children, wore similar clothes, and conducted most of her social life within the same socioeconomic class, but she remained the maid's daughter—and learned the limitations of that position. Teresa watched her mother uphold higher standards for her and apply a different set of standards to the employers' children; most of the time, however, it appeared to Teresa as if they had no rules at all.

Sharing stories about the Smiths and other employers in a female, Mexican, and worker-dominated social setting provided Teresa with a clear image of the people she lived with as employers rather than as family members. Seeing the employers through the eyes of the employees forced Teresa to question their kindness and benevolence and to recognize their use of manipulation to obtain additional physical and emotional labor from the employees. She became aware of the workers' struggles and the long list of grievances, including no annual raises, no paid vacations, no social security or health benefits, little if any privacy, and sexual harassment. Teresa was also exposed to the price that working-class immigrant women employed as live-in maids paid in maintaining white, middle-class, patriarchal communities. Employers' careers and lifestyles, particularly the everyday rituals affirming male privilege, were made possible through the labor women provided for men's physical, social, and emotional needs. Female employers depended on the maid's labor to assist in the reproduction of their gendered class status. Household labor was expanded in order to accommodate the male members of the employers' families and to preserve their privilege. Additional work was created by rearranging meals around men's work and recreation schedules and by waiting on them and serving them. Teresa's mother was frequently called upon to provide emotional labor for the wife, husband, mother, and father within an employer's family, thus freeing members to work or increase their leisure time.

Discussion

Teresa's account offers insight into the ways racial ethnic women gain knowledge about the social order and use the knowledge to develop survival strategies. As the college-educated daughter of an immigrant Mexican woman employed as a live-in maid, Teresa's experiences in the employers' homes, neighborhood, and school and her experiences in the homes of working-class Mexicano families and barrios provided her with the skills to cross the class and cultural boundaries separating the two worlds. The process of negotiating social boundaries involved an evaluation of Euro-American culture and its belief system in light of an intimate knowledge of white, middle-class families. Being in the position to compare and contrast behavior within different communities, Teresa debunked notions of "American family values" and resisted efforts toward assimilation. Learning to function in the employers' world was accomplished without internalizing its belief system, which defined ethnic culture as inferior. Unlike the employers' families, Teresa's was not able to assume the taken-for-granted reality of her mother's employers because her experiences provided a different kind of knowledge about the social order.

While the employers' children were surrounded by positive images of their race and class status, Teresa faced negative sanctions against her culture and powerless images of her race. Among employers' families she quickly learned that her "mother tongue" was not valued and that her culture was denied. All the Mexican adults in the neighborhood were in subordinate positions to the white adults and were responsible for caring for and nurturing white children. Most of the female employers were full-time homemakers who enjoyed the financial security provided by their husbands, whereas the Mexican immigrant women in the neighborhood all worked as maids and were financially independent; in many cases they were supporting children, husbands, and other family members. By directly observing her mother serve, pick up after, and nurture employers and their families, Teresa learned about white, middle-class privileges. Her experiences with other working-class Mexicans were dominated by women's responsibility for their children and extended families. Here the major responsibility of mothering was financial; caring and nurturing were secondary and were provided by the extended family or children did without. Confronted with a working mother who was too tired to spend time with her, Teresa learned about the racial, class, and gender parameters of parenthood, including its privileges, rights, responsibilities, and obligations. She also learned that the role of a daughter included helping her mother with everyday household tasks and, eventually, with the financial needs of the extended family. Unlike her uncles and male cousins, Teresa was not exempt from cooking and housework, regardless of her financial contributions. Within the extended family Teresa was subjected to standards of beauty strongly weighted by male definitions of women as modest beings, many times restricted in her dress and physical movements. Her social worlds became clearly marked by race, ethnic, class, and gender differences.

Successfully negotiating movement from a white, male, and middle-class setting to one dominated by working-class, immigrant, Mexican women involved a socialization process that provided Teresa with the skills to be bicultural. Since neither setting was bicultural, Teresa had to become that in order to be a competent social actor in each. Being bicultural included having the ability to assess the rules governing each setting and to understand her ethnic, class, and gender position. Her early socialization in the employers' households was not guided by principles of creativity, independence, and leadership but, rather, was based on conformity and accommodation. Teresa's experiences in two different cultural groups allowed her to separate each and to fulfill the employers' expectations

without necessarily internalizing the meaning attached to the act. Therefore, she was able to learn English without internalizing the idea that English is superior to Spanish or that monolingualism is normal. The existence of a Mexican community within the employers' neighborhood provided Teresa with a collective experience of class-based racism, and the maids' support system affirmed and enhanced their own belief system and culture. As Philomena Essed (1991, 294) points out, "The problem is not only how knowledge of racism is acquired but also what kind of knowledge is being transmitted."

Teresa's life story lends itself to a complex set of analyses because the pressures to assimilate were challenged by the positive interactions she experienced within her ethnic community. Like other bilingual persons in the United States, Teresa's linguistic abilities were shaped by the linguistic practices of the social settings she had access to. Teresa learned the appropriate behavior for each social setting, each marked by different class and cultural dynamics and in which women's economic roles and relationships to men were distinct. An overview of Teresa's socialization illustrates the process of biculturalism—a process that included different sets of standards and rules governing her actions as a woman, as a Chicana, and as the maid's daughter. . . .

NOTES

This essay was originally presented as a paper at the University of Michigan, "Feminist Scholarship: Thinking through the Disciplines," 30 January 1992. I want to thank Abigail J. Stewart and Donna Stanton for their insightful comments and suggestions.

1. The names are pseudonyms.

REFERENCE

Essed, Philomena. 1991. *Understanding Everyday Racism.* Newbury Park, Calif.: Sage Publications.

THINKING ABOUT THE READING

Teresa's childhood is unique in that she and her mother lived in several employers' homes, requiring her to learn different sets of rules and to adjust her behavior to these new expectations each time they moved. Unlike most children, who are free to explore the world around them, her childhood was shaped by the need to read signals from others to determine her position in each social setting. What were some of the different influences in Teresa's early socialization? Did she accept people's attempts to mold her, or did she resist? How did she react to her mother's employers' referring to her as "one of the family"? Teresa came from a poor family, but she spent her childhood in affluent households. With respect to socialization, what advantages do you think these experiences provided her? What were the disadvantages? How do you think these experiences would have changed if she was a *son* of a live-in maid rather than a daughter? If she was a poor *white* girl rather than Latina?

Boyhood, Organized Sports, and the Construction of Masculinities

Michael A. Messner

(1990)

The rapid expansion of feminist scholarship in the past two decades has led to fundamental reconceptualizations of the historical and contemporary meanings of organized sport. In the nineteenth and twentieth centuries, modernization and women's continued movement into public life created widespread "fears of social feminization," especially among middle-class men (Hantover, 1978; Kimmel, 1987). One result of these fears was the creation of organized sports as a homosocial sphere in which competition and (often violent) physicality were valued, while "the feminine" was devalued. As a result, organized sport has served to bolster a sagging ideology of male superiority, and has helped to reconstitute masculine hegemony (Bryson, 1987; Hall, 1988; Messner, 1988; Theberge, 1981).

The feminist critique has spawned a number of studies of the ways that women's sport has been marginalized and trivialized in the past (Greendorfer, 1977; Oglesby, 1978; Twin, 1978), in addition to illuminating the continued existence of structural and ideological barriers to gender equality within sport (Birrell, 1987). Only recently, however, have scholars begun to use feminist insights to examine men's experiences in sport (Kidd, 1987; Messner, 1987; Sabo, 1985). This article explores the relationship between the construction of masculine identity and boyhood participation in organized sports.

I view gender identity not as a "thing" that people "have," but rather as a *process of construction* that develops, comes into crisis, and changes as a person interacts with the social world. Through this perspective, it becomes possible to speak of "gendering" identities rather than "masculinity" or "femininity" as relatively fixed identitiesor statuses.

There is an agency in this construction; people are not passively shaped by their social environment. As recent feminist analyses of the construction of feminine gender identity have pointed out, girls and women are implicated in the construction of their own identities and personalities, both in terms of the ways that they participate in their own subordination and the ways that they resist subordination (Benjamin, 1988; Haug, 1987). Yet this self construction is not a fully conscious process. There are also deeply woven, unconscious motivations, fears, and anxieties at work here. So, too, in the construction of masculinity. Levinson (1978) has argued that masculine identity is neither fully "formed" by the social context, nor is it "caused" by some internal dynamic put into place during infancy. Instead, it is shaped and constructed through the interaction between the internal and the social. The internal gendering identity may set developmental "tasks," may create thresholds of anxiety and ambivalence, yet it is only through a concrete examination of people's interactions with others within social institutions that we can begin to understand both the similarities and differences in the construction of gender identities.

In this study I explore and interpret the meanings that males themselves attribute to their boyhood participation in organized sports. In what ways do males construct masculine identities within the institution of organized sports? In what ways do class and racial differences mediate this relationship and perhaps lead to the construction of different meanings, and perhaps different masculinities? And what are some of the problems and contradictions within these constructions of masculinity?

Description of Research

Between 1983 and 1985, I conducted interviews with 30 male former athletes. Most of the men I interviewed had played the (U.S.) "major sports"—football, basketball, baseball, track. At the time of the interview, each had been retired from playing organized sports for at least five years. Their ages ranged from 21 to 48, with the median, 33; 14 were black, 14 were white, and two were Hispanic; 15 of the 16 black and Hispanic men had come from poor or working-class families, while the majority (9 of 14) of the white men had come from middle-class or professional families. All had at some time in their lives based their identities largely on their roles as athletes and could therefore be said to have had "athletic careers." Twelve had played organized sports through high school, 11 through college, and seven had been professional athletes. Though the sample was not randomly selected, an effort was made to see that the sample had a range of difference in terms of race and social class backgrounds, and that there was some variety in terms of age, types of sports played, and levels of success in athletic careers. Without exception, each man contacted agreed to be interviewed.

The tape-recorded interviews were semi-structured and took from one and one-half to six hours, with most taking about three hours. I asked each man to talk about four broad eras in his life: (1) his earliest experiences with sports in boyhood, (2) his athletic career, (3) retirement or disengagement from the athletic career, and (4) life after the athletic career. In each era, I focused the interview on the meanings of "success and failure," and on the boy's/man's relationships with family, with other males, with women, and with his own body.

In collecting what amounted to life histories of these men, my overarching purpose was to use feminist theories of masculine gender identity to explore how masculinity develops and changes as boys and men interact within the socially constructed world of organized sports. In addition to using the data to move toward some generalizations about the relationship between "masculinity and sport," I was also concerned with sorting out some of the variations among boys, based on class and racial inequalities that led them to relate differently to athletic careers. I divided my sample into two comparison groups. The first group was made up of 10 men from higher-status backgrounds, primarily white, middle-class, and professional families. The second group was made up of 20 men from lower-status backgrounds, primarily minority, poor, and working-class families.

Boyhood and the Promise of Sports

Zane Grey once said, "All boys love baseball. If they don't they're not real boys" (as cited in Kimmel, 1990). This is, of course, an ideological statement. In fact, some boys do *not* love baseball, or any other sports, for that matter. There are millions of males who at an early age are rejected by, become alienated from, or lose interest in organized sports. Yet all boys are, to a greater or lesser extent, judged according to their ability, or lack of ability, in competitive sports (Eitzen, 1975; Sabo, 1985). In this study I focus on those males who did become athletes—males who eventually poured thousands of hours into the development of specific physical skills. It is in boyhood that we can discover the roots of their commitment to athletic careers.

How did organized sports come to play such a central role in these boys' lives? When asked to recall how and why they initially got into playing sports, many of the men interviewed for this study seemed a bit puzzled: after all, playing sports was "just the thing to do." A 42-year old black man who had played college basketball put it this way:

> It was just what you did. It's kind of like, you went to school, you played athletics, and if you didn't, there was something wrong with you. It was just like brushing your teeth: it's just what you did. It's part of your existence.

Spending one's time playing sports with other boys seemed as natural as the cycle of the seasons: baseball in the spring and summer, football in the fall, basketball in the winter—and then it was time get out the old baseball glove and begin again. As a black 35-year-old former professional football star said:

> I'd say when I wasn't in school, 95% of the time was spent in the park playing. It was the only thing to do. It just came as natural.

And a black, 34-year-old professional basketball player explained his early experiences in sports:

> My principal and teacher said, "Now if you work at this you might be pretty damned good." So it was more or less a community thing—everybody in the community said, "Boy, if you work hard and keep your nose clean, you gonna be good." Cause it was natural instinct.

"It was natural instinct." "I was a natural." Several athletes used words such as these to explain their early attraction to sports. But certainly there is nothing "natural" about throwing a ball through a hoop, hitting a ball with a bat, or jumping over hurdles. A boy, for instance, may have amazingly dexterous inborn hand-eye coordination, but this does not predispose him to a career of hitting baseballs any more than it predisposes him to a life as a brain surgeon. When one listens closely to what these

men said about their early experiences in sports, it becomes clear that their adoption of the self-definition of "natural athlete" was the result of what Connell (1990) has called "a collective practice" that constructs masculinities. The boyhood development of masculine identity and status—truly problematic in a society that offers no official rite of passage into adulthood—results from a process of interaction with people and social institutions. Thus, in discussing early motivations in sports, men commonly talk of the importance of relationships with family members, peers, and the broader community.

Family Influences

Though most of the men in this study spoke of their mothers with love, respect, even reverence, their descriptions of their earliest experiences in sports are stories of an exclusively male world. The existence of older brothers or uncles who served as teachers and athletic role models—as well as sources of competition for attention and status within the family—was very common. An older brother, uncle, or even close friend of the family who was a successful athlete appears to have acted as a sort of standard of achievement against whom to measure oneself. A 34-year-old black man who had been a three-sport star in high school said:

> My uncles—my Uncle Harold went to the Detroit Tigers, played pro ball—all of 'em, everybody played sports, so I wanted to be better than anybody else. I knew that everybody in this town knew them—their names were something. I wanted my name to be just like theirs.

Similarly, a black 41-year-old former professional football player recalled:

> I was the younger of three brothers and everybody played sports, so consequently I was more or less forced into it. 'Cause one brother was always better than the next brother and then I came along and had to show them that

I was just as good as them. My oldest brother was an all-city ballplayer, then my other brother comes along and he's all-city and all-state, and then I have to come along.

For some, attempting to emulate or surpass the athletic accomplishments of older male family members created pressures that were difficult to deal with. A 33-year-old white man explained that he was a good athlete during boyhood, but the constant awareness that his two older brothers had been better made it difficult for him to feel good about himself, or to have fun in sports:

I had this sort of reputation that I followed from the playgrounds through grade school, and through high school. I followed these guys who were all-conference and all-state.

Most of these men, however, saw their relationships with their athletic older brothers and uncles in a positive light; it was within these relationships that they gained experience and developed motivations that gave them a competitive "edge" within their same-aged peer group. As a 33-year-old black man describes his earliest athletic experiences:

My brothers were role models. I wanted to prove—especially to my brothers—that I had heart, you know, that I was a man.

When asked, "What did it mean to you to be 'a man' at that age?" he replied:

Well, it meant that I didn't want to be a so-called scaredy-cat. You want to hit a guy even though he's bigger than you to show that, you know, you've got this macho image. I remember that at that young an age, that feeling was exciting to me. And that carried over, and as I got older, I got better and I began to look around me and see, well hey! I'm competitive with these guys, even though I'm younger, you know? And then of course all the compliments come—and I began to notice a change, even in my parents—especially in my father—he was

proud of that, and that was very important to me. He was extremely important . . . he showed me more affection, now that I think of it.

As this man's words suggest, if men talk of their older brothers and uncles mostly as role models, teachers, and "names" to emulate, their talk of their relationships with their fathers is more deeply layered and complex. Athletic skills and competition for status may often be learned from older brothers, but it is in boys' relationships with fathers that we find many of the keys to the emotional salience of sports in the development of masculine identity.

Relationships With Fathers

The fact that boys' introductions to organized sports are often made by fathers who might otherwise be absent or emotionally distant adds a powerful emotional charge to these early experiences (Osherson, 1986). Although playing organized sports eventually came to feel "natural" for all of the men interviewed in this study, many needed to be "exposed" to sports, or even gently "pushed" by their fathers to become involved in activities like Little League baseball. A white, 33-year-old man explained:

I still remember it like it was yesterday—Dad and I driving up in his truck, and I had my glove and my hat and all that—and I said, "Dad, I don't want to do it." He says, "What?" I says, "I don't want to do it." I was nervous. That I might fail. And he says, "Don't be silly. Lookit: There's Joey and Petey and all your friends out there." And so Dad says, "You're gonna do it, come on." And in my memory he's never said that about anything else; he just knew I needed a little kick in the pants and I'd do it. And once you're out there and you see all the other kids making errors and stuff, and you know you're better than those guys, you know: Maybe I *do* belong here. As it turned out, Little League was a good experience.

Some who were similarly "pushed" by their fathers were not so successful as the aforementioned man had been in Little League baseball, and thus the experience was not altogether a joyous affair. One 34-year-old white man, for instance, said he "inherited" his interest in sports from his father, who started playing catch with him at the age of four. Once he got into Little League, he felt pressured by his father, one of the coaches, who expected him to be the star of the team:

> I'd go 0-for-four sometimes, strike out three times in a Little League game, and I'd dread the ride home. I'd come home and he'd say, "Go in the bathroom and swing the bat in the mirror for an hour," to get my swing level. . . . It didn't help much, though, I'd go out and strike out three or four times again the next game too [laughs ironically].

When asked if he had been concerned with having his father's approval, he responded:

> Failure in his eyes? Yeah, I always thought that he wanted me to get some kind of [athletic] scholarship. I guess I was afraid of him when I was a kid. He didn't hit that much, but he had a rage about him—he'd rage, and that voice would just rattle you.

Similarly, a 24-year-old black man described his awe of his father's physical power and presence, and his sense of inadequacy in attempting to emulate him:

> My father had a voice that sounded like rolling thunder. Whether it was intentional on his part or not, I don't know, but my father gave me a sense, an image of him being the most powerful being on earth, and that no matter what I ever did I would never come close to him. . . . There were definite feelings of physical inadequacy that I couldn't work around.

It is interesting to note how these feelings of physical inadequacy relative to the father lived on as part of this young man's permanent internalized image. He eventually became a "feared" high school football player and broke school records in weight-lifting, yet,

> As I grew older, my mother and friends told me that I had actually grown to be a larger man than my father. Even though in time I required larger clothes than he, which should have been a very concrete indication, neither my brother nor I could ever bring ourselves to say that I was bigger. We simply couldn't conceive of it.

Using sports activities as a means of identifying with and "living up to" the power and status of one's father was not always such a painful and difficult task for the men I interviewed. Most did not describe fathers who "pushed" them to become sports star. The relationship between their athletic strivings and their identification with their fathers was more subtle. A 48-year-old black man, for instance, explained that he was not pushed into sports by his father, but was aware from an early age of the community status his father had gained through sports. He saw his own athletic accomplishments as a way to connect with and emulate his father:

> I wanted to play baseball because my father had been quite a good baseball player in the Negro leagues before baseball was integrated, and so he was kind of a model for me. I remember, quite young, going to a baseball game he was in—this was before the war and all—I remember being in the stands with my mother and seeing him on first base, and being aware of the crowd. . . . I was aware of people's confidence in him as a serious baseball player. I don't think my father ever said anything to me like "play sports." . . . [But] I knew he would like it if I did well. His admiration was important . . . he mattered.

Similarly, a 24-year-old white man described his father as a somewhat distant "role model" whose approval mattered:

> My father was more of an example . . . he definitely was very much in touch with and still had very fond memories of being an athlete

and talked about it, bragged about it.... But he really didn't do that much to teach me skills, and he didn't always go to every game I played like some parents. But he approved and that was important, you know. That was important to get his approval. I always knew that playing sports was important to him, so I knew implicitly that it was good and there was definitely a value on it.

First experiences in sports might often come through relationships with brothers or older male relatives, and the early emotional salience of sports was often directly related to a boy's relationship with his father. The sense of commitment that these young boys eventually made to the development of athletic careers is best explained as a process of development of masculine gender identity and status in relation to same-sex peers.

Masculine Identity and Early Commitment to Sports

When many of the men in this study said that during childhood they played sports because "it's just what everybody did," they of course meant that it was just what *boys* did. They were introduced to organized sports by older brothers and fathers, and once involved, found themselves playing within an exclusively male world. Though the separate (and unequal) gendered worlds of boys and girls came to appear as "natural," they were in fact socially constructed. Thorne's observations of children's activities in schools indicated that rather than "naturally" constituting "separate gendered cultures," there is considerable interaction between boys and girls in classrooms and on playgrounds. When adults set up legitimate contact between boys and girls, Thorne observed, this usually results in "relaxed interactions." But when activities in the classroom or on the playground are presented to children as sex-segregated activities and gender is marked by teachers and other adults ("boys line up here, girls over there"), "gender boundaries are heightened, and mixed-sex interaction

becomes and explicit arena of risk" (Thorne, 1986, p. 70). Thus sex-segregated activities such as organized sports, as structured by adults, provide the context in which gendered identities and separate "gendered cultures" develop and come to appear natural. For the boys in this study, it became "natural" to equate masculinity with competition, physical strength, and skills. Girls simply did not (could not, it was believed) participate in these activities.

Yet it is not simply the separation of children, by adults, into separate activities that explains why many boys came to feel such strong connection with sports activities, while so few girls did. As I listened to men recall their earliest experiences in organized sports, I heard them talk of insecurity, loneliness, and especially a need to connect with other people as a primary motivation in their early sports strivings. As a 42-year-old white man stated, "The most important thing was just being out there with the rest of the guys—being friends." Another 32-year-old interviewee was born in Mexico and moved to the United States at a fairly young age. He never knew his father, and his mother died when he was only nine years old. Suddenly he felt rootless, and threw himself into sports. His initial motivations, however, do not appear to be based on a need to compete and win:

> Actually, what I think sports did for me is it brought me into kind of an instant family. By being on a Little League team, or even just playing with all kinds of different kids in the neighborhood, it brought what I really wanted, which was some kind of closeness. It was just being there, and being friends.

Clearly, what these boys needed and craved was that which was most problematic for them: connection and unity with other people. But why do these young males find *organized sports* such an attractive context in which to establish "a kind of closeness" with others? Comparative observations of young boys' and girls' game-playing behaviors yield important insights into this question. Piaget (1965) and Lever (1976) both observed that girls tend to have more "pragmatic" and "flexible" orientations to the rules of games; they are more prone to make exceptions and innovations in the middle of a game in order to make the game more "fair." Boys, on the other hand, tend to have a more firm, even [in]flexible orientation to the rules of a game; to them, the rules are what protect any fairness. This difference, according to Gilligan (1982), is based on the fact that early developmental experiences have yielded deeply rooted differences between males' and females' developmental tasks, needs, and moral reasoning. Girls, who tend to define themselves primarily through connection with others, experience highly competitive situations (whether in organized sports or in other hierarchical institutions) as threats to relationships, and thus to their identities. For boys, the development of gender identity involves the construction of positional identities, where a sense of self is solidified through separation from others (Chodorow, 1978). Yet feminist psychoanalytic theory has tended to oversimplify the internal lives of men (Lichterman, 1986). Males do appear to develop positional identities, yet despite their fears of intimacy, they also retain a human need for closeness and unity with others. This ambivalence toward intimate relationships is a major thread running through masculine development throughout the life course. Here we can conceptualize what Craib (1987) calls the "elective affinity" between personality and social structure: For the boy who both seeks and fears attachment with others, the rule-bound structure of organized sports can promise to be a safe place in which to seek nonintimate attachment with others within a context that maintains clear boundaries, distance, and separation.

Competitive Structures and Conditional Self-Worth

Young boys may initially find that sports give them the opportunity to experience "some kind of closeness" with others, but the structure of sports and athletic careers often undermines the possibility of boys learning to transcend their fears of intimacy, thus becoming able to develop truly close intimate relationships with others (Kidd, 1990; Messner, 1987). The sports world is extremely hierarchical, and an incredible amount of importance is placed on winning, on "being number one." For instance, a few years ago I observed a basketball camp put on for boys by a professional basketball coach and his staff. The youngest boys, about eight years old (who could barely reach the basket with their shots) played a brief scrimmage. Afterwards, the coaches lined them up in a row in front of the older boys who were sitting in the grandstands. One by one, the coach would stand behind each boy, put his had on the boy's head (much in the manner of a priestly benediction), and the older boys in the stands would applaud and cheer, louder or softer, depending on how well or poorly the young boy was judged to have performed. The two or three boys who were clearly the exceptional players looked confident that they would receive the praise they were due. Most of the boys, though, had expressions ranging from puzzlement to thinly disguised terror on their faces as they awaited the judgments of the older boys.

This kind of experience teaches boys that it is not "just being out there with the guys— being friends" that ensures the kind of attention and connection that they crave; it is being *better* than the other guys—*beating* them—that is the key to acceptance. Most of the boys in this study did have some early successes in sports, and thus their ambivalent need for connection with others was met, at least for a time. But the institution of sport tends to encourage the development of what Schafer (1975) has called "conditional self-worth" in boys. As boys become aware that acceptance by others is contingent upon being good—a "winner"—narrow definitions of success, based upon performance and winning, become increasingly important to them. A 33-year-old black man said that by the time he was in his early teens:

It was expected of me to do well in all my contests—I mean by my coaches, my peers, and my family. So I in turn expected to do well, and if I didn't do well, then I'd be very disappointed.

The man from Mexico, discussed above, who said that he had sought "some kind of closeness" in his early sports experiences began to notice in his early teens that if he played well, was a *winner,* he would get attention from others:

It got to the point where I started realizing, noticing that people were always there for me, backing me all the time—sports got to be really fun because I always had some people there backing me. Finally my oldest brother started going to all my games, even though I had never really seen who he was [laughs]—after the game, you know, we never really saw each other, but he was at all my baseball games, and it seemed like we shared a kind of closeness there, but only in those situations. Off the field, when I wasn't in uniform, he was never around.

By high school, he said, he felt "up against the wall." Sports hadn't delivered what he had hoped it would, but he thought if he just tried harder, won one more championship trophy, he would get the attention he truly craved. Despite his efforts, this attention was not forthcoming. And, sadly, the pressures he had put on himself to excel in sports had taken most of the fun out of playing.

For many of the men in this study, throughout boyhood and into adolescence, this conscious striving for successful achievement became the primary means through which they sought connection with other people (Messner, 1987). But it is important to recognize that young males' internalized ambivalence about intimacy do not fully determine the contours and directions of their lives. Masculinity continues to develop through interaction with the social world—and

because boys from different backgrounds are interacting with substantially different familial, educational, and other institutions, these differences will lead them to make different choices and define situations in different ways. Next, I examine the differences in the ways that boys from higher- and lower-status families and communities related to organized sports.

Status Differences and Commitments to Sports

In discussing early attractions to sports, the experiences of boys from higher- and lower-status backgrounds are quite similar. Both groups indicate the importance of fathers and older brothers in introducing them to sports. Both groups speak of the joys of receiving attention and acceptance among family and peers for early successes in sports. Note the similarities, for instance, in the following descriptions of boyhood athletic experiences of two men. First, a man born in a white, middle-class family:

I loved playing sports so much from a very early age because of early exposure. A lot of the sports came easy at an early age, and because they did, and because you were successful at something, I think that you're inclined to strive for that gratification. It's like, if you're good, you like it, because it's instant gratification. I'm doing something that I'm good at and I'm gonna keep doing it.

Second, a black man from a poor family:

Fortunately I had some athletic ability, and, quite naturally, once you start doing good in whatever it is—I don't care if it's jacks—you show off what you do. That's your ability, that's your blessing, so you show it off as much as you can.

For boys from both groups, early exposure to sports, the discovery that they had some "ability," shortly followed by some sort of family, peer, and community recognition, all eventually led to the commitment of hundreds and thousands of hours of playing, practicing, and dreaming of future stardom. Despite these similarities, there are also some identifiable differences that begin to explain the tendency of males from lower-status backgrounds to develop higher levels of commitment to sports careers. The most clear-cut difference was that while men from higher-status backgrounds are likely to describe their earliest athletic experiences and motivations almost exclusively in terms of immediate family, men from lower-status backgrounds more commonly describe the importance of a broader community context. For instance, a 46-year-old man who grew up in a "poor working class" black family in a small town in Arkansas explained:

> In that community, at the age of third or fourth grade, if you're a male, they expect you to show some kind of inclination, some kind of skill in football or basketball. It was an expected thing, you know? My mom and my dad, they didn't push at all. It was the general environment.

A 48-year-old man describes sports activities as a survival strategy in his poor black community:

> Sports protected me from having to compete in gang stuff, or having to be good with my fists. If you were an athlete and got into the fist world, that was your business, and that was okay—but you didn't have to if you didn't want to. People would generally defer to you, give you your space away from trouble.

A 35-year-old man who grew up in "a poor black ghetto" described his boyhood relationship to sports similarly:

> Where I came from, either you were one of two things: you were in sports or you were out on the streets being a drug addict, or breaking into

places. The guys who were in sports, we had it a little easier, because we were accepted by both groups. . . . So it worked out to my advantage, cause I didn't get into a lot of trouble—some trouble, but not a lot.

The fact that boys in lower-status communities faced these kinds of realities gave salience to their developing athletic identities. In contrast, sports were important to boys from higher-status backgrounds, yet the middle-class environment seemed more secure, less threatening, and offered far more options. By the time most of these boys got into junior high or high school, many had made conscious decisions to shift their attentions away from athletic careers to educational and (nonathletic) career goals. A 32-year-old white college athletic director told me that he had seen his chance to pursue a pro baseball career as "pissing in the wind," and instead, focused on education. Similarly, a 33-year-old white dentist who was a three-sport star in high school, decided not to play sports in college, so he could focus on getting into dental school. As he put it,

> I think I kind of downgraded the stardom thing. I thought it was small potatoes. And sure, that's nice in high school and all that, but on a broad scale, I didn't think it amounted to all that much.

This statement offers an important key to understanding the construction of masculine identity within a middle-class context. The status that this boy got through sports had been *very* important to him, yet he could see that "on a broad scale," this sort of status was "small potatoes." This sort of early recognition is more than a result of the oft-noted middle-class tendency to raise "future-oriented" children (Rubin, 1976; Sennett and Cobb, 1973). Perhaps more important, it is that the *kinds* of future orientations developed by boys from higher-status backgrounds are consistent with the middle-class context. These men's descriptions of their boyhoods reveal that they grew up immersed in a wide range of institutional frameworks, of which organized sports was just one. And—importantly—they could see that the status of adult males around them was clearly linked to their positions within various professions, public institutions, and bureaucratic organizations. It was clear that access to this sort of institutional status came through educational achievement, not athletic prowess. A 32-year-old black man who grew up in a professional-class family recalled that he had idolized Wilt Chamberlain and dreamed of being a pro basketball player, yet his father discouraged his athletic strivings:

> He knew I liked the game. I *loved* the game. But basketball was not recommended; my dad would say, "That's a stereotyped image for black youth. . . . When your basketball is gone and finished, what are you gonna do? One day, you might get injured. What are you gonna look forward to?" He stressed education.

Similarly, a 32-year-old man who was raised in a white, middle-class family, had found in sports a key means of gaining acceptance and connection in his peer group. Yet he was simultaneously developing an image of himself as a "smart student," and becoming aware of a wide range of non-sports life options:

> My mother was constantly telling me how smart I was, how good I was, what a nice person I was, and giving me all sorts of positive strokes, and those positive strokes became a self-motivating kind of thing. I had this image of myself as smart, and I lived up to that image.

It is not that parents of boys in lower-status families did not also encourage their boys to work hard in school. Several reported that their parents "stressed books first, sports second." It's just that the broader social context—education, economy, and community—was more likely to *narrow* lower-status boys' perceptions of real-life options, while boys from higher-status backgrounds faced an expanding world of options. For instance, with a different socioeconomic background, one 35-year-old black man might have become a great musician instead of a star professional football running back. But he did not. When he was a child, he said, he was most interested in music:

> I wanted to be a drummer. But we couldn't afford drums. My dad couldn't go out and buy me a drum set or a guitar even—it was just one of those things; he was just trying to make ends meet.

But he *could* afford, as could so many in his socioeconomic condition, to spend countless hours at the local park, where he was told by the park supervisor

> that I was a natural—not only in gymnastics or baseball—whatever I did, I was a natural. He told me I shouldn't waste this talent, and so I immediately started watching the big guys then.

In retrospect, this man had potential to be a musician or any number of things, but his environment limited his options to sports, and he made the best of it. Even within sports, he, like most boys in the ghetto, was limited:

> We didn't have any tennis courts in the ghetto—we used to have a lot of tennis balls, but not racquets. I wonder today how good I might be in tennis if I had gotten a racquet in my hands at an early age.

It is within this limited structure of opportunity that many lower-status young boys found sports to be *the* place, rather than *a* place, within which to construct masculine identity, status, and relationships. A 36-year-old white man explained that his father left the family when he was very young and this mother faced a very difficult struggle to make ends meet. As his words suggest, the more limited a boy's options, and the more insecure his family situation, the more likely he is to make an early commitment to an athletic career:

> I used to ride my bicycle to Little League practice—if I'd waited for someone to pick me up and take me to the ball park I'd have never played. I'd get to the ball park and all the other kids would have their dad bring them to practice or games. But I'd park my bike to the side and when it was over I'd get on it and go home. Sports was the way for me to move everything to the side—family problems, just all the embarrassments—and think about one thing, and that was sports. . . . In the third grade, when the teacher went around the classroom and asked everybody, "What do you want to be when your grow up?" I said, "I want to be a major league baseball player," and everybody laughed their heads off.

This man eventually did enjoy a major league baseball career. Most boys from lower-status backgrounds who make similar early commitments to athletic careers are not so successful. As stated earlier, the career structure of organized sports is highly competitive and hierarchical. In fact, the chances of attaining professional status in sports are approximately 4:100,000 for a white man, 2:100,000 for a black man, and 3:1 million for a Hispanic man in the United States (Leonard and Reyman, 1988). Nevertheless, the immediate rewards (fun, status, attention), along with the constricted (nonsports) structure of opportunity, attract disproportionately large numbers of boys from lower-status backgrounds to athletic careers as their major means of constructing a masculine identity. These are the boys who later, as young men, had to struggle with "conditional self-worth," and, more often than not, occupational dead ends. Boys from higher-status backgrounds, on the other hand, bolstered their boyhood, adolescent, and early adult status through their athletic accomplishments. Their wide range of experiences and life changes led to an early shift away from sports careers as the major basis of identity (Messner, 1989).

Conclusion

The conception of the masculinity-sports relationship developed here begins to illustrate the idea of an "elective affinity" between social structure and personality. Organized sports is a "gendered institution"—an institution constructed by gender relations. As such, its structure and values (rules, formal organization, sex composition, etc.) reflect dominant conceptions of masculinity and femininity. Organized sports is also a "gendering institution"—an institution that helps to construct the current gender order. Part of this construction of gender is accomplished through the "masculinizing" of male bodies and minds.

Yet boys do not come to their first experiences in organized sports as "blank slates," but arrive with already "gendering" identities due to early developmental experiences and previous socialization. I have suggested here that an important thread running through the development of masculine identity is males' ambivalence toward intimate unity with others. Those boys who experience early athletic success find in the structure of organized sports an affinity with this masculine ambivalence toward intimacy: The rule-bound, competitive, hierarchical world of sport offers boys an attractive means of establishing an emotionally distant (and thus "safe") connection with others. Yet as boys begin to define themselves as "athletes," they learn that in order to be accepted (to have connection) through sports, they must be winners. And in order to be winners, they must construct relationships with others (and with themselves) that are consistent with the competitive and hierarchical values and structure of the sports world. As a result, they often develop a "conditional self-worth" that leads them to construct more instrumental relationships with themselves and others. This ultimately exacerbates their difficulties in constructing intimate relationships with others. In effect, the interaction between the young male's preexisting internalized ambivalence toward intimacy with the competitive hierarchical institution of sports has resulted in the construction of a masculine personality that is characterized by instrumental rationality, goal-orientation, and difficulties with intimate connection and expression (Messner, 1987).

This theoretical line of inquiry invites us not simply to examine how social institutions "socialize" boys, but also to explore the ways that boys' already-gendering identities interact with social institutions (which, like organized sports, are themselves the product of gender relations). This study has also suggested that it is not some singular "masculinity" that is being constructed through athletic careers. It may be correct, from a psychoanalytic perspective, to suggest that all males bring ambivalences toward intimacy to their interaction with the world, but "the world" is a very different place for males from different racial and socioeconomic backgrounds. Because males have substantially different interactions with the world, based on class, race, and other differences and inequalities, we might expect the construction of masculinity to take on different meanings for boys and men from differing backgrounds (Messner, 1989). Indeed, this study has suggested that boys from higher-status backgrounds face a much broader range of options than do their lower-status counterparts. As a result, athletic careers take on different meanings for these boys. Lower-status boys are likely to see athletic careers as *the* institutional context for the construction of their masculine status and identities, while higher-status males make an early shift away from athletic careers toward other institutions (usually education and nonsports careers). A key line of inquiry for future studies might begin by exploring this irony of sports careers: Despite the fact that "the athlete" is currently an example of an exemplary form of

masculinity in public ideology, the vast majority of boys who became most committed to athletic careers are never well-rewarded for their efforts. The fact that class and racial dynamics lead boys from higher status backgrounds, unlike their lower-status counterparts, to move into nonsports careers illustrates how the construction of different kinds of masculinities is a key component of the overall construction of the gender order.

REFERENCES

Benjamin, J. (1988) *The Bounds of Love: Psychoanalysis, Feminism, and the Problem of Domination.* New York: Pantheon.

Birrell, S. (1987) "The woman athlete's college experience: knowns and unknowns." *J. of Sport and Social Issues* 11:82–96.

Bryson, L. (1987) "Sport and the maintenance of masculine hegemony." *Women's Studies International Forum* 10:349–360.

Chodorow, N. (1978) *The Reproduction of Mothering.* Berkeley: Univ. of California Press.

Connell, R. W. (1990) "An iron man: the body and some contradictions of hegemonic masculinity," in M. A. Messner and D. F. Sabo (eds.) *Sport, Men and the Gender Order: Critical Feminist Perspectives.* Champaign, IL: Human Kinetics.

Craib, I. (1987) "Masculinity and male dominance." *Soc. Rev.* 38:721–743.

Eitzen, D. S. (1975) "Athletics in the status system of male adolescents: a replication of Coleman's *The Adolescent Society.*" *Adolescence* 10:268–276.

Gilligan, C. (1982) *In a Different Voice: Psychological Theory and Women's Development.* Cambridge, MA: Harvard Univ. Press.

Greendorfer, S. L. (1977) "The role of socializing agents in female sport involvement." *Research Q.* 48:304–310.

Hall, M.A. (1988) "The discourse on gender and sport: from femininity to feminism." *Sociology of Sport J.* 5:330–340.

Hantover, J. (1978) "The boy scouts and the validation of masculinity." *J. of Social Issues* 34:184–195.

Haug, F. (1987) *Female Sexualization.* London: Verso.

Kidd, B. (1987) "Sports and masculinity," pp. 250–265 in M. Kaufman (ed.) *Beyond Patriarchy: Essays by Men on Pleasure, Power, and Change.* Toronto: Oxford Univ. Press.

Kidd, B. (1990) "The men's cultural centre: sports and the dynamic of women's oppression/men's repression," in M. A. Messner and D. F. Sabo (eds.) *Sport, Men and the Gender Order: Critical Feminist Perspective.* Champaign, IL: Human Kinetics.

Kimmel, M. S. (1987) "Men's responses to feminism at the turn of the century." *Gender and Society* 1:261–283.

Kimmel, M. S. (1990) "Baseball and the reconstitution of American masculinity: 1880–1920," in M. A. Messner and D. F. Sabo (eds.) *Sport, Men and the Gender Order: Critical Feminist Perspectives.* Champaign, IL: Human Kinetics.

Leonard, W. M. II and J. M. Reyman (1988) "The odds of attaining professional athlete status: refining the computations." *Sociology of Sport J.* 5:162–169.

Lever, J. (1976) "Sex differences in the games children play." *Social Problems* 23:478–487.

Levinson, D. J. et al. (1978) *The Seasons of a Man's Life.* New York: Ballantine.

Lichterman, P. (1986) "Chodorow's psychoanalytic sociology: a project half-completed." *California Sociologist* 9:147–166.

Messner, M. (1987) "The meaning of success: the athletic experience and the development of male identity," pp. 193–210 in H. Brod (ed.) *The Making of Masculinities: The New Men's Studies.* Boston: Allen & Unwin.

Messner, M. (1988) "Sports and male domination: the female athlete as contested ideological terrain." *Sociology of Sport J.* 5:197–211.

Messner, M. (1989) "Masculinity and athletic careers." *Gender and Society* 3:71–88.

Oglesby, C. A. (ed.) (1978) *Women and Sport: From Myth to Reality.* Philadelphia: Lea & Farber.

Osherson, S. (1986) *Finding our Fathers: How a Man's Life Is Shaped by His Relationship with His Father.* New York: Fawcett Columbine.

Piaget, J. H. (1965) *The Moral Judgment of the Child.* New York: Free Press.

Rubin, L. B. (1976) *Worlds of Pain: Life in the Working Class Family.* New York: Basic Books.

Sabo, D. (1985) "Sport, patriarchy and male identity: new questions about men and sport." *Arena Rev.* 9:2.

Schafer, W. E. (1975) "Sport and male sex role socialization." *Sport Sociology Bull.* 4:47–54.

Sennett, R. and J. Cobb (1973) *The Hidden Injuries of Class.* New York: Random House.

Theberge, N. (1981) "A critique of critiques: radical and feminist writings on sport." *Social Forces* 60:2.

Thorne, B. (1986) "Girls and boys together . . . but mostly apart: gender arrangements in elementary schools," pp. 167–184 in W. W. Hartup and Z. Rubin (eds.) *Relationships and Development.* Hillsdale, NJ: Lawrence Erlbaum.

Twin, S. L. (ed.) (1978) *Out of the Bleachers: Writings on Women and Sport.* Old Westbury, NY: Feminist Press.

THINKING ABOUT THE READING

What does Messner mean when he calls organized sports a "gendered" as well as a "gendering" institution? In what ways do sports provide men with opportunities to establish their masculinity? How does the rule-bound structure of organized sports provide boys with a "safe place" to express feelings of closeness to other boys? Why do you suppose athletic success is such an important source of masculine identity for adolescent boys? Why do you suppose adolescent boys aren't able to achieve as much esteem from academic success as they are from athletic success? What role do you think the media play in perpetuating this ideal? How does social class influence the relationship between sports and masculine self-worth? As girls' athletics become more popular and a more visible feature in the culture, what is the likelihood that girls will begin to define their self-worth in terms of athletic success?

The Gospel Hour

Liminality, Identity, and Religion in a Gay Bar

Edward R. Gray and Scott Thumma

(1997)

WE SQUEEZE THROUGH A CROWD thick with gay men. Some ignore us; others greet us with smiles. Everyone is animated. Bartenders race back and forth opening bottles of beer and mixing gin tonics for the hot and thirsty assembly. Dance music is playing loudly. Suddenly, the music changes incongruously to a stirring orchestral version of the "Hallelujah" chorus. This is Morticia Deville's cue. Unnoticed in the rear of the darkened room, Morticia starts to navigate her large figure through the audience slowly toward the dance floor. The crowd begins to applaud. A spotlight—after what seems a long moment—strikes her sequined gown, perfectly made-up face, and blond wig. She looks the perfect Southern Gospel singer on a televised revival hour as she takes the stage. With all eyes on her, Morticia begins to sing, "Living in the Presence of the King." The song is a popular contemporary Christian hymn. The Gospel Hour at this midtown Atlanta gay bar has begun.

Morticia is a gay man in drag in her early thirties. She sings as a member of "The Gospel Girls" with a popular black drag queen and a straight black woman. Each week they and their audience use Christian symbols and song to create a unique gay gospel cabaret, The Gospel Hour. It is a two-hour-long gospel performance and sing-along. Performers sing or lip-sync traditional gospel hymns and contemporary numbers. Morticia and other Gospel Girls perform in drag for a mostly white gay male audience. Many in this audience are from Evangelical backgrounds and many are Christian still.

Morticia DeVille is the founder and star of the Gospel Hour. She is also a make-believe character; an identity created by a man we call Paul. As Morticia, Paul combines religious sensibilities and songs learned as a child in the mountains of north Georgia with the art of high drag learned as a gay man in the bars of Atlanta. Even as a child, Paul was drawn to both drag and religion. He told us how he would sneak into his grandmother's bedroom to steal her lipstick. Afterwards he retreated to the loneliness and safety of an empty mountain hollow. Robed in a bedsheet, he preached to the winds, pretending he was Billy Graham. Paul has exchanged bedsheets for sequined frocks and covert wearing of lipstick in rural Georgia for a public identity as a drag queen in Atlanta. . . .

Evangelical gospel music blends with drag not for parody but for purpose at the Gospel Hour. The performance challenges everyday categories of experience by absorbing these categories and transforming them. The Gospel Hour merges gospel performance models with high drag. It also blends southern Evangelical Christian sensibilities and cultural norms with urban gay ones. Its audience of gays, straights, blacks, and whites has multiple experiences of the Gospel Hour. Participants have differential encounters to the Gospel Hour based on individual and shared experiences. . . . Nonetheless, for the segment of the audience we observed— and for the performers themselves—the Gospel Hour is a ritual of identity negotiation. Southern gay men reconcile their newly achieved modern urban gay identity with their childhood and young adult Evangelical Christian formation. The Gospel Hour—a drag show—is the setting for this identity work. Its product is a model that defies dominant cultural norms and establishes new ways to organize social relations.

The Gospel Hour generates what Victor Turner (1969) has called "templates or models" that reclassify social relationships. They provide motives and guides to action. We examine how the model or template of gay drag gospel performance allows participants to reclassify ordinary, taken-for-granted social relationships and cultural categories framing Christianity and gay sexuality. Turner described modern "social life as a type of dialectical process involving successive experience of high and low, *communitas* and structure, homogeneity and differentiation, equality and inequality" (Turner 1969: 96). Our investigation employs Turner's insight to show how culturally marginal groups create new cultural forms and practices through ritual. His theory illumines how our informants use the ritual template generated by the Gospel Hour to negotiate their identity as southern gay Christian men. The performance is a liminal time and space set apart from the everyday. It is betwixt and between dominant cultural and subcultural norms. Being gay and Christian, within this liminal moment, is not exceptional or odd. It is normal.

Singing gospel songs in a gay bar led by men in drag defies most norms and experiences of both urban gay culture and Evangelical Christianity. Because it is a drag show in a gay bar, the Gospel Hour is alien to the Evangelical world. Because it is a Christian gospel music performance, it falls outside the expected parameters of gay drag. Yet the Gospel Hour is a gay drag show and a gospel music performance. Morticia DeVille *is* a gospel singer *and* a drag queen. Singing gospel hymns in drag is a ritual act redefining everyday classifications of experience and creating a new model for

identity. This model or template has a normative function. It reconciles being gay and Christian. "All rituals have this exemplary, model displaying character," according to Turner. Rituals create society "in much the same way as Oscar Wilde held life to be 'an imitation of art'" (1969: 117). A young man, a former Christian charismatic, may have said it best to us one night after the Gospel Hour.

It's hard [to get used to at first] because you grow up and you believe that these are praises to God and you see this big drag queen camping it up, and you are thinking "Oh no, something is really wrong here and we can't let this go on. . . ." It clashes with all the preconceived ideas you have. . . . Later on, you realize that it can be this way, too. . . .

The Gospel Hour as Ritual: Fully Gay and Altogether Southern Evangelical

Twice each Sunday the Gospel Girls conduct what they call "services" for their "congregation." During the first half of the nearly two-hour performance, they sing solo numbers. Some of these are signature pieces. Special guests often sing during this time from a repertoire of classic and contemporary gospel music. The songs differ at each service, but they are selected from a circumscribed range of a few dozen pieces. The quality of performance, nonetheless, is uniformly high week-to-week. "That's the good thing about us," Morticia told us one day in a slow drawl. "The music is so powerful. It's so good. And Southern."

Morticia is sweet and warm—grandmotherly in a Sunday school teacher sort of way. She can stir the audience with her singing. For some songs, like "Standing in the Presence of the King," she lip-syncs to another performer. Most often, however, she sings well-known hymns in her own strong and beautiful voice. Audience members place dollar bills in her hands and kiss her on the cheek.

Morticia introduces Ramona Dugger after her opening segment. Ramona is the number two Gospel Girl. She has a remarkable vocal range. When she sings "Amazing Grace"—a signature number for her—you begin to fear for the glassware in the bar. Her songs are emotional and passionate. Ramona is straight, young, and African American. She favors contemporary gospel music. Her background is Episcopalian. Many songs in the Gospel Hour repertoire, therefore, were unfamiliar. When she does sing traditional Evangelical hymns, she favors the classics like "Amazing Grace" and "How Great Thou Art." Sometimes she sings, "If You're Happy and You Know it, Clap Your Hands" changing the words to "If you're happy and gay, clap your hands!"

Ramona became a Gospel Girl in 1994. She had been a regular guest performer for five years—most of the ensemble's career. When Morticia announced that Ramona would become "official," one owner of the bar objected. He said that bartenders were getting complaints about the explicitly religious nature of Ramona's onstage comments. The barkeep's description of the usual thrust of Ramona's remarks—explicitly Christian—struck us as accurate. Soon after, the Gospel Hour moved. We asked Ramona about proselytizing during her performance. She said,

We're treading a fine line as it is. You know, it's a very fine line. And I quite frankly identify with it probably most strongly more than anyone else in the show on a higher spiritual level. And because of that I probably step over that line. Tish never says "God." She never says "Jesus." I will. I don't do it on a regular basis because I don't want people to feel like "I'm coming into a bar and I'm just getting preached at" because I'm not preaching to anybody. But I do think there are so many people who are so hungry to know that God does love them, you know, and that they're under so much stress and so much trouble in their lives that they need to be reminded that it's just not

all here and now. There's more to that. You got to look up and know you are not alone in all this. . . . And try to give them some comfort. So I do, I admit I do cross that line a bit.

After her initial song—usually "Friends Are Friends Forever" sung powerfully and warmly with Morticia—Ramona invites an American sign language interpreter to the stage. He reported to us that deaf people come regularly. As he signs, Ramona moves to the rear. Under the spotlight, his hands sing gracefully and energetically for the unhearing. The beauty and grace of the signing captures the audience.

Alicia Kelly is the most recent Gospel Girl. She is a young muscular black man. Ramona and others report she does an amazingly realistic Patti LaBelle. We believe it. She lip-syncs her numbers but everything else about her performance is authentic. She pours a fantastic amount of energy into her dancing, or "shouting." Kelly imitates a Pentecostal devotee possessed by the Holy Spirit. The congregation watches her transport herself acrobatically across the stage and they respond with loud applause. Many toss crumbled bills onto the stage and shout "Amen, Sister!" Alicia dramatically concludes by throwing her wig into the crowd and dousing herself with a bottle of beer or mineral water grabbed from a startled member of the audience. They roar.

Alicia, Ramona told us, "is doing the style she grew up with. They're the women that she saw in church. Often she will say, 'Well, this is Sister so-and-so,' and she'll become Sister so-and-so." The manager of the group—echoing an assessment that could have come from anyone in the audience—said, "If [Alicia Kelly] doesn't light your fire, your wood's wet!" Her electrifying performance concludes the first half of the hour.

Immediately, Morticia introduces the "Greeting Portion" of the service, a time, she says, for the congregation to meet and greet one another. She invites strangers to introduce themselves. Morticia leads the way and begins to mingle with the crowd. Most people do not follow her example, but some do. Romances have started at the Gospel Hour, including some lasting ones. Morticia takes this portion of the service seriously.

> I really want them to meet each other. The greeting portion . . . I mean, it's very difficult for them to talk to each other. Nobody will go up and speak to a stranger. And at Drakes I'd make a point to go all the way around the entire room. I don't do that so much anymore. I really do try to push. . . .

Gospel music continues to play during the quarter-of-an-hour break. The service resumes with the crowd eagerly anticipating the "High Church Sing-Along"—the highlight of the performance. Morticia, Ramona, Alicia, and guest singers sit on bar stools. They lead the crowd in favorite hymns like "When the Roll Is Called Up Yonder," "Because He Lives, I Can Face Tomorrow," and "There Is Power in the Blood of the Lamb." The volume, quality, and passion of the singing would be the envy of any church. During these hymns, participants occasionally close their eyes, some bow their heads. A few others raise their hands. "I really missed gospel music," Gary, a tall, handsome son of a famous Pentecostal minister told us. "There is a part of me that likes to sing," Gary continued, "so now I sing gospel music in a gay bar." Like so many at the Gospel Hour, Gary loves to sing, and he loves to sing *these* songs.

The Gospel Girls then invite individual members of the audience to sing a verse of "Amazing Grace." The ability of the audience participants covers a wide range. On Easter Sunday, 1995, a young man in a wheelchair sang. He chose the verse including the line "I once was lost but now I'm found, was blind but now I see." The bar fell silent straining to hear his weak voice. Later, Morticia DeVille confided

that she wanted to cry because she found the young man's singing so sweet.

Although weeping is not *supposed* to happen in a gay bar, tears are no strangers at these services. We have seen men cry during the Gospel Hour, caught up in the music and the emotion of the evening. One Sunday, a young man began to sob after the mention of the many who have died of AIDS, sometimes abandoned by family at their deaths but often surrounded by friends. The man—who we assumed was mourning the loss of a loved one—was embraced and comforted by his circle of friends. He did not hide his tears. No one made any move to the door. The emotion was very public—like at a revival meeting.

Participants have reacted emotionally since Morticia began to sing gospel songs in the gay bars of Atlanta. She recalled how her first audience responded in 1984.

> I did a show at Doug's. And it was just me and this piano player. And it just went so well. All those leather men like, had tears, they were all singing, they were crying. It was, it was really moving. . . .

The Gospel Girls and participants behave themselves during the hour. They sometimes openly enforce a standard of conduct on the audience. Morticia once chastised some rowdy participants with the rebuke, "As my Mamma used to say to me, 'Girl, you can give one hour a week back (to God)!'" They avoid the kind of bawdy sexual remarks typical of drag performances. Morticia, however, can be sexually suggestive but subtly. The hour never seems so sexually charged as when Alicia Kelly dances her ecstatic black Pentecostal shouts. Yet none of this sexuality is overt. Like church, there may be undertones of sexuality, but the worship service is not the place to act on these feelings.

One Sunday, a male stripper danced between services. The bar scene before, between, and after each performance is indistinguishable from any other drag show. In that regard, a male stripper was not out of place. Morticia said that while there is nothing wrong with strippers, they are inappropriate as part of the Gospel Hour or in proximity with it. She explained this to the crowd. The stripper never returned.

Restrained sexual expression is just one of the several informal rules at the Gospel Hour. The Gospel Girls never charge a cover. They never make fun of religious personalities. When the audience chooses to, however, they do not object. One recording popular with the audience captures Jimmy Swaggert giving a warm welcome to some unidentified religious group. He encourages them to hug, embrace, and show how they love each other. Participants enjoy the irony (or perhaps the ambiguity) of the liminal setting. Although they perform almost exclusively in bars, the Gospel Girls are careful not to drink in public. Seeing anyone drunk during the performance, for that matter, is rare although the bar does a brisk business. Almost no one cruises overtly. Audience members, however, get picked-up on occasion.

The two other bars in the immediate area attract their own crowds. One fills when the Gospel Hour ends. Many participants go there afterwards rather than stay at Prism after singing "See You in the Rapture." The transition from its concluding notes to dance music is abrupt but most people seem to prefer to go elsewhere to dance. They maintain the distinction between sacred time and secular entertainment. One comment summarized the attitude of many participants. "I don't normally do here what I do in a bar. I just feel funny about doing it. . . . I don't chase men when I come to the Gospel Girls. That's not the purpose of coming here." Participants separate from the straight world by coming to the gay bar. They actively set themselves apart from norms of the gay world, too. They do this by making the choice to listen to and sing gospel music. . . .

Many participants are out with their friends, having a good time. The performance dominates, but it does not monopolize. Participants and the singers alike combine behaviors learned in church and in bars. They have created a new model or template of identity mixing Evangelical and gay forms seamlessly.

The Participants: Identity Negotiation in a Modern Fragmented World

The first time visitor to the Gospel Hour immediately notices the predominantly young white crowd. A second glance, however, uncovers the approximately 10 percent who are African Americans, along with a few Hispanics and Asians. On any given night ten to fifteen women attend. Perhaps 20 percent are older than fifty-five years of age. Several of those interviewed attested to this unique diversity. One person claimed that Gospel Hour participants were "not your normal S and M gays . . . you know 'Stand and Model' gays." One fourth of our informants insisted they were not "bar people." Not only was this an older and more mature group, most did not have gym-perfected bodies. Many, in fact, were overweight, short, bald, or unattractive. The youngest, most handsome participants whom you might see in any popular gay bar often gather in small groups hugging the railing around the large stage. Directly in front, a group of regulars, many of them members of the MCC [Metropolitan Community Church], enthusiastically sing along. Most of the audience crams into the space behind these clusters. A middle-aged mother of a gay man or a sympathetic minister may sit at the few small tables to one side of the bar. Morticia is careful to greet and introduce them and other special guests each week. When she does, the audience receives the newcomers warmly. . . .

Donald, a former Southern Baptist and middle-aged man with no current church affiliation, reported that "at the Gospel Hour we can feel safe, like we won't be condemned." Regular participation allows him and others to identify more openly as Christian to gay friends. "We can say, 'Come go to the Gospel Hour.' We could never say 'Come go to church,'" he explained. "The Gospel Hour is fine because it's in a bar." "Going here I now can realize that I can be gay and still be with God," Mark, another regular participant, said. "God can reach out and say, 'I love you!'" For him, a man in his twenties from South Carolina, this was a significant realization. Mark was raised, like many we spoke with, as a Southern Baptist. He grew up knowing that he couldn't be both gay and Christian at the same time. By the time he came out he had been an ordained minister for five years. Since then, Mark has left institutional religion. "I was very fearful of incorporating the two concepts together," he confided. "I was told by most organized religion that I was wrong and damned to hell."

Mark was not the only one to believe and fear the message of nonacceptance and condemnation from American religious institutions. Nearly three-quarters of the respondents to the 1984 General Social Survey considered same-sex relations to be always or almost always wrong (Roof and McKinney 1987: 213). Likewise, most Gospel Hour participants know all too well the historic incompatibility of Christianity and homosexuality. Their childhood and adult experiences of the church, its ministers, and indirectly of the Christian God are ample proof. What takes place at the Gospel Hour is not important for participants alone. Nonetheless, the Gospel Hour provides a model for the place of gay people in the church contrary to dominant Christian practices and beliefs.

For gays and lesbians of Evangelical Christian heritage, religious support and advocacy have been nearly nonexistent. A few tolerant churches and support groups exist. For the most part, however, gay Evangelical and Pentecostal Christians face hard choices. They must remain closeted in their conservative churches, switch into a liberal denomination, or leave organized Christianity all together (Thumma 1987: 125). With the two latter options, the gay Evangelical Southern man must leave behind the symbols, rituals, hymns, and religious culture in which he was raised. The Gospel Hour is another option. It offers a setting in which participants can be both gay and Christian openly. High drag (an art form to which urban gay men become acculturated) combines with the familiar and cherished worship style of participants' early religious formation.

Our informants report considerable early religious formation as Evangelical Christians. Six were raised Southern Baptist, two Methodist, three Pentecostal or charismatic, and one Presbyterian (one person did not answer). Evangelical churches and institutions educated and employed these men. Three attended Christian colleges, three attended seminaries or Bible schools. Four spoke of being "called" to the ministry. One person sang at Jerry Falwell's Liberty University. Gary sang at Church of God congregations throughout the South. One person was currently a minister. Mark and another man were former clergy; a third was a former Southern Baptist missionary. The remainder reported their earliest religious formation in moderate and liberal Protestant Christian churches. We encountered few who were Catholics, Jews, non-Christians, or not religiously identified at all. . . .

Almost every person spoke of nonacceptance of gays and lesbians by religious groups. Many said they had experienced animosity from religious persons. Hostility is the normal, everyday posture of Christianity toward gays and lesbians. Our informants believe that gays have been, as one said, "shut off from Christianity." "If you are gay, you are going to hell!" said another, summarizing the prevailing message of the church of his youth. This older message sharply contrasts with what gay men see, hear, and do at the Gospel Hour.

"I realized that the God that the Baptists preached hated me," Shannon, the former missionary, said one Sunday between services. "I was told for so long that [as a gay man] I was hated by God." Many told us of their personal negative experiences. "I always thought that God completely hated me. I was told, 'You are gay and you are going to hell.'" Another informant told of his church friends' reactions after he shared his sexual orientation with them. "My best friends in the world turned their backs on me," he remembered. In the face of overt rejection by the Christian community, many gays decide to have nothing further to do with religion. Gary described his response plainly but with some of the cadence of an Evangelical preacher. "I jumped out of the closet and slammed the door right behind me. I left in the closet my family, my religion, and my God." . . .

In spite of almost always negative, frequently hostile, and occasionally violent responses to homosexuality in and outside the church, many at the Gospel Hour are still Christian—when construed in broad, cultural terms—although not active church members. For many Southern gay men, Evangelical churches provided important models of identity. Many at the Gospel Hour are still the choirboys, testifying and witnessing lay members, and even clerical leaders that they were in the Evangelical churches of their youth and young adult lives. As children and youths, these churches taught them their religious identity and helped prepare them to be (white) Christian men in the South. In the more diverse and tolerant cultural spaces of the city where they have learned to be gay, they are mastering how to be Christian again too—on their own terms.

Some Gospel Hour participants attending for the first time are hostile, ambiguous, or conflicted about Christianity. Others still respect the church or cherish a childhood memory of it. For six of the thirteen interviewed, the Gospel Girls' performance initially seemed wrong, even disgusting. Ben, a former fundamentalist Southern Baptist who attended Jerry Falwell's University, recalled his first impression. "I thought it was hypocritical and blasphemous." Guy, deeply involved in the charismatic movement, left after his initial visit and did not return for six years. "The first time I came, I was just totally disgusted. I thought, 'How could they be doing this in a gay place—singing gospel music and trying to be religious?'" Gregory recalled for us his first visceral reaction. "At first I was appalled. I just knew the ground was going to open up and we'd be sucked straight into hell . . . *but* after a while I began to notice the look of joy on people's faces."

These participants no longer find the Gospel Hour appalling or hypocritical. To the contrary, they spoke of feeling the presence of God. "I do, many times, sense the presence of the Spirit," one said. Another commented, "I never feel like I leave here without getting something out of this." The Gospel Hour stands in stark contrast to the message that gay life and Christianity are irreconcilable. The Gospel Hour does more than send a countervailing message. It enacts in a specific time and space a new model of gay Christian identity and a new template for cultural and social relations between Evangelicalism and gay life. . . .

For our informants, the drag show is a moving spiritual experience. "Everybody gets something out of (the Gospel Hour)," Gregory said in this subtle southern accent, "even if it is just that God doesn't hate them. It is a good and positive outlet." "It is a form of ministry," another maintained. Paul, however, is reluctant to talk about his work as Morticia DeVille as anything approximating a religious calling. In fact, he explicitly denies it. Paul, who earns his living as Morticia, speaks of her as a different person, someone apart and different from himself. Morticia is "jovial and funny and loving and trying to be grandmotherish" in Paul's description. He acknowledges that the *character* of Morticia DeVille might be ministerial, but not the person we call Paul. Other Gospel Girls and regular participants, however, are not hesitant to claim that Paul is following his calling. One Sunday, Morticia read a card from a MCC minister, a regular at the services. "You wear makeup and a wig," he wrote to her. "I wear a robe. But we both serve the same person."

That Morticia does wear a dress, however, is essential to the ritual. Drag is an ambiguous art. The drag performer embodies a picture of the gay man—as the feminine—rejected by many gays. Drag erases symbolically in a particular subcultural setting the gender lines created and maintained symbolically and socially in the dominant culture. Urban gay men must rehearse these daily in some segments of their lives. They are increasingly free in the American urban milieu, however, to ignore dominant gender lines in others.

The Gospel Hour functions differently for each person, and sometimes on multiple levels. For core participants it was their church. One said, "I always call it 'coming to church' . . . my friends and I call it 'coming to services.'" Another participant stated, "It is just an extension of church." Some participants have attended the Gospel Hour regularly for years, but have not stepped foot in a church.

For others the Gospel Hour gave them an opportunity for spiritual reconnection and restoration. Shannon (the former missionary) said, "Many (gays) are scared to go back to church because [it] turned them away. This is their one touch with God." James, a Presbyterian from New Jersey who is an Episcopal church organist, stated, "Gay anger against God is dealt with here." Hurt, too. A gay man visiting from Minnesota broke down during the singing. Regaining some composure, he confessed, "I can still identify with God, there is hope for me, a backslidden Christian. . . . I really want to get involved in church again," he tearily told Ramona. The comments of other participants echoed this sentiment.

> The Gospel Hour has helped me find an outlet to develop my spirituality.

> It showed me a void. A need in my life . . . it created a hunger for (church) again.

> The Gospel Hour made me aware of the longing I had for a relationship with God that I had turned away from.

For these and other informants the Gospel Hour offers fellowship and a sense of community. James, the organist, stated plainly, "It's a time of fellowship, that is what it is all about." Ben, the former fundamentalist, added, "I look forward to this as much as I do Sunday morning. . . . This is the fellowship portion." Finally, Mark, the former Southern Baptist preacher, found intimacy and an acceptance of his spirituality. "I could talk to others about what I feel and it was at the deepest, most intimate spiritual level." At the Gospel Hour new norms and new classifications of social relations take hold.

The Gospel Hour is most overtly a structured time for singing the old gospel songs. The act of singing these hymns has its own power, fulfilling a deep need created during early years of church life for our informants (Clark 1993: 105–6). One reported that part of him likes to sing, another attested that "music communicates in a way that words cannot." Some missed gospel music because singing it reminded them of home and family. Singing gospel music, Shannon said, is "my way of showing my religion, my relationship to God." Singing these songs, he continued, "is when I feel closest to God." Guy, the former charismatic, told us that "the music makes you feel real good about yourself."

Above all, almost every informant found the combination of gay and Christian cultural templates the most compelling feature of the Gospel Hour. It is a time and space they can be fully gay and altogether evangelical—on their own terms. Informants saw it as "our own place," a place of security and divine acceptance. Mark exclaimed, "I am able to be myself . . . I can do both [be gay and Christian] and be happy!" Shannon, his friend, explained,

> Here were people who knew "the songs" . . . knew what I had been raised with. I could identify all of a sudden. I was in a bar and it was not a sexual thing, not a social thing, it was a spiritual thing. . . . I could talk to others about what I feel and it was at the deepest and most intimate spiritual level.

Conclusion: Gay Liminality and Christian Identity

This ethnography has described how an urban gay bar becomes each week a religious space. The Gospel Hour transforms the bar into a liminal setting. High drag blends with southern Evangelical Christian music and song to create a new model or template for the relationship between being Christian and gay. Some embrace the exemplary template enacted ritually at this gay drag gospel cabaret to negotiate their identity as Christian and gay. . . .

The Gospel Hour provides a model of identity and a template for social relations. But the liminal space it creates is not a simple egalitarian communitas. It is a structured social setting, an institution with its own norms. Its ritual enactments of liminal identities and social roles are contingent on a wider social and institutional surround. In modern cities like Atlanta residents have the opportunity to create and sustain liminal rituals—and to choose from among them. Liminality may comprise an entire ritual event. It may involve an entire segment of an audience. The models and templates created may be more durable than fleeting communitas. Such durability makes ritual a richer source for normative, exemplary behaviors and practices. It also demonstrates that liminality, although ritually generated, is institutionally sustained in wider settings. The Gospel Hour ritually creates a "make believe" picture of gay and Christian social relations and turns the make believe into reality by replacing dominant norms with its own and institutionalizing them.

The Gospel Hour provides a safe haven for gays coming from Evangelical and other Christian traditions. The songs remind them of the comfort they once found in their faith. The drag performance marks the space and time as uniquely gay. Our informants used cultural models extant in gay and Evangelical subcultures as tools to negotiate a new identity and a new set of relationships with Christianity, gay culture, and even God. The Gospel Hour fuses both gay and Evangelical realities. It is gay and Christian, cabaret and revival.

At the Gospel Hour life imitates art.

REFERENCES

Clark, Linda J. 1993. "Songs My Mother Taught me: Hymns as Transmitters of Faith." In *Beyond Establishment*, edited by J. Carroll and W. Clark Root. Louiseville, KY: Westminister John Knox Press.

Thumma, Scott. 1987. "Straightening Identities: Evangelical Approaches to Homosexuality." Master's Thesis. Emory University, Atlanta, GA.

Turner, Victor. 1969. *The Ritual Process*. Ithaca, NY: Cornell University Press.

THINKING ABOUT THE READING

What do the authors mean by a "liminal space"? How does a liminal space provide an opportunity to engage in new and unique forms of self expression? What is the importance of physical space or venues in this identity performance? Consider some spaces in your own life in which you feel you can be "completely myself." What are some of the characteristics of these spaces? Why do you think it's important for the gay men in this article to be able to express both their religious identities and their sexual identities in the same place? Consider some identity conflicts in your own life. What are the underlying sources of these conflicts?

6 Supporting Identity

The Presentation of Self

A significant portion of social life is influenced by the images we form of others. We typically form impressions of people based on an initial assessment of their social group membership (race, age, gender, and so on), their personal attributes (for example, physical attractiveness), and the verbal and nonverbal messages they provide. Such assessments are usually accompanied by a set of expectations we've learned to associate with members of certain social groups or people with certain attributes. Such judgments allow us to place people in broad categories and provide a degree of predictability in interactions.

Though most of us would probably wish otherwise, our physical bodies dramatically influence the impressions others form of us. As Sharlene Hesse-Biber explains in "Becoming a Certain Body," this phenomenon is especially restrictive and potentially destructive for girls and women in this society. "Body watching" is a prime concern of most American girls, and one that is encouraged directly and indirectly by parents, siblings, peers, and even family doctors. Before they've even reached puberty, girls have learned the difference between the "right" body and the "wrong" body and have incorporated that distinction into their own self-image.

While we are forming impressions of others, we are fully aware that they are doing the same thing with us. Early in life, most of us learn that it is to our advantage to have people think highly of us. Hence, through a process called *impression management,* we attempt to control and manipulate information about ourselves to influence the impressions others form of us. Impression management provides the link between the way we perceive ourselves and the way we want others to perceive us. We've all been in situations—a first date, a job interview, meeting a girlfriend's or boyfriend's family for the first time—in which we've felt compelled to "make a good impression." What we often fail to realize, however, is that personal impression management may be influenced by larger organizational and institutional forces.

In "Frederick the Great or Frederick's of Hollywood," sociologist Melissa Embser-Herbert shows us how impression management in some institutional settings is made especially difficult by conflicting expectations. She draws from her research interviews to explore the different impression management strategies of women in the military. These women are under constant pressure to present themselves as tough soldiers who are capable of doing work that has been traditionally considered a "man's job." They must be able to prove to their fellow soldiers that they are up to the task and can be counted on in life-or-death situations. At the same time, they must take care to maintain the impression that they are still feminine. Military women use a variety of strategies to manage this double-bind, although their choice of strategy can have important implications regarding the perpetuation of gender stereotypes.

Men face different self-presentational dilemmas. In "Sisyphus in a Wheelchair," Tom Gerschick focuses on some of the ways in which performances of masculinity are based on assumptions of able-bodiedness. In particular, the men in his study find that the identities others impose on them are strongly connected to impressions regarding the physical body. Men with disabilities struggle to be seen as whole persons, but sometimes this means reconsidering their own social ideals regarding masculinity.

Something to Consider as You Read:

As you read these selections on the presentation of self and identity, consider where people get their ideas about who and what they can be in various settings. Consider a setting in which everyone present may be trying to create a certain impression because that's what they all think everyone else wants. What would have to happen in order for the "impression script" to change in this setting? In what ways do material resources and authority influence the impression we can make? Are there certain types of people who needn't be concerned about their impression in a given setting?

Becoming a Certain Body

Sharlene Hesse-Biber

(1996)

"My parents were always complimenting me on how I looked. It was such a big deal. I remember my father would say 'you look good, you lost weight.' And he also commented on other women, more than me. If there was a waitress, he'd say, 'Boy, is she beautiful!' Always commenting on pretty young girls. So I knew it was very important for him that I looked good too. When I'd dress up, I wanted him to see that I could be just as pretty as all those women he was commenting on."

—Jane, college sophomore

As part of membership in our society, young women have to learn how "to be a body." And, for the most part, what a woman observes in the mirror is what she uses as a measure of her worth as a human being. . . .

The food, diet, and fitness industries, aided by the media, have systematically convinced women that independence means self-improvement, self-control, and the responsibility for achieving the ultra slender body ideal. But the family, school, and peer group also have a role. They reflect and frequently amplify societal norms. These social influences often take the form of rewards and punishments to urge women's bodies toward thinness. The result creates vast differences in how men and women feel about their bodies.

Seeing the Self

Growing up in American society, we are taught, of course, to value what our society values. We learn to see ourselves as others see us, in terms of social standards. Self-image develops through social interaction. According to noted social psychologist George Herbert Mead, "The self

has a character which is different from that of the physiological organism, with a development all its own. The self is not even present at birth but arises later in the process of social experience and activity."

Mead adds that we experience ourselves as both subjects and objects. "The individual experiences himself as such, not directly, but only indirectly, from the particular standpoints of other individual members of the same group or from the generalized standpoint of the social group as a whole to which he belongs." Sociologist Charles Horton Cooley refers to this as the "looking-glass" self. Our significant others, such as family and friends, are the mirrors that reflect us. What others value in us provides the basic building blocks of selfhood.

Unlike personality, tastes, and social values, our physical appearance is always visible to others. It is a critical factor in the development of self-concept for women, especially during adolescence and young adulthood.

Weight is an important aspect of appearance, affecting young women's sense of social and psychological well-being. Many women experience even a few extra pounds as a major issue in their lives; they tend to weigh themselves frequently and report seeking medical help for weight problems more often than men. Although physical appearance is important for men, their traditional socialization stresses the importance of achievement (the mind) as a primary determinant of self image and self-esteem.

Women's bodily focus arises from their discussions with their friends, their interactions with family and social groups, and the messages they receive from outside this intimate circle. It is reinforced by the everyday practices that make the body central to their identity as a female—from clothing, hairstyle, and makeup; to speech, walk, and gesture. The Cult of Thinness becomes a powerful lure as society decides which is the "right" or the "wrong" body and treats women accordingly. . . .

Joining the Cult of Thinness

"I was raised by a domineering mother and also a strong father who didn't give me very much personal space to develop, so I was really used to being told what to do. I learned from a very young age to surrender myself to other people's will, desire, and wants . . . to really set myself aside."

—Anna, former
religious cult member

"I see commercials with these bodies and I want to look like that. I have this collage in my room of just beautiful bodies, beautiful women. And at the bottom it says 'THIN PROMISES' in really big letters. I have it up on my mirror, so I look at it every morning, just to pump me up a little bit, motivate me, dedicate me."

—Elena, college sophomore

For Elena, the pursuit of thinness has taken on the qualities of a religion. She makes a collage out of media images, paragons of female beauty. These are the "totems" that she worships; the inspiration for her quest for an ideal body. Her mirror can be compared to an altar, where she examines herself and fervently prays that she will be able to attain her ideal through practicing the rituals of dieting and exercising. Her daily mantra, "Thin Promises," keeps her dedicated and focused on a physical self that must be continually improved.

The college-age women I interviewed related their struggles and rewards and disappointments as they learned the culturally accepted ways of "being a body." They told me about the body watching and food monitoring practices they followed. These ritual aspects serve as powerful anchors to membership in the Cult of Thinness.

One of the most common practices is body monitoring—carefully scrutinizing the mirror for one's own physical flaws, or examining "the competition" for comparisons and defects. This involves treating the body as an object, in fact, experiencing oneself as "unembodied."

Body measuring techniques and incentives, along with food watching rituals, keep women like Elena "pumped up" and dedicated to the cause. In some cases these rituals can be painful reminders that one is not meeting these standards, a failure akin to eternal damnation. They require a great deal of time and energy, even a reorganization of daily life, not unlike the practices that religious cultists like Anna followed. "We would get up at 4 a.m. to meditate and do yoga for 2 ½ hours every morning," she told me. "It was hard, and everybody watched to see who showed up, who stayed awake, who practiced correctly. People felt guilty and did self penance if they didn't follow the practice."

Many Ways to Measure Up: Mirrors, Clothing, Photographs, and Scales

Methods of evaluating the body can be precisely quantitative—the reading on the scale, the image in the mirror, or the inch in the waistband of one's skirt. There are also more subtle indications, such as the admiring or critical glances and remarks from friends, relatives, or boyfriends.

Body comparisons are also ways of measuring. Very often such comparisons serve only to increase a sense of competition and insecurity in women. Do they measure up to other women in their immediate circle of friends and relations? Then there are the more global measures of comparison that are present in the wider society. Women may judge themselves according to the perfect images used in advertising or the media, or compare themselves to high profile women in beautiful-body professions, such as acting, modeling, ballet, or gymnastics.

Many of the women I interviewed looked into the mirror and believed they did not measure up to the societal expectations of the correct body image. "Not measuring up" sometimes led to strong feelings of self-hatred.

Cathleen reacted to these feelings by going on an extreme diet that led to anorexia: "I will never be satisfied with what's in the mirror. When I see other women I want to be better, thinner, than them. I would rather be anorexic than not."

Other women look in the mirror and enter the purgatory of self blame, for not being able to control their appetites. Lisa said: "I think the real problem is my whole self image—the way I see myself—never being able to achieve the goal of looking like those women body builders or being able to control myself. I feel so weak—'there you go again giving into your eating problem.' I'm just so powerless. I feel awful about myself, pretty much hate myself if I don't look a certain way. When I'm home and I'm gaining all that weight, I feel like shit. I avoid mirrors."

Roberta told me: "One day this week I woke up in the morning and I looked in the mirror, and I just was disgusting looking. And I just went right back to bed. I missed class, I could not get up. I can look in the mirror and just go, 'Yikes!' I guess I really feel like if anyone's going to like me I'm going to have to be beautiful."

Many of the women I talked with used the fit of their clothes as a way to watch their bodies, as well as an incentive to maintain or to improve their shape. When the clothing was loose, it was a time for celebration; when the fit felt tight, it was source of emotional pain. Getting into the right size can be an aid in losing weight for, as one woman put it, "You've got to find yourself some incentive clothes." Many expressed certain measurements they would tolerate in clothing and swore to stay within these sizes.

"You know there are limits," said Angela. "I don't want to go above size 10 or whatever—I'd like to stay at my size 8."

Jane said, "When I notice that my pants fit a little tighter or something like that, then I'll stop and go to my conventional diet where I just don't eat as much as I have been."

Judy noted that when her skirt was tight or her pants no longer fit, "I snap at everyone and I'm cranky and miserable. And when my clothes fit right and I walk down the street and I know my ass wiggles—I feel great. Everything's right. It's like a high."

Another important yardstick for body measuring comes from photographs taken over a period of time. Women examine these pictures in excruciating detail and evaluate their body shape over the months and years. Several students I interviewed frequently compared their pictures from high school with their current college pictures.

For instance, when Tina, a freshman, returned home for Thanksgiving, her father "just looked at me and said, 'I can't believe you're this heavy.' And my mother too. I looked like a totally different person. Within a matter of one semester my face was plump. Lately I've been looking at my high school pictures. I had my best year senior year—I was the best body. Now I just look at those pictures and I think, 'I could get down to that weight if I really wanted to.'"

"When I picture the body that I want," Rita said, "I picture myself during my freshman year in high school. I have a picture at home. It was of me standing there in a move from a cheerleading routine. You could see the bones. I wasn't anorexic looking, I was just tight. I was thin, but everything was in place. Tight and muscular."

One of the most obvious body measuring devices is the scale. In a sense it is the totem of all totems, encountered at gyms, fitness clubs, and diet centers. It is often a household shrine as well, with its own prescribed daily ritual. Most women disrobe before going on the scale, stripping themselves of any excess weight like jewelry or hair clips in hopes that they will "measure up" to certain weight expectations.

Joan noted: "The big thing at my house is getting on the scale every day. My mother will ask 'What do you weigh?' and it's a big thing. We weigh ourselves separately, but the question always comes up during the day."

Ruth told me: "I get on the scale five times a day. I just get really nervous. I panic when I get above 120. A lot of times, like last night, I'll go out and exercise right then."

For Marina, seeing extra pounds on the scale was like a death warrant: "I gained weight and I didn't feel good about myself. I gained four pounds. Doesn't that sound stupid? I say that to myself, but when you see it on a scale, it's like death. It's like someone scraping their nails on a chalkboard. It's like you can't go up there."

Measuring Up to the "Pros"

Certain body-conscious occupations create other sub-cults, whose participants find that they must continually work at the "right" body.

For most of Cindy's life, wanting to be a gymnast meant constant attention to body work. A college junior, she told me she had been extra conscious of her body image in high school because this sport demanded a certain height and weight limit.

"In gymnastics, they made us so weight conscious. Every single day we weighed in. Once, the day before an important competition, one of my friends weighed in over five pounds. The coach told her that if she didn't lose the weight by the next morning, she couldn't compete. She did everything she could. She put on a [sweat]suit and ran all night. She had beautiful long hair but she just chopped it all off, and the coach didn't care—as long as she lost the weight. Whenever there was a weigh-in, if you walked into the bathroom there was someone puking or on Ex-Lax."

Cindy started gymnastics when she was five. She practiced for four hours a day, six days a week, and on most weekends she was away at competitions. Ultimately, such an obsessive focus destroyed her pleasure and interest in the sport, but not before it had also stunted her physical growth.

"My father is over six feet. My mother is 5 foot 9 inches and my sister is also tall. I was supposed to be tall too—I wear a size eight and a half shoe. But my doctor said the hard training stunted my growth. I am only 5 foot 3 inches."

During her long years as a gymnast Cindy ate what she wanted. Her mother never objected to this since she was getting exercise. "Typically, I would get home from school and have dinner about 3:30 P.M. by myself. Then I'd go to the gym. So I never really ate with my family. On weekends we tried to get together on Sundays and sit down and eat. If I hadn't been in that kind of active sport, burning everything up so fast, I think my body would have been like a normal person. I never thought about food when I was younger, because it was never something that I wasn't allowed to have. I was the good girl and I stayed in gymnastics for two years longer than I wanted because my parents wanted me to. If it had been up to me I would have quit sooner, a lot sooner. I started to burn out. My freshman year of high school was my peak."

When Cindy got a bit older, around sophomore year, her coach started to take food away from her. "My coach was saying 'You have to lose weight before you compete, or you can't work out.' He was taking it away and when my mother found out about that she would just oversee it herself. She would say, 'You can't have this, you can't have that.' I'd find a way to binge. I'd go into my room with a bag of cookies and I'd shove them all in my mouth. She never knew. This was a big problem for me because I am a binger. I'll binge and then I'll starve myself the next day. I've been through it all. I've been through the bulimic stage. I've been through the Ex-Lax and I've been through bingeing and starving. When I was really thin, my junior year of high school, I looked good. I got compliments from everyone." Cindy's years of rigid discipline and practice backfired into an eating disorder, and has continued to be an issue for her in college.

Family Input and Peer Pressure

Early on, parents, siblings, peers, and even family doctors and diet clubs are important "guides and gurus" in the process of body watching. The women I interviewed told me that what their parents thought of them had quite an impact on how they perceived themselves. Helene felt her mother was always monitoring her:

> My mother wanted me to have everything she never had, like a college education. She wanted me to have more than she did. But she was critical of my body. If she didn't like what I was wearing she'd tell me right off the bat, 'Don't you know how to dress?' Last year she called

me a moose, and that hurt. Sometimes I think I need that, like just to make me aware so that I do something about my weight. I can see that all her pushing me has gotten me where I am. At my house we get on the scale every day. And my mother will ask, 'What do you weigh?'

> When I'm home I drop weight, because my mother is always on my back. When we go out to eat she tells me what I should order. When I look fine, my mother says nothing about my body, not even a compliment. But when I start gaining weight, the criticism begins.

Peggy's mother took her to the doctor when she was not getting rid of her baby fat. Her mother put a high premium on looking good, and expected her daughter to do the same:

> You know, my mother thought I was fat. I was 11 years old at the time. She took me to her weight doctor. She put me on extensive diets and I didn't like that. She gave me these amino tablets and she'd search around and make sure I didn't take cookies with me to school. She watched me. I actually remember the moment when I first felt shame. I was undressing, and all of a sudden, I jumped away from the window, and suddenly realized I should cover myself up.

Andrea's mother was also concerned about her daughter's weight. Andrea admits that she was, and still is, pudgy. Her baby pictures show her as a chubby little kid. She said:

> When I was smaller it was overlooked. You know, you're cute and dimply. But then as I got into grammar school I became heavier. From that point my mother was always concerned that I was heavy. She'd say, 'Couldn't you go on a diet?' And she tried her best to be nice about it, but when you're heavy you don't care to hear it from anybody. I joined a diet club when I was in high school because my mother said I had to. I was practically physically dragged to this place, totally against my will. I was so embarrassed. But I looked at everyone else who was

there, and thought, "Well at least someone's bigger than me."

Many women felt that peer group interaction was an important indicator of how their bodies measured up. June relates her discomfort during the transition from elementary to middle school:

> Because I was taller than all the guys in middle school, this one kid used to call me 'Amazon.' When I look back on it, the reason he called me that was because of my height, but I thought it was because I was fat. I really was never overweight as a kid, just the tallest. But then, when I went into 7th grade, I had this incredible will power. I just didn't eat.

Dangerous Comparison and Deadly Competition

. . . My interview subjects reported that they constantly compared themselves to their sisters, mothers, and girlfriends. When they felt they didn't measure up to the competition, [they experienced] anger [and] resentment. . . .

Cory felt her body did not conform to the standards of beauty set by her culture, and was angry and despairing that the mirror did not tell her what she wanted to hear.

> I think I am not attractive . . . I hate my skin and I hate my body. I'm small-chested, and have big hips and cellulite on the back of my thighs. It's disgusting. I see girls in my classes and I think they are very pretty. They've got gorgeous long hair, blue eyes. I tried to change myself in addition to my weight. I've tried to comb my hair long, and it doesn't look good. I've changed the color of my hair. Nothing is right. I don't like my nose, I don't like my face and I hate my double chin.

Beauty pageants are a good example of how society fuels the fires of competition and envy. While giving a passing nod to talent contests and oral interviews, pageants still focus on the ritual line-up of bodies in swimsuits and gowns. One student related her experience:

> Last year I won the local competition and I went on to compete in the state competition. My agent said I had a chance. As soon as I got to the contest, I realized that girls just enter year after year until they win. And I was one of the few people who was there for the first time. The girls were so bitchy and so catty and not friendly at all. A big part of winning is showmanship. It's how you approach the judges.

Some women described their transition to college as also involving a heightened need to compete with yet another set of beauty expectations.

Molly said, "I feel the competition here to look good. I mean you've got some incredibly good looking women that go to this school. They call it 'the beautiful school.' I never felt like I had to compete until I came here and people put all this pressure on you."

Sometimes the competition for male attention brings confrontation and the threat of violence. Mary was at a bar with her roommate, and narrowly avoided a fight.

> I was at a bar hanging out, and there were a couple of guys on the other side. My roommate called me over to introduce me to a couple of her friends. I didn't look good, I had a bandanna in my hair. My makeup was all over the place. I mean, I'd been through a lot that night. So I was talking to these guys, and this girl comes over and nudges me. She was made-up, her hair beautiful. She said, 'Excuse me, but are you with this party? Cause if you're not, would you mind moving?' That was it. I completely lost it. The next thing I knew, I was in this girl's face and said 'Who the hell do you think you are?' And my roommate just pulled me out of the bar because there was going to be trouble. This girl thought she was so much better than me. The guys just stood there. They were all like, 'You don't want to mess with her, you know?'

Sometimes the competition hits close to home, when mothers, daughters, siblings, and peers are comparing their bodies. "My mother was a model," Lucy told me. "She was always Little Miss Beauty Queen. And there was pressure for me to follow in her footsteps. But my mother was jealous of me. I could feel that tension between us. She would often say, 'Well, you look a little scruffy today.'"

Irene was competitive with both her mother and her sister:

When I was in high school my mom dyed her hair blonde, and was skinnier than I, and I was incredibly jealous. It drove me crazy. I didn't want guys I liked to meet her. I didn't really tell her, but on the beach she'd wear bikinis, and I hated it. I thought my mother was trying to be a teenager when she was older, and I was really jealous of her. I like being with my father alone rather than with my mother, because I guess I feel that I'm still competing with her.

What got Irene particularly upset was that her mother could eat almost anything and never put on weight. Irene's sister was also thin and had her mother's metabolism. Irene was built more like her father, who was big-boned, tall, and somewhat overweight.

"My father used to say that I had no style. My sister had all the style. She could wear anything because she was so thin. I always got A's in school, and I was in Honor Society, whereas my sister did badly. But that was the least of my concern, getting A's. I wanted to be thin. I would just look at my sister, and think, 'My god, if I could only be thin like her.'"

Peer competition intensifies in a closed community like a boarding school. Maria talked at length about her experiences at the school she attended in France before coming to college. The girls in this boarding school practiced body and food watching rituals with great concentration, as befitted their exclusive cult subculture.

The first year there, when I was fifteen, I didn't have any problem with my eating. The second year, Sandra came along. Sandra is German and very pretty. She and I became good friends. We had both been friends with Claire, who had steadily become anorexic at school, then died that summer. It really didn't hit Sandra and me. We had gone on a diet the previous year and continued this at school the next year. First of all we started purging (vomiting). We'd actually gotten this idea from Claire. And it got to the point where it would come naturally. I was bulimic for six months. It was horrible. My housemaster noticed, and sent me to the doctor. I had a lot of chest pains at the time—I had just destroyed the lining of my stomach. They gave me this awful white liquid. And I wasn't necessarily thin—I was pretty much the same weight. Then the following year, as seniors, Sandra and I started with this vicious competition about losing weight. I ate only carrots and this low fat cream with diet crackers. I started losing weight and Sandra was losing weight faster, because she was thinner than I was to begin with, and taller. So everyone was yelling at me, "Why are you letting Sandra do this to you!"

At this boarding school, appearance is everything. Everyone there was gorgeous. People look at my yearbook and say 'wow!' And I think that's the way the school wanted us to be—glamorous and gorgeous and intelligent. The perfect girl at this boarding school would be someone with long blonde hair, terribly skinny, big blue eyes, some sort of affected accent, and no makeup. Everyone tried to put makeup on to look like there was nothing there. They would color their cheeks, or whatever. Girls wore colored contact lenses at the age of 13. Everyone also definitely tried to be skinny. The girl next door to me was anorexic. She used diuretics. Another friend upstairs was also anorexic and she had to go to the hospital because she had used laxatives for so long her body would no longer function normally. Last year when I went back for a reunion I found out that another good friend of mine, Carla, had died of an eating disorder.

At this school, if you had dinner at the table and ate the entire meal, you were considered a pig, and you were going to be talked about. The biggest thing was to just run around with the salad bowl and ask if any one had any extra salad.

We lived in a girls' house but there were guys there as well. That's who you had to look good for. It doesn't hit you how bizarre something is until someone from the outside says something. We lived in such a closed community. You weren't allowed to go into the city, you weren't even allowed to go to any of the towns. You had to stay there.

Measured by Men

One all-important indication that a woman has the culturally correct body image is the attention she gets from men. This may take the form of getting a date or merely prompting a nice remark from a male concerning her appearance.

Virginia was sure that her weight problem was responsible for her empty social life: "Now, looking back at pictures, I looked fine, I was never even overweight. But at that time I thought, 'Oh I'm horrible and that must be the reason I don't have a boyfriend.'"

Judy felt pleased to be recognized as attractive by one of the waiters at a restaurant she frequented with her college friends: "The host called me over last night, and he said, 'You know the waiter thinks you're very attractive. Is there a chance you'd say yes if he asked you out?' So if he calls I will go out with him. It really made me feel good last night because I was out with five other very pretty girls, and he picked me, thought I was attractive. It's usually my roommate that gets the guys."

Food Watching Rituals

The ritual of food watching goes hand in hand with body watching. It is often practiced on a daily basis, either alone or with the help of another individual (usually a family member) or with a group such as a diet club. Food watching ranges from calorie counting, to full scale dieting, to the behavioral symptoms of anorexia or bulimia.

Almost all women in my sample of college students had been on what they termed "a diet" during their teenage years. They consider dieting normal behavior.

For example: "I would do just normal dieting and then exercising, nothing crazy, but just cutting down, maybe more than I should actually. I'd just eat very little from each food group, and exercise a lot. I was always hungry."

And: "I never went to Weight Watchers or anything. I went on the Sherry Vitti diet a couple of times. You know, no junk, nothing between meals, don't eat after supper, that kind of thing. I would eat three times a day but small amounts. And sometimes like at night, I remember the room would start to spin a little bit, and then I'd have to get some whole milk or something to put in my stomach."

Some dieting behavior consists of fasting for days at a time. Georgia went on a fast after her boyfriend made a comment concerning her weight. "I was so hurt at the time, so mad at him. What I did was just not eat anything. I went to aerobics every night. And of course there was nothing else in my life. I had my school work, but I had no other interests. I'd go out on weekends with my friends, but I didn't even want to do that much because that was always sitting around food. It was great while I looked good and I got all the compliments, but I don't think it was worth all the anguish and deprivation I went through. And I hadn't changed my eating problems, I had just suppressed them for 8 weeks. I lost 30 pounds. I remember being exhausted when I got home from school. I wouldn't feel like doing anything. Once I started eating, I gained the weight back again."

Parents, friends, and diet organizations can also be involved in "helping" women food watch. Judy said:

> My mother was very critical of my appearance. I was always the fat one and she was the thin one. She would say that I have the fattest thighs in the world, and that I'd better watch what I'm eating. She would always make sarcastic remarks. She would say, 'If you want to diet, I'll help you. I'll make special meals for you. I'll do anything I can for you.' She was good in that aspect, but in the back of my mind I knew she was always going to say something when I picked up that Twinkie.

· · ·

Thin Promises: The Rewards of the Right Body

Women continue to follow the standards of the ideal thin body because of how they are rewarded by being in the right body. Thinness gives women access to a number of important resources: feelings of power, self-confidence, even femininity; male attention or protection; and the social and economic benefits that can

follow. The students I interviewed knew exactly what thinness meant to them. Julia commented on how becoming thinner really made a difference in getting men to respond to her.

> Last summer when I lost a lot of weight, men were much more receptive to me, and it's flattering. I kind of like the feeling how a woman can tease men almost, you know, just a look, or what you're wearing, or the way you look at them, and that's exciting. I mean, it could be dangerous, and you don't want to push things too far, but again it's exciting. Because I've never experienced that before, you know?

And Elizabeth said, "When I lose weight, I have a wonderful feeling of power. It's like I am in control of my body. I'm thin, and it's so great. I even commented on it one time to this friend of mine. I said 'Charlie, it's so funny, you lose 30 pounds and guys really want to pay a lot of attention to you,' and Charlie said, 'Yeah, it's kind of lame' and it is kind of lame, but it doesn't surprise me at all. Losing weight was great for my ego."

For so many women whose bodies are their primary identities, the Cult of Thinness promises the rewards of cultural acceptance.

THINKING ABOUT THE READING

Historically, women have been much more concerned about body image than men. Why? What rewards have women been taught to believe they will receive if they maintain the ideal weight? What are some of the consequences of the "cult of thinness" for women? How are cultural ideals of beauty connected to self-expectations, self-expression, and self-esteem? Why are men, in general, less concerned about body image than women? Consider how media imagery reinforces these gender differences. Are circumstances changing? If so, in what ways? Are men becoming more concerned about body image than they were in the past? Are women becoming less concerned?

Frederick the Great or Frederick's of Hollywood

The Accomplishment of Gender Among Women in the Military

Melissa Sheridan Embser-Herbert

(1998)

Introduction

In an article on military culture, Karen Dunivin writes, "the combat, masculine-warrior paradigm is the essence of military culture" (1994: 534). For military women, this may pose something of a contradiction. Women are often expected, by virtue of the perceived relationship between sex and gender, to display societal norms of femininity. What is expected when women fill an occupational role whose defining characteristics are inexorably linked with masculinity? While these women, by virtue of being in the military, fill a masculine work-role, it is quite possible that they are also penalized for being "too masculine," or, in essence, violating the societal expectations that they maintain some degree of femininity.

Masculinity in military men is not only rewarded, but is the primary construct around which resocialization as a soldier takes place. It is not surprising that femininity, or characteristics believed to be associated with femininity, would be discouraged. On the other hand, the military, reflecting the broader society, may find that women's femininity serves "to validate male identity and both individual and collective male power" (Lenskyj 1986: 56). This is, I believe, illustrated by the recently abandoned Marine Corps policy of requiring female Marines to undergo make-up and etiquette training and in current regulations that require women's hair not be cut "so short as to appear masculine." Additionally, the military is

highly traditional, primarily conservative, institution in which we may expect the expression, "men are men and women are women" to be taken seriously. Exactly how are women in the military supposed to "be women?"....

Perceptions of women and their "fit" with what is believed to be gender appropriate may be critical to the ability of women to become accepted as members of the military. The integration of women into an institution *defined* by its association with masculinity may pose an interesting dilemma for military women. Can one truly be a soldier[1] and a woman and not be viewed as deviating either from what it means to be a soldier, or from what it means to be a woman? I can recall being asked by a fellow soldier why I, and other women, didn't "dress up" when we were off duty. It struck me then, as it does now, that we were expected to do our jobs "like the men," and transform "into women" once we removed our flak jackets and helmets and turned in our rifles and ammunition. One respondent spoke to these contradictions when, addressing men's perceptions, she wrote, "If you're too feminine, then you're not strong enough to command respect and lead men into battle, but if you're strong and aggressive you're not being a woman."

Those in the military, but particularly women, must "do gender." In their article, "Doing Gender," West and Zimmerman argue that gender is "a routine accomplishment embedded in everyday interaction" (1987: 125)....Gender is "the local management of conduct in relation to normative conceptions of appropriate attitudes and activities for particular sex categories" (West and Fenstermaker 1993: 156). Although women in the military are clearly recognized as women, that is, as belonging to both the female sex (i.e., physiologically female) and female sex category (i.e., perceived as physiologically female; what others might call gender), given their role as members of the military, these women must constantly create and manage their gendered identities. While all women must do so, it should be noted that men also "do gender," on a daily basis. As Ronnie Steinberg notes, men "actively recreate their dominance every day" (1992: 576).

The military, I believe, is a particularly good site in which to examine the "everyday" ways in which women negotiate a world in which they must simultaneously be recognized and accepted as women, but must perform a job that has been perceived by many as appropriate only for men. Not only has the "soldier" been constructed, both ideologically and historically, as male, but soldiering has been the very means by which men have "become" men. Thus, the masculinity of soldiering is not "just" masculinity, but hypermasculinity. . . . While women and men throughout society must "do gender," the increased salience of gender within the military makes it possible that it may be even more true within that setting, at least with regard to traditional conceptions of gender.

. . . [In this article I focus on the interactional processes related to the performance of gender in institutional settings.] "Interaction between individuals and groups is the medium for much institutional functioning, for decision making and image production" (Acker 1992: 568). It is through this process that gender is created and re-created. Goffman, addressing the "interactional field" and the interactions themselves, argues that "these scenes do not so much allow for the expression of natural differences between the sexes as for the production of that difference itself" (1977: 324). Gender is not accomplished solely on the basis of specific actions (e.g., wearing a skirt instead of pants), but it requires that interactions occur in which the action is recognized as placing the actor in a particular gendered context. West and Zimmerman write:

> While it is individuals who do gender, the enterprise is fundamentally interactional and institutional in character, for accountability is a feature of social relationships and its idiom is drawn from the institutionalized arena in which those relationships are enacted (1987: 136–137).

. . . West and Zimmerman (1987) pose three central questions: "If, for example, individuals strive to achieve gender in encounters with others, how does a culture instill the need to achieve it? What is the relationship between the production of gender at the level of interaction and such institutional arrangements as the division of labor in society? And, perhaps most important, how does doing gender contribute to the subordination of women by men?" (140). In this [article] I respond to these questions by examining the place of gender in the lives of women in the United States military. . . .

Methodology

The findings in this paper are based on 256 surveys collected from women who are veterans of, or currently serving in, the United States military. I used a variety of avenues to identify potential respondents including posting notices at women's bookstores, gay and lesbian community centers, on computer bulletin boards, in publications such as *Minerva's Bulletin Board*, *The Register* (the newsletter of the Women in Military Service for America Project), and at college and university veterans' program offices around the nation. The 15-page questionnaire contained seven sections with items in formats varying among yes/no questions, multiple choice questions, open-ended questions, check off items, and Likert-scale items. Each section has a different focus. The sections of the questionnaire assess the following: (1) personal information, (2) military service, (3) education, (4) personal assessment of military service, (5) personal resources, (6) gender, and (7) sexuality. The surveys were used to create a computerized data set as well as text files of the answers to open-ended questions. I should note that my own military service formed the basis for many of the questions. Though my experience is limited to the Army, I was able to formulate questions about uniforms, on-post and off-post activities, chain of command, etc., on the basis of not only familiarity with scholarship on women in the military, but with the aid of 15 years experience in both the active and reserve components of the U.S. Army as both enlisted and officer.

The women who answered the survey came from over 40 states, all branches, all ranks except flag officer (i.e., General/Admiral), and served as early as the 1950s. . . .

The survey asked respondents to indicate whether they believed that penalties exist for women who are perceived as "too feminine." In a separate question, it asked whether they believe that penalties exist for women who are perceived as "too masculine" and to provide examples of what the penalties might be. The results presented here are based on descriptive statistics and analyses of the open-ended responses about types of penalties.

The survey also included a list of 28 behaviors. Respondents were asked to "check any of the following that you believe applied to yourself" (while on active duty). These items consisted of behaviors such as polishing one's fingernails, wearing cologne on duty, keeping one's hair trimmed above the collar, socializing with the men in the unit, and so on. Respondents were then asked, "Do you believe that any of those behaviors checked . . . were

part of a conscious attempt to insure that others perceived you as feminine?" The survey also asked, "Do you believe that any of those behaviors checked . . . were part of a conscious attempt to insure that others perceived you as masculine?"

Respondents were asked the question: "Are there other things that you did that you believe were a conscious attempt to insure that others perceived you as feminine/masculine?" This question was included in the survey because it was impossible to identify a list of all possible strategies. Answers to questions, both closed-ended and open-ended, illuminate how women strategize about gender.

By examining if and/or how military women believe that gender is policed and what they do in response, we can begin to understand how women engage in the accomplishment of gender as opposed to simply "being" feminine or masculine. By "policed," I mean that their behaviors are monitored or censured by other members of the military, female and male and at all levels, to insure that women are not seen as violating norms of gender appropriateness. The strategies that women employ are both interactional and internal. . . . The strategies are interactional in that their existence, and perpetuation, is dependent upon the response that the individual receives from others. And, they are internal in that, to some degree, they become incorporated into the persona of the person deploying them.

. . . In this research . . . I wanted to see if women would recognize and acknowledge their consciously engaging in strategies to manage gender.

Perceptions of Femininity

Do women believe that they are penalized for being perceived as "too feminine" or "too masculine"? Findings indicate that there is very little latitude for women when it comes to perceptions of gender. Sixty-four percent believe there are penalties for being perceived as "too feminine," while 60 percent of respondents indicate that they believe there are penalties for being perceived as "too masculine." . . .

Those women who believed there are penalties were asked to describe what they believed such penalties to be. One-hundred and sixty-five women described penalties for femininity. One hundred and fifty-seven described penalties for masculinity. Rather than starting with expected categories and coding the answers for whether or not they "fit" a particular category, I conducted a content analysis on the responses to see what categories emerged. Some answers could be coded into more than one category, as some respondents provided numerous examples, sometimes just listing words (e.g., "being perceived as an airhead, bimbo, or slut"). . . .

Though the penalties for femininity were quite varied, six common themes emerged: (1) ostracism or disapproval from other women, (2) being viewed as a slut or sexually available, (3) being perceived as weak, (4) being perceived as incompetent or incapable, (5) not being taken seriously, and (6) career limitations. While some of these categories overlap and might even be perceived as one and the same (e.g., weak vs. incompetent), the specific words were used enough, and often within the same response, that it seemed as though they had different meanings for the respondents and should be coded accordingly.

The first five penalties are related to the sixth, and most frequently mentioned penalty: that of career limitations. This is true almost by definition, in that if there were no potentially negative impact on one's performance or career aspirations, one might question the way in which a given situation constituted a penalty. It is difficult to think of a situation in which a woman is penalized that does not carry with it the potential to damage one's work relationships and/or career.

"Career limitations" is actually a catch-all phrase for a number of career penalties. As

illustrated by the respondents, they include, but are certainly not limited to, obvious limitations such as not being allowed to perform the job for which one was trained, not being promoted, not sent to a school needed for promotion, not getting choice assignments, etc. One woman wrote, "They are not assigned to 'career building' areas such as pilots, maintenance, security police—the generally thought of 'male jobs.'" Another woman wrote:

> I was a long haired blonde, outstanding figure, long beautiful nails (my own!) etc., etc. I was constantly told I couldn't do my job (working on aircraft) as I was a dumb blonde, I'd get my nails dirty, I was a danger to the guys working on aircraft because I distracted them, etc., etc. My first rating was not a favorable one even though I scored higher on the OJT [on-the-job-training] tests than anyone had ever scored in that shop!

Another indicated that "you don't get the tough jobs you need to be in good shape for promotion, and women who are too feminine usually get ignored or put in office jobs with no troops." Command positions, leading troops, are critical to the promotion of those in the officer ranks. Many women mentioned the penalty of being "removed from position[s] of authority and placed in somebody's office," or being "given more feminine jobs to do." Command positions are definitely not considered "feminine." One woman expressed her opinion on this issue:

> It is a great privilege as an officer to be in a command position. Part of being a commander is having a "command presence." I greatly doubt that women who wear lots of perfume, make-up, speak softly, and/or make strong efforts to appear feminine are considered frequently as serious contenders for command positions.

The categories of penalties clearly overlap. Especially in a military that "has no place for weakness," it is difficult to discuss attributions of weakness without discussing incompetence as well. It is difficult to discuss perceptions of incompetence without noting its relationship to not being taken seriously and suffering career limitations. In sum, while about one-quarter of the respondents mentioned career limitations explicitly ("Not selected for schools, promotion."), virtually all the penalties discussed are related, whether directly or indirectly, to the ability of women to be treated equally with men and, therefore, to achieve the same degree of success as their male counterparts. While the penalties for being perceived as too feminine are varied, they do share a common theme. Whether at the informal (e.g., perceived as a slut by other members of the unit) or formal level (e.g., not selected to attend leadership training), each of these penalties serves as a mechanism for insuring that women remain "outsiders" to the boys' club of the military.

Perceptions of Masculinity

If women who are perceived as too feminine experience penalties, what happens to those women who are perceived as too masculine? Are they polar opposites on some scale of acceptability? One might argue that the best mechanism for combating penalties for being too feminine is to insure that one is perceived as masculine. Examination of the data reveals that this is not the case.

Of the 157 women who described the penalties for being perceived as too masculine, over half indicated that such women would be labeled as lesbians. There were a number of responses that seemed as though that was what was being inferred, but because it wasn't stated explicitly I opted for a conservative approach and did not code them as such. Consider these examples: "Comments," "Many lewd remarks were made about 'masculine' type women," "I think they may have to prove themselves more especially if not married," and "'Too masculine' tends to be equated with 'man hating.'" If descriptions of this type were

included, about two-thirds of the responses could be considered to address lesbianism.

Although the label "lesbian" emerges as a single category of penalty, it is illustrative to look at the different ways in which the issue is addressed. In many cases women stated very plainly, "Perceived as being a lesbian," "Perceived as lesbians," "Lesbo, dyke, etc.— Need I say more!" In other cases their descriptions were much more colorful or detailed. Consider the following description:

> Being teased by other service members... called "butch," "bitch," "dyke," a lesbian. If a female can't be told apart visually, at first glance, from a male she *will* be subjected to being called sir vs. ma'am and may be kicked out of a few female restrooms, at first glance.[2]

A number of respondents, as was the case when a woman is perceived as too feminine, indicated that penalties also came from other women. One woman wrote:

> If you go past gender neutral (the "ideal" woman officer), past masculine (conspicuous), to too masculine, you were courting being labeled a lesbian. Too masculine made men and women nervous. Me, too.

Another indicated that "they are often avoided by both male and female soldiers. They are the outcasts of the unit."

One of the most revealing findings regarding the penalty of being labeled a lesbian is the understanding that this label was often applied to women regardless of sexual orientation. This fact serves as a wonderful illustration of the way in which homophobia and perceptions of sexual orientation serve as mechanisms for the subjugation of all women. "I believe they are labeled as homosexuals, 'dykes,' whether they are or not." "Of course, they are tagged or stereotyped as lesbians, whether they are or not." The impact of such allegations can extend well beyond having to tolerate "talk." As one woman writes:

One of the women in the unit who had a masculine appearance was accused of being a lesbian even though she wasn't. When her time was up she got out because of the accusations she was gay. She was a good soldier.

Being labeled a lesbian was the only category that clearly emerged from a content analysis of these items. Some answers occurred more frequently than others, but none so much as the penalty of being labeled a lesbian. Other penalties that respondents described included: (1) ostracism and ridicule and, (2) career limitations. Though they each constituted only about 10 percent of the descriptions, in these "non-sexualized" instances women are receiving social and career penalties for exhibiting behavior that is highly desirable in male soldiers. It is critical to understand that women are being penalized for exhibiting gendered behaviors that are consistent with the work-role of "soldier."

Bearing in mind that I am talking about the military, consider this description of how, and for what, women are penalized. "Women who were seen as too aggressive—too much focus on aggressive or violent activities were not seen as 'normal' or to be 'trusted.'" Exhibiting interests in activities that many would agree form the core of military ideology (i.e., aggression and violence) results in the penalty of not being considered "normal" or "trustworthy." Another respondent indicated the "women were discouraged from being aggressive, displaying leadership skills, being self-assured and independent."

The ostracism that women describe is often, but not always, linked to the subject of lesbianism. While some women offered comments such as, "They are shunned, called names (e.g. dyke)," others were less specific in their remarks. "Rejected by both male and female peers," or "A woman who appears too masculine may be ridiculed for it." One woman wrote, "Yeah, everybody hates them." Whether explicitly related to sexual orientation or not, it

seems apparent that women who violate gender norms of femininity are "outsiders" to the same degree, albeit in a different fashion, as are women who violate the masculine work-role of the military by being too feminine.

By understanding that women receive career penalties for being perceived as too masculine, as well as too feminine, we begin to understand the degree to which women are required to walk a fine line. One woman's comments capture this contradiction beautifully:

> [I] knew a female airman [sic] who could do her job on the flight line better than most of the guys in her unit. This convinced some people she was a "dyke"—just had to be a lesbian otherwise she wouldn't have been so good at a "man's job."

Although cast in the light of sexual orientation, such a description illustrates the difficulties women face when simply trying to do the job for which they were recruited. Another wrote:

> A female commander who does the exact same discipline as a male commander is probably seen as a bitch on a power trip. You're derided and not respected for playing tough by the rules. . . . You play by their rules but then you lose because they didn't consider you part of their game.

In other instances, the examples described specific career penalties such as "not selected for 'high profile' jobs," "poor evaluations or less than deserved marks," and "overlooked for awards/promotions." As one woman described, "I believe it can affect performance reviews, assignments, and coaching or counseling which is provided for developmental growth." While the cynic might argue that women "just have to tough it out," it is clear that there are plenty of formal mechanisms by which women can be penalized if they are perceived as gender deviant, regardless of the direction of the alleged deviance. What, then, do women do?

Conscious Strategies—Femininity

... Forty-one percent, or close to half, of the sample indicated that they engaged in some form of gender management, or strategizing. ...

Of those respondents who indicated employing strategies to be perceived as feminine, at least one-third chose each of the following strategies: wearing make-up on duty (40 percent), wearing long hair (38 percent), wearing earrings while in uniform when permitted (37 percent) (this figure may have been even higher if women had always been permitted to wear earrings; it was only in the 1980s that women were granted permission to wear earrings with certain dress uniforms), wearing cologne or perfume (35 percent), and wearing make-up off duty (34 percent). Slightly less than one-third indicated that they wore pumps instead of flat shoes (low quarters) with the dress uniform (32 percent) and that they wore skirt uniforms instead of pants uniforms (28 percent) as strategies to be perceived as feminine. The fact that these items focus on clothing is primarily a function of the choices that were provided in the survey.

One of the most interesting aspects of clothing as a strategy for being perceived as feminine was the *way* in which clothing was often worn. This is of interest not only because it goes beyond the issue of clothing *choice*, but because the way in which an item was worn was often in violation of the regulations. Consider the following examples of strategies that women described: "My uniform skirt was always too short," "[I] did not wear a t-shirt under fatigues," and "I wore my BDU cap and Class A cap way back on my head to look more like a female." Such violations could lead to formal punishment, such as receiving a counseling statement, or to informal punishment, such as being the subject of negative comments. In my military experience, women were frequently ridiculed for not wearing their uniforms properly. Such women were viewed as

not being serious soldiers and as being more concerned about their appearance than doing their job. Thus, women may highlight femininity as a means of being viewed more favorably, but to do so they may choose a strategy that has negative repercussions as well.

Women not only strategize with props such as clothing, jewelry, and make-up, but they also used their bodies to highlight femininity. One example of this is seen in the closed-ended item regarding hair length. As indicated above, 38 percent of those who indicated strategizing said that they wore their hair long as a strategy for being perceived as feminine. In the open-ended question, others referred to hair styling in general: "I tried to keep my hair in a feminine style that suited me. This involved getting a perm every 3–4 months."

Another strategy was the intentional avoidance of swearing. One woman wrote that she "never used bad language like many other women in [the] military do," while another wrote that she simply, "did not swear much." Other strategies that appeared repeatedly included home and office décor ("Flowers on my desk, my Noritake coffee cup, and picture frames on my desk"), and watching one's weight ("I kept a close watch on my weight because I was under the false assumption that 'thinness' and feminine were related"). In sum, conscious manipulation of one's appearance and engaging in behaviors traditionally marked as "female" were common strategies for managing the perceptions others had about one's status as feminine.

All of the strategies discussed thus far focus on appearance, personal space, and personal habits. None of these strategies are particularly surprising, nor can most immediately be labeled as detrimental to one's physical or emotional well-being. The same cannot be said of the last group of strategies.

It is evident from the data that both men and women not only shape ideas of femininity, but also mete out the penalties for gender violations. While men were not surveyed or interviewed, the women gave many examples of how both women and men let women know when they were seen as deviating from accepted norms of gender. Most strategies, while influenced by others, were engaged in on an individual basis. That is, they did not involve the active participation of another individual, but could be accomplished alone (e.g., wearing make-up or a knife). In the last group of strategies addressing femininity, discussed below, men play a key role. These strategies are those in which women intentionally engaged in social or sexual relations with men.

The closed-ended question revealed that anywhere from 6 to 10 percent of those who strategized either socialized with the men in their units (seven percent), dated men in their units (11 percent), or married while on active duty (six percent) as a conscious attempt to be perceived as feminine. Four percent indicated that, as a strategy for being perceived as feminine, when they had a boyfriend they "made sure people knew it." These numbers may seem inconsequential until we realize that this means that people are intentionally engaging in personal relationships as strategies for altering or enhancing the perceptions that others have of them.

One woman wrote, "I believe I did a little 'indiscriminate' dating, more than I should have, maybe to feel more feminine." Another "Made up stories re: boyfriends, [heterosexual] sex, dates; even slept with man/men (when I was drunk) to cover for myself and the company." One woman said that she "tried to date civilian men," while another said, "I felt that I *had* to have a boyfriend." The relationship between femininity and heterosexuality is a key element to understanding why such social and sexual relations with men would serve as strategies. As one woman said, "I mostly made conscious attempts to appear heterosexual v. feminine." Another woman

answered, "Hanging around with nothing but males and having sex with them to prove I wasn't a lesbian." Because of the obvious link to displays of heterosexuality, it is worth noting at this point that there was an entirely separate question, not analyzed here, about strategies to avoid being perceived as lesbian. The responses provided here are specifically in response to the question about being perceived as feminine. This is powerful evidence of the link between the ways gender and sexuality have been constructed.

Conscious Strategies—Masculinity

Although a majority of women who strategized did so toward femininity, this was not true for everyone. Twelve percent of those who employed strategies aimed some or all of their efforts at masculinity. Seventy-four percent of the respondents who indicated employing at least one masculine strategy said they wanted to be considered "one of the guys." Forty-one percent said that they "socialized with men" in their unit as a strategy. Thirty-one percent wore pants uniforms rather than skirt uniforms as a strategy and 30 percent indicated that their preference for work uniforms (e.g., camouflage uniforms) to dress uniforms was a strategy for being perceived as more masculine. Thus, clothing was also a strategy for being perceived as masculine, but not nearly as frequently as it was a strategy for being perceived as feminine. Clearly, being seen as "one of the guys" and/or socializing with men were key strategies for women wishing to be perceived as masculine.

Analysis of the open-ended items revealed strategies similar to those above. The four main strategies identified in the qualitative data are: swearing, drinking, working out, and doing other "guy things." In the findings concerning feminine strategies we saw that avoidance of swearing was considered by some to be a strategy for being perceived as feminine. In the results presented here we see the opposite approach. In answer to the open-ended question about strategies, one woman wrote, "My favorite cuss word is 'shit.' I cussed when I wanted to make a point." Other examples include: "Started cursing," "Swearing," "Perhaps a bit cruder, earthier way of talking," "Talk nasty like guys, swear and stuff," "Use foul language to the extent men did," and "Used profanity when around men." Clearly, the expression "the mouth of a sailor" held some meaning for these women, as a number of them put the cliché to work.

A number of women indicated that drinking also served as a strategy. One woman said that she drank more than she should have. Another said, "Drinking with the guys—trying to keep up." One woman, however, did not acknowledge employing strategies, but then wrote, "Maybe—I tried beer because all of the guys were drinking it." Yet another mentioned "the amount of substance abuse" as a strategy for being perceived as masculine. As one woman wrote, "Foul language, smoking, drinking, joking—I am undeniably feminine—but I tried in many ways to 'compensate' (unfortunately)." While not all would agree, many would argue that swearing and drinking are more acceptable in men, relative to women, especially in the military.[3] Thus, it is not surprising that if women wished to emphasize masculinity, they would seize on these "available" behaviors as strategies for doing so.

A third strategy described by respondents was "working out" or concentrating on physical fitness. In the military, especially in recent years, we would expect this to be a "positive" strategy because of the military's emphasis on physical fitness. Additionally, if feminine women are perceived as weak, then it makes sense that some women might try to ensure that they are perceived as physically fit. As one woman described, "I made sure that I was physically fit to avoid being perceived as a weak female." Another wrote, "[I] Thought many other women were weak and pathetic. Made sure I

was *very strong* physically." Several made specific mention of training in weight lifting, a stereotypically masculine mode of working out.

In a related vein, a number of women mentioned not allowing co-workers to help them with physical tasks. Typical responses included: "Not asking assistance of others when lifting heavy things" and [I] "lifted heavier things on the job than I should have." Another wrote:

> I did not let others (men) help me, unless a job normally required 2 people, and the guy was *assigned* to work with me. I only asked other women to help me, or went to great lengths to use leverage and improvise.

Demonstration of physical strength, whether through physical development or task accomplishment, is apparently one mechanism by which women try to be perceived as masculine and, as such, to fit in.

Though the last decade has led to significant change in this arena, the strategy of "working out," especially weight lifting, is viewed by some as "doing guy things." Some would say the same of swearing and drinking. If this weren't the case then it is unlikely that these would be identified as strategies for being perceived as masculine. Yet, the frequency with which these behaviors were mentioned warranted their being considered separate categories. The fourth strategy, "doing guy things," is distinct. Women mentioned a variety of behaviors, apart from those discussed above, that they exhibited as a means of being perceived as masculine. In some cases, these were specific behaviors (e.g., "learned to scuba and skydive"); in others they were general statements (e.g., "Go out with the guys and do the types of things they like to do"). The following comments illustrate these findings: "I drove a Pinto station wagon with a tool box in the back. I did my own oil changes." "Talked about stuff I did as a civilian—played in rock band, rode motorcycle, etc." "Auto hobby shop—fixed guys' cars—took flying lessons and mechanics with the guys." Again, certain behaviors, hobbies, etc., are culturally defined as masculine. If participation in these events is readily available then it is understandable that they would be part of the behavioral repertoire of those women who wish to be perceived as masculine.

"Demeanor" is another strategy of "doing guy things." One woman discussed "using the language and mannerisms of men," while another said she "became more assertive/aggressive." One woman said she "learned to be aggressive when necessary," while another said, "High assertiveness; low exhibited emotionality." As one woman described it, "Developed a tougher attitude and tried to hide my softer side at work."

Related to the strategy of "doing guy things" was the strategy of *not* doing "female things." One woman "attempted to downplay feminine 'traits' such as gossiping, flowers on desk, being emotional" while another wrote:

> Whenever I deployed, I reduced my attachment to "feminine" stuff; no contacts, no make-up, no complaints if I couldn't shower/wash hair, no perfume—made fun of women who continued these trappings while deployed.

In some instances, and as would be the case with some weight lifters, such behaviors involved physical change. One woman said, "I didn't wear make-up, I never swayed my hips, I strode along." Another said, "I kept my fingernails short and never polished them!" To some degree, the absence of the feminine may be seen, by default, as an approximation of the masculine. . . .

Results show that the types of strategies employed by women seeking to manage gender are numerous and diverse. Whether one is trying to be perceived as feminine or masculine there is an available repertoire of strategies from which one may choose. As I have shown, close to half of the women in this sample acknowledge the employment of strategies to manage gender. While most opt toward femininity, some do strategize toward masculinity. . . .

Doing Gender/Doing Sexuality

The first question posed by West and Zimmerman addressed the question of how a culture instills the need to achieve gender. . . . By establishing ideas about what is essentially female or male, what is "normal" or "natural" the culture instills within us a need to maintain these gendered identities. That is, we must continually create and recreate our identities as gendered beings.

I believe that this analysis is accurate, but fails to consider another important mechanism for insuring that we feel compelled to engage in the active accomplishment of gender. I argue that the link between gender and sexuality also serves to reinforce our need to "do gender." There are at least two ways in which sexuality functions to reinforce our need to do gender. First, notions of what types of sexual behavior are appropriate are used to insure that women work to be seen as "good women." For example, a woman who does not want to be viewed as a "whore," or a "tramp," must modify her appearance, and possibly demeanor, so that she fits "acceptable" ideas of how a "good woman" looks or acts. Similarly, men who have a certain "look" are assumed to possess, or not posses, a degree of sexual prowess. And, sexuality is viewed as being composed of the good vs. the bad. If all sexuality were viewed positively, there would be no negative connotations to labels such as whore or tramp. Homosexuality would not be viewed as bad; homophobia would not exist. If there were nothing "wrong" with being labeled a whore or a lesbian the labels would not be threatening.

Second, perceptions of gender are used to make assessments of one's sexual orientation.

In women, femininity implies heterosexuality, masculinity implies homosexuality. And conversely, a woman known to be a lesbian may be assumed to possess more masculine traits than her heterosexual counterpart. Thus, perceptions about gender are used to make inferences about sexuality, and vice versa. This research provides ample evidence for the way that "masculinity" is used to "determine" that a woman is a lesbian.

Our culture instills the need to achieve gender not only by creating a sense of the "natural" or the "normal," but also by threatening social actors with penalties for violating prescribed notions of acceptable gendered behavior and acceptable sexual behavior. By linking the two together, we insure that violations in either arena result in penalties. Specifically, and because gendered behaviors are the more visible, the threat of being labeled sexually deviant may function to insure that we "do gender" in the appropriate fashion. That is, women enact femininity, and men enact masculinity. West and Fenstermaker make clear that "doing gender does not always mean living up to normative conceptions of femininity or masculinity" (1993: 157). But, they also note that "To the extent that members of society know their actions are accountable, they will design their actions in relation to how they might be seen and described by others" (1993: 157). They write:

> First, and perhaps most important, conceiving of gender as an ongoing accomplishment, accountable to interaction, implies that we must locate its emergence in *social situations*, rather than within the individual or some ill-defined set of role expectations. . . . What it involves is crafting conduct that can be evaluated in relation to normative conceptions of manly and womanly natures (Fenstermaker and Berk 1985, p. 203), and assessing conduct in light of those conceptions—given the situation at hand (West and Zimmerman 1987, p. 139–140). (157)

Thus, it is not simply that women, for example, seek to enact femininity because it is expected of them, but also that situations call for such enactment. The social situation in which femininity serves as an indicator of heterosexuality can only compel one to enact femininity if there is some reason to want to insure that one is perceived to be heterosexual. Sociocultural attitudes toward homosexuality function to insure that this is the case. But, some situations are especially strongly marked, or call more strongly for gendered behavior. The military is one such situation.

The ban on lesbians, gay men, and bisexuals exacerbates this situation even further. As of this writing, military policy "allows" lesbians, gay men, and bisexuals to serve as long as they "don't tell." This, of course, requires that lesbians in the military do what they can to mask all potential "markers" of homosexuality. While the policymakers claim that they would not "ask" about sexual orientation and service-members could "be" homosexual as long as they didn't "tell" the military has not upheld their end of the bargain. People continue to be harassed, investigated, and discharged for being lesbian, gay, or bisexual. While there are many instances outside the military where this is so, there are few, if any, places where federal law supports such discrimination. Federal law may not *protect* civilians, but neither does it compel an employer to fire them if it is discovered that they are lesbian, gay, or bisexual.

As was addressed earlier, to be perceived as masculine may result in one being labeled a lesbian. Not only may women be "shunned," or lose the respect of their peers, but the institutional requirement that lesbians be discharged may result in investigation and, ultimately, discharge. One way of avoiding such charges is to insure that one is perceived as feminine, and thus, heterosexual. While I would not argue that this is the sole explanation for women enacting femininity, I do believe that it is a significant factor. As a number of women indicated, it was more important to be perceived as heterosexual than feminine, but the latter helps insure the former. Remember, one woman wrote, "I mostly made conscious attempts to appear heterosexual v. feminine." . . .

. . . For women in the military, women must "do femininity" to insure that they are perceived as heterosexual and, as such, are somewhat protected from potential stigma and/or expulsion.

Gender and the Institution

The second question posed by West and Zimmerman (1987) is : "What is the relationship between the production of gender at the level of interaction and such institutional arrangements as the division of labor in society?" In the case of the military, gender is produced at the level of interaction, but the result is the reinforcement of perceptions of women as unfit for military service. These perceptions are not merely micro-level assessments, but perceptions that permeate the broader institution. When the majority of women can be labeled "feminine," and anything feminine is viewed as inappropriate for military service, women, as a group, can become viewed as "inconsistent" with, or less than capable of performing, military service. Thus, by producing gender at the level of interaction (e.g., enacting femininity), a broader ideology, as well as institutional arrangements (e.g., job restrictions) in which women are perceived to be second class soldiers is maintained.

If women were aggressive they were seen as lesbians; if women were not aggressive enough they were seen as incapable of leading troops and could receive poor evaluation reviews. In either case, the ultimate penalty could be discharge. At the least, women as a group are subject to the label of "unfit." Women have to prove themselves the exception to the rule. One interesting example of this is the experience of the male sergeant who, together with a female flight surgeon, was captured by the Iraqis during Desert Storm. After their experience as prisoners of war, he acknowledged that she could go into battle with him anytime, but that he wasn't prepared to say the same for all women. SGT Troy Dunlap stated, "I was really amazed . . . I was overwhelmed by the way she handled herself. . . . She can go to combat with me anytime" (Pauley 1992). He made it clear that she was the exception. One woman had proven herself; women as a group remained questionable. As MAJ Rhonda Cronum said in response, "I don't think I'll ever change his mind that says that women as a category of people shouldn't go to combat, but I think I did change his mind that this one individual person who happens to be female can go" (Pauley 1992).

When women "produce enactments of their 'essential' femininity" (West and Zimmerman 1987: 144), they are not being good soldiers. When they are "good soldiers," they often risk being labeled as lesbians. As Navy Vice Admiral Joseph S. Donnell wrote in 1990, lesbian sailors are "generally hard-working, career-oriented, willing to put in long hours on the job and among the command's top performers" (Gross, 1990: 24). It is not difficult to imagine how women who fit this description, regardless of sexual orientation, may be labeled as lesbian (Shilts 1993). Thus, the enactment of gender at the interactional level has the potential to reinforce perceptions of women as inappropriate for military service for a number of reasons. Such a perception of women then reinforces the belief that men are somehow uniquely suited to serving in the nation's military. Thus, the production of gender at the interactional level reinforces both ideological and institutional arrangements that place women at the margins of military participation.

It should be noted that stereotypical gay men do not fit the model of "soldier," in that they are not seen as masculine "enough." If gay male soldiers, or *any* male soldier for that matter, were not seen as appropriately masculine they would risk censure. The paradox is that the stereotypical lesbian *does* fit the model of "soldier," and, yet, risks censure for being "gender appropriate" to the work role of soldier. While a gay man can "pass" by "doing masculinity" in the appropriate fashion, women are faced with the contradiction that "doing masculinity" results in being perceived as a lesbian.

Gender as a Tool of Male Dominance

The third question posed by West and Zimmerman (1987) is "how does doing gender contribute to the subordination of women by men?" If, as described above, women in the military are perceived as second class soldiers, or as less than capable, it is not farfetched to argue that women are being subordinated by men. It is important to reiterate that clearly not all women, as individuals, are seen as second rate or unsuccessful. There are thousands of women who have served admirably and have earned the respect of their male co-workers, peers and superiors alike.[4] The case I am making here is that military women *as a group* are viewed as second class and are subordinated by the male institution of the military. Whether women are sexually harassed, denied assignments, or prohibited from performing particular jobs, we must realize that it is not simply the case of a poor performing individual that allows such incidents to occur. The social and institutional arrangements (e.g., the prohibition of women from most combat jobs) which permit women to be viewed as poor substitutes for male soldiers subordinate women to men and limit their participation as full members of the military. In some cases, attributions of inadequacy have followed women to their deaths.

LT Kara Hultgreen was one of the first women to qualify to fly a Naval fighter jet, the

F-14. LT Hultgreen died on October 25, 1994 when she crashed in the Pacific during a training exercise. The Navy rumor mill immediately spun into action with some going "so far as to send out false information in anonymous phone calls and faxes purporting that Hultgreen was unqualified and received special treatment by a politically correct Navy. In fact, Hultgreen was third out of seven flyers in her class" (*Minerva's Bulletin Board* Fall/Winter, 1994: 3). Subsequent investigation revealed that the aircraft had lost an engine and that even skilled pilots would have had a difficult time landing successfully. CDR Trish Beckman, president of Women Military Aviators, writes:

> A combination of factors and limited time to recognize and correct them, put Kara in a "deep hole" which cost her life (and would have done the same to skilled Test Pilots in the same situation). What is different in this circumstance is that unnamed Navy men have attempted to slander and libel her reputation publicly (something that has never been done to a deceased male aviator, no matter how incompetent he was known to be or how many lives he took with him)." (*Minerva's Bulletin Board* Fall/Winter, 1994: 3–4)

In contrast, when two Navy pilots flew their helicopter past the demilitarized zone into North Korea in December 1994, resulting in the death of one and the capture of the other, no mention was made of blame or incompetence. No one suggested that perhaps permitting men to fly was a mistake.

Does the above question address the issue of the relationship between doing gender in the military and the subordination of women to men? I believe so. When military women enact femininity, they are subject to accusations that they are not capable of performing tasks, etc., that have been labeled as "masculine." When military women enact masculinity, they are subject to accusations of lesbianism. Doing gender results in women being subjected to an endless range of accusations which together result in the subordination of women as a class of citizens. The question, however, remains, is it possible to avoid doing gender?

West and Zimmerman (1987) write:

> If we do gender appropriately, we simultaneously sustain, reproduce, and render legitimate the institutional arrangements that are based on sex category. If we fail to do gender appropriately, we as individuals—not the institutional arrangements—may be called to account (for our character, motives, and predispositions). (146)

While it is unlikely, given the existing social order, that we can avoid doing gender, we can begin to tackle the resulting inequities in a number of ways. "Social change, then, must be pursued both at the institutional and cultural level of sex category and at the interactional level of gender" (West and Zimmerman 1987: 147). That is, we must challenge the institutional and cultural arrangements that perpetuate distinctions made on the basis of sex, or sex category. In the military, one way to accomplish this would be to eliminate prohibitions of women in combat. Another would be to eliminate the ban on lesbians, gay men, and bisexuals in the military. If we eliminate the importance of sex category in the "politics of sexual-object choice" (Connell 1985: 261) we eliminate the need for compulsory heterosexuality. That is, if whether a potential mate is female or male is irrelevant, heterosexuality loses it hegemonic stranglehold on society and its institutions. Thus, eliminating compulsory heterosexuality would do much to reduce the pressures women feel to be seen as feminine as well as the fear of being seen as too masculine, and not without significance, the fear men have of being seen as too feminine.

Conclusion

... There are some very real implications for women's day-to-day participation in the military. Women are likely to be subjected to a variety of unpleasantries ranging from sexual harassment to being shunned, from being denied access to schooling to being denied promotions. While the penalties are varied, they share one potential outcome. All of the penalties discussed in this research may lead to women being discharged or feeling compelled to leave the service. Thus, the major implication of this research is that the perpetuation of an ideology in which soldiering and masculinity are closely bound results in the perpetuation of a military which is not only ideologically, but numerically, male as well.

There are several mechanisms which function to keep the military "male." In addition to women leaving the service, whether by force or choice, perceptions of the military as male also limit the numbers of women who will consider the military as a career option. As of late 1993, the proportion of enlistees who were women was, in fact, on the rise (*Minerva's Bulletin Board* Spring, 1994: 1–2). As of this writing, the Army had experienced a slight drop in women recruits after widespread sexual harassment was exposed in late 1996. Whether this will have any long term effect on Army recruiting is not yet known. It is impossible, at this point, to determine if women are finding the military more attractive than has been true in the past, or whether smaller numbers of male recruits are inflating the proportion of female recruits.

In addition, the ideology of the "male military" and restrictions on the participation of women function together to limit the number of positions open to women. Thus, fewer women, compared to men, can enter the service. That is, even if huge numbers of women wished to enlist, their numbers would be suppressed by the comparatively fewer numbers of available positions, especially in the Army where large numbers of jobs are classified as combat arms and, as such, are off limits to women.

As long as the military is viewed as the domain of men, women will be outsiders and their participation will be challenged. Thus, a cycle of male dominance is perpetuated. The military is defined as male, a small proportion of women are allowed to participate, the participation of these women is challenged and penalized, the military remains ideologically and numerically male dominated, the numbers of women remain small. How can this cycle be broken? First, we can challenge cultural constructions of sex/gender. Second, we can challenge institutional arrangements which allow the perpetuation of distinctions on the basis of sex/sex category. That is, reduce the importance of being feminine or masculine and female or male.

The first of these institutional arrangements is the classification of military job eligibility by sex. That is, one is eligible for a particular job only if one is male. In the military this is the case for jobs coded as having a high likelihood of engaging the enemy. Women, as a group, are thus excluded from some specific occupations and some specific assignments. Barriers are being broken, but many remain. As long as women are eligible only for some jobs they will be viewed as second class soldiers (or sailors, "airmen," etc.). If we eliminate such barriers and assign individuals on the basis of their performance, ability, etc., it is highly likely that we will see a corresponding increase in the acceptance of women as participants in the military.

The second arrangement which will improve the ability of women to participate on equal terms with men is the repeal of the laws prohibiting the participation of lesbians, gay men, and bisexuals in the United States military. It is painfully apparent that this ban hurts many lesbians, gay men, and bisexuals. Many wish to serve in the military, but know that to do so is not without risk. Many do join the military only to have their careers ended prematurely. But, as I have indicated, the ban on lesbians, gay men, and bisexuals also impacts negatively on all women and men, regardless of sexual orientation. If the confirmation of

heterosexuality were not imperative, women would be free to engage in a much wider range of behaviors, particularly those labeled as masculine. If women did not feel compelled to ensure that they are seen as heterosexual, there would be less pressure to enact femininity, a marker of heterosexuality.

By having to confirm heterosexuality, women enact femininity, thereby ensuring that they will be perceived as less capable than their male counterparts. The link between gender and sexuality, situated in an organization which has an institutional mandate for heterosexuality, ensures the subordination of women. To eliminate compulsory heterosexuality would greatly enhance the more equal participation of women. To be sure, eliminating the degree to and manner in which women deploy gender at the interactional level would also enhance equal participation. But, without corresponding changes at the institutional level such changes are unlikely to occur. By understanding: (1) how gender is produced at the interactional level, (2) how the interactional level is related to existing institutional arrangements, and (3) how the link between gender and sexuality empowers this relationship, we can offer a new vision for the equal participation of women and men in the military and, more importantly, throughout society.

NOTES

1. Members of the military are also referred to as airmen [sic], sailors, Marines, etc., depending upon their branch. For ease of discussion I use the term soldiers, as the Army is the largest branch and in common parlance many often refer to all members of the military as soldiers, regardless of branch.

2. For an interesting, non-military, account of the experiences of androgynous women see Holly Devor's *Gender Blending: Confronting the Limits of Duality*, Bloomington, IN: Indiana University Press, 1989.

3. In the past swearing was not viewed as inappropriate or unprofessional and drinking was

not only tolerated, but encouraged. New policies on sexual harassment and alcohol abuse have led to significant changes in recent years.

4. Of course, one could argue as well that while women have to *earn* the respect of the men with whom they work, men begin with that respect and must do something to lose it.

REFERENCES

Acker, Joan. 1992. "Gendered Institutions." *Contemporary Sociology* 21(5): 565–569.

Connell, Robert W. 1985. "Theorizing Gender." *Sociology* 19(2) 260–272.

Dunivin, Karen. 1994. "Military Culture: Change and Continuity." *Armed Forces & Society* 20(4): 531–547.

"Freedom of Press Seen on Trial Now." 1942. *New York Times,* 17 April, 8.

Goffman, Erving. 1977. "The Arrangement Between the Sexes." *Theory and Society* 4(3): 301–331.

Gross, Jane, 1990. "Navy Is Urged to Root Out Lesbians Despite Abilities." *New York Times,* 2 September, 24.

Lenskyj, Helen. 1986. *Out of Bounds: Women, Sport and Sexuality.* Toronto: The Women's Press.

The MINERVA Center. Spring, 1994. "Proportion of Women Growing Among New Recruits." *Minerva's Bulletin Board,* 1–2.

———. Fall/Winter, 1994. "Second Woman to Qualify as F-14 Pilot Dies in Crash." *Minerva's Bulletin Board,* 3–4.

Pauley, Jane. 1992. *Dateline NBC:* Interview with MAJ Rhonda L. Cornum. New York.

Shilts, Randy. 1993. *Conduct Unbecoming: Lesbians and Gays in the U.S. Military Vietnam to the Persian Gulf.* New York, NY: St. Martin's Press.

Steinberg, Ronni. 1992. "Gender on the Agenda: Male Advantage in Organizations." *Contemporary Sociology* 21(5): 576–581.

Veterans Administration. 1985. *Survey of Female Veterans: A Study of the Needs, Attitudes, and Experiences of Women Veterans.* Office of Information Management and Statistics, IM & SM 70–85–7.

West, Candace and Sarah Fenstermaker. 1993. "Power, Inequality and the Accomplishment of Gender: An Ethnomethodological View," in *Theory on Gender/Feminism on Theory,* P. England (ed.). Hawthorne, NY: Aldine de Gruyter, 151–174.

West, Candace and Don H. Zimmerman. 1987. "Doing Gender." *Gender & Society* 1(2): 125–151.

THINKING ABOUT THE READING

Which do you think is worse for female soldiers: being perceived as "too masculine" or being perceived as "too feminine"? How is female soldiers' need to "walk a fine line" between masculinity and femininity related to impression management? Can you think of a comparable situation for men—one in which an occupation requires a certain degree of femininity, while at the same time demanding that they present an image of themselves as "real men"? Given the extreme, potentially life-and-death demands of military combat, do you think that female soldiers will ever be accepted as equals to male soldiers?

Sisyphus in a Wheelchair

Physical Disabilities and Masculinity

Thomas J. Gerschick

(1998)

Sisyphus, the King of Corinth in Greek mythology, has been condemned for all eternity by the Judges of the Dead to roll a large boulder up a mountain. Each time he approaches the summit, after much bitter toil, he inevitably loses control and the rock returns to the plains below. He repeatedly retrieves it and wearily begins the climb anew. The myth of Sisyphus captures the struggle and frustration men with physical disabilities experience as they seek to create and maintain masculine gender identities in a culture that views them as "not men."

This article focuses specifically on the ways in which men with physical disabilities experience gender domination by the temporarily-able-bodied[1] in the United States.[2] This domination depends upon a double-bind: men with physical disabilities are judged according to the standards of hegemonic masculinity which are difficult to achieve due to the limitations of their bodies. Simultaneously, these men are blocked in everyday interactions from opportunities to achieve this form of masculinity. The most significant barriers they face occur in the key domains of hegemonic masculinity: work, the body, athletics, sexuality, and independence and control.[3] Because men with physical disabilities cannot enact hegemonic standards in these realms, they are denied recognition as men. As "failed" men, they are marginalized and occupy a position in the gender order similar to gay men, men of color, and women. Successfully creating and

maintaining self-satisfactory masculine gender identities under these circumstances is an almost Sisyphean task. Men with physical disabilities, at times, act complicit in their domination by internalizing the dominant group's stereotypes and images of them. Hence these men's struggle against gender domination occurs not only with others, but also with themselves. The effort to resist gender domination has led some men with physical disabilities to develop counter-hegemonic gender identities.

In order to explore the struggle that men with physical disabilities undergo to create a realistic and positive self-image as men, I address the following three questions. First, how are men with physical disabilities dominated due to their inability to meet the demands of hegemonic masculinity? Second, how do they act complicit with, or resist, hegemonic masculinity? Third, what can be learned from the struggles of men with physical disabilities, especially from the alternative gender identities that some men with physical disabilities develop as a result of these struggles?

Data to address these questions come from two sources. First, an associate and I conducted in-depth, semi-structured interviews with 11 men with physical disabilities. Initial interviews lasted an average of an hour. We provided informants with their transcripts and asked them to read them carefully to ensure that they were accurately represented. We then conducted follow-up interviews with most of these men to clarify statements and to ask questions which were stimulated in the first round of interviews. All of the interviews were tape recorded and transcribed verbatim. Correspondence with several informants continues and has been added, with permission, to the transcripts. Most of the informants had paraplegia and sustained their disabilities through either accidents or disease. None of the men we interviewed has a congenital disability. Their ages ranged from 16 to 72. Nine of these men were white, two were Black. Seven were professionally employed, one was a retired business-owner, two were full-time students, and one was a service-sector worker. The second source of data is ten autobiographies, semi-autobiographies, and collections of essays.[4] None of these books were expressly about masculinity and disability, however, all of them addressed issues related to these topics at least implicitly. Extensive notes were taken from these accounts which were then treated as fieldnotes.

The lives of men with physical disabilities provide an instructive arena in which to study gender domination for three reasons. First, men with physical disabilities contravene many of the beliefs associated with being a man. Studying their gender identity struggles provides valuable insight into the struggles that all men experience in this realm. Second, men with physical disabilities occupy a unique subject position in what Patricia Hill Collins (1990: 225–7) calls the matrix of domination and privilege.[5] These men have gender privilege by virtue of being men, yet this privilege is significantly eroded due to their disability, which leaves them subject to domination and marginalization. Their marginal position in the gender order provides access to knowledge that is obscured from those in the mainstream (Beisser 1989; Janeway 1980). One of the goals of this article is to elucidate their "fugitive information," as writer Kay Hagan (1993) calls the knowledge of the marginalized, and how it

can be used to construct counter-hegemonic masculine gender identities. Third, little has been written about the intersection of disability and gender. Where gender has been explored with reference to disability, the research has primarily focused on women. Consequently, this research addresses a lacuna in the literature.

Life at the Crossroads: Physical Disability and Masculinity

In order to contextualize the gender domination that men with physical disabilities experience, three sets of social dynamics need to be woven together. The first involves the stigma associated with having a physical disability, the second concerns gender as an interactional process, and the third is the hegemonic gender standard to which men with physical disabilities are held.

To have a disability is not only a physical or mental condition, it is also a social and stigmatized one (Goffman 1963; Kriegel 1991; Zola 1982). As anthropologist Robert Murphy (1990: 113) observed:

> Whatever the physically impaired person may think of himself [sic], he is attributed a negative identity by society, and much of his social life is a struggle against this imposed image. It is for this reason that we can say that stigmatization is less a by-product of disability than its substance. The greatest impediment to a person's taking full part in this society are not his physical flaws, but rather the tissue of myths, fears, and misunderstandings that society attaches to them.

This stigma is embodied in the popular stereotypes of people with disabilities; they are perceived to be weak, passive, and dependent (Shapiro 1993). Our language exemplifies this stigmatization: people with disabilities are de-formed, dis-eased, dis-abled, dis-ordered, ab-normal, and in-valid (Zola 1982: 206).

This stigma is also embedded in the daily interactions between people with disabilities and the temporarily-able-bodied. People with disabilities are evaluated in terms of normative expectations and are, because of their disability, frequently found wanting. As a consequence, they experience a range of reactions from those without disabilities from subtle indignities and slights to overt hostility and outright cruelty. More commonly people with disabilities are avoided, ignored, and marginalized (Fine and Asch 1988; Shapiro 1993). This treatment creates formidable physical, economic, psychological, architectural, and social obstacles to their participation in all aspects of social life. Having a disability also becomes a primary identity which overshadows almost all other aspects of one's identity. As a consequence, it influences all interactions with the temporarily-able-bodied, including gendered interactions.

In order to accomplish gender, each person in a social situation needs to be recognized by others as appropriately masculine or feminine. Those with whom we interact continuously assess our gender performance and decide whether we are "doing gender" appropriately in that situation. Our "audience" or interaction partners then hold us accountable and sanction us in a variety of ways in order to encourage compliance (West and Zimmerman 1987). Our need for social approval and validation as gendered beings further encourages conformity. Much is at stake in this process, as one's sense of self rests precariously upon the audience's decision to validate or reject one's gender performance. Successful enactment bestows status and acceptance, failure invites embarrassment and humiliation (West and Zimmerman 1987).

In the contemporary United States, men's gender performance tends to be judged using the standard of hegemonic masculinity which represents the optimal attributes, activities, behaviors, and values expected of men in a culture (Connell 1990). Social scientists have identified career-orientation, activeness, athleticism, sexual desirability and virility, independence, and self-reliance as exalted masculine attributes in the United States (Connell 1995; Gerschick and Miller 1994; Kimmel 1994). Consequently, the body is central to the attainment of hegemonic masculinity. Men whose bodies allow them to evidence the identified characteristics are differentially rewarded in U.S. dominant culture over those who cannot. Despite the fact that attaining these attributes is often unrealistic and more based in fantasy than reality, men continue to internalize them as ideals and strive to demonstrate them as well as judge themselves and other men using them. Women also tend to judge men using these standards.

Arenas of Gender Domination, Complicity and Resistance

Work

The prejudice and discrimination that many men with physical disabilities face in the labor market threaten to undermine an important measure of self-determination and a key component of their masculine gender identity. Despite being qualified, these men report being discriminated against in hiring, work-place accommodations, retention, and promotion. They encounter a particular form of double-bind. Due to the actions of the temporarily-able-bodied, men with physical disabilities are discouraged or prevented from competing for highly remunerated or prestigious jobs and are then devalued as men because they do not have them. Given the importance of work to a masculine identity, this situation reinforces their marginalized status as men.

Many men with physical disabilities have internalized the importance of work to enacting masculinity, realizing that in our culture the type of job a man has and the income he earns contribute significantly to his status and power. For instance, after contracting polio as a teenager, Leo realized "I didn't want to be weak. I wanted to be strong. I wanted to have a regular job, bring in income, be a success." When asked what being a man meant to him, Michael, an Independent Living Skills Specialist who has paraplegia, replied, "being able to work, to pay my own way . . . It [having a job] enhances my self image."

Due to ignorance and prejudice, many temporarily-able-bodied people do not perceive men with physical disabilities as valuable employees; instead they are perceived to have high rates of absenteeism, to have low rates of productivity, and to be expensive to accommodate and insure (Shapiro 1993). Brent, an administrator of a university's disability program who has paraplegia, observed that:

> In this culture there is a quite a bit of stereotypical attitudes about people with disabilities, about who we are, what we can do, why we do what we do, and I think that makes it difficult for me to be, to have job flexibility. I don't think that I have the same access to jobs that other people do. I don't think I have the same access to promotions that other people do.

Having tired of being tracked into jobs which lacked recognition and opportunities for advancement, Brent recently took early retirement. Another of my informants, Jerry, a high school junior with Juvenile Rheumatoid Arthritis, lamented, "I know I have had a hard time finding part-time jobs, just because it seems like people are really intimidated and sort of afraid." Attitudes like these on the part of the temporarily-able-bodied contribute significantly to the 41 percent unemployment rate for men with physical disabilities (McNeil 1993, table 24: 62).

Men with physical disabilities are frequently steered into low status, low paying, low prestige white collar or service sector jobs. Generally these involve some type of social service work, most frequently disability-related, which is deemed more culturally appropriate. Harold, for instance, noted that people who are temporarily-able-bodied "want to pigeonhole you. They see a disabled guy and they go, oh, the only thing you can write about is, you know, covering the disability scene. But that's not always true." Harold's example reveals how the temporarily-able-bodied subtly attach conditions to the employment of men with physical disabilities which impede their ability to compete for higher-status jobs, which in turn hinders their ability to be recognized as "real" men. The segregation in the labor force that many of these men face is similar to that experienced by people of color and women (Amott and Matthaei 1991) and gay men (Levine 1992) and demonstrates the similarity of their subject positions.

Several of my informants report cooperating in their labor force segregation. Of the eight informants who held jobs at the time of their interviews, six worked in disability-related occupations. Three noted that they gravitated to their occupations because they "knew it would be easier to find work" or it "seemed appropriate." Perhaps unconsciously they turned to disability-related jobs because they knew they would face less prejudice and discrimination.

Given their generally low status and low power position in society, men with physical disabilities do not control how they are perceived among the temporarily-able-bodied. As a consequence, they face formidable barriers in the labor market. The prejudice and discrimination they face make it difficult for them to achieve economic success, which is a key characteristic of hegemonic masculinity. Consequently, their difficulties in the labor market contribute to their marginalized position within the hegemonic gender order.

The Body

Men with physical disabilities do not meet mainstream notions of what is athletic, physically attractive, or sexually desirable. Instead, because of their bodies, they "contravene all the values of youth, virility, activity, and physical beauty that Americans cherish" (Murphy 1990: 116). As a result, men with physical disabilities are significantly less likely than temporarily-able-bodied men to be publicly recognized as athletes and/or potential sexual partners. These are two of the bedrocks upon which masculine gender identities are built. Consequently, masculinity is threatened when corporeal appearance and performance are discordant with hegemonic expectations, such as in the case of having a physical disability (Connell 1995; Gerschick and Miller 1994).

Bodies are important in contemporary social life. One's body and relationship to it provide a way to apprehend the world and one's place in it (Gerschick and Miller 1994). When one is alienated from one's body, one is alienated from one's sense of self. Psychiatrist Arnold Beisser (1989: 166–7), who had polio, explains:

> I felt as though I were cut off from the elemental functions and activities which had grounded me. I was quite literally separated from the earth, for while I spent my time in an iron lung, in a bed, or in a wheelchair, my feet almost never touched the ground. But more important, I believe, was being separated from so many of the elemental routines that occupy people. Even if I would work, I did not have any experience of physical exertion. I could not, on my own, assume the familiar positions of standing, sitting, and lying down. I was even separated from my breathing, as it was done by a machine. I felt no longer connected with the familiar roles I had known in family, work, and sports. My place in the culture was gone.

Thus having a physical disability compromises men's connection to one of the key sources of their identity: their bodies.

In U.S. culture, bodies are simultaneously symbolic, kinetic, and social (Connell 1995). They are kinetic in that they allow us to move, to accomplish physical tasks, to perform. Bodies are also social; people respond to one another's bodies which initiates social processes such as

validation and the assignment of status (Goffman 1963). Finally, bodies are symbolic. They are a form of self-presentation; one's body signifies one's worth. Bodies, then, are essential to the performance and achievement of gender. This becomes clear when one investigates men with physical disabilities' experiences with athletics, sexuality, and independence and control.

Athletics

In our sports-obsessed culture, ability, especially athletic ability, has become a key way for men to embody their masculinity. Sports provides men with an opportunity to exhibit key characteristics of hegemonic masculinity such as endurance, strength, and competitive spirit (Goffman 1977). The institutional organization of sports also embeds social relations such as competition, hierarchy, exclusion, and domination (Connell 1995: 54).

The athletic performances of men with physical disabilities tend not to be socially recognized and validated but instead are trivialized and devalued (Taub and Greer 1997). One of Taub and Greer's (1997: 13–4) informants, a 23-year-old student, described temporarily-able-bodied people's reactions to encountering him in the gym:

> It's people's perceptions [that] kill me . . . it doesn't seem like it's respect . . . it's just like a pat on the head type thing . . . "you're so courageous . . . you're overcoming all these boundaries . . . that's so good what you're doing." I wish people would . . . just look at wheelchair basketball as a sport . . . instead of just like a human interest story.

Because athletic performance embodies gender performance, not being taken seriously as an athlete symbolizes not being taken seriously as a man.

When men with physical disabilities are recognized as athletes, that recognition is conditional. This is represented by the qualifiers attached to titles such as "Special" Olympics, "wheelchair" basketball, and "disabled" athletes. Scott, a paraplegic, explained:

> Softball, I play it now from a wheelchair. I play in a regular city league, so it's able bodied, everyone else in the league is able-bodied. Um, I find that I do pretty well and everybody seems to think that I'm, the guys I play with now have never seen me play before my disability, and so they are all impressed. For me sometimes, it bothers me because I know I'm not the player that I used to be, but I do still enjoy it, but occasionally I have those frustrated times where I feel like, you know, everybody is impressed that I'm a good player, for a gimp, where I just want to be a good player.

Qualifying men with physical disabilities' athletic performances is condescending and patronizing. The devaluation of these men's efforts reveals that social acceptance and recognition are based both on the ability to perform and on the quality of the performance. Men who cannot perform to the hegemonic standard, due to a disability for instance, are marginalized as feminine or sissies (Messner 1992). The lack of recognition of men with physical disabilities as athletes undermines their ability to establish and maintain self-satisfactory gender identities.

Sexuality

Similar to athletic marginalization, men with physical disabilities tend not to be perceived as sexually attractive. "What bothers me more than anything else is the stereotypes, and, even more so, in terms of sexual desirability," Brent complained in his interview, "because I had a disability, I was less desirable than able bodied people and that I found very frustrating." Men with physical disabilities have a difficult time being recognized as potential life/sexual partners because they do not meet societal standards of beauty. Political scientist Harlan Hahn (1989: 54) explains:

Much as they would prefer to deny it, the unavoidable reality is that men with disabilities are significantly devalued in modern society. This devaluation occurs not only in the labor force, where disabled men are often prevented from fulfilling the traditional role of "breadwinner," but also in the social marketplace, where they frequently are deprived of romantic partners and lasting companionship. Both forms of exclusion may result as much from aesthetic aversion to a different physical appearance as from limitations on functional capabilities.

One of my informants noted that the emphasis on the body is particularly costly for gay men with physical disabilities like himself because the body is so central to conceptions of beauty and sexuality in gay male culture.

Not only are men with physical disabilities frequently perceived as undesirable, they are also perceived to be asexual (Zola 1982). While there are exceptions, the sex lives of men with physical disabilities symbolize the passivity and dependency that is pervasive in their lives which contravenes what most men strive for: activity, initiative and control (Murphy 1990).

Like in other arenas of domination, men with physical disabilities act complicit in this one. In the following quote, Billy Golfus (1997: 420), who was disabled due to a motorcycle accident, illustrates the insidiousness of internalizing asexual stereotypes about people with disabilities when he discusses a potential relationship:

> Even though she is attractive, I don't really think about her that way partly because the [wheel] chair makes me not even see her and because after so many years of being disabled you quit thinking about it as an option.

The woman in this illustration was as invisible to him as his own sexuality was. This example reveals how deeply some men with physical disabilities internalize hegemonic standards of desirability and sexuality which make them complicit in their own domination.

Similarly, many men with physical disabilities internalize the value associated with hegemonic masculinity that men's sexuality and sexual desirability determine their self-worth as men. Author and cartoonist John Callahan (1990: 121) explained:

> I can remember looking at my body with loathing and thinking, Boy, if I ever get to heaven, I'm not going to ask for a new pair of legs like the average quad does. I'm going to ask for a dick I can feel. The idea promoted in rehab of the socially well-adjusted, happily married quad made me sick. This was the cruelest thing of all. Always, I felt humiliated. Surely a man with any self-respect would pull the plug on himself.

The lack of self-esteem in this crucial masculine arena leads men with physical disabilities to withdraw further into the margins as a form of self-protection, as the late sociologist Irving Zola (1982: 215) described: "We do not express or even show our wishes, because we have learned that in our condition of disablement or disfigurement, no one could (or should) find us sexually attractive."

Yet another strategy to deal with one's compromised sexuality is to enact hypersexuality as Michael attests:

> My sexuality and being able to please my partner . . . is my most masculine, the thing most endearing to my masculinity . . . It's probably the thing I feel most vulnerable about . . . I think that my compensation for my feelings of vulnerability is I overcompensate and trying to please my partner and leave little room to allow my partner to please me . . . Some of my greatest pleasure is exhausting my partner, while having sex.

Through his sexual behavior, Michael seeks validation of himself as a man. This is especially important to him because he has internalized the hegemonic standard and feels vulnerable that he will not be able to meet it. Michael's accordance with hegemonic masculinity in this example comes from sacrificing himself and his pleasure while pursuing an unobtainable ideal.

It is hard to be masculine if people restrict the opportunities to earn the recognition as a man. This is the difficulty that men with physical disabilities face in a culture where bodies are a type of social currency. Men's bodies become validated in two key arenas: athletics and sexuality. Due to temporarily-able-bodied people's stigmatization of men with physical disabilities, these arenas of self-expression and self-validation are largely closed to them. This situation further undermines men with physical disabilities' opportunities to establish and maintain satisfactory gender identities and reveals the pervasiveness of the domination they experience from the temporarily-able-bodied.

Independence and Control

Self-reliance is extremely important in the presentation of self to others in social interaction. As Jerry noted, this is especially true for men:

> If I ever have to ask someone for help, it really makes me, like, feel like less of a man. I don't like asking for help at all. You know, like even if I could use some I'll usually not ask just because I can't, I just hate asking . . . [A man is] fairly self-sufficient in that you can sort of handle just about any situation, in that you can help other people, and that you don't need a lot of help.

The independence and control that most men take for granted is compromised for men with physical disabilities due to the response of temporarily-able-bodied people. In cultures like the United States where few accommodations are made for people with disabilities, dependency is synonymous with powerlessness and powerlessness is antithetical to masculinity. Arnold Beisser (1989: 21–2), paralyzed from the neck down and forced to rely on an iron lung after a bout of polio, describes how being dependent undermined his masculinity:

> I had been thrust backward in the developmental scale, and my dependence was now as profound as that of a newborn. Once again I had to deal with all of the overwhelming, degrading conditions of dependency that belong with infancy and childhood—at the same time that I considered myself a mature adult. I did not adjust easily to my new dependence, and despised giving up what I had won years ago in long-forgotten battles. The baby and the man were in conflict.

Through their actions, temporarily-able-bodied people subtly, and at times unconsciously, undermine the independence of men with physical disabilities and replace it with dependency. The following examples illustrate this process and the double-bind in which it places these men. The first example involves Irving Zola (1982: 52) who contracted polio at age 15, which weakened his back and legs. As a consequence, he utilized several braces. He described the change in his status when he took on the role of a wheelchair user in order to do participant observation:

> As soon as I sat in the wheelchair I was no longer seen as a person who could fend for himself. Although Metz had known me for nine months, and had never before done anything physical for me without asking, now he took over without permission. Suddenly in his eyes I was no longer able to carry things, reach for objects, or even push myself around. Though I was perfectly capable of doing all of these things, I was being wheeled around, and things were brought to me—all without my

asking. Most frightening was my own compliance, my alienation from myself and from the process.

Metz had worked closely with Zola and was cognizant of his use of braces and a cane. Interacting with Zola in a wheelchair, however, immediately transformed Metz's sense of Zola's capabilities and initiated a profound change in the status of their relationship. Zola was no longer an independent and accomplished man, but rather a dependent child.

One of my informants, Robert, who has paraplegia, helped explain Zola's compliance when he noted that having people do things you can do for yourself "kind of strips you of your independence. But it's a Catch-22 because a lot of times people do it with good intentions, you know, not recognizing that this guy really wants to [do it] by himself." This double-bind was felt most acutely by Jerry who provided the second example. He noted that his friends were "uncomfortable" about his disability and his use of a wheelchair. "They feel like you need to be sort of helped all the time, even when you don't." he said. This led to an unspoken social contract between he and his friends. When together socially, he would allow them to push him in his wheelchair, thereby making them feel more comfortable in the interaction, and they would in turn, hang around with him. Thus Jerry was forced to make a difficult decision: surrender his independence and remain in the group, or retain his autonomy at the expense of his friendships. Jerry acquiesced to his domination, but, given his lack of alternatives, one can clearly understand why.

These examples reveal the domination and complicity inherent in the social relations between the temporarily-able-bodied and men with physical disabilities. By doing something for men with physical disabilities that they could do for themselves, the temporarily-able-bodied deny these men of a sense of agency, independence, and control. Through this treatment, they infantilize men with disabilities.

In a similar way, the actions of the temporarily-able-bodied make it difficult for men with physical disabilities to control their public gender performance. For instance, Michael noted in his interview that:

> I'm confronted with my disability because someone blocks the curb and then I, um, try and get up over the curb and I end up, you know, not doing it very, with very much style. I look pretty awkward at it, and I don't like looking awkward, so I have a hard time.

By not being able to control his immediate physical environment, Michael was not able to control his public gender performance. According to the dictates of hegemonic masculinity, Michael should be in control of himself and his image at all times. But the carelessness of the temporarily-able-bodied can quickly and easily undercut these pretensions (Murphy 1990: 121).

Michael reveals the importance of control to many men with physical disabilities' sense of their masculinity in an additional example:

> If I fall in public, it's difficult, if not virtually impossible, for me to get back into my chair and I find it embarrassing. It makes me feel . . . if I am laying on the ground because I can't walk, I feel more disabled that way than I do if I'm just up and about in my chair. I feel crippled.

This helpless and dependent position is antithetical to hegemonic masculinity. To be a cripple, is not to be a man.

Philosopher Susan Wendell (1997: 273) has observed that "dependence on the help of others is humiliating in a society which prizes independence." Yet in U.S. culture, dependency and lack of control are thrust upon men with physical disabilities. Temporarily-able-bodied people infantilize these men through their attitudes and actions. This keeps men with physical disabilities marginalized and subordinated within the gender order.

Confronting Sisyphus: The Denial of Masculinity

When one considers the entire set of impediments: the stigmatization, marginalization, limited economic opportunities, rejection of athleticism, barriers to sexual expression and relations, and obstacles to cherished independence and control, it becomes apparent that the primary way that men with physical disabilities are dominated is through not being recognized or validated as men. As Jerry observed, they are figuratively emasculated: "I think you're not looked upon as much as a, you know, like you're, like I might be a really nice person, but not like a guy per se . . . you're sort of genderless to them." This lack of recognition occurs because the temporarily-able-bodied block access to the crucial arenas of masculine accomplishment.

The lack of recognition makes it difficult for men with physical disabilities to think of themselves as men. Jerry explained:

> I think it [others' definition of what it means to be a man] is very important because if they don't think of you as one, it is hard to think of yourself as one or it really doesn't matter if you think of yourself as one if no one else does . . . You're sort of still a boy even if you think of yourself as a man and you would be a man if you weren't disabled . . . It's so awful if no one else thinks of you as one, even if it doesn't affect how you think of yourself. It limits you so much to what you can do and how others regard you as opposed to how they regard other people that it makes it hard. It doesn't really matter if you do as much as they do.

Despite Jerry's youth, he had already experienced and clearly understood how others invalidate his masculinity and the masculinity of other men with physical disabilities.

The denial of gender identity leads men with physical disabilities to experience what Robert Murphy (1990) calls embattled identities. They are not perceived as men and they know that they are not women. Yet they inhabit a similar social space, as the following quote illustrates:

> Whoever I was, whatever I had, there was always a sense that I should be grateful to someone for allowing it to happen, for like women, I, a handicapped person, was perceived as dependent on someone else's largesse for my happiness, or on someone else to *let* me achieve it for myself. (Zola 1982: 213)

This gender domination and resulting marginalization make it exceedingly difficult for men with physical disabilities to create and maintain self-satisfactory masculine gender identities. Because of the power of hegemonic masculinity, many men with physical disabilities act as modern day Sisyphi struggling with the social, economic, and physical barriers; the temporarily-able-bodied; and themselves to enact a form of masculinity which is recognized and validated.

Men with physical disabilities respond to their gender domination in a variety of ways. One response is to heed the siren call of hegemonic masculinity and to continually try to prove one's masculinity to oneself and to others. This leads to hyper-masculinity (Gerschick and Miller 1994) as Michael illustrates:

> I had just begun dating again after an eighteen month break while adjusting to being paralyzed. The girl I was dating lived on the second floor of an apartment complex without an elevator. I was so determined to see her and didn't want to ask for help that I tried to wheel myself up the stairs. I knew that it was impossible, but I tried anyway. I had been working out extensively since just after my accident and had good upper body strength. By popping the front wheels of my chair in the air while simultaneously rolling forward, I got up five stairs. It was hard work. By the time I reached the fifth stair, my strength gave out and my chair tipped back and I skidded back down the stairs on the back of my head. My girlfriend heard the noise and found me. I was never so embarrassed in all my life.

By trying to get up the stairs and maintain his independence and control, and thus his masculinity, all the while realizing the futility of it, Michael personified a modern day Sisyphus. As with Sisyphus, he was destined to fail. By taking hegemonic masculinity's demand for independence to an extreme, he resisted the limitations of his disability but he did so in a way that made him complicit with the demands of hegemonic masculinity to a point where he almost killed himself.

Escaping Sisyphus' Fate: Reconstructing Gender Identity

A resistant, and more healthy, response to gender domination comes from distancing oneself from hegemonic masculinity and the expectations of others while redefining masculinity for oneself. Ironically, for men with physical disabilities, being marginalized creates a social space where expectations are reduced, scrutiny is diminished, and there is more latitude for action. In this space counter-hegemonic masculine gender identities can be constructed, performed, and revised with minimum interference from the temporarily-able-bodied. In order for this reconstruction to occur, men with physical disabilities must resist the stigmatization associated with having a disability, change their primary reference group, and reject or redefine the hegemonic standards of career orientation, activeness, physical strength and athleticism, sexual desirability and virility, and independence and control.

Men with physical disabilities tend to internalize the hegemonic standard of career-orientation, however, they resist the labor market and workplace barriers associated with gender dominance. Rather than being governed by the prejudice and discrimination of others, they create work opportunities for themselves. Aaron, for instance, described how he begot his first job after a gunshot accident left him with paraplegia: "[I was] watching television one night and said, Wow! What a great vehicle for educating the public, and changing attitudes. I could do that . . . I think I will do that." The next day he arranged a meeting with a television station manager and convinced him that he should be hired as a reporter who focused on people's abilities, not their disabilities. Aaron later founded a social service agency dedicated to assisting people with disabilities. Three additional informants demonstrated a similar sense of vocation by working in disability-related positions. By defining their occupation for themselves, these men resisted the domination embodied in the prejudice and discrimination that steers others toward work that they would not otherwise do.

There are a variety of strategies that men with physical disabilities use to resist the activity and athletic ideals embodied in hegemonic masculinity. Some of these men reject temporarily-able-bodied persons' perceptions of them as non-athletes. Taub and Greer (1997), for instance, report that their informants did not internalize temporarily-able-bodied people's negative assessments of them because these men looked to alternative reference groups for their recognition. Other men with physical disabilities counter the hegemonic masculine ideal of physical strength and athleticism by rejecting it. Brent noted:

> I think that I am probably insolent by the cultural norms that say that manhood is, that physical strength and physical well being is [sic] important. But, um, to me I don't think

that's what makes me a, makes me who I am, as how strong I am or how weak I am physically . . . So physical strength is not, or ability is low down on the scale for me.

Yet others replace physical strength and athleticism with other forms of strength. For instance, Harold focused on his mental acuity: "I think the greatest thing a man can do is to develop his mind and think." Harold's conception of masculinity also privileged mental fortitude:

> Strength is a very vague term . . . you can lack physical strength in the power sense or the soldier of fortune sense and you can be very strong in other areas . . . Disabled men can be very, very strong without even being able to, you know, do anything physically active, okay? It's the amount of crap that you can tolerate.

Attention to the mind as a place for demonstrating masculine strength leads to more emphasis on emotional connection to others. For some men with physical disabilities, this connection takes precedence over activity and ability. Brent explained:

> Emotionally more than anything else, is the most important. You know, for me that is my measure of who I am as an individual and who I am as a man, is my ability to be able to be honest with my wife, be able to be close with her, to be able to ask for help, provide help, um, to have a commitment, to follow through and to do all those things that I think are important.

The attention to the emotional side of relationships reveals that some men with physical disabilities are incorporating traditional "feminine" characteristics into their counter-hegemonic masculine identities. For instance, Aaron remarked that, "Manhood today means, um, being responsible for one's actions, being considerate of another's feelings, being sensitive to individuals who are more vulnerable than yourself to what their needs would be."

Resistance to hegemonic masculine sexuality is based on rejecting the ideal standards and replacing them with more realistic ones. Alex, a college student with quadriplegia, exemplifies this:

> There is a part of me that, you know, has been conditioned and acculturated and knows those [hegemonic] values, but my practical experience . . . keeps my common sense in order. You know, . . . because I may have to do something different or non-standard or difficult sexually, I don't think makes me less of a man, or even if I couldn't have sex at all, because I've learned that there's definitely a difference between fucking and making love and that even within the range of sexual behavior, there's a lot of different ways to give a partner that you care about pleasure and to receive pleasure.

While Alex demonstrates a willingness to enact his sexuality in a non-traditional way, his resistance is only successful if he can find a partner who shares his approach. This is possible, but difficult due to the cultural devaluation of men with physical disabilities.

In place of the unobtainable hegemonic demand for independence and control, some men with physical disabilities privilege interdependence and cooperation. Brent, for instance, shared that: "One of the values I have for myself, though, is to be more cooperative and to be able to help and to be helped in turn." This reflects a very different understanding of what it means to be a man.

The ramifications of rejecting the unobtainable ideals embodied in hegemonic masculinity and embracing new ways of performing gender are not limited solely to men with physical disabilities. The gender practices of men with physical disabilities who have developed counter-hegemonic identities provide viable models for new forms of masculinity for all men to practice. As a consequence, the struggles that men with physical disabilities experience have implications for all men regarding their masculinity and all people regarding gender relations.

Conclusion: Sisyphus in a Wheelchair

Returning to the metaphor with which I opened this article, for men with physical disabilities, Sisyphus' mountain represents hegemonic masculinity and his boulder their domination. The exertion of pushing the boulder to the summit represents the struggle that men with physical disabilities experience as they seek to gain recognition of themselves as men within the hostile hegemonic gender order that is largely controlled by the temporarily-able-bodied. Many men with physical disabilities act complicit with this domination and continue their Sisyphean struggle for acceptance according to the hegemonic standards.

There are limits, however, to this metaphor. While Sisyphus's struggle is futile and eternal, men with physical disabilities' exertions need not be. Despite the pervasive dominance that they face, they have an agency that Sisyphus lacks. They have the power to resist this domination. By rejecting hegemonic masculinity, changing their reference groups, and asserting their agency, it is possible for men with physical disabilities largely to escape their gender domination and to construct counter-hegemonic alternatives. In so doing, these men become models for all men who struggle with their masculinity.

NOTES

1. Among those who identify with the Disability Rights Movement, the use of this term acknowledges that almost everyone will experience a disability before death. The term underscores the similarities between those who currently have a disability and those who are likely to have one in the future. For more on the importance of language in this context, see Zola 1993.

2. Relatively little research has been done comparing the experiences of men and women with disabilities. For accounts of the challenges that women with disabilities face, see Fine and Asch 1988.

3. The type and severity of a person's disability interact with other social characteristics to influence the kind and extent of domination they experience. As a consequence, the domination experienced by men with physical disabilities varies depending on their social class, race and ethnicity, age, and sexual orientation.

4. These are: Beisser 1989; Callahan 1989; Dubus 1992; Fries 1997; Hockenberry 1995; Kovic 1976; Kriegel 1991; Murphy 1990; Puller 1991; and Zola 1982.

5. The key axes of this matrix are race, social class, gender, ethnicity, sexual orientation, age, and ability/disability.

REFERENCES

Altman, Barbara M. and Sharon Barnartt. 1996. "Implications of Variations in Definitions of Disability Used in Policy Analysis: The Case of Labor Force Outcomes." Paper presented at the annual meeting of the Society for Disability Studies, June 13, Washington, DC.

Amott, Teresa and Julie A. Matthaei. 1991. *Race, Gender, and Work: A Multicultural Economic History of Women in the United States*. Boston, MA: South End.

Beisser, Arnold. 1989. *Flying Without Wings: Personal Reflections on Being Disabled*. New York, NY: Doubleday.

Callahan, John. 1989. *Don't Worry, He Won't Get Far on Foot*. New York, NY: Vintage Books.

Connell, R. W. 1990. "An Iron Man: The Body and Some Contradictions of Hegemonic Masculinity," in *Sport, Men, and the Gender Order*, M. Messner and D. Sabo (eds). Champaign, IL: Human Kinetics, 83–96.

——. 1995. *Masculinities*. Berkeley, CA: University of California Press.

Denzin, Norman. 1989. *The Research Act: A Theoretical Introduction to Sociological Methods*. Englewood Cliffs, NJ: Prentice Hall.

Dubus, Andre. 1992. *Broken Vessels*. Boston, MA: David R. Godine.

Fine, Michelle and Adrienne Asch, (eds). 1988. *Women with Disabilities: Essays in Psychology, Culture, and Politics*. Philadelphia, PA: Temple University Press.

Fries, Kenny. 1997. *Body, Remember*. New York, NY: Dutton.

Gerschick, Thomas J. and Adam S. Miller. 1994. "Gender Identities at the Crossroads of Masculinity and Physical Disability." *Masculinities* 2(1): 32–53.

Goffman, Erving. 1963. *Stigma: Notes on the Management of Spoiled Identity*. New York, NY: Simon and Schuster.

——. 1977. "The Arrangement Between the Sexes." *Theory and Society* 4(3): 301–31.

Golfus, Billy. 1997. "Sex and the Single Gimp," in *The Disability Studies Reader*, L. J. Davis (ed.). New York: Routledge, 419–28.

Hagan, Kay Leigh. 1993. *Fugitive Information: Essays from a Feminist Hothead*. New York, NY: HarperCollins.

Hahn, Harlan. 1989. "Masculinity and Disability." *Disability Studies Quarterly* 9(1): 54–6.

Hill Collins, Patricia. 1990. *Black Feminist Thought*. Boston, MA: Unwin Hyman.

Hockenberry, John. 1995. *Moving Violations: War Zones, Wheelchairs, and Declarations of Independence*. New York, NY: Hyperion.

Janeway, Elizabeth. 1980. *Powers of the Weak*. New York, NY: Alfred A. Knopf.

Kimmel, Michael S. 1994. "Consuming Manhood: The Feminization of American Culture and the Recreation of the Male Body, 1832–1920," in *The Male Body*, L. Goldstein (ed.). Ann Arbor, MI: The University of Michigan Press, 12–41.

Kovic, Ron. 1976. *Born on the Fourth of July*. New York, NY: Pocket Books.

Kriegel, Leonard. 1991. *Falling into Life*. San Francisco, CA: North Point Press.

Levine, Martin P. 1992. "The Status of Gay Men in the Workplace," in *Men's Lives*, 2nd ed., M. S. Kimmel and M. Messner (eds). New York, NY: Macmillan, 251–66.

McNeil, John M. 1993. *Americans with Disabilities 1991–92*. U.S. Bureau of the Census. Current Population Reports, P70–33. Washington, DC: U.S. Government Printing Office.

Messner, Michael A. 1992. *Power at Play: Sports and the Problem of Masculinity.* Boston, MA: Beacon Press.

Murphy, Robert F. 1990. *The Body Silent.* New York, NY: Norton.

Newby, Robert. 1992. "Review Symposium: Black Feminist Thought." *Gender and Society* 6(3): 508–11.

Puller, Lewis B. Jr. 1991. *Fortunate Son.* New York, NY: Bantam.

Shapiro, Joseph P. 1993. *No Pity: People with Disabilities Forging a New Civil Rights Movement.* New York, NY: Random House.

Taub, Diane E. and Kimberly R. Greer. 1997. "Sociology of Acceptance Revisited: Males with Physical Disabilities Participating in Sport and Physical Fitness Activity." Paper presented at the annual meeting of the Midwest Sociological Society, April 4, Des Moines, IA.

Wendell, Susan. 1997. "Toward a Feminist Theory of Disability," in *The Disability Studies Reader,* L. J. Davis (ed.). New York, NY: Routledge, 260–78.

West, Candace and Don H. Zimmerman. 1987. "Doing Gender." *Gender and Society* 1(2): 125–51.

Zola, Irving Kenneth. 1982. *Missing Pieces: A Chronicle of Living with a Disability.* Philadelphia, PA: Temple University Press.

——. 1993. "Self, Identity, and the Naming Question: Reflections on the Language of Disability," in *Perspectives on Disability,* 2nd ed., M. Nagler (ed.). Palo Alto, CA: Health Markets Research, 15–23.

THINKING ABOUT THE READING

Whether we're physically disabled or not, all of us have to "do gender." What are some of the culturally valued gender expectations women must live up to when they "do gender"? How might these expectations be affected by physical disabilities? In other words, is being in a wheelchair a threat to femininity in the same way that it's a threat to masculinity? Is it possible to disagree with these gender expectations and still act in ways that perpetuate them? This article illustrates one way in which the body is used as a form of self-presentation. Think of various messages conveyed by the body and how we work to shape this aspect of our identity. How important are the reactions of those around you in your efforts to shape a physical presentation that conforms to gender expectations? What are some ways in which men can enact "counter-hegemonic masculinities"? Are some of these techniques more or less culturally acceptable than others? Why?

7

Building Social Relationships

Intimacy and Family

In this culture, close, personal relationships are the standard by which we judge the quality and happiness of our everyday lives. Yet in a complex, individualistic society like ours, these relationships are becoming more difficult to establish and sustain. Although we like to think that the things we do in our relationships are completely private experiences, they are continually influenced by large-scale political interests and economic pressures. Like every other aspect of our lives, close relationships are best understood within the broader social context. Laws, customs, and social institutions often regulate the form relationships can take, our behavior in them, and even the ways in which we can exit them. At a more fundamental level, societies determine which relationships can be considered "legitimate" and therefore entitled to cultural and institutional recognition. Relationships that lack societal validation are often scorned and stigmatized.

Social validation is particularly difficult to obtain for homosexual couples, who are often portrayed by others as a threat to the institution of family. In "No Place Like Home," sociologist Christopher Carrington describes how lesbians and gay men construct and sustain a sense of family in their own lives. From his research, Carrington argues that *family* isn't necessarily determined by blood or law, but by a consistent pattern of loving and caring. *Family* resides in the unremarkable, everyday things that partners do with and for each other. In that sense, same-sex couples establish extensive life-long bonds, just like those found in long-term heterosexual couples.

One of the most pressing dilemmas that all types of families face these days is how to balance the demands of their work lives with those of their home lives. In "Coping With Commitment," Kathleen Gerson examines the strategies men and women use to emphasize one sphere of their lives over the other. Two of these strategic responses—the stay-at-home mother and breadwinner father—are quite traditional and, historically, have had tremendous cultural support. Two other strategies—the working mother and the caretaking father—are distinctly non-traditional and often carry extra burdens. Although many people believe that the choice to emphasize the domestic component or the work component of one's life is a matter of moral conviction, Gerson points out that these choices are often influenced by broader cultural barriers, economic shifts, and occupational opportunities.

Achieving a balance between work and family is especially difficult for poor people in developing countries. As Arlie Russell Hochschild points out in "Love and Gold," many destitute mothers in places like the Philippines, Mexico, and Sri Lanka leave their own children for long periods of time to work abroad because they cannot make ends meet at home. Ironically, the jobs these women typically take when they leave their families—nannies, maids, service workers—involve caring for and nurturing other people's families. So while migrant women provide much needed income for their own families and valuable "care work" for their employers, they leave an emotional vacuum in their home countries. Hochschild asks as to consider the toll this phenomenon is taking on the children of these absent mothers. Not surprisingly, most of the women feel a profound sense of guilt and remorse that is largely invisible to the families they work for.

Something to Consider as You Read:

Each of these selections emphasizes the significance of external or structural components in shaping the family life. As you read, keep track of factors such as income level and job opportunities and consider how these factors affect the choices families make. Consider some of the ways in which household income might be related to family choices. For example, consider what choices a family with a high income might have regarding how best to assist an ailing grandparent or how to deal with an unexpected teen pregnancy or in providing children with extracurricular activities. Consider how these choices are related to the appearance of "traditional family values."

No Place Like Home

Christopher Carrington

(1999)

This was a law developed for the purpose of ensuring that people can care for their families. It's inappropriate for a senator to cheapen the meaning of family by saying family is a "fill in the blank."

—Kristi Hamrick, spokesperson for
the Family Research Council, commenting on
New Jersey Sen. Robert Torricelli's decision to
voluntarily extend some of the provisions of the 1993
Family and Medical Leave Act to lesbian and gay
members of his staff (www. glinn.com March 13, 1997)

As I write these words, a cultural debate in the United States rages over the status of lesbian and gay families, most notably in the struggles over lesbian and gay marriage, as well as in the struggles to gain "domestic partnership" benefits. Much of the current debate about lesbian and gay families stems from the threat that such families are perceived to pose to the dominant organization of family practices in contemporary Western societies (Mohr 1994; Stacey 1996). However, a pervasive sense of crisis in the American family has existed throughout much of American history (Skolnick 1991; Coontz 1992), and the national debate concerning lesbian and gay families is but the latest grist for the mill. This sense of family crisis pervades the political efforts to block lesbian and gay people from attaining legal marriage and benefits of domestic partnership. The sense of crisis, and the rhetorical overkill that accompanies it, not only makes it difficult for political debate to focus on the everyday realities of

lesbian and gay families but insures that many people will both understand such families in stereotypical ways and impede efforts to improve the quality of lesbian and gay family life. The quotation at the beginning of this chapter from Ms. Hamrick denies the possibility that lesbian and gay families exist, much less acknowledges that they should enjoy any kind of cultural recognition.

... Actual lesbigay families, like most other American families, face the struggles of balancing work and family commitments, of managing the stresses and strains of waxing and waning sexual desires, of maintaining open and honest communication, of fighting over household responsibilities, and, most frequently, of simply trying to make ends meet. The latter point deserves much more attention, for if any phantom lurks in the lives of lesbian and gay families, it is their inability to achieve financial security, the foundation of a happy, communicative, and stable relationship (Voydanoff 1992).

This is a study of "family life" among a group of fifty-two lesbian and gay families (twenty-six female and twenty-six male). This study provides an ethnographic and empirical account of how lesbians and gay men actually construct, sustain, enhance, or undermine a sense of family in their lives. . . . I use the term *lesbigay,* which is coming into wider use, because it includes lesbians, bisexuals, and gay men, all of whom participate in the families I studied. Of the fifty-two adult women participants, two consider themselves bisexual, as does one of the fifty-three adult men.

In this study I reflect upon the *details* of everyday life in the households of the lesbigay families, and explore the relationship of such detail to the actual experience of and creation of family in the lives of lesbigay people. The participants in this research, similar to many other citizens, use the term *family* in diverse and often contradictory ways. At one moment a participant will conceive of family as a legal and biological category, a category that they reject, and might even define themselves as over and against. In a different place and time that same participant will conceive of family in favor of an understanding that emphasizes the labors involved and not the socially sanctioned roles. And at yet another place and time that same participant will embrace the legal and biological definitions of family with the hopes of achieving lesbigay inclusion into those categorizations (for example, advocating lesbigay legal marriage or attempting to secure custody of a child on the basis of biological linkage).

In my analysis the crucial element for defining what or who constitutes a family derives from whether the participants engage in a consistent and relatively reciprocal pattern of loving and caring activities and understand themselves to be bound to provide for, and entitled to partake of, the material and emotional needs and/or resources of other family members. I understand family as consisting of people who love and care for one another. This makes a couple a family. In other words, through their loving and caring activities, and their reflections upon them, people conceive of, construct, and maintain social relationships that they come to recognize and treat as family (Schneider 1984). In this sense a family, any family, is a social construction, or set of relationships recognized, edified, and sustained through human initiative. People "do" family.

This research ponders the deceptively simple activities that constitute love and care, activities that frequently go unnoticed in most families, including most lesbigay families. These may entail trips to the store to pick up something special for dinner, phoning an order to a catalog company for someone's birthday, tallying the money owed to friends, sorting the daily mail, remembering a couple's anniversary, finishing up the laundry before one's spouse returns home, maintaining a photo album, remembering the vegetables that family members dislike, or attending to myriad other small, often hidden, seemingly insignificant matters. Decidedly not insignificant, these small matters form the fabric of our daily lives as participants in families. Moreover, the proliferation of these small matters produces a stronger and more pervasive sense of the relationship(s) as a family, both in the eyes of the participants and in the eyes of others. . . .

Kin Work Among Lesbigay Families

In recent years, scholars of family life have begun to document the forms of work that heterosexual women do in order to establish and sustain family relations. Some of this research reveals the forms of hidden and frequently unrecognized labor involved in maintaining kin relations (Rosenthal 1985; Di Leonardo 1987; Gerstel and Gallagher 1993 1994). Di Leonardo refers to these kinds of activities as "kin work":

The conception, maintenance, and ritual celebration of cross-household kin ties, including visits, letters, telephone calls, presents and cards to kin; the organization of holiday gatherings; the creation and maintenance of quasi-kin relations; decisions to neglect or to intensify particular ties; the mental work of reflection about all of these activities; and the creation and communication of altering images of family and kin vis-à-vis the images of others, both folk and mass media. (1987, 442–43)

The forms of kin work Di Leonardo delineates appear in lesbigay families as well, although much of the aforementioned empirical research fails to include such families. In writing letters, making phone calls, organizing holiday and social occasions, selecting and purchasing gifts, as well as the forethought and decisions about how to do these things, how much to do, and for whom to do them, lesbigay families engage in a great deal of kin work. In fact, engaging in kin work is essential to creating lesbigay family life.

Kith as Family

In most respects, lesbigay families engage in forms of kin work quite similar to heterosexual families, though many do so among intimate friends rather than among biologically defined relatives (Weston 1990; Nardi 1992; Nardi and Sherrod 1994). In contrast to the traditional Anglo-Saxon distinction made between kith (friends and acquaintances) and kin (relatives), many lesbigay families operate with a different set of distinctions where kith become kin and, sometimes, kin become kith. For example, Mary Ann Callihan, a thirty-eight-year-old artist now living in Oakland, reflects:

I do consider my close friends as my family. They are my real family, I mean, my other family lives back East, and I don't have much to do with them and they don't have much to do with me. They really aren't a family, not at least in how I think a family should be. The people who care for me, listen to me, and love me are right here. They are my kin.

And while Mary Ann's comments diminishing the importance of biolegally defined kin reflect the views of roughly a third of the sample, her sentiments regarding the definition of family capture a common theme found in many lesbigay households: a normative sense of family as a voluntary association, as *chosen*. Sociologist Judith Stacey identifies this pattern of chosen kin and voluntary family ties as the "postmodern family" (Stacey 1990, 17, 270). Many lesbigay households operate with this postmodern conception of kin. Many respondents use the phrase "gay family" to designate their chosen family.

This conception of friends as family notwithstanding, lesbigay families make clear distinctions among friends. Anthropologist Kath Weston notes, "Although many gay families included friends, not just any friend would do" (1991, 109). Weston argues that "gay families differed from networks to the extent that they quite consciously incorporated symbolic demonstrations of love, shared history, material and emotional assistance and other signs of enduring solidarity" (109). Bringing the perspectives and findings of the literature on kin work to bear on Weston's findings raises a number of questions: What activities constitute symbolic demonstrations of love? What kind of work does material and emotional assistance involve and who performs that work? What activities/behaviors serve as signs of enduring solidarity and what forms of work come to play in those activities? Peter Nardi, describing the role of friendships in lives of gay people, points out that

in addition to providing opportunities for expressions of intimacy and identity, friendships for gay men and lesbians serve as sources for various kinds of social support (ranging from the monetary to health care) and provide them with a network of people with whom they can share celebrations, holidays, and other transitional rituals. (1992, 112)

Nardi's delineation of activities crucial to friendship suggests the presence of kin work: planning, provisioning, and coordinating visits, celebrations, holidays, and transitional rituals; making phone calls and sending e-mail on a consistent basis; sending notes, cards, and flowers at the appropriate times; selecting, purchasing, and wrapping gifts; providing or arranging for the provision of healthcare (not a minor matter given the HIV/AIDS epidemic); and reflecting upon and strategizing about relationships. All of these activities constitute kin work, and performing these activities *creates* and sustains family.

When laying claim to the term *family* to describe lesbigay relationships, most respondents point to particular phenomena as evidence of family: sharing meals, sharing leisure, sharing holidays, sharing religious community, sharing resources, relying on someone for emotional or medical care, turning to someone in an emergency, and/or sharing a common history. For example, many lesbians and gay men point to the sharing of holiday meals as indicative of the presence of family in their lives. Susan Posner, reflecting on those people with whom she and her partner, Camille, spend their holidays, comments:

> Well, we have them over to eat or they have us over. We have been together through thick and thin for so long from when we first came out of the closet, through our commitment ceremony, and through buying this house. That makes us family. I have known one of them for a very long time, that's a lot of eating and sharing and crying and stuff.

Susan began to cry as she reflected on these events in her life. She then recounted several holiday gatherings where the joy that she experienced with her lesbigay family was so overwhelming that she began to cry during the events. Many lesbigay people can recount similar stories. In part, these are tears of exile from biolegal kin, but they are more than that. They are also tears of joy—joy in the discovery of a new home and a new family.

In addition to sharing holiday meals, other participants pointed to other kinds of kin work as evidence of family. Daniel Sen Yung, a twenty-eight-year-old accountant for a small nonprofit agency, offers another instance of kith becoming kin via various forms of kin work. Daniel, responding to my question about whether he considers his close friends as family, replies:

> Oh, yes, I know that I can depend on them for certain things that you would get from a family. If I were to get really ill, they would take care of me, house me, provide for me. We eat together, just like families should. I consider friends as family, especially as a gay person, I think that way. I definitely have a gay family. They look out for me and check in on me. They are the people who pay my bills when I go overseas for work, or who were with me when I had to take my cat to the veterinary hospital. They are the ones who came and visited me in the hospital, for God's sake.

Another participant, Raquel Rhodes, a thirty-one-year-old woman working as an assistant manager for a rental car agency, identified those who had loaned her money as central to her conception of family:

> I think you know who your real family is when you fall on hard times. My friends Rebecca and Sue, they came through for me when I lost my job. They lent me the money I needed to keep going. My own mother wouldn't because of all of her homophobic bullshit. That tells you who really counts and for me—Rebecca and Sue really count.

Loaning people money involves kin work. Managing and negotiating the feelings incumbent in such lending, particularly when a couple is doing the lending, as well as managing the money itself are both forms of kin work. Other forms of lesbigay kin work include all the efforts that people put into recognizing and celebrating their own and other people's relationships. The recent work by anthropologist Ellen Lewin (1998) exploring the commitment ceremonies of lesbian and gay couples reveals the extensive work entailed in creating these ceremonies. Lewin chronicles the efforts these couples put into selecting invitations, attire, and locations for the ceremony, as well as making arrangements for out-of-town guests. She also reveals the extensive emotional labor that goes into deciding who to invite—a sometimes gut-wrenching and potentially combative enterprise. When we do these things, we create family.

The Lesbigay Family Kin Keepers

Quite frequently, relationships function as a center for extended kinship structures. To use an astronomical metaphor, these relationships become planets around whom a series of moons (frequently, single individuals) revolve. The planning, organization, and facilitation of social occasions (picnics, holiday gatherings, vacations, commitment ceremonies/holy unions, birthday parties, gay-pride celebrations, hiking trips) bring these individuals into an orbit around lesbigay relationships. These occasions often take place in the homes of couples, as contrasted with individuals, and one member of the couple often performs the work involved. In answering questions about holiday gatherings, lesbigay families frequently recount stories of shared Thanksgiving meals, Jewish Sedarim, gay-pride celebrations, and Christmas Eve gatherings. Many speak of the importance of making sure that everyone "has a place to go" on such occasions.

For example, Matthew Corrigan and his partner, Greg Fuss, have been together for

thirteen years and live in San Francisco's Castro district. Matthew works as an administrator in a nearby hospital and Greg works as a salesperson for a large pharmaceutical company. Matthew responds to my question about how he decides whom to invite for holiday occasions by saying:

> We have a lot of single friends. Many of them would like to be in couples, but they just haven't found Mr. or Mrs. Right yet. So, we are kind of their family. I mean, we will still be family after they find someone, but right now, they come here for holidays. I try to make sure that no one spends their Christmas alone. When we talk about who to invite, we always think about who doesn't have a place to go.

Matthew's comments capture a common dynamic where lesbigay families function as the center of kin relations for many single individuals. The lesbigay families can also function as a place where single individuals come into contact with one another and begin new relationships (Harry 1984, 143). These families become the center due to a number of socioeconomic factors. First, the formation of lesbigay families leads to pooling of resources. The shared resources of family groupings allow for larger residences, larger meal expenditures, and, interestingly, more time for kin work. Family status brings with it the possibility of at least one member in a family reducing the number of hours they work at paid labor and spending more time on family/household matters. Second, as lesbigay couples and threesomes come to perceive of their relationship in familial terms, they begin to act in familial ways: inviting others over for dinner, and creating holiday occasions, among other things. Third, it seems that unpartnered individuals view couples in familial ways and hold expectations that these individuals will act in familial terms. Angela DiVincenzo, a thirty-three-year-old elementary school teacher, felt this expectation from her lesbigay family:

I think that our friends have a stake in our relationship. A lot of them are single and they kind of view us as the ideal family. I mean, partly, I think, it's about their hopes of having their own relationship, but also, it's about the fact that we are their family. They look to us to act like a family. We all do things together, go on little trips or hiking or whatever. We are kind of a stabilizing influence in their lives. They know we are here and are interested in their lives, unlike many of their real families, that is, *supposedly* real families. We are the real family.

Moreover, in a number of the longer-term and more affluent lesbigay families, there emerges a person who becomes a family "kinkeeper" (Rosenthal 1985). This person functions as a sort of center for an extended lesbigay family. This individual actually coordinates some of the kin work across families. For example, Randy Ambert, a forty-two-year-old flight attendant, plans and coordinates many joint occasions for an extended kin group who he and his partner, Russ Pena, both consider their extended family. They include in this extended family a lesbian couple, another gay-male couple, a single lesbian, and two single gay men. In talking with Randy about these activities, he observes:

I am sort of the family mom, if you get my drift. I tend to be the first person who thinks about what is coming up. I get everyone thinking about what we're going to do for summer travel, and I like to make sure that we don't forget anyone's birthday. With the other couples, that's not too much of an issue because they keep on top of each other's birthdays. But sometimes, the couples seem pretty busy and too worn out to make plans for things, you know, so I try to keep us all together. I plan a big celebration for Gay Pride each year that brings us all together.

In addition to planning these joint occasions, Randy reports making calls to gay family members who now live out of town and keeping them abreast of the news of the various people in the extended kin group. Randy's work sustains kinship; it makes real the claim of many lesbigay people, the claim to chosen family. Yet the work and the claim to family status occurs under a particular set of social conditions. Randy's relatively flexible work schedule and the relative affluence of his household allow Randy to invest more time in kin work, and to become a kinkeeper.

Arranging for such gatherings takes a great deal of kin work. In addition to the actual planning, provisioning and preparation of the food—all examples of feeding work—a number of other less observed labors make such family meals possible. Someone must envision such occasions and make decisions about whom to invite and when. Some people tend to think of the envisioning of such meals as a form of leisure, but in fact, this envisioning entails various hidden forms of labor. The envisioning of shared meals requires one to think and act in response to a number of different factors: individual, corporate, and societal calendars; whom to invite and how frequently; who gets along with whom and what mix of people would work; making phone calls or sending invitations; knowledge of social etiquette; and learning what foods guests like or dislike. Rich Niebuhr, a forty-one-year-old attorney working part-time, reveals the mental effort involved in deciding which people to invite to dinner:

Well, it can be kind of awkward sometimes deciding whom to invite. Usually, I handle it because Joe doesn't like dealing with that kind of stuff. But, sometimes, I find myself torn because I know that we owe someone dinner, either we haven't seen them in a while and we run into them in Castro or at a movie, but I don't really feel like inviting them. Usually, I break down and invite them because I feel like a worm if I don't. I will think about whom to invite over at the same time—sort of to take the edge off, to make it a little less intense. It's okay. But, I kind of get mad that Joe just sort of expects me to negotiate all this stuff. Sometimes, I put my foot down, and make him call them. It can be real draining trying to stay on top of all this stuff.

Rich exemplifies the kinds of considerations that constitute kin work. Note how Rich bears responsibility for managing the interpersonal conflict and for strategizing the occasion because "Joe doesn't like dealing with that kind of stuff." Participant observation in Joe and Rich's home reveals that Rich performs much of the kin work, both in its visible forms (making calls and planning events), as well as in its invisible forms (thinking about whom they should call and planning when to make the calls).

Variations in Kin Work Patterns

Not surprisingly the character and extent of kin work varies dramatically depending on a number of different social factors. Class identities, . . . the presence or absence of children, gender identities, . . . and ethnic and racial identities all influence the context in which kin work happens and the character of that kin work.

Social class and lesbigay kin work. While most lesbigay families in this study fall into the middle and upper middle class, clear distinctions emerge between these groups in terms of kin work. More affluent, upper-middle-class lesbigay households engage in significantly more kin work and much more frequently conceive of friends as family than their middle-class counterparts. Those families earning more than the median annual household income ($61,500) report twice as many close friends (twelve per household) as those households earning below the median (five). This pattern conforms to other empirical research revealing that patterns of informal association become more extensive as one moves up the socioeconomic hierarchy (Hodges 1964; Curtis and Jackson 1977). Among the ten most affluent

households, all family members conceive of friends as family. In contrast, among the ten least affluent, only within four households does even one family member conceive of friends as family. In part this pattern may reflect the relatively younger age of the less affluent families. It also appears that among the more affluent, friendship/family networks become more strongly lesbigay. Less affluent respondents' friendship/family networks, while smaller, consist of a greater proportion of straight people. Overall, more affluent households maintain larger family structures and they do family with other lesbigay people.

This means that the work of creating and sustaining such relationships becomes more extensive and requires more labor for more affluent lesbigay families. For instance, they invite others over for shared meals more often, entertain larger numbers of people at dinner parties and other occasions, and go out to dinner with others more consistently. These activities require extensive kin work in the form of planning for such occasions, deciding whom to invite, extending invitations, deciding where to go out to eat, and maintaining a record (mental or written) of previous engagements.

Lawrence Sing and Henry Goode, together as a family for over two decades, live in a restored Edwardian flat in a rapidly gentrifying neighborhood in San Francisco. Lawrence works part-time as a real estate agent, and Henry works as a physician. They both possess postgraduate degrees. Lawerence, who performs much of the kin-related work in the family, makes the following comments about some of that work:

I'm the keeper of the social calendar. I decide whom to invite over and when. I keep a mental record of who came last and whom we would like to see. I ask Henry if there is anyone he would like to see, but generally, I know how he feels about certain people. I keep up our obligations. Some people we see once a year, but there is a core of twenty-five to thirty people who I maintain contact with and whom we see with some frequency.

Lawrence, speaking with great enthusiasm and affection for his family of gay friends, denotes other forms of kin work in the effort to maintain those family relationships:

> I write letters to our closest friends who live farther away, and we always send them birthday presents and cards and, of course, presents at Christmastime. We try to plan holiday travel and our vacations with some of them. I often call them on Sundays; that's the day I make many of the long-distance calls to everybody. It's a lot of effort to keep it all together, but I think it's worth it. They're our family.

Lawrence's observations reflect common forms of kin work among more affluent lesbigay households. In contrast to less affluent lesbigay families, the affluent ones engage in some forms of kin work much more frequently: writing letters; buying and mailing gifts for birthdays and holidays; sending flowers; sending birthday, anniversary, and get-well cards; and sending a larger number of holiday greeting cards. When dividing up the sample into thirds, the most affluent one-third sent an average of seventy-five cards; and the lower one-third, fifteen cards per household. The more affluent families keep in contact with out-of-town friends and biolegal relatives much more frequently than less affluent families. The affluent make more long-distance calls and spend more time talking. All of these efforts constitute kin work: deciding upon and purchasing gifts and cards, writing and mailing the gifts and cards, remembering to call and write and deciding for whom to do these things.

In like manner, the more affluent households report more extensive holiday celebrations, and they often point to the sharing of holidays together as evidence of the family status of their intimate friends. Kathy Atwood and Joan Kelsey live in the Oakland hills in an Arts

and Crafts style cottage in a neighborhood with many other lesbian families. Kathy works as an accountant for a prominent bank headquartered in downtown San Francisco. Joan works part-time as a finance manager for a local savings and loan. Together they earn slightly over $100,000 per year. Joan has a master's degree in accounting from a prestigious college in the East and Kathy has a bachelor's degree from the University of California. Kathy expresses her conception of friends as constituting family:

> I consider my friends as family. I see them as often as I see my biolegal family. I discuss our relationship with them. They come here for holidays or we go to their house. Our shared holidays are symbolic of our familiness. We share personal experiences. I would want them here for significant events, like Christmas or our Holy Union or whatever.

Joan, who does much of the kin work in the family, engages in a great deal of effort to make the holidays pleasant and meaningful to her chosen family:

> I put quite a bit of effort into getting the house together for Christmas. We had a lot of people over at different times, and our chosen family over on Christmas Eve, and we went to their house on Christmas day. I mean, I planned out the meals, a very special one for Christmas Eve. I bought and mailed invitations for a Sunday afternoon holiday party. I went to the Flowermart in the city and bought greens and stuff like that. I bought a new tablecloth with a holiday theme. We chose presents for them together, but I had the time to wrap them and stuff like that.

Nearly a dozen individuals from more affluent families conceive of shared holidays as constitutive of family, while only two individuals from families earning below the median speak in these terms.

Conversely, in most cases, less affluent households more often conceive of family in biolegally defined terms, they engage in less kin work and to some extent they do different kinds of kin work. In terms of household income, most respondents perceiving of family as uniquely consisting of biolegal relatives fall below the median. I would characterize many of them as "minimal families" (Dizard and Gadlin 1990). They do not create and sustain large kin structures, either biolegally defined or lesbigay defined, and their conceptions of family emphasize biolegal links. Although these families afford less time and energy to maintaining kin relations, the efforts they do make often focus on biolegal relatives. These families often feel isolated and spend more time alone. Social researchers made the discovery long ago that the wealthy and the poor maintain stronger ties to kin for economic reasons than do middle-class Americans (Schneider and Smith 1973; Stack 1974). Most of those lesbigay families falling below the median income in this sample clearly fall into the middle or the lower middle class, as opposed to the working class or the poor. For instance, Amy Gilfoyle and Wendy Harper, a lesbian family living in a distant suburb north of San Francisco, a place where they could afford to buy a home, spend much of their time alone. They spend major holidays "alone together," without the presence of others. They both conceive of family as consisting of their own relationship and possibly Amy's biolegal parents. They report one close friend between the two of them, and both express disappointment about this. They would like more friends, but they seem conflicted. Wendy, a student and landscape gardener, feels somewhat threatened by new friends:

> I would worry about getting too close to a lot of other lesbians. There are always issues about falling in love with friends and that ruining your relationship. And, we live so far away from the places where we might meet friends. I suppose we could become friends with some gay men, but they don't live out here, or at least we don't have any way of finding those who do.

Wendy's comments point to issues partly beyond social class, to concerns about gender and sexuality. But the fact that Wendy and Amy live so far away from San Francisco speaks clearly of social class and the ability of more affluent families to buy and rent homes in the city. Interview questions focusing on the reasons for living in suburban communities almost always point to the cost of housing in the city as a factor in deciding where to live. Wendy and Amy bring in a household income of $35,000 per year. This places them somewhat below the Bay Area median household income of $41,459 (U.S. Census 1991). Like many other middle- and lower middle-class lesbigay families, they exert less effort in the maintenance of kinship structures than do more affluent families. They infrequently call friends or biolegal relatives. They rarely send cards of any sort. Together they sent eight holiday greeting cards in 1993. They rarely invite people over, though they actually have the space to entertain. Only once every few months do they go out to dinner, and then usually just the two of them go. They lead relatively isolated lives and feel ambiguous about changing this. . . .

In sum, social class appears to play a central role in the extent and the character of kin work among lesbigay families. As one ascends the social-class hierarchy of lesbigay families in this sample from lower middle class to upper middle class, the intensity of kin work increases. The character of kin work shifts from concerns about establishing kin relationships to managing and sustaining kin relationships. The flow of material exchange intensifies with affluent lesbigay families buying more gifts, throwing more parties, hosting more dinners, making more phone calls, and sending more cards. Explaining why more affluent households do more kin work than less affluent ones involves several interrelated influences. First, more affluent families live closer to the lesbigay enclaves due to the higher cost of living in the city. Proximity to other lesbigay people leads to larger kin networks. Yet, some lower middle-class lesbigay families live in the center of lesbigay enclaves and engage in significantly less kin work than their more affluent neighbors. Second, more affluent lesbigay families turn to the marketplace for other forms of domestic labor (for example, laundry and housekeeping) thus freeing these families to invest more energy in kin work. . . .

Lesbigay parenting and kin work. The presence of children diminishes the conception of friends as family in lesbian and gay households. In four of the five households with children present in this study, neither primary partner conceives of their close friends as family. Rather, these households limit family to the primary couple, the children, and to bio-legal relatives. Emily Fortune and Alice Lauer, parents of two young infants, understand family in strongly biolegal terms. Emily states: "Some people use the term *family* very loosely. I don't call friends that. The kids and our relatives, they feel like family to me. To me, my family is my biolegal family. We have a natural bond to one another." Her partner, Alice:

> My concept of family has changed a great deal in the past few months. I think before the children were born I might have considered my friends as family. My relationship with my own sister has changed since the kids were born. I have more of a sense of this family right here. I have a new appreciation for my family of origin. We can turn to them in a crisis, even though they may not be that comfortable with our sexuality.

Gay and lesbian parents appear more vested in biolegal conceptions of family, perhaps for very concrete reasons. To establish biolegal links in the American kinship structure often also establishes and legitimates economic links. Three of the lesbian families, all with infants, report relying on biolegal kin for

resources, either in the form of providing housing, making loans, lending automobiles, or providing daycare. Anthropologist Ellen Lewin suggests that the pattern of intensifying relations to blood kin among lesbian parents expresses an attempt to legitimate the claim to family and to provide a stable socioeconomic environment for the children (1993, 91–94).

Moreover, the presence of children within some families distracts from the ability to maintain friends. Clarice Perry, a college professor who is also deaf, expresses her feelings about family:

> My experience with family is strange. It's not easy to draw the line since I have Cheryl's children. I share responsibility for the kids, that's my idea of family. As an individual, my close friends, mostly deaf, we can't share that much because of the kids. The kids have changed my relationship with my friends. I have mixed feelings about it. I resent the kids sometimes. They took my friends away. It was not my plan to have kids, but they are now my family and I love them.

The addition of children changes one's social circumstances, both for lesbigay people and for heterosexuals. However, given that relatively few lesbigay families have children, and that parents often befriend parents in American culture, lesbigay parents may find it quite difficult to establish social links. This further encourages lesbigay families with kids to establish stronger relations with biolegal kin. The possibility exists that lesbian and gay friends may also intentionally diminish relationships with friends who have children. Some scholars find a fairly strong sentiment against children, especially among some gay men (Newton 1993).

Gender identities and lesbigay kin work. Gender appears central to explaining kin work in many settings. For instance, Di Leonardo posits that kin work reflects the influence of gender much more strongly than the influence of social class in heterosexual families (1987, 449). I can make no such unilateral claim about gender within lesbigay families. I detect gender-related concerns in terms of how lesbians and gay men both portray and do kin work, but this is complicated by the impact of socioeconomic factors. Interestingly, in this study, gay men do significantly more kin work than lesbian women. This parallels the finding of Blumstein and Schwartz (1983, 149–50) and my own research that gay men do more housework than lesbian women do. Blumstein and Schwartz argue this emerges from an effort among lesbians to avoid the low-status role assigned to housework in American society. I think additional factors play a role here.

While Blumstein and Schwartz find lesbian women shunning domestic work to avoid the low-status stigma attached to it, in the case of kin work I find both patterns of avoidance and a significantly diminished rationale for the generally less affluent lesbian families to engage in extensive kin work. When considering the economic affluence, educational level, and occupational prestige of all lesbigay households, the more affluent the household, the more educated and the more prestigious the career, the more extensive the kin work becomes regardless of gender. Dividing the lesbian families on the basis of household income into three groups (high, medium, and low) shows that those with high income report twice as many friends as those with low incomes. The same holds for males. Affluent families, regardless of gender, engage in much more extensive kin work. Due to the persistence of gender inequality, and the barriers women face in achieving higher-status, higher-paid employment, the resources necessary to sustain larger kin structures do not exist for many lesbian households as much as they do for gay men. Nor does maintaining such a network provide any economic advantage, as it does for those in occupational categories where extensive networks provide business and client contacts (lawyers, private-practice physicians, and psychologists).

Nonetheless, I am not suggesting that gender has no relevance here, but its relevance eludes easy classification. On the one hand, lesbian women may well avoid kin work activity in order to escape the devalued status associated with doing the work. After all, who wants to be "just a housewife" (Matthews 1987)? On the other hand, if one hopes to create and live within a family, then someone has to do this work. And in most lesbigay families these forms of work do occur. However, doing kin work, or failing to do it, carries different risks for gay men and lesbians. For the men, engaging in kin work produces threats to gender identity. Making calls to family, sending cards, buying presents, inviting dinner guests and worrying about soured relationships with family all carry the potential to become gender-producing phenomena (Berk 1985; West and Zimmerman 1987). A woman failing to engage in these nurturing/caring activities runs the risk of stigma. This "nurturing imperative" exists for women regardless of sexual orientation (Westkott 1986). I suspect that many lesbian women answering questions about kin work felt an obligation to do kin work. For instance, Melinda Rodriguez, a twenty-seven-year-old human resources administrator comments when I ask about making phone calls to biolegal relatives:

> Should I answer that the way I am supposed to or should I be more honest about it? [Laughter] I don't call too much. I feel guilty about it. But hey, my brothers don't call my parents. My mother complains to me about that, but not to my brothers. Why should I be judged differently? I guess it's not a very feminine attitude, but I don't care. Well, I do care, but I wish they would have more realistic expectations. You know, I work a lot, as much as my brothers do. So I don't have that much time. Not like my mother, who doesn't work. She has time to call people.

Meanwhile, men engaging in extensive kin work frequently struggle with even more intense concerns about gender identity. Lance Meyter and Mike Tuzin, both in their late twenties, together for three years, and both working in the healthcare field (one in clerical, the other in higher administration), illustrate the dilemma some male couples face in negotiating kin work. Mike does most of the limited amount of kin work for their relationship. Lance feels that because Mike works at a less stressful job and has more time at home, he should do more of the "arranging of the social life." Mike, while accepting Lance's calculus, comments:

> I feel kind of weird about doing this stuff sometimes. I mean, I work, basically, as a secretary because I can't decide what to do with my life. That's already kind of embarrassing and hard on my self-esteem. I like to do a lot of social-type stuff, like talking to our friends, and arranging for things, but you know, it's hard. I was talking to my mother recently, and she wanted to know what we were doing that weekend and I told her everything I had planned and she said: "My, aren't you the little housewife." She was just joshing me, but I sort of, I wanted to puke. I mean, I think it's important to do this stuff, but it's kind of embarrassing, you know? *I do go to the gym quite a bit, so I guess that sort of makes up for it* (emphasis added).

Here we see the potential for the stigmatization of men who do these activities. Mike, in attempting to manage both a feminine-defined occupation and responsibility for kin work (among other forms of domestic work), turns to the realm of athletics "to make up for it." Many gay-male families must manage the threatening character of domestic work (including kin work) to male gender identity. Let it suffice to say that there are many ways to resolve this issue, including constructing myths, using rhetorical strategies that hide the true division of domestic labor, and, for a few, simply violating conventional expectations. . . .

Ethnic and racial distinctions and lesbigay kin work. The influence of ethnic and racial identity upon kin work eludes easy analysis. The confluence of class and race in American culture often conceals distinctions between race and class (Steinberg 1989). This study captures the diversity of lesbigay families in terms of ethnic/racial identity, with over 40 percent of the respondents identifying themselves as Latino-, African-, or Asian-American. However, comparisons are limited by the fact that many of these same respondents are middle class. I know from my attempts to identify lower middle-class and working-class respondents within these groups and among Euro-Americans that lesbigays with fewer economic resources are far more hesitant to participate in this kind of research due to concerns about exposure of sexual identity. That said, let me turn to some discussion of the possible influence of ethnic/racial identity upon the extent and character of kin work.

On the one hand, because most of these families' household earnings, education and occupational identities place them in the middle class, they exhibit kin work patterns similar to their Euro-American middle-class counterparts. Most live in what Dizard and Gadlin would characterize as "minimal families" (1990). Similar to many middle-class families, and in contrast to more affluent families, these families report fewer close friends, they invite nonbiolegal kin over less often, they send fewer cards, write fewer letters, make fewer visits, make fewer long-distance calls, buy, send and give fewer presents, and organize fewer social occasions. On the other hand, Latino/Asian/African-identified lesbigay families recurrently report more extensive connections to biolegal relatives than do Euro-American families, and further, they more often than not conceive of family in strongly biolegal terms. For instance, they report greater exchange of money and material goods with biolegal relatives. A number of factors help to explain these dynamics.

First, the wide majority of African-, Asian- and Latino-American lesbigays grew up in California. This contrasts markedly with the Euro-Americans, 90 percent of whom grew up elsewhere and relocated to California. This means that, because Asian-, African- and Latino-American biolegal kin live in the area, kin relations become more extensive and more pressing. This dynamic appears more strongly related to geographical proximity than to ethnic/racial distinction. Euro-Americans who grew up in this region also exhibit stronger ties to biolegal kin. However, many lesbigay people of color strongly link conceptions of racial/ethnic identity with conceptions of kinship, something not heard among Euro-Americans. Deborah James, an African-American woman, and her partner, Elsa Harding, also African-American, both speak of their connections to biolegal family as a component of their racial identity. Deborah, who works as a daycare provider, states:

> I think that Anglo-Americans don't value family as much as Black people do. I mean, I know some lesbians who think of each other as their family, but I really don't get that. I mean, I think you gotta love your family, even if they aren't that accepting of you. For us, part of being African-American is keeping your connections to your family and your church and stuff like that.

Barbara Cho, a thirty-eight-year-old Chinese-American woman working as a hotel clerk, holds a similar view: "I think of my family as my relatives. I love Barbara [her partner], but she is not really a part of my relatives. I don't want to say she isn't like family to me, but she's not my family. My mother and father, and my sisters, they are my family."

Although most Asian-, African-, and Latino-American lesbigay families conceive of family in biolegal terms (many respondents use the phrase "blood is thicker than water"), not all share this conception. Ceasar Portes and Andy Yanez, together for seventeen years and living in San Francisco's Mission district, a predominantly Latino neighborhood, exhibit an alternative pattern. Ceasar comes from a large Mexican-American family, most of whom live within a half-day's drive. Andy comes from a somewhat smaller, though equally close, Filipino-American family. Ceasar, diminishing the distinction between biolegal and lesbigay kin, asserts:

> We try to include all of our family, I mean both our gay family and our blood family, who live in San Jose or in Pacifica, in our lives. We also have our religious family, you know, many brothers and sisters in the faith, who are a part of our community. We invite everyone to be here. At first, it was hard. I don't think my blood relatives really understood gay people. But they have really changed. My mother loves all of our gay family now, and so we are all family together.

Andy reports that his family, while less accepting of his sexual identity than Ceasar's family, remains strongly committed to "keeping the family together," and includes Ceasar in family activities. Ceasar says that one of his sisters thinks of Andy as a "padrino," or godfather, to her children and makes an effort to include him in family activities.

Derrick Harding and Andrew Joust, both African-American men, provide another counterexample to the notion that "blood is thicker than water." Derrick mentions two heterosexual couples at their local church whom he considers family. In response to a question as to why he considers them such, he reflects: "Why yes, without a doubt, they care about us. They are like our godparents. They adopted us. We are real close with them. They are our family." His partner, Andrew, comments on the same heterosexual couples: "They took us under their wing when we first got here. I think of them as our family, I don't know what else you would call them." These competing views of the importance of ethnic/racial distinctions upon family that exist among African-, Asian-, and Latino-American lesbigay families point to the influence of factors related to but different from ethnicity that play a role in conceptions and constructions of family life. In the case of Andrew and Derrick, they migrated to the Bay Area and established connections to a church community. Their biolegal relatives remain in the East and far away from their day-to-day lives. Andrew reports that he last spoke with a biolegal relative more than a year ago. What really seems to divide those African-, Asian-, and Latino-American lesbigay families who redefine family in non-biolegal terms from those who do is social class. All of those families who blur the distinctions between biolegal and chosen families possess bachelor's degrees, work in professional careers, and earn higher incomes. Ceasar and Derrick both work as social workers, Andrew works as a secondary education teacher, and Andy works in higher education administration.

Kin Work and the Creation of Family

In its extensiveness, its focused character, and its reflection of genuine bonds of love and affection, kin work contributes much to the creation and sustenance of lesbigay life. The family that results from this kin work is not, as many opponents of lesbigay people would have one believe, a rough approximation of the real thing or a sad substitute for genuine biolegal relations. Nor is it just a group of friends. Far from it. The bonds created within and among these families are far more extensive than what most middle-class Americans would conventionally view as friendship bonds (Rapp 1992). Middle-class Americans infrequently take in their friends and provide them housing, food, and medical care while they are dying. Moreover, any number of the lesbigay families in this study would not dream of sacrificing the lesbigay kin

ties they have created in favor of some biolegally defined entity. Not to mention that many lesbigay families don't have to make that choice because their biolegal kin have not excluded them, and therein they have been able to integrate biolegal and lesbigay kin into a greater whole. Surely, many lesbigay families are struggling to create and sustain kin ties against socioeconomic conditions that deter them, but the effort is paradoxical and often threatening to the broader culture. These families are struggling to create and sustain kin relations with the qualities associated with family ideals in American culture, but not necessarily with the forms most citizens associate with family.

REFERENCES

Badgett, L., and M. King. 1997. Lesbian and gay occupational strategies. In A. Gluckman and B. Reed, eds., *Homo Economics: Capitalism, Community and Lesbian and Gay Life.* New York: Routledge.

Berk, S. Fenstermacher. 1985. *The Gender Factory: The Apportionment of Work in American Households.* New York: Plenum Press.

Blumstein, P., and P. Schwarz. 1983. *American Couples.* New York: Morrow.

Coontz, S. 1992. *The Way We Never Were: American Families and the Nostalgia Trap.* New York: Basic Books.

Curtis, R., and E. Jackson. 1977. *Inequality in American Communities.* New York: Academic Press.

D'Emilio, J. 1983. Capitalism and gay identity. In Ann Snitow, ed., *Powers of Desire: The Politics of Sexuality.* New York: Monthly Press Review.

Di Leonardo, M. 1987. The female world of cards and holidays: Women, families, and the work of kinship. *Signs* 12 (Summer): 440–52.

Dizard, J., and H. Gadlin. 1990. *The Minimal Family.* Amherst: University of Massachusetts Press.

Gerstel, N., and S. Gallagher. 1993. Kinkeeping and distress: Gender, recipients of care, and work-family conflict. *Journal of Marriage and Family* 55 (Aug.): 598–607.

Gerstel, N., and S. Gallagher. 1994. Caring for kith and kin: Gender, employment, and privatization of care. *Social Problems* 41 (4): 519–39.

Harry, J. 1984. *Gay couples.* New York: Praeger.

Hodges, H. 1964. *Social Stratification: Class in America.* Cambridge, Mass.: Schenkman.

Lewin, E. 1993. *Lesbian Mothers: Accounts of Gender in American Culture.* Ithaca, N.Y.: Cornell University Press.

———. 1998. *Recognizing Ourselves: Ceremonies of Lesbian and Gay Commitment.* New York: Columbia University Press.

Matthews, G. 1987. *Just a Housewife: The Rise and Fall of Domesticity in America.* New York: Oxford.

Mohr, R. 1994. *A More Perfect Union: Why Straight America Must Stand Up for Gay Rights.* Boston: Beacon.

Nardi, P. 1992. That's what friends are for: Friends as family in the gay and lesbian community. In K. Plummer, ed., *Modern Homosexualities.* London: Routledge.

Nardi, P., and D. Sherrod. 1994. Friendship in the lives of gay men and lesbians. *Journal of Social and Personal Relationships* 11:185–99.

Newton, E. 1993. *Cherry Grove, Fire Island: Sixty Years in America's First Gay and Lesbian Town.* Boston: Beacon.

Rosenthal, C. 1985. Kinkeeping in the family division of labor. *Journal of Marriage and the Family* 47 (4): 965–74.

Schneider, D. 1984. *A Critique of the Study of Kinship.* Ann Arbor: University of Michigan Press.

Schneider, D., and R. Smith. 1973. *Class Differences and Sex Roles in American Kinship and Family Structure.* Englewood Cliffs, N.J.: Prentice Hall.

Skolnick, A. 1991. *Embattled Paradise: The American Family in an Age of Uncertainty.* New York: Basic Books.

Stacey, J. 1990. *Brave New Families: Stories of Upheaval in the Late Twentieth Century.* New York: Basic Books.

———. 1996. *In the Name of the Family: Rethinking Family Values in the PostModern Age.* Boston: Beacon.

Stack, C. 1974. *All Our Kin: Strategies for Survival in a Black Community.* New York: Harper and Row.

Steinberg, Stephen. 1989. *The Ethnic Myth: Race, Ethnicity, and Class in America.* Boston: Beacon.

U.S. Bureau of the Census. 1991. *Money Income of Households, Families, and Persons in the United States: 1990.* Series P-60, no. 174. Washington, D.C.

Voydanoff, P. 1992. Economic distress and family relations: A review of the eighties. *Journal of Marriage and the Family* 52:1099–1115.

West, C., and D. Zimmerman. 1987. Doing gender. *Gender and Society* I (2): 125–51.

Westkott, M. 1986. *The Feminist Legacy of Karen Horney.* New Haven, Conn.: Yale University Press.

Weston, K. 1990. *Families We Choose: Lesbians, Gays, Kinship.* New York: Columbia University Press.

THINKING ABOUT THE READING

What is "kin work"? Do you agree that kin work is what creates and sustains families? Should two people who consistently love and care for each other and who engage in the day-to-day tasks necessary to maintain a household be considered a family and be eligible for all the benefits that legal families are entitled to? If, as Carrington argues, the family-defining activities that gay and lesbian couples engage in are no different from those that heterosexual couples engage in, why is there such strong public opposition to the legal recognition of gay couples as families? Carrington implies that individuals should have the freedom to define their own living arrangements as a family. Do you agree? Does society have an interest in controlling who can and can't be considered a family?

Coping With Commitment

Dilemmas and Conflicts of Family Life

Kathleen Gerson

(1992)

Since 1950, when the breadwinner-homemaker household accounted for almost two-thirds of all American households, widespread changes have occurred in the structure of American family life. Rising rates of divorce, separation, and cohabitation outside of marriage have created a growing percentage of single-parent and single-adult households. The explosion in the percentage of employed women, and especially employed mothers, has produced a rising tide of dual-earner couples whose patterns of child rearing differ substantially from the 1950s' norm of the stay-at-home mother. . . . The breadwinner-homemaker model of family life has become only one of an array of alternatives that confront men and women as they build (and often change) their lives over the course of an expanded adulthood.

As changes in family structure have become apparent to intellectuals, politicians, and ordinary citizens, a national debate has arisen over their nature and significance. The most widely embraced interpretation of family change is one of alarm and condemnation. Analysts and social critics across the political spectrum routinely blame "the breakdown of the family" for a host of modern social ills, extending from the drug epidemic and increases in violent crime to teenage pregnancy, child abuse and neglect, the decline of educational standards, and even the birth dearth. But a competing and less pessimistic perspective emphasizes the resilience of families, which are adapting rather than disintegrating in the face

of social change, and the resourcefulness of individuals, who are able to build meaningful interpersonal bonds amid the uncertainty and fragility of modern relationships. . . .

Incomplete and unequal social change has created new personal dilemmas over how to balance parental and employment commitments and new social conflicts between those who have developed "traditional" and "nontraditional" resolutions to the intransigent conflicts between family and workplace demands. These dilemmas and conflicts pose the central challenges to which new generations of women, men, and children must respond.

Personal Dilemmas and Family Diversity: The Consequences of Unequal Social Change

Social change in family structure remains inconsistent in two consequential ways. First, some social arrangements have changed significantly, but others have not. Even though an increasing percentage of families depend on the earnings of wives and mothers, women continue to face discrimination at the workplace and still retain responsibility for the lion's share of household labor. Similarly, despite the growth of dual-earner and single-parent households, the structural conflicts between family and work continue to make it difficult for either women or men to combine child rearing with sustained employment commitment. The combination of dramatic change in some social arrangements (for example, women's influx into the labor force) and relatively little change in others (for example, employers' continuing expectation that job responsibilities should take precedence over family needs) has created new forms of gender inequality and new dilemmas for both women and men who confront the dual demands of employment and parenthood.

Second, social change is inconsistent because social groups differ greatly in how and to what degree they have been exposed to change. Not only are the alternatives that women and men face structured differently, but within each gender group, the alternatives vary significantly. A growing group of women, for example, have gained access to highly rewarded professional and managerial careers, but most women remain segregated in relatively ill-rewarded, female-dominated occupations. Similarly, the stagnation of real wages has eroded many men's ability to support wives and children on their paycheck alone, but most men still enjoy significant economic advantages. This variation in opportunities and constraints has, in turn, promoted contrasting orientations toward family change among differently situated groups of women and men.

This chapter draws on two studies of how differently situated groups of women and men are responding to the dilemmas posed by unequal social change. . . . Women and men have developed a range of strategic responses to cope with the contrasting dilemmas they confront. We can compare the "coping strategies" of those who developed a "traditional orientation" with the strategies that grew out of two alternative orientations—an orientation that stresses the avoidance of parental commitments and, finally, an orientation based on seeking a balance between work and family commitments. Since the conflicts and dilemmas inherent in each family pattern vary according to gender, women's and men's strategic responses are analyzed separately.

Women and men confront a different set of opportunities and constraints, but each group must respond to the dilemmas posed by unequal and uneven social change. Their contending resolutions to these family dilemmas shape the terms of political conflict as well as the contours of social change.

Choosing Between Employment and Motherhood

Although most women, including most mothers, now participate in the paid labor force, this apparent similarity masks important differences in women's responses to the conflicts between employment and motherhood. Not only do some mothers continue to stay home to rear children, but many employed women work part time or intermittently and continue to emphasize family over employment commitments.—These "domestically oriented" women stand in contrast to a growing group of "nondomestic" women, who have developed employment ties that rival, and or some surpass, family commitments. Women develop "domestic" or "nondomestic" orientations in response to specific sets of occupational and interpersonal experiences. These contrasting orientations to family life are not only rooted in different social circumstances; they also represent opposing responses to the conflict between motherhood and employment. . . .

All women face an altered social context, but they differ in how and to what extent they have been exposed to structural change. This uneven exposure to new opportunities and constraints has produced contrasting orientations toward employment and motherhood. . . .

Exposure to expanded opportunities outside the home (for example, upward employment mobility) and unanticipated insecurities within it (for example, marital instability or economic squeezes in the household) tends to promote a nondomestic orientation, even among women who once planned for full-time motherhood. Exposure to a more traditional package of opportunities and constraints (such as constricted employment options and stable marriage) tends, in contrast, to promote a domestic orientation even among those who felt ambivalent toward motherhood and domesticity as children. Both orientations reflect contextually sensible, if unexpected and largely unconscious, responses to the structural conflicts between employment and motherhood.

Uneven exposure to structural change, like the partial nature of change, promotes contrasting family orientations among women. Some women remain dependent on a traditional family structure that emphasizes sharp social differences between the sexes along with male economic support for women's mothering. Others increasingly depend on social and economic supports outside the home—which can be guaranteed only if women are accorded the same rights, responsibilities, and privileges as men. Rising marital instability and stagnant male wages have eroded the structural supports for female domesticity, but persistent gender inequality at the workplace and in the home also make domesticity an inviting alternative to those who still face limited options in the paid labor force. In the context of this ambiguous mix of expanded options and new insecurities, the choices of both domestically oriented and work-committed women remain problematic, however personally fulfilling they may be.

Strategies of Domestically Oriented Women

Despite the forces leading other women out of the home, domestically oriented women confront ample reasons to avoid such a fate. Blocked occupational opportunities leave these women poorly positioned to enjoy the benefits of work outside the home. They have concluded that domestic pursuits offer significant advantages over workplace commitment. A homemaker and mother of two declared:

> I never plan to go back [to work]. I'm too spoiled now. I'm my own boss. I have independence; I have control; I have as much freedom as anyone is going to have in our society. No [paid] job can offer me those things.

Since their "freedom" depends on someone else's paycheck, domestically oriented women are willing to accept responsibility for the care of home and children in exchange for male economic support. As this disillusioned ex-schoolteacher and full-time mother of two pointed out, they have little desire to change places with their breadwinning husbands:

> I have met guys who were housepersons, but I can't see any reason [for it]. It would turn it all crazy for me to come home around five thirty, and he'd have to have things ready for me. I think if I thought that [bringing in a paycheck] was my role for the rest of my life, I would hate it. I don't want to be [my husband]; then I would have to go and fight the world. I don't want the pressures that he has to bear— supporting a family, a mortgage, putting in all those hours at the office. Ugh!

Whether or not they work, domestically oriented women put their family commitments first. When employed, they carefully define their work attachments as a discretionary choice that can be curtailed if necessary and that always comes second to their children's needs. A part-time clerk and mother of two defined paid work as a "job," not a career:

> I would never want to get us in a situation where I would *have* to work, because then I would really hate it. I don't work to have a career. Without a career, I can quit a job whenever I want. To have a career, you have to stick with it, and it takes a lot. I'd have to give up a lot of things my kids need, and it's not worth it to me. A job, I don't have to give up anything.

Although relatively insulated from the pushes and pulls that lead other women toward strong labor force attachment, domestically oriented women are nevertheless affected by the social changes taking place around them. The erosion of structural and ideological supports for a traditional arrangement has made their commitment to a family form based on a strict sexual division of labor problematic. The increased fragility of marriage, for example, poses an abiding, if unspoken, threat to domestic women's security. In the context of high divorce rates, homemaking women cannot assume that the relationships they depend on will last. This ex-clerk and mother of a young daughter complained:

> [Having a child] has made me more dependent on my husband. I think he was attracted to me because I was very independent, and now I'm very dependent. I don't know what I would do if things didn't work out between [us] and we had to separate and I had to go to work to support my child. I think I'd be going bananas. It's scary to me.

Even when their marriages are secure, domestically oriented women face other incursions on their social position. The rise of work-commitment among other women has not only provided an alternative to domesticity, it has also eroded the ideological hegemony that homemakers once enjoyed. Domestically oriented women feel unfairly devalued by others, as these ex-clerical workers explained:

> There are times when I have some trouble with my identity; that has to do with being a mother. Because of society, sometimes the recognition or lack of it bothers me.
> People put no value on a housewife. If you have a job, you're interesting. If you don't you're really not very interesting, and sometimes I think people turn you off.

This ex-nurse added that even when economic pressures are weak, the social pressures to seek employment make domesticity a difficult choice:

> I have been feeling a lot of pressure . . . there's a lot of pressure on women now that you should feel like you want to work. Sometimes it's hard to know what you feel, because I really don't feel like I want to [work], but I think I *should* feel like I want to.

The erosion of the structural and ideological supports for domesticity has left domestically oriented women feeling embattled. They are now forced to defend a personal choice and family arrangement that was once considered sacrosanct. For these reasons, domestically oriented women cannot afford to take a neutral stance toward social change, and many have developed ideologies of opposition to other people's choices. Domestically oriented women tend to view employed mothers as either selfish and dangerous to children or overburdened and miserable, as these two homemakers suggested:

> I have a neighbor with young children who works just because she wants to. I get sort of angry . . . I think I resent the unfairness to the child. I don't know how to answer the argument that men can have families and work, but women can't. Maybe it's not fair, but that's the way it is.
> Most of the time all I hear from them is griping, and they're tired, and they're frantic to get everything done. It's a shame. I hate hurrying like that.

They viewed career-committed women as selfish, unattractive, and, at least in the case of childless women, unfulfilled:

> Women can [take on men's jobs], but it's a blood-and-guts type of a thing. Those who make it are witches because they found out what they had to do to get there. [ex-saleswoman planning first child]
> I feel like they're missing out on something. If they're going to make a long-term thing of it

and never have children, I think they're missing something.

Finally, domestically oriented women support men's right and duty to be primary breadwinners. They frown on men who shirk their duties to support women and children. This homemaker and mother of two could not understand why "undependable" men were considered glamorous:

> There's this mystique about the charismatic, not decent and dependable, sort of man. They're movie types. . . . My husband goes to work at eight and comes home at five, and [people] say, "Isn't that boring?" And I say, "No. Not at all," because it gives me time to do what I want.

Although their strategies have unfolded against the tide of social change, domestically oriented women illustrate the forces that not only limit the change but provide a powerful opposition to it. Their personal circumstances give them ample reason to view change as a dangerous threat to their own and their children's well-being, even when it leads in the direction of greater gender equality.

Strategies of Work-Committed Women

Work-committed women lack the option of domesticity, or the desire to opt for it, but they nevertheless face significant obstacles. Persistent wage inequality and occupational sex segregation continue to deny most employed women an equal opportunity to succeed at the workplace. In addition, limited change in the organization of work, especially in male-dominated occupations, combines with the "stalled revolution" in the sexual division of domestic work to make it difficult for employed women to integrate career-commitment with motherhood. Work-committed women have responded in several ways to this predicament. A small

but significant proportion have decided to forgo childbearing altogether, but the majority of work-committed women are attempting to balance child rearing with strong labor force attachment.

Childless women have concluded that childbearing is an unacceptably dangerous choice in a world where marriage is fragile and motherhood threatens to undermine employment prospects. A strong skepticism regarding the viability of marriage led a divorced executive to reject childbearing:

> [Having children] probably would set back my career . . . irretrievably. The real thing that fits in here is my doubts about men and marriage, because if I had real faith that the marriage would go on, and that this would be a family unit and be providing for these children, being set back in my career wouldn't be that big a deal. But I have a tremendous skepticism about the permanency of relationships, which makes me want to say, "Don't give anything up, because you're going to lose something that you're going to need later on, because [the man] won't be there.

Childless women also have considerable skepticism about men's willingness to assume the sacrifices and burdens of parenthood. Since gender equality in parenting seems out of reach, so does motherhood. For this childless physician, even avowedly egalitarian men appeared untrustworthy:

> I would *never* curtail my career goals for a [child] . . . I would not subjugate my career any more than a man would subjugate his career. . . . [And] I don't know anybody who says he wants an egalitarian relationship. Among the married ones with children, everybody says, "Sure, we'll share with children equally." But nobody does.

Given the lack of structural supports for combining career commitment and childbearing, these women are convinced they must choose between the two. They have decided that the continuing obstacles to integrating employment and child rearing leave women facing a curiously "old-fashioned" choice between mutually exclusives alternatives:

> I think you either do one or the other. . . . You could have children and work, but you wouldn't really be a very senior sort of involved person. Although men can be presidents of companies and have children, women can't. [single interior designer]
>
> I just think that [children] are a responsibility, and you have to be willing to devote all your time to them. If you can't do that, I don't think you should have them. I know that's really old-fashioned, but I tend to believe it. [high school-educated secretary]

Most work-committed women, however, do eventually have children. Many hold the beliefs this lawyer voiced:

> I don't think it's fair that [working] women can't have kinds. They make things fuller, more complete. I think it rounds out your life.

Work-committed mothers must create strategies to meet the competing demands of child rearing and employment. However, their strategic choices are severely limited by intransigence in the workplace. This aspiring banker lamented:

> [My bosses] figure that I'm to have my career, and what I do at home is my own business, but it better not interrupt the job. I've been pushed as far forward as I have because I was a maniac and I never went home.

Since most employers continue to penalize workers, regardless of gender, for parental involvement that interferes with the job, employed mothers have had to look elsewhere for relief from the competing demands of employment and child rearing. Three strategies, in particular, offer hope of easing their plight.

First, employed mothers limit their demands by limiting family size. Although the two-child family remains the preferred alternative, the one-child family is gaining acceptance. This upwardly mobile office worker concluded:

> I know one child won't drive me crazy, and two might. I know I couldn't work and have two. . . . I don't think [one child] would affect [my work plans] at all. More than one would. That's one of the reasons I only want one.

Employed mothers must also reevaluate and alter the beliefs about child rearing they inherited from earlier generations, who frowned on working mothers. One work-committed office worker rejected the idea that children suffer when mothers work, despite having been raised by a full-time mother:

> I liked my mother being home, but I think it's okay for a mother to work. As long as she doesn't make her children give things up, and I don't think I'd make my children give anything up by me working.

Finally, work-committed mothers have engaged in a protracted struggle to bring men into the process of parenting. Their male partner's support of their independence gives them leverage to demand sharing, even if it doesn't guarantee that such sharing will be equal. A professor acknowledged:

> [My husband] respects my accomplishments. He wants me to keep doing something I enjoy. He wants me to be fairly independent, and he also wants his own independence . . . as long as he can support himself and half a child.

Some have decided that male parental involvement is a precondition to childbearing, as these upwardly mobile workers explained:

> I want [equal] participation, and without it I don't want children. I want it for the children, for myself. Without two people doing it, I think it would be a burden on one person. It's no

longer a positive experience. [lawyer engaged to be married, in her early thirties]

I think it's going to come to the point that if we're willing to have children, we work things out pretty much [equally] between ourselves. And I think he would rather help out than to not have [children] at all. It's a two-way thing. [office manager in her late twenties]

In rejecting childlessness, most work-committed women have developed strategies to cope with the dual burdens of employment and motherhood. In addition to having smaller families, developing new ideologies about child rearing and mothering, and pressuring men to become involved fathers, work-committed mothers are challenging traditional work and family arrangements based on the assumption of a male worker with a wife at home or, at most, loosely tied to paid employment. Like their domestically oriented counterparts, the need to defend their choices against other people's disapproval encourages them to denigrate different resolutions to the conflict between employment and motherhood. From this perspective, it becomes tempting to define domestically oriented women as:

 . . . kind of mentally underdeveloped and not too interesting. Let's face it, it's kind of boring. I guess I don't consider just having children as doing something.

Inconsistent and unequal social change has promoted differing strategic reactions among women that leave them socially divided and politically opposed. The contours of change, however, also depend on men's reactions to the emerging conflicts and dilemmas of family life.

Choosing Between Privilege and Sharing: Men's Responses to Gender and Family Change

While the transformation in women's lives has garnered the most attention, significant changes have also occurred in men's family patterns. The primary breadwinner who emphasizes economic support and constricted participation in child rearing persists, but this model—like its female counterpart, the homemaker—no longer predominates. Alongside this pattern, several alternatives have gained adherents. An increasing proportion of men have moved away from family commitments—among them single and childless men who have chosen to forgo parenthood and divorced fathers who maintain weak ties to their offspring. Another group of men, however, has become more involved in the nurturing activities of family life. Although these "involved fathers" rarely assume equal responsibility for child rearing, they are nevertheless significantly more involved with their children than are primary breadwinners, past or present. Change in men's lives, while limited and contradictory, is nonetheless part of overall family change.

As with women's choices, men's family patterns reflect uneven exposure to structural change in family and work arrangements. In my research on men's changing patterns of parental involvement, I found that men who established employment stability in highly rewarded but demanding jobs, and who experienced unexpected marital stability with a domestically oriented spouse, were pushed and pulled toward primary breadwinning even when they had originally hoped to avoid such a fate. In contrast, men who experienced employment instability and dissatisfaction with the "rat race" of high-pressure, bureaucratically controlled jobs tended to turn away from primary breadwinning. When these experiences were coupled with instability in heterosexual relationships and dissatisfying experiences with children, many rejected parental involvement altogether—opting instead for personal independence and freedom from children. When declining work commitments were coupled with unexpected pleasure in committed, egalitarian heterosexual relationships and unexpected fulfillment through involvement with children, men tended to become oriented toward involved fatherhood. . . .

Among men (as among women), different experiences and orientations promote contrasting strategies to cope with the tensions between maintaining male privilege and easing traditional male burdens.

Strategies of Primary Breadwinning Men

Just as domestically oriented women interpret the meaning of work through the lens of their family commitments, whether or not they are employed, so primary breadwinning men define their parental involvement in terms of income, whether or not their wives work. First, these men emphasize money, not time, in calculating their contributions to the household. For this surveyor, "good fathering" means being a good provider—that is providing financial support, not participating in child rearing:

> What is a good father? It's really hard to say. I always supported my children, fed them, gave them clothes, a certain amount of love when I had time. There was always the time factor. Maybe giving them money doesn't make you a good father, but not giving it probably makes you a bad father. I guess I could have done maybe a little more with them if financially I wasn't working all the time, but I've never hit my kids. I paid my daughter's tuition. I take them on vacation every year. Am I a good father? Yes, I would say so.

Even when their wives are employed, primary breadwinning men de-value the importance of wives' earnings. They define this income as "extra" and nonessential and thus also define a woman's job as secondary to her domestic responsibilities. Even though his wife worked hard as a waitress, this architect did not believe that she shared the duties of breadwinning:

> She took care of [our son], and I did all the breadwinning. When we got the house, she started working for extra money. She worked weekends, but her job doesn't affect us at all. Financially, my job takes care of everything plus. Her income is gravy, I guess you'd call it.

By defining fatherhood in terms of financial support and wives' income as supplementary and nonessential, primary breadwinners relieve themselves of the responsibility for domestic chores and of a sense of guilt that such an arrangement might generate. A park worker was proud to announce:

> I do nothing with the cooking or cleaning. I do no household, domestic anything. I could, but I won't, because I feel I shouldn't have to. If my wife's not sick, I see no reason why I should do it. I feel my responsibility is to bring home the money and her responsibility is to cook and clean.

And like the domestically oriented women who felt fortunate not to *have* to work, primary breadwinners see their wives as the fortunate recipients of personal freedom and material largesse. The park worker continued:

> My wife's got it made. The cat's got it made, too. I'm very good to my wife. She drives a new car, has great clothes, no responsibilities. She's very happy to be just around the house, do what she wants. She's got her freedom; what more could you want?

Although primary breadwinning men, like domestically oriented women, have been relatively insulated from the social-structural incentives that promote nontraditional choices among others, they, too, are affected by changes in others' lives. Despite stable employment and marriages, these men fear the erosion of the material and ideological supports for male privilege that their fathers could take for granted. As women have fought for equal rights at the workplace and other men have moved away from family patterns that emphasize separate spheres, those who remain committed to the "good provider" ethic feel embattled and threatened. Even the small gains made by women at the workplace are perceived as unfair as the historic labor market advantages of men undergo reconsideration, if not drastic alteration. A plumber and father of five resented the incursions some women are making into his field of expertise:

> Women have it a little easier as far as job-related [matters] is concerned [sic]. The tests are getting easier, classifications are going down [to let women in]. From what I hear in plants with women, they *can't* do the job. This isn't chauvinistic guys talking; this is guys talking in general. We pick up a 250-pound motor, but there's no way a young lady will pick it up unless she's a gorilla, a brute. But when she's got to do the job, two other guys have got to come along to help. I'm not saying women can't handle the job, [but] a woman comes to work for us, and they [the bosses] have got five men covering for her. Usually it's a hardship, but the guys bend over backwards for her. If she can't handle her job, why should she be there?

Similarly, primary breadwinners make a distinction between their situation and that of other men—especially childless, single men who, presumably, do not share their heavy economic responsibilities. They define their interests not just in terms of being a man, but a particular type of man who sacrifices for the good of his family and therefore needs to protect his interests in a hostile, changing world. The park worker explained:

> Being a father is a responsibility. If you don't have a wife, don't have children—you get fired, who cares? When you have someone who's depending on your salary, you protect your interest on the job more. You become more afraid, and you become more practical. You realize you're out in the ocean, and nobody's going to help you. You're on your own, and you grow up real quick and start behaving like an adult.

In response to this perceived need to protect their interests, primary breadwinning men, like domestically oriented women, hold tightly to a set of social and political beliefs that emphasize the natural basis and moral superiority of gender differences and inequalities. Primary breadwinners argue that their own sexual division of labor is both natural and normal, as the plumber maintained:

> As far as bread and butter is concerned, the man should have a little more [of] the responsibility than the woman. I'm not chauvinistic or anything, but it's basic, normal [that] it's a man. There aren't many men where the wife works full-time.
> *Who should take care of the children?*
> Again, you go back to whoever's home and whoever's working. Primary would be the mother. It's natural; it comes natural. In my house, it's my wife. She's doing it all.

If their own choices are viewed as natural and normal, then other patterns appear abnormal, unhealthy, and dangerous. Men who are unable or unwilling to meet the demands of breadwinning are judged to be moral and social failures, as the park worker pointed out.

> The husband may not be able to provide. Just because he's a man, doesn't mean he can provide. There's a lot of losers out there, a lot of guys have a thirty-dollar-an-hour drug habit. How are they going to work? The wife might have to. Considering both people are normal, the breadwinner in my opinion should be the man.

Primary breadwinners hold similar beliefs about nondomestic patterns for women. Along with domestically oriented women, they tend to argue that career and motherhood are mutually exclusive alternatives for women and that responsible mothering requires forgoing a career. With five children and his own wife a homemaker, the plumber had little sympathy for mothers who feel the need for a life outside the home:

> A career is a career; a family is a family. When you have a career, you donate your whole self to your career. If you have a family, you donate yourself to your family. [If a woman] has a career and no children, that's different. If she's a mother, her place should be at home. If she doesn't need the money, she has to have an ulterior motive for going to work. She's either tired of the kids or she's tired of being around the kids. If she's trying to keep her sanity, if she's unhappy at home, then she's got nobody to blame but herself, because she created that.

If a strict sexual division of caretaking and breadwinning is morally correct, it follows that current social changes are dangerous. Primary breadwinners tend to view these changes as hazardous for women as well as for men and children. Like their domestically oriented female counterparts, they argue, according to the park worker, that the decline of inequality threatens the historic protections women have enjoyed:

> The woman should be protected, have a higher place. A mother is the most cherished thing you could be on this earth, and the woman should be respected and cared for. Equality would reduce that. A woman should be put on a pedestal above the man, and equality would put them on the same level. Why would they want to be equal with men who are dying earlier, under stress, who are really in the firing position? They already got it all. Equality for a woman would be the worst thing, because she already has the advantage. Women would lose from equality. Why would they want it? What is the need for it?

Despite their contrasting commitments, primary breadwinning men and domestically oriented women are interdependent in ways that lead their world views and political ideologies to converge. Their outlooks contrast not only with those of nondomestic women, but with those developed by nontraditional men as well.

Alternatives to Primary Breadwinning Among Men

Men who eschew primary breadwinning have concluded that the privileges afforded "good providers" are not worth the price that privilege entails. They view breadwinning responsibilities as burdensome and constricting, but their rejection of breadwinning poses its own dilemmas. The loosening bonds of marriage allow these men greater latitude to avoid parental responsibilities, both economic and social. On the other hand, the increasing number of work-committed women encourages and, indeed, pressures some nontraditional men to become more involved in the noneconomic aspects of family life than was typical of men a generation ago. These two patterns—forgoing parental commitments and becoming involved in caretaking—represent increasingly popular, if quite different, responses to the search for an alternative to traditional masculinity amid a contradictory and ambiguous set of options.

Forgoing Parental Commitments

Like permanently childless women, some men have opted to forgo parental responsibilities. This group includes childless men who do not wish or plan to become fathers and divorced fathers who have significantly curtailed their economic and social ties to their offspring in the wake of marital disruption. These men have come to value autonomy over commitment and to view children as a threat to their freedom of choice. A social service director, for example, was convinced that childlessness opened vocational options he would not have enjoyed as a breadwinning father:

> *What do you think things would be like if you did have kids?*
>
> Vocationally, I would have had to make other choices because the field I'm in just doesn't pay a terrific amount of money, and with children, you have expenses, and you have to look forward to a lot more future planning than I have to do with my current situation. So I've been able to sort of play with my career, and really just have a lot of fun in doing what I do, without having that responsibility.

Permanently childless men have decided that the potential benefits of fatherhood are not worth its risks. A childless psychologist admitted with some discomfort:

> *Does seeing other men with young children bring out any response in you?*
>
> Relief! [laughs] I don't just see the good parts; I see it all. I see the shit they have to wade through literally and figuratively, and very often I say to myself, "There but for the grace of God go I." It's a very ambivalent position I have about it.

This ambivalence toward fatherhood is not necessarily confined to childless men. Some divorced fathers also develop a relatively weak emotional and social attachment to their children. Whether their reaction is a defense against the pain of loss or an extension of their lack of involvement in child rearing prior to divorce, divorced fathers who become distant from their children tend to discount the importance of parenthood. A truck driver and divorced father of two, who sees his children and pays their child support sporadically, explained:

> *How would you feel if you had never had kids?*
>
> I don't think that would bother me. Being that I do have them, it's okay. I enjoy them when I see them. But if I never had them, I don't think I'd really miss them. I don't think it would be that important if they weren't there.

And even though this divorced dentist spent little time with his school-age daughter, who resided with her mother in another city, he envied his childless counterparts:

> Men who don't have any children just seem to have more time to do the things they want to do and don't have to deal with the trials and tribulations of raising a child.

In contrast to traditional women and men, these men agree with work-committed women that traditional arrangements are neither inherently superior nor more natural family forms. Instead, they argue that primary breadwinning is oppressive to men and harmful to society. Though more vociferous than most, the psychologist, who at age 43 had never married, painted a vivid picture of the personal and social costs these men attach to male breadwinning:

> At this particular period in history, the woman is getting all the sympathy for her desperate position in the home by herself, lonely and isolated, taking care of these kids. I also have sympathy for the guy who has to be out getting his ass kicked by industrial tyrants and corporate assholes and the whole competitive complex. I think it's a tough life, and very often the man is tremendously underestimated, underrated.

Another confirmed bachelor, a childless free-lance writer, equated the woes of materialism with the "trap" of primary breadwinning:

> I just see these people, and they seem so closed and so materialistic, and it makes me sad for them. Because all this free spirit seems to go down the drain and they're trapped. I wrote a song called "When You're My Age, You'll Be Selling Insurance." It makes me happy that I managed to avoid it, that I haven't been trapped by that.

Although permanently childless men and uninvolved fathers have rejected the "good provider" ethos, they are less certain about what to put in its place. They reject traditional beliefs about gender, but they are also ambivalent about what gender equality should mean.

In contrast to primary breadwinners and domestically oriented women, these men argue that gender differences are smaller, more malleable, and less desirable than traditional views suggest. A single, childless physician argued that perceived gender differences are socially constructed and reflect social evaluations of behavior rather than essential, sex-related characteristics:

> To me, the key to being a man, the same thing as being a woman, is being a good human being. For me, there's nothing that really defines being a man. It doesn't mean you can't cry. I could stay at home and be happy and have a lot of what would be quote feminine characteristics. In some situations, it helps to be macho, but a lot of that just reflects stereotypes. If it's a guy, he's aggressive; if it's a woman, she's a ball buster. One's negative; one's positive. And it can be the same behavior. Sometimes I wish it was a little clearer, but basically you've got to say, "What are you as an individual?"

If gender is socially constructed and thus malleable, it follows that it can be reconstructed in a different way. He believed that a change in the social definitions of gender is desirable:

> I look at the grief and anxiety my father had by being the sole provider. So if being a man is being the rock and support of your family, let's change that definition of being a man. Because that doesn't look very good to me.

Although men who have opted for freedom from parental commitments argue that gender differences are neither natural nor necessarily desirable, they remain ambivalent about what gender does or should mean. They believe that gender equality is a desirable goal, but equality defined in a specific and limited way. They emphasize women's equal responsibilities in the context of equal rights. For these men, equality means exactly what domestically oriented women fear it will mean—that women should relinquish the economic and legal "protections" that have accompanied their second-class status. As the divorced truck driver, quoted earlier, argued:

> [If] women want equal rights, let them pay child support, alimony. Let them get drafted. You want to be equal, you do everything equal not just certain things. They got girls now in the sanitation department. God bless them if that's what [they] want to do, but when it comes down to it, you've got to pick up that pail and dump it in the truck. I'm not going to go over and help you. You want the job, you do what I do and that's it.

Similarly, these men support women's economic self-sufficiency, for their own ability to remain autonomous is closely linked to women's independence. A systems analyst who had never married declared:

> I'm not really big on women who stay at home and just raise kids. I think everybody should be a fully functioning, self-supporting adult, and certainly economically that's necessity now. I believe, in terms of women's issues, that if they prepared themselves for the idea that they have to assume their financial burdens and responsibilities, they won't have to be emotional hostages to toxic relationships. And men won't either.

This vision of economic and social equality does not, however, easily extend to the domestic sphere. Because these men place a high value on their freedom, they resist applying the principle of equality to child rearing. Indeed, the paradox of espousing the equal right to be free while resisting the equal responsibility for parenthood leads them to avoid parental commitments. The systems analyst feared he would be drawn into what he deemed the least attractive aspects of parenting:

> [If I had a child,] I could see that I would want to take a role in playing with the child, overseeing its training and schooling, providing that type of thing. I don't really see me wanting to do a lot in the way of getting up in the middle of the night, formulas, changing diapers. I'm not at all into that.

And so, these men are able to resolve the dilemma between their support of some aspects of gender equality and their resistance to its more threatening implications only by forgoing both the burdens and the joys of raising a child.

Caretaking Fathers

A more equal sharing of both earning income and rearing children provides another alternative to primary breadwinning. While complete equality remains rare even among dual-earner couples, male participation in caretaking is nevertheless on the rise. Men who are married to work-committed women and divorced fathers who have retained either joint or sole custody of their children are particularly likely to participate in child rearing. In contrast to childless men, these men have placed family at the center of their lives. In contrast to primary breadwinners, they value spending time with their families as much as contributing money to them. A utility worker with a young daughter and a wife employed as a marketing manager insisted:

> For me, being with my family is the major, the ultimate in my life—to be with them and share things with them. Money is secondary, but time with them is the important thing in life. That's why I put up with this job—because I can get home early. To me, spending time with

[my daughter] makes up for it. I'm home at 3:40 and spend a lot of time with her, just like the long days when she was young and I was on unemployment.

Some involved fathers view the time spent in child care not as simply helping out, but as an incomparably pleasurable activity and an essential component of good parenting. This thirty-seven-year-old construction worker chose to work the night shift so that he could spend his days with his newborn daughter while his wife pursued a dancing career:

> I take care of [my daughter] during the morning and the day. [My wife] takes care [of her] in the evenings. I work from three to eleven P.M. and wake up with the morning ahead of me, and that's important with a little one. Even if I'm pretty tired when I get up, all I have to do is look at that little face, and I feel good. It's not just a case of doing extra things. I'm not doing extra things. This is what has to be done when you have a baby. . . . You learn so much too. It's a thrill to watch the various senses start to come into play. She'll make a gurgling noise that's close to a vowel sound or an actual syllable, and I'll repeat it. I love the communication. The baby smiles more around me than she does around [her mother].

Unlike primary breadwinners or childless men, these "involved fathers" do not draw distinct boundaries between the tasks of mothers and fathers. The time constraints on their wives combine with their own need and preference for economic sharing to promote financial and social interdependence. Neither breadwinning nor nurturing is defined as one person's domain. As the utility worker pointed out:

> It's not like, "Give me your money, and I hold it; or you take my money and hold it." We put it in one pot and take care of whatever we need. . . . We pull the same weight. . . . As far as time and being around the house is concerned, I can stay home more than [my wife] can stay

home. I come home in the afternoon, and I'm here with [my daughter] after school. [My wife] can come home at night to be with her. She likes her job, and she likes the sharing. She's got both worlds. So it has worked out good.

Like employed mothers, involved fathers must juggle the dual demands of employment and parenthood. While men do not generally jeopardize their chances for workplace success by becoming fathers, those men who wish to spend time with their children must trade off between work and family in much the same kinds of ways that employed mothers do. A bank vice-president, married to a woman with a career in public relations, began to relax his obsessive work habits when his daughter was born:

They changed immediately, which is exactly what I expected would happen, and I've never really gone back to my old habits of working all the time. I still work long days in the office, but I get home every night to relieve the babysitter by six. I hardly ever work on weekends, and I don't work at home. So, yes, my habits have changed.

These involved fathers come closest to embracing the "interdependent" vision of gender equality upheld by work-committed mothers. They see moral and practical advantages to shared caretaking. According to the construction worker quoted earlier, domestic as well as workplace equality is not only the most practical response to changed economic conditions but also the best way to avoid the resentment and conflict that too often occur between husbands and wives:

With the baby, we do everything even-steven. What other way can you go nowadays, the whole economy being what it is? But that's also the way it should be. Even if I had the money to take of things [myself], [my wife] has a calling, a vocation, that she needs to fulfill and I

want her to fulfill. We're in this together; we both want to be an influence on the child. The next logical step is for both of us to spend time with her. . . . I feel there won't be any of this women-against-men in our marriage.

If work-committed women face numerous obstacles in their search for ways to combine career and motherhood, then nurturing fathers also face deeply rooted structural barriers to full equality in parenting. Even when the desire to participate in parenting is strong, these men encounter significant constraints on implementing their preferences. Role reversal, for example, is rarely a realistic option, since men's wages remain essential to the survival of the vast majority of households and few couples are comfortable with an arrangement in which a woman supports a man. The utility worker found being a "househusband" unacceptable, despite his preference for not working:

Is there an ideal job for you?
Staying home. But, it's just not possible. I couldn't just quit and say, "You work, and I'll stay home." But if we were put into the situation where we didn't have to work, I could tell her we could both quit. When I hit the Lotto . . . but right now, I'm stuck.

Were it not for the economic and psychological need to earn a steady income through paid employment, these men might be far more involved in child rearing than is currently possible. Yet, as the supports for homemaking mothers erode, supports for homemaking fathers have not arisen to offset the growing imbalance between children's needs and families' resources. Like domestically oriented women, a rehabilitation counselor defined paid work in terms of a "job," not a "career." Unlike such women, however, he lacked the option to trade his paid but tiresome job for the more personally fulfilling work of parenting:

I don't like to work. I work because I need the money, and I want to give my family the best I could [*sic*], but work's not that important to me. I'm not the type that has career aspirations and [is] very goal-oriented. To tell you the truth, if I won the lottery, and I didn't have to work, I wouldn't. But I would volunteer. I would work in a nursery school. I would do a lot more volunteer work with my daughter's school. I would love to go on trips that the mothers who don't work get a chance go to on. I would like to be more active in the PTA, get my hands into a lot of different volunteer organizations. I would *love* that. But I can't.

In sum, while women grapple with the choice between motherhood and committed employment, men are generally denied such a choice. Even when a man wishes to be an involved father, rarely is he able to trade full-time employment for parental involvement. The primary breadwinning surveyor noted, with some envy, that although women remain disadvantaged, many still retain the option not to work—an option few men enjoy:

> Women can have the best of both worlds, whereas men can only have one choice. A woman has a choice of which way she wants to go. If she wants to be a successful lawyer, she has that choice. If she wants to stay home, she also has that choice most of the time. Women have doors opened for them and their meals paid for. They have the best of both worlds; men are just stuck with one.

Structural and ideological barriers to men's participation in child rearing inhibit the prospects for genuine equality in parental and employment options. Limits on men's options constrain even the most feminist men's ability and willingness to embrace genuine symmetry in gender relations. The truncated range of choices available to men restricts the options open to women as well.

Beyond the Debate on the Family

Social change in family arrangements has expanded the range of options adult women and men encounter, but the inconsistent nature of change has also created new personal dilemmas, more complex forms of gender inequality, and a growing social and ideological cleavage between more traditional family forms and the emerging alternatives. Since people have different exposure to changes in the structure of marriage, the economy, and the workplace, they have developed contrasting responses. Some have developed new patterns of family life that emphasize either greater freedom from family commitments (for example, childless women and men and uninvolved divorced fathers) or more equal sharing of breadwinning responsibilities (for example, work-committed women and involved fathers). Others have endeavored to re-create a more traditional model of gender exchange in spite of the social forces promoting change (for example, women who are domestically oriented and men who are primary breadwinners). The growth of alternative patterns of family life amid the persistence of more traditional forms has not produced a new consensus to replace the old, but rather an increasing competition among a diverse range of family types. This range cuts across gender, as different groups of women and of men find themselves in opposing positions. The complex landscape of emerging family patterns defies generalizations about either the decline or persistence of American families. Instead, men and women are developing multiple "family strategies" and contradictory directions of change to cope with the contrasting dilemmas they confront.

If the uneven and inconsistent nature of change has produced social division and political conflict in the short run, then the long-run fate of American family life depends on finding genuine resolutions to the dilemmas and conflicts that make all family choices problematic. Such an approach would move beyond a "zero-sum" politics of the family to acceptance of and support for diversity in family life; it would reduce the barriers to integrating work and family for employed parents of either sex; and it would promote gender equality in rights, responsibilities, and options regarding parenting and employment. The conflicts and dilemmas spawned by uneven social change can only be resolved by striving to make change itself more equal and consistent. . . .

In this context, the central political challenge should not be defined as how to halt the so-called decline of the family. Instead, we need to find a way to transcend the conflicts among the emerging array of "family groups." Surely, the first step is to abandon the search for one, and only one, correct family form in favor of addressing the full range of dilemmas and needs spawned by inevitable but unequal change. Only then will citizens and policymakers be able to forge a humane and just set of opportunities for all parents and their children.

THINKING ABOUT THE READING

Make a list of the factors that Gerson offers to explain the different choices people make about work and family. According to Gerson, do people usually end up taking the family role they planned, or do their lives shift as they cope with unexpected choices? Discuss the relationship between "family values" and economic structure. In your estimation, who benefits most from a traditional family arrangement? What kind of arrangement do you think would be most beneficial to all family members? What kind of employment and economic situation would support this arrangement? Do you think the current structure of the labor force in the United States reflects the realistic lives of most families? Explore some of the different arrangements in other countries. Do these differing arrangements suggest anything about the connection between cultural ideologies and law and economics?

Love and Gold

Arlie Russell Hochschild

(2004)

Whether they know it or not, Clinton and Princela Bautista, two children growing up in a small town in the Philippines apart from their two migrant parents, are the recipients of an international pledge. It says that a child "should grow up in a family environment, in an atmosphere of happiness, love, and understanding," and "not be separated from his or her parents against their will ..." Part of Article 9 of the United Nations Declaration on the Rights of the Child (1959), these words stand now as a fairy-tale ideal, the promise of a shield between children and the costs of globalization.

At the moment this shield is not protecting the Bautista family from those human costs. In the basement bedroom of her employer's home in Washington, D.C., Rowena Bautista keeps four pictures on her dresser: two of her own children, back in Camiling, a Philippine farming village, and two of her children she has cared for as a nanny in the United States. The pictures of her own children, Clinton and Princela, are from five years ago. As she recently told *Wall Street Journal* reporter Robert Frank, the recent photos "remind me how much I've missed." She has missed the last two Christmases, and on her last visit home, her son Clinton, now eight, refused to touch his mother. "Why," he asked, "did you come back?"

The daughter of a teacher and an engineer, Rowena Bautista worked three years toward an engineering degree before she quit and went abroad for work and adventure. A few years later, during her travels, she fell in love with a Ghanaian construction worker, had two children with him, and returned to the Philippines with them. Unable to find a job in the Philippines, the father of her children went to Korea in search of work and, over time, he faded from his children's lives.

Rowena again traveled north, joining the growing ranks of Third World mothers who work abroad for long periods of time because they cannot make ends meet at home. She left her children with her mother, hired a nanny to help out at home, and flew to Washington, D.C., where she took a job as a nanny for the same pay that a small-town doctor would make in the Philippines. Of the 792,000 legal household workers in the United States, 40 percent were born abroad, like Rowena. Of Filipino migrants, 70 percents, like Rowena, are women.

Rowena calls Noa, the American child she tends, "my baby." One of Noa's first words was "Ena," short for Rowena. And Noa has started babbling in Tagalog, the language Rowena spoke in the Philippines. Rowena lifts Noa from her crib mornings at 7:00 A.M., takes her to the library, pushes her on the swing at the playground, and curls up with her for naps. As Rowena explained to Frank, "I give Noa what I can't give to my children." In turn, the American child gives Rowena what she doesn't get at home. As Rowena puts it, "She makes me feel like a mother."

Rowena's own children live in a four-bedroom house with her parents and twelve other family members—eight of them children, some of whom also have mothers who work abroad. The central figure in the children's lives—the person they call "Mama"—is Grandma, Rowena's mother. But Grandma works surprisingly long hours as a teacher—from 7:00 A.M. to 9:00 P.M. As Rowena tells her story to Frank, she says little about her father, the children's grandfather (men are discouraged from participating actively in child rearing in the Philippines). And Rowena's father is not much involved with his grandchildren. So, she has hired Anna de la Cruz, who arrives daily at 8:00 A.M. to cook, clean, and care for the children. Meanwhile, Anna de la Cruz leaves her teenage son in the care of her eighty-year-old mother-in-law.

Rowena's life reflects an important and growing global trend: the importation of care and love from poor countries to rich ones. For some time now, promising and highly trained professionals have been moving from ill-equipped hospitals, impoverished schools, antiquated banks, and other beleaguered workplaces of the Third World to better opportunities and higher pay in the First World. As rich nations become richer and poor nations become poorer, this one-way flow of talent and training continuously widens the gap between the two. But in addition to this brain drain, there is now a parallel but more hidden and wrenching trend, as women who normally care for the young, the old, and the sick in their own poor countries move to care for the young, the old, and the sick in rich countries, whether as maids and nannies or as day-care and nursing-home aides. It's a care drain.

The movement of care workers from south to north is not altogether new. What is unprecedented, however, is the scope and speed of women's migration to these jobs.

Many factors contribute to the growing feminization of migration. One is the growing split between the global rich and poor. . . .

[For example] domestic workers [who] migrated from the Philippines to the United States and Italy [in the 1990s] had averaged $176 a month, often as teachers, nurses, and administrative and clerical workers. But by doing less skilled—though no less difficult—work as nannies, maids, and care-service workers, they can earn $200 a month in Singapore, $410 a month in Hong Kong, $700 a month in Italy, or $1,400 a month in Los Angeles. To take one example, as a fifth-grade dropout in Colombo, Sri Lanka, a woman could earn $30 a month plus room and board as a housemaid, or she could earn $30 a month as a salesgirl in a shop, without food or lodging. But as a nanny in Athens she could earn $500 a month, plus room and board.

The remittances these women and send home provide food and shelter for their families and often a nest egg with which to start a small business. Of the $750 Rowena Bautista earns each month in the United States, she mails $400 home for her children's food, clothes, and schooling, and $50 to Anna de la Cruz, who shares some of that with her mother-in-law and her children. As Rowena's story demonstrates, one way to respond to the gap between rich and poor countries is to close it privately—by moving to a better paying job. . . .

The International Organization for Migration estimates that 120 million people moved from one country to another, legally or illegally, in 1994. Of this group, about 2 percent of the world's population, 15 to 23 million are refugees and asylum seekers. Of the rest, some move to join family members who have previously migrated. But most move to find work.

As a number of studies show, most migration takes place through personal contact with networks of migrants composed of relatives and friends and relatives and friends of relatives and friends. One migrant inducts another. Whole networks and neighborhoods leave to work abroad, bringing back stories, money, know-how, and contacts. Just as men form networks along which information about jobs are passed, so one domestic worker in New York, Dubai, or Paris passes on information to female relatives or friends about how to arrange papers, travel, find a job, and settle. Today, half of all the world's migrants are women. . . .

The trends outlined above—global polarization, increasing contact, and the establishment of transcontinental female networks—have caused more women to migrate. They have also changed women's motives for migrating. Fewer women move for "family reunification" and more move in search of work. And when they find work, it is often within the growing "care sector," which, according to the economist Nancy Folbre, currently encompasses 20 percent of all American jobs.

A good number of the women who migrate to fill these positions seem to be single mothers. After all, about a fifth of the world's households are headed by women: 24 percent in the industrial world, 19 percent in Africa, 18 percent in Latin America and the Caribbean, and 13 percent in Asia and the Pacific. . . .

Many if not most women migrants have children. The average age of women migrants into the United States is twenty-nine, and most come from countries, such as the Philippines and Sri Lanka, where female identity centers on motherhood, and where the birth rate is high. Often migrants, especially the undocumented ones, cannot bring their children with them. Most mothers try to leave their children in the care of grandmothers, aunts, and fathers, in roughly that order. An orphanage is a last resort. A number of nannies working in rich countries hire nannies to care for their own children back home either as solo caretakers or as aides to the female relatives left in charge back home. Carmen Ronquillo, for example, migrated from the Philippines to Rome to work as a maid for an architect and single mother of two. She left behind her husband, two teenagers—and a maid.

Whatever arrangements these mothers make for their children, however, most feel the separation acutely, expressing guilt and remorse to the researchers who interview them. Says one migrant mother who left her two-month-old baby in the care of a relative. "The first two years I felt like I was going crazy. You have to believe me when I say that it was like I was having intense psychological problems. I would catch myself gazing at nothing, thinking about my child." Recounted another migrant nanny through tears, "When I saw my children again, I thought, 'Oh children do grow up even without their mother.' I left my youngest when she was only five years old. She was already nine when I saw her again, but she still wanted me to carry her."

Many more migrant female workers than migrant male workers stay in their adopted countries—in fact, most do. In staying, these mothers remain separated from their children, a choice freighted, for many, with a terrible sadness. Some migrant nannies, isolated in their employers' homes and faced with what is often depressing work, find solace in lavishing their affluent charges with the love and care they wish they could provide their own children. In an interview with Rhacel Parreñas, Vicky Diaz, a college-educated school teacher who left behind five children in the Philippines, said, "the only thing you can do is to give all your love to the child [in your care]. In my absence from my children, the most I could do with my situation was to give all my love to that child." Without intending it, she has taken part in a global heart transplant.

As much as these mothers suffer, their children suffer more. And there are a lot of them. An estimated 30 percent of Filipino children—some eight million—live in households where at least one parent has gone overseas. These children have counterparts in Africa, India, Sri Lanka, Latin America, and the former Soviet Union. How are these children doing? Not very well, according to a survey Manila's Scalabrini Migration Center conducted with more than seven hundred children in 1996. Compared to their classmates, the children of migrant workers more frequently fell ill; they were more likely to express anger, confusion, and apathy; and they performed particularly poorly in school. Other studies of this population show a rise in delinquency and child suicide. When such children were asked whether they would also migrate when they grew up, leaving their own children in the care of others, they all said no.

Faced with these facts, one senses some sort of injustice at work, linking the emotional deprivation of these children with the surfeit of affection their First World counterparts enjoy. In her study of native-born women of color who do domestic work, Sau-Ling Wong argues that the time and energy these workers devote to the children of their employers is diverted from their own children. But time and energy are not all that's involved; so, too, is love. In this sense, we can speak about love as an unfairly distributed resource—extracted from one place and enjoyed somewhere else.

Is love really a "resource" to which a child has a right? Certainly the United Nations Declaration on the Rights of the Child asserts all children's right to an "atmosphere of happiness, love, and understanding." Yet in some ways, this claim is hard to make. The more we love and are loved, the more deeply we can love. Love is not fixed in the same way that most material resources are fixed. Put another way, if love is a resource, it's a *renewable* resource; it creates more of itself. And yet Rowena Bautista can't be in two places at once. Her day has only so many hours. It may also be true that the more love she gives to Noa, the

less she gives to her own three children back in the Philippines. Noa in the First World gets more love, and Clinton and Princela in the Third World get less. In this sense, love does appear scarce and limited, like a mineral extracted from the earth.

Perhaps, then, feelings *are* distributable resources, but they behave somewhat differently from either scarce or renewable material resources. According to Freud, we don't "withdraw" and "invest" feeling but rather *displace* or redirect it. The process is an unconscious one, whereby we don't actually give up a feeling of, say, love or hate, so much as we find a new object for it—in the case of sexual feeling, a more appropriate object than the original one, whom Freud presumed to be our opposite-sex parent. While Freud applied the idea of displacement mainly to relationships within the nuclear family, it seems only a small stretch to apply it to relationships like Rowena's to Noa. As Rowena told Frank, the *Wall Street Journal* reporter, "I give Noa what I can't give my children."

Understandably, First World parents welcome and even invite nannies to redirect their love in this manner. The way some employers describe it, a nanny's love of her employer's child is a natural product of her more loving Third World culture, with its warm family ties, strong community life, and long tradition of patient maternal love of children. In hiring a nanny, many such employers implicitly hope to import a poor country's "native culture," thereby replenishing their own rich country's depleted culture of care. They import the benefits of Third World "family values." Says the director of a coop nursery in the San Francisco Bay Area, "This may be odd to say, but the teacher's aides we hire from Mexico and Guatemala know how to love a child better than the middle-class white parents. They are more relaxed, patient, and joyful. They enjoy the kids more. These professional parents are pressured for time and anxious to develop their kids' talents. I tell the parents that they can really learn how to love from the Latinas and the Filipinas."

When asked why Anglo mothers should relate to children so differently than do Filipina teacher's aides, the nursery director speculated, "The Filipinas are brought up in a more relaxed, loving environment. They aren't as rich as we are, but they aren't so pressured for time, so materialistic, so anxious. They have a more loving, family-oriented culture." One mother, an American lawyer, expressed a similar view:

> Carmen just enjoys my son. She doesn't worry whether . . . he's learning his letters, or whether he'll get into a good preschool. She just enjoys him. And actually, with anxious busy parents like us, that's really what Thomas needs. I love my son more than anyone in this world. But at this stage Carmen is better for him.

Filipina nannies I have interviewed in California paint a very different picture of the love they share with their First World charges. Theirs is not an import of happy peasant mothering but a love that partly develops on American shores, informed by an American ideology of mother-child bonding and fostered by intense loneliness and longing for their own children. If love is a precious resource, it is not one simply extracted from the Third World and implanted in the First; rather, it owes its very existence to a peculiar cultural alchemy that occurs in the land to which it is imported.

For María Gutierrez, who cares for the eight-month-old baby of two hardworking professionals (a lawyer and a doctor, born in the Philippines but now living in San Jose, California), loneliness and long work hours feed a love for her employers' child. "I love Ana more than my own two children. Yes, more! It's strange, I know. But I have time to be with her. I'm paid. I am lonely here. I work ten hours a

day, with one day off. I don't know any neighbors on the block. And so this child gives me what I need."

Not only that, but she is able to provide her employer's child with a different sort of attention and nurturance than she could deliver to her own children. "I'm more patient," she explains, "more relaxed. I put the child first. My kids, I treated them the way my mother treated me."

I asked her how her mother had treated her and she replied:

> "My mother grew up in a farming family. It was a hard life. My mother wasn't warm to me. She didn't touch me or say 'I love you.' She didn't think she should do that. Before I was born she had lost four babies—two in miscarriage and two died as babies. I think she was afraid to love me as a baby because she thought I might die too. Then she put me to work as a 'little mother' caring for my four younger brothers and sisters. I didn't have time to play."

Fortunately, an older woman who lived next door took an affectionate interest in María, often feeding her and even taking her in overnight when she was sick. María felt closer to this woman's relatives than she did to her biological aunts and cousins. She had been, in some measure, informally adopted—a practice she describes as common in the Philippine countryside and even in some towns during the 1960s and 1970s.

In a sense, María experienced a premodern childhood, marked by high infant mortality, child labor, and an absence of sentimentality, set within a culture of strong family commitment and community support. Reminiscent of fifteenth-century France, as Philippe Ariès describes it in *Centuries of Childhood*, this was a childhood before the romanticization of the child and before the modern middle-class ideology of intensive mothering. Sentiment wasn't the point; commitment was.

María's commitment to her own children, aged twelve and thirteen when she left to work abroad, bears the mark of that upbringing. Through all of their anger and tears, María sends remittances and calls, come hell or high water. The commitment is there. The sentiment, she has to work at. When she calls home now, María says, "I tell my daughter 'I love you.' At first it sounded fake. But after a while it became natural. And now she says it back. It's strange, but I think I learned that it was okay to say that from being in the United States."

María's story points to a paradox. On the one hand, the First World extracts love from the Third World. But what is being extracted is partly produced or "assembled" here: the leisure, the money, the ideology of the child, the intense loneliness and yearning for one's own children. In María's case, a premodern childhood in the Philippines, a postmodern ideology of mothering and childhood in the United States, and the loneliness of migration blend to produce the love she gives to her employers' child. That love is also a product of the nanny's freedom from the time pressure and school anxiety parents feel in a culture that lacks a social safety net—one where both parent and child have to "make it" at work because no state policy, community, or marital tie is reliable enough to sustain them. In that sense, the love María gives as a nanny does not suffer from the disabling effects of the American version of late capitalism.

If all this is true—if, in fact, the nanny's love is something at least partially produced by the conditions under which it is given—is María's love of a First World child really being extracted from her own Third World children? Yes, because her daily presence has been removed, and with it the daily expression of her love. It is, of course, the nanny herself who is doing the extracting. Still, if her children suffer the loss of her affection, she suffers with them. This, indeed, is globalization's pound of flesh.

Curiously, the suffering of migrant women and their children is rarely visible to the First World beneficiaries of nanny love. Noa's mother focuses on her daughter's relationship with Rowena. Ana's mother focuses on her daughter's relationship with María. Rowena loves Noa, María loves Ana. That's all there is to it. The nanny's love is a thing in itself. It is unique, private—fetishized. Marx talked about the fetishization of things, not feelings. When we make a fetish of an object—an SUV, for example—we see that object as independent of its context. We disregard, he would argue, the men who harvested the rubber latex, the assembly-line workers who bolted on the tires, and so on. Just as we mentally isolate our idea of an object from the human scene within which it was made, so, too, we unwittingly separate the love between nanny and child from the global capitalist order of love to which it very much belongs.

The notion of extracting resources from the Third World in order to enrich the First World is hardly new. It harks back to imperialism in its most literal form: the nineteenth-century extraction of gold, ivory, and rubber from the Third World. . . . Today, as love and care become the "new gold," the female part of the story has grown in prominence. In both cases, through the death or displacement of their parents, Third World children pay the price.

Imperialism in its classic form involved the north's plunder of physical resources from the south. Its main protagonists were virtually all men: explorers, kings, missionaries, soldiers, and the local men who were forced at gunpoint to harvest wild rubber latex and the like. . . .

Today's north does not extract love from the south by force: there are no colonial officers in tan helmets, no invading armies, no ships bearing arms sailing off to the colonies. Instead, we see a benign scene of Third World women pushing baby carriages, elder care workers patiently walking, arms linked, with elderly clients on streets or sitting beside them in First World parks.

Today, coercion operates differently. While the sex trade and some domestic service is brutally enforced, in the main the new emotional imperialism does not issue from the barrel of a gun. Women choose to migrate for domestic work. But they choose it because economic pressures all but coerce them to. That yawning gap between rich and poor countries is itself a form of coercion, pushing Third World mothers to seek work in the First for lack of options closer to home. But given the prevailing free market ideology, migration is viewed as a "personal choice." Its consequences are seen as "personal problems." . . .

Some children of migrant mothers in the Philippines, Sri Lanka, Mexico, and elsewhere may be well cared for by loving kin in their communities. We need more data if we are to find out how such children are really doing. But if we discover that they aren't doing very well, how are we to respond? I can think of three possible approaches. First, we might say that all women everywhere should stay home and take care of their own families. The problem with Rowena is not migration but neglect of her traditional role. A second approach might be to deny that a problem exists: the care drain is an inevitable outcome of globalization, which is itself good for the world. A supply of labor has met a demand—what's the problem? If the first approach condemns global migration, the second celebrates it. Neither acknowledges its human costs.

According to a third approach—the one I take—loving, paid child care with reasonable hours is a very good thing. And globalization brings with it new opportunities, such as a nanny's access to good pay. But it also introduces painful new emotional realities for Third World children. We need to embrace the needs of Third World societies, including their children. We need to develop a global sense of ethics to match emerging global economic realities. If we go out to buy a pair of Nike shoes, we want to know how low the wage and how long the hours were for the Third World worker who made them. Likewise, if Rowena is taking care of a two-year-old six thousand miles from her home, we should want to know what is happening to her own children.

If we take this third approach, what should we or others in the Third World do? One obvious course would be to develop the Philippine and other Third World economies to such a degree that their citizens can earn as much money inside their countries as outside them. Then the Rowenas of the world could support their children in jobs they'd find at home. While such an obvious solution would seem ideal—if not easily achieved—Douglas Massey, a specialist in migration, points to some unexpected problems, at least in the short run. In Massey's view, it is not underdevelopment that sends migrants like Rowena off to the First World but development itself. The higher the percentage of women working in local manufacturing, he finds, the greater the chance that any one woman will leave on a first, undocumented trip abroad. Perhaps these women's horizons broaden. Perhaps they meet others who have gone abroad. Perhaps they come to want better jobs and more goods. Whatever the original motive, the more people in one's community migrate, the more likely one is to migrate too.

If development creates migration, and if we favor some form of development, we need to find more humane responses to the migration such development is likely to cause. For those women who migrate in order to flee abusive husbands, one part of the answer would be to create solutions to that problem closer to home—domestic-violence shelters in these women's home countries, for instance. Another might be to find ways to make it easier for migrating nannies to bring their children with them. Or as a last resort, employers could be required to finance a nanny's regular visits home.

A more basic solution, of course, is to raise the value of caring work itself, so that whoever does it gets more rewards for it. Care, in this case, would no longer be such a "pass-on" job. And now here's the rub: the value of the labor of raising a child—always low relative to the value of other kinds of labor—has, under the impact of globalization, sunk lower still. Children matter to their parents immeasurably, of course, but the labor of raising them does not earn much credit in the eyes of the world. When middle-class housewives raised children as an unpaid, full-time role, the work was dignified by its aura of middle-classness. That was the one upside to the otherwise confining cult of middle-class, nineteenth- and early-twentieth-century American womanhood. But when the unpaid work of raising a child became the paid work of child-care workers, its low market value revealed the abidingly low value of caring work generally—and further lowered it.

The low value placed on caring work results neither from an absence of a need for it nor from the simplicity or ease of doing it. Rather, the declining value of child care results from a cultural politics of inequality. It can be compared with the declining value of basic food crops relative to manufactured goods on the international market. Though clearly more necessary to life, crops such as wheat and rice fetch low and declining prices, while manufactured goods are more highly valued. Just as the market price of primary produce keeps the Third World low in the community of nations, so the low market value of care keeps the status of the women who do it—and, ultimately, all women—low.

One excellent way to raise the value of care is to involve fathers in it. If men shared the care of family members worldwide, care would spread laterally instead of being passed down a social class ladder. In Norway, for example, all employed men are eligible for a year's paternity leave at 90 percent pay. Some 80 percent of Norwegian men now take over a month of parental leave. In this way, Norway is a model to the world. For indeed it is men who have for the most part stepped aside from caring work, and it is with them that the "care drain" truly begins.

In all developed societies, women work at paid jobs. According to the International Labor Organization, half of the world's women between ages fifteen and sixty-four do paid work. Between 1960 and 1980, sixty-nine out of eighty-eight countries surveyed showed a growing proportion of women in paid work. Since 1950, the rate of increase has skyrocketed in the United States, while remaining high in Scandinavia and the United Kingdom and moderate in France and Germany. If we want developed societies with women doctors, political leaders, teachers, bus drivers, and computer programmers, we will need qualified people to give loving care to their children. And there is no reason why every society should not enjoy such loving paid child care. It may even be true that Rowena Bautista or María Guttierez are the people to provide it, so long as their own children either come with them or otherwise receive all the care they need. In the end, Article 9 of the United Nations Declaration on the Rights of the Child—which the United States has not yet signed—states an important goal. . . . It says we need to value care as our most precious resource, and to notice where it comes from and ends up. For, these days, the personal is global.

THINKING ABOUT THE READING

Why do women leave their own families to work in other countries? Why is there such great demand for nannies and other care workers in some countries? Discuss the concept of carework as a commodity available for sale on a global market. What other services are available on a global market that used to be considered something one got "for free" from family members? Before such services were hired out, who, traditionally, was expected to provide them? What has changed? Discuss some reasons why women make up so much of the global labor force today. If these trends in global labor continue, what do you think families will look like in the near future?

Constructing Difference

Social Deviance

According to most sociologists, deviance is not an inherent feature or personality trait. Instead, it is a consequence of a definitional process. Like beauty, it is in the eye of the beholder. Deviant labels can impede everyday social life by forming expectations in the minds of others. Some sociologists argue that the definition of deviance is a form of social control exerted by more powerful people and groups over less powerful ones.

At the structural level, the treatment of people defined as deviant is often more a function of *who* they are than of *what* they did. In particular, sex, age, class, ethnic, and racial stereotypes often combine to influence social reactions to individuals who have broken the law. In "Watching the Canary," Lani Guinier and Gerald Torres provide several explanations for the disproportionate number of black and Latino young men in American prisons. They examine the intersection of racial profiling tactics, the war on drugs, and our mass incarceration policies to illustrate why these men are at greater risk for arrest. On the basis of race, these men are already defined as deviant and often expected to be engaged in criminal activity.

Similarly, our perceptions of deviant social problems can also be influenced by the identities of people most closely associated with the behavior in question. Justin Tuggle and Malcolm Holmes examine this issue in their article, "Blowing Smoke." When we think of legal attempts at criminalizing the use of certain substances, we usually assume that the desire to ban such use emerges from the inherent danger of the substance itself. Tuggle and Holmes show that efforts to impose smoking bans are informed not only by medical concerns, but more importantly, by perceptions of smokers. Smokers are commonly depicted as lower-class social misfits whose behavior is unclean and intrusive. A lifestyle associated with the less educated, less affluent, lower occupational strata eventually becomes stigmatized as a public health hazard and targeted for coercive reform.

Sociologists also tell us that behavior commonly attributed to individual personality traits or even physiological processes can be better understood by examining the broader social context within which it takes place. Consider illegal drug use. Why do some people merely experiment with drugs while others become habitual users? Howard Becker addresses this question in "Becoming a Marihuana User." He concludes that those who continue smoking marijuana do so, not because they have become physically dependent on the drug, but because they have "learned" to define the experience and the effects as enjoyable. People "learn" to respond to events and experiences through their interactions with others. They learn how to engage with things (in this case how to actually smoke marijuana to produce effects) and how to recognize experiences (knowing whether you're high). And when they introduce the drug to friends, they pass along this positive information.

Something to Consider as You Read:

In reading and comparing these selections, consider who has the power to define others as deviant. Think about the role of social institutions in establishing definitions of deviance. For example, how does medicine or religion or law participate in describing certain behaviors as abnormal and/or immoral and/or illegal? Does is make a difference which social institution defines certain behaviors as deviant? Why do you think some deviant behaviors fall under the domain of medicine and others fall under the domain of the law? For instance, over time, alcohol use has moved from being an illegal activity to being a medical condition. Who makes the decisions to define certain behaviors not only as deviant, but as deviant within a particular social domain?

Watching the Canary

Lani Guinier and Gerald Torres

(2002)

"To my friends, I look like a black boy. To white people who don't know me I look like a wanna-be punk. To the cops I look like a criminal." Niko, now fourteen years old, is reflecting on the larger implications of his daily journey, trudging alone down Pearl Street, backpack heavy with books, on his way home from school. As his upper lip darkens with the first signs of a moustache, he is still a sweet, sometimes kind, unfailingly polite upper-middle-class black boy. To his mom and dad he looks innocent, even boyish. Yet his race, his gender, and his baggy pants shout out a different, more alarming message to those who do not know him. At thirteen, Niko was aware that many white people crossed the street as he approached. Now at fourteen, he is more worried about how he looks to the police. After all, he is walking while black.

One week after Niko made these comments to his mom, the subject of racial profiling was raised by a group of Cambridge eighth graders who were invited to speak in a seminar at Harvard Law School. Accompanied by their parents, teachers, and the school principal, the students read essays they had written in reaction to a statement of a black Harvard Law School student whose own arrest the year before in New York City had prompted him to write about racial profiling.[1] One student drew upon theories of John Locke to argue that "the same mindset as slavery provokes police officers to control black people today." Another explained a picture he had drawn showing a black police officer hassling a black woman because the officer assumed she was a prostitute. Black cops harass black people too, he said aloud. "It just seems like all the police are angry and have a lot of aggression coming out." A third boy concluded that when the cops see a black person they see "the image of a thug." Proud that he knew the *American Heritage Dictionary*'s definition of a thug—a "cut-throat or ruffian"—he concluded that the cops are not the key to understanding racial profiling. Nor did he blame the white people who routinely crossed the street as he approached. If what these white people see is a thug, "they would normally want to pull their purse away." He blamed the media for this "psychological enslavement," as well as those blacks who allowed themselves to be used to "taint our image."

One boy spoke for fifteen minutes in a detached voice, showing little emotion; but he often strayed from his prepared text to describe in great detail the story of relatives who had been stopped by the police or to editorialize about what he had written. Only after all the students left did the professor discover why the boy had talked so long—and why so many adults had shown up for this impromptu class.

Several of the boys, including the one who had spoken at length, had already had personal encounters with the police. Just the week before, two of the boys had been arrested and had spent six hours locked in separate cells. . . .

Watching the Canary

Rashid and Jonathan (not their real names) are the sons of a lawyer and a transit employee, respectively. "Why don't you arrest *them*?" one of the boys asked the officer, referring to the white kids walking in the same area. "We only have two sets of cuffs," the officer replied. These cops knew whom to take in: the white kids were innocent; the black boys were guilty.

In the words of one of their classmates, black boys like Rashid and Jonathan are viewed as thugs, despite their class status. Aided by the dictionary and the media, our eighth-grade informant says this is racial profiling. Racial profiling, he believes, is a form of "psychological enslavement." . . .

But these black boys are not merely victims of racial profiling. They are canaries. And our political-race project asks people to pay attention to the canary. The canary is a source of information for all who care about the atmosphere in the mines—and a source of motivation for changing the mines to make them safer. The canary serves both a diagnostic and an innovative function. It offers us more than a critique of the way social goods are distributed. What the canary lets us see are the hierarchical arrangements of power and privilege that have naturalized this unequal distribution.

. . . We have urged those committed to progressive social change to watch the canary—and to assure the most vulnerable among us a space to experiment with democratic practice and discover their own power. Even though the canary is in a cage, it continues to have agency and voice. If the miners were watching the canary, they would not wait for it to fall off its perch, legs up. They would notice that it is talking to them. "I can't breathe, but you know what? You are being poisoned too. If you save me, you will save yourself. Why is that mine owner sending all of us down here to be poisoned anyway?" The miners might then realize that they cannot escape this life-threatening

social arrangement without a strategy that disrupts the way things are.

What would we learn if we watched these particular two black boys? First, we would discover that from the moment they were born, each had a 30 percent chance of spending some portion of his life in prison or jail or under the supervision of the criminal justice system. . . . Among black men between the ages of 18 and 30 who drop out of high school, more become incarcerated than either go on to attend college or hold a job.[2] . . .

In the United States, if young men are not tracked to college and they are black or brown, we wait for their boredom, desperation, or sense of uselessness to catch up with them. We wait, in other words, for them to give us an excuse to send them to prison. The criminal justice system has thus become our major instrument of urban social policy.

David Garland explains that imprisonment has ceased to be the incarceration of individual offenders and has instead become "the systematic imprisonment of whole groups of the population"—in this case, young black and Latino males in large urban municipalities. Or as the political scientist Mary Katzenstein observes, "Policies of incarceration in this country are fundamentally about poverty, about race, about addiction, about mental illness, about norms of masculinity and female accommodation among men and women who have been economically, socially, and politically demeaned and denied."[3] . . .

But how does this "race to incarcerate" happen disproportionately to young black and Latino boys? Why is it that increasingly the nation's prisons and jails have become temporary or permanent cages for our canaries? One reason is that white working-class youth enjoy greater opportunities in the labor market than do black and Latino boys, owing in part to lingering prejudice. . . .

A second reason for the disproportionate impact of incarceration on the black and brown communities is the increased discretion given to prosecutors and police officers and the decreased discretion given to judges, whose decisions are exposed to public scrutiny in open court, unlike the deals made by prosecutors and police. Media sensationalism and political manipulation around several high profile cases (notably Willy Horton and Polly Klaas) led to mandatory minimum sentences in many states. Meanwhile, laws such as "three strikes and you're out" channeled unreviewable discretion to prosecutors, who decide which strikes to call and which to ignore. . . .

A third and, according to some commentators, the most important explanation for the disproportionate incarceration of black and Latino young men is the war on drugs. In this federal campaign—one of the most volatile issues in contemporary politics—drug users and dealers are routinely painted as black or Latino, deviant and criminal. This war metaphorically names drugs as the enemy, but it is carried out in practice as a massive incarceration policy focused on black, Latino, and poor white young men. It has also swept increasing numbers of black and Latina women into prison. . . .

Presidents Ronald Reagan and George Bush had a distinct agenda, according to Marc Mauer: "to reduce the powers of the federal government," to "scale back the rights of those accused of crime," and to "diminish privacy rights."[4] Their goal was to shrink one branch of government (support for education and job training), while enlarging another (administration of criminal justice). Mauer concludes that the political and fiscal agendas of both the Reagan and first Bush administrations were quite successful. They reduced the social safety net and government's role in helping the least well off. Their success stemmed, in part, from their willingness to "polarize the debate" on a variety of issues, including drugs and prison.

Racial targeting by police (racial profiling) works in conjunction with the drug war to criminalize black and Latino men. Looking for drug couriers, state highway patrols use a profile, developed ostensibly at the behest of federal drug officials, that suggests black and Latinos are more likely to be carrying drugs. The disproportionate stops of cars driven by blacks or Latinos as well as the street sweeps of pedestrians certainly helps account for some of the racial disparity in sentencing and conviction rates. And because much of the drug activity in the black and Latino communities takes place in public, it is easier to target. . . .

A fourth explanation for the high rates of incarceration of black and brown young men is the economic boon that prison-building has brought to depressed rural areas. Prison construction has become—next to the military—our society's major public works program. And as prison construction has increased, money spent on higher education has declined, in direct proportion. Moreover, federal funds that used to go to economic or job training programs now go exclusively to building prisons. . . .

A fifth explanation is the need for a public enemy after the Cold War. Illegal drugs conveniently fit that role. President Nixon started this effort, calling drugs "public enemy number one." George Bush continued to escalate the rhetoric, declaring that drugs are "the greatest domestic threat facing our nation" and are turning our cities "into battlegrounds." By contrast, the use and abuse of alcohol and prescription drugs, which are legal, rarely result in incarceration. . . .

When drunk drivers do serve jail time, they are typically treated with a one- or two-day sentence for a first offense. For a second offense they may face a mandatory sentence of two to ten days. Compare that with a person arrested and convicted for *possession* of illegal drugs. Typical state penalties for a first-time offender are up to five years in prison and one to ten years for a second offense. . . .

We do not, by any means, claim to have exhaustively researched the criminal justice implications of racial profiling, the war on drugs, or our nation's mass incarceration policies. What we do claim is that canary watchers should pay attention to these issues if they want to understand what is happening in the United States. The cost of these policies is being subsidized by all taxpayers; one immediate result is that government support for other social programs has become an increasingly scarce resource.

NOTES

1. Bryonn Bain, "Walking While Black," *The Village Voice*, April 26, 2000, at 1, 42. Bain and his brother and cousin were arrested, held overnight and then released, with all charges eventually dropped, after the police in New York City, looking for young men who were throwing bottles on the Upper West Side, happened upon Bain et al. as they exited a Bodega. Bain, at the time, had his laptop and law books in his backpack, because he was enroute to the bus station where he intended to catch a bus back to Cambridge. Bain's essay in *The Voice* generated 90,000 responses.

2. Bruce Western and Becky Pettit, "Incarceration and Racial Inequality in Men's Employment," 54 *Industrial and Labor Relations Review* 3 (2000).

3. "Remarks on Women and Leadership: Innovations for Social Change," sponsored by Radcliffe Association, Cambridge, Massachusetts, June 8, 2001. In her talk, Katzenstein cities David Garland. "Introduction: The Meaning of Mass Imprisonment," 3(1) *Punishment and Society* 5–9 (2001).

4. Marc Mauer. (1999) *Race to Incarcerate*, New York: New Press.

THINKING ABOUT THE READING

Make a list of the social factors that Guinier and Torres link to the high incarceration rate of African American and Latino men. Discuss why these factors may affect these men more than white men. Do you think economic opportunity is related to these factors? In other words, are all African American and Latino men equally at risk for incarceration? What other factors do you think might be part of this equation? Groups who oppose the death penalty often argue that it is applied unevenly and discriminates among certain groups of people. Discuss this argument in light of what you have just read. As you think about this, consider each of the phases of the judicial process: processes of arrest, the decision to charge with a crime, availability of legal defense, jury selection, and sentencing guidelines. Who or what is making the decisions in each of these instances? Do you think the different people and agencies involved in each step of the process are all in agreement, or might there be disagreement between say, the police, judges, and lawmakers? How might these relationships affect the likelihood of a defendant being treated "justly"?

Blowing Smoke

Status Politics and the Smoking Ban

Justin L. Tuggle and Malcolm D. Holmes

(1997)

Over the past half century, perceptions of tobacco and its users have changed dramatically. In the 1940s and 1950s, cigarette smoking was socially accepted and commonly presumed to lack deleterious effects (see, e.g., Ram 1941). Survey data from the early 1950s showed that a minority believed cigarette smoking caused lung cancer (Viscusi 1992). By the late 1970s, however, estimates from survey data revealed that more than 90% of the population thought that this link existed (Roper Organization 1978). This and other harms associated with tobacco consumption have provided the impetus for an antismoking crusade that aims to normatively redefine smoking as deviant behavior (Markle and Troyer 1979).

There seems to be little question that tobacco is a damaging psychoactive substance characterized by highly adverse chronic health effects (Steinfeld 1991). In this regard, the social control movement probably makes considerable sense in terms of public policy. At the same time, much as ethnicity and religion played a significant role in the prohibition of alcohol (Gusfield 1963), social status may well play a part in this latest crusade.

Historically, attempts to control psychoactive substances have linked their use to categories of relatively powerless people. Marijuana use was associated with Mexican Americans (Bonnie and Whitebread 1970), cocaine with African Americans (Ashley 1975), opiates with Asians (Ben-Yehuda 1990), and alcohol with immigrant Catholics (Gusfield 1963). During the heyday of cigarette smoking, it was thought that

> Tobacco's the one blessing that nature has left for all humans to enjoy. It can be consumed by both the "haves" and "have nots" as a common leveler, one that brings all humans together from all walks of life regardless of class, race, or creed. (Ram 1941, p. 125)

But in contrast to this earlier view, recent evidence has shown that occupational status (Ferrence 1989; Marcus et al. 1989; Covey et al. 1992), education (Ferrence 1989; Viscusi 1992) and family income (Viscusi 1992) are related negatively to current smoking. Further, the relationships of occupation and education to cigarette smoking have become stronger in later age cohorts (Ferrence 1989). Thus we ask, *is the association of tobacco with lower-status persons a factor in the crusade against smoking in public facilities?* Here we examine that question in a case study of a smoking ban implemented in Shasta County, California.

Status Politics and the Creation of Deviance

Deviance is socially constructed. Complex pluralistic societies have multiple, competing symbolic-moral universes that clash and negotiate (Ben-Yehuda 1990). Deviance is relative, and social morality is continually restructured. Moral, power, and stigma contests are ongoing, with competing symbolic-moral universes striving to legitimize particular lifestyles while making others deviant (Schur 1980; Ben-Yehuda 1990).

The ability to define and construct reality is closely connected to the power structure of society (Gusfield 1963). Inevitably, then, the distribution of deviance is associated with the system of stratification. The higher one's social position, the greater one's moral value (Ben-Yehuda 1990). Differences in lifestyles and moral beliefs are corollaries of social stratification (Gusfield 1963; Zurcher and Kirkpatrick 1976; Luker 1984). Accordingly, even though grounded in the system of stratification, status conflicts need not be instrumental; they may also be symbolic. Social stigma may, for instance, attach to behavior thought indicative of a weak will (Goffman 1963). Such moral anomalies occasion status degradation ceremonies, public denunciations expressing indignation not at a behavior per se, but rather against the individual motivational type that produced it (Garfinkel 1956). The denouncers act as public figures, drawing upon communally shared experience and speaking in the name of ultimate values. In this respect, status degradation involves a reciprocal element: Status conflicts and the resultant condemnation of a behavior characteristic of a particular status category symbolically enhances the status of the abstinent through the degradation of the participatory (Garfinkel 1956; Gusfield 1963).

Deviance creation involves political competition in which moral entrepreneurs originate moral crusades aimed at generating reform (Becker 1963; Schur 1980; Ben-Yehuda 1990). The alleged deficiencies of a specific social group are revealed and reviled by those crusading to define their behavior as deviant. As might be expected, successful moral crusades are generally dominated by those in the upper social strata of society (Becker 1963). Research on the antiabortion (Luker 1984) and antipornography (Zurcher and Kirkpatrick 1976) crusades has shown that activists in

these movements are of lower socioeconomic status than their opponents, helping explain the limited success of efforts to redefine abortion and pornography as deviance.

Moral entrepreneurs' goals may be either assimilative or coercive reform (Gusfield 1963). In the former instance, sympathy to the deviants' plight engenders integrative efforts aimed at lifting the repentant to the superior moral plane allegedly held by those of higher social status. The latter strategy emerges when deviants are viewed as intractably denying the moral and status superiority of the reformers' symbolic-moral universe. Thus, whereas assimilative reform may employ educative strategies, coercive reform turns to law and force for affirmation.

Regardless of aim, the moral entrepreneur cannot succeed alone. Success in establishing a moral crusade is dependent on acquiring broader public support. To that end, the moral entrepreneur must mobilize power, create a perceived threat potential for the moral issue in question, generate public awareness of the issue, propose a clear and acceptable solution to the problem, and overcome resistance to the crusade (Becker 1963; and Ben-Yehuda 1990).

The Status Politics of Cigarette Smoking

The political dynamics underlying the definition of deviant behaviors may be seen clearly in efforts to end smoking in public facilities. Cigarettes were an insignificant product of the tobacco industry until the end of the 19th century, after which they evolved into its staple (U.S. Department of Health and Human Services 1992). Around the turn of the century, 14 states banned cigarette smoking and all but one other regulated sales to and possession by minors (Neuhring and Markle 1974). Yet by its heyday in the 1940s and 1950s, cigarette smoking was almost universally accepted, even considered socially desirable (Neuhring and

Markle 1974; Steinfeld 1991). Per capita cigarette consumption in the United States peaked at approximately 4,300 cigarettes per year in the early 1960s, after which it declined to about 2,800 per year by the early 1990s (U.S. Department of Health and Human Services 1992). The beginning of the marked decline in cigarette consumption corresponded to the publication of the report to the surgeon general on the health risks of smoking (U.S. Department of Health, Education and Welfare 1964). Two decades later, the hazards of passive smoking were being publicized (e.g., U.S. Department of Health and Human Services 1986).

Increasingly, the recognition of the apparent relationship of smoking to health risks has socially demarcated the lifestyles of the smoker and nonsmoker, from widespread acceptance of the habit to polarized symbolic-moral universes. Attitudes about smoking are informed partly by medical issues, but perhaps even more critical are normative considerations (Neuhring and Markle 1974); more people have come to see smoking as socially reprehensible and deviant, and smokers as social misfits (Markle and Troyer 1979). Psychological assessments have attributed an array of negative evaluative characteristics to smokers (Markle and Troyer 1979). Their habit is increasingly thought unclean and intrusive.

Abstinence and bodily purity are the cornerstones of the nonsmoker's purported moral superiority (Feinhandler 1986). At the center of their symbolic-moral universe, then, is the idea that people have the right to breathe clean air in public spaces (Goodin 1989). Smokers, on the other hand, stake their claim to legitimacy in a precept of Anglo-Saxon political culture—the right to do whatever one wants unless it harms others (Berger 1986). Those sympathetic to smoking deny that environmental tobacco smoke poses a significant health hazard to the nonsmoker (Aviado 1986). Yet such arguments have held little sway

in the face of counterclaims from authoritative governmental agencies and high status moral entrepreneurs.

The development of the antismoking movement has targeted a lifestyle particularly characteristic of the working classes (Berger 1986). Not only has there been an overall decline in cigarette smoking, but, as mentioned above, the negative relationships of occupation and education to cigarette smoking have become more pronounced in later age cohorts (Ferrence 1989). Moreover, moral entrepreneurs crusading against smoking are representatives of a relatively powerful "knowledge class," comprising people employed in areas such as education and the therapeutic and counseling agencies (Berger 1986).

Early remedial efforts focused on publicizing the perils of cigarette smokers, reflecting a strategy of assimilative reform (Neuhring and Markle 1974; Markle and Troyer 1979). Even many smokers expressed opposition to cigarettes and a generally repentant attitude. Early educative efforts were thus successful in decreasing cigarette consumption, despite resistance from the tobacco industry. Then, recognition of the adverse effects of smoking on nonusers helped precipitate a turn to coercive reform measures during the mid 1970s (Markle and Troyer 1979). Rather than a repentant friend in need of help, a new definition of the smoker as enemy emerged. Legal abolition of smoking in public facilities became one focus of social control efforts, and smoking bans in public spaces have been widely adopted in recent years (Markle and Troyer 1979; Goodin 1989).

The success of the antismoking crusade has been grounded in moral entrepreneurs' proficiency at mobilizing power, a mobilization made possible by highly visible governmental campaigns, the widely publicized health risks of smoking, and the proposal of workable and generally acceptable policies to ameliorate the problem. The success of this moral crusade has been further facilitated by the association of deviant characteristics with those in lower social strata, whose stigmatization reinforces existing relations of power and prestige. Despite the formidable resources and staunch opposition of the tobacco industry, the tide of public opinion and policy continues to move toward an antismoking stance.

Research Problem

The study presented below is an exploratory examination of the link between social status and support for a smoking ban in public facilities. Based on theorizing about status politics, as well as evidence about patterns of cigarette use, it was predicted that supporters of the smoking ban would be of higher status than those who opposed it. Further, it was anticipated that supporters of the ban would be more likely to make negative normative claims denouncing the allegedly deviant qualities of smoking, symbolically enhancing their own status while lowering that of their opponents.

The site of this research was Shasta County, California. The population of Shasta County is 147,036, of whom 66,462 reside in its only city, Redding (U.S. Bureau of the Census 1990). This county became the setting for the implementation of a hotly contested ban on smoking in public buildings.

In 1988, California voters passed Proposition 99, increasing cigarette taxes by 25 cents per pack. The purpose of the tax was to fund smoking prevention and treatment programs. Toward that end, Shasta County created the Shasta County Tobacco Education Program. The director of the program formed a coalition with officials of the Shasta County chapters of the American Cancer Society and American Lung Association to propose a smoking ban in all public buildings. The three groups formed an organization to promote that cause, Smoke-Free Air For Everyone (SAFE). Unlike other bans then in effect in California, the proposed ban included restaurants and bars, because its

proponents considered these to be places in which people encountered significant amounts of secondhand smoke. They procured sufficient signatures on a petition to place the measure on the county's general ballot in November 1992.

The referendum passed with a 56% majority in an election that saw an 82% turnout. Subsequently, the Shasta County Hospitality and Business Alliance, an antiban coalition, obtained sufficient signatures to force a special election to annul the smoking ban. The special election was held in April 1993. Although the turnout was much lower (48%), again a sizable majority (58.4%) supported the ban. The ordinance went into effect on July 1, 1993.

Analytic Strategy

. . . [D]ata were analyzed in our effort to ascertain the moral and status conflicts underlying the Shasta County smoking ban . . . [based on] interviews with five leading moral entrepreneurs and five prominent status quo defenders.[1] These individuals were selected through a snowball sample, with the original respondents identified through interviews with business owners or political advertisements in the local mass media. The selected respondents repeatedly surfaced as the leading figures in their respective coalitions. Semi-structured interviews were conducted to determine the reasons underlying their involvement. These data were critical to understanding how the proposed ban was framed by small groups of influential proponents and opponents; it was expected that their concerns would be reflected in the larger public debate about the ban.

Findings

Moral Entrepreneur/Status Quo Defender Interviews

The moral entrepreneurs and status quo defenders interviewed represented clearly different interests. The former group included three high-level administrators in the county's chapters of the American Cancer Society and American Lung Association. A fourth was an administrator for the Shasta County Tobacco Education Project. The last member of this group was a pulmonary physician affiliated with a local hospital. The latter group included four bar and/or restaurant owners and an attorney who had been hired to represent their interests. Thus the status quo defenders were small business owners who might see their economic interests affected adversely by the ban. Importantly, they were representatives of a less prestigious social stratum than the moral entrepreneurs.

The primary concern of the moral entrepreneurs was health. As one stated,

> I supported the initiative to get the smoking ban on the ballot because of all the health implications that secondhand smoke can create. Smoking and secondhand smoke are the most preventable causes of death in this nation.

Another offered that

> On average, secondhand smoke kills 53,000 Americans each year. And think about those that it kills in other countries! It contains 43 cancer-causing chemical agents that have been verified by the Environmental Protection Agency. It is now listed as a Type A carcinogen, which is the same category as asbestos.

Every one of the moral entrepreneurs expressed concern about health issues during the interview. This was not the only point they raised, however. Three of the five made negative normative evaluations of smoking, thereby implicitly degrading the status of smokers. They commented that "smoking is no longer an acceptable action," that "smoke stinks," or that "it is just a dirty and annoying habit." Thus, whereas health was their primary concern, such comments revealed the moral entrepreneurs' negative view of smoking irrespective of any medical issues. Smokers were

seen as engaging in unclean and objectionable behavior—stigmatized qualities defining their deviant social status.

The stance of the status quo defenders was also grounded in two arguments. All of them expressed concern about individual rights. As one put it,

> I opposed that smoking ban because I personally smoke and feel that it is an infringement of my rights to tell me where I can and cannot smoke. Smoking is a legal activity, and therefore it is unconstitutional to take that right away from me.

Another argued that

> Many people have died for us to have these rights in foreign wars and those also fought on American soil. Hundreds of thousands of people thought that these rights were worth dying for, and now some small group of people believe that they can just vote away these rights.

Such symbolism implies that smoking is virtually a patriotic calling, a venerable habit for which people have been willing to forfeit their lives in time of war. In the status quo defenders' view, smoking is a constitutionally protected right.

At the same time, each of the status quo defenders was concerned about more practical matters, namely business profits. As one stated, "my income was going to be greatly affected." Another argued,

> If these people owned some of the businesses that they are including in this ban, they would not like it either. By taking away the customers that smoke, they are taking away the mainstay of people from a lot of businesses.

The competing viewpoints of the moral entrepreneurs and status quo defenders revealed the moral issues—health versus individual rights—at the heart of political conflict over the smoking ban. Yet it appears that status issues also fueled the conflict. On the one hand, the moral entrepreneurs denigrated smoking, emphasizing the socially unacceptable qualities of the behavior and symbolically degrading smokers' status. On the other hand, status quo defenders were concerned that their livelihood would be affected by the ban. Interestingly, the occupational status of the two groups differed, with the moral entrepreneurs representing the new knowledge class, the status quo defenders a lower stratum of small business owners. Those in the latter group may not have been accorded the prestige and trust granted those in the former (Berger 1986). Moreover, the status quo defenders' concern about business was likely seen as self-aggrandizing.

Summary and Discussion

This research has examined the moral and status politics underlying the implementation of a smoking ban in Shasta County, California. Moral entrepreneurs crusading for the ban argued that secondhand smoke damages health, implicitly grounding their argument in the principle that people have a right to a smoke-free environment. Status quo defenders countered that smokers have a constitutional right to indulge wherever and whenever they see fit. Public discourse echoed these themes, as seen in the letters to the editor of the local newspaper. Thus debate about the smoking ban focused especially on health versus smokers' rights; yet evidence of social status differences between the competing symbolic-moral universes also surfaced. Competing symbolic-moral universes are defined not only by different ethical viewpoints on a behavior, but also by differences in social power—disparities inevitably linked to the system of stratification (Ben-Yehuda 1990). Those prevailing in moral and stigma contests typically represent the higher socioeconomic echelons of society.

The moral entrepreneurs who engineered the smoking ban campaign were representatives of the prestigious knowledge class, including among their members officials from the local chapters of respected organizations at the forefront of the national antismoking crusade. In contrast, the small business owners who were at the core of the opposing coalition, of status quo defenders, represented the traditional middle class. Clearly, there was an instrumental quality to the restaurant and bar owners' stance, because they saw the ban as potentially damaging to their business interests. But they were unable to shape the public debate, as demonstrated by the letters to the editor.

In many respects, the status conflicts involved in the passage of the Shasta County smoking ban were symbolic. The moral entrepreneurs focused attention on the normatively undesirable qualities of cigarette smoking, and their negative normative evaluations of smoking were reflected in public debate about the ban. Those who write in support of the ban more frequently offered negative normative evaluations than antiban writers; their comments degraded smoking and, implicitly, smokers. Since the advent of the antismoking crusade in the United States, smoking has come to be seen as socially reprehensible, smokers as social misfits characterized by negative psychological characteristics (Markle and Troyer 1979).

Ultimately, a lifestyle associated with the less educated, less affluent, lower occupational strata was stigmatized as a public health hazard and targeted for coercive reform. Its deviant status was codified in the ordinance banning smoking in public facilities, including restaurants and bars. The ban symbolized the deviant status of cigarette smokers, the prohibition visibly demonstrating the community's condemnation of their behavior. Further, the smoking ban symbolically amplified the purported virtues of the abstinent lifestyle. A political victory such as the passage of a law is a prestige-enhancing symbolic triumph that is perhaps even more rewarding than its end result (Gusfield 1963). The symbolic nature of the ban serendipitously surfaced in another way during one author's unstructured observations in 42 restaurants and 21 bars in the area: Whereas smoking was not observed in a single restaurant, it occurred without sanction in all but one of the bars. Although not deterring smoking in one of its traditional bastions, the ban called attention to its deviant quality and, instrumentally, effectively halted it in areas more commonly frequented by the abstemious.

Although more systematic research is needed, the findings of this exploratory case study offer a better understanding of the dynamics underlying opposition to smoking and further support to theorizing about the role of status politics in the creation of deviant types. Denunciation of smoking in Shasta County involved not only legitimate allegations about public health, but negative normative evaluations of those engaged in the behavior. In the latter regard, the ban constituted a status degradation ceremony, symbolically differentiating the pure and abstinent from the unclean and intrusive. Not coincidentally, the stigmatized were more likely found among society's lower socioeconomic strata, their denouncers among its higher echelons.

Certainly the class and ethnic antipathies underlying attacks on cocaine and opiate users earlier in the century were more manifest than those revealed in the crusade against cigarette smoking. But neither are there manifest status conflicts in the present crusades against abortion (Luker 1984) and pornography (Zurcher and Kirkpatrick 1976); yet the underlying differences of status between opponents in those movements are reflected in their markedly different symbolic-moral universes, as was the case in the present study.

This is not to suggest that smoking should be an approved behavior. The medical evidence seems compelling: Cigarette smoking is harmful to the individual smoker and to those exposed to secondhand smoke. However, the objective harms of the psychoactive substance in question are irrelevant to the validity of our analysis, just as they were to Gusfield's (1963) analysis of the temperance movement's crusade against alcohol use. Moreover, it is not our intention to imply that the proban supporters consciously intended to degrade those of lower social status. No doubt they were motivated primarily by a sincere belief that smoking constitutes a public health hazard. In the end, however, moral indignation and social control flowed down the social hierarchy. Thus we must ask: Would cigarette smoking be defined as deviant if there were a positive correlation between smoking and socieconomic status?

NOTE

1. Although the term moral entrepreneur is well established in the literature on deviance, there seems to be little attention to or consistency in a corresponding term for the interest group(s) opposing them. Those that have been employed, such as "forces for the status quo" (Markle and Troyer 1979), tend to be awkward. "Status quo defenders" is used here for lack of a simpler or more common term.

REFERENCES

Ashley, Richard. 1975. *Cocaine: Its History, Uses, and Effects.* New York: St. Martin's Press.

Aviado, Domingo M. 1986. "Health Issues Relating to 'Passive' Smoking." Pp. 137–165 in *Smoking and Society: Toward a More Balanced Assessment,* edited by Robert D. Tollison. Lexington, MA: Lexington Books.

Becker, Howard S. 1963. *Outsiders: Studies in the Sociology of Deviance.* New York: Free Press.

Ben-Yehuda, Nachman. 1990. *The Politics and Morality of Deviance: Moral Panics, Drug Abuse, Deviant Science, and Reversed Stigmatization.* Albany, NY: State University of New York Press.

Berger, Peter L. 1986. "A Sociological View of the Antismoking Phenomenon." Pp. 225–240 in *Smoking and Society: Toward a More Balanced*

Assessment, edited by Robert D. Tollison. Lexington, MA: Lexington Books.

Bonnie, Richard J., and Charles H. Whitebread II. 1970. "The Forbidden Fruit and the Tree of Knowledge: An Inquiry into the Legal History of American Marihuana Prohibition." *Virginia Law Review* 56: 971–1203.

Covey, Lirio S., Edith A. Zang, and Ernst L. Wynder. 1992. "Cigarette Smoking and Occupational Status: 1977 to 1990." *American Journal of Public Health* 82: 1230–1234.

Feinhandler, Sherwin J. 1986. *The Social Role of Smoking.* Pp. 167–187 in *Smoking and Society: Toward a More Balanced Assessment,* edited by Robert D. Tollison. Lexington, MA: Lexington Books.

Ferrence, Roberta G. 1989. *Deadly Fashion: The Rise and Fall of Cigarette Smoking in North America.* New York: Garland.

Garfinkel, Harold. 1956. "Conditions of Successful Degradation Ceremonies." *American Journal of Sociology* 61: 402–424.

Goffman, Erving. 1963. *Stigma: Notes on the Management of Spoiled Identity.* Englewood Cliffs, NJ: Prentice Hall.

Goodin, Robert E. 1989. *No Smoking: The Ethical Issues.* Chicago: University of Chicago Press.

Gusfield, Joseph R. 1963. *Symbolic Crusade: Status Politics and the American Temperance Movement.* Urbana, IL: University of Illinois Press.

Luker, Kristin. 1984. *Abortion and the Politics of Motherhood.* Berkeley, CA: University of California.

Marcus, Alfred C., Donald R. Shopland, Lori A. Crane, and William R. Lynn. 1989. "Prevalence of Cigarette Smoking in United States: Estimates from the 1985 Current Population Survey." *Journal of the National Cancer Institute* 81: 409–414.

Markle, Gerald E., and Ronald J. Troyer. 1979. "Smoke Gets in Your Eyes: Cigarette Smoking as Deviant Behavior." *Social Problems* 26: 611–625.

Neuhring, Elane, and Gerald E. Markle. 1974. "Nicotine and Norms: The Re-Emergence of a Deviant Behavior." *Social Problems* 21: 513–526.

Ram, Sidney P. 1941. *How to Get More Fun Out of Smoking.* Chicago: Cuneo.

Roper Organization. 1978, May. *A Study of Public Attitudes Toward Cigarette Smoking and the Tobacco Industry in 1978, Volume 1.* New York: Roper.

Schur, Edwin M. 1980. *The Politics of Deviance: Stigma Contests and the Uses of Power.* New York: Random House.

Steinfeld, Jesse. 1991. "Combating Smoking in the United States: Progress Through Science and Social Action." *Journal of the National Cancer Institute* 83: 1126–1127.

U.S. Bureau of the Census. 1990. *General Population Characteristics.* Washington, DC: U.S. Government Printing Office.

U.S. Department of Health, Education and Welfare. 1964. *Smoking and Health: Report of the Advisory Committee to the Surgeon General of the Public Health Service.* Washington, DC: U.S. Government Printing Office.

U.S. Department of Health and Human Services. 1986. *The Health Consequences of Involuntary Smoking. A Report of the Surgeon General.* Washington, DC: U.S. Government Printing Office.

U.S. Department of Health and Human Services. 1992. *Smoking and Health in the Americas. A 1992 Report of the Surgeon General, in Collaboration with the Pan American Health Organization.* Washington, DC: U.S. Government Printing Office.

Viscusi, W. Kip. 1992. *Smoking: Making the Risky Decision.* New York: Oxford University Press.

Zurcher, Louis A. Jr., and R. George Kirkpatrick. 1976. *Citizens for Decency: Antipornography Crusades as Status Defense.* Austin, TX: University of Texas Press.

THINKING ABOUT THE READING

Tuggle and Holmes contend that the antismoking movement developed for reasons beyond the health risks of tobacco. What were those reasons? How are smokers usually portrayed by those who want public smoking banned? Contrast this portrayal with other drugs and those who use them, such as alcohol, marijuana, pain killers, and diet drugs. Why are some of these substances considered legal and others deviant? When considering alcohol users, are there different portrayals of different kinds of drinkers? Which kinds of drinkers are considered "deviant"? Which kinds are "normal"? What are the typical images of people addicted to cocaine and people addicted to pain killers? Does social class play a role in these definitions? Do agencies such as law enforcement treat different kinds of smokers/drinkers/drug users differently? Discuss the meaning of a "moral entrepreneur" and consider other instances where groups of people try to "sell" a particular definition of deviance.

Becoming a Marihuana User

Howard S. Becker

(1953)

The use of marihuana is and has been the focus of a good deal of attention on the part of both scientists and laymen. One of the major problems students of the practice have addressed themselves to has been the identification of those individual psychological traits which differentiate marihuana users from nonusers and which are assumed to account for the use of the drug. That approach, common in the study of behavior categorized as deviant, is based on the premise that the presence of a given kind of behavior in an individual can best be explained as the result of some trait which predisposes or motivates him to engage in the behavior.[1]

This study is likewise concerned with accounting for the presence or absence of marihuana use in an individual's behavior. It starts, however, from a different premise: that the presence of a given kind of behavior is the result of a sequence of social experiences during which the person acquires a conception of the meaning of the behavior, and perceptions and judgments of objects and situations, all of which make the activity possible and desirable. Thus, the motivation or disposition to engage in the activity is built up in the course of learning to engage in it and does not antedate this learning process. For such a view it is not necessary to identify those "traits" which "cause" the behavior. Instead, the problem becomes one of describing the set of changes in the person's conception of the activity and of the experience it provides for him.[2]

This paper seeks to describe the sequence of changes in attitude and experience which lead to *the use of marihuana for pleasure.* Marihuana does not produce addiction, as do alcohol and the opiate drugs; there is no withdrawal sickness and no ineradicable craving for the drug.[3] The most frequent pattern of use might be termed "recreational." The drug is used occasionally for the pleasure the user finds in it, a relatively casual kind of behavior in comparison with the connected use of addicting drugs. The term "use for pleasure" is meant to emphasize the noncompulsive and casual character of the behavior. It is also meant to eliminate from consideration here those few cases in which marihuana is used for its prestige value only, as a symbol that one is a certain kind of person, with no pleasure at all being derived from its use.

The analysis presented here is conceived of as demonstrating the greater explanatory usefulness of the kind of theory outlined above as opposed to the predispositional theories now current. This may be seen in two ways: (1) predispositional theories cannot account for that group of users (whose existence is admitted)[4] who do not exhibit the trait or traits considered to cause the behavior and (2) such theories cannot account for the great variability over time of a given individual's behavior with reference to the drug. The same person will at one stage be unable to use the drug for pleasure, at a later stage be able and willing to do so, and still later, again be unable to use it in this way. These changes, difficult to explain from a predispositional or motivational theory, are readily understandable in terms of changes in the individual's conception of the drug as is the existence of "normal" users.

The study attempted to arrive at a general statement of the sequence of changes in individual attitude and experience which have always occurred when the individual has become willing and able to use marihuana for pleasure and which have not occurred or not been permanently maintained when this is not the case. This generalization is stated in universal terms in order that negative cases may be discovered and used to revise the explanatory hypothesis.[5]

Fifty interviews with marihuana users from a variety of social backgrounds and present positions in society constitute the data from which the generalization was constructed and against which it was tested.[6] The interviews focused on the history of the person's experience with the drug, seeking major changes in his attitude toward it and in his actual use of it, and the reasons for these changes. The final generalization is a statement of that sequence of changes in attitude which occurred in every case known to me in which the person came to use marihuana for pleasure. Until a negative case is found, it may be considered as an explanation of all cases of marihuana use for pleasure. In addition, changes from use to non-use are shown to be related to similar changes in conception, and in each case it is possible to explain variations in the individual's behavior in these terms.

This paper covers only a portion of the natural history of an individual's use of marihuana,[7] starting with the person having arrived at the point of willingness to try marihuana. He knows that others use it to "get high," but he does not know what this means in concrete terms. He is curious about the experience, ignorant of what it may turn out to be, and afraid that it may be more than he has bargained for.

The steps outlined below, if he undergoes them all and maintains the attitudes developed in them, leave him willing and able to use the drug for pleasure when the opportunity presents itself.

I

The novice does not ordinarily get high the first time he smokes marihuana, and several attempts are usually necessary to induce this state. One explanation of this may be that the drug is not smoked "properly," that is, in a way that ensures sufficient dosage to produce real symptoms of intoxication. Most users agree that it cannot be smoked like tobacco if one is to get high:

> Take in a lot of air, you know, and . . . I don't know how to describe it, you don't smoke it like a cigarette, you draw in a lot of air and get it deep down in your system and then keep it there. Keep it there as long as you can.

Without the use of some such technique[8] the drug will produce no effects, and the user will be unable to get high:

> The trouble with people like that [who are not able to get high] is that they're just not smoking it right, that's all there is to it. Either they're not holding it down long enough, or they're getting too much air and not enough smoke, or the other way around or something like that. A lot of people just don't smoke it right, so naturally nothing's gonna happen.

If nothing happens, it is manifestly impossible for the user to develop a conception of the drug as an object which can be used for pleasure, and use will therefore not continue. The first step in the sequence of events that must occur if the person is to become a user is that he must learn to use the proper smoking technique in order that his use of the drug will produce some effects in terms of which his conception of it can change.

Such a change is, as might be expected, a result of the individual's participation in groups in which marihuana is used. In them the individual learns the proper way to smoke the drug. This may occur through direct learning:

> I was smoking like I did an ordinary cigarette. He said, "No, don't do it like that." He said, "Suck it, you know, draw in and hold it in your lungs till you . . . for a period of time."
>
> I said, "Is there any limit of time to hold it?"
>
> He said, "No, just till you feel that you want to let it out, let it out." So I did that three or four times.

Many new users are ashamed to admit ignorance and, pretending to know already, must learn through the more indirect means of observation and imitation:

> I came on like I had turned on [smoked marihuana] many times before, you know. I didn't want to seem like a punk to this cat. See, like I didn't know the first thing about it—how to smoke it, or what was going to happen, or what. I just watched him like a hawk—I didn't take my eyes off him for a second, because I wanted to do everything just as he did it. I watched how he held it, how he smoked it, and everything. Then when he gave it to me I just came on cool, as though I knew exactly what the score was. I held it like he did and took a poke just the way he did.

No person continued marihuana use for pleasure without learning a technique that supplied sufficient dosage for the effects of the drug to appear. Only when this was learned was it possible for a conception of the drug as an object which could be used for pleasure to emerge. Without such a conception marihuana use was considered meaningless and did not continue.

II

Even after he learns the proper smoking technique, the new user may not get high and thus not form a conception of the drug as something which can be used for pleasure. A remark made by a user suggested the reason for this difficulty in getting high and pointed to the next necessary step on the road to being a user:

> I was told during an interview, "As a matter of fact, I've seen a guy who was high out of his mind and didn't know it."
>
> I expressed disbelief: "How can that be, man?"
>
> The interviewee said, "Well, it's pretty strange, I'll grant you that, but I've seen it. This guy got on with me, claiming that he'd never got high, one of those guys, and he got completely stoned. And he kept insisting that he wasn't high. So I had to prove to him that he was."

What does this mean? It suggests that being high consists of two elements: the presence of symptoms caused by marihuana use and the recognition of these symptoms and their connection by the user with his use of the drug. It is not enough, that is, that the effects be present; they alone do not automatically provide the experience of being high. The user must be able to point them out to himself and consciously connect them with his having smoked marihuana before he can have this experience. Otherwise, regardless of the actual effects produced, he considers that the drug has had no effect on him: "I figured it either had no effect on me or other people were exaggerating its effect on them, you know. I thought it was probably psychological, see." Such persons believe that the whole thing is an illusion and that the wish to be high leads the user to deceive himself into believing that something is happening when, in fact, nothing is. They do not continue marihuana use, feeling that "it does nothing" for them.

Typically, however, the novice has faith (developed from his observation of users who do get high) that the drug actually will produce some new experience and continues to experiment with it until it does. His failure to get high worries him, and he is likely to ask more experienced users or provoke comments from them about it. In such conversations he is made aware of specific details of his experience which he may not have noticed or may have noticed but failed to identify as symptoms of being high.

> I didn't get high the first time . . . I don't think I held it in long enough. I probably let it out, you know, you're a little afraid. The second time I wasn't sure, and he [smoking companion] told me, like I asked him for some of the symptoms or something, how would I know, you know. . . . So he told me to sit on a stool. I sat on—I think I sat on a bar stool—and he said. "Let your feet hang," and then when I got down my feet were real cold, you know.
>
> And I started feeling it, you know. That was the first time. And then about a week after that, sometime pretty close to it, I really got on. That was the first time I got on a big laughing kick, you know. Then I really knew I was on.

One symptom of being high is an intense hunger. In the next case the novice becomes aware of this and gets high for the first time:

> They were just laughing the hell out of me because like I was eating so much. I just scoffed [ate] so much food, and they were just laughing at me, you know. Sometimes I'd be looking at them, you know, wondering why they're laughing, you know, not knowing what I was doing. [Well, did they tell you why they were laughing eventually?] Yeah, yeah, I come back, "Hey, man, what's happening?" Like, you know, like I'd ask, "What's happening?" and all of a sudden I feel weird, you know. "Man, you're on you know. You're on pot [high on marihuana]." I said, "No, am I?" Like I don't know what's happening.

The learning may occur in more indirect ways:

> I heard little remarks that were made by other people. Somebody said, "My legs are rubbery," and I can't remember all the remarks that were made because I was very attentively listening for all these cues for what I was supposed to feel like.

The novice, then, eager to have this feeling, picks up from other users some concrete referents of the term "high" and applies these notions to his own experience. The new concepts make it possible for him to locate these symptoms among his own sensations and to point out to himself a "something different" in his experience that he connects with drug use. It is only when he can do this that he is high. In the next case, the contrast between two successive experiences of a user makes clear the crucial importance of the awareness of the symptoms in being high and re-emphasizes the important role of interaction with other users in acquiring the concepts that make this awareness possible:

> [Did you get high the first time you turned on?] Yeah, sure. Although, come to think of it, I guess I really didn't. I mean, like that first time it was more or less of a mild drunk. I was happy, I guess, you know what I mean. But I didn't really know I was high, you know what I mean. It was only after the second time I got high that I realized I was high the first time. Then I knew that something different was happening.
>
> [How did you know that?] How did I know? If what happened to me that night would of happened to you, you would've known, believe me. We played the first tune for almost two hours—one tune! Imagine, man! We got on the stand and played this one tune, we started at nine o'clock. When he got finished I looked at my watch, it's a quarter to eleven. Almost two hours on one tune. And it didn't seem like anything. I mean, you know, it does that to you. It's like you have much more time or something. Anyway, when I saw that, man, it was too much. I knew I must really be high or something if anything like that could happen. See, and then they explained to me that that's what it did to you, you had a different sense of time and everything. So I realized that's what it was. I knew then. Like the first time, I

probably felt that way, you know, but I didn't know what's happening.

It is only when the novice becomes able to get high in this sense that he will continue to use marihuana for pleasure. In every case in which use continued, the user had acquired the necessary concepts with which to express to himself the fact that he was experiencing new sensations caused by the drug. That is, for use to continue, it is necessary not only to use the drug so as to produce effects but also to learn to perceive these effects when they occur. In this way marihuana acquires meaning for the user as an object which can be used for pleasure.

With increasing experiencing the user develops a greater appreciation of the drug's effects; he continues to learn to get high. He examines succeeding experiences closely, looking for new effects, making sure the old ones are still there. Out of this there grows a stable set of categories for experiencing the drug's effects whose presence enables the user to get high with ease.

The ability to perceive the drug's effects must be maintained if use is to continue; if it is lost, marihuana use ceases. Two kinds of evidence support this statement. First, people who become heavy users of alcohol, barbiturates, or opiates do not continue to smoke marihuana, largely because they lose the ability to distinguish between its effects and those of the other drugs.[9] They no longer know whether the marihuana gets them high. Second, in those few cases in which an individual uses marihuana in such quantities that he is always high, he is apt to get this same feeling that the drug has no effect on him, since the essential element of a noticeable difference between feeling high and feeling normal is missing. In such a situation, use is likely to be given up completely, but temporarily, in order that the user may once again be able to perceive the difference.

III

One more step is necessary if the user who has now learned to get high is to continue use. He must learn to enjoy the effects he has just learned to experience. Marihuana-produced sensations are not automatically or necessarily pleasurable. The taste for such experience is a socially acquired one, not different in kind from acquired tastes for oysters or dry martinis. The user feels dizzy, thirsty; his scalp tingles; he misjudges time and distances; and so on. Are these things pleasurable? He isn't sure. If he is to continue marihuana use, he must decide that they are. Otherwise, getting high, while a real enough experience, will be an unpleasant one he would rather avoid.

The effects of the drug, when first perceived, may be physically unpleasant or at least ambiguous:

> It started taking effect, and I didn't know what was happening, you know, what it was, and I was very sick. I walked around the room, walking around the room trying to get off, you know; it just scared me at first, you know. I wasn't used to that kind of feeling.

In addition, the novice's naive interpretation of what is happening to him may further confuse and frighten him, particularly if he decides, as many do, that he is going insane:

> I felt I was insane, you know. Everything people done to me just wigged me. I couldn't hold a conversation, and my mind would be wandering, and I was always thinking, oh, I don't know, weird things, like hearing music different. . . . I get the feeling that I can't talk to anyone. I'll goof completely.

Given these typically frightening and unpleasant first experiences, the beginner will not continue use unless he learns to redefine the sensations as pleasurable:

It was offered to me, and I tried it. I'll tell you one thing. I never did enjoy it at all. I mean it was just nothing that I could enjoy. [Well, did you get high when you turned on?] Oh, yeah, I got definite feelings from it. But I didn't enjoy them. I mean I got plenty of reactions, but they were mostly reactions of fear. [You were frightened?] Yes, I didn't enjoy it. I couldn't seem to relax with it, you know. If you can't relax with a thing, you can't enjoy it, I don't think.

In other cases the first experiences were also definitely unpleasant, but the person did become a marihuana user. This occurred, however, only after a later experience enabled him to redefine the sensations as pleasurable:

[This man's first experience was extremely unpleasant, involving distortion of spatial relationships and sounds, violent thirst, and panic produced by these symptoms.] After the first time I didn't turn on for about, I'd say, ten months to a year. . . . It wasn't a moral thing; it was because I'd gotten so frightened, bein' so high. An' I didn't want to go through that again, I mean, my reaction was, "Well, if this is what they call bein' high, I don't dig [like] it." . . . So I didn't turn on for a year almost, accounta that. . .

Well, my friends started, an' consequently I started again. But I didn't have any more, I didn't have that same initial reaction, after I started turning on again.

[In interaction with his friends he became able to find pleasure in the effects of the drug and eventually became a regular user.]

In no case will use continue without such a redefinition of the effects as enjoyable.

This redefinition occurs, typically, in interaction with more experienced users who, in a number of ways, teach the novice to find pleasure in this experience which is at first so frightening.[10] They may reassure him as to the temporary character of the unpleasant sensations and minimize their seriousness, at the same time calling attention to the more enjoyable aspects. An experienced user describes how he handles newcomers to marihuana use:

Well, they get pretty high sometimes. The average person isn't ready for that, and it is a little frightening to them sometimes. I mean, they've been high on lush [alcohol], and they get higher that way than they've ever been before, and they don't know what's happening to them. Because they think they're going to keep going up, up, up till they lose their minds or begin doing weird things or something. You have to like reassure them, explain to them that they're not really flipping or anything, that they're gonna be all right. You have to just talk them out of being afraid. Keep talking to them, reassuring, telling them it's all right. And come on with your own story, you know: "The same thing happened to me. You'll get to like that after awhile." Keep coming on like that; pretty soon you talk them out of being scared. And besides they see you doing it and nothing horrible is happening to you, so that gives them more confidence.

The more experienced user may also teach the novice to regulate the amount he smokes more carefully, so as to avoid any severely uncomfortable symptoms while retaining the pleasant ones. Finally, he teaches the new user that he can "get to like it after awhile." He teaches him to regard those ambiguous experiences formerly defined as unpleasant as enjoyable. The older user in the following incident is a person whose tastes have shifted in this way, and his remarks have the effect of helping others to make a similar redefinition:

A new user had her first experience of the effects of marihuana and became frightened and hysterical. She "felt like she was half in and half out of the room" and experienced a number of alarming physical symptoms. One of the more experienced users present said, "She's dragged because she's high like that. I'd give anything to get that high myself. I haven't been that high in years."

In short, what was once frightening and distasteful becomes, after a taste for it is built up, pleasant, desired, and sought after. Enjoyment is introduced by the favorable definition of the experience that one acquires from others. Without this, use will not continue, for marihuana will not be for the user an object he can use for pleasure.

In addition to being a necessary step in becoming a user, this represents an important condition for continued use. It is quite common for experienced users suddenly to have an unpleasant or frightening experience, which they cannot define as pleasurable, either because they have used a larger amount of marihuana than usual or because it turns out to be a higher-quality marihuana than they expected. The user has sensations which go beyond any conception he has of what being high is and is in much the same situation as the novice, uncomfortable and frightened. He may blame it on an overdose and simply be more careful in the future. But he may make this the occasion for a rethinking of his attitude toward the drug and decide that it no longer can give him pleasure. When this occurs and is not followed be a redefinition of the drug as capable of producing pleasure, use will cease.

The likelihood of such a redefinition occurring depends on the degree of the individual's participation with other users. Where this participation is intensive, the individual is quickly talked out of his feeling against marihuana use. In the next case, on the other hand, the experience was very disturbing, and the aftermath of the incident cut the person's participation with other users to almost zero. Use stopped for three years and began again only when a combination of circumstances, important among which was a resumption of ties with users, made possible a redefinition of the nature of the drug:

It was too much, like I only made about four pokes, and I couldn't even get it out of my mouth, I was so high, I got real flipped. In the basement, you know, I just couldn't stay in there anymore. My heart was pounding real hard, you know, and I was going out of my mind; I thought I was losing my mind completely. So I cut out of this basement, and this other guy, he's out of his mind, told me, "Don't, don't leave me, man. Stay here." And I couldn't.

I walked outside, and it was five below zero, and I thought I was dying, and I had my coat open; I was sweating. I was perspiring. My whole insides were all . . . , and I walked about two blocks away, and I fainted behind a bush. I don't know how long I laid there. I woke up, and I was feeling the worst, I can't describe it at all, so I made it to a bowling alley, man, and I was trying to act normal, I was trying to shoot pool, you know, trying to act real normal, and I couldn't lay and I couldn't stand up and I couldn't sit down, and I went up and laid down where some guys that spot pins lay down, and that didn't help me, and I went down to a doctor's office. I was going to go in there and tell the doctor to put me out of my misery . . . because my heart was pounding so hard, you know. . . . So then all weekend I started flipping, seeing things there and going through hell, you know, all kinds of abnormal things. . . . I just quit for a long time then.

[He went to a doctor who defined the symptoms for him as those of a nervous breakdown caused by "nerves" and "worries." Although he was no longer using marihuana, he had some recurrences of the symptoms which led him to suspect that "it was all his nerves."] So I just stopped worrying, you know; so it was about thirty-six months later I started making it again. I'd just take a few pokes, you know. [He first resumed use in the company of the same user-friend with whom he had been involved in the original incident.]

A person, then, cannot begin to use marihuana for pleasure, or continue its use for pleasure, unless he learns to define its effects as enjoyable, unless it becomes and remains an object which he conceived of as capable of producing pleasure.

IV

In summary, an individual will be able to use marihuana for pleasure only when he goes through a process of learning to conceive of it as an object which can be used in this way. No one becomes a user without (1) learning to smoke the drug in a way which will produce real effects; (2) learning to recognize the effects and connect them with drug use (learning, in other words, to get high); and (3) learning to enjoy the sensations he perceives. In the course of this process he develops a disposition or motivation to use marihuana which was not and could not have been present when he began use, for it involves and depends on conceptions of the drug which could only grow out of the kind of actual experience detailed above. On completion of this process he is willing and able to use marihuana for pleasure.

He has learned, in short, to answer "Yes" to the question: "Is it fun?" The direction his further use of the drug takes depends on his being able to continue to answer "Yes" to this question and, in addition, on his being able to answer "Yes" to other questions which arise as he becomes aware of the implications of the fact that the society as a whole disapproves of the practice: "Is it expedient?" "Is it moral?" Once he has acquired the ability to get enjoyment out of the drug, use will continue to be possible for him. Considerations of morality and expediency, occasioned by the reactions of society, may interfere and inhibit use, but use continues to be a possibility in terms of his conception of the drug. The act becomes impossible only when the ability to enjoy the experience of being high is lost, through a change in the user's conception of the drug occasioned by certain kinds of experience with it.

In comparing this theory with those which ascribe marihuana use to motives or predispositions rooted deep in individual behavior, the evidence makes it clear that marihuana use for pleasure can occur only when the process described above is undergone and cannot occur without it. This is apparently so without reference to the nature of the individual's personal makeup, or psychic problems. Such theories assume that people have stable modes of response which predetermine the way they will act in relation to any particular situation or object and that, when they come in contact with the given object or situation, they act in the way in which their makeup predisposes them.

This analysis of the genesis of marihuana use shows that the individuals who come in contact with a given object may respond to it at first in a great variety of ways. If a stable form of new behavior toward the object is to emerge, a transformation of meanings must occur, in which the person develops a new conception of the nature of the object.[11] This happens in a series of communicative acts in which others point out new aspects of his experience to him, present him with new interpretations of events, and help him achieve a new conceptual organization of his world, without which the new behavior is not possible. Persons who do not achieve the proper kind of conceptualization are unable to engage in the given behavior and turn off in the direction of some other relationship to the object or activity.

This suggests that behavior of any kind might fruitfully be studied developmentally, in terms of changes in meanings and concepts, their organization and reorganization, and the way they channel behavior, making some acts possible while excluding others.

NOTES

1. See, as examples of this approach, the following: E. Marcovitz & H. J. Meyers (1944, December), "The marihuana addict in the army," *War Medicine, 6,* 382–391; H. S. Gaskill (1945, September), "Marihuana, an intoxicant," *American Journal of Psychiatry, 102,* 202–204; S. Charen &

L. Perelman (1946, March), "Personality studies of marihuana addicts," *American Journal of Psychiatry, 102,* 674–682.

2. This approach stems from George Herbert Mead's (1934) discussion of objects in *Mind, self, and society,* Chicago: University of Chicago Press, pp. 277–280.

3. Cf. R. Adams (1942, November), "Marihuana," *Bulletin of the New York Academy of Medicine, 18,* 705–730.

4. Cf. L. Kolb (1938, July), "Marihuana," *Federal Probation, 2,* 22–25; and W. Bromberg (1939, July 1), "Marihuana: A psychiatric study," *Journal of the American Medical Association, 113,* 11.

5. The method used is that described in A. R. Lindesmith (1947), *Opiate addiction,* Bloomington, IN: Principia, chap. i. I would like also to acknowledge the important role Lindesmith's work played in shaping my thinking about the genesis of marihuana use.

6. Most of the interviews were done by the author. I am grateful to Solomon Kobrin and Harold Finestone for allowing me to make use of interviews done by them.

7. I hope to discuss elsewhere other stages in this natural history.

8. A pharmacologist notes that this ritual is in fact an extremely efficient way of getting the drug into the blood stream. R. P. Walton (1938), *Marihuana: America's new drub problem,* Philadelphia: J. B. Lippincott, p. 48.

9. "Smokers have repeatedly stated that the consumption of whiskey while smoking negates the potency of the drug. They find it very difficult to get 'high' while drinking whiskey and because of that smokers will not drink while using the 'weed.'" Cf. New York City Mayor's Committee on Marihuana (1944), *The marihuana problem in the city of New York,* Lancaster, PA: Jacques Cattel, p. 13.

10. Charen & Perelman (1946), p. 679.

11. Cf. A. Strauss (1952, June), "The development and transformation of monetary meanings in the child," *American Sociological Review, 17,* 275–286.

THINKING ABOUT THE READING

This article illustrates that our responses to things are based on the social meaning they hold for us and highlights the power of social groups in teaching us what to enjoy. Is Becker's argument applicable only to illegal drug use or can it be applied to the process by which we learn to enjoy more mundane activities, such as eating certain foods and drinking certain beverages? Can his argument also be used to explain how we come to fear certain activities? What are some things that you are afraid of? Think about whether you have had direct experience that has created these fears or whether you learned them from others. Likewise, consider also some of the routines you engage in at work, school, and home. How did you learn these routines? Can you recall specific individuals or groups from whom you learned them? What about your beliefs and ideals? Can you trace these to their various social sources?

PART III

Social Structure, Institutions, and Everyday Life

The Structure of Society

Organizations and Social Institutions

One of the great sociological paradoxes of our existence is that in a society that so fiercely extols the virtues of rugged individualism and personal accomplishment, we spend most of our lives responding to the influence of larger organizations and social institution. From the nurturing environments of our churches and schools to the cold depersonalization of massive bureaucracies, organizations and institutions are a fundamental part of our everyday lives.

No matter how powerful and influential they are, organizations are more than structures, rules, policies, goals, job descriptions, and standard operating procedures. Each organization, and each division within an organization, develops its own norms, values, and language. This is usually referred to as organizational culture. Organizational cultures are usually pervasive and entrenched, yet, even so, individuals often find ways to exert some control over their lives within the confines of these organizations. Accordingly, organizations are dynamic entities in which individuals struggle for personal freedom and expression while also existing under the rules and procedures that make up the organization. Given this dynamic activity, an organization is rarely what it appears to be on the surface.

In larger organizations, distinct cultures develop where similar meanings and perspectives are cultivated. As in society as a whole, however, distinct subcultures can develop. In "The Smile Factory," John Van Maanen examines the organizational culture of one of American society's most enduring icons: Disney theme parks. Disneyland and Disney World have a highly codified and strict set of conduct standards. Variations from tightly defined employee norms are not tolerated. You'd expect in such a place that employees would be a rather homogeneous group. However, Van Maanen discovers that beneath the surface of this self-proclaimed "Happiest Place on Earth" lies a mosaic of distinct groups that have created their own status system and that work hard to maintain the status boundaries between one another.

One type of organization that most of us are familiar with in one way or another are hospitals. We usually see them for that they are fundamentally designed to be: places where sick people go to get better. Likewise, we are inclined to see the professionals who work in them—particularly doctors and nurses—as people who are dedicated to helping patients who are ailing. In "The Routinization of Disaster," Dan Chambliss shows us that the enormous pressures of such a pursuit can create in hospital employees a unique and surprising approach to their jobs. Chambliss focuses on the process by which nurses routinize and render "matter of fact" experiences that to the rest of us are among the most traumatic and catastrophic of our lives: sickness and death. Far from being cold and unfeeling, such an approach is a necessary personal and organizational adaptation to the tragedy that nurses see on a daily basis in large hospitals.

Something to Consider as You Read:

As you read these selections, think about a job you've had and the new procedures you had to learn when you started. Was the job just about the procedures, or did you also have to learn new (and perhaps informal) cultural norms? Think about some of the ways in which the organizational environment induces you to behave in ways that are very specific to that situation. As you read, compare some of these organizational environments to others you've read about in previous sections, including the military, domestic service, law enforcement, and so on.

The Smile Factory
Work at Disneyland

John Van Maanen

(1991)

Part of Walt Disney Enterprises includes the theme park Disneyland. In its pioneering form in Anaheim, California, this amusement center has been a consistent money maker since the gates were first opened in 1955. Apart from its sociological charm, it has, of late, become something of an exemplar for culture vultures and has been held up for public acclaim in several best-selling publications as one of America's top companies. . . . To outsiders, the cheerful demeanor of its employees, the seemingly inexhaustible repeat business it generates from its customers, the immaculate condition of park grounds, and, more generally, the intricate physical and social order of the business itself appear wondrous.

Disneyland as the self-proclaimed "Happiest Place on Earth" certainly occupies an enviable position in the amusement and entertainment worlds as well as the commercial world in general. Its product, it seems, is emotion—"laughter and well-being." Insiders are not bashful about promoting the product. Bill Ross, a Disneyland executive, summarizes the corporate position nicely by noting that "although we focus our attention on profit and loss, day-in and day-out we cannot lose sight of the fact that this is a feeling business and we make our profits from that."

The "feeling business" does not operate, however, by management decree alone. Whatever services Disneyland executives believe they are providing to the 60 to 70 thousand visitors per day that flow through the park during its peak summer season, employees at the bottom of the organization are the ones who most provide them. The work-a-day practices that employees adopt to amplify or dampen customer spirits are therefore a core concern of this feeling business. The happiness trade is an interactional one. It rests partly on the symbolic resources put into place by history and park design but it also rests on an animated workforce that is more or less eager to greet the guests, pack the trams, push the buttons, deliver the food, dump the garbage, clean the streets, and, in general, marshal the will to meet and perhaps exceed customer expectations. False moves, rude words, careless disregard, detected insincerity, or a sleepy and bored presence can all undermine the enterprise and ruin a sale. The smile factory has its rules.

Author's Note: This paper has been cobbled together using three-penny nails of other writings. Parts come from a paper presented to the American Anthropological Association Annual Meetings in Washington, D.C., on November 16, 1989 called "Whistle While You Work." Other parts come from J. Van Maanen and G. Kunda, 1989. "Real feelings: Emotional expressions and organization culture." In B. Staw & L. L. Cummings (Eds.), *Research in Organization Behavior* (Vol. 11, pp. 43–103). Greenwich, CT: JAI Press. In coming to this version, I've had a good deal of help from my friends Steve Barley, Nicloe Biggart, Michael Owen Jones, Rosanna Hertz, Gideon Kunda, Joanne Martin, Maria Lydia Spinelli, Bob Sutton, and Bob Thomas.

It's a Small World

... This rendition is of course abbreviated and selective. I focus primarily on such matters as the stock appearance (vanilla), status order (rigid), and social life (full), and swiftly learned codes of conduct (formal and informal) that are associated with Disneyland ride operators. These employees comprise the largest category of hourly workers on the payroll. During the summer months, they number close to four thousand and run the 60-odd rides and attractions in the park.

They are also a well-screened bunch. There is—among insiders and outsiders alike—a rather fixed view about the social attributes carried by the standard-make Disneyland ride operator. Single, white males and females in their early twenties, without facial blemish, of above average height and below average weight, with straight teeth, conservative grooming standards, and a chin-up, shoulder-back posture radiating the sort of good health suggestive of a recent history in sports are typical of these social identifiers. There are representative minorities on the payroll but because ethnic displays are sternly discouraged by management, minority employees are rather close copies of the standard model Disneylander, albeit in different colors.

This Disneyland look is often a source of some amusement to employees who delight in pointing out that even the patron saint, Walt himself, could not be hired today without shaving off his trademark pencil-thin mustache. But, to get a job in Disneyland and keep it means conforming to a rather exacting set of appearance rules. These rules are put forth in a handbook on the Disney image in which readers learn, for example, that facial hair or long hair is banned for men as are aviator glasses and earrings and that women must not tease their hair, wear fancy jewelry, or apply more than a modest dab of makeup. Both men and women are to look neat and prim, keep their uniforms fresh, polish their shoes, and maintain an upbeat countenance and light dignity to complement their appearance—no low spirits or cornball raffishness at Disneyland.

The legendary "people skills" of park employees, so often mentioned in Disneyland publicity and training materials, do not amount to very much according to ride operators. Most tasks require little interaction with customers and are physically designed to practically insure that is the case. The contact that does occur typically is fleeting and swift, a matter usually of only a few seconds. In the rare event sustained interaction with customers might be required, employees are taught to deflect potential exchanges to area supervisors or security. A Training Manual offers the proper procedure: "On misunderstandings, guests should be told to call City Hall. . . . In everything from damaged cameras to physical injuries, don't discuss anything with guests . . . there will always be one of us nearby." Employees learn quickly that security is hidden but everywhere. On Main Street security cops are Keystone Kops; in Frontierland, they are Town Marshalls; on Tom Sawyer's Island, they are Cavalry Officers, and so on.

Occasionally, what employees call "line talk" or "crowd control" is required of them to explain delays, answer direct questions, or provide directions that go beyond the endless stream of recorded messages coming from virtually every nook and cranny of the park. Because such tasks are so simple, consisting of little more than keeping the crowd informed and moving, it is perhaps obvious why management considers the sharp appearance and wide smile of employees so vital to park operations. There is little more they could ask of ride operators whose main interactive tasks with visitors consist of being, in their own terms, "information booths," "line signs," "pretty props," "shepherds," and "talking statues."

A few employees do go out of their way to initiate contact with Disneyland customers but, as a rule, most do not and consider those who do to be a bit odd. In general, one need do little more than exercise common courtesy while looking reasonably alert and pleasant. Interactive skills that are advanced by the job have less to do with making customers feel warm and welcome than they do with keeping each other amused and happy. This is, of course, a more complex matter.

Employees bring to the job personal badges of status that are of more than passing interest to peers. In rough order, these include: good looks, college affiliation, career aspirations, past achievements, age (directly related to status up to about age 23 or 24 and inversely related thereafter), and assorted other idiosyncratic matters. Nested closely alongside these imported status badges are organizational ones that are also of concern and value to employees.

Where one works in the park carries much social weight. Postings are consequential because the ride and area a person is assigned provide rewards and benefits beyond those of wages. In-the-park stature for ride operators turns partly on whether or not unique skills are required. Disneyland neatly complements labor market theorizing on this dimension because employees with the most differentiated skills find themselves at the top of the internal status ladder, thus making their loyalties to the organization more predictable.

Ride operators, as a large but distinctly middle-class group of hourly employees on the floor of the organization, compete for status not only with each other but also with other employee groupings whose members are hired for the season from the same applicant pool. A loose approximation of the rank ordering among these groups can be constructed as follows:

1. The upper-class prestigious Disneyland Ambassadors and Tour Guides (bilingual young women in charge of ushering—some say rushing—little bands of tourists through the park);

2. Ride operators performing coveted "skilled work" such as live narrations or tricky transportation tasks like those who symbolically control customer access to the park and drive the costly entry vehicles (such as the antique trains, horse-drawn carriages, and Monorail);

3. All other ride operators;

4. The proletarian Sweepers (keepers of the concrete grounds);

5. The sub-prole or peasant status Food and Concession workers (whose park sobriquets reflect their lowly social worth— "pancake ladies," "peanut pushers," "coke blokes," "suds divers," and the seemingly irreplaceable "soda jerks").

Pay differentials are slight among these employee groups. The collective status adheres, as it does internally for ride operators, to assignment or functional distinctions. As the rank order suggests, most employee status goes to those who work jobs that require higher degrees of special skill, [offer] relative freedom from constant and direct supervision, and provide the opportunity to organize and direct customer desires and behavior rather than to merely respond to them as spontaneously expressed.

The basis for sorting individuals into these various broad bands of job categories is often unknown to employees—a sort of deep, dark secret of the casting directors in personnel. When prospective employees are interviewed, they interview for "a job at Disneyland," not a specific one. Personnel decides what particular job they will eventually occupy. Personal contacts are considered by employees as crucial in this job-assignment process as they are in the hiring decision. Some employees, especially those who wind up in the lower ranking jobs, are quite disappointed with their assignments as is the case when, for example, a would-be Adventureland guide is posted to a New Orleans Square restaurant as a pot scrubber.

Although many of the outside acquaintances of our pot scrubber may know only that he works at Disneyland, rest assured, insiders will know immediately where he works and judge him accordingly.

Uniforms are crucial in this regard for they provide instant communication about the social merits or demerits of the wearer within the little world of Disneyland workers. Uniforms also correspond to a wider status ranking that casts a significant shadow on employees of all types. Male ride operators on the Autopia wear, for example, untailored jump-suits similar to pit mechanics and consequently generate about as much respect from peers as the grease-stained outfits worn by pump jockeys generate from real motorists in gas stations. The ill-fitting and homogeneous "whites" worn by Sweepers signify lowly institutional work tinged, perhaps, with a reminder of hospital orderlies rather than street cleanup crews. On the other hand, for males, the crisp, officer-like Monorail operator stands alongside the swashbuckling Pirate of the Caribbean, the casual cowpoke of Big Thunder Mountain, or the smartly vested Riverboat pilot as carriers of valued symbols in and outside the park. Employees lust for these higher status positions and the rights to small advantages such uniforms provide. A lively internal labor market exists wherein there is much scheming for the more prestigious assignments.

For women, a similar market exists although the perceived "sexiness" of uniforms, rather than social rank, seems to play a larger role. To wit, the rather heated antagonisms that developed years ago when the ride "It's a Small World" first opened and began outfitting the ride operators with what were felt to be the shortest skirts and most revealing blouses in the park. Tour Guides, who traditionally headed the fashion vanguard at Disneyland in their above-the-knee kilts, knee socks, tailored vests, black English hats, and smart riding crops were apparently appalled at being upstaged by their social inferiors and lobbied actively (and, judging by the results, successfully) to lower the skirts, raise the necklines, and generally remake their Small World rivals.

Important, also, to ride operators are the break schedules followed on the various rides. The more the better. Work teams develop inventive ways to increase the number of "time-outs" they take during the work day. Most rides are organized on a rotational basis (e.g., the operator moving from a break, to queue monitor, to turnstile overseer, to unit loader, to traffic controller, to driver, and, again, to a break). The number of break men or women on a rotation (or ride) varies by the number of employees on duty and by the number of units on line. Supervisors, foremen, and operators also vary as to what they regard as appropriate break standards (and, more importantly, as to the value of the many situational factors that can enter the calculation of break rituals—crowd size, condition of ride, accidents, breakdowns, heat, operator absences, special occasions, and so forth). Self-monitoring teams with sleepy supervisors and lax (or savvy) foremen can sometimes manage a shift comprised of 15 minutes on and 45 minutes off each hour. They are envied by others, and rides that have such a potential are eyed hungrily by others who feel trapped by their more rigid (and observed) circumstances.

Movement across jobs is not encouraged by park management, but some does occur (mostly within an area and job category). Employees claim that a sort of "once a sweeper, always a sweeper" rule obtains but all know of at least a few exceptions to prove the rule. The exceptions offer some (not much) hope for those working at the social margins of the park and perhaps keep them on the job longer than might otherwise be expected. Dishwashers can dream of becoming Pirates, and with persistence and a little help from their friends, such dreams just might come true next season (or the next).

These examples are precious, perhaps, but they are also important. There is an intricate pecking order among very similar categories of employees. Attributes of reward and status tend to cluster, and there is intense concern about the cluster to which one belongs (or would like to belong). To a degree, form follows function in Disneyland because the jobs requiring the most abilities and offering the most interest also offer the most status and social reward. Interaction patterns reflect and sustain this order. Few Ambassadors or Tour Guides, for instance, will stoop to speak at length with Sweepers who speak mostly among themselves or to Food workers. Ride operators, between the poles, line up in ways referred to above with only ride proximity (i.e., sharing a break area) representing a potentially significant intervening variable in the interaction calculation. . . .

Paid employment at Disneyland begins with the much renowned University of Disneyland whose faculty runs a day-long orientation program (Traditions I) as part of a 40-hour apprenticeship program, most of which takes place on the rides. In the classroom, however, newly hired ride operators are given a very thorough introduction to matters of managerial concern and are tested on their absorption of famous Disneyland fact, lore, and procedure. Employee demeanor is governed, for example, by three rules:

First, we practice the friendly smile.

Second, we use only friendly and courteous phrases.

Third, we are not stuffy—the only Misters in Disneyland are Mr. Toad and Mr. Smee.

Employees learn too that the Disneyland culture is officially defined. The employee handbook put it in this format:

Dis-ney Cor-po-rate Cul-ture (diz'ne kor'pr'it kul'cher) *n* 1. Of or pertaining to the Disney organization, as *a:* the philosophy underlying all business decisions; *b:* the commitment of top leadership and management to that philosophy; *c:* the actions taken by individual cast members that reinforce the image.

Language is also a central feature of university life, and new employees are schooled in its proper use. Customers at Disneyland are, for instance, never referred to as such, they are "guests." There are no rides at Disneyland, only "attractions." Disneyland itself is a "Park," not an amusement center, and it is divided into "back-stage," "on-stage," and "staging" regions. Law enforcement personnel hired by the park are not policemen, but "security hosts." Employees do not wear uniforms but check out fresh "costumes" each working day from "wardrobe." And, of course, there are no accidents at Disneyland, only "incidents." . . .

The university curriculum also anticipates probable questions ride operators may someday face from customers, and they are taught the approved public response. A sample:

Question (posed by trainer): What do you tell a guest who requests a rain check?

Answer (in three parts): We don't offer rain checks at Disneyland because (1) the main attractions are all indoors; (2) we would go broke if we offered passes; and (3) sunny days would be too crowded if we gave passes.

Shrewd trainees readily note that such an answer blissfully disregards the fact that waiting areas of Disneyland are mostly outdoors and that there are no subways in the park to carry guests from land to land. Nor do they miss the economic assumption concerning the apparent frequency of Southern California rains. They discuss such matters together, of course, but rarely raise them in the training classroom. In most respects, these are recruits who easily take the role of good student.

Classes are organized and designed by professional Disneyland trainers who also instruct a well-screened group of representative hourly employees straight from park operations on the approved newcomer training methods and materials. New-hires seldom see professional trainers in class but are brought on board by enthusiastic peers who concentrate on those aspects of park procedure thought highly general matters to be learned by all employees. Particular skill training (and "reality shock") is reserved for the second wave of socialization occurring on the rides themselves as operators are taught, for example, how and when to send a mock bobsled caroming down the track or, more delicately, the proper ways to stuff an obese adult customer into the midst of children riding the Monkey car on the Casey Jones Circus Train or, most problematically, what exactly to tell an irate customer standing in the rain who, in no uncertain terms, wants his or her money back and wants it back now.

During orientation, considerable concern is placed on particular values the Disney organization considers central to its operations. These values range from the "customer is king" verities to the more or less unique kind, of which "everyone is a child at heart when at Disneyland" is a decent example. This latter piety is one few employees fail to recognize as also attaching to everyone's mind as well after a few months of work experience. Elaborate checklists of appearance standards are learned and gone over in the classroom and great efforts are spent trying to bring employee emotional responses in line with such standards. Employees are told repeatedly that if they are happy and cheerful at work, so, too, will the guests be at play. Inspirational films, hearty pep talks, family imagery, and exemplars of corporate performance are all representative of the strong symbolic stuff of these training rites. . . .

Yet, like employees everywhere, there is a limit to which such overt company propaganda can be effective. Students and trainers both seem to agree on where the line is drawn, for there is much satirical banter, mischievous winking, and playful exaggeration in the classroom. As young seasonal employees note, it is difficult to take seriously an organization that provides its retirees "Golden Ears" instead of gold watches after 20 or more years of service. All newcomers are aware that the label "Disneyland" has both an unserious and artificial connotation and that a full embrace of the Disneyland role would be as deviant as its full rejection. It does seem, however, because of the corporate imagery, the recruiting and selection devices, the goodwill trainees hold toward the organization at entry, the peer-based employment context, and the smooth fit with real student calendars, the job is considered by most ride operators to be a good one. The University of Disneyland, it appears, graduates students with a modest amount of pride and a considerable amount of fact and faith firmly ingrained as important things to know (if not always accept).

Matters become more interesting as new hires move into the various realms of Disneyland enterprise. There are real customers "out there" and employees soon learn that these good folks do not always measure up to the typically well mannered and grateful guest of the training classroom. Moreover, ride operators may find it difficult to utter the prescribed "Welcome Voyager" (or its equivalent) when it is to be given to the 20-thousandth human being passing through the Space Mountain turnstile on a crowded day in July. Other difficulties present themselves as well, but operators learn that there are others onstage to assist or thwart them.

Employees learn quickly that supervisors and, to a lesser degree, foremen are not only on the premises to help them, but also to catch them when they slip over or brazenly violate set procedures or park policies. Because most rides are tightly designed to eliminate human judgment and minimize operational disasters, much of the supervisory monitoring is directed at activities ride operators consider trivial: taking too long a break; not wearing parts of one's official uniform such as a hat, standard-issue belt, or correct shoes; rushing the ride (although more frequent violations seem to be detected for the provision of longer-than-usual rides for lucky customers); fraternizing with guests beyond the call of duty; talking back to quarrelsome or sometimes merely querisome customers; and so forth. All are matters covered quite explicitly in the codebooks ride operators are to be familiar with, and violations of such codes are often subject to instant and harsh discipline. The firing of what to supervisors are "malcontents," "trouble-makers," "bumblers," "attitude problems," or simply "jerks" is a frequent occasion at Disneyland, and among part-timers, who are most subject to degradation and being fired, the threat is omnipresent. There are few workers who have not witnessed firsthand the rapid disappearance of a co-worker for offenses they would regard as "Mickey Mouse." Moreover, there are few employees who themselves have not violated a good number of operational and demeanor standards and anticipate, with just cause, the violation of more in the future.

In part, because of the punitive and what are widely held to be capricious supervisory practices in the park, foremen and ride operators are usually drawn close and shield one another from suspicious area supervisors. Throughout the year, each land is assigned a number of area supervisors who, dressed alike in short-sleeved white shirts and ties with walkie-talkies hitched to their belts, wander about their territories on the lookout for deviations from park procedures (and other signs of disorder). Occasionally, higher level supervisors pose in "plainclothes" and ghost-ride the various attractions just to be sure everything is up to snuff. Some area supervisors are well-known among park employees for the variety of surreptitious techniques they employ when going about their monitoring duties. Blind observation posts are legendary, almost sacred,

sites within the park ("This is where Old Man Weston hangs out. He can see Dumbo, Storybook, the Carousel, and the Tea Cups from here"). Supervisors in Tomorrowland are, for example, famous for their penchant of hiding in the bushes above the submarine caves, timing the arrivals and departures of the supposedly fully loaded boats making the 8½ minute cruise under the polar icecaps. That they might also catch a submarine captain furtively enjoying a cigarette (or worse) while inside the conning tower (his upper body out of view of the crowd on the vessel) might just make a supervisor's day—and unmake the employee's. In short, supervisors, if not foremen, are regarded by ride operators as sneaks and tricksters out to get them and representative of the dark side of park life. Their presence is, of course, an orchestrated one and does more than merely watch over the ride operators. It also draws operators together as cohesive little units who must look out for one another while they work (and shirk). . . .

Employees are also subject to what might be regarded as remote controls. These stem not from supervisors or peers but from thousands of paying guests who parade daily through the park. The public, for the most part, wants Disneyland employees to play only the roles for which they are hired and costumed. If, for instance, Judy of the Jets is feeling tired, grouchy, or bored, few customers want to know about it. Disneyland employees are expected to be sunny and helpful; and the job, with its limited opportunities for sustained interaction, is designed to support such a stance. Thus, if a ride operator's behavior drifts noticeably away from the norm, customers are sure to point it out—"Why aren't you smiling?" "What's wrong with you?" "Having a bad day?" "Did Goofy step on your foot?" Ride operators learn swiftly from the constant hints, glances, glares, and tactful (and tactless) cues sent by their audience what their role in the park is to be, and as long as they keep to it, there will be no objections from those passing by.

I can remember being out on the river looking at the people on the Mark Twain looking down on the people in the Keel Boats who are looking up at them. I'd come by on my raft and they'd all turn and stare at me. If I gave them a little wave and a grin, they'd all wave back and smile; all ten thousand of them. I always wondered what would happen if I gave them the finger? (Ex-ride operator, 1988)

Ride operators also learn how different categories of customers respond to them and the parts they are playing on-stage. For example, infants and small children are generally timid, if not frightened, in their presence. School-age children are somewhat curious, aware that the operator is at work playing a role but sometimes in awe of the role itself. Nonetheless, these children can be quite critical of any flaw in the operator's performance. Teenagers, especially males in groups, present problems because they sometimes go to great lengths to embarrass, challenge, ridicule, or outwit an operator. Adults are generally appreciative and approving of an operator's conduct provided it meets their rather minimal standards, but they sometimes overreact to the part an operator is playing (positively) if accompanied by small children. . . .

The point here is that ride operators learn what the public (or, at least, their idealized version of the public) expects of their role and find it easier to conform to such expectations than not. Moreover, they discover that when they are bright and lively others respond to them in like ways. This . . . balancing of the emotional exchange is such that ride operators come to expect good treatment. They assume, with good cause, that most people will react to their little waves and smiles with some affection and perhaps joy. When they do not, it can ruin a ride operator's day.

With this interaction formula in mind, it is perhaps less difficult to see why ride operators detest and scorn the ill-mannered or unruly guest. At times, these grumpy, careless, or otherwise unresponsive characters insult the very role the operators play and have come to

appreciate—"You can't treat the Captain of the USS Nautilus like that!" Such out-of-line visitors offer breaks from routine, some amusement, consternation, or the occasional job challenge that occurs when remedies are deemed necessary to restore employee and role dignity.

By and large, however, the people-processing tasks of ride operators pass good naturedly and smoothly, with operators hardly noticing much more than the bodies passing in front of view (special bodies, however, merit special attention as when crew members on the subs gather to assist a young lady in a revealing outfit on board and then linger over the hatch to admire the view as she descends the steep steps to take her seat on the boat). Yet, sometimes, more than a body becomes visible, as happens when customers overstep their roles and challenge employee authority, insult an operator, or otherwise disrupt the routines of the job. In the process, guests become "dufusses," "ducks," and "assholes" (just three of many derisive terms used by ride operators to label those customers they believe to have gone beyond the pale). Normally, these characters are brought to the attention of park security officers, ride foremen, or area supervisors who, in turn, decide how they are to be disciplined (usually expulsion from the park).

Occasionally, however, the alleged slight is too personal or simply too extraordinary for a ride operator to let it pass unnoticed or merely inform others and allow them to decide what, if anything, is to be done. Restoration of one's respect is called for, and routine practices have been developed for these circumstances. For example, common remedies include: the "seatbelt squeeze," a small token of appreciation given to a deviant customer consisting of the rapid cinching-up of a required seatbelt such that the passenger is doubled-over at the point of departure and left gasping for the duration of the trip; the "break-toss," an acrobatic gesture of the Autopia trade whereby operators jump on the outside of a norm violator's car, stealthily unhitching the safety belt, then slamming on the brakes, bringing the car to an almost instant stop while the driver flies on the hood of the car (or beyond); the "seatbelt slap," an equally distinguished (if primitive) gesture by which an offending customer receives a sharp, quick snap of a hard plastic belt across the face (or other parts of the body) when entering or exiting a seat-belted ride; the "break-up-the-party" gambit, a queuing device put to use in officious fashion whereby bothersome pairs are separated at the last minute into different units, thus forcing on them the pain of strange companions for the duration of a ride through the Haunted Mansion or a ramble on Mr. Toad's Wild Ride; the "hatch-cover ploy," a much beloved practice of Submarine pilots who, in collusion with mates on the loading dock, are able to drench offensive guests with water as their units pass under a waterfall; and, lastly, the rather ignoble variants of the "Sorry-I-didn't-see-your-hand" tactic, a savage move designed to crunch a particularly irksome customer's hand (foot, finger, arm, leg, etc.) by bringing a piece of Disneyland property to bear on the appendage, such as the door of a Thunder Mountain railroad car or the starboard side of a Jungle Cruise boat. This latter remedy is, most often, a "near miss" designed to startle the little criminals of Disneyland.

All of these unofficial procedures (and many more) are learned on the job. Although they are used sparingly, they are used. Occasions of use provide a continual stream of sweet revenge talk to enliven and enrich colleague conversation at break time or after work. Too much, of course, can be made of these subversive practices and the rhetoric that surrounds their use. Ride operators are quite aware that there are limits beyond which they dare not pass. If they are caught, they know that restoration of corporate pride will be swift and clean.

In general, Disneyland employees are remarkable for their forbearance and polite good manners even under trying conditions. They are taught, and some come to believe, for

a while at least, that they are really "on-stage" at work. And, as noted, surveillance by supervisory personnel certainly fades in light of the unceasing glances an employee receives from the paying guests who tromp daily through the park in the summer. Disneyland employees know well that they are part of the product being sold and learn to check their more discriminating manners in favor of the generalized countenance of a cheerful lad or lassie whose enthusiasm and dedication is obvious to all.

At times, the emotional resources of employees appear awesome. When the going gets tough and the park is jammed, the nerves of all employees are frayed and sorely tested by the crowd, din, sweltering sun, and eyeburning smog. Customers wait in what employees call "bullpens" (and park officials call "reception areas") for up to several hours for a 3½ minute ride that operators are sometimes hell-bent on cutting to 2½ minutes. Surely a monument to the human ability to suppress feelings has been created when both users and providers alike can maintain their composure and seeming regard for one another when in such a fix.

It is in this domain where corporate culture and the order it helps to sustain must be given its due. Perhaps the depth of a culture is visible only when its members are under the gun. The orderliness—a good part of the Disney formula for financial success—is an accomplishment based not only on physical design and elaborate procedures, but also on the low-level, part-time employees who, in the final analysis, must be willing, even eager, to keep the show afloat. The ease with which employees glide into their kindly and smiling roles is, in large measure, a feat of social engineering. Disneyland does not pay well; its supervision is arbitrary and skin-close; its working conditions are chaotic; its jobs require minimal amounts of intelligence or judgment; and asks a kind of sacrifice and loyalty of its employees that is almost fanatical. Yet, it attracts a particularly able workforce whose personal backgrounds suggest abilities far exceeding those required of a Disneyland traffic cop, people stuffer, queue or line manager, and button pusher. As I have suggested, not all of Disneyland is covered by the culture put forth by management. There are numerous pockets of resistance and various degrees of autonomy maintained by employees. Nonetheless, adherence and support for the organization are remarkable. And, like swallows returning to Capistrano, many part-timers look forward to their migration back to the park for several seasons.

The Disney Way

Four features alluded to in this unofficial guide to Disneyland seem to account for a good deal of the social order that obtains within the park. First, socialization, although costly, is of a most selective, collective, intensive, serial, sequential, and closed sort. These tactics are notable for their penetration into the private spheres of individual thought and feeling. . . . Incoming identities are not so much dismantled as they are set aside as employees are schooled in the use of new identities of the situational sort. Many of these are symbolically powerful and, for some, laden with social approval. It is hardly surprising that some of the more problematic positions in terms of turnover during the summer occur in the food and concession domains where employees apparently find little to identify with on the job. Cowpokes on Big Thunder Mountain, Jet Pilots, Storybook Princesses, Tour Guides, Space Cadets, Jungle Boat Skippers, or Southern Belles of New Orleans Square have less difficulty on this score. Disneyland, by design, bestows identity through a process carefully set up to strip away the job relevance of other sources of identity and learned response and replace them with others of organizational relevance. It works.

Second, this is a work culture whose designers have left little room for individual experimentation. Supervisors, as apparent in their focused wandering and attentive looks, keep very close tabs on what is going on at any moment in all the lands. Every bush, rock, and tree in Disneyland is numbered and checked continually as to the part it is playing in the park. So too are employees. Discretion of a personal sort is quite limited while employees are "on-stage." Even "back-stage" and certain "off-stage" domains have their corporate monitors. Employees are indeed aware that their "off-stage" life beyond the picnics, parties, and softball games is subject to some scrutiny, for police checks are made on potential and current employees. Nor do all employees discount the rumors that park officials make periodic inquiries on their own as to a person's habits concerning sex and drugs. Moreover, the sheer number of rules and regulations is striking, thus making the grounds for dismissal a matter of multiple choice for supervisors who discover a target for the use of such grounds. The feeling of being watched is, unsurprisingly, a rather prevalent complaint among Disneyland people, and it is one that employees must live with if they are to remain at Disneyland.

Third, emotional management occurs in the park in a number of quite distinct ways. From the instructors at the university who beseech recruits to "wish every guest a pleasant good day," to the foremen who plead with their charges to, "say thank you when you herd them through the gate," to the impish customer who seductively licks her lips and asks, "what does Tom Sawyer want for Christmas?" appearance, demeanor, and etiquette have special meanings at Disneyland. Because these are prized personal attributes over which we normally feel in control, making them commodities can be unnerving. Much self-monitoring is involved, of course, but even here self-management has an organizational side. Consider ride operators who may complain of being "too tired to smile" but, at the same time, feel a little guilty for uttering such a confession. Ride operators who have worked an early morning shift on the Matterhorn (or other popular rides) tell of a queasy feeling they get when the park is opened for business and they suddenly feel the ground begin to shake under their feet and hear the low thunder of the hordes of customers coming at them, oblivious of civil restraint and the small children who might be among them. Consider, too, the discomforting pressures of being "on-stage" all day and the cumulative annoyance of having adults ask permission to leave a line to go to the bathroom, whether the water in the lagoon is real, where the well-marked entrances might be, where Walt Disney's cryogenic tomb is to be found, or—the real clincher—whether or not one is "really real."

The mere fact that so much operator discourse concerns the handling of bothersome guests suggests that these little emotional disturbances have costs. There are, for instance, times in all employee careers when they put themselves on "automatic pilot," "go robot," "can't feel a thing," "lapse into a dream," "go into a trance," or otherwise "check out" while still on duty. Despite a crafty supervisor's (or curious visitor's) attempt to measure the glimmer in an employee's eye, this sort of willed emotional numbness is common to many of the "on-stage" Disneyland personnel. Much of this numbness is, of course, beyond the knowledge of supervisors and guests because most employees have

little trouble appearing as if they are present even when they are not. It is, in a sense, a passive form of resistance that suggests there still is a sacred preserve of individuality left among employees in the park.

Finally, taking these three points together, it seems that even when people are trained, paid, and told to be nice, it is hard for them to do so all of the time. But, when efforts to be nice have succeeded to the degree that is true of Disneyland, it appears as a rather towering (if not always admirable) achievement. It works at the collective level by virtue of elaborate direction. Employees—at all ranks—are stage-managed by higher ranking employees who, having come through themselves, hire, train, and closely supervise those who have replaced them below. Expression rules are laid out in corporate manuals. Employee time-outs intensify work experience. Social exchanges are forced into narrow bands of interacting groups. Training and retraining programs are continual. Hiding places are few. Although little sore spots and irritations remain for each individual, it is difficult to imagine work roles being more defined (and accepted) than those at Disneyland. Here, it seems, is a work culture worthy of the name.

THINKING ABOUT THE READING

What is the significance of the title, "The Smile Factory"? What, exactly, is the factory-made product that Disney sells in its theme parks? How does the Disney organizational culture shape the lives of employees? Disney is frequently criticized for its strict—some would say oppressive—employee rules and regulations. But would it be possible to run a "smile factory" with a more relaxed code of conduct where employees could regularly make their own decisions and act as they pleased? Explain. Disney theme parks abroad (in Japan and France, for instance) have not been nearly as successful as Disneyland and Disney World. Why has it been so difficult to export the "feeling business" to other countries? Consider also how Van Maanen describes the ways in which employees define the social rank of different positions within Disneyland. Describe an organizational situation you've been in where such a ranking of members occurred. What were the criteria upon which such rankings were made?

The Routinization of Disaster

Daniel F. Chambliss

(1996)

How the Hospital Is Different

... Much [in a hospital] is the same as in other organizations: the daily round of paper processing, answering the phone, making staffing decisions, collecting bills, ordering supplies, stocking equipment rooms; there are fights between departments, arguments with the boss, workers going home tired or satisfied. And medical sociology has made much of these similarities, using its research to create broader theories of, for instance, deviance or of the structure of professions.

But in one crucial respect the hospital remains dramatically different from other organizations: *in hospitals, as a normal part of the routine, people suffer and die.* This is unusual. "[A] good working definition of a hospital is that place where death occurs and no one notices; or, more sharply, the place where others agree to notice death as a social fact only so far as it fits their particular purposes." Only combat military forces share this feature. To be complete, theories of hospital life need to acknowledge this crucial difference, since adapting themselves to pain and death is for hospital workers the most distinctive feature of their work. It is that which most separates them from the rest of us. In building theories of organizational life, sociologists must try to see how hospitals resemble other organizations ... but we should not make a premature leap to the commonalities before appreciating the unique features of hospitals

that make a nurse's task so different from that of a teacher or a businessman or a bureaucrat.[1]

A quick survey of typical patients in one Surgical Intensive Care Unit on one Saturday evening should make the point. The words in brackets are additions to my original field notes:

Room 1. 64-year-old white woman with an aortic valve replacement: five separate IMEDs [intravenous drip-control devices] feeding in nitroglycerine, vasopressors, Versed [a pain killer which also blocks memory]. Chest tube [to drain off fluids]. On ventilator [breathing machine], Foley [catheter in the bladder], a pulse oximeter on her finger, a[rterial monitoring] line. Diabetic. In one 30-second period during the night, her blood pressure dropped from 160/72 to 95/50, then to 53/36, before the nurse was able to control the drop. N[urse]s consider her "basically healthy."

Room 2. Man with pulmonary artresia, pulmonary valvotomy [heart surgery].

Room 3. Woman with CABG [coronary artery bypass graft; a "bypass operation"]. Bleeding out [i.e., hemorrhaging] badly at one point during the night, they sent her back to the OR [Operating Room]. On heavy vasopressors [to keep blood pressure up].

Room 4. Older woman with tumor from her neck up to her temple. In OR from 7 a.m. until 2 a.m. the next morning having it removed. Infarct [dead tissue] in the brain.

Room 5. 23-year old woman. MVA [motor vehicle accident]. ICP [intracranial pressure—a measure of brain swelling] measured—terrible. Maybe organ donor. [Patient died next day.]

Room 6. Don't know.

Room 7. Abdominal sepsis, possibly from surgery. DNR [Do Not Resuscitate] today.

Room 8. Big belly guy [an old man with a horribly distended abdomen, uncontrollable. Staff says it's from poor sterile technique in surgery by Doctor M., who is notoriously sloppy. This patient died within the week.] [Field Notes]

This is a typical patient load for an Intensive Care Unit. Eight beds, three patients dead in a matter of days. "Patients and their visitors often find the ICU to be a disturbing, even terrifying place. Constant artificial light, ceaseless activity, frequent emergencies, and the ever-present threat of death create an atmosphere that can unnerve even the most phlegmatic of patients. Some are so sick that they are unaware of their surroundings or simply forget the experience, but for others the ICU is a nightmare remembered all too well."[2] On floors—the larger, less critical care wards of the hospital—fatalities are less common, and patients are not so sick; even so, one-third of the patients may have AIDS, another one-third have cancer, and the rest suffer a variety of serious if not immediately lethal diseases. The ICUs just get patients whose deaths are imminent.

It is interesting that this density of disease presents one of the positive attractions of nursing. People don't become nurses to avoid seeing suffering or to have a quiet day. Every day nurses respond to and share the most intense emotions with total strangers. "People you don't know are going through the most horrible things, and you are supposed to help them. That's intense," says one nurse. And another enthuses about coming home as the sun is coming up; the rest of the world thinks things are just starting, and here you're coming off a big emergency that lasted half the night: "[T]here's a real adrenaline kick in all this

stuff. If you deny that, you're denying a big part of [nursing]."

The abnormality of the hospital scene liberates the staff from some niceties of everyday life and allows them a certain freedom. . . . Two small, even silly, examples may illustrate the point. (1) Many nurses wear scrub suits—the pajama-like pants and tops worn in operating rooms and on some units. Written on the suits are phone numbers, vital statistics, or even doodles drawn during surgery. It's more convenient than finding a piece of paper. One observer, Judith André, has commented, "It's like a childhood fantasy" to scribble things on your clothes. (2) During a "code," as a patient was being resuscitated, one nurse who was having her period began to leak menstrual fluid. She ran into the patient's bathroom to change her sanitary pad. When she came out, another nurse, seeing the stain on her pants, yelled, "Well, J. got her period!"—a comment unthinkable in the everyday world. But this isn't the everyday world. As Everett Hughes wrote, "All occupations—most of all those considered professions and perhaps those of the underworld—include as part of their very being a license to deviate in some measure from common modes of behavior."[3] In this sense, the hospital is like a war zone, in which common niceties and rules of decorum are discarded in the pursuit of some more immediate, desperate objective. There is an excitement, and a pressure, that frees hospital workers in the "combat zone" from an array of normal constraints on what they say and do.

And yet, for them their work has become normal, routine. On a medical floor, with perhaps two-thirds of the patients suffering eventually fatal diseases, I say to a nurse, "What's happening?" and she replies, walking on down the hall, "Same ol' same ol'." Nothing new, nothing exciting. Or in an Intensive Care Unit in the same hospital, "What's going on?" The resident replies, with a little shrug of the shoulders, "People are living, people are dying." Again, no surprises, nothing new. The routine goes on.

As other writers have noted, the professional treats routinely what for the patient is obviously not routine. For the health worker, medical procedures happen to patients every day, and the hospital setting is quite comfortable: "The staff nurse . . . belongs to a world of relative health, youth, and bustling activity. She may not yet have experienced hospitalization herself for more than the removal of tonsils or the repair of a minor injury. Although she works in an environment of continuous sickness, she has been so conditioned to its external aspects that she often expresses surprise when someone suggests that the environment must be anxiety evoking."[4] Everett Hughes's formulation of this divergence of experience is classic: "In many occupations, the workers or practitioners . . . deal routinely with what are emergencies to the people who receive their services. This is a source of chronic tension between the two." Or, more precisely, "[O]ne man's routine of work is made up of the emergencies of other people."[5]

To the patient, though, the hospital world is special, frightening, a jarring break from the everyday world. For the nurse, it's just the "same ol' same ol'." How extreme the gap is was observed in an ICU one evening:

> Three residents were attempting an LP [lumbar puncture—a "spinal tap" in which a long needle is inserted into the spinal column to draw out spinal fluid]. This is a very painful procedure and is difficult to perform. The television over the foot of the patient's bed was turned on, and "LA Law" was playing. While the resident was inserting the needle, she kept glancing up at the television, trying to simultaneously watch the show and do the LP. The patient, curled into the fetal position to separate the vertebrae, was unaware of this. The other two residents as well were glancing back and forth from procedure to television. The resident tried for several minutes drawing out

> blood instead of fluid. Eventually, she called the head resident, who came in and successfully finished the LP. [Field Notes].

This illustrates how casual staff can become, to the point of malfeasance.

How do staff, nurses in particular, routinize the abnormal? Or more fundamentally, what do we even mean by routinization?

What Routinization Entails: The Operating Room

The most egregious violation of commonsense morality—the profound physical violation of another person's body—is made completely routine in the hospital operating room. To help the reader understand routinization, we will consider this example in some detail.

In large teaching hospitals like Northern General or Southwest Regional, there are some twelve to twenty operating rooms in the "OR suite," with the rooms organized in a long hallway around a central equipment and supply area. The entire suite is "sterile," that is, everyone coming in and out wears scrub suits and face masks, shoe covers, and hair bonnets. Each operating room is furnished with a narrow padded table on which the patient lies during surgery, as well as with huge movable overhead lights and rolling tables for equipment of all sorts. Certain rooms are typically reserved for cardiac, neurological, orthopedic, and other special types of surgery, and the peculiar equipment for each of these is always available in those rooms. There are also one or two "crash rooms," for emergency surgery of the sort associated with the automobile wrecks or shootings frequently seen in large urban medical centers. Each room may be scheduled for one to six operations in a day; several dozen surgeries are scheduled for the hospital each weekday morning, usually starting at 6:00 and running until 2:00 or so in the afternoon.

Nurses manage these rooms between operations, supervising the flow of patients and the resupply of equipment (sponges, surgical tools, clean linens, etc.), answering the telephone or intercom and letting the physicians know when it is time to begin. There are typically at least two such nurses, the "scrub nurse" who assists the surgeon, handing tools and dealing directly with the sterile field, and the "circulating nurse" who can move in and out of the OR, touch nonsterile areas (such as the telephone), and keep the supplies flowing as needed to the surgical team. The circulating nurse is a kind of stage manager and fills in as needed, solving problems arising outside the surgery itself.

During surgery, the circulating nurse has several duties. First, she must document everything that happens: the time when surgery begins, what specific procedures are being conducted, what personnel are participating, when the procedure is done and "closing" begins, and when the patient is wheeled out of the room. Working together with the scrub nurse, she repeatedly counts and recounts the number of "sponges" (absorbent pads) used in the operation (there may be dozens). She must account for all of them both before and after the operation, to ensure that none are mistakenly left in the patient's body. She does the same for the surgical needles used, making certain that all are accounted for and disposed of properly, a serious concern since the advent of AIDS. The best circulating nurses, it would seem, are precise to the point of obsessiveness. The scrub nurse shares in these duties, counting sponges and accounting for all equipment, as well as passing to the surgeon, quickly and reliably, the specific tools needed at different stages of the operation. The scrub nurse also "preps" the patient: she drapes the patient with sterile cloths, leaving bare then shaving the area to be cut open, disinfecting the body surface with an iodine solution, and covering the skin with a clear plastic film called "Opsite"

which protects the uncut area. A screen of cloth is usually set up between the patient's head and the rest of the body, so conscious patients will not see what's going on. This also means that the operating area is detached from the patient as a person, an important feature of the scene. The nurses carry out routine tasks dozens of times in a single day—for instance, the one-by-one counting of sponges, carried with tongs from a table to a waste bucket, perhaps two dozen of them counted aloud. The failure to perform these tasks conscientiously could be disastrous.

Once both room and patient are "prepped," the medical team can begin. The patient's body, fundamentally, is transformed into an object. An anesthesiologist (a physician), or a nurse anesthetist, will administer either a spinal anesthetic, which numbs the body below the injection point on the spinal cord, or a general anesthetic, which puts the patient to sleep. From then on, the operative area, screened from the patient's head and deadened of all feeling, effectively becomes to the surgeons a piece of nonhuman meat. The target area is isolated and immobilized; the patient is either asleep or, with a spinal, may be chatting away up at the head of the table with the anesthesiologist. In one case, a man's leg was being removed at one end of the table while at the other he was telling the anesthesiologist about his recent vacation trip. Looking at the operating area, the skin being cut or bone being sawed, you think, "No one I know has ever looked like this." Anesthetized flesh doesn't respond as the flesh of a living human being would. In amputations, the flesh being removed is usually dead and looks it—dark, hard, lifeless. But living flesh, too, on the table, looks more like what it "objectively" is, that is, meat. Human fat looks like the chicken fat you see on the stove; human skin peels back the way a chicken's does when peeled. An old man's tanned skin, when cut, looks like leather—which, precisely speaking, it is: old, tanned, animal skin. Surgeons working inside the body cavity remind one of cooks stuffing the Thanks-giving turkey, pulling open a section here, pushing a hand deep inside, feeling around for something there, stretching back tendons, trim-ming the fat, snipping pieces here and there with a small pair of scissors. The fine details of surgery are remarkably complex and refined, but its basic principles are brutally simple:

> To amputate this diabetic lady's toes, Dr. R., a small woman, used a thing like a big pair of bolt cutters to actually cut the bones, one toe at a time—with the big toe she had some diffi-culty, and she was almost lifted off the floor squeezing the big handles together before the "crunch" and the blades snapped through the toe. Then the last flesh was snipped away and five toes, all together, like a section of beef or chicken, came off in a single piece, and the scrub nurse laid it into a specimen tray. [Field Notes]

This primitive business is executed with simple tools: a razor-edge knife to cut open the skin (the scalpel); scissors to trim away flesh inside the body; smooth hooks to pull back the skin while the operation is under way (retrac-tors); needle-nose pliers to shut off blood ves-sels (hemostats); and a small electric probe, essentially a soldering iron, used to cauterize the open ends of small blood vessels (the "Bovie"). Tools come in many sizes and spe-cialized shapes, but this is the basic array. Orthopedic surgery adds its various saws, drills, and bits; the equipment table looks like a bench in an immaculate hobbyist's work-shop, which in a sense it is.

To the senior staff, these tools and their uses become commonplace. During one rou-tine orthopedic operation (routine for the staff, not for the patient), a group of young residents were working on a teenage patient's shoulder. The supervising attending physician, nomi-nally in charge, popped in occasionally during the three-hour operation to see how things were going. On one visit he stopped for fifteen minutes to flip through the "swimsuit issue" of *Waterski* magazine, which one of the residents had brought. His pointed air of "no big deal" was more than casual; it seemed almost an assertion of his own power and sophistication, contrasted with the barely concealed anxiety of the residents he was monitoring. When he left, the residents visibly relaxed and resumed openly discussing how to perform the opera-tion. One actually shuttled back and forth to a table against the wall to look at the diagrams in his textbook to see how the surgery should be done. Then the attending anesthesiologist came in to check on his resident and to sign a form ("So I'll get my cut," he said smiling) and walked out again. Music by popular musicians Phil Collins and Los Lobos was on a portable tape cassette player as the residents worked. The residents were learning to do highly skilled surgery and how to regard it as part of every-day life.

Routinization in the OR or elsewhere in the hospital seems to mean several things: that actions are repeated, that they violate normal taboos, and that routine is embedded in behavior. Consider each in turn, drawing on further examples from other settings in the hospital:

1. *Repeatability.* Each operation is not the first of its kind; most in fact are done several times each day and hundreds of times each year, even by a single team of surgeons, nurses, and tech-nical aides. What the team sees, they have seen many times. Gallbladder removals, hernia repairs and shoulder operations on athletes—these are all very common procedures in the major medical center.[6]

And those repeated procedures take place against the even less dramatic background of the repeated daily events of the nurse's work: start-ing intravenous lines, taking blood pressures four times a day on every patient on the floor, drawing blood samples, charting vital signs, writing nurses' progress notes, passing food trays, helping patients on and off the bedpan. Both trivial and consequential activities are repeated over and over until each one becomes much like the next; indeed, as Hughes says, the professional's "very competence comes from having dealt with a thousand cases of what the client likes to consider his unique experience."[7] Says one nurse, "You get to the point where you don't really care for the patients anymore, and one GI [gastrointestinal] bleeder gets to be the same as the next GI bleeder."

In a Medical Intensive Care Unit, death itself becomes an often-repeated event:

> Another MICU patient just coded and died; that's five in the past six days. Incredible. The docs are here one month—N[urse]s are here for good . . .
>
> I just came in unit; first N[urse] says, "You just missed it." They said that to me a few days ago. It's not that I "just miss," I think, but rather that so much [is] going on. You'll always "just miss" something. [Field Notes]

Death becomes a routinized part of daily life, incorporated into the flow. "Mr. Smith died last night," says one nurse to another. "Oh, that's too bad. He was such a nice man"; a casual exchange. One day is like another, if not for Mr. Smith, then at least for the rest of us. For the nurses, Mr. Smith will be replaced by another man, a Mr. Jones, with similar ailments and a similar end. . . .

The repeatability of the events—the sense that the same things happen over and over—is part of what is meant by routinization.

2. *Profanation.* Normally, we experience our bodies and the bodies of others as sacred, as areas to be approached with reverence or even with awe. To the healthy person outside the hospital, the body is special, a thing distinct from other things in the world, and must be treated as different. Physical contact with other bodies is emotionally provocative, in ways good and bad. A touch, a hug, a kiss arouse some sensitivity; a

slap, however light, provokes humiliation or perhaps rage. But for patients in the hospital, their bodies are dramatically profaned. The body is often exposed to strangers, older and younger, male and female, even in groups. Many times a day the patient's body is punctured by injection needles. It is the object of teachers' lectures to their students. It is touched frequently, often without special preliminaries. It is probed with fingers and hands and tools in ways that are sometimes brutal, with little respect for the body as a sacred object. Even when professionals are respectful (and many of them always are), the effect on patients is one of the secularization of their own flesh. . . .

3. *Existentiality.* Routinization of the abnormal involves not so much a mental leap as an existential action; creating a routine is not some trick of the conscious mind but rather a whole way of acting that involves physical as well as mental components. It comprises embodied habits. Routinization is not "all in the head"; it is something one does. It is carried out in the way a nurse walks and talks while in the presence of abnormal events. It entails that "matter of factness" with which she inserts a bladder catheter or cleans up feces; it is evidenced in the full range of emotions she shows, laughing with a dying man, chatting and even laughing with colleagues during a code (a resuscitation effort), glancing casually through a nursing journal filled with full-color advertisements for ileostomy appliances and crèmes for cancer lesions. After a middle-aged woman died late one night in room 5 of a medical ICU, her family, loudly crying and hugging each other, came into the room to see their dead mother. Outside the room, three nurses who had tried for thirty minutes to resuscitate the patient sat around a table eating corn chips and gossiping, as if nothing had happened. One of those nurses said to me, "We're pretty dehumanized, huh?" But it wasn't true: if she were dehumanized no such comment would even be made.

She knew what was happening, and eating corn chips, even then, is in fact quite human. In a unit where three patients die each week, to get upset with every death would be humanly unacceptable.

So in the Operating Room and elsewhere events are repeated over and over, in an attitude of secularized treatment of the body, and this repeated attitude is built into and expressed in the very ordinary doings of the staff. Sometimes routinization goes beyond mere commonplace into an attitude of detachment, unconcern, or sheer boredom—one of the more common emotions of the nurse's life, to the surprise of laypersons. Indeed, one of the most frequent questions nurses asked me during my research was, "Aren't you bored?" . . .

How Routinization Is Accomplished: Creating Conditions for Ordinary Life

Thus, for the nurse, hospital life is ordinary—not extraordinary, or mystical, or even an object of thoughtful scrutiny. We saw in the last section how the nurse's ordinary daily life consists largely of repeated, secular activities. Things happen, time and time again, in essentially the same way; these happenings are for the most part devoid of any special, sacred character; and they are carried out in the working world, through concrete actions, not merely (or not even) thought about in any conscious way. "The ambience of nursing units is not tragic, but mundane and businesslike. The work of nurses and aides is largely repetitive and is carried on largely in a habitual manner . . . For the most part, nursing personnel seem to be hardly perturbed at the graphic condition of their patients . . . When they enter the presence of a sorely afflicted patient, their countenances are not likely to betray more than a flicker of emotion."[8] This is what we mean by saying the nurse has routinized the world of the hospital. Her life here has taken on a quality of mundane sameness, often to the point of sheer boredom.

> The first time I had to interview a patient in my first year of nursing school, he said he had a scar [on his chest]. I asked to see it, he just pulled up his gown [around his neck; she gestures to show how he was bare]. I was . . . [rolls her eyes, embarrassed] "Oh, my God." And now . . . [waves her hand, flutters eyes to indicate her totally blasé attitude]. [Field Notes]

No layperson would experience such exposure so casually. And nudity is simple; witnessing open heart surgery, or an endotracheal intubation, or CPR, is far more threatening to one's everyday reality. But nurses see these events every day, without becoming upset. The nurse's view—or more accurately, the nurse's very way of *living* here and dealing with such trauma—is different from ours.

How does this casual attitude develop? How does the abnormal become routine? The conventional answer is that "you just get used to it." This implies that over time, with enough exposure, one adapts, willy-nilly, to whatever is happening in the environment. This may be true, but it is insufficient. "Getting used to it" suggests that routinization is purely a matter of the passage of time, with repetition as the implied causative agent. Yes, routinization happens "over time," but time alone is insufficient to cause routinization. Some nurses never become accustomed, as we will see, to deformed newborns, or psychotic teenagers, or incontinent geriatric patients. Then, too, some people "get used to it" virtually immediately. Before my own first witnessing of surgery, I conscientiously followed all the head nurse's instructions to avoid physical or emotional upset: I rose early, ate a full breakfast, and was wide awake before going to the OR suite. After donning the scrub suit, bonnet, and shoe covers, I went into the OR and asked the circulating nurse what the first case would be, hoping for something "easy," maybe a wrist or ankle operation. She looked at the chart and said, without missing a beat, "leg amputation." I nearly panicked, but I stayed. To my own amazement, I was not in the least upset by the amputation or any of the surgeries I witnessed, including the repair of a ruptured ectopic pregnancy that drove at least two experienced nurses from the OR in dismay. For some reason, there seemed to be no period of "getting used to it" at all. So repeated exposure as a means of routinization is insufficient; more is at work.

At least four phenomenological tasks go into the routinization of the hospital world: learning one's geographical surroundings, so that the routine is physically manageable; learning the language so one can meet and work with other people; learning the technique of the work being done (if you don't know how to start an IV, it's hard to be casual about it); and learning the "types" of patients and the standard procedures for recognizing and dealing with them. . . . There is also, harder to define, a fifth task, a perceptual "leap," which I will describe after presenting these components. . . .

1. *Learning the geography.* The first step in the routinization of a world is simply to learn one's way around the physical setting. It's difficult to be casual when rooms are unfamiliar, hallways look long and forbidding, and one can't find the bathroom. Supplies are often kept in unexpected places, telephones sometime work in strange ways ("You have to dial 8 first"), even chairs may have traditional claims on them (until recently in American hospitals, nurses stood while physicians sat). Hospital beds come in various models, and working them isn't always easy.

This geography has social meanings and implications, too, which must be learned. One has to know that "this is Joanne's chair," or that the clerk always gets the phone, or that everyone cleans their own coffee cup. The physical setting, that is, must be known in its social ramifications. . . .

2. *Learning the language.* To move easily in the world of the hospital, the nurse must learn its peculiar language, the technical jargon, and the informal slang. The jargon is technically complex, even daunting. DNR: an order to Do Not Resuscitate a terminal patient when his or her breathing or heartbeat stops. CABG: pronounced "Cabbage," a coronary artery bypass graft, what the layperson calls bypass surgery. Or consider this description of the possible causes of one common symptom.

> [It is found] accompanying diaphragmatic pleurisy, pneumonia, uremia, or alcoholism . . . abdominal causes include disorders of the stomach, and esophagus, bowel diseases, pancreatitis, pregnancy, bladder irritation, hepatic metastases, or hepatitis. Thoracic and mediastinal lesions or surgery may be responsible. Posterior fossa tumors or infarcts may stimulate centers in the medulla oblongata . . .[9]

Pity the poor layperson who overhears such language to discuss his or her symptom—which in this case is hiccups.

Besides medical jargon, informal slang is highly developed, as the staff live in an experiential world far different than the layperson. Here, a dying patient is "going down the tubes," "circling the drain." The dead have "bought the farm," "straight-lined," or perhaps "Marshalled"—a reference to the name of the building that houses the morgue. An older patient who violently resists the nurses is "confused" and after drug sedation become much more "appropriate." Every emergency room has its "Gomers"—one of the most ubiquitous cases of hospital slang, derived from "Grand Old Man of the ER," or variants, and referring generically to old people with no treatable problems who are virtually permanent residents of the hospital.[10] On the acute psychiatric unit, there is the "quiet room": what once was called a padded cell, where a suicidal teenage girl huddles in a corner, crying, visible through the peephole in the door. The patient is regularly technicized in discussions of "input" and "output" (of food and waste). Learning the peculiar language is a vital part of becoming an insider. To understand what people are talking about, much less to become comfortable here, you need to learn the slang.[11] And even when no special jargon is used, the very matter-of-factness of the talk can be disarming: "Well, he had a stool; it was soft, but he said there was some diarrhea." Most of us simply don't talk in that way with fellow workers.

3. *Learning the techniques.* Routinization requires learning the techniques of one's work: the job itself must be familiar. One reason that I was immediately "used to" seeing surgery was that I was only observing it, not participating. Observing is a skill at which, as a sociologist, I have had much practice. There was no further technical learning necessary.

Nursing entails a great number of specific technical skills, and until one learns them the job can be overwhelming. "Being organized" is a prime job skill for nurses. The staff nurse dispenses hundreds of pills a day to dozens of patients, starts and maintains intravenous lines, gives bed baths, documents on paper virtually everything she does, monitors temperatures, blood pressures, and urine "outputs," delivers food trays, and responds more or less to all the miscellaneous patient and family requests that, from her point of view, often get in the way of her finishing her basic required work. Simply getting through an eight-hour shift without mistakenly giving Mrs. Jones the pills for Ms. Smith, or forgetting to check Mr. Martin's IV line, or not helping Miss Garcia eat her lunch is challenge enough. And these are the everyday, nonemergency tasks, the basics of the job. In the operating room, a circulating nurse is responsible for setting up tables with hundreds of small tools, stocking the correct combination of gauze sponges, suture kits, sterile gowns, and all the rest, knowing that surgeons are notoriously demanding; the scrub nurse sequentially passes the surgeon dozens of tools, when it matters most. Indeed,

the mass of details that nurses organize can appear overwhelming. And each detail, so apparently innocuous, can have enormous implications—as when a single sponge, one out of dozens used, is left inside the patient after surgery, or when one wrong pill goes to a heavily medicated patient. Thus, outstanding nurses often are described as "really well organized." . . .

4. *Learning the patients.* Patient types, too, become routine to the nurse. Despite an outsider's first impression of a multitude of different medical problems, most patients suffer one of a fairly small number of predictable ailments: cancer, heart disease, COPD (chronic obstructive pulmonary disease, such as emphysema or bronchitis), and now AIDS. These cover most of the severe cases. Treatments are relatively predictable as well, from the nursing staff's perspective: surgery, intravenous therapy, the usual medications. In heart disease, there are perhaps a half-dozen routinely used drugs; for cancer, there is surgery and the usual chemotherapy or radiation. So patients quickly become typed: the COPD lady in room 8, the AIDS guy in 2. . . .

An advantage of being used to seeing pain is that one can then work with suffering people. The "detached concern" that Merton writes about allows a nurse to lose the embarrassment many of us feel in front of sick people and allows her to talk with sick or dying patients. A dying woman can tell a nurse her fears; she may hesitate to burden a friend with them. A nurse, one may believe, has seen it all, so seeing one more thing perhaps won't upset her. It's probably true. One nurse told me that a friend said to her, "My dad is on oxygen!" and she, the nurse, thought to herself, "What would these people think if they saw someone in the unit with IV lines, an NG [nasogastric] tube, chest tubes, a catheter stuck in the bladder, and another tube stuck up the rectum? Ye gods, everyone I *know* is on oxygen!" She has become familiar with patients.

Having learned the geography of the hospital, the language, the techniques of work, and the types of patient, a nurse is well prepared to convert what was a chaos of disasters into a routine, well-organized round of daily activities.

5. *Routinization of the world.* But learning the specifics of the job—the geography, the jargon, the techniques, the patients—does not automatically produce an acceptance of the hospital world as normal. Some nurses learn the techniques but still never accept the daily disasters; they leave the profession, or move to less acute care settings, working in a school, a physician's office, or perhaps a home health care agency. More is demanded than simply accruing new information about work, or people, or the setting. Routinization itself demands a qualitative transformation in one's thinking, an entirely new way of relating to events and people. It can happen suddenly. Some nurses say that after six months or so on the job, having struggled through the heavy demands, often near to despair, one day they realize that the work no longer bothers them; they are "into" it.

> When I [first] walked into that unit, I had never seen any of these machines...there are 15,000 machines, they all have different alarms, they all have different ways to work them, different trouble-shooting things, and here you are expected to take care of this patient who's crumping every minute...it's just overwhelming.
>
> And then all of a sudden, one day, you say, Gee, I've survived this shift, and all of these things happened, and it was OK....
>
> [So what happened that you got used to it?]
>
> You know, I have absolutely no idea...You go in and you do it again and again, and your patient codes for the fifth time...I can't even tell you when it happens, it's different for different people...
>
> Then the scary thing happens. You start to *like* it. [Field Notes]

What this nurse describes is not just a gradual transition over time, not a simple

accumulation of experiences that finally equal "getting used to it." The accumulation of experiences is part of it, to be sure. But these only make possible the major shift, a qualitative transformation of consciousness, a *routinization of the world*. It is as if one takes the proverbial journey of a thousand single steps and discovers that the final step is in fact a fifteen-foot jump over a deep mountain gorge. Without that final leap, the journey is incomplete, almost a waste. But even that analogy doesn't quite fit, since many nurses "jump the gorge" without every realizing what they have done. Usually, it just happens ("How did you get used to it?" "I have absolutely no idea."). Still, it is the nurse who "does" this happening, who makes the leap, even if unconsciously. . . .

NOTES

1. On the routinization of dying, see David Sudnow, *Passing On: The Social Organization of Dying.* (Englewood Cliffs, NJ: Prentice-Hall, 1967).

2. Arnold S. Relman, "Intensive Care Units: Who Needs Them?" *New England Journal of Medicine* 302 (April 1980), p. 965.

3. Hughes, E. C. *Men and Their Work* (Westport, CT: Greenwood Press, 1958), p. 79.

4. Esther Lucile Brown, "Nursing and Patient Care," in Fred Davis, *The Nursing Profession: Five Sociological Essays* (New York: John Wiley & Sons, 1966), p. 202.

5. Hughes, E. C. *Men and Their Work* (Westport, CT: Greenwood Press, 1958), pp. 54, 88.

6. Some physicians have astonishing numbers of routinized operations to their credit. For example, Dr. Denton Cooley of Houston has performed over 75,000 open heart surgeries with his team. Over two-thirds were personally performed by Dr. Cooley. *Guinness Book of World Records* (New York: Bantam Books, 1988).

7. Hughes, E. C. *Men and Their Work* (Westport, CT: Greenwood Press, 1958), p. 54.

8. Ronald Philip Preston, *The Dilemmas of Care: Social and Nursing Adaptations to the Deformed, the Disabled and the Aged* (New York: Elsevier, 1979), p. 93.

9. *The Merck Manual of Diagnosis and Therapy*, 15th ed. (Rahway, NJ: Merck Sharp & Dohme Research Laboratories, 1987). pp. 1356–1357.

10. See Samuel Shem, M.D. *The House of God* (New York: Dell Publishing Co., 1978), for many more examples.

11. "No profession can do its work without licence to talk in shocking terms about clients and their problems." Hughes, *Men and their Work*, p. 82.

THINKING ABOUT THE READING

Describe the techniques nurses use to routinize pain, suffering, and tragedy in the hospital. Why is such routinization necessary? Answer this question both in terms of personal survival and the institutional needs of the field of medicine. It is ironic that at precisely those moments when sick patients want their nurse to take a deep personal interest in them, that nurses must work hard to maintain emotional distance. What would happen to the U.S. health care system if nurses (as well as doctors) had ordinary emotional responses to misery and death? Contrast this work to the care work that nannies and other care givers are hired to perform. Do you see differences as well as similarities in strategies that both sets of workers might use to get the job done and also maintain personal detachment?

The Architecture of Stratification

Social Class and Inequality

Inequality is woven into the fabric of all societies through a structured system of *social stratification*. Social stratification is a ranking of entire groups of people that perpetuates unequal rewards and life chances in society. The structural-functionalist explanation of stratification is that the stability of society depends on all social positions being filled—that is, there are people around to do all the jobs that need to be done. Higher rewards, such as prestige and large salaries, are afforded to the most important positions, thereby ensuring that the most qualified individuals will occupy the highest positions. In contrast, conflict theory argues that stratification reflects an unequal distribution of power in society and is a primary source of conflict and tension.

Social class is the primary means of stratification in American society. Contemporary sociologists are likely to define one's class standing as a combination of income, wealth, occupational prestige, and educational attainment. It is tempting to see class differences as simply the result of an economic stratification system that exists at a level above the individual. Although inequality is created and maintained by larger social institutions, it is often felt most forcefully and is reinforced most effectively in the chain of interactions that take place in our day-to-day lives.

The media play a significant role in shaping people's perceptions of class. But instead of providing accurate descriptive information about different classes, the media—especially the news media—give the impression that the United States is largely a classless society. According to Gregory Mantsios in "Making Class Invisible," when different classes are depicted in the media, the images tend to hover around stereotypes that reinforce the cultural belief that people's position in society is largely a function of their own effort and achievement, or in the case of "the poor," lack of effort and achievement.

Whether accurately portrayed or not, social class affects virtually every aspect of our daily lives. In "Branded With Infamy: Inscriptions of Poverty and Class in America," Vivyan Adair describes the various ways in which poor women's bodies are marked as "unclean" or "unacceptable." These markings are the result of a life of poverty: lack of access to adequate health care, lack of proper nutrition and shelter, and a consequence of difficult and demanding physical labor. But more affluent people often come to view these women (and their children), not as victims of economic circumstances, but as members of an undesirable class who deserve to be disciplined, controlled, and punished.

The face of American poverty has changed somewhat over the past several decades. The economic status of single mothers and their children has deteriorated while that of people over age 65 has improved somewhat. What hasn't changed is the ever widening gap between the rich and the poor. Poverty persists because in a free-market and competitive society it serves economic and social functions. In addition, poverty receives institutional "support" in the form of segmented labor markets and inadequate educational systems. The ideology of competitive individualism—that to succeed in life all one has to do is work hard and win in competition with others—creates a belief that poor people are to blame for their own suffering. So although the problem of poverty remains serious, public attitudes toward poverty and poor people are frequently indifferent or even hostile.

Furthermore, important social institutions can perpetuate the problem. In "Savage Inequalities in America's Schools," Jonathan Kozol provides a troubling portrait of inequality in the American educational system by comparing the school experiences of children in two very different cities. Although the children of destitute East St. Louis, Illinois, and affluent Rye, New York, are citizens of the same country, they live in two very different worlds. Kozol draws compelling contrasts between the broken-down classrooms, outdated textbooks, and faulty plumbing in East St. Louis and the sparkling new auditoriums and up-to-date computers in Rye. These vastly different educational experiences make it difficult to sustain the myth that all children, no matter where they live, are competing in a fair race for society's resources.

Something to Consider as You Read:

In reading these selections, pay careful attention to the small ways in which economic resources affect everyday choices and behavior. For instance, how might poverty, including the lack of access to nice clothing, affect one's ability to portray the best possible image at a job interview? Consider further the connection between media portrayals and self-image. Where do people get their ideas about their own self-worth, their sense of entitlement, and how they fit into society generally? Some observers have suggested that people in the United States don't know how to talk about class, except in stereotypical terms. How might this lack of "class discourse" perpetuate stereotypes and the myth that the poor deserve their fate?

Making Class Invisible

Gregory Mantsios

(1998)

Of the various social and cultural forces in our society, the mass media is arguably the most influential in molding public consciousness. Americans spend an average twenty-eight hours per week watching television. They also spend an undetermined number of hours reading periodicals, listening to the radio, and going to the movies. Unlike other cultural and socializing institutions, ownership and control of the mass media is highly concentrated. Twenty-three corporations own more than one-half of all the daily newspapers, magazines, movie studios, and radio and television outlets in the United States. The number of media companies is shrinking and their control of the industry is expanding. And a relatively small number of media outlets is producing and packaging the majority of news and entertainment programs. For the most part, our media is national in nature and single-minded (profit-oriented) in purpose. This media plays a key role in defining our cultural tastes, helping us locate ourselves in history, establishing our national identity, and ascertaining the range of national and social possibilities. In this essay, we will examine the way the mass media shapes how people think about each other and about the nature of our society.

The United States is the most highly stratified society in the industrialized world. Class distinctions operate in virtually every aspect of our lives, determining the nature of our work, the quality of our schooling, and the health and safety of our loved ones. Yet remarkably, we, as a nation, retain illusions about living in an egalitarian society. We maintain these illusions, in large part, because the media hides gross inequities from public view. In those instances when inequities are revealed, we are provided with messages that obscure the nature of class realities and blame the victims of class-dominated society for their own plight. Let's briefly examine what the news media, in particular, tells us about class.

About the Poor

The news media provides meager coverage of poor people and poverty. The coverage it does provide is often distorted and misleading.

The Poor Do Not Exist

For the most part, the news media ignores the poor. Unnoticed are forty million poor people in the nation—a number that equals the entire population of Maine, Vermont, New Hampshire, Connecticut, Rhode Island, New Jersey, and New York combined. Perhaps even more alarming is that the rate of poverty is increasing twice as fast as the population growth in the United States. Ordinarily, even a calamity of much smaller proportion (e.g., flooding in the Midwest) would garner a great deal of coverage and hype from a media usually eager to declare a crisis, yet less than one in five hundred articles in the *New York Times* and one in one thousand articles listed in the

Readers Guide to Periodic Literature are on poverty. With remarkably little attention to them, the poor and their problems are hidden from most Americans.

When the media does turn its attention to the poor, it offers a series of contradictory messages and portrayals.

The Poor Are Faceless

Each year the Census Bureau releases a new report on poverty in our society and its results are duly reported in the media. At best, however, this coverage emphasizes annual fluctuations (showing how the numbers differ from previous years) and ongoing debates over the validity of the numbers (some argue the number should be lower, most that the number should be higher). Coverage like this desensitizes us to the poor by reducing poverty to a number. It ignores the human tragedy of poverty—the suffering, indignities, and misery endured by millions of children and adults. Instead, the poor become statistics rather than people.

The Poor Are Undeserving

When the media does put a face on the poor, it is not likely to be a pretty one. The media will provide us with sensational stories about welfare cheats, drug addicts, and greedy panhandlers (almost always urban and Black). Compare these images and the emotions evoked by them with the media's treatment of middle-class (usually white) "tax evaders," celebrities who have a "chemical dependency," or wealthy businesspeople who use unscrupulous means to "make a profit." While the behavior of the more affluent offenders is considered an "impropriety" and a deviation from the norm, the behavior of the poor is considered repugnant, indicative of the poor in general, and worthy of our indignation and resentment.

The Poor Are an Eyesore

When the media does cover the poor, they are often presented through the eyes of the middle class. For example, sometimes the media includes a story with panhandlers. Rather than focusing on the plight of the poor, these stories are about middle-class opposition to the poor. Such stories tell us that the poor are an inconvenience and an irritation.

The Poor Have Only Themselves to Blame

In another example of media coverage, we are told that the poor live in a personal and cultural cycle of poverty that hopelessly imprisons them. They routinely center on the Black urban population and focus on perceived personality or cultural traits that doom the poor. While the women in these stories typically exhibit an "attitude" that leads to trouble or a promiscuity that leads to single motherhood, the men possess a need for immediate gratification that leads to drug abuse or an unquenchable greed that leads to the pursuit of fast money. The images that are seared into our mind are sexist, racist, and classist. Census figures reveal that most of the poor are white not Black or Hispanic, that they live in rural or suburban areas not urban centers, and hold jobs at least part of the year. Yet, in a fashion that is often framed in an understanding and sympathetic tone, we are told that the poor have inflicted poverty on themselves.

The Poor Are Down on Their Luck

During the Christmas season, the news media sometimes provides us with accounts of poor individuals or families (usually white) who are down on their luck. These stories are often linked to stories about soup kitchens or other charitable activities and sometimes call for charitable contributions. These "Yule time" stories are as much about the affluent as they are about the poor: they tell us that the affluent in our society are a kind, understanding, giving people—which we are not.* The series of unfortunate circumstances that have led to impoverishment are presumed to be a temporary condition that will improve with time and a change in luck.

Despite appearances, the messages provided by the media are not entirely disparate. With each variation, the media informs us what poverty is not (i.e., systemic and indicative of American society) by informing us what it is. The media tells us that poverty is either an aberration of the American way of life (it doesn't exist, it's just another number, it's unfortunate but temporary) or an end product of the poor themselves (they are a nuisance, do not deserve better, and have brought their predicament upon themselves).

By suggesting that the poor have brought poverty upon themselves, the media is engaging in what William Ryan has called "blaming the victim." The media identifies in what ways the poor are different as a consequence of deprivation, then defines those differences as the cause of poverty itself. Whether blatantly hostile or cloaked in sympathy, the message is that there is something fundamentally wrong with the victims—their hormones, psychological makeup, family environment, community, race, or some combination of these—that accounts for their plight and their failure to lift themselves out of poverty.

But poverty in the United States is systemic. It is a direct result of economic and political policies that deprive people of jobs, adequate wages, or legitimate support. It is neither natural nor inevitable: there is enough wealth in our nation to eliminate poverty if we chose to redistribute existing wealth or income. The plight of the poor is reason enough to make the elimination of poverty the nation's first priority. But poverty also impacts dramatically on the non-poor. It has a dampening effect on wages in general (by maintaining a reserve army of unemployed and underemployed anxious for any job at any wage) and breeds crime and violence (by maintaining conditions that invite private gain by illegal means and rebellion-like behavior, not entirely unlike the urban riots of the 1960s). Given the extent of poverty in the nation and the impact it has on us all, the media must spin considerable magic to keep the poor and the issue of poverty and its root causes out of the public consciousness.

About Everyone Else

Both the broadcast and the print news media strive to develop a strong sense of "we-ness" in their audience. They seek to speak to and for an audience that is both affluent and like-minded. The media's solidarity with affluence, that is, with the middle and upper class, varies little from one medium to another. Benjamin DeMott points out, for example, that the *New York Times* understands affluence to be intelligence, taste, public spirit, responsibility, and a readiness to rule and "conceives itself as spokesperson for a readership awash in these qualities." Of course, the flip side to creating a

---

* American households with incomes of less than $10,000 give an average of 5.5 percent of their earning to charity or to a religious organization, while those making more than $100,000 a year give only 2.9 percent. After changes in the 1986 tax code reduced the benefits of charitable giving, taxpayers earning $500,000 or more slashed their average donation by nearly one-third. Furthermore, many of these acts of benevolence do not help the needy. Rather than provide funding to social service agencies that aid the poor, the voluntary contributions of the wealthy go to places and institutions that entertain, inspire, cure, or educate wealthy Americans—art museums, opera houses, theaters, orchestras, ballet companies, private hospitals, and elite universities.

sense of "we," or "us," is establishing a perception of the "other." The other relates back to the faceless, amoral, undeserving, and inferior "underclass." Thus, the world according to the news media is divided between the "underclass" and everyone else. Again the messages are often contradictory.

The Wealthy Are Us

Much of the information provided to us by the news media focuses attention on the concerns of a very wealthy and privileged class of people. Although the concerns of a small fraction of the populace, they are presented as though they were the concerns of everyone. For example, while relatively few people actually own stock, the news media devotes an inordinate amount of broadcast time and print space to business news and stock market quotations. Not only do business reports cater to a particular narrow clientele, so do the fashion pages (with $2,000 dresses), wedding announcements, and the obituaries. Even weather and sports news often have a class bias. An all news radio station in New York City, for example, provides regular national ski reports. International news, trade agreements, and domestic policies issues are also reported in terms of their impact on business climate and the business community. Besides being of practical value to the wealthy, such coverage has considerable ideological value. Its message: the concerns of the wealthy are the concerns of us all.

The Wealthy (as a Class) Do Not Exist

While preoccupied with the concerns of the wealthy, the media fails to notice the way in which the rich as a class of people create and shape domestic and foreign policy. Presented as an aggregate of individuals, the wealthy appear without special interests, interconnections, or unity in purpose. Out of public view are the class interests of the wealthy, the interlocking business links, the concerted actions to preserve their class privileges and business interests (by running for public office, supporting political candidates, lobbying, etc.). Corporate lobbying is ignored, taken for granted, or assumed to be in the public interest. (Compare this with the media's portrayal of the "strong arm of labor" in attempting to defeat trade legislation that is harmful to the interests of working people.) It is estimated that two-thirds of the U.S. Senate is composed of millionaires. Having such a preponderance of millionaires in the Senate, however, is perceived to be neither unusual nor antidemocratic; these millionaire senators are assumed to be serving "our" collective interests in governing.

The Wealthy Are Fascinating and Benevolent

The broadcast and print media regularly provide hype for individuals who have achieved "super" success. These stories are usually about celebrities and superstars from the sports and entertainment world. Society pages and gossip columns serve to keep the social elite informed of each others' doings, allow the rest of us to gawk at their excesses, and help to keep the American dream alive. The print media is also fond of feature stories on corporate empire builders. These stories provide an occasional "insider's" view of the private and corporate life of industrialists by suggesting a rags to riches account of corporate success. These stories tell us that corporate success is a series of smart moves, shrewd acquisitions, timely mergers, and well thought out executive suite shuffles. By painting the upper class in a positive light, innocent of any wrongdoing (labor leaders and union organizations usually get the opposite treatment), the media assures us that wealth and power are benevolent. One person's capital accumulation is presumed to be good for all. The elite, then, are portrayed as investment wizards, people of special talent and skill, who even their victims (workers and consumers) can admire.

The Wealthy Include a Few Bad Apples

On rare occasions, the media will mock selected individuals for their personality flaws. Real estate investor Donald Trump and New York Yankees owner George Steinbrenner, for example, are admonished by the media for deliberately seeking publicity (a very un-upper class thing to do); hotel owner Leona Helmsley was caricatured for her personal cruelties; and junk bond broker Michael Milkin was condemned because he had the audacity to rob the rich. Michael Parenti points out that by treating business wrongdoing as isolated deviations from the socially beneficial system of "responsible capitalism," the media overlooks the features of the system that produce such abuses and the regularity with which they occur. Rather than portraying them as predictable and frequent outcomes of corporate power and the business system, the media treats abuses as if they were isolated and atypical. Presented as an occasional aberration, these incidents serve not to challenge, but to legitimate, the system.

The Middle Class Is Us

By ignoring the poor and blurring the lines between the working people and the upper class, the news media creates a universal middle class. From this perspective, the size of one's income becomes largely irrelevant: what matters is that most of "us" share an intellectual and moral superiority over the disadvantaged. As *Time* magazine once concluded, "Middle America is a state of mind." "We are all middle class," we are told, "and we all share the same concerns": job security, inflation, tax burdens, world peace, the cost of food and housing, health care, clean air and water, and the safety of our streets. While the concerns of the wealthy are quite distinct from those of the

middle class (e.g., the wealthy worry about investments, not jobs), the media convinces us that "we [the affluent] are all in this together."

The Middle Class Is a Victim

For the media, "we" the affluent not only stand apart from the "other"—the poor, the working class, the minorities, and their problems—"we" are also roles, minorities (who commit crimes against us), and by workers (who are greedy and drive companies out and prices up). Ignored are the subsidies to the rich, the crimes of corporate America, and the policies that wreak havoc on the economic well-being of middle America. Media magic convinces us to fear, more than anything else, being victimized by those less affluent than ourselves.

The Middle Class Is Not a Working Class

The news media clearly distinguishes the middle class (employees) from the working class (i.e., blue collar workers) who are portrayed, at best, as irrelevant, outmoded, and a dying breed. Furthermore, the media will tell us that the hardships faced by blue collar workers are inevitable (due to progress), a result of bad luck (chance circumstances in a particular industry), or a product of their own doing (they priced themselves out of a job). Given the media's presentation of reality, it is hard to believe that manual, supervised, unskilled, and semiskilled workers actually represent more than 50 percent of the adult working population. The working class, instead, is relegated by the media to "the other."

In short, the news media either lionizes the wealthy or treats their interests and those of the middle class as one and the same. But the upper class and the middle class do not share the same interests or worries. Members of the upper class worry about stock dividends (not employment), they profit from inflation and global militarism, their children attend exclusive private schools, they eat and live in a royal fashion, they call on (or are called upon by) personal physicians, they have few consumer problems, they can escape whenever they want from environmental pollution, and they live on streets and travel to other areas under the protection of private police forces.*

The wealthy are not only a class with distinct life-styles and interests, they are a ruling class. They receive a disproportionate share of the country's yearly income, own a disproportionate amount of the country's wealth, and contribute a disproportionate number of their members to governmental bodies and decision-making groups—all traits that William Domhoff, in his classic work *Who Rules America*, defined as characteristic of a governing class.

This governing class maintains and manages our political and economic structures in such a way that these structures continue to yield an amazing proportion of our wealth to a minuscule upper class. While the media is not above referring to ruling classes in other countries (we hear, for example, references to Japan's ruling elite), its treatment of the news proceeds as though there were no such ruling class in the United States.

Furthermore, the news media inverts reality so that those who are working class and middle class learn to fear, resent, and blame those below, rather than those above them in the class structure. We learn to resent welfare, which accounts for only two cents out of every dollar in the federal budget (approximately $10 billion) and provides financial relief for the needy,** but learn little about the $11 billion the federal government spends on individuals with incomes in excess of $100,000 (not needy), or the $17 billion in farm subsidies, or the $214 billion (twenty times the cost of welfare) in interest payments to financial institutions.

Middle-class whites learn to fear African Americans and Latinos, but most violent crime occurs within poor and minority communities and is neither interracial[†] nor interclass. As horrid as such crime is, it should not mask the destruction and violence perpetrated by corporate America. In spite of the fact that 14,000 innocent people are killed on the job each year, 100,000 die prematurely, 400,000 become seriously ill, and 6 million are injured from work-related accidents and diseases, most Americans fear government regulation more than they do unsafe working conditions.

Through the media, middle-class—and even working-class—Americans learn to blame blue collar workers and their unions for declining purchasing power and economic security. But while workers who managed to keep their jobs and their unions struggled to keep up with inflation, the top 1 percent of American families saw their average incomes soar 80 percent in the last decade. Much of the wealth at the top was accumulated as stockholders and corporate executives moved their companies abroad to employ cheaper labor (56 cents per hour in El Salvador) and avoid paying taxes in the United

---

*The number of private security guards in the United States now exceeds the number of public police officers. (Robert Reich, "Secession of the Successful." *New York Times Magazine,* February, 1991)

**A total of $20 billion is spent on welfare when you include all state funding. But the average state funding also comes to only two cents per state dollar.

[†]In 92 percent of the murders nationwide the assailant and the victim are of the same race (46 percent are white/white, 46 percent are black/black), 5.6 percent are black on white, and 2.4 percent are white on black. (FBI and Bureau of Justice Statistics, 1985–1986, quoted in Raymond S. Franklin. *Shadows of Race and Class,* University of Minnesota Press, Minneapolis, 1991, p. 108.)

States. Corporate America is a world made up of ruthless bosses, massive layoffs, favoritism and nepotism, health and safety violations, pension plan losses, union busting, tax evasions, unfair competition, and price gouging, as well as fast buck deals, financial speculation, and corporate wheeling and dealing that serve the interests of the corporate elite, but are generally wasteful and destructive to workers and the economy in general.

It is no wonder Americans cannot think straight about class. The mass media is neither objective, balanced, independent, nor neutral. Those who own and direct the mass media are themselves part of the upper class, and neither they nor the ruling class in general have to conspire to manipulate public opinion. Their interest is in preserving the status quo, and their view of society as fair and equitable comes naturally to them. But their ideology dominates our society and justifies what is in reality a perverse social order—one that perpetuates unprecedented elite privilege and power on the one hand and widespread deprivation on the other. A mass media that did not have its own class interests in preserving the status quo would acknowledge that inordinate wealth and power undermines democracy and that a "free market" economy can ravage a people and their communities.

THINKING ABOUT THE READING

What kinds of messages do people get about wealth and social position from the media? What do these messages suggest about who is deserving and who is not? If these messages are based on inaccurate stereotypes, where can people get more accurate information? Do you think that people in different social classes view themselves and their lives differently based on how they are portrayed in the news and on television? If these portrayals are a significant source of information about one's place in society, do you think these media images affect a person's sense of self-worth and opportunity?

Branded With Infamy

Inscriptions of Poverty and Class in America

Vivyan Adair

(2002)

"My kids and I been chopped up and spit out just like when I was a kid. My rotten teeth, my kids' twisted feet. My son's dull skin and blank stare. My oldest girl's stooped posture and the way she can't look no one in the eye no more. This all says we got nothing and we deserve what we got. On the street good families look at us and see right away what they'd be if they don't follow the rules. They're scared too, real scared."

—Welfare recipient and
activist, Olympia, Washington, 1998

I begin with the words of a poor, White, single mother of three. Although officially she has only a tenth-grade education, she expertly reads and articulates a complex theory of power, bodily inscription, and socialization that arose directly from material conditions of her own life. She sees what many far more "educated" scholars and citizens fail to recognize: that the bodies of poor women and children are produced and positioned as texts that facilitate the mandates of a . . . profoundly brutal and mean-spirited political regime. . . .

Over the past decade or so, a host of inspired feminist welfare scholars and activists have addressed and examined the relationship between state power and the lives of poor women and children. As important and insightful as these exposés are, with few exceptions, they do not get at the closed circuit that fuses together systems of power, the material conditions of poverty, and the bodily experiences that allow for the perpetuation—and

indeed the justification—of these systems. They fail to consider what the speaker of my opening passage recognized so astutely: that systems of power produce and patrol poverty through the reproduction of both social and bodily markers. . . .

. . . [In this article I employ the theory of Michel Foucault to describe how the body is] the product of historically specific power relations. Feminists have used this notion of social inscription to explain a range of bodily operations from cosmetic surgery (Brush 1998, Morgan 1991), prostitution (Bell 1994), and Anorexia Nervosa (Hopwood 1995, Bordo 1993) to motherhood (Chandler 1999, Smart 1992), race (Stoler 1995, Ford-Smith 1995), and cultural imperialism (Desmond 1991). As these analyses illustrate, Foucault allows us to consider and critique the body as it is invested with meaning and inserted into regimes of truth via the operations of power and knowledge. . . .

Foucault clarifies and expands on this process of bodily/social inscription in his early work. In "Nietzsche, Genealogy, History," he positions the physical body as virtual text, accounting for the fact that "the body is the inscribed surface of events that are traced by language and dissolved by ideas" (1977, 83).... For Foucault, the body and [power] are inseparable. In his logic, power constructs and holds bodies....

In *Discipline and Punish* Foucault sets out to depict the genealogy of torture and discipline as it reflects a public display of power on the body of subjects in the 17th and 18th centuries. In graphic detail Foucault begins his book with the description of a criminal being tortured and then drawn and quartered in a public square. The crowds of good parents and their growing children watch and learn. The public specta-cle works as a patrolling image, socializing and controlling bodies within the body politic. Eighteenth century torture "must mark the victim: it is intended, either by the scar it leaves on the body or by the spectacle that accompa-nies it, to brand the victim with infamy . . . it traces around or rather on the very body of the condemned man signs that can not be effaced" (1984, 179). For Foucault, public exhibitions of punishment served as a socializing process, writing culture's codes and values on the minds and bodies of its subjects. In the process pun-ishment . . . rearranged bodies.

. . . Foucault's point in *Discipline and Punish* is . . . that public exhibition and inscrip-tion have been replaced in contemporary society by a much more effective process of socialization and self-inscription. According to Foucault, today discipline has replaced torture as the privileged punishment, but the body continues to be written on. Discipline produces "subjected and practiced bodies, docile bodies" (1984, 182). We become subjects . . . of ideol-ogy, disciplining and inscribing our own bodies/minds in the process of becoming stable and singular subjects. . . . The body continues to be the site and operation of ideology. . . .

Indeed, while we are all marked discur-sively by ideology in Foucault's paradigm, in the United States today poor women and children of all races are multiply marked with signs of both discipline and punishment that cannot be erased or effaced. They are systemat-ically produced through both 20th century forces of socialization and discipline and 18th century exhibitions of public mutilation. In addition to coming into being as disciplined and docile bodies, poor single welfare mothers and their children are physically inscribed, punished, and displayed as dangerous and pathological "other." It is important to note when considering the contemporary inscrip-tion of poverty as moral pathology etched onto the bodies of profoundly poor women and children, that these are more than metaphoric and self-patrolling marks of discipline. Rather on myriad levels—sexual, social, material and physical—poor women and their children, like the "deviants" publicly punished in Foucault's scenes of torture, are marked, mutilated, and made to bear and transmit signs in a public spectacle that brands the victim with infamy.

. . .

The (Not So) Hidden Injuries of Class

Recycled images of poor, welfare women per-meate and shape our national consciousness.[1] Yet—as is so often the case—these images and narratives tell us more about the culture that spawned and embraced them than they do about the object of the culture's obsession. . . .

These productions orchestrate the story of poverty as one of moral and intellectual lack and of chaos, pathology, promiscuity, illogic, and sloth, juxtaposed always against the order, progress, and decency of "deserving" citizens. . . .

I am, and will probably always be, marked as a poor woman. I was raised by a poor, sin-gle, White mother who had to struggle to keep her four children fed, sheltered, and clothed by working at what seemed like an endless stream of minimum wage, exhausting, and demeaning jobs. As a child poverty was written onto and into my being at the level of private and public thought and body. At an early age my body bore witness to and emitted signs of the painful devaluation carved into my flesh; that same devaluation became integral to my being in the world. I came into being as disciplined body/mind while at the same time I was taught to read my abject body as the site of my own punishment and erasure. In this excess of meaning the space between private body and public sign was collapsed.

For many poor children this double exposure results in debilitating . . . shame and lack. As Carolyn Kay Steedman reminds us in *Landscape for a Good Woman,* the mental life of poor children flows from material deprivation. Steedman speaks of the "relentless laying down of guilt" she experienced as a poor child living in a world where identity was shaped through envy and unfulfilled desire and where her own body "told me stories of the terrible unfairness of things, of the subterranean culture of longing for that which one can never have" (1987, 8). For Steedman, public devaluation and punishment "demonstrated to us all the hierarchies of our illegality, the impropriety of our existence, our marginality within the social system" (1987, 9). Even as an adult she recalls that:

> . . . the baggage will never lighten for me or my sister. We were born, and had no choice in the matter; but we were social burdens, expensive, unworthy, never grateful enough. There was nothing we could do to pay back the debt of our existence. (1987, 19)

Indeed, poor children are often marked with bodily signs that cannot be forgotten or erased. Their bodies are physically inscribed as "other" and then read as pathological, dangerous, and undeserving. What I recall most vividly about being a child in a profoundly poor family was that we were constantly hurt and ill, and

because we could not afford medical care, small illnesses and accidents spiraled into more dangerous illnesses and complications that became both a part of who we were and written proof that we were of no value in the world.

In spite of my mother's heroic efforts, at an early age my brothers and sister and I were stooped, bore scars that never healed properly, and limped with feet mangled by illfitting, used Salvation Army shoes. When my sister's forehead was split open by a door slammed in frustration, my mother "pasted" the angry wound together on her own, leaving a mark of our inability to afford medical attention, of our lack, on her very forehead. When I suffered from a concussion, my mother simply put borrowed ice on my head and tried to keep me awake for a night. And when throughout elementary school we were sent to the office for mandatory and very public yearly checks, the school nurse sucked air through her teeth as she donned surgical gloves to check only the hair of poor children for lice.

We were read as unworthy, laughable, and often dangerous. Our school mates laughed at our "ugly shoes," our crooked and ill-serviced teeth, and the way we "stank," as teachers excoriated us for inability to concentrate in school, our "refusal" to come to class prepared with proper school supplies, and our unethical behavior when we tried to take more than our allocated share of "free lunch."[2] Whenever backpacks or library books came up missing, we were publicly interrogated and sent home to "think about" our offences, often accompanied by notes that reminded my mother that as a poor single parent she should be working twice as hard to make up for the discipline that allegedly walked out the door with my father. When we sat glued to our seats, afraid to stand in front of the class in ragged and ill-fitting hand-me-downs, we were held up as examples of unprepared and uncooperative children. And when our grades reflected our otherness, they were used to justify even more elaborate punishment. . . .

Friends who were poor as children, and respondents to a survey I conducted in 1998,[3] tell similar stories of the branding they received at the hands of teachers, administrators, and peers. An African-American woman raised in Yesler Terrace, a public housing complex in Seattle, Washington, writes:

> Poor was all over our faces. My glasses were taped and too weak. My big brother had missing teeth. My mom was dull and ashy. It was like a story of how poor we were that anyone could see. My sister Evie's lip was bit by a dog and we just had dime store stuff to put on it. Her lip was a big scar. Then she never smiled and no one smiled at her cause she never smiled. Kids called her "Scarface." Teachers never smiled at her. The principle put her in detention all the time because she was mean and bad (they said).

And, a White woman in the Utica, New York, area remembers:

> We lived in dilapidated and unsafe housing that had fleas no matter how clean my mom tried to be. We had bites all over us. Living in our car between evictions was even worse— then we didn't have a bathroom so I got kidney problems that I never had doctor's help for. When my teachers wouldn't let me got to the bathroom every hour or so I would wet my pants in class. You can imagine what the kids did to me about that. And the teachers would refuse to let me go to the bathroom because they said I was willful.

Material deprivation is publicly written on the bodies of poor children in the world. In the United States poor families experience violent crime, hunger, lack of medical and dental care, utility shut-offs, the effects of living in unsafe housing and/or of being homeless, chronic illness, and insufficient winter clothing (Lein and Edin 1996, 224–231). According to Jody Raphael of the Taylor Institute, poor women and their children are also at five times the risk of experiencing domestic violence (Raphael, 2000).

As children, our disheveled and broken bodies were produced and read as signs of our inferiority and undeservedness. As adults our mutilated bodies are read as signs of inner chaos, immaturity, and indecency as we are punished and then read as proof of need for further discipline and punishment. When my already bad teeth started to rot and I was out of my head with pain, my choices as an adult welfare recipient were to either let my teeth fall out or have them pulled out. In either case the culture would then read me as a "toothless illiterate," as a fearful joke. In order to pay my rent and to put shoes on my daughter's feet I sold blood at two or three different clinics on a monthly basis until I became so anemic that they refused to buy it from me. A neighbor of mine went back to the man who continued to beat her and her children after being denied welfare benefits, when she realized that she could not adequately feed, clothe and house her family on her own minimum wage income. My good friend sold her ovum to a fertility clinic in a painful and potentially damaging process. Other friends exposed themselves to all manner of danger and disease by selling their bodies for sex in order to feed and clothe their babies.

Exhaustion also marks the bodies of poor women in indelible script. Rest becomes a privilege we simply cannot afford. After working full shifts each day, poor mothers trying to support themselves at minimum wage jobs continue to work to a point of exhaustion that is inscribed on their faces, their bodies, their posture, and their diminishing sense of self and value in the world. My former neighbor recently recalled:

> I had to take connecting buses to bring and pick up my daughters at childcare after working on my feet all day. As soon as we arrived at home, we would head out again by bus to do

laundry. Pick up groceries. Try to get to the food bank. Beg the electric company to not turn off our lights and heat again. Find free winter clothing. Sell my blood. I would be home at nine or ,ten o'clock at night. I was loaded down with one baby asleep and one crying. Carrying lots of heavy bags and ready to drop on my feet. I had bags under my eyes and no shampoo to wash my hair so I used soap. Anyway I had to stay up to wash diapers in the sink. Otherwise they wouldn't be dry when I left the house in the dark with my girls. In the morning I start all over again.

This bruised and lifeless body, hauling sniffling babies and bags of dirty laundry on the bus, was then read as a sign that she was a bad mother and a threat that needed to be disciplined and made to work even harder for her own good. Those who need the respite less go away for weekends, take drives in the woods, take their kids to the beach. Poor women without education are pushed into minimum wage jobs and have no money, no car, no time, no energy, and little support, as their bodies are made to display marks of their material deprivation as a socializing and patrolling force.

Ultimately, we come to recognize that our bodies are not our own; that they are rather public property. State mandated blood tests, interrogation of the most private aspects of our lives, the public humiliation of having to beg officials for food and medicine, and the loss of all right to privacy, teach us that our bodies are only useful as lessons, warnings, and signs of degradation that everyone loves to hate. In "From Welfare to Academe: Welfare Reform as College-Educated Welfare Mothers Know It," Sandy Smith-Madsen describes the erosion of her privacy as a poor welfare mother:

> I was investigated. I was spied upon. A welfare investigator came into my home and after thoughtful deliberation, granted me permission to keep my belongings. . . . Like the witch hunts of old, if a neighbor reports you as a welfare queen, the guardians of the state's compelling interest come into your home and interrogate you. While they do not have the right to set your body ablaze on the public square, they can forever devastate heart and soul by snatching away children. Just like a police officer, they may use whatever they happen to see against you, including sexual orientation. Full-fledged citizens have the right to deny an officer entry into their home unless they possess a search warrant; welfare mothers fork over citizenship rights for the price of a welfare check. In Tennessee, constitutional rights go for a cash value of $185 per month for a family of three. (2000, 185)

Welfare reform policy is designed to publicly expose, humiliate, punish and display "deviant" welfare mothers. "Workfare" and "Learnfare"—two alleged successes of welfare reform—require that landlords, teachers, and employers be made explicitly aware of the second class status of these very public bodies. In Ohio, the Department of Human Services uses tax dollars to pay for advertisements on the side of Cleveland's RTA busses that show a "Welfare Queen" behind bars with a logo that proclaims "Crime does not pay. Welfare fraud is a crime" (Robinson 1999). In Michigan a pilot program mandating drug tests for all welfare recipients began on October 1, 1999. Recipients who refuse the test will lose their benefits immediately (Simon 1999). In Buffalo, New York, a County Executive proudly announced that his county will begin intensive investigation of all parents who refuse minimum wage jobs that are offered to them by the state. He warned: "We have many ways of investigating and exposing these errant parents who choose to exploit their children in this way" (Anderson 1999). And, welfare reform legislation enacted in 1996 as the Personal Responsibility and Work Opportunities Reconciliation Act (PRWORA), requires that poor mothers work full-time, earning minimum wage salaries with which they cannot support their children.

Often denied medical, dental, and childcare benefits, and unable to provide their families with adequate food, heat, or clothing, through this legislation the state mandates child neglect and abuse. The crowds of good parents and their growing children watch and learn. . . .

Reading and Rewriting the Body . . .

The bodies of poor women and children, scarred and mutilated by state mandated material deprivation and public exhibition, work as spectacles, as patrolling images socializing and controlling bodies within the body politic. . . .

Spectacular cover stories of the "Welfare Queen" play and re-play in the national mind's eye, becoming a prescriptive lens through which the American public as a whole reads the individual dramas of the bodies of poor women and their place and value in the world. These dramas produce "normative" citizens as singular, stable, rational, ordered, and free. In this dichotomous, hierarchical frame the poor welfare mother is juxtaposed against a logic of "normative" subjectivity as the embodiment of disorder, disarray, and other-ness. Her broken and scarred body becomes proof of her inner pathology and chaos, suggesting the need for further punishment and discipline.

In contemporary narrative welfare women are imagined to be dangerous because they refuse to sacrifice their desires and fail to participate in legally sanctioned heterosexual relationships; theirs is read, as a result, as a selfish, "unnatural," and immature sexuality. In this script, the bodies of poor women are viewed as being dangerously beyond the control of men and are as a result construed as the bearers of perverse desire. In this androcentric equation fathers become the sole bearers of order and of law, defending poor women and children against their own unchecked sexuality and lawlessness.

For Republican Senator [now Attorney General] John Ashcroft writing in *The St. Louis Dispatch*, the inner city is the site of "rampant illegitimacy" and a "space devoid of discipline" where all values are askew. For Ashcroft, what is insidious is not material poverty, but an entitlement system that has allowed "out-of-control" poor women to rupture traditional patriarchal authority, valuation, and boundaries (1995, A:23). Impoverished communities then become a site of chaos because without fathers they allegedly lack any organizing or patrolling principle. George Gilder agrees with Ashcroft when he writes in the conservative *American Spectator* that:

> The key problem of the welfare culture is not unemployed women and poor children. It is the women's skewed and traumatic relationships with men. In a reversal of the pattern of civilized societies, the women have the income and the ties to government authority and support. . . . This balance of power virtually prohibits marriage, which is everywhere based on the provider role of men, counterbalancing the sexual and domestic superiority of women. (1995, B:6)

For Gilder, the imprimatur of welfare women's sordid bodies unacceptably shifts the focus of the narrative from a male presence to a feminized absence.

In positioning welfare mothers as sexually chaotic, irrational, and unstable, their figures are temporarily immobilized and made to yield meaning as a space that must be brought under control and transformed through public displays of punishment. Poor single mothers and children who have been abandoned, have fled physical, sexual, and/or psychological abuse, or have in general refused to capitulate to male control within the home are mythologized as dangerous, pathological, out of control, and selfishly unable—or unwilling—to sacrifice their "naturally" unnatural desires. They are understood and punished as a danger to a culture resting on a foundation of inviolate male authority and absolute privilege in both public and private spheres.

William Raspberry disposes of poor women as selfish and immature, when in "Ms. Smith Goes After Washington," he warrants that:

> ... unfortunately AFDC is paid to an unaccountable, accidental and unprepared parent who has chosen her head of household status as a personal form of satisfaction, while lacking the simple life skills and maturity to achieve love and job fulfillment from any other source. I submit that all of our other social ills—crime, drugs, violence, failing schools ... are a direct result of the degradation of parenthood by emotionally immature recipients. (1995, A:19)

Raspberry goes on to assert that like poor children, poor mothers must be made visible reminders to the rest of the culture of the "poor choices" they have made. He claims that rather than "coddling" her, we have a responsibility to "shame her" and to use her failure to teach other young women that it is "morally wrong for unmarried women to bear children," as we "cast single motherhood as a selfish and immature act" (1995, A:19).

Continuous, multiple, and often seamless public inscription, punishing policy, and lives of unbearable material lack leave poor women and their children scarred, exhausted, and confused. As a result their bodies are imagined as an embodiment of decay and cultural dis-ease that threatens the health and progress of our nation. . . . In a 1995 *USA Today* article entitled "America at Risk: Can We Survive Without Moral Values?" for example, the inner city is portrayed as a "*dark*" realm of "*decay* rooted in the *loss* of values, the *death* of work ethics, and the *deterioration* of families and communities." Allegedly here, "all morality has *rotted* due to a *breakdown* in gender discipline." This space of disorder and disease is marked with tropes of race and gender. It is also associated with the imagery of "communities of women

without male leadership, cultural values and initiative [emphasis added]" (1995, C:3). In George Will's *Newsweek* editorial he proclaims that "*illogical* feminist and racial *anger* coupled with *misplaced* American emotion may be part or a cause of the *irresponsible* behavior *rampant* in poor neighborhoods." Will continues, proclaiming that here "mothers *lack* control over their children and have *selfishly* taught them to embrace a *pathological* ethos that values *self-need* and *self-expression* over self-control [emphasis added]" (1995, 23).

Poor women and children's bodies, publicly scarred and mutilated by material deprivation, are read as expressions of an essential lack of discipline and order. In response to this perception, journalist Ronald Brownstein of the *L.A. Times* proposed that the *Republican Contract with America* will "*restore* America to its path, *enforcing* social *order* and common *standards* of behavior, and replacing *stagnation* and *decay* with *movement* and *forward* thinking *energy* [emphasis added]" (1994, A:20). In these rhetorical fields poverty is . . . linked to lack of progress that would allegedly otherwise order, stabilize, and restore the culture. What emerges from these diatribes is the positioning of patriarchal, racist, capitalist, hierarchical, and heterosexist "order" and movement against the alleged stagnation and decay of the body of the "Welfare Queen."

Race is clearly written on the body of the poor single mother. The welfare mother, imagined as young, never married, and Black (contrary to statistical evidence[4]), is framed as dangerous and in need of punishment because she "naturally" emasculates her own men, refuses to service White men, and passes on—rather than appropriate codes of subservience and submission—a disruptive culture of resistance, survival, and "misplaced" pride to her children (Collins 1991). In stark contrast, widowed women with social security and divorced women with child support and alimony are imaged as White, legal, and propertied mothers whose value rests on their abilities to stay in their homes, care for their own children, and impart traditional cultural morals to their offspring, all for the betterment of the culture. In this narrative welfare mothers have only an "outlaw" culture to impart. Here the welfare mother is read as both the product and the producer of a culture of disease and disorder. These narratives imagine poor women as powerful contagion capable of, perhaps even lying in wait to infect their own children as raced, gendered, and classed agents of their "diseased" nature. In contemporary discourses of poverty racial tropes position poor women's bodies as dangerous sites of "naturalized chaos" and as potentially valuable economic commodities who refuse their proper role.

Gary McDougal in "The Missing Half of the Welfare Debate" furthers this image by referring to the "crab effect of poverty" through which mothers and friends of individuals striving to break free of economic dependency allegedly "pull them back down." McDougal affirms—again despite statistical evidence to the contrary—that the mothers of welfare recipients are most often themselves "generational welfare freeloaders lacking traditional values and family ties who can not, and will not, teach their children right from wrong." "These women" he asserts "would be better off doing any kind of labor regardless of how little it pays, just to get them out of the house, to break their cycles of degeneracy" (1996, A:16).

In this plenitude of images of evil mothers, the poor welfare mother threatens not just her own children, but all children. The Welfare Queen is made to signify moral aberration and economic drain; her figure becomes even more impacted once responsibility for the destruction of the "American Way of Life" is attributed to her. Ronald Brownstein reads her "spider web of dependency" as a "crisis of character development that leads to a morally bankrupt American ideology" (1994, A:6).

These representations position welfare mothers' bodies as sites of destruction and as catalysts for a culture of depravity and disobedience; in the process they produce a reading of the writing on the body of the poor woman that calls for further punishment and discipline. In New York City, "Workfare" programs force *lazy* poor women to take a job—"any job"—including working for the city wearing orange surplus prison uniforms picking up garbage on the highway and in parks for about $1.10 per hour (Dreier 1999). "Bridefare" programs in Wisconsin give added benefits to *licentious* welfare women who marry a man—"any man"—and publish a celebration of their "reform" in local newspapers (Dresang 1996). "Tidyfare" programs across the nation allow state workers to enter and inspect the homes of poor *slovenly* women so that they can monetarily sanction families whose homes are deemed to be appropriately tidied.[5] "Learnfare" programs in many states publicly expose and fine *undisciplined* mothers who for any reason have children who don't (or can't) attend school on a regular basis (Muir 1993). All of these welfare reform programs are designed to expose and publicly punish the *misfits* whose bodies are read as proof of their refusal or inability to capitulate to androcentric, capitalist, racist, and heterosexism values and mores.

The Power of Poor Women's Communal Resistance

Despite the rhetoric and policy that mark and mutilate our bodies, poor women survive. Hundreds of thousands of us are somehow good parents despite the systems that are designed to prohibit us from being so. We live on the unlivable and teach our children love, strength, and grace. We network, solve irresolvable dilemmas, and support each other and our families. If we somehow manage to find a decent pair of shoes, or save our foodstamps to buy our children a birthday cake, we are accused of being cheats or living too high. If our children suffer, it is read as proof of our inferiority and bad mothering; if they succeed we are suspect for being too pushy, for taking more than our share of free services, or for having too much free time to devote to them. Yet, as former welfare recipient Janet Diamond says in the introduction to *For Crying Out Loud:*

> In spite of public censure, welfare mothers graduate from school, get decent jobs, watch their children achieve, make good lives for themselves . . . welfare mothers continue to be my inspiration, not because they survive, but because they dare to dream. Because when you are a welfare recipient, laughter is an act of rebellion. (1986, 1)

. . . Because power is diffuse, heterogeneous, and contradictory, poor women struggle against the marks of their degradation. . . .

Poor women rebel by organizing for physical and emotional respite, and eventually for political power. My own resistance was born in the space between self-loathing and my love of and respect for poor women who were fighting together against oppression. In the throes of political activism (at first I was dragged blindly into such actions, ironically, in a protest that required, according to the organizer, just so many poor women's bodies) I became caught up in the contradiction between my body's meaning as despised public sign, and our shared sense of communal power, knowledge, authority, and beauty. Learning about labor movements, fighting for rent control, demanding fair treatment at the welfare office, sharing the costs, burdens, and joys of raising children, forming good cooperatives, working with other poor women to go to college, and organizing for political change, became addictive and life affirming acts of resistance.

Communal affiliation among poor women is discouraged, indeed in many cases prohibited, by those with power over our lives. Welfare offices, for example, are designed to prevent poor women from talking together; uncomfortable plastic chairs are secured to the ground in arrangements that make it difficult to communicate, silence is maintained in waiting rooms, case workers are rotated so that they do not become too "attached" to their clients, and, reinforced by "Welfare Fraud" signs covering industrially painted walls, we are daily reminded not to trust anyone with the details of our lives for fear of further exposure and punishment. And so, like most poor women, I had remained isolated, ashamed, and convinced that I was alone in, and responsible for, my suffering.

Through shared activism we became increasingly aware of our individual bodies as sites of contestation and of our collective body as a site of resistance and as a source power.

Noemy Vides in "Together We Are Getting Freedom," reminds us that "by talking and writing about learned shame together, [poor women] pursue their own liberation" (305). Vides adds that it is through this process that she learned to challenge the dominant explanations that decree her value in the world,

> provoking an awareness that the labels— ignorant peasant, abandoned woman, broken-English speaker, welfare cheat—have nothing to do with who one really is, but serve to keep women subjugated and divided. [This communal process] gives women tools to understand the uses of power; it emboldens us to move beyond the imposed shame that silences, to speak out and join together in a common liberatory struggle. (305)

In struggling together we contest the marks of our bodily inscription, disrupt the use of our bodies as public sign, change the conditions of our lives, and survive. In the process we come to understand that the shaping of our bodies is not coterminous with our beings or abilities as a whole. Contestation and the deployment of new truths cannot erase the marks of our poverty, but the process does transform the ways in which we are able to interrogate and critique our bodies and the systems that have branded them with infamy. As a result these signs are rendered fragile, unstable, and ultimately malleable.

NOTES

1. Throughout this paper I use the terms "welfare recipients," and "poor working women" interchangeably because as the recent *Urban Institute* study made clear, today these populations are, in fact, one and the same. (Loprest 1999)

2. As recently as 1995, in my daughter's public elementary school cafeteria, "free lunchers" (poor children who could not otherwise afford to eat lunch, including my daughter) were reminded with a large and colorful sign to "line up last."

3. The goal of my survey was to measure the impact of the 1996 welfare reform legislation on the lives of profoundly poor women and children in the United States. Early in 1998 I sent fifty questionnaires and narrative surveys to four groups of poor women on the West and the East coasts; thirty-nine were returned to me. I followed these surveys with forty-five minute interviews with twenty of the surveyed women.

4. In the two years directly preceding the passage of the PRWORA, as a part of sweeping welfare reform, in the United States the largest percentage of people on welfare were white (39%) and fewer than 10% were teen mothers. (1994. U.S. Department of Health and Human Services, "An Overview of Entitlement Programs")

5. *Tidyfare* programs additionally required that caseworkers inventory the belongings of AFDC recipients so that they could require them to "sell-down" their assets. In my own case, in 1994 a HUD inspector came into my home, counted my daughter's books, checked them against his list to see that as a nine year old she was only entitled to have twelve books, calculated what he perceived to be the value of the excess books, and then had my AFDC check reduced by that amount in the following month.

REFERENCES

Abramovitz, Mimi. 1989. *Regulating the lives of women, social welfare policy from colonial times to the present.* Boston: South End Press.

———. 2000. *Under attack, fighting back.* New York: Monthly Review Press.

Albelda, Randy. 1997. *Glass ceilings and bottomless pits: Women's work, women's poverty.* Boston: South End Press.

"America at risk; can we survive without moral values." 1995. *USA Today.* October, Sec. C: 3.

Amott, Teresa. 1993. *Caught in the crises: women and the U.S. economy today.* New York: Monthly Review Press.

Anderson, Dale. 1999. "County to investigate some welfare recipients." *The Buffalo News.* August 18, Sec. B: 5.

Ashcroft, John. 1995. "Illegitimacy rampant." *The St. Louis Dispatch.* July 2, Sec. A: 23.

Bell, Shannon. 1994. *Reading, writing and rewriting the prostitute body.* Bloomington and Indianapolis: Indiana University Press.

Bordo, Susan, 1993. *Unbearable Weight: Feminism, western culture and the body.* Berkeley: University of California Press.

Brownstein, Ronald. 1994. "GOP welfare proposals more conservative." *Los Angeles Times,* May 20, Sec. A: 20.

———1994. "Latest welfare reform plan reflects liberals' priorities." *Los Angeles Times.* May 20, Sec. A: 6.

Chandler, Mielle. 1999. "Queering maternity." *Journal of the Association for Research on Mothering.* Vol. 1, no. 2, (21–32).

Collins, Patricia Hill. 2000. *Black feminist thought: Knowledge, consciousness, and the politics of empowerment.* New York: Routledge.

Crompton, Rosemary. 1986. *Gender and stratification.* New York: Polity Press.

Desmond, Jane. 1991. "Dancing out the difference; cultural imperialism and Ruth St. Denis's Radna of 1906." *Signs.* Vol. 17, no. 1, Autumn, (28–49).

Diamond, Janet. 1986. *For crying out loud: Women and poverty in the United States.* Boston: Pilgrim Press.

Dreier, Peter. 1999. "Treat welfare recipients like workers." *Los Angeles Times.* August 29, Sec. M: 6.

Dresang, Joel. 1996. "Bridefare designer, reform beneficiary have role in governor's address." *Milwaukee Journal Sentinel.* August 14, Sec. 9.

Dujon, Diane and Ann Withorn. 1996. *For crying out loud: Women's poverty in the Unites States.* South End Press.

Edin, Kathryn and Laura Lein. 1997. *Making ends meet: how single mothers survive welfare and low wage work.* Russell Sage Foundation.

Ford-Smith, Honor. 1995. "Making white ladies: race, gender and the production of identity in late colonial Jamaica." *Resources for Feminist Research,* Vol. 23, no. 4, Winter, (55–67).

Foucault, Michel. 1984. Discipline and punish. In P. Rabinow (ed.) *The Foucault reader.* New York: Pantheon Books.

———. 1978. *The history of sexuality: An introduction.* Trans. R. Hurley. Harmondsworth: Penguin.

———. 1984. "Nietzsche, genealogy, history." In P. Rabinow (ed.) *The Foucault reader.* New York Pantheon Books.

———. 1980. *Power/knowledge: Selected interviews and other writings 1972–1977.* C. Gordon (ed.) Brighton: Harvester.

Funiciello, Theresa. 1998. "The brutality of bureaucracy." *Race, class and gender: An anthology,* 3rd ed. Eds. Margaret L. Andersen and Patricia Hill Collins. Belmont: Wadsworth Publishing Company, (377–381).

Gilder, George. 1995. "Welfare fraud today." *American Spectator.* September 5, Sec. B: 6.

Gordon, Linda. 1995. *Pitied, but not entitled: Single mothers and the history of welfare.* New York: Belknap Press, 1995.

hooks, bell. "Thinking about race, class, gender and ethics" 1999. Presentation at Hamilton College, Clinton, New York.

Hopwood, Catherine. 1995. "My discourse/myself: therapy as possibility (for women who eat compulsively)." *Feminist Review.* No. 49, Spring, (66–82).

Langston, Donna. 1998. "Tired of playing monopoly?" *In Race, class and gender: An anthology,* 3rd ed. Eds. Margaret L. Andersen and Patricia Hill Collins. Belmont: Wadsworth Publishing Company, (126–136).

Lerman, Robert. 1995. "And for fathers?" *The Washington Post.* August 7, Sec. A: 19.

Loprest, Pamela. 1999. "Families who left welfare: Who are they and how are they doing?" *The Urban Institute,* Washington, D.C. August, No. B-1.

McDougal, Gary. 1996. "The missing half of the welfare debate." *The Wall Street Journal.* September 6, Sec. A: 16 (W).

McNay, Lois. 1992. *Foucault and feminism: Power, gender and the self.* Boston: Northeastern University Press.

Mink, Gwendoly. 1998. *Welfare's end.* Cornell University Press.

———. 1996. *The wages of motherhood: Inequality in the welfare state 1917–1942.* Cornell University Press.

Morgan, Kathryn. 1991. "Women and the knife: Cosmetic surgery and the colonization of women's bodies." *Hepatia.* V6, No 3. Fall, (25–53).

Muir, Kate. 1993. "Runaway fathers at welfare's final frontier. *The Times.* Times Newspapers Limited. July 19, Sec. A: 2.

"An overview of entitlement programs." 1994. U.S. Department of Health and Human Services. Washington, DC: U.S. Government Printing Office.

Piven, Frances Fox and Richard Cloward. 1993. *Regulating the poor: The functions of public welfare.* New York: Vintage Books.

Raspberry, William. 1995. "Ms. Smith goes after Washington." *The Washington Post.* February 1, Sec. A: 19.

———. 1996. "Uplifting the human spirit." *The Washington Post.* August 8, Sec. A: 31.

Robinson, Valerie. 1999. "State's ad attacks the poor." *The Plain Dealer,* November 2, Sec. B: 8.

Sennett, Richard and Jonathan Cobb. 1972. *The hidden injuries of class.* New York: Vintage Books.

Sidel, Ruth. 1998. *Keeping women and children last: America's war on the poor.* New York: Penguin Books.

Simon, Stephanie. 1999. "Drug tests for welfare applicants." *The Los Angeles Times.* December 18, Sec. A: 1. National Desk.

Smart, Carol. 1997. *Regulating womanhood: Essays on marriage, motherhood and sexuality.* New York: Routledge.

———. "Disruptive bodies and unruly sex: the regulation of reproduction and sexuality in the nineteenth century." New York: Routledge, (7–32).

Smith-Madsen, Sandy. 2000. "From welfare to academe: Welfare reform as college-educated welfare mothers know it." *And still we rise: women, poverty and the promise of education in America.* Forthcoming. Vivyan Adair and Sandra Dahlber, Eds. Philadelphia: Temple University Press, (160–186).

Steedman, Carolyn Kay. 1987. *Landscape for a good woman.* New Brunswick, N.J., Rutgers University Press.

Stoler, Ann Laura. 1995. *Race and the education of desire: Foucault's history of sexuality and the colonial order of things.* Durham: Duke University Press.

Sylvester, Kathleen. 1995. "Welfare debate." *The Washington Post.* September 3, Sec. E: 15.

Tanner, Michael. 1995. "Why welfare pays." *The Wall Street Journal.* September 28, Sec. A: 18 (W).

Vides, Noemy and Victoria Steinitz. 1996. "Together we are getting freedom." *For crying out loud.* Diane Dujon and Ann Withorn (eds.) Boston: South End Press, (295–306).

Will, George. 1995. "Welfare gate." *Newsweek.* February 5, Sec. 23.

THINKING ABOUT THE READING

When we think of people's bodies being labeled as deviant, we usually assume the bodies in question either deviate from cultural standards of shape and size or are marked by some noticeable physical handicap. However, Adair shows us that poor women's and children's bodies are tagged as undesirable in ways that are just as profound and just as hard to erase. What does she mean when she says that the illnesses and accidents of youth became part of a visible reminder of who poor people are in the eyes of others? How do the public degradations suffered by poor people (for instance, having a school nurse wear surgical gloves to check only the hair of poor children for lice) reinforce their subordinate status in society? Why do you think Adair continually evokes the images of "danger," "discipline," and "punishment" in describing the ways non-poor people perceive and respond to the physical appearance of poor people? Explain how focusing on the "deviance" of poor people deflects public attention away from the harmful acts committed by more affluent citizens.

Savage Inequalities in American Schools
Life on the Mississippi: East St. Louis, Illinois

Jonathan Kozol

(1991)

"East of anywhere," writes a reporter for the *St. Louis Post-Dispatch*, "often evokes the other side of the tracks. But, for a first-time visitor suddenly deposited on its eerily empty streets, East St. Louis might suggest another world." The city, which is 98 percent black, has no obstetric services, no regular trash collection, and few jobs. Nearly a third of its families live on less than $7,500 a year; 75 percent of its population lives on welfare of some form. The U.S. Department of Housing and Urban Development describes it as "the most distressed small city in America."

Only three of the 13 buildings on Missouri Avenue, one of the city's major thoroughfares, are occupied. A 13-story office building, tallest in the city, has been boarded up. Outside, on the sidewalk, a pile of garbage fills a ten-foot crater.

The city, which by night and day is clouded by the fumes that pour from vents and smokestacks at the Pfizer and Monsanto chemical plants, has one of the highest rates of child asthma in America.

It is, according to a teacher at the University of Southern Illinois, "a repository for a non-white population that is now regarded as expendable." The *Post-Dispatch* describes it as "America's Soweto."

Fiscal shortages have forced the layoff of 1,170 of the city's 1,400 employees in the past 12 years. The city, which is often unable to buy heating fuel or toilet paper for the city hall, recently announced that it might have to cashier all but 10 percent of the remaining work force of 230. In 1989 the mayor announced that he might need to sell the city hall and all six fire stations to raise needed cash. Last year the plan had to be scrapped after the city lost its city hall in a court judgment to a creditor. East St. Louis is mortgaged into the next century but has the highest property-tax rate in the state.

Since October 1987, when the city's garbage pickups ceased, the backyards of residents have been employed as dump sites. In the spring of 1988 a policeman tells a visitor that 40 plastic bags of trash are waiting for removal from the backyard of his mother's house. Public health officials are concerned the garbage will attract a plague of flies and rodents in the summer. The policeman speaks of "rats as big as puppies" in his mother's yard. They are known to the residents, he says, as "bull rats." Many people have no cars or funds to cart the trash and simply burn it in their yards. The odor of smoke from burning garbage, says the *Post-Dispatch*, "has become one of the scents of spring" in East St. Louis.

Railroad tracks still used to transport hazardous chemicals run through the city. "Always present," says the *Post-Dispatch*, "is the threat of chemical spills. . . . The wail of sirens warning residents to evacuate after a spill is common." The most recent spill, the paper says, "was at the Monsanto Company plant. . . . Nearly 300 gallons of phosphorous trichloride spilled when a railroad tank was overfilled. About 450 residents were taken to St. Mary's

Hospital. . . . The frequency of the emergencies has caused Monsanto to have a 'standing account' at St. Mary's." . . .

The dangers of exposure to raw sewage, which backs up repeatedly into the homes of residents in East St. Louis, were first noticed, in the spring of 1989, at a public housing project, Villa Griffin. Raw sewage, says the *Post-Dispatch,* overflowed into a playground just behind the housing project, which is home to 187 children, "forming an oozing lake of . . . tainted water." Two schoolgirls, we are told, "experienced hair loss since raw sewage flowed into their homes."

While local physicians are not certain whether loss of hair is caused by the raw sewage, they have issued warnings that exposure to raw sewage can provoke a cholera or hepatitis outbreak. A St. Louis health official voices her dismay that children live with waste in their backyards. "The development of working sewage systems made cities livable a hundred years ago," she notes. "Sewage systems separate us from the Third World."

The sewage, which is flowing from collapsed pipes and dysfunctional pumping stations, has also flooded basements all over the city. The city's vacuum truck, which uses water and suction to unclog the city's sewers, cannot be used because it needs $5,000 in repairs. Even when it works, it sometimes can't be used because there isn't money to hire drivers. A single engineer now does the work that 14 others did before they were laid off. By April the pool of overflow behind the Villa Griffin project has expanded into a lagoon of sewage. Two million gallons of raw sewage lie outside the children's homes. . . .

The Daughters of Charity, whose works of mercy are well known in the Third World, operate a mission at the Villa Griffin homes. On an afternoon in early spring of 1990, Sister Julia Huiskamp meets me on King Boulevard and drives me to the Griffin homes.

As we ride past blocks and blocks of skeletal structures, some of which are still inhabited,

she slows the car repeatedly at railroad crossings. A seemingly endless railroad train rolls past us to the right. On the left: a blackened lot where garbage has been burning. Next to the burning garbage is a row of 12 white cabins, charred by fire. Next: a lot that holds a heap of auto tires and a mountain of tin cans. More burnt houses. More trash fires. The train moves almost imperceptibly across the flatness of the land.

Fifty years old, and wearing a blue suit, white blouse, and blue head-cover, Sister Julia points to the nicest house in sight. The sign on the front reads MOTEL. "It's a whorehouse," Sister Julia says.

When she slows the car beside a group of teen-age boys, one of them steps out toward the car, then backs away as she is recognized.

The 99 units of the Villa Griffin homes—two-story structures, brick on the first floor, yellow wood above—form one border of a recessed park and playground that were filled with fecal matter last year when the sewage mains exploded. The sewage is gone now and the grass is very green and looks inviting. When nine-year-old Serena and her seven-year-old brother take me for a walk, however, I discover that our shoes sink into what is still a sewage marsh. An inch-deep residue of fouled water still remains.

Serena's brother is a handsome, joyous little boy, but troublingly thin. Three other children join us as we walk along the marsh: Smokey, who is nine years old but cannot yet tell time; Mickey, who is seven; and a tiny child with a ponytail and big brown eyes who talks a constant stream of words that I can't always understand.

"Hush, Little Sister," says Serena. I ask for her name, but "Little Sister" is the only name the children seem to know.

"There go my cousins," Smokey says, pointing to two teen-age girls above us on the hill.

The day is warm, although we're only in the second week of March; several dogs and cats are playing by the edges of the marsh. "It's a lot of squirrels here," says Smokey. "There go one!"

"This here squirrel is a friend of mine," says Little Sister.

None of the children can tell me the approximate time that school begins. One says five o'clock. One says six. Another says that school begins at noon.

When I ask what song they sing after the flag pledge, one says "Jingle Bells."

Smokey cannot decide if he is in the second or third grade.

Seven-year-old Mickey sucks his thumb during the walk.

The children regale me with a chilling story as we stand beside the marsh. Smokey says his sister was raped and murdered and then dumped behind his school. Other children add more details: Smokey's sister was 11 years old. She was beaten with a brick until she died. The murder was committed by a man who knew her mother.

The narrative begins when, without warning, Smokey says, "My sister has got killed."

"She was my best friend," Serena says.

"They had beat her in the head and raped her," Smokey says.

"She was hollering out loud," says Little Sister.

I ask them when it happened. Smokey says, "Last year." Serena then corrects him and she says, "Last week."

"It scared me because I had to cry," says Little Sister.

"The police arrested one man but they didn't catch the other," Smokey says.

Serena says, "He was some kin to her."

But Smokey objects, "He weren't no kin to me. He was my momma's friend."

"Her face was busted," Little Sister says.

Serena describes this sequence of events: "They told her go behind the school. They'll give her a quarter if she do. Then they knock her down and told her not to tell what they had did."

I ask, "Why did they kill her?"

"They was scared that she would tell," Serena says.

"One is in jail," says Smokey. "They can't find the other."

"Instead of raping little bitty children, they should find themselves a wife," says Little Sister.

"I hope," Serena says, "her spirit will come back and get that man."

"And *kill* that man," says Little Sister.

"Give her another chance to live," Serena says.

"My teacher came to the funeral," says Smokey.

"When a little child dies, my momma say a star go straight to Heaven," says Serena.

"My grandma was murdered," Mickey says out of the blue. "Somebody shot two bullets in her head."

I ask him, "Is she really dead?"

"She dead all right," says Mickey. "She was layin' there, just dead."

"I love my friends," Serena says. "I don't care if they no kin to me. I care for them. I hope his mother have another baby. Name her for my friend that's dead."

"I have a cat with three legs," Smokey says.

"Snakes hate rabbits," Mickey says, again for no apparent reason.

"Cats hate fishes," Little Sister says.

"It's a lot of hate," says Smokey.

Later, at the mission, Sister Julia tells me this: "The Jefferson School, which they attend, is a decrepit hulk. Next to it is a modern school, erected two years ago, which was to have replaced the one that they attend. But the construction was not done correctly. The roof is too heavy for the walls, and the entire structure has begun to sink. It can't be occupied. Smokey's sister was raped and murdered and dumped between the old school and the new one."

As the children drift back to their homes for supper, Sister Julia stands outside with me and talks about the health concerns that trouble people in the neighborhood. In the setting sun, the voices of the children fill the evening air. Nourished by the sewage marsh, a field of wild daffodils is blooming. Standing here, you wouldn't think that anything was wrong. The street is calm. The poison in the soil can't be seen. The sewage is invisible and only makes the grass a little greener. Bikes thrown down by children lie outside their kitchen doors. It could be an ordinary twilight in a small suburban town.

Night comes on and Sister Julia goes inside to telephone a cab. In another hour, the St. Louis taxis will not come into the neighborhood. . . .

East St. Louis—which the local press refers to as "an inner city without an outer city"—has some of the sickest children in America. Of 66 cities in Illinois, East St. Louis ranks first in fetal death, first in premature birth, and third in infant death. Among the negative factors listed by the city's health director are the sewage running in the streets, air that has been fouled by the local plants, the high lead levels noted in the soil, poverty, lack of education, crime, dilapidated housing, insufficient health care, unemployment. Hospital care is deficient too. There is no place to have a baby in East St. Louis. The maternity ward at the city's Catholic hospital, a 100-year-old structure, was shut down some years ago. The only other hospital in town was forced by lack of funds to close in 1990. The closest obstetrics service open to the women here is seven miles away. The infant death rate is still rising.

As in New York City's poorest neighborhoods, dental problems also plague the children here. Although dental problems don't command the instant fears associated with low birth weight, fetal death or cholera, they do have the consequence of wearing down the stamina of children and defeating their ambitions. Bleeding gums, impacted teeth and rotting teeth are routine matters for the children I have interviewed in the South Bronx. Children get used to feeling constant pain. They go to sleep with it. They go to school with it. Sometimes their teachers are alarmed and try to get them to a clinic. But it's

all so slow and heavily encumbered with red tape and waiting lists and missing, lost or canceled welfare cards, that dental care is often long delayed. Children live for months with pain that grown-ups would find unendurable. The gradual attrition of accepted pain erodes their energy and aspiration. I have seen children in New York with teeth that look like brownish, broken sticks. I have also seen teenagers who were missing half their teeth. But, to me, most shocking is to see a child with an abscess that has been inflamed for weeks and that he has simply lived with and accepts as part of the routine of life. Many teachers in the urban schools have seen this. It is almost commonplace.

Compounding these problems is the poor nutrition of the children here—average daily food expenditure in East St. Louis is $2.40 for one child—and the underimmunization of young children. Of every 100 children recently surveyed in East St. Louis, 55 were incompletely immunized for polio, diphtheria, measles and whooping cough. In this context, health officials look with all the more uneasiness at those lagoons of sewage outside public housing.

On top of all else is the very high risk of death by homicide in East St. Louis. In a recent year in which three cities in the state of roughly the same size as East St. Louis had an average of four homicides apiece, there were 54 homicides in East St. Louis. But it is the heat of summer that officials here particularly dread. The heat that breeds the insects bearing polio or hepatitis in raw sewage also heightens asthma and frustration and reduces patience. "The heat," says a man in public housing, "can bring out the beast. . . ."

The fear of violence is very real in East St. Louis. The CEO of one of the large companies out on the edge of town has developed an "evacuation plan" for his employees. State troopers are routinely sent to East St. Louis to put down disturbances that the police cannot control. If the misery of this community explodes someday in a real riot (it has happened in the past), residents believe that state and federal law-enforcement agencies will have no hesitation in applying massive force to keep the violence contained. . . .

The problems of the streets in urban areas, as teachers often note, frequently spill over into public schools. In the public schools of East St. Louis this is literally the case.

"Martin Luther King Junior High School," notes the *Post-Dispatch* in a story published in the early spring of 1989, "was evacuated Friday afternoon after sewage flowed into the kitchen. . . . The kitchen was closed and students were sent home." On Monday, the paper continues, "East St. Louis Senior High School was awash in sewage for the second time this year." The school had to be shut because of "fumes and backed-up toilets." Sewage flowed into the basement, through the floor, then up into the kitchen and the students' bathrooms. The backup, we read, "occurred in the food preparation areas."

School is resumed the following morning at the high school, but a few days later the overflow recurs. This time the entire system is affected, since the meals distributed to every student in the city are prepared in the two schools that have been flooded. School is called off for all 16,500 students in the district. The sewage backup, caused by the failure of two pumping stations, forces officials at the high school to shut down the furnaces.

At Martin Luther King, the parking lot and gym are also flooded. "It's a disaster," says a legislator. "The streets are underwater; gaseous fumes are being emitted from the pipes under the schools," she says, "making people ill."

In the same week, the schools announce the layoff of 280 teachers, 166 cooks and cafeteria workers, 25 teacher aides, 16 custodians and 18 painters, electricians, engineers and plumbers. The president of the teachers' union says the cuts, which will bring the size of kindergarten and primary classes up to 30 students, and the size of fourth to twelfth grade classes up to 35, will have "an unimaginable impact" on the students. "If you have a high school teacher with five classes each day and between 150 and 175 students . . . , it's going to have a devastating effect." The school system, it is also noted, has been using more than 70 "permanent substitute teachers," who are paid only $10,000 yearly, as a way of saving money.

Governor Thompson, however, tells the press that he will not pour money into East St. Louis to solve long-term problems. East St. Louis residents, he says, must help themselves. "There is money in the community," the governor insists. "It's just not being spent for what it should be spent for."

The governor, while acknowledging that East St. Louis faces economic problems, nonetheless refers dismissively to those who live in East St. Louis. "What in the community," he asks, "is being done right?" He takes the opportunity of a visit to the area to announce a fiscal grant for sewer improvement to a relatively wealthy town nearby.

In East St. Louis, meanwhile, teachers are running out of chalk and paper, and their paychecks are arriving two weeks late. The city warns its teachers to expect a cut of half their pay until the fiscal crisis has been eased.

The threatened teacher layoffs are mandated by the Illinois Board of Education, which, because of the city's fiscal crisis, has been given supervisory control of the school budget. Two weeks later the state superintendent partially relents. In a tone very different from that of the governor, he notes that East St. Louis does not have the means to solve its education problems on its own. "There is no natural way," he says, that "East St. Louis can bring itself out of this situation." Several cuts will be required in any case—one quarter of the system's teachers, 75 teacher aides, and several dozen others will be given notice—but, the state board notes, sports and music programs will not be affected.

East St. Louis, says the chairman of the state board, "is simply the worst possible place I can imagine to have a child brought up. . . . The community is in desperate circumstances." Sports and music, he observes, are, for many children here, "the only avenues of success." Sadly enough, no matter how it ratifies the stereotype, this is the truth; and there is a poignant aspect to the fact that, even with class size soaring and one quarter of the system's teachers being given their dismissal, the state board of education demonstrates its genuine but skewed compassion by attempting to leave sports and music untouched by the overall austerity.

Even sports facilities, however, are degrading by comparison with those found and expected at most high schools in America. The football field at East St. Louis High is missing almost everything—including goalposts. There are a couple of metal pipes—no crossbar, just the pipes. Bob Shannon, the football coach, who has to use his personal funds to purchase footballs and has had to cut and rake the football field himself, has dreams of having goalposts someday. He'd also like to let his students have new uniforms. The ones they wear are nine years old and held together somehow by a patchwork of repairs. Keeping them clean is a problem, too. The school cannot afford a washing machine. The uniforms are carted to a corner laundromat with fifteen dollars' worth of quarters. . . .

In the wing of the school that holds vocational classes, a damp, unpleasant odor fills the halls. The school has a machine shop, which cannot be used for lack of staff, and a woodworking shop. The only shop that's occupied this morning is the auto-body class. A man with long blond hair and wearing a white sweat suit swings a paddle to get children in their chairs. "What we need the most is new equipment," he reports. "I have equipment for alignment, for example, but we don't have money to install it. We also need a better form

of egress. We bring the cars in through two other classes." Computerized equipment used in most repair shops, he reports, is far beyond the high school's budget. It looks like a very old gas station in an isolated rural town.

The science labs at East St. Louis High are 30 to 50 years outdated. John McMillan, a soft-spoken man, teaches physics at the school. He shows me his lab. The six lab stations in the room have empty holes where pipes were once attached. "It would be great if we had water," says McMillan. . . .

Leaving the chemistry labs, I pass a double-sized classroom in which roughly 60 kids are sitting fairly still but doing nothing. "This is supervised study hall," a teacher tells me in the corridor. But when we step inside, he finds there is no teacher. "The teacher must be out today," he says.

Irl Solomon's history classes, which I visit next, have been described by journalists who cover East St. Louis as the highlight of the school. Solomon, a man of 54 whose reddish hair is turning white, has taught in urban schools for almost 30 years. A graduate of Brandeis University in 1961, he entered law school but was drawn away by a concern with civil rights. "After one semester, I decided that the law was not for me. I said, 'Go and find the toughest place there is to teach. See if you like it.' I'm still here. . . .'"

Teachers like Mr. Solomon, working in low-income districts such as East St. Louis, often tell me that they feel cut off from educational developments in modern public schools. "Well, it's amazing," Solomon says. "I have done without so much so long that, if I were assigned to a suburban school, I'm not sure I'd recognize what they are doing. We are utterly cut off."

"Very little education in the school would be considered academic in the suburbs. Maybe 10 to 15 percent of students are in truly academic programs. Of the 55 percent who graduate, 20 percent may go to four-year colleges: something like 10 percent of any entering class.

Another 10 to 20 percent may get some other kind of higher education. An equal number join the military. . . .

"Sometimes I get worried that I'm starting to burn out. Still, I hate to miss a day. The department frequently can't find a substitute to come here, and my kids don't like me to be absent."

Solomon's advanced class, which soon comes into the room, includes some lively students with strong views.

"I don't go to physics class, because my lab has no equipment," says one student. "The typewriters in my typing class don't work. The women's toilets. . . ." She makes a sour face. "I'll be honest," she says. "I just don't use the toilets. If I do, I come back into class and I feel dirty."

"I wanted to study Latin," says another student. "But we don't have Latin in this school."

"We lost our only Latin teacher," Solomon says.

A girl in a white jersey with the message DO THE RIGHT THING on the front raises her hand. "You visit other schools," she says. "Do you think the children in this school are getting what we'd get in a nice section of St. Louis?"

I note that we are in a different state and city.

"Are we citizens of East St. Louis or America?" she asks. . . .

Clark Junior High School is regarded as the top school in the city. I visit, in part, at the request of school officials, who would like me to see education in the city at its very best. Even here, however, there is a disturbing sense that one has entered a backwater of America.

"We spend the entire eighth grade year preparing for the state exams," a teacher tells me in a top-ranked English class. The teacher seems devoted to the children, but three students sitting near me sleep through the entire period. The teacher rouses one of them, a girl in the seat next to me, but the student promptly lays her head back on her crossed arms and is soon asleep again. Four of the 14 ceiling lights are broken. The corridor outside the room is filled with voices. Outside the window, where I see no schoolyard, is an empty lot.

In a mathematics class of 30 children packed into a space that might be adequate for 15 kids, there is one white student. The first white student I have seen in East St. Louis, she is polishing her nails with bright red polish. A tiny black girl next to her is writing with a one-inch pencil stub.

In a seventh grade social studies class, the only book that bears some relevance to black concerns—its title is *The American Negro*—bears a publication date of 1967. The teacher invites me to ask the class some questions. Uncertain where to start, I ask the students what they've learned about the civil rights campaigns of recent decades.

A 14-year-old girl with short black curly hair says this: "Every year in February we are told to read the same old speech of Martin Luther King. We read it every year. 'I have a dream. . . . ' It does begin to seem—what is the word?" She hesitates and then she finds the word: "perfunctory."

I ask her what she means.

"We have a school in East St. Louis named for Dr. King," she says. "The school is full of sewer water and the doors are locked with chains. Every student in that school is black. It's like a terrible joke on history."

It startles me to hear her words, but I am startled even more to think how seldom any press reporter has observed the irony of naming segregated schools for Martin Luther King. Children reach the heart of these hypocrisies much quicker than the grown-ups and the experts do.

Public Education in New York

The train ride from Grand Central Station to suburban Rye, New York, takes 35 to 40 minutes. The high school is a short ride from the station. Built of handsome gray stone and set in a landscaped campus, it resembles a New England prep school. On a day in early June of 1990, I enter the school and am directed by a student to the office.

The principal, a relaxed, unhurried man who, unlike many urban principals, seems gratified to have me visit in his school, takes me in to see the auditorium, which, he says, was recently restored with private charitable funds ($400,000) raised by parents. The crenellated ceiling, which is white and spotless, and the polished dark-wood paneling contrast with the collapsing structure of the auditorium at Morris High. The principal strikes his fist against the balcony: "They made this place extremely solid." Through a window, one can see the spreading branches of a beech tree in the central courtyard of the school.

In a student lounge, a dozen seniors are relaxing on a carpeted floor that is constructed with a number of tiers so that, as the principal explains, "they can stretch out and be comfortable while reading."

The library is wood-paneled, like the auditorium. Students, all of whom are white, are seated at private carrels, of which there are approximately 40. Some are doing homework; others are looking through the *New York Times*. Every student that I see during my visit to the school is white or Asian, though I later learn there are a number of Hispanic students and that 1 or 2 percent of students in the school are black.

According to the principal, the school has 96 computers for 546 children. The typical student, he says, studies a foreign language for four or five years, beginning in the junior high school, and a second foreign language (Latin is available) for two years. Of 140 seniors, 92 are now enrolled in AP classes. Maximum teacher salary will soon reach $70,000. Per-pupil funding is above $12,000 at the time I visit.

The students I meet include eleventh and twelfth graders. The teacher tells me that the class is reading Robert Coles, Studs Terkel, Alice Walker. He tells me I will find them more than willing to engage me in debate, and this turns out to be correct. Primed for my visit, it appears, they arrow in directly on the dual questions of equality and race.

Three general positions soon emerge and seem to be accepted widely. The first is that the fiscal inequalities "do matter very much" in shaping what a school can offer ("That is obvious," one student says) and that any loss of funds in Rye, as a potential consequence of future equalizing, would be damaging to many things the town regards as quite essential.

The second position is that racial integration—for example, by the busing of black children from the city or a nonwhite suburb to this school—would meet with strong resistance, and the reason would not simply be the fear that certain standards might decline. The reason, several students say straightforwardly, is "racial" or, as others say it, "out-and-out racism" on the part of adults.

The third position voiced by many students, but not all, is that equity is basically a goal to be desired and should be pursued for moral reasons, but "will probably make no major difference" since poor children "still would lack the motivation" and "would probably fail in any case because of other problems."

At this point, I ask if they can truly say "it wouldn't make a difference" since it's never been attempted. Several students then seem to rethink their views and say that "it might work, but it would have to start with preschool and the elementary grades" and "it might be 20 years before we'd see a difference."

At this stage in the discussion, several students speak with some real feeling of the present inequalities, which, they say, are "obviously unfair," and one student goes a little further and proposes that "we need to change a lot more than the schools." Another says she'd favor racial integration "by whatever means—including busing—even if my parents disapprove." But a contradictory opinion also is expressed with a good deal of fervor and is stated by one student in a rather biting voice: "I don't see why we should do it. How could it be of benefit to us?"

Throughout the discussion, whatever the views the children voice, there is a degree of unreality about the whole exchange. The children are lucid and their language is well chosen and their arguments well made, but there is a sense that they are dealing with an issue that does not feel very vivid, and that nothing that we say about it to each other really matters since it's "just a theoretical discussion." To a certain degree, the skillfulness and cleverness that they display seem to derive precisely from this sense of unreality. Questions of unfairness feel more like a geometric problem than a matter of humanity or conscience. A few of the students do break through the note of unreality, but, when they do, they cease to be so agile in their use of words and speak more awkwardly. Ethical challenges seem to threaten their effectiveness. There is the sense that they were skating over ice and that the issues we addressed were safely frozen underneath. When they stop to look beneath the ice they start to stumble. The verbal competence they have acquired here may have been gained by building walls around some regions of the heart.

"I don't think that busing students from their ghetto to a different school would do much good," one student says. "You can take them out of the environment, but you can't take the environment out of *them*. If someone grows up in the South Bronx, he's not going to be prone to learn." His name is Max and he has short black hair and speaks with confidence. "Busing didn't work when it was tried," he says. I ask him how he knows this and he says he saw a television movie about Boston.

"I agree that it's unfair the way it is," another student says. "We have AP courses and they don't. Our classes are much smaller." But, she says, "putting them in schools like ours is not the answer. Why not put some AP classes into *their* school? Fix the roof and paint the halls so it will not be so depressing."

The students know the term "separate but equal," but seem unaware of its historical associations. "Keep them where they are but make it equal," says a girl in the front row.

A student named Jennifer, whose manner of speech is somewhat less refined and polished than that of the others, tells me that her parents came here from New York. "My family is originally from the Bronx. Schools are hell there. That's one reason that we moved. I don't think it's our responsibility to pay our taxes to provide for *them*. I mean, my parents used to live there and they wanted to get out. There's no point in coming to a place like this, where schools are good, and then your taxes go back to the place where you began."

I bait her a bit: "Do you mean that, now that you are not in hell, you have no feeling for the people that you left behind?"

"It has to be the people in the area who want an education. If your parents just don't care, it won't do any good to spend a lot of money. Someone else can't want a good life for you. You have got to want it for yourself." Then she adds, however, "I agree that everyone should have a chance at taking the same courses. . . ."

I ask her if she'd think it fair to pay more taxes so that this was possible.

"I don't see how that benefits me," she says.

It occurs to me how hard it would have been for anyone to make that kind of statement, even in the wealthiest suburban school, in 1968. Her classmates would have been unsettled by the voicing of such undisguised self-interest. Here in Rye, in 1990, she can say this with impunity. She's an interesting girl and I reluctantly admire her for being so straightforward.

Max raises a different point. "I'm not convinced," he says, "that AP courses would be valued in the Bronx. Not everyone is going to go to college."

Jennifer picks up on this and carries it a little further. "The point," she says, "is that you cannot give an equal chance to every single person. If you did it, you'd be changing the whole economic system. Let's be honest. If you equalize the money, someone's got to be short-changed. I don't doubt that children in the Bronx are getting a bad deal. But do we want *everyone* to get a mediocre education?"

"The other point," says Max, "is that you need to match the money that you spend to whether children in the school can profit from it. We get twice as much as kids in the South Bronx, but our school is *more* than twice as good and that's because of who is here. Money isn't the whole story...."

"In New York," says Jennifer, "rich people put their kids in private school. If we equalize between New York and Rye, you would see the same thing happen here. People would pull out their kids. Some people do it now. So it would happen a lot more."

An eleventh grader shakes her head at this. "Poor children need more money. It's as simple as that," she says. "Money comes from taxes. If we have it, we should pay it."

It is at this point that a boy named David picks up on a statement made before. "Someone said just now that this is not our obligation, our responsibility. I don't think that that's the question. I don't think you'd do it, pay more taxes or whatever, out of obligation. You would do it just because . . . it is unfair the way it is." He falters on these words and looks a bit embarrassed. Unlike many of the other students who have spoken, he is somewhat hesitant and seems to choke up on his words. "Well, it's easy for me to be sitting here and say I'd spend my parents' money. I'm not working. I don't earn the money. I don't need to be conservative until I do. I can be as open-minded and unrealistic as I want to be. You can be a liberal until you have a mortgage."

I ask him what he'd likely say if he were ten years older. "Hopefully," he says, "my values would remain the same. But I know that having money does affect you. This, at least, is what they tell me."

Spurred perhaps by David's words, another student says, "The biggest tax that people pay is to the federal government. Why not take some money from the budget that we spend on armaments and use it for the children in these urban schools?"

A well-dressed student with a healthy tan, however, says that using federal taxes for the poor "would be like giving charity," and "charitable things have never worked. . . . Charity will not instill the poor with self-respect."

Max returns to something that he said before: "The environment is everything. It's going to take something more than money." He goes on to speak of inefficiency and of alleged corruption in the New York City schools. "Some years ago the chancellor was caught in borrowing $100,000 from the schools. I am told that he did not intend to pay it back. These things happen too much in New York. Why should we pour money in, when they are wasting what they have?"

I ask him, "Have we *any* obligations to poor people?"

"I don't think the burden is on us," says Jennifer again. "Taxing the rich to help the poor—we'd be getting nothing out of it. I don't understand how it would make a better educational experience for me."

"A child's in school only six hours in a day," says Max. "You've got to deal with what is happening at home. If his father's in the streets, his mother's using crack . . . how is money going to make a difference?"

David dismisses this and tells me, "Here's what we should do. Put more money into preschool, kindergarten, elementary years. Pay college kids to tutor inner-city children. Get rid of the property tax, which is too uneven, and use income taxes to support these schools. Pay teachers more to work in places like the Bronx. It has to come from taxes. Pay them extra to go into the worst schools. You could forgive their college loans to make it worth their while."

"Give the children Head Start classes," says another student. "If they need more buildings, give them extra money so they wouldn't need to be so crowded."

"It has got to come from taxes," David says again.

"I'm against busing," Max repeats, although this subject hasn't been brought up by anybody else in a long while.

"When people talk this way," says David, "they are saying, actually—" He stops and starts again: "They're saying that black kids will never learn. Even if you spend more in New York. Even if you bring them here to Rye. So what it means is—you are writing people off. You're just dismissing them. . . ."

"I'd like it if we had black students in this school," the girl beside him says.

"It seems rather odd," says David when the hour is up, "that we were sitting in an AP class discussing whether poor kids in the Bronx deserve to get an AP class. We are in a powerful position."

THINKING ABOUT THE READING

What do you suppose would happen if a student from a place like East St. Louis were to attend a school in a place like Rye? Or vice versa? At one point in the reading, one of the students from Rye says, "You can take them [that is, poor, underprivileged students] out of the environment, but you can't take the environment out of them." Do you agree or disagree with that assessment of the problem of unequal education? Do you think this is a common attitude in U.S. society? Does it enhance or impede progress regarding inequality in this country? In addition to regular aspects of education, what other lessons and resources do young people pick up in school? Consider some of the forms of "cultural capital" that schools convey. How might this affect life chances?

The Architecture of Inequality

Race and Ethnicity

The history of race in the United States is an ambivalent one. Cultural beliefs about equality conflict with the experiences of most racial and ethnic minorities: oppression, violence, and exploitation. Opportunities for life, liberty, and the pursuit of happiness have always been distributed along racial and ethnic lines. U.S. society is built on the assumption that different immigrant groups will ultimately assimilate, changing their way of life to conform to that of the dominant culture. But the increasing diversity of the population has shaped people's ideas about what it means to be an American and has influenced our relationships with one another and with our social institutions.

Racial inequality is both a personal and structural phenomenon. On the one hand, it is lodged in individual prejudice and discrimination. On the other hand, it resides in our language, collective beliefs, and important social institutions. This latter manifestation of racism is more difficult to detect than personal racism, hence it is more difficult to change. Because such racism exists at a level beyond personal attitudes, it will not disappear simply by reducing people's prejudices.

Sociologists tell us that race is not a biological characteristic but rather a social construction that can change across time and from culture to culture. The socially constructed nature of race is illustrated in the question Min Zhou poses in the title of her article: "Are Asian Americans Becoming 'White'?" Such a question might strike you as odd. Clearly she isn't asking if the skin color of Asian Americans is lightening. Instead she is exploring the way racial categories change and, more importantly, how they intersect with social class. Indeed, the suggestion that Asians are becoming "white" has more to do with social position, status and wealth, and access to privilege than with any biological markers of race. The same analysis has been applied to the question of how the Irish, Italians, Jews, and other ethnic groups became "white."

It has been said that white people in the United States have the luxury of "having no color." When someone is described with no mention of race, the default assumption is that he or she is white. In other words, "white" is used far less often as a modifying adjective than "Black," "Asian," or "Latino." As a result, "whiteness" is rarely questioned or examined as a racial category. Only recently have scholars begun to explore the origins and characteristics of whiteness. In "Blinded by Whiteness," Mark Chesler, Melissa Peet, and Todd Sevig describe the racial identities and attitudes of white students attending a major public university. These students have lived most of their lives in segregated environments, so coming to a racially diverse college for the first time forces them to examine their "whiteness" in new and sometimes challenging ways. As the title of this article suggests, their own racial history often obscures their understanding of the important racial issues they and their fellow students face in college.

Maxine Thompson and Verna Keith explore the complex nuances of "blackness" in "The Blacker the Berry." They examine the highly emotional issue of skin color prejudice *among* African Americans and the different effects such prejudice has for men and women. They analyzed the responses of a sample of over 2,000 African Americans to questions on the *National Survey of Black Americans* to draw conclusions about how gender and skin tone combine to influence evaluations of self-worth and self-competence among African Americans.

Something to Consider as You Read:

As you read these selections consider the differences between individual prejudice and institutional racism. Is it possible for someone not to be racist and still participate in practices that perpetuate racism? Compare these readings with those in other sections. Consider the connections between access to economic resources, social class, and race.

Think also about how you identify your own race or ethnicity. When you filll out a questionnaire that asks you to select a racial/ethnic category, do you think the category adequately reflects you? When you go somewhere, do you assume you will easily find others of your own race? When you watch television or a movie, how likely is it that the stars will be people who share your racial background? Practice asking yourself similar questions as a way of enhancing your racial awareness.

Are Asian Americans Becoming "White"?

Min Zhou

(2004)

"I never asked to be white. I am not literally white. That is, I do not have white skin or white ancestors. I have yellow skin and yellow ancestors, hundreds of generations of them. But like so many other Asian Americans of the second generation, I find myself now the bearer of a strange new status: white, by acclimation. Thus it is that I have been described as an 'honorary white,' by other whites, and as a 'banana' by other Asians . . . to the extent that I have moved away from the periphery and toward the center of American life, I have become white inside."

—*Eric Liu*, The Accidental Asian (p. 34)

Are Asian Americans becoming "white"? For many public officials the answer must be yes, because they classify Asian-origin Americans with European-origin Americans for equal opportunity programs. But this classification is premature and based on false premises. Although Asian Americans as a group have attained the career and financial success equated with being white, and although many have moved next to or have even married whites, they still remain culturally distinct and suspect in a white society.

At issue is how to define Asian American and white. The term "Asian American" was coined by the late historian and activist Yuji Ichioka during the ethnic consciousness movements of the late 1960s. To adopt this identity was to reject the western-imposed label of "Oriental." Today, "Asian American" is an umbrella category that includes both U.S. citizens and immigrants whose ancestors came from Asia, east of Iran. Although widely used

in public discussions, most Asian-origin Americans are ambivalent about this label, reflecting the difficulty of being American and still keeping some ethnic identity: Is one, for example, Asian American or Japanese American?

Similarly, "white" is an arbitrary label having more to do with privilege than biology. In the United States, groups initially considered nonwhite, such as the Irish and Jews, have attained "white" membership by acquiring status and wealth. It is hardly surprising, then, that nonwhites would aspire to becoming "white" as a mark of and a tool for material success. However, becoming white can mean distancing oneself from "people of color" or disowning one's ethnicity. Pan-ethnic identities—Asian American, African American, Hispanic American—are one way the politically vocal in any group try to stem defections. But these group identities may restrain individual members' aspirations for personal advancement.

Varieties of Asian Americans

Privately, few Americans of Asian ancestry would spontaneously identify themselves as Asian, and fewer still as Asian American. They instead link their identities to specific countries of origin, such as China, Japan, Korea, the Philippines, India or Vietnam. In a study of Vietnamese youth in San Diego, for example, 53 percent identified themselves as Vietnamese, 32 percent as Vietnamese American, and only 14 percent as Asian American. But they did not take these labels lightly; nearly 60 percent of these youth considered their chosen identity as very important to them.

Some Americans of Asian ancestry have family histories in the United States longer than many Americans of Eastern or Southern European origin. However, Asian-origin Americans became numerous only after 1970, rising from 1.4 million to 11.9 million (4 percent of the total U.S. population), in 2000. Before 1970, the Asian-origin population was largely made up of Japanese, Chinese and Filipinos. Now, Americans of Chinese and Filipino ancestries are the largest subgroups (at 2.8 million and 2.4 million, respectively), followed by Indians, Koreans, Vietnamese and Japanese (at more than one million). Some 20 other national-origin groups, such as Cambodians, Pakistanis, Laotians, Thai, Indonesians and Bangladeshis, were officially counted in government statistics only after 1980; together they amounted to more than two million Americans in 2000.

The sevenfold growth of the Asian-origin population in the span of 30-odd years is primarily due to accelerated immigration following the Hart-Celler Act of 1965, which ended the national origins quota system, and the historic resettlement of Southeast Asian refugees after the Vietnam War. Currently, about 60 percent of the Asian-origin population is foreign-born (the first generation), another 28 percent are U.S.-born of foreign-born parents (the second generation), and just 12 percent were born to U.S.-born parents (the third generation and beyond).

Unlike earlier immigrants from Asia or Europe, who were mostly low-skilled laborers looking for work, today's immigrants from Asia have more varied backgrounds and come for many reasons, such as to join their families, to invest their money in the U.S. economy, to fill the demand for highly skilled labor, or to escape war, political or religious persecution and economic hardship. For example, Chinese, Taiwanese, Indian, and Filipino Americans tend to be over-represented among scientists, engineers, physicians and other skilled professionals, but less educated, low-skilled workers are more common among Vietnamese, Cambodian, Laotian, and Hmong Americans, most of whom entered the United States as refugees. While middle-class immigrants are able to start their American lives with high-paying professional careers and comfortable suburban lives, low-skilled immigrants and refugees often have to endure low-paying menial jobs and live in inner-city ghettos.

Asian Americans tend to settle in large metropolitan areas and concentrate in the West. California is home to 35 percent of all Asian Americans. But recently, other states such as Texas, Minnesota and Wisconsin, which historically received few Asian immigrants, have become destinations for Asian American settlement. Traditional ethnic enclaves, such as Chinatown, Little Tokyo, Manilatown, Koreatown, Little Phnom Penh, and Thaitown, persist or have emerged in gateway cities, helping new arrivals to cope with cultural and linguistic difficulties. However, affluent and highly-skilled immigrants tend to bypass inner-city enclaves and settle in suburbs upon arrival, belying the stereotype of the "unacculturated" immigrant. Today, more than half of the Asian-origin population is spreading out in suburbs surrounding traditional gateway cities, as well as in new urban centers of Asian settlement across the country.

Differences in national origins, timing of immigration, affluence and settlement patterns profoundly inhibit the formation of a pan-ethnic identity. Recent arrivals are less likely than those born or raised in the United States to identify as Asian American. They are also so busy settling in that they have little time to think about being Asian or Asian American, or, for that matter, white. Their diverse origins include drastic differences in languages and dialects, religions, cuisines and customs. Many national groups also bring to America their histories of conflict (such as the Japanese colonization of Korea and Taiwan, Japanese attacks on China, and the Chinese invasion of Vietnam).

Immigrants who are predominantly middle-class professionals, such as the Taiwanese and Indians, or predominantly small business owners, such as the Koreans, share few of the same concerns and priorities as those who are predominantly uneducated, low-skilled refugees, such as Cambodians and Hmong. Finally, Asian-origin people living in San Francisco or Los Angeles among many other Asians and self-conscious Asian Americans develop a stronger ethnic identity than those living in predominantly Latin Miami or predominantly European Minneapolis. A politician might get away with calling Asians "Oriental" in Miami but get into big trouble in San Francisco. All of these differences create obstacles to fostering a cohesive pan-Asian solidarity. As Yen Le Espiritu shows, pan-Asianism is primarily a political ideology of U.S.-born, American-educated, middle-class Asians rather than of Asian immigrants, who are conscious of their national origins and overburdened with their daily struggles for survival.

Underneath the Model Minority: "White" or "Other"

The celebrated "model minority" image of Asian Americans appeared in the mid-1960s, at the peak of the civil rights and the ethnic consciousness movements, but before the rising waves of immigration and refugee influx from Asia. Two articles in 1966—"Success Story, Japanese-American Style," by William Petersen in the *New York Times Magazine*, and "Success of One Minority Group in U.S.," by the *US News & World Report* staff—marked a significant departure from how Asian immigrants and their descendants had been traditionally depicted in the media. Both articles congratulated Japanese and Chinese Americans on their persistence in overcoming extreme hardships and discrimination to achieve success, unmatched even by U.S.-born whites, with "their own almost totally unaided effort" and "no help from anyone else." (The implicit contrast to other minorities was clear.) The press attributed their winning wealth and respect in American society to hard work, family solidarity, discipline, delayed gratification, nonconfrontation and eschewing welfare.

This "model minority" image remains largely unchanged even in the face of new and diverse waves of immigration. The 2000 U.S. Census shows that Asian Americans continue to score remarkable economic and educational achievements. Their median household income in 1999 was more than $55,000—the highest of all racial groups, including whites—and their poverty rate was under 11 percent, the lowest of all racial groups. Moreover, 44 percent of all Asian Americans over 25 years of age had at least a bachelor's degree, 18 percentage points more than any other racial group. Strikingly, young Asian Americans, including both the children of foreign-born physicians, scientists, and professionals and those of uneducated and penniless refugees, repeatedly appear as high school valedictorians and academic decathlon winners. They also enroll in the freshman classes of prestigious universities in disproportionately large numbers. In 1998, Asian Americans, just 4 percent of the nation's population, made up more than 20 percent of the undergraduates at universities such as

Berkeley, Stanford, MIT and Cal Tech. Although some ethnic groups, such as Cambodians, Lao, and Hmong, still trail behind other East and South Asians in most indicators of achievement, they too show significant signs of upward mobility. Many in the media have dubbed Asian Americans the "new Jews." Like the second-generation Jews of the past, today's children of Asian immigrants are climbing up the ladder by way of extraordinary educational achievement.

One consequence of the model-minority stereotypes is that it reinforces the myth that the United States is devoid of racism and accords equal opportunity to all, fostering the view that those who lag behind do so because of their own poor choices and inferior culture. Celebrating "model minorities" can help impede other racial minorities' demands for social justice by pitting minority groups against each other. It can also pit Asian Americans against whites. . . . [The] model-minority image implicitly casts Asian Americans as different from whites. By placing Asian Americans above whites, this image still sets them apart from other Americans, white or nonwhite, in the public mind.

There are two other less obvious effects. The model-minority stereotype holds Asian Americans to higher standards, distinguishing them from average Americans. "What's wrong with being a model minority?" a black student once asked, in a class I taught on race, "I'd rather be in the model minority than in the downtrodden minority that nobody respects." Whether people are in a model minority or a downtrodden minority, they are still judged by standards different from average Americans. Also, the model-minority stereotype places particular expectations on members of the group so labeled, channeling them to specific avenues of success, such as science and engineering. This, in turn, makes it harder for Asian Americans to pursue careers outside these designated fields. Falling into this trap, a Chinese immigrant father gets upset when his

son tells him he has changed his major from engineering to English. Disregarding his son's talent for creative writing, such a father rationalizes his concern, "You have a 90 percent chance of getting a decent job with an engineering degree, but what chance would you have of earning income as a writer?" This thinking represents more than typical parental concern; it constitutes the self-fulfilling prophecy of a stereotype.

The celebration of Asian Americans rests on the perception that their success is unexpectedly high. The truth is that unusually many of them, particularly among the Chinese, Indians and Koreans, arrive as middle-class or upper middle-class immigrants. This makes it easier for them and their children to succeed and regain their middle-class status in their new homeland. The financial resources that these immigrants bring also subsidize ethnic businesses and services, such as private after-school programs. These, in turn, enable even the less fortunate members of the groups to move ahead more quickly than they would have otherwise.

Not so Much Being "White" as Being American

Most Asian Americans seem to accept that "white" is mainstream, average and normal, and they look to whites as a frame of reference for attaining higher social position. Similarly, researchers often use non-Hispanic whites as the standard against which other groups are compared, even though there is great diversity among whites, too. Like most immigrants to the United States, Asian immigrants tend to believe in the American Dream and measure their achievements materially. As a Chinese immigrant said to me in an interview, "I hope to accomplish nothing but three things: to own a home, to be my own boss, and to send my children to the Ivy League." Those with sufficient education, job skills and money manage to move into white middle-class suburban [areas and] accumulate enough savings to move their families up and out of inner-city ethnic enclaves. Consequently, many children of Asian ancestry have lived their entire childhood in white communities, made friends with mostly white peers, and grown up speaking only English. In fact, Asian Americans are the most acculturated non-European group in the United States. By the second generation, most have lost fluency in their parents' native languages (see "English-Only Triumphs, but the Costs are High," *Contexts*, Spring 2002). David Lopez finds that in Los Angeles, more than three-quarters of second-generation Asian Americans (as opposed to one-quarter of second-generation Mexicans) speak only English at home. Asian Americans also intermarry extensively with whites and with members of other minority groups. Jennifer Lee and Frank Bean find that more than one-quarter of married Asian Americans have a partner of a different racial background, and 87 percent of those marry whites; they also find that 12 percent of all Asian Americans claim a multiracial background, compared to 2 percent of whites and 4 percent of blacks.

Even though U.S.-born or U.S.-raised Asian Americans are relatively acculturated and often intermarry with whites, they may be more ambivalent about becoming white than their immigrant parents. Many only cynically agree that "white" is synonymous with "American." A Vietnamese high school student in New Orleans told me in an interview, "An American is white. You often hear people say, hey, so-and-so is dating an 'American.' You know she's dating a white boy. If he were black, then people would say he's black." But while they recognize whites as a frame of reference, some reject the idea of becoming white themselves: "It's not so much being white as being American," commented a Korean-American student in my class on the new second generation. This aversion to becoming white is particularly common among second-generation

college students who have taken ethnic studies courses, and among Asian-American community activists. However, most of the second generation continues to strive for the privileged status associated with whiteness, just like their parents. For example, most U.S.-born or U.S.-raised Chinese-American youth end up studying engineering, medicine, or law in college, believing that these areas of study guarantee a middle-class life.

Second-generation Asian Americans are also more conscious of the disadvantages associated with being nonwhite than their parents, who as immigrants tend to be optimistic about overcoming the disadvantages of this status. As a Chinese-American woman points out from her own experience, "The truth is, no matter how American you think you are or try to be, if you have almond-shaped eyes, straight black hair, and a yellow complexion, you are a foreigner by default. . . . You can certainly be as good as or even better than whites, but you will never become accepted as white." This remark echoes a commonly-held frustration among second-generation, U.S.-born Asians who detest being treated as immigrants or foreigners. Their experience suggests that whitening has more to do with the beliefs of white America, than with the actual situation of Asian Americans. Speaking perfect English, adopting mainstream cultural values, and even intermarrying members of the dominant group may help reduce this "otherness" for particular individuals, but it has little effect on the group as a whole. New stereotypes can emerge and un-whiten Asian Americans, no matter how "successful" and "assimilated" they have become. For example, Congressman David Wu once was invited by the Asian-American employees of the U.S. Department of Energy to give a speech in celebration of Asian-American Heritage Month. Yet, he and his Asian-American staff were not allowed into the department building, even after presenting their Congressional identification, and were repeatedly asked about their citizenship and country of origin. They were told that this was standard procedure for the Department of Energy and that a congressional ID card was not a reliable document. The next day, a congressman of Italian descent was allowed to enter the same building with his congressional ID, no questions asked.

The stereotype of the "honorary white" or model minority goes hand-in-hand with that of the "forever foreigner." Today, globalization and U.S.-Asia relations, combined with continually high rates of immigration, affect how Asian Americans are perceived in American society. Many historical stereotypes, such as the "yellow peril" and "Fu Manchu" still exist in contemporary American life, as revealed in such highly publicized incidents as the murder of Vincent Chin, a Chinese American mistaken for Japanese and beaten to death by a disgruntled white auto worker in the 1980s; the trial of Wen Ho Lee, a nuclear scientist suspected of spying for the Chinese government in the mid-1990s; the 1996 presidential campaign finance scandal, which implicated Asian Americans in funneling foreign contributions to the Clinton campaign; and most recently, in 2001, the Abercrombie & Fitch t-shirts that depicted Asian cartoon characters in stereotypically negative ways, with slanted eyes, thick glasses and heavy Asian accents. Ironically, the ambivalent, conditional nature of their acceptance by whites prompts many Asian Americans to organize pan-ethnically to fight back—which consequently heightens their racial distinctiveness. So becoming white or not is beside the point. The bottom line is: Americans of Asian ancestry still have to constantly prove that they truly are loyal Americans.

REFERENCE

Liu, Eric. 1988. *The Accidental Asian*. New York: Random House.

THINKING ABOUT THE READING

What is assimilation? What is the relationship between social class and the "whiteness" of an ethnic group? According to Zhou, what are the advantages and disadvantages of being considered "white"? Discuss the idea of the Asian "model minority" and compare this idea with cultural stereotypes of other racial or ethnic minorities. What are some of the factors that explain why some minority immigrant groups "get ahead" more easily than others in the United States?

"White supremacy" is the notion that whiteness is associated with power, prestige, and belonging. Does assimilation perpetuate the idea of "white supremacy"?

Blinded by Whiteness

The Development of White College Students' Racial Awareness

Mark A. Chesler, Melissa Peet, and Todd Sevig

(2003)

Racial identity is the meaning attached to self as a member of a group or collectivity in racial situations, and individuals may express this . . . identity differently in different circumstances (Cornell and Hartman 1998). Since identity is formed by class and gender as well as race, there are many ways of being white or any other race/ethnicity. Racial attitudes and changing attitudes are the statements of a person's preferred views or positions about others and about contemporary (or historic) policies and events. Attitudes are also shaped by one's social location and are expressed differently in different circumstances. Social and institutional structures and cultures provide the limits and opportunities for both the creation of racial identities and the formation and expression of racial attitudes.

Throughout, we present the voices of white students attending the University of Michigan, a university with a tradition of student, faculty, and administrative engagement with issues of racism and affirmative action. Recently, Michigan has become one of the nation's battlegrounds for competing narratives and institutional policies around racial matters. The data reported here were gathered from white students of varied backgrounds in individual and small-group interviews conducted between 1996 and 2000. Although they are not geographically, temporally, or in terms of cohort representative of other white students' racial consciousness, they are useful windows into the ways in which racial processes become visible and are expressed.

Background

The social and cultural context of the modern university is one of racial plurality but also of racial separatism and tension. Students come to these settings from racially separated and often segregated neighborhoods and communities (Bonilla-Silva and Forman 2000; Massey and Denton 1993). For many, the university is the first place in which they have sustained contact with a substantial number of students of another race. Although there are more numerous formal and informal opportunities for racial interaction and growth in the university than in most secondary educational environs, white students' lives in these environs are often not very different from their separated lives in previous home and school communities (Hurtado et al. 1994).

In these collegiate circumstances, white students are often confronted for the first time with the need to think about their own racial location. Having been socialized and educated at home, in their neighborhoods, through the media, and in previous schooling to expect people of color to be different, less competent, and potentially threatening, most young white people are ignorant, curious, and awkward in the presence of "others." Some may be aware of their racial group membership and identity, but others may be relatively unaware. Furthermore, during this developmental stage of late adolescence and early adulthood, students' identities as racial beings, as well as their racial attitudes, are subject to challenge and change. Hence it is important to understand the potential developmental trajectory of students' views as they move from their communities of origin to and through diverse collegiate experiences.

Recent explorations of whiteness suggest that changes in the economic, political, and cultural landscape have promoted greater self-consciousness about race. As a result, for many students the invisibility of whiteness, the notion that white is normal and natural, has become harder to sustain. Challenges to white ignorance and/or privilege have also increased some whites' sense of threat to their place in the social order and to their assumptions about their lives and society (Feagin and Vera 1995; Pincus 2000; Winant 1997). Discussions of historic privilege, structural inequality, and racial oppression have caused some white students (and college administrators and faculties as well) to question their enmeshment in pervasive (if unintended) patterns of institutional discrimination. In addition, institutions that now see the education of a diverse citizenry as integral to their missions of education and public service are struggling to make changes in the demographics of their faculty and student bodies, curricular designs, pedagogical tactics, student financial aid programs, and support services.

Contemporary Theories of White Racial Attitudes and Identities

In the context of these shifts and struggles, scholars have described and explained the genesis and nature of whiteness and white racial attitudes and experiences as well as the developmental aspects of white racial identity and consciousness. When understood in the context of larger patterns of institutional racism and changing cultural narratives about race, these identity and attitude frames are useful guides—heuristic devices—to understanding white racial consciousness and conceptions of whiteness itself. However, almost all interpretations and typologies of white attitudes and identities focus on their views of "the other" rather than on views of oneself or one's own racial group. That is, surveys of racial attitudes generally ask white people about their views of or prospective behavior toward people of color or race-related policies, seldom inquiring into whites' views of their own racial selves or of their earned/unearned status (i.e., privileges).

Similarly, most white identity development models focus on how whites view people of color rather than themselves; thus their racial identity is conceived as a reflection of their views of "the other." The stance that overlooks one's own race and focuses on others' can itself be seen as a manifestation of the "naturalness" and dominance of whiteness. Certainly one's views of the other and of the self are interactive, and people learn about their racial identity and attitudes in an interactive context, but one's views of others (or of the meaning of others' race) and one's view of themselves (or of the meaning of their own race) are not the same thing. . . .

The notion of white racial "identity stages" suggests a developmental process that generally proceeds as follows (Helms 1990; Rowe et al. 1994; Tatum 1992): 1) from racial unawareness or conformity to traditional racial stereotypes, sometimes called an "unachieved" racial identity; 2) through questioning of these prior familial and societal messages, with attendant confusion, dissonance, and perhaps even "overidentification" with the other and attendant rebellion; 3) to retrogressive reintegration, where white culture is idealized, others are rejected, and a racially "dominative" ideology holds forth; 4) into a generally liberal (sometimes called pseudo-) acceptance or tolerance of people of color, often accompanied by adherence to notions of "color blindness" or denial and conflict around remaining prejudices; and 5) it is hoped to an antiracist stance, wherein understanding of others' oppression and one's own privilege is (more or less) fully integrated into a personal worldview called an "autonomous" or "integrative" white racial identity. . . .

Given increased collegiate attention to racial injustice and the desire of some people and advocacy groups to challenge institutional racism, it is not surprising that some young white collegians are becoming more conscious of their racial membership and its privileges. Such consciousness is likely to be painful, as it requires acknowledging both systemic advantage and personal privilege and enmeshment (historically and contemporarily) in structural or institutional discrimination and oppression. A few scholars have pointed to the emergence of a "liberationist" or "antiracist" form of white racial attitudes, wherein white people acknowledge and grapple with their accumulated racial privilege and their role (intentional or not) in sustaining white advantage and the domination over people of color. The racial identity literature refers to this belief/action system as an integrated, autonomous, introspective, or antiracist racial consciousness. . . .

What Do White Students Bring With Them to the University?

In interviews, white students [we interviewed] discussed the neighborhood and schools in which they grew up and the effect these largely segregated experiences had on their conceptions of themselves, race, and racism. The major themes that characterize their precollege experience are lack of exposure, subtle and overt racism, racial tokenism, and lack of successful role models of people of color:

I never really think about the fact that I am white. I just think that it is fortunate that we don't have to think about it, you know what I mean? It is one of the perks of being white.

I consider myself white, but I don't think about it. The only time I think about it is when we have to do these dumb forms and think about what race we are.

According to Janet Helms (1990:3), racial identity is "a sense of group or collective identity based on one's perception that he or she shares a common racial heritage with a particular group." If the students above never thought about being white and didn't feel a sense of shared racial heritage, they could not possibly develop a self-conscious racial identity; they were at the unaware stage.

White students consistently indicated that their lack of prior contact with people of color, even in the midst of liberal rhetoric, failed to prepare them to engage meaningfully about race:

I grew up in a very white community, and the church was really white. We talked about other cultures, but it was all about boys and girls are equal and worthy and so are people of different colors. It was all about "everything's OK."

Where I grew up, everybody was white, and even though I knew (on some level) that not everyone was white, we never really had to deal with it, and so we didn't.

A few students reported coming from more diverse neighborhoods and schools, but they too indicated a relatively low level of sustained interaction or conscious educational attention to issues of diversity and intergroup relations. In these "more diverse" settings, racial segregation was still the normative experience for white students (as well as for students of color):

[The city] is very segregated in terms of housing, and there's all different kinds of people who live here. But there isn't a tremendous amount of communication and social interaction between the groups . . . unless you played sports or you were involved in something else, because it was tracked. Almost all of the kids on the college track were white and almost all of the kids on the other tracks were black . . . and then there were also Asian kids and they were generally in the white track.

This lack of meaningful contact with people from other races was often coupled with various forms of both subtle and overt racism. If fact, many students' comments indicate that intergroup separation supported the home and media-based racism they were exposed to, creating and sustaining conditions wherein remnants of "old-fashioned racism" and an identity stage of unawareness and acceptance of stereotypes could be maintained:

So I grew up with my dad particularly being really racist, he didn't really say much about any other group except Black people. "Nigger" was a common word in my family. I knew that that was not a good thing in terms of race. I knew that there was the black side of town, there was the black neighborhood, and then the rest of it was white, and that's what I grew up in. . . . But we never had any personal interactions with anybody [from the black neighborhood].

My whole town was white except for a few families who migrated from Mexico to work. I had the clear sense that they weren't supposed to be there. They were like some unspoken exception that was supposed to be invisible.

In addition to the lack of contact in school and neighborhood and the various forms of racism that students were exposed to, several students indicated that when they did learn about people from other races, they were usually token efforts of inclusion:

The only thing I learned in school was that [George] Washington Carver was a black man

and he discovered peanuts or something like that. I think we might have peripherally dealt with Martin Luther King. But four years, two years of history, two years of government, we really didn't touch on African-American or any other issues at all . . . that just didn't even exist as far as anybody was concerned. In elementary school we dealt with the Indians. You know, you put your hand on a piece of paper and you draw around it and you cut it out and you make a turkey, or you make little Indian hats and things like that with feathers.

Finally, even students who experienced token efforts of inclusion as unsatisfactory found little opportunity to formulate openly meaningful questions about race. Several students commented that when they did have racial questions and concerns during their high school years, they were simply told that there was "nothing to talk about":

The message that I got from the white teachers at the school and other people was that the way not to be racist was to just pretend that you don't see any differences between people. And so everybody had feelings about race, but nobody talked, there was no place to talk about those things. And you only have to just treat everybody as an individual and everything will be fine.

In my high school government class I asked a question about the Civil Rights movement and racism. The answer I got was basically that it was bad back then, but now everything was fine.

Growing up with everyday processes of segregation, lacking contact with racially (or socioeconomically) different peers, being exposed to various forms of racism and racial tokenism, and not being educated meaningfully about race and racism deeply affect white students' social identity—their sense of themselves as well as their relations with others. In their homes, schools, and communities these students acquired habitual attitudes, expectations, and ways of making meaning about their world. White students were socialized to not see themselves as having a race and did not understand their own (and their communities') exclusionary attitudes and behaviors. . . .

White Students' Experiences on Campus: New Challenges to Whiteness

Students' precollege socialization forms a grid of attitudes and expectations about race and whiteness that is often reenacted and reified through their collegiate experience. As several white students reported, once in college they still did not think about themselves as being white— even in the presence of diversity; no one and no program invited or required them to. Hence, as the racial majority on campus and the dominant group within the larger society, the experience of knowing themselves as white was primarily reactive. That is, white students' numerical and cultural dominance protected them from having to know or understand others' experiences. Consequently, in order to "see" their race, they had to have a critical encounter or be consciously challenged to think and reflect about the particular experiences (perhaps privileges) that they had as a result of their racial position. Unless this challenge occurs at a conscious level, their own racial identity remains unknown and invisible during their college years.

Even when white students do have a critical encounter that raises their awareness of their race, they may not have the skills and consciousness (or instructional and experiential assistance) to deal with or act on it productively. Compare, for instance, the level of insight conveyed in these two excerpts:

> I don't understand why all the black students sit together in the dining hall. They complain about people being racist, but isn't that racist?

> Something I see is that the different races tend to stick with people like themselves. Once, in a class, I asked why all the black students sit together in the dormitory cafeteria. A black student then asked: "Well, why do you think all the white kids sit together?" I was speechless. I thought that was a dumb question until I realized that I see white people sitting together as normal and black people sitting together as a problem. . . .

These comments reflect larger social assumptions about race relations on campus, wherein the prevailing myth has been that minority students are "self-segregating" and the exclusionary behaviors of the majority white group remain unseen (Elfin and Burke 1993; Tatum 1997). However, longitudinal research with over 200,000 students from 172 institutions found that it was white students who displayed the most exclusionary behaviors—particularly when it came to dating (Hurtado et al. 1994). Thus the view that minority students are self-segregating is clearly a skewed perspective that does not take into consideration the separatist and/or exclusionary behaviors of white students. It also fails to account for the ways in which institutional norms and cultures help students misinterpret patterns of interracial interaction.

Other white behaviors took the form of promoting or reacting to patterns of racial marginalization and separation in daily interactions in classrooms, social events, or casual encounters. The result, of course, continues to be minimal opportunity for sustained interaction:

> My black friend invited me to a party with her. And the first thing I could think of was how many white people are usually there. I remembered thinking, this is probably going to be uncomfortable, and I would rather just go out with my white friends. I'm feeling apprehensive about meeting their friends and therefore spending time with them.

I used to feel very guilty thinking I don't have many diverse friends. I thought: "I have to go out and get a black friend."

Some white students reported finding these and other situations so discomforting that they began to express resentment against students of color. This type of resentment is supported by the discourse of whites as victims:

I think white males have a hard time because we are constantly blamed for being power-holding oppressors, yet we are not given many concrete ways to change. Then we just feel guilty or rebel.

I think that black people use their race to get jobs. I've seen it happen. My friend should have had this job as a resident advisor, but a black guy got it instead. There's no way the black guy was qualified.

. . . Views such as these, expressing the emergence of a self-interested form of racial awareness, are consistent with Lawrence Bobo's (1999) discussion of the group-position frame of racial attitudes.

Hence we encounter the view of the white person as the "new victim" of racism or as the target of "reverse discrimination" (Gallagher 1995; Pincus 2000). Victimhood, like all racial identities and views, is historically situated, and current public discourse about affirmative action and other race-based remedies stimulates and supports its development and expression. A lack of understanding of one's own prejudices, the realities of racial discrimination, and the advantages whites have leads to the view that minority advance is unmerited and a reflection of special privilege. The result often is aversive or self-interested racism that facilitates the interpretation of interracial encounters or circumstances as overprivileging minorities and victimizing whites. This also is referred to as the reintegrative or dominative stage of white racial identity.

The inability to understand racial membership is compounded by denial of any racial prejudice or racism. As a result of professed innocence about the meaning and implications of their own racial status and privileges, white students are often "blind" to the reality and status of students of color and regard themselves as "color-blind." If white students do not understand the personal or structural implications of being white and are unable to see how their racial behaviors affect others, they blindly negotiate racial encounters with the sense that all that matters is their good intentions. Their structural position of racial dominance, together with precollege socialization and color-blind ideology, makes it very difficult to distinguish between good intentions (or innocence) and a reflective consciousness that can enact just racial encounters:

I am a pretty open person and someone who wouldn't even think about race, who would try to be color-blind.

When I was asked in a class to describe my beliefs about race, it was easy. I said that I think that the whole idea of race has gone too far, that we need to stop thinking about race and start remembering that everyone is an individual.

Robert Terry (1981) identifies this pervasive color-blind ideology as an attempt to ignore or deny the relevance of race by emphasizing everyone's "humanness." Others have pointed out that the changing discourse of affirmative action—from a need to remediate past injustice to a concern about reverse discrimination—has affected how white people construct racial meaning (Gamson and Modigliani 1987). The new discourse of white victimhood not only acts to obscure the experiences of students of color but also further reinforces barriers to white students' ability to acknowledge their own racial identity as members of the dominant or privileged group.

Despite these reports of unawareness, negativity, blindness, and victimhood, there are also signs that some white students develop more sophisticated and progressive views of race. As they encounter themselves and others, some white students report moving out of the stage of "conformity" or "dissonance," going [out of] stereotyped assumptions or expectations. This occurs partly as a function of structured educational experiences and informal contacts:

> It took me a long time to be able to get to a point where I can say that I have prejudices.

> Something I learned is that people have stereotypes. I learned that having stereotypes about other groups is part of the environment that we grow up in.

For a number of white students, these realizations led to a sense of shame or guilt: several scholars have also referred to these responses as the symbolic or emotional "costs" of white racism (Feagin and Vera 1995; Rose 1991);

> But I was so guilt-ridden, just horribly liberal guilt-ridden, paralyzed and unable to act. I was totally blowing every little minor interaction that I had with people of color way out of proportion and thinking that this determines whether or not I'm a good white person or a bad white person, and whether I'm racist or not. I saw how hard it was for me to stop doing that and start being more productive. And how hard it was for me to not be scared.

Such strong feelings, when combined in sensitive ways (as contrasted with self-pitying or defensive ways) with new educational input, helped some white students understand some of the privileges that were normally accorded them as a function of their white skin color (and associated socioeconomic and educational status):

> I learned that being white, they're so many privileges that I didn't even know of . . . like loans from the bank, not being stopped by the police, and other things me and white kids can get away with.

> I had not noticed the extent to which white privilege has affected and continues to affect many aspects of my everyday life. I thought "I" had accomplished so much, but how much of where I am is due to my accumulated privilege—my family, economic status, school advantages? . . .

Innovative educational programs must be designed and implemented to address these issues in students' racial identities and attitudes. However, even such innovations will not be effective or sustained without parallel changes in the operations of departments and the larger collegiate or university environment. Without changes in this broader organizational landscape, it is unlikely that individual white students' attitudes will change or that their racial identities will continue to "progress"—or that such change programs, if initiated, can be maintained. Moreover, students' consciousness and the academy itself are enmeshed in our society's continuing struggle with racial discrimination and racial privilege. There are real limits for any change toward more liberationist or antiracist white identities or racial attitudes within a highly racialized and racist society and higher educational system.

REFERENCES

Bonilla-Silva, Eduardo, and Tyrone A. Forman, 2000. "'I Am Not a Racist But . . .': Mapping White College Students' Racial Ideology in the USA." *Discourse & Society* 11: 50–85.

Cornell, Stephen and D. Hartman, 1998. *Ethnicity and Race: Making Identities in a Changing World.* Thousand Oaks, CA: Pine Forge.

Helms, Janet E., ed. 1990. *Black and White Racial Identity: Theory, Research and Practice.* New York: Greenwood.

Hurtado, S., Dey, E., & L. Trevino, 1994. "Exclusion or Self-Segregation: Interaction Across Racial/Ethnic Groups on Campus." Presented to meetings of the American Educational Research Association. New Orleans, LA.

Massey, Douglas S., and Nancy A. Denton, 1993. *American Apartheid: Segregation and the Making of the Underclass.* Cambridge, MA: Harvard University Press.

Terry, Robert W. 1981. "The Negative Impact on White Values." Pp. 119–151 in *Impacts of Racism on White Americans*, ed. Benjamin P. Bowser and Raymond G. Hunt. Beverly Hills, CA: Sage.

THINKING ABOUT THE READING

How do the authors define "white"? Think about the various ways people identify themselves racially and ethnically. Of the following groups, who are most likely to be considered white: Arabs, Greeks, Jews, Irish, Italians? Can blacks be white? What are the similarities and differences between categories such as Norwegian-American and Mexican-American? Why did the white students in this article have such difficulty understanding the concerns of other ethnoracial groups? The authors suggest that "colorblindness" is actually a form of racism. Discuss this contention. When you hear the words "American citizen" whom do you visualize?

The Blacker the Berry

Gender, Skin Tone, Self-Esteem, and Self-Efficacy

Maxine S. Thompson and Verna M. Keith

(2001)

She should have been a boy, then color of skin wouldn't have mattered so much, for wasn't her mother always saying that a Black boy could get along, but that a Black girl would never know anything but sorrow and disappointment? But she wasn't a boy; she was a girl, and color did matter, mattered so much that she would rather have missed receiving her high school diploma than have to sit as she now sat, the only odd and conspicuous figure on the auditorium platform of the Boise high school . . .

Get a diploma?—What did it mean to her? College?—Perhaps. A job?—Perhaps again. She was going to have a high school diploma, but it would mean nothing to her whatsoever.

—Thurman 1929, 4–5

Wallace Thurman (1929) speaking through the voice of the main character, Emma Lou Morgan, in his novel, "The Blacker the Berry," about skin color bias within the African American community, asserts that the disadvantages and emotional pain of being "dark skinned" are greater for women than men and that skin color, not achievement, determines identity and attitudes about the self. Thurman's work describes social relationships among African Americans that were shaped by their experiences in the white community during slavery and its aftermath. In the African American community, skin color, an ascribed status attribute, played an integral role in determining class distinctions. Mulattoes, African Americans with white progenitors, led a more privileged existence when compared with their Black counterparts, and in areas of the Deep South (i.e., most notably Louisiana and South Carolina), mulattoes served as a buffer class between whites and Blacks (Russell, Wilson, and Hall 1992). In the *Black Bourgeoisie*, Frazier (1957) describes affluent organized clubs within the Black community called "blue vein" societies. To be accepted into these clubs, skin tone was required to be lighter than a "paper bag" or light enough for visibility of "blue veins" (Okazawa Rey, Robinson, and Ward 1987). Preferential treatment given by both Black and white cultures to African Americans with light skin have conveyed to many Blacks that if they conformed to the white, majority standard of beauty, their lives would be more rewarding (Bond and Cash 1992; Gatewood 1988).

Although Thurman's novel was written in 1929, the issue of *colorism* (Okazawa Rey, Robinson, and Ward 1987), intraracial discrimination based on skin color, continues to divide and shape life experiences within the African American community. The status advantages afforded to persons of light complexion continue despite the political preference for dark skin tones in the Black awareness movement during the 1960s. No longer an unspoken taboo, color prejudice within the African American community has been a "hot" topic of talk shows, novels, and movies and an issue in a court case on discrimination in the workplace (Russell, Wilson, and Hall 1992). In addition to discussions within lay communities, research scholars have had considerable interest in the importance of skin color. At the structural levels, studies have noted that skin color is an important determinant of educational and occupational attainment: Lighter skinned Blacks complete more years of schooling, have more prestigious jobs, and earn more than darker skinned Blacks (Hughes and Hertel 1990; Keith and Herring 1991). In fact, one study notes that the effect of skin color on earnings of "lighter" and "darker" Blacks is as great as the effect of race on the earnings of whites and all Blacks (Hughes and Hertel 1990). The most impressive research on skin tone effects is studies on skin tone and blood pressure. Using a reflectometer to measure skin color, research has shown that dark skin tone is associated with high blood pressure in African Americans with low socioeconomic status (Klag et al. 1991; Tryoler and James 1978). And at the social-psychological level, studies find that skin color is related to feelings of self-worth and attractiveness, self-control, satisfaction, and quality of life (Bond and Cash 1992; Boyd Franklin 1991; Cash and Duncan 1984; Chambers et al. 1994; Neal and Wilson 1989; Okazawa Rey, Robinson, and Ward 1987).

It is important to note that skin color is highly correlated with other phenotypic features—eye color, hair texture, broadness of nose, and fullness of lips. Along with light skin, blue and green eyes, European-shaped noses, and straight as opposed to "kinky" hair are all accorded higher status both within and beyond the African American community.

Colorism embodies preference and desire for both light skin as well as these other attendant features. Hair, eye color, and facial features function along with color in complex ways to shape opportunities, norms regarding attractiveness, self-concept, and overall body image. Yet, it is color that has received the most attention in research on African Americans.[1] The reasons for this emphasis are not clear, although one can speculate that it is due to the fact that color is the most visible physical feature and is also the feature that is most enduring and difficult to change. As Russell, Wilson, and Hall (1992) pointed out, hair can be straightened with chemicals, eye color can be changed with contact lenses, and a broad nose can be altered with cosmetic surgery. Bleaching skin to a lighter tone, however, seldom meets with success (Okazawa Rey, Robinson, and Ward 1987). Ethnographic research also suggests that the research focus on skin color is somewhat justified. For example, it played the central role in determining membership in the affluent African American clubs.

Although colorism affects attitudes about the self for both men and women, it appears that these effects are stronger for women than men. In early studies, dark-skinned women were seen as occupying the bottom rungs of the social ladder, least marriageable, having the fewest options for higher education and career advancement, and as more color conscious than their male counterparts (Parrish 1944; Warner, Junker, and Adams 1941). There is very little empirical research on the relationship between gender, skin color, and self-concept development. In this article, we evaluate the relative importance of skin color to feelings about the self for men and women within the African American community. . . .

. . . Using an adult sample of respondents who are representative of the national population, we examine[d] the relationship of skin tone to self-concept development. . . . More important, we examine[d] the way in which gender socially constructs the impact of skin tone on self-concept development. . . .

The Sample

Data for this study come from the National Survey of Black Americans (NSBA) (Jackson and Gurin 1987). . . . Only self-identified Black American citizens were eligible for the study. Face-to-face interviews were carried out by trained Black interviewers, yielding a sample of 2,107 respondents. The response rate was approximately 69 percent. For the most part, the NSBA is representative of the national Black population enumerated in the 1980 census, with the exception of a slight over-representation of women and older Blacks and a small under-representation of southerners (Jackson, Tucker, and Gurin 1987). . . . [Using these data we were able to study the relationship between skin tone, gender, and self-evaluation. (For a description of the methods and results, see the complete article.)]

Skin Tone and Gender

Issues of skin color and physical attractiveness are closely linked and because expectations of physical attractiveness are applied more heavily to women across all cultures, stereotypes of attractiveness and color preference are more profound for Black women (Warner, Junker, and Adams 1941). In the clinical literature (Boyd Franklin 1991; Grier and Cobbs 1968; Neal and Wilson 1989; Okazawa Rey, Robinson, and Ward 1987), issues of racial identity, skin color, and attractiveness were central concerns of women. The "what is beautiful is good" stereotype creates a "halo" effect for light-skinned persons. The positive glow generated by physical attractiveness includes a host of desirable personality traits. Included in these positive judgments are beliefs that attractive people would be significantly more intelligent, kind, confident, interesting, sexy, assertive, poised, modest, and successful, and

they appear to have higher self-esteem and self-worth (Dion, Berscheid, and Walster 1972). When complexion is the indicator of attractiveness, similar stereotypic attributes are found. There is evidence that gender difference in response to the importance of skin color to attractiveness appears during childhood. Girls as young as six are twice as likely as boys to be sensitive to the social importance of skin color (Porter 1971; Russell, Wilson, and Hall 1992, 68). In a study of facial features, skin color, and attractiveness, Neal (cited in Neal and Wilson 1989, 328) found that

> unattractive women were perceived as having darker skin tones than attractive women and that women with more Caucasoid features were perceived as more attractive to the opposite sex, more successful in their love lives and their careers than women with Negroid features.

Frequent exposure to negative evaluations can undermine a woman's sense of self. "A dark skinned Black woman who feels herself unattractive, however, may think that she has nothing to offer society no matter how intelligent or inventive she is" (Russell, Wilson, and Hall 1992, 42).

Several explanations are proffered for gender differences in self-esteem among Blacks. One is that women are socialized to attend to evaluations of others and are vulnerable to negative appraisals. Women seek to validate their selves through appraisal from others more than men do. And the media has encouraged greater negative self-appraisals for dark-skinned women. A second explanation is that colorism and its associated stressors are not the same for dark-skinned men and women. For men, stereotypes associated with perceived dangerousness, criminality, and competence are associated with dark skin tone, while for women the issue is attractiveness (Russell, Wilson, and Hall 1992, 38). Educational attainment is a vehicle by which men might overcome skin color bias, but changes in physical features are difficult to accomplish. Third, women may react more strongly to skin color bias because they feel less control of their lives. Research studies show that women and persons of low status tend to feel fatalistic (Pearlin and Schooler 1978; Turner and Noh 1983) and to react more intensely than comparable others to stressors (Kessler and McLeod 1984; Pearlin and Johnson 1977; Thoits 1982, 1984; Turner and Noh 1983). This suggests a triple jeopardy situation: black women face problems of racism and sexism, and when these two negative status positions—being Black and being female—combine with colorism, a triple threat lowers self-esteem and feelings of competence among dark Black women.

Skin Tone and Self-Evaluation

William James (1890) conceived of the self as an integrating social product consisting of various constituent parts (i.e., the physical, social, and spiritual selves). Body image, the aspect of the self that we recognize first, is one of the major components of the self and remains important throughout life. One can assume that if one's bodily attributes are judged positively, the impact on one's self is positive. Likewise, if society devalues certain physical attributes, negative feelings about the self are likely to ensue. Body image is influenced by a number of factors including skin color, size, and shape. In our society, dark-skinned men and women are raised to believe that "light" skin is preferred. They see very light-skinned Blacks having successful experiences in advertisements, in magazines, in professional positions, and so forth. They are led to believe that "light" skin is the key to popularity, professional status, and a desirable marriage. Russell, Wilson, and Hall (1992) argue that the African American gay and lesbian community is also affected by colorism because a light-skinned or even white mate confers status. Whether heterosexual, gay, or lesbian, colorism may lead to negative self-evaluations among African Americans with dark skin.

Self-evaluations are seen as having two dimensions, one reflecting the person's moral worth and the other reflecting the individual's competency or agency (Gecas 1989). The former refers to self-esteem and indicates how we feel about ourselves. The latter refers to self-efficacy and indicates our belief in the ability to control our own fate. These are two different dimensions in that people can feel that they are good and useful but also feel that what happens to them is due to luck or forces outside themselves.

Self-esteem and skin tone. Self-esteem consists of feeling good, liking yourself, and being liked and treated well. Self-esteem is influenced both by the social comparisons we make of ourselves with others and by the reactions that other people have toward us (i.e., reflected appraisals). The self-concept depends also on the attributes of others who are available for comparison. Self-evaluation theory emphasizes the importance of consonant environmental context for personal comparisons; that is, Blacks will compare themselves with other Blacks in their community. Consonant environmental context assumes that significant others will provide affirmation of one's identity and that similarity between oneself and others shapes the self. Thus, a sense of personal connectedness to other African Americans is most important for fostering and reinforcing positive self-evaluations. This explains why the personal self-esteem of Blacks, despite their lower status position, was as high as that of whites (Porter and Washington 1989, 345; Rosenberg and Simmons 1971).[2] It does not explain the possible influence of colorism on self-esteem within the African American community. Evidence suggests that conflictual and dissonant racial environments have negative effects on self-esteem, especially within the working class (Porter and Washington 1989, 346; Verna and Runion 1985). The heterogeneity of skin tone hues and colorism create a dissonant racial environment and become a source of negative self-evaluation.

Self-efficacy and skin tone. Self-efficacy, as defined by Bandura (1977, 1982), is the belief that one can master situations and control events. Performance influences self-efficacy such that when faced with a failure, individuals with high self-efficacy generally believe that extra effort or persistence will lead to success (Bandura 1982). However, if failure is related to some stable personal characteristic such as "dark skin color" or social constraints such as blocked opportunities resulting from main-streaming practices in the workplace, then one is likely to be discouraged by failure and to feel less efficacious than his or her lighter counter-parts. In fact, Pearlin and colleagues (1981) argue that stressors that seem to be associated with inadequacy of one's efforts or lack of success are implicated in a diminished sense of self. Problems or hardships "to which people can see no end, those that seem to become fixtures of their existence" pose the most sustained affront to a sense of mastery and self-worth (Pearlin et al. 1981, 345). For Bandura, however, individual agency plays a role in sustaining the self. Individuals actively engage in activities that are congenial with a positive sense of self. Self-efficacy results not primarily from beliefs or attitudes about performance but from undertaking challenges and succeeding. Thus, darker skinned Blacks who experience success in their everyday world (e.g., work, education, etc.) will feel more confident and empowered.

Following the literature, we predict a strong relationship between skin tone and self-esteem and self-efficacy, but the mechanisms are different for the two dimensions. The effect of skin tone on self-efficacy will be partially mediated by occupation and income. The effect will be direct for self-esteem. That is, the direct effect will be stronger for self-esteem than for self-efficacy. Furthermore, we expect a stronger relationship between skin tone and self-esteem for women than men because women's self-esteem is conditioned by the appraisals of others, and the media has encouraged negative appraisals for dark-skinned women.

Discussion [of the Study]

The data in this study indicate that gender—mediated by socioeconomic status variables such as education, occupation, and income—socially constructs the importance of skin color evaluations of self-esteem and self-efficacy. Self-efficacy results not primarily from beliefs or attitudes about performance but rather reflects an individual's competency or agency from undertaking challenges and succeeding at overcoming them. Self-esteem consists of feeling good about oneself and being liked and treated favorably by others. However, the effect of skin color on these two domains of self is different for women and men. Skin color is an important predictor of perceived efficacy for Black men but not Black women. And skin color predicts self-esteem for Black women but not Black men. This pattern conforms to traditional gendered expectations (Hill Collins 1990, 79–80). The traditional definitions of masculinity demand men specialize in achievement outside the home, dominate in interpersonal relationships, and remain rational and self-contained. Women, in contrast, are expected to seek affirmation from others, to be warm and nurturing. Thus, consistent with gendered characteristics of men and women, skin color is important in self-domains that are central to masculinity (i.e., competence) and femininity (i.e., affirmation of the self).[3]

Turning our attention to the association between skin color and self-concept for Black men, the association between skin color and self-efficacy increases significantly as skin color lightens. And this is independent of the strong positive contribution of education—and ultimately socioeconomic status—to feelings of competence of men. We think that the effect of skin tone on self-efficacy is the result of widespread negative stereotyping and fear associated with dark-skinned men that pervade the larger society and operates independent of social class. Correspondingly, employers view darker African American men as violent, uncooperative, dishonest, and unstable (Kirschenman and Neckerman, 1998). As a consequence, employers exclude "darker" African American men from employment and thus block their access to rewards and resources.

Evidence from research on the relationship between skin tone and achievement supports our interpretation. The literature on achievement and skin tone shows that lighter skinned Blacks are economically better off than darker skinned persons (Hughes and Hertel 1990; Keith and Herring 1991). Hughes and Hertel (1990), using the NSBA data, present findings that show that for every dollar a light-skinned African American earns, the darker skinned person earns 72 cents. Thus, it seems colorism is operative within the workplace. Lighter skinned persons are probably better able to predict what will happen to them and what doors will open and remain open, thus leading to a higher sense of control over their environment. Our data support this finding and add additional information on how that process might work, at least in the lives of Black men. Perhaps employers are looking to hire African American men who will assimilate into the work environment, who do not alienate their clients (Kirschenman and Neckerman 1998), and who are nonthreatening. One consequence of mainstreaming the workplace is that darker skinned Black men have fewer opportunities to demonstrate competence in the breadwinner role. It is no accident that our inner cities where unemployment is highest are filled with darker skinned persons, especially men (Russell, Wilson, and Hall 1992, 38). During adolescence, lighter skinned boys discover that they have better job prospects, appear less threatening to whites, and have a clearer sense of who they are and their competency (Russell, Wilson, and Hall 1992, 67). In

contrast, darker skinned African American men may feel powerless and less able to affect change through the "normal" channels available to light skinned African American men (who are able to achieve a more prestigious socioeconomic status).

While skin color is an important predictor of self-efficacy for African American men, it is more important as a predictor of self-esteem for African American women. These data confirm much of the anecdotal information from clinical studies of clients in psychotherapy that found that dark-skinned Black women have problems with self-worth and confidence. Our findings suggest that this pattern is not limited to experiences of women who are in therapy but that colorism is part of the everyday reality of black women. Black women expect to be judged by their skin tone. No doubt messages from peers, the media, and family show a preference for lighter skin tones. Several studies cited in the literature review point out that Black women of all ages tend to prefer lighter skin tones and believe that lighter hues are perceived as most attractive by their Black male counterparts (Bond and Cash 1992; Chambers et al. 1994; Porter 1971; T. L. Robinson and Ward 1995).

Evidence from personal accounts reported by St. John and Feagin (1998, 75) in research on the impact of racism in the everyday lives of Black women supports this interpretation. One young woman describes her father's efforts to shape her expectations about the meaning of beauty in our society and where Black women entered this equation.

> Beauty, beauty standards in this country, a big thing with me. It's a big gripe, because I went through a lot of personal anguish over that, being Black and being female, it's a real big thing with me, because it took a lot for me to find a sense of self . . . in this white-male-dominated society. And just how beauty standards are so warped because like my daddy always tell me, "white is right." The whiter you are, somehow the better you are, and if you

look white, well hell, you've got your ticket, and anything you want, too.

Nevertheless, the relationship between skin color and self-esteem among African American women is moderated by socioeconomic status. For example, there is no correlation between skin color and self-esteem among women who have a more privileged socioeconomic status. Consequently, women who are darker and "successful" evaluate themselves just as positively as women of a lighter color. On the other hand, the relationship between skin color and self-esteem is stronger for African American women from the less privileged socioeconomic sectors. In other words, darker skinned women with the lowest incomes display the lowest levels of self-esteem, but self-esteem increases as their skin color lightens. Why does skin color have such importance for self-regard in the context of low income or poverty? Low income shapes self-esteem because it provides fewer opportunities for rewarding experiences or affirming relationships. In addition, there are more negative attributes associated with behaviors of individuals from less privileged socioeconomic status than with those of a more prestigious one. For example, the derisive comment "ghetto chick" is often used to describe the behaviors, dress, communication and interaction styles of women from low-income groups. Combine stereotypes of classism and colorism, and you have a mixture that fosters an undesirable if not malignant context for self-esteem development. An important finding of this research is that skin color and income determine self-worth for Black women and especially that these factors can work together. Dark skin and low income produce Black women with very low self-esteem. Accordingly, [our study] help[s] refine [the] understanding of gendered racism and of "triple oppression" involving race, gender, and class that places women of color in a subordinate social and economic position relative to

men of color and the larger white population as well (Segura 1986). More important, the data suggest that darker skinned African American women actually experience a "quadruple" oppression originating in the convergence of social inequalities based on gender, class, race, and color. . . . We noted the absence of an interaction effect between skin tone and education, and we can only speculate on the explanation for this nonfinding. Perhaps education does not have the same implications for self-esteem as income because it is a less visible symbol of success. Financial success affords one the ability to purchase consumer items that tell others, even at a distance, that an individual is successful. These visible symbols include the place where we live, the kind of car we drive, and the kind of clothing that we wear. Educational attainment is not as easily grasped, especially in distant social interactions— passing on the street, walking in the park, or attending a concert event. In other words, for a dark-skinned African American woman, her M.A. or Ph.D. may be largely unknown outside her immediate friends, family, and coworkers. Her Lexus or Mercedes, however, is visible to the world and is generally accorded a great deal of prestige.

Finally, the data indicate that self-esteem increases as skin color becomes lighter among African American women who are judged as having "low and average levels of attractiveness." There is no relationship between skin color and self-esteem for women who are judged "highly attractive," just as there is no correlation between skin color and self-esteem for women of higher socioeconomic status. That physical attractiveness influenced feelings of self-worth for Black women is not surprising. Women have traditionally been concerned with appearance, regardless of ethnicity. Indeed, the pursuit and preoccupation with beauty are central features of female sex-role socialization. Our findings suggest that women who are judged "unattractive" are more vulnerable to color bias than those judged attractive.

NOTES

1. Skin color bias has also been investigated among Latino groups, although more emphasis has been placed on the combination of both color and European phenotype facial characteristics. Studies of Mexican Americans have documented that those with lighter skin and European features attain more schooling (Telles and Murguia 1990) and generally have higher socioeconomic status (Acre, Murguia, and Frisbie 1987) than those of darker complexion with more Indian features. Similar findings have been reported for Puerto Ricans (Rodriguez 1989), a population with African admixture.

2. Self-concept theory argued that the experience of social inequality would foster lower self-concept of persons in lower status positions compared with their higher status counterparts. However, when comparing the self-concept of African American schoolboys and schoolgirls, Rosenberg and Simmons (1971) found that their self-feelings were as high and in some instances higher than those of white schoolchildren. This "unexpected" finding was explained by strong ties and bonds within the African American community as opposed to identifying with the larger community.

3. These findings also reflect the dual nature of colorism as it pertains to Black women. Colorism is an aspect of racism that results in anti-Black discrimination in the wider society and, owing to historical patterns, also occurs within the Black community. The finding that the effects of skin tone on self-efficacy become nonsignificant when socioeconomic status variables are added suggests that the interracial discrimination aspect of colorism is more operational for Black women's self-efficacy via access to jobs and income. The finding that the effect of skin tone is more central to Black women's self-esteem indicates that colorism within the Black community is the more central mechanism. Self-esteem is derived from family, friends, and close associates.

REFERENCES

Acre, Carlos, Edward Murguia, and W. P. Frisbie, 1987. Phenotype and life chances among Chicanos. *Hispanic Journal of Behavioral Sciences* 9(1): 19–32.

Aiken, Leona S., and Stephen G. West. 1991. *Multiple regression: Testing and interpreting interactions.* Newbury Park, CA: Sage.

Bachman, J. G., and Johnson. 1978. *The monitoring the future project: Design and procedures.* Ann Arbor: University of Michigan, Institute for Social Research.

Bandura, A. 1977. Self efficacy: Towards a unifying theory of behavioral change. *Psychological Review* 84: 191–215.

———. 1982. Self efficacy mechanism in human agency. *American Psychologist* 37: 122–47.

Bond, S., and T. F. Cash. 1992. Black beauty: Skin color and body images among African-American college women. *Journal of Applied Social Psychology* 22 (11): 874–88.

Boyd Franklin, N. 1991. Recurrent themes in the treatment of African-American women in group psychotherapy. *Women and Therapy* 11 (2): 25–40.

Cash, T. S., and N. C. Duncan. 1984. Physical attractiveness stereotyping among Black American college students. *Journal of Social Psychology* 1:71–77.

Chambers, J. W., T. Clark, L. Dantzler, and J. A. Baldwin. 1994. Perceived attractiveness, facial features, and African self-consciousness. *Journal of Black Psychology* 20 (3): 305–24.

Dion, K., E. Berscheid, and E. Walster. 1972. What is beautiful is good. *Journal of Personality and Social Psychology* 24:285–90.

Frazier, E. Franklin. 1957. *Black bourgeoisie: The rise of the new middle class.* New York: Free Press.

Freeman, H. E., J. M. Ross, S. Armor, and R. F. Pettigrew. 1966. Color gradation and attitudes among middle class income Negroes. *American Sociological Review* 31: 365–74.

Gatewood, W. B. 1988. Aristocrat of color: South and North and the Black elite, 1880–1920. *Journal of Southern History* 54: 3–19.

Gecas, Viktor. 1989. The social psychology of self-efficacy. *Annual Review of Sociology* 15: 291–316.

Grier, W., and P. Cobbs. 1968. *Black rage.* New York: Basic Books.

Hill Collins, Patricia. 1990. *Black feminist thought: Knowledge, consciousness, and the politics of empowerment.* Boston: Unwin Hyman.

Hughes, M., and B. R. Hertel. 1990. The significance of color remains: A study of life chances, mate selection, and ethnic consciousness among Black Americans. *Social Forces* 68(4): 1105–20.

Hughes, Michael, and David H. Demo. 1989. Self perceptions of Black Americans: Self-esteem and personal efficacy. *American Journal of Sociology* 95: 132–59.

Jackson, J., and G. Gurin. 1987. *National Survey of Black Americans, 1979–1980* (machine-readable codebook). Ann Arbor: University of Michigan, Inter-University Consortium for Political and Social Research.

Jackson, J. S., B. Tucker, and G. Gurin. 1987. *National Survey of Black Americans 1979–1980* (MRDF). Ann Arbor, MI: Institute for Social Research.

James, W. 1890. *The principles of psychology.* New York: Smith.

Keith, V. M., and C. Herring. 1991. Skin tone and stratification in the Black community. *American Journal of Sociology* 97 (3): 760–78.

Kessler, R. C., and J. D. McLeod. 1984. Sex differences in vulnerability to undesirable life events. *American Sociological Review* 49: 620–31.

Kirschenman, J., and K. M. Neckerman. 1998. We'd love to hire them, but . . . In *The meaning of race for employers in working American: Continuity, conflict, and change,* edited by Amy S. Wharton. Mountain View, CA: Mayfield.

Klag, Michael, Paul Whelton, Josef Coresh, Clarence Grim, and Lewis Kuller. 1991. The association of skin color with blood pressure in U.S. Blacks with low socioeconomic status. *Journal of the American Medical Association* 65(5): 599–602.

Miller, Herman P. 1964. *Rich man, poor man.* New York: Corwell.

Neal, A., and M. Wilson. 1989. The role of skin color and features in the Black community: Implications for Black women in therapy. *Clinical Psychology Review* 9 (3): 323–33.

Okazawa Rey, Margo, Tracy Robinson, and Janie V. Ward. 1987. *Black women and the politics of skin color and hair.* New York: Haworth.

Parrish, Charles. 1944. The significance of skin color in the Negro community. Ph.D. diss., University of Chicago.

Pearlin, L. I., and J. S. Johnson. 1977. Marital status, life strains, and depression. *American Sociological Review* 42: 704–15.

Pearlin, L. I., M. A. Liberman, E. G. Meneghan, and J. T. Mullan. 1981. The stress process. *Journal of Health and Social Behavior* 22 (December): 337–56.

Pearlin, L. I., and C., Schooler. 1978. The structure of coping. *Journal of Health and Social Behavior* 19: 2–21.

Porter, J. 1971. *Black child, white child: The development of racial attitudes.* Cambridge, MA: Harvard University Press.

Porter, J. R., and R. E. Washington. 1989. Developments in research on black identity and self esteem: 1979–88. *Review of International Psychology and Sociology* 2:341–53.

Ransford, E. H. 1970. Skin color, life chances and anti-white attitudes. *Social Problems* 18:164–78.

Robinson, J. P., and P. R. Shaver. 1969. *Measures of social psychological attitudes.* Ann Arbor: University of Michigan, Institute of Social Research.

Robinson, T. L., and J. V. Ward. 1995. African American adolescents and skin color. *Journal of Black Psychology* 21 (3): 256–74.

Rodriguez, Clara. 1989. *Puerto Ricans: Born in the USA.* Boston: Unwin Hyman.

Rosenberg, M. 1979. *Conceiving the self.* New York: Basic Books.

Rosenberg, M., and R. Simmons. 1971. *Black and white self-esteem: The urban school child.* Washington, DC: American Sociological Association.

Russell, Kathy, Midge Wilson, and Ronald Hall. 1992. *The color complex: The politics of skin color among African Americans.* New York: Harcourt Brace Jovanovich.

Segura, Denise. 1986. Chicanas and triple oppression in the labor force. In *Chicana voices: Intersections of class, race, and gender,* edited by Teresa Cordova and the National Association of Chicana Studies Editorial Committee. Austin, TX: Center for Mexican American Studies.

St. John, Y., and J. R. Feagin. 1998. *Double burden: Black women and everyday racism.* New York: M. E. Sharpe.

Telles, Edward E., and Edward Murguia. 1990. Phenotypic discrimination and income differences among Mexican Americans. *Social Science Quarterly* 71 (4): 682–95.

Thoits, Peggy A. 1982. Life stress, social support, and psychological vulnerability: Epidemiological considerations. *Journal of Community Psychology* 10: 341–62.

———. 1984. Explaining distributions of psychological vulnerability: Lack of social support in the face of life stress. *Social Forces* 63: 452–81.

Thurman, Wallace. 1929. *The blacker the berry: A novel of Negro life.* New York: Macmillan.

Tryoler, H. A., and S. A. James. 1978. Blood pressure and skin color. *American Journal of Public Health* 58: 1170–72.

Turner, R. J., and S. Noh. 1983. Class and psychological vulnerability among women: The significance of social support and personal control. *Journal of Health and Social Behavior* 24: 2–15.

Udry, J. R., K. E. Baumann, and C. Chase. 1969. Skin color, status, and mate selection. *American Journal of Sociology* 76: 722–33.

Verna. G., and K. Runion. 1985. The effects of contextual dissonance on the self concept of youth from high vs. low socially valued groups. *Journal of Social Psychology* 125: 449–58.

Warner, W. L., B. H. Junker, and W. A. Adams. 1941. *Color and human nature.* Washington, DC: American Council on Education.

Wright, B. 1976. *The dissent of the governed: Alienation and democracy in America.* New York: Academic Press.

THINKING ABOUT THE READING

Describe the different effects skin tone has on black men and women. How can you explain the gender differences in the relationship between skin tone and self-esteem and between skin tone and self-efficacy? What role does socioeconomic status play in mediating these relationships? What are the long-term economic and political consequences of skin color bias? Thompson and Keith state that *colorism*—intraracial discrimination based on skin color—still divides and shapes the lives of African Americans. How does this skin color bias within the African American community compare to the prejudice and discrimination Blacks are subjected to by non-Blacks? Is there comparable *within-group* prejudice among other races? If so, how does it compare to what Thompson and Keith describe? If not, why is such prejudice unique to the African American community?

12 The Architecture of Inequality

Sex and Gender

I n addition to racial and class inequality, gender inequality—and the struggle against it—has been a fundamental part of the historical development of our national identity. Gender ideology has influenced the lives and dreams of individual people, shaped popular culture, and created or maintained social institutions. Gender is a major criterion for the distribution of important economic, political, and educational resources in most societies. Gender inequality is perpetuated by a dominant cultural ideology that devalues women on the basis of presumed biological differences between them and men. This ideology overlooks the equally important role of social forces in determining male and female behavior.

One example of persistent gender difference and inequality is the way young people are socialized to understand their own emerging sexuality. We tend to think of sexuality as something that just happens to us. In fact, we are continuously socialized about how we should think, feel, and behave sexually. Boys and girls receive very different messages about what kind of sexual feelings and behavior they should have. When you understand the gender differences in sexual socialization, you begin to see why men and women have such a difficult time relating to one another. In "Dilemmas of Desire," Deborah Tolman examines how conceptions of male and female sexuality drastically and dangerously diverge in adolescence. Throughout their teen years, boys and girls are exposed to different rules and principles about sexuality. For boys, sexual desire is "natural and healthy," their ticket to normal manhood; for girls, sexual desire is "bad" and framed in terms of its risks and dangerous consequences. These distinctive ideals ultimately alienate boys and girls from one another and from the development of a healthy and socially responsible understanding of sexual desire. In her interviews with adolescent girls, Tolman finds a discrepancy between how girls' sexuality has been portrayed and what they actually reveal about their own sexual desires. While some resist and suppress their desires, others see these desires with a sense of entitlement. The complicated ways in which these girls talk about their own sexuality tells us that girls' feelings are very much at odds with what society expects of them. Girls recognize this, and as a consequence, often experience tremendous conflict between cultural expectations for what girls are supposed to feel and do, and how they really feel.

Like the article, "The Blacker the Berry . . ." in the previous chapter, Bart Landry explores the intersections of race and gender in "Black Women and a New Definition of Womanhood." Landry examines the difficulties black women have faced throughout history in being seen by others as virtuous and moral. This article provides a fascinating picture of women's struggle for equality from the perspective of black women, a group that is often ignored and marginalized in discussions of the women's movement. Although much of the article focuses on black women's activism in the 19th century, it provides important insight into the intersection of race and gender today. Landry raises an important contrast between the way in which 19th-century middle-class white women and middle-class black women framed the relationship between family and public life,

Gender inequality exists at the institutional level as well, in the law, in the family (in terms of such things as the domestic division of labor), and in economics. Not only are social institutions sexist, in that women are systematically segregated, exploited, and excluded, they are also gendered. Institutions themselves are structured along gender lines so that traits associated with success are usually stereotypically male characteristics: tough-mindedness, rationality, assertiveness, competitiveness, and so forth.

Women have made significant advances politically, economically, educationally, and socially over the past decades. The traditional obstacles to advancement continue to fall. Women have entered the paid labor force in unprecedented numbers. Yet despite their growing presence and their entry into historically male occupations, rarely do women work alongside men or perform the same tasks and functions.

Jobs within an occupation still tend to be divided into "men's work" and "women's work." Such gender segregation has serious consequences for women in the form of blocked advancement and lower salaries. But looking at gender segregation on the job as something that happens only to women gives us an incomplete picture of the situation. It is just as important to examine what keeps men out of "female" jobs as it is to examine what keeps women out of "male" jobs. The proportion of women in male jobs has increased over the past several decades, but the proportion of men in female jobs has remained virtually unchanged. In "Still a Man's World," Christine Williams looks at the experiences of male nurses, social workers, elementary school teachers, and librarians. She finds that although these men do feel somewhat stigmatized by their nontraditional career choices, they still enjoy significant gender advantages.

Something to Consider as You Read:

While reading these selections, think about the significance of gender as a social category. A child's gender is the single most important thing people want to know when it is born. "What is it?" is a commonly understood shorthand for "is it a boy or a girl?" From the time children are born, they learn that certain behaviors, feelings, and expectations are associated with the gender category to which they have been assigned. Think about some of the behaviors associated with specific gender categories. Make a list of stereotypical gender expectations. Upon reflection, do these seem reasonable to you? What are some recollections you have about doing something that was considered inappropriate for your gender? Think about ways in which these stereotypical expectations affect people's perceptions, especially in settings such as school or jobs.

Dilemmas of Desire
Teenage Girls Talk About Sexuality

Deborah L. Tolman

(2002)

On a May morning when the warmth of the sun seemed to be finally winning out over the last chilly breeze of a New England winter, I met Inez, a seventeen-year-old Latina junior in a public high school, who agreed to participate in my study of adolescent girls' sexual desire. Sitting in an out-of-the-way, sun-filled corner of a seldom-used corridor, I listen to Inez's voice as she speaks about her experiences of her sexuality. Our heads bend down around the quiet whirling of my tape recorder, shielding us both from intrusions and from being overheard. In the hour and a half that we talk, Inez seems to find it easy to respond to my questions. Her stories are detailed, punctuated with reflections on what she thought and how she felt. One of the first stories she chooses to tell me is about the first time she had sexual intercourse, with a boy with whom she was "in love":

> The first time I ever had sex, it was something that I least expected it. I didn't actually go to his house and expect something to happen, because it, he was kissing me, and I felt like I wasn't there, it was like my body just went limp. It was like, I had went out with him for a year, and I was like, I was like wow, and um, he was just kissing me, and I was like, and then all of a sudden like, just, like my body just went limp, and then everything just happened. To me, I feel like I didn't notice anything.

There are several ways to hear Inez's story. Developmental psychologists might explain it as evidence of her immaturity, because it demonstrates that she has not yet constructed a sexual self. Since Inez never says directly that she wanted to have sex, some might think that this story reflects an experience of victimization and coercion. Yet Inez offers this experience as one of sexual pleasure, which to her means the pleasure of "being wanted" and "show[ing] him that I loved him more, in a physical way." And so another way to think about Inez's story is as a condoned version: The main theme, that sex "just happened," is an explanation girls frequently offer for how they come to have sex. Having sex "just happen" is one of the few acceptable ways available to adolescent girls for making sense of and describing their sexual experiences; and, given the power of such stories to shape our experiences of our bodies, it may tell us what their sexual experiences actually are like. In a world where "good," nice, and normal girls do not have sexual feelings of their own, it is one of the few decent stories that a girl can tell. That is, "it just happened" is a story about desire (Plummer, 1995).

"It just happened," then, can also be understood as a cover story. It is a story about the necessity for girls to cover their desire. It is also a story that covers over active choice, agency, and responsibility, which serves to "disappear" desire, in the telling and in the living. But "it just happened" is much more than a story told by yet another girl to describe her individual experience. Focusing on Inez's individually unfolding sexual development leaves out the fact that girls' sexuality does not develop in a vacuum. It leaves out the ways in which girls are under systematic pressure not to feel, know, or act on their sexual desire. It covers up both our consistent refusal to offer girls any guidance for acknowledging, negotiating, and integrating their own sexual desire and the consequences of our refusal: sexual intercourse—most often unprotected, that "just happens" to girls. "It just happened" is undoubtedly one of a multitude of stories that a girl can tell about any single experience. Its veracity is not on the line; the wisdom of telling and living this story about female adolescent sexuality is. I suggest that "it just happened" is an unsafe and unhealthy story for girls. . . .

Victims and Victors: Two Roads to Sexual Maturity

How far our conceptions of male and female adolescent sexuality diverge came into startling focus one night at a dinner party I attended with some friends who have teenage children. A man I had not met before began bragging about how his teenage son showed every sign of being a "ladies' man." He beamed with pride as he described his son's ability to elude the "grasp" of any single girl, how his boy was so successful at "playing the field." The father winked at another man at the table, hinting that, by the age of sixteen, his son had "gotten" plenty of sexual experience, showing all the signs of having the "raging hormones" that he appeared to believe was normal for his son. His pleasure that his son was a heartbreaker was evident.

Later in the evening, this same man spoke about his fifteen-year-old daughter. A different picture of the terrain of adolescent sexuality came to the fore. On the one hand, he was clearly proud that his daughter was considered an attractive and desirable date by her male peers; on the other, he was uncomfortable when she actually went out with them. While

he understood that she wanted to have a boyfriend, which he ascribed to her desire to be like her friends, he preferred that she bring boys home rather than be out with them. He worried that "things might happen to her" that she would "regret." His fear that she would be sexually victimized or "taken advantage of" by boys was palpable.

Several things struck me about this conversation. It was clear this man had two entirely different ideas about appropriate and normal sexuality for male and female adolescents. It was also clear he did not see how they were connected. His belief that boys are sexual predators and his encouragement and approval of this behavior in his own son fueled his conviction that girls, including his daughter, need to be protected *from* boys while also being attractive *for* boys. Unstated but eminently implicit in his formulation was the assumption that girls are the objects of boys' sexual desire and have no desires of their own. This man's perspectives on his son and his daughter illustrate the ways in which our beliefs about sexuality are gendered.

As a society, we parcel sexuality out, assuming that normal boys but not girls have "raging hormones"—and that normal girls but not boys long for emotional connection and relationships. We assume that adolescent boys are burgeoning sexual beings. We believe that they are obsessed with their sexuality and expect them not only to feel sexual desire but to be compelled to act on it, or at the very least to make the attempt. In many circles, if a boy reaches mid-adolescence without having shown any perceptible sexual interest in girls, those around him may become concerned about his masculinity and sexual orientation. In contrast, when it comes to girls, what we still expect, and in many ways continue to encourage, is their yearning for love, relationships, and romance. Acknowledgment of their sexual longings as an anticipated part of their adolescence is virtually nonexistent. We have effectively desexualized girls' sexuality, substituting the desire for relationship and emotional connection for sexual feelings in their bodies. . . .

As early as middle school (Tolman et al., 2002) or even the waning moments of elementary school (Thorne, 1993), girls and boys are relentlessly exposed to a set of rules, principles, and roles that are mapped out for the production of "normal" heterosexual adolescent relationships and sexual behavior, in which gender is the most salient factor. Teenage girls continue to be denied entitlement to their own sexuality, and girls who do defy the irrepressible double standard continue to do so at their own risk.

Despite the incessant flow of sexual images and relationship advice, girls do not get many positive messages about their sexuality. They are barraged with an ever more confusing and contradictory set of guidelines for how they should manage their developing sexuality: don't be a prude but don't be a slut; have (or fake) orgasms to ensure that your boyfriend is not made to feel inadequate, if you want to keep him. Ultimately, though subtly, the media continue to represent the belief that adolescent girls should be sexy for boys and not have their *own* sexual desires. . . .

Teen magazines, movies, and television contribute to the pervasive paradox: They offer advice on how to provide pleasure to boys juxtaposed with stories of sexual violation and harassment. Madonna powerfully models female sexual freedom; yet, despite their admiration and even awe at her willingness to defy social norms, few teenage girls feel that they themselves—ordinary girls, not gorgeous celebrities—could "get away with it" without a besmirched reputation (Kitzinger, 1995, p. 193). Music directed at adolescent girls continues to mix the message. At the same time Christina Aguilera sings about "what a girl wants, what a girl needs," she presents herself as a sex symbol, consciously turning her body into a commodity, an object of admiration and desire for others, obscuring how or even whether her own desires figure in her willingness to do "whatever keeps me in your arms." In her memoir *Promiscuities* (1997) Naomi Wolf observed that even today "girls must speak in a world where they are expected to be sexually available but not sexually in charge of themselves" (p. 136). And so the conundrum: while *sexualized images* of adolescent girls are omnipresent, *their* sexual feelings are rarely if ever portrayed. . . .

When I searched the literature to find out what psychologists knew about adolescent girls' sexual desire, I found that no one had asked about it. In the many hundreds of studies that have been done to determine what predicts adolescent girls' sexual behavior, only a handful had identified girls' sexual desire as a potential factor. We tend to conflate adolescent sexuality with risky behavior, to define "sex" only in terms of sexual intercourse without distinguishing its various component parts, such as sexual feelings and desire, and the different types of behavior that express those feelings. This tendency, an artifact of public policy and funded research geared toward avoiding the risks of sexuality, leads us to single out girls as the receptacle of our concerns. Our fear about girls' sexual behavior thus conceptualized has understandable roots, since it is still girls who suffer overwhelmingly the physical, social, psychological, and material consequences of unprotected intercourse. . . .

An examination of our conception of male adolescent sexual desire sheds light on this tendency to deny girls' sexuality. It is, indeed, a frightening conception. We believe that desire is a demanding physical urge, instinct, or drive, embedded so deeply in the body that it gains a life of its own once ignited. It is impossible to control, absolutely necessary to satisfy (through sexual intercourse), and aggressive to the point of violence. It is the unstoppable artifact of testosterone overload. In our worst scenarios, we think of desire as a kind of selfish, exploitative monster, as a force that demands its bearer find satisfaction at the expense of or without concern for someone else. Desire is uncivilized.

It is all about individual needs and has nothing to do with relationships. It is male, and it is masculine. Thus conceived, desire is not only incompatible but at odds with society's conceptions of femininity, precluding it from being part of the array of feelings and behaviors that we expect from girls who are developing in an acceptable fashion. Given these beliefs, no wonder we think of those first stirrings of adult sexual desire in adolescence—either "healthy" boys' sexual desire or "bad" girls' sexual desire—as dangerous. . . .

The obsessive quality of our focus on teenage girls' sexual behavior and vulnerability calls attention to less obvious motives for our intense anxiety about them. Recall the Spur Posse case in Lakewood, California: A group of high school boys who were discovered to be competing for how many girls they could manipulate into having sex. Although many people criticized their behavior as an example of unchecked adolescent sexuality, the boys' parents were publicly untroubled by their sons' actions. But try to substitute "girls" for "boys": Can anyone imagine a girl who coerced a boy to have sex being shrugged off or even defended and admired by her parents on national television because of her "raging hormones" or because of their belief that "girls will be girls"? Such concerns about boys are glossed over by the assumption that adolescent boys not only are sexual beings but are overwhelmed by their sexuality, and that such intense sexual desire is a *natural and normal part of male adolescence and male sexuality*. A gendered perspective on adolescent sexuality offers more explanation for what is behind the urgency of resisting girls' sexual desire: Girls' *lack* of desire serves as the necessary linchpin in how adolescent sexuality is organized and managed. To the extent that we believe that adolescent sexuality is under control, it is adolescent girls whom we hold responsible, because we do not believe boys can or will be. We are left with a circuitous argument that fails to include the reality or importance of female adolescents' own sexuality: Boys will be boys ergo sexuality is dangerous for girls. Our impulse to keep girls safe by keeping them under control seems so necessary that the cost of denying them the right to live fully in their own bodies appears unavoidable. Just as impossible standards of thinness serve to curtail girls' and women's hunger for food, this seemingly justified worry about their sexuality fuels denial and demonization of female adolescent sexual desire. In essence, we let boys off the hook for a wide array of consequences *for girls* because of what we denote and perceive to be their inevitable and uncontainable sexuality, as was so blatantly conveyed by my dinner companion. In the process, we also make it hard for adolescent boys to experience a full range of emotions and connections. In the wake of these beliefs, how could we not worry about girls? Why would we want to acknowledge *their* desire? . . .

If I listen to Inez from the perspective that girls have sexual feelings and can or should act on them, I listen for her acknowledgment of her own sexual feelings, for the presence and absence of her own desire in her description of her sexual experiences. Prior to telling this story, Inez has told me that she is capable of feeling sexual desire and can describe those embodied feelings: When she gets in the "pleasure mood," she explains, her "body says yes, yes, yes." She identifies herself as Latina, and the specific qualities associated with acceptable feminine demeanor and behavior for Latina girls suffuse everything she says. In this story, I listen specifically for what Inez says about herself and her body—"I felt like I wasn't there, it was like my body just went limp . . . I feel like I didn't notice anything." Inez describes a body that is present yet not feeling; a self that is not there, that does not act but is acted upon, that does not contribute or even "notice"; a body that is "limp" rather than alive or engaged. From this perspective, Inez's story is about how *she* disappears when she has sex for the first time—literally and figuratively. Her body is silent—and consequently, (unprotected) sex "just happened." In this story, there is no hint that her own sexual desire was part of her first experience of sexual intercourse.

Inez's story illustrates how, by disallowing female sexual desire, we manufacture danger and risk by throwing a roadblock in the pathway of girls' psychosocial development, psychological health, and ability to form authentic relationships. We create an impossible situation for girls: Healthy sexuality means having sexual desire, but there is little if any safe space—physically, socially, psychologically—for these forbidden and dangerous feelings. Girls who embrace or even resist the stories we offer about female and male sexuality inevitably face dilemmas when they feel sexual desire: Do they feel and act on their desire and risk the negative, even punitive, possibly disastrous consequences, or do they deny, discount, or distract others from their desire and suffer a profound disconnection from themselves? . . .

By equating and confounding sexuality with sexual intercourse, we limit how all adolescents learn to conceptualize their romantic relationships and themselves as sexual beings. We also undermine our efforts to educate them and to learn more ourselves about adolescent sexuality through research. Sexual desire is not the same as sexual intercourse or even desire for sexual intercourse. Intercourse is one of an array of behaviors with which a person can respond to such feelings. By focusing on sexual intercourse, which is an act or a behavior, we have left out and glossed over another key aspect of sexuality and sexual development: *sexual feelings*.

With this distinction in mind, rather than designing yet another study to investigate girls' sexual activity, behavior, or attitudes, I organized my research around a new line of inquiry: When asked in a straightforward and safe way about their own sexual desire, what do adolescent girls say? . . .

Hearing an Erotic Voice

. . . I was struck by the discrepancy between how adolescent girls are generally portrayed, studied, and discussed and what these girls said. The belief that girls' sexuality is focused exclusively on relationships and that their own sexual feelings are nonexistent or irrelevant did not match these girls' descriptions of desire. While some said the feeling of desire leads them into adventure and explorations of themselves, they also said that it can lead them into risky situations and thus is sometimes a warning. Sexual desire is, for these girls, a feature of being in a relationship with someone else and, in so doing, knowing themselves. These girls made a key distinction, however, between their sexual desire and their wish for a relationship. While their feelings of sexual desire most often arise in relationships, they are not the same as or a substitute for wanting a relationship.

What comes across powerfully in the narratives of the girls who said they feel sexual desire is that they experience it as having an unmistakable power and intensity. Inez knows she is feeling desire when "my body says yes yes yes yes." Lily calls feeling desire "amazing." Rochelle feels it "so, so bad . . . I wanna have sex so bad, you know"; she adds, "you just have this feeling, you just have to get rid of it." Liz explains: "I just wanted to have sex with him really badly and I just, and we just took off our bathing suits really fast [she laughs] and um, it was almost like really rushed and really quick." For Barbara it is "very strong . . . an overwhelming longing" and "a wicked [strong] urge." Paulina's heart "would really beat fast"; she is "extremely aware of every, every touch and everything." Alexandra speaks of being "incredibly attracted" to her friend. Jane calls the power of her desire "demanding" and says, "the feelings are so strong inside you that they're just like ready to burst." These direct acknowledgments of the power of sexual desire came from girls of different geography, race, and sexual orientation.

Some girls also conveyed the intensity of their desire by the strength of their voiced resistance to it; in response to her body's "yes yes yes yes," Inez explains that "my mind says no no no, you stop kissing him." Cassandra evidences the strength and the urgency of her feeling in narrating what she does not want to do, "stop": "he just like stopped all of a sudden and I was like what are you doing? 'cause I didn't want to stop at all"; she says that for her, desire is "powerful." Lily contrasts not being "in the mood to do anything . . . because I just have all my clothes on . . . because it's just too inconvenient" with the power of her desire when she feels it, "once in a while": "even though it's inconvenient for me, sometimes I just have this feeling, well I just don't care, if I have to put my pantyhose on or not," the power of her desire overriding the normally paramount concern she has for maintaining a proper appearance.

Whereas these girls spoke about feelings in their stomachs, shoulders, necks, and legs, as well as sensations all over their bodies, Megan was one of the few girls to connect her desire to her vagina. Very few girls named the sexual parts of their bodies in these interviews about their sexual desire. Megan speaks of knowing she is feeling sexual desire for boys because of what she feels in her body; as she says, "kind of just this feeling, you know? Just this feeling inside my body . . . my vagina starts to kinda like act up and it kinda like quivers and stuff, and um, like I'll get like tingles and and you can just feel your hormones [laughs] doing something weird, and you just, you get happy and you just get, you know, restimulated kind of and it's just, and oh! Oh!" and "your nerves feel good."

Hearing Dilemmas of Desire

. . . As girls' descriptions of their desire illustrate, they did indeed experience powerful sexual feelings. But the secret life of sexuality that I had imagined did not materialize. What I heard instead was how the social dilemma that

societal constructions of female and male sexuality set up for girls, a choice between their sexual feelings or their safety, was experienced as a personal dilemma by them. Given that this dilemma is framed *as if* it were an individual rather than a social problem—if a girl has desire, she is vulnerable to personal physical, social, material, or relational consequences—it is in a way not especially surprising that girls would experience their desire and these resulting difficulties as their own personal problem. Although girls themselves did not use the word "dilemma" in narrating their experiences, they described dilemmas and private efforts to solve what they perceived to be personal problems, since talking about and thus revealing their own desire is itself taboo.

This dilemma of desire takes different forms for different girls, with certain consequences or potential bad outcomes more evident or salient to some than to others. In telling their stories of desire, and of not having desire, these girls articulated the various consequences they were aware their sexual desire could invite. Their stories illuminate how dealing with desire makes important normative adolescent developmental processes difficult. Specifically, these adolescents reveal how their experiences of desire get in the way of their relationships with peers, romantic partners, parents, and other important adults in their lives. They tell stories elaborating how their desire challenges their ability to develop identities as "good," acceptable, moral, and normal women, and how confusing it is to develop a sexual identity that leaves their sexuality out. Their desire narratives show how the girls juggle and at the same time integrate the logistics of being an adolescent and the belief systems of their religions, their cultures, and their communities, including the specific communities of their schools.

Ellen feared that her own desire could lead to risking pregnancy, a fear intensified by her perception that she must choose between her own sexuality and the material consequence of losing her chance of getting an education as a way out of poverty. Kim internalized her father's stated belief that a desiring girl is more likely to be considered at fault by others if she is raped. Jane described her guilt at having betrayed her boyfriend by kissing another boy, her confusion about her own culpability in this choice, and her fear about how her boyfriend, her mother, or her sisters would judge her if they found out. Lily acted on her desire and was thrown out of her mother's house. Nikki's stories reflected the not unlikely possibility of male violence. Emily, confused by the social mandate to appear sexy, was afraid of being used. Magda did not want her sexual feelings to prevent her from fulfilling her immigrant mother's expectations that she would be the first in her family to go to college. Megan worried that her desire would lead her to lose control of herself and make choices she might later regret. Zoe found waiting for a boy to figure out and take the initiative to satisfy her desire frustrating but the only possibility she could imagine for herself. Sophie managed to work around her perception that girls were not supposed to want or initiate sexual encounters. Julia believed that if she were to act on her desire, she would be considered "just as promiscuous" as the girls whose behavior she herself frowned upon. Melissa was highly aware that her desire for girls could lead to rejection and violence as well as constant disappointment. Barbara talked about the risk of embarrassment and frustration when her feelings were not returned or when someone considered her "perverted" because of her desires. Charlene was afraid that her desire would make her seem like a "slut."

A few girls were able to skirt, resist, or even transform such denial and demonizing of their desire in some contexts but experienced their desire as a dilemma in other situations. For instance, while Megan resisted the formulation of her desire as problematic in heterosexual relationships, her desire for girls was "blocked"

by her awareness of homophobia and compulsory heterosexuality. Eugenia felt safe as a desiring girl in a long-term monogamous heterosexual relationship but worried about judging herself and being judged by friends and family as "bad" because of sexual desires that did not fit neatly into that specific configuration. Beverly related her concern about hurting a boy's feelings or having to deal with his violent reaction if she had told him that he could not please her. Virtually all of the girls spoke about how girls who act on their desire leave themselves open to getting a bad reputation, though not all of them were worried about this outcome for themselves. None of these examples is exclusive to any single girl; even the few girls who were aware of and fully rejected the sexual double standard and refused to accept the conditions that make their own sexual feelings appear to be "the problem," even the girls who articulated the positive possibilities that may result from acting on the basis of their sexual desire and talked about their sexuality in more nuanced and complex ways, could not shake the shadows of these unrelenting threats of what can happen to a desiring girl.

These remain reasonable fears, *under current gender arrangements*. Not being able to find a comfortable fit for desire in their sexual identities or their social and relational terrains made it hard or sometimes impossible for these girls to be aware of or feel, let alone accept or validate, their own sexual feelings. What came through all of their stories of desire was how their acute and astute awareness of the dangers associated with their sexuality, the denigration of their sexual feelings, and their expectations about boys' sexuality led most of them to consider the source of danger to be *their own sexuality*. In effect, these girls described how social processes and meanings that clearly originate outside the body end up incorporated into its physiological demeanor and both unconscious and conscious behaviors. As Lynn Philips

(2000) has so succinctly put it, "we do not simply live inside our cultures. In many ways our cultures live inside of us" (p. 17).

Embedded in the stories about desire that these girls told was a multitude of strategies, more and less conscious, for negotiating the tricky terrain of their own sexual feelings. It turned out that my question about desire was often a question the girls themselves had already been struggling with in some form, always in silence and isolation, outside any relationship with other girls or adult women, sometimes consciously and sometimes not. For some, this question was like a low-grade fever, making them a little bit uncomfortable, but not really a major problem. For other girls, the question of their desire was crucial, an important clue to their identity that remained elusive for them. As girls tried to sort out their feelings on their own, the question of their sexual desire remained both unspoken and unresolved until we began talking about it. Sometimes the question itself had never been articulated. Instead, they essentially lived the question. . . .

Disappearing Desire

Some girls resist their sexual feelings by making them go away. The girls who thus "disappear" desire may or may not be conscious they are engaging in this process. Some, . . . juggle various kinds of desire—the desire to achieve, the desire not to get pregnant, the desire to protect relationships—and seem unaware they are describing the disappearance of their sexual desire. Others . . . narrate a semiconscious resistance to their own sexual feelings, with awareness of the power and importance of desire but not of the multiple dimensions of the trade-offs they are making. And some, like Inez, talk about a conscious decision to stifle their desire; aware of the power, pleasure, and danger associated with their desire, they choose safety above

all else, with an understanding of the costs involved in this choice. . . .

Ambivalent Desires

The girls who "disappear" their desire sacrifice their sexuality for the sake of safety in a realm of their lives that feels suffused with danger. None of them questions this approach; the notion that it is unsafe for girls to have sexual feelings, premised on an assumption of male entitlement to unbridled sexuality, is deeply embedded in their response to their own desire. The other group of girls who resist their own sexual desire do not sound as decisive, nor do they sacrifice their desire in the same fashion. Both Emily and Megan have some awareness that they should be entitled to their sexual desire and so do not cut themselves off as a solution. However, they describe an uneasy balance between the power of desire and the threat of consequences. As they feel desire, apprehend how it connects them with themselves, and appreciate a mutual connection with another person, they worry about the price they will have to pay. In the circumscribed space they have allotted to their sexual subjectivity, vulnerability to being objectified and ostracized looms large. These girls also evidence a glimmer of a critical perspective on the institution of heterosexuality, which unfairly punishes desiring girls, yet they do not go so far as to push "good" girls off their pedestals or to elevate "sluts." Emily, who has a vague sense of her right to sexual feelings, is especially fearful of social consequences, while Megan, whose critique of the double standard is more evolved yet still falls short of rejection, has more comfort with her desire for boys. For Megan, the recent acceptance of her sexual feelings for girls is the front line of her struggle. . . .

[These girls] negotiate their own personal dilemmas of desire by resisting their sexual feelings. While they are aware—some more, some less—of the power, pleasure, and possibility embedded in their sexual desire, they feel acutely vulnerable to its dangers. The more dangerous they feel desire to be for them, the more unequivocally they resist their desire. Working within the institution of heterosexuality, they do not hold boys or social conventions accountable for making sexuality dangerous; rather, it is *their own sexual feelings* that constitute both the problem and the answer. These girls all evidence awareness, at some level, that if they bring their desire forthrightly into their relationships, they will be in conflict with others in their lives, and with themselves. Some, like Inez, resist consciously: she tells her body no. Others, . . . respond more psychologically and reflexively, as when her own desire frightens her to the point of tears. Still others . . . vacillate between recognition of their own desire and a painful discomfort with accepting it as a normal feature of who they are. . . .

Why is their formulation of their desire as a route to danger a problem? Why should we worry, for example, that Ellen and Inez silence their bodies in response to their own desire? After all, for Ellen, this is the road to staying safe until she completes her education, and for Inez, it is a way to gain respect and avoid sexual intercourse. Given current arrangements, this strategy not only makes sense, it even conveys a certain wisdom. But if we anchor our assessment in the belief that having sexual desire is normal, we ask a different question: Why should the girls' responses have to be so extreme? Why should they have to cut themselves off from themselves simply to stay safe, complete their education, maintain their reputations? . . .

Entitlement Maneuvers

To claim safe spaces for their desire one group of girls utilizes the degrees of freedom they find within the conventions of romance, maneuvering into secure spots and around minefields that go along with that territory. Some seek refuge in long-term heterosexual relationships with boys who defy characterization as sexual predators; others consciously manipulate the role available to them. All make choices that allow them to express their sexual desire but only in circumstances where the dangers of desire can be muted. These girls speak of a kind of freedom to question and to get to know their own bodies and the parameters of their own pleasure, and they also describe experiences of both equality and mutuality in their different manifestations of this kind of relationship. Entitled to their sexual feelings, they strain against the limits of the good-girl category without shattering it. In a sense, these girls are figuring out how to have it both ways. They reach the limits of this arrangement and find that it affords only partial protection for certain forms of desire rather than for the full range of their feelings. Yet they also reproduce the distinction between girls whose desire is "worthy" and those who should be demonized and devalued for not living up to their standards of "purity." Without an explicit politicized perspective on their sexual subjectivity, their stories reflect how the parameters of pleasure thus remain constrained for them. . . .

Desire Politics

A third and very small group of girls stand apart from the others in . . . the study as a whole. While making unapologetic claims on their desire, these girls also speak about desire in a matter-of-fact way, as an aspect of their experience that they simply expect to have. They offer sophisticated and critical analyses of gendered sexuality as the context in which they deal with their own sexual desire. Fully aware that they are not supposed to be desiring girls, and fully aware of the consequences for doing so, they simply refuse to deny their feelings. Not only do they feel entitled to their own sexual feelings, since they believe such feelings are normal and acceptable, they think that the "reality" of gendered sexuality is a con of immense proportions. Thus, there is a conscious political edge to their resistance to gendered sexuality, tinged with their outrage at being unjustly muzzled. They understand how their sexuality is perceived from a "male gaze" but do not embody it. Instead, they embody sexual subjectivity as a form of resistance with both psychological and political contours. They are agile at consciously "working within the system," as a kind of guerrilla tactic to maintain their integrity, or just rejecting it as unfair and oppressive. Their resistance is thus both overt and political.

Rather than accept the limits of unreliable pseudosafe spaces for their desire, these girls defy the very categories of good and bad, recognizing how this hierarchy separates girls from one another and diminishes and undermines them all. They are outspoken, irate, and defiant about their right to their own desire and pleasure in mutually acceptable circumstances. The girls tell stories about balancing pleasure and danger, refusing to be hemmed in by the fear of a bad reputation, insisting on taking appropriate precautions to protect themselves from physical consequences, and making active decisions about what sexual experiences they want to have and doing so in the relational contexts that make them comfortable. They not only are aware of the double standard but also know what is wrong with it; and they not only see that it is unfair but also pinpoint what is unfair about it. Though they do not use the word themselves, these girls are adamant *political* resisters. That is, they are engaging in a conscious refusal to comply with constrained constructions of who they can be and insisting on breaking rules they know to be unfair in order to be authentic and have integrity with themselves and others (Brown & Gilligan, 1992). In the realm of sexuality, overt political resistance constitutes a girl's unabashed claim to her own sexual desire and sexual subjectivity. And it risks dangerous reactions from people or institutions that are threatened by such a refusal to accept condoned conceptions of normality and morality (Freire, 1970; Lorde, 1984; Taylor, Gilligan, & Sullivan, 1995). Refusing to engage with the framing of their desire as a personal dilemma, these girls understand that the problem they are dealing with is not simply their own but one with deep social roots. . . .

The stories told by these desiring girls illustrate how feeling entitled to their own sexual desire can enable them to make active choices in their relationships. Comfortable with their own embodiment, they narrate sexual subjectivities that are compelling and enlightening. These girls' stories clarify how sexual desire, like all other forms of desire, can be empowering, instrumental for girls' confidence in themselves, and essential to their overall ability to act on their own terms. Sexual desire becomes a compass for making decisions about relationships and sexuality, and a road to knowledge about oneself and relationships, an empowering force in girls' lives. The more entitled they feel to desire, the more they speak of balancing pleasure and danger. These girls exude a vitality and a psychological robustness not seen in many of the other girls in the study. . . . These girls are happy to be alive, connected to themselves and to others through their embodied feelings. . . .

Finding New Ways to Think About Sexual Desire

As Amber Hollibaugh has said, "it is always dangerous to refuse the knowledge of your own acts and wishes, to create a sexual amnesia, to deny how and who you desire, allowing others the power to name it, be its engine or its brake. As long as I lived afraid of what I would discover about my own sexuality and my fantasies, I had always to wait for another person to discover and give me the material of my own desires" (1984, p. 406). . . .

The dilemma of desire is not going to be easily eliminated. What is required is that we make our schools, neighborhoods, and other public and private spaces safer for girls and women. As a society, we need to commit to eradicating sexual violence and its roots in the oppression of girls and women, as well as dismantling sexual hierarchies among girls and women and creating equitable access to reliable methods of contraception and disease protection.

Although adolescents would like to have honest conversations with their parents about sexuality, few feel able to (Satcher, 2001). . . . They end up feeling they are supposed to learn this information through osmosis rather than direct talk. Whether out of fear for their children or their own discomfort with sexuality, the ways in which adults do speak to adolescents about sexuality are impoverished. School is an institution in which most adolescents spend a lot of time. As Michelle Fine (1988) observed, underlying sex education in school is the assumption that girls have to learn to protect themselves from boys, to say no. Girls are taught to talk about sexuality only in terms of learning how to say no to sexual behavior rather than in terms of communicating about what both partners do and do not want as part of their relationship.

Sex education is an obvious arena where changes can and should be made. The surgeon general recommended comprehensive sexuality education that is both developmentally and culturally appropriate (Satcher, 2001). Yet little of what teachers are able to say or do is grounded in research, and policy about sex education is fueled by politics and polemic rather than what the science tells us about girls' or boys' sexual health. The current federal regulations demanding the teaching of "abstinence only" or "abstinence only until marriage" are a case in point. Sexuality education does not "cause" adolescents to have sexual intercourse, and abstinence-only "education" does not

prevent it. For those who do have sexual intercourse, comprehensive sexuality education is associated with an increased use of contraception and condoms, whereas students who have had abstinence education, many of whom subsequently have sex after the short-term effect of the abstinence-only message wanes, are much less likely to take these precautions. . . .

Consider how "abstinence" is a truly insidious cover story that puts girls at risk. Abstinence implies an absence of (girls') sexuality, which denies the fact that we are all sexual beings. To deny adolescents their sexuality and information about it, rather than to educate them about the intricacies and complexities and nuances of their feelings, choices, and behaviors, is to deny them a part of their humanity. What "choice" do girls have when their own sexual feelings are not supposed to exist? This study underscores the importance of comprehensive sexuality education that actually informs adolescents about their *sexuality*. As Sophie suggests, "the way that you can help girls is if you let them know that everything they feel and think is normal." . . .

If we really care about adolescents' sexual safety and health, then adults—parents, teachers, social workers, physicians, youth workers, therapists—need to speak to adolescents about the realities of sexuality: that girls as well as boys have sexual desire, which should be acknowledged and respected by both partners; that boys can be responsible for their sexual behavior; that sexual intercourse is not the only "adult" form of sexual expression; that sex is not a commodity or thing to get but a way to express one's feelings for another person; that masturbation and phone sex are safe sex.

Encouraging girls to "just say no" is what yields the cover story of "it just happened." As Megan astutely asked, why is it the girl who has to say no? And to what and whom is she saying no? This mantra does not help girls figure out what they do and do not wish to do, nor the conditions under which some choices are acceptable to them and others are not. Until girls can say yes and not be punished or suffer negative consequences, until girls have access to alternatives to the romance narrative—which offers them one line only, "no"—girls will continue to have their "no" mistaken for "token resistance." Sharon Thompson (1990) offers the slogan "Just Say Not until I Know I Want To" as a much needed corrective to the kinds of advice we give girls. Michelle Fine has explained that "a genuine discourse of desire would invite adolescents to explore what feels good and bad, desirable and undesirable, grounded in experience, needs, and limits . . . would enable an analysis of the dialectics of victimization and pleasure, and would pose female adolescents as subjects of sexuality" (1988, p. 33). . . .

This is a social problem that demands change at a societal level, in how we think and talk as a society about adolescent sexuality, both girls' and boys'. Boys also face limited social constructions of their sexuality. We need to know more about boys' sexuality, in particular, how boys deal with our society's conviction that their desire is monstrous and uncontrollable. We need to learn about boys' wishes to be authentic with themselves and in relationships, given the pressures they are under to commodify sex, objectify girls and women, and not be vulnerable or out of control. We need to examine how different discourses about male sexuality that demonize some boys (for instance, black boys, Latino boys, homosexual boys) may constrain them and enable others. We cannot underestimate the importance of offering and nurturing a critical perspective on how current gender arrangements and the institution of heterosexuality are unfair and diminish the humanity of boys and girls.

REFERENCES

Fine, M. (1988). "Sexuality, Schooling, and Adolescent Females: The Missing Discourse of Desire." *Harvard Educational Review,* 58(1), 29–53.

Fine, M. (1991). *Framing Dropouts: Notes on the Politics of an Urban High School.* Albany: State University of New York Press.

Freire, P. (1970). *Pedagogy of the oppressed.* New York: Continuum.

Hollibaugh, A. (1984). "Desire for the Future: Radical Hope in Passion and Pleasure." In C. S. Vance (ed.), *Pleasure and Danger: Exploring Female Sexuality.* Boston: Routledge and Kegan Paul.

Kitzinger, J. (1995). "'I'm Sexually Attractive but I'm Powerful': Young Women Negotiating Sexual Reputation." *Women's Studies International Forum,* 18(2), 187–196.

Lorde, A. (1984). *Sister Outsider: Essays and Speeches.* Trumansburg, N.Y.: Crossing Press.

Phillips, L. M. (2000). *Flirting with Danger: Young Women's Reflections on Sexuality and Domination.* New York: New York University Press.

Plummer, K. (1995). *Telling Sexual Stories.* London: Routledge.

Satcher, D. (2001). *The Surgeon General's Call to Action to Promote Sexual Health and Responsible Sexual Behavior.* Washington, D.C.: U.S. Department of Health and Human Services.

Thompson, S. (1995). *Going All the Way: Teenage Girls' Tales of Sex, Romance, and Pregnancy.* New York: Hill and Wang.

Thorne, B. (1993). *Gender Play: Girls and Boys in School.* New Brunswick, N.J.: Rutgers University Press.

Tolman, D. (2002). "Female Adolescent Sexuality: An Argument for a Developmental Perspective on the New View of Women's Sexual Problems." In E. Kaschak & L. Tiefer (eds.), *A New View of Women's Sexual Problems* (pp. 195–210). Binghamton, N.Y.: Haworth Press.

THINKING ABOUT THE READING

Make a list of different sexual behaviors and sexual feelings associated with being female or male. Think about your own sexual socialization. What messages do you remember receiving about the kind of sexual being you were expected to be? Consider the impact these cultural messages have on young people whose personal feelings are in conflict with social expectations. How might such a conflict affect their self esteem? What messages do young people get about how to talk about their sexual confusion and with whom to talk about their concerns? Some observers have said that in the U.S. we are simultaneously sexually obsessed, repressed, and depressed. In other words, sexual imagery and messages are everywhere, but we don't have healthy venues for talking about all this imagery. The result is a lot of confusion and low self-esteem as both men and women think their feelings are out of line with cultural expectations. Discuss what "healthy" sexuality education would look like and which social institutions should be responsible for doing it.

Black Women and a New Definition of Womanhood

Bart Landry

(2000)

A popular novel of 1852 chirped that the white heroine, Eoline, "with her fair hair, and celestial blue eyes bending over the harp . . . really seemed 'little lower than the angels,' and an aureola of purity and piety appeared to beam around her brow."[1] By contrast, in another popular antebellum novel, *Maum Guinea and Her Plantation Children* (1861), black women are excluded from the category of true womanhood without debate: "The idea of modesty and virtue in a Louisiana colored-girl might well be ridiculed; as a general thing, she has neither."[2] Decades later, in 1902, a commentator for the popular magazine *The Independent* noted, "I sometimes hear of a virtuous Negro woman, but the idea is absolutely inconceivable to me. . . . I cannot imagine such a creature as a virtuous Negro woman."[3] Another writer, reflecting early-twentieth-century white male stereotypes of black and white women, remarked that, like white women, "Black women had the brains of a child, [and] the passions of a woman" but, unlike white women, were "steeped in centuries of ignorance and savagery, and wrapped about with immoral vices."[4]

Faced with the prevailing views of white society that placed them outside the boundaries of true womanhood, black women had no choice but to defend their virtue. Middle-class black women led this defense, communicating their response in words and in the actions of their daily lives. In doing so they went well beyond defending their own virtue to espouse a broader conception of womanhood that anticipated modern views by more than half a century. Their vision of womanhood combined the public and the private spheres and eventually took for granted a role for women as paid workers outside the home. More than merely an abstract vision, it was a philosophy of womanhood embodied in the lives of countless middle-class black women in both the late nineteenth and the early twentieth centuries.

Virtue Defended

Although black women were seen as devoid of all four of the cardinal virtues of true womanhood—piety, purity, submissiveness, and domesticity—white attention centered on purity. As Hazel Carby suggests, this stemmed in part from the role assigned to black women in the plantation economy. She argues that "two very different but interdependent codes of sexuality operated in the antebellum South, producing opposite definitions of motherhood and womanhood for white and black women which coalesce in the figures of the slave and the mistress."[5] In this scheme, white mistresses gave birth to heirs, slave women to property. A slave woman who attempted to preserve her virtue or sexual autonomy was a threat to the plantation economy. In the words of Harriet Jacobs's slave narrative, *Incidents in the Life of a Slave Girl* (1861), it was "deemed a crime in her [the slave woman] to wish to be virtuous."[6]

Linda Brent, the pseudonym Jacobs used to portray her own life, was an ex-slave struggling to survive economically and protect herself and her daughter from sexual exploitation. In telling her story, she recounts the difficulty all black women faced in practicing the virtues of true womanhood. The contrasting contexts of black and white women's lives called for different, even opposite, responses. While submissiveness and passivity brought protection to the white mistress, these characteristics merely exposed black women to sexual and economic exploitation. Black women, therefore, had to develop strength rather than glory in fragility, and had to be active and assertive rather than passive and submissive.

Though "conventional principles of morality were rendered impossible by the conditions of the slave," as Jacobs argued,[7] Linda Brent embodied the virtues required by black women to survive with dignity in a hostile environment. It was a world in which "Freedom replaced and transcended purity."[8] In the conventional sentimental novels of the period, white heroines who lost their purity chose death or went mad. Black women saw death as an alternative to slavery. "As I passed the wreck of the old meeting house," Linda Brent mused, "where, before Nat Turner's time, the slaves had been allowed to meet for worship, I seemed to hear my father's voice come from it, bidding me not to tarry till I reached freedom or the grave."[9] Painfully aware of her inability to meet the standards of conventional white womanhood ("I do not sit with my children in a home of my own. I still long for a hearthstone of my own, however humble."[10]), Linda Brent nevertheless represented a fundamental challenge to this ideology and the beginnings of an alternative, broader definition of womanhood, one that incorporated resourcefulness and independence.

Three decades later, in the 1890s, black women found reasons to defend their moral integrity with new urgency against attacks from all sides. Views such as those in *The Independent* noted earlier were given respectability by a report of the Slater Fund, a foundation that supported welfare projects for blacks in this period. The foundation asserted without argument, "The negro women of the South are subject to temptations . . . which come to them from the days of their race enslavement. . . . To meet such temptations the negro woman can only offer the resistance of a low moral standard, an inheritance from the system of slavery, made still lower from a lifelong residence in a one-room cabin."[11]

At the 1893 World Columbian Exposition in Chicago, where black women were effectively barred from the exhibits on the achievements of American women, the few black women allowed to address a women's convention there felt compelled to publicly challenge these views. One speaker, Fannie Barrier Williams, shocked her audience by her forthrightness. "I regret the necessity of speaking of the moral question of our women," but "the morality of our home life has been commented on so disparagingly and meanly that we are placed in the unfortunate position of being defenders of our name."[12] She went on to emphasize that black women continued to be the victims of sexual harassment by white men and chided her white female audience for failing to protect their black sisters. In the same vein, black activist and educator Anna Julia Cooper told the audience that it was not a question of "temptations" as much as it was "the painful, patient, and silent toil of mothers to gain title to the bodies of their daughters."[13] Williams was later to write on the same theme. "It is a significant and shameful fact that I am constantly in receipt of letters from the still unprotected women in the South, begging me to find employment for their daughters . . . to save them from going into the homes of the South as servants as there is nothing to save them from dishonor and degradation."[14] Another black male writer was moved to reveal in *The Independent*: "I know of more than one colored woman who was openly importuned by

White women to become the mistress of their husbands, on the ground that they, the white wives, were afraid that, if their husbands did not associate with colored women they would certainly do so with outside white women. . . . And the white wives, for reasons which ought to be perfectly obvious, preferred to have all their husbands do wrong with colored women in order to keep their husbands *straight!*"[15] The attacks on black women's virtue came to a head with a letter written by James Jacks, president of the Missouri Press Association, in which he alleged, "The Negroes in this country were wholly devoid of morality, the women were prostitutes and all were natural thieves and liars."[16] These remarks, coming from such a prominent individual, drew an immediate reaction from black women throughout the country. The most visible was Josephine St. Pierre Ruffin's invitation to black club women to a national convention in Boston in 1895; one hundred women from ten states came to Boston in response. In a memorable address to representatives of some twenty clubs, Ruffin directly attacked the scurrilous accusations:

Now for the sake of the thousands of self-sacrificing young women teaching and preaching in lonely southern backwoods, for the noble army of mothers who gave birth to these girls, mothers whose intelligence is only limited by their opportunity to get at books, for the cultured women who have carried off the honors at school here and often abroad, for the sake of our own dignity, the dignity of our race and the future good name of our children, it is "meet, right and our bounden duty" to stand forth and declare ourselves and our principles, to teach an ignorant and suspicious world that our aims and interests are identical with those of all good, aspiring women. Too long have we been silent under unjust and unholy charges. . . . It is to break this silence, not by noisy protestations of what we are not, but by a dignified showing of what we are and hope to become, that we are impelled to take this step,

to make of this gathering an object lesson to the world.[17]

At the end of three days of meetings, the National Federation of Afro-American Women was founded, uniting thirty-six black women's clubs in twelve states.[18] The following year, the National Federation merged with the National League of Colored Women to form the National Association of Colored Women (NACW).

Racial Uplift: In Defense of the Black Community

While the catalyst for these national organizations was in part the felt need of black women to defend themselves against moral attacks by whites, they soon went beyond this narrow goal. Twenty years after its founding, the NACW had grown to fifty thousand members in twenty-eight federations and more than one thousand clubs.[19] The founding of these organizations represented a steady movement by middle-class black women to assume more active roles in the community. Historian Deborah Gray White argues that black club women "insisted that only black women could save the black race," a position that inspired them to pursue an almost feverish pace of activities.[20]

These clubs, however, were not the first attempts by black women to participate actively in their communities. Since the late 1700s black women had been active in mutual-aid societies in the North, and in the 1830s northern black women organized anti-slavery societies. In 1880 Mary Ann Shadd Cary and six other women founded the Colored Women's Progressive Franchise Association in Washington, D.C. Among its stated goals were equal rights for women, including the vote, and the even broader feminist objective of taking "an aggressive stand against the assumption that men only begin and conduct industrial and other things."[21] Giving expression to this goal were a growing number of black women professionals, including the first female physicians to practice in the South.[22] By the turn of the twentieth century, the National Business League, founded by Booker T. Washington, could report that there were "160 Black female physicians, seven dentists, ten lawyers, 164 ministers, assorted journalists, writers, artists, 1,185 musicians and teachers of music, and 13,525 school instructors."[23]

Black women's activism was spurred by the urgency of the struggle for equality, which had led to a greater acceptance of black female involvement in the abolitionist movement. At a time when patriarchal notions of women's domestic role dominated, historian Paula Giddings asserts, "There is no question that there was greater acceptance among Black men of women in activist roles than there was in the broader society."[24] This is not to say that all black men accepted women as equals or the activist roles that many were taking. But when faced with resistance, black women often *demanded* acceptance of their involvement. In 1849, for example, at a black convention in Ohio, "Black women, led by Jane P. Merritt, threatened to boycott the meetings if they were not given a more substantial voice in the proceedings."[25]

In the postbellum period black women continued their struggle for an equal voice in activities for racial uplift in both secular and religious organizations. Historian Evelyn Brooks Higginbotham has offered a detailed account of the successful struggle of black women in the Baptist Church during the late nineteenth century to win acceptance of independent organizations led by themselves.[26] These women's organizations then played a significant role not only in missionary activities, but also in general racial uplift activities in both rural and urban areas.[27] . . .

Black Women and the Suffrage Movement

In their struggle for their own rights, black women moved into the political fray and eagerly joined the movement for passage of a constitutional amendment giving women the right to vote. Unlike white women suffragists, who focused exclusively on the benefits of the vote for their sex, black women saw the franchise as a means of improving the condition of the black community generally. For them, race and gender issues were inseparable. As historian Rosalyn Terborg-Penn emphasizes, black feminists believed that by "increasing the black electorate" they "would not only uplift the women of the race, but help the children and the men as well."[28]

Prominent black women leaders as well as national and regional organizations threw their support behind the suffrage movement. At least twenty black suffrage organizations were founded, and black women participated in rallies and demonstrations and gave public speeches.[29] Ironically, they often found themselves battling white women suffragists as well as men. Southern white women opposed including black women under a federal suffrage as a matter of principle. Northern white women suffragists, eager to retain the support of southern white women, leaned toward accepting a wording of the amendment that would have allowed the southern states to determine their own position on giving black women the vote, a move that would have certainly led to their exclusion.[30]

After the Nineteenth Amendment was ratified in 1920 in its original form, black women braved formidable obstacles in registering to vote. All across the South white registrars used "subterfuge and trickery" to hinder them from registering, including a "grandmother clause" in North Carolina, literacy tests in Virginia, and a $300 poll tax in Columbia, South Carolina. In Columbia, black women "waited up to twelve hours to register" while white women were registered first.[31] In their struggle to register, black women appealed to the NAACP, signed affidavits against registrars who disqualified them, and finally asked for assistance from national white women suffrage leaders. They were especially disappointed in this last attempt. After fighting side by side with white women suffragists for passage of the Nineteenth Amendment, they were rebuffed by the National Woman's Party leadership with the argument that theirs was a race rather than a women's rights issue.[32] Thus, white women continued to separate issues of race and sex that black women saw as inseparable.

Challenging the Primacy of Domesticity

A conflicting conception of the relationship between gender and race issues was not the only major difference in the approaches of black and white women to their roles in the family and society. For most white women, their domestic roles as wives and mothers remained primary. In the late nineteenth century, as they began increasingly to argue for acceptance of their involvement on behalf of child-labor reform and growing urban problems, white women often defended these activities as extensions of their housekeeping role. Historian Barbara Harris comments, "The [white women] pioneers in women's education, who probably did more than anyone else in this period to effect change in the female sphere, advocated education for women and their entrance into the teaching profession on the basis of the values proclaimed by the cult of true womanhood. In a similar way, females defended their careers as authors and their involvement in charitable, religious, temperance, and moral reform societies."[33] Paula Giddings notes that in this way white women were able "to become more active outside the home while still preserving the probity of 'true womanhood.'"[34] From the birth of white feminism at the Seneca Falls Convention in 1848, white feminists had a difficult time advancing their goals. Their numbers were few and their members often divided over the propriety of challenging the cult of domesticity. . . .

In the late nineteenth century the cult of domesticity remained primary even for white women graduates of progressive women's colleges such as Vassar, Smith, and Wellesley. For them, no less than for those with only a high-school education, "A Woman's Kingdom" was "a well-ordered home."[35] In a student essay, one Vassar student answered her rhetorical question, "Has the educated woman a duty towards the kitchen?" by emphasizing that the kitchen was "exactly where the college woman belonged" for "the orderly, disciplined, independent graduate is the woman best prepared to manage the home, in which lies the salvation of the world."[36] This essay reflects the dilemma faced by these young white women graduates. They found little support in white society to combine marriage and career. In *Beyond Her Sphere* historian Barbara Harris comments, "To a degree that is hard for us to appreciate, a [white] woman had to make a choice: she either married and had children, or she remained single and had a career. . . . Yet, after their exhilarating years at college, many women were far too committed to the pursuit of knowledge or the practical application of their education to retreat willingly to the narrow confines of Victorian domesticity. And so, in surprising numbers, they chose the other alternative and rejected marriage."[37] Historian Carl Degler estimates that in 1900 25 percent of white women college graduates and 50 percent of those receiving Ph.D.s remained single. Graduates of elite women's colleges in the East were even less likely to marry: 45 and 57 percent, respectively, of Bryn Mawr and Wellesley graduates between 1889 and 1909. While the increasing numbers of white women receiving college degrees did contribute to the ranks of activists, this did not result in a frontal attack on the cult of domesticity. In fact, a number of prominent feminists such as Angelina Grimké and Antoinette Brown Blackwell "disappeared from the ranks of feminist leaders after their marriage," and Alice Freeman Palmer, the president of Wellesley College, resigned after her marriage in 1887 to Herbert Palmer, a philosophy professor at Harvard.[38] Society sanctioned only three courses for the middle-class white woman in the Progressive period: "marriage, charity work or teaching."[39] Marriage and motherhood stood as the highest calling. If there were no economic need for them to work, single women were encouraged to do volunteer charity work. For those who needed an independent income, teaching was the only acceptable occupation.

Historian John Rousmaniere suggests that the white college-educated women involved in the early settlement house movement saw themselves as fulfilling the "service norm" so prominent among middle-class women of the day. At the same time, he argues, it was their sense of uniqueness as college-educated women and their felt isolation upon returning home that led them to this form of service. The settlement houses, located as they were in white immigrant, working-class slums, catered to these women's sense of noblesse oblige; they derived a sense of accomplishment from providing an example of genteel middle-class virtues to the poor. Yet the settlement houses also played into a sense of adventure, leading one resident to write, "We feel that we know life for the first time."[40] For all their felt uniqueness, however, with some notable exceptions these women's lives usually offered no fundamental challenge to the basic assumptions of true womanhood. Residency in settlement houses was for the most part of short duration, and most volunteers eventually embraced their true roles of wife and mother without significant outside involvement. The exceptions were women like Jane Addams, Florence Kelley, Julia Lathrop, and Grace Abbott, who became major figures in the public sphere. Although their lives disputed the doctrine of white women's confinement to the private sphere, the challenge was limited in that most of them did not themselves combine the two spheres of marriage and a public life. Although Florence Kelley was a divorced mother, she nevertheless upheld "the American tradition that men support their families, their wives throughout life," and bemoaned the "retrograde movement" against man as the breadwinner.[41]

Most college-educated black middle-class women also felt a unique sense of mission. They accepted Lucy Laney's 1899 challenge to lift up their race and saw themselves walking in the footsteps of black women activists and feminists of previous generations. But their efforts were not simply "charity work"; their focus was on "racial uplift" on behalf of themselves as well as of the economically less fortunate members of their race.[42] The black women's club movement, in contrast to the white women's, tended to concern themselves from the beginning with the "social and legal problems that confronted both black women and men."[43] While there was certainly some elitism in the NACW's motto, "Lifting as We Climb," these activists were always conscious that they shared a common experience of exploitation and discrimination with the masses and could not completely retreat to the safe haven of their middle-class homes.[44] On the way to meetings they shared the black experience of riding in segregated cars or of being ejected if they tried to do otherwise, as Ida B. Wells did in 1884.[45] Unlike white women for whom, as black feminist Frances Ellen Watkins Harper had emphasized in 1869, "the priorities in the struggle for human rights were sex, not race,"[46] black women could not separate these twin sources of their oppression. They understood that, together with their working-class sisters, they were assumed by whites to have "low animalistic urges." Their exclusion from the category of true womanhood was no less complete than for their less educated black sisters.

It is not surprising, therefore, that the most independent and radical of black female activists led the way in challenging the icons of true womanhood, including on occasion motherhood and marriage. Not only did they chafe under their exclusion from true womanhood, they viewed its tenets as strictures to their efforts on behalf of racial uplift and their own freedom and integrity as women. In 1894 *The Woman's Era* (a black women's magazine) set forth the heretical opinion that "not all women are intended for mothers. Some of us have not the temperament for family life. . . . Clubs will make women think seriously of their future lives, and not make girls think their only alternative is to marry."[47] Anna Julia Cooper, one of the most dynamic women of the period, who had been married and widowed, added that a woman was not "compelled to look to sexual love as the one sensation capable of giving tone and relish, movement and vim to the life she leads. Her horizon is extended."[48] Elsewhere Cooper advised black women that if they married they should seek egalitarian relationships. "The question is not now with the woman 'How shall I so cramp, stunt, and simplify and nullify myself as to make me eligible to the honor of being swallowed up into some little man?' but the problem . . . rests with the man as to how he can so develop . . . to reach the ideal of a generation of women who demand the noblest, grandest and best achievements of which he is capable."[49]

. . . Black activists were far more likely to combine marriage and activism than white activists. . . . Historian Linda Gordon found this to be the case in her study of sixty-nine black and seventy-six white activists in national welfare reform between 1890 and 1945. Only 34 percent of the white activists had ever been married, compared to 85 percent of the black activists. Most of these women (83 percent of blacks and 86 percent of whites) were college educated.[50] She also found that "The white women [reformers], with few exceptions, tended to view married women's economic dependence on men as desirable, and their employment as a misfortune. . . ."[51] On the other hand, although there were exceptions, Gordon writes, " . . . most black women activists projected a favorable view of working women and women's professional aspirations."[52] Nor could it be claimed that these

black activists worked out of necessity, since the majority were married to prominent men "who could support them."[53]

Witness Ida B. Wells-Barnett (married to the publisher of Chicago's leading black newspaper) in 1896, her six-month-old son in tow, stumping from city to city making political speeches on behalf of the Illinois Women's State Central Committee. And Mary Church Terrell dismissing the opinion of those who suggested that studying higher mathematics would make her unappealing as a marriage partner with a curt, "I'd take a chance and run the risk."[54] She did eventually marry and raised a daughter and an adopted child. Her husband, Robert Terrell, a Harvard graduate, was a school principal, a lawyer, and eventually a municipal court judge in Washington, D.C. A biographer later wrote of Mary Terrell's life, "But absorbing as motherhood was, it never became a full-time occupation."[55] While this could also be said of Stanton, perhaps what most distinguished black from white feminists and activists was the larger number of the former who unequivocally challenged domesticity and the greater receptivity they found for their views in the black community. As a result, while the cult of domesticity remained dominant in the white community at the turn of the twentieth century, it did not hold sway within the black community.

Rejection of the Public/Private Dichotomy

Black women of the nineteenth and early twentieth centuries saw their efforts on behalf of the black community as necessary for their own survival, rather than as noblesse oblige. "Self preservation," wrote Mary Church Terrell in 1902, "demands that [black women] go among the lowly, illiterate and even the vicious, to whom they are bound by ties of race and sex . . . to reclaim them."[56] These women rejected the confinement to the private sphere mandated by the cult of domesticity. They felt women could enter the public sphere without detriment to the home. As historian Elsa Barkley Brown has emphasized, black women believed that "Only a strong and unified community made up of both women and men could wield the power necessary to allow black people to shape their own lives. Therefore, only when women were able to exercise their full strength would the community be at its full strength. . . ."[57]

In her study of black communities in Illinois during the late Victorian era (1880–1910), historian Shirley Carlson contrasts the black and white communities' expectations of the "ideal woman" at that time:

The black community's appreciation for and development of the feminine intellect contrasted sharply with the views of the larger society. In the latter, intelligence was regarded as a masculine quality that would "defeminize" women. The ideal white woman, being married, confined herself almost exclusively to the private domain of the household. She was demure, perhaps even self-effacing. She often deferred to her husband's presumably superior judgment, rather than formulating her own views and vocally expressing them, as black women often did. A woman in the larger society might skillfully manipulate her husband for her own purposes, but she was not supposed to confront or challenge him directly. Black women were often direct, and frequently won community approval for this quality, especially when such a characteristic was directed toward achieving racial uplift. Further, even after her marriage, a black woman might remain in the public domain, possibly in paid employment. The ideal black woman's domain, then, was both the private and public spheres. She was wife and mother, but she could also assume other roles such as schoolteacher, social activist, or businesswoman, among others. And she was intelligent.[58]

In their struggle for an expansion of roles beyond the domestic sphere, black women sometimes had to contend with opposition from within the black community, especially from men, as well as with the larger society's definition of women's proper role. When Ida Wells-Barnett was elected financial secretary of the Afro-American Council, the *Colored American* newspaper suggested that a man should hold the position. While recognizing that "She is a woman of unusual mental powers," the newspaper argued that "the proprieties would have been observed by giving her an assignment more in keeping with the popular idea of women's work and which would not interfere so disastrously with her domestic duties."[59]

Feminist Maggie Lena Walker, the first woman in the nation (and the first African American, male or female) to establish and head a bank and founder of the Richmond Council of Colored Women in Virginia, also met with male opposition in her efforts for racial uplift and expanded women's roles. She too opposed these limitations to the domestic sphere, contending, "Men should not be so pessimistic and down on women's clubs. They don't seek to destroy the home or disgrace the race."[60] The Woman's Union, a Richmond female insurance company founded in 1898, took as its motto, "The Hand That Rocks the Cradle Rules the World." As Brown has clarified, however, "unlike nineteenth-century white women's rendering of that expression to signify the limitation of woman's influence to that which she had by virtue of rearing her sons, the idea as these women conceived it transcended the separation of private and public spheres and spoke to the idea that women, while not abandoning their roles as wives and mothers, could also move into economic and political activities in ways that would support rather than conflict with family and community."[61]

Although many black males, like most white males, opposed the expansion of black women's roles, many other black males supported women's activism and even criticized their brethren for their opposition. Echoing Maggie Walker's sentiments, T. Thomas Fortune wrote, "The race could not succeed nor build strong citizens, until we have a race of women competent to do more than hear a brood of negative men."[62] Support for women's suffrage was especially strong among black males. . . . Black men saw women's suffrage as advancing the political empowerment of the race. For black women, suffrage promised to be a potent weapon in their fight for their rights, for education and jobs.[63]

A Threefold Commitment

An expanded role for black women did not end at the ballot box or in activities promoting racial uplift. Black middle-class women demanded a place for themselves in the paid labor force. Theirs was a threefold commitment to family, career, and social movements. According to historian Rosalyn Terborg-Penn, "most black feminists and leaders had been wives and mothers who worked yet found time not only to struggle for the good of their sex, but for their race." Such a threefold commitment "was not common among white women."[64]

In her study of eighty African American women throughout the country who worked in "the feminized professions" (such as teaching) between the 1880s and the 1950s, historian Stephanie Shaw comments on the way they were socialized to lives dedicated to home, work, and community. When these women were children, she indicates, "the model of womanhood held before [them] was one of achievement in *both* public and private spheres. Parents cast domesticity as a complement rather than a contradiction to success in public arenas."[65] Later, in her discussion of one woman whose husband opposed her desire to work outside the home, Shaw observes, "It seems, then, that Henry Riddick subscribed to an old tradition (which was becoming less and less influential in general, and which *had never been a real tradition among most black families*) wherein the wife of a 'good' husband did not need to work for pay."[66]

An analysis of the lives of 108 of the first generation of black clubwomen bears this out. "The career-oriented clubwomen, comments Paula Giddings, "seemed to have no ambivalence concerning their right to work, whether necessity dictated it or not."[67] According to Giddings, three-quarters of these 108 early clubwomen were married, and almost three-quarters worked outside the home, while one-quarter had children.

A number of these clubwomen and other black women activists not only had careers but also spoke forcefully about the importance of work, demonstrating surprisingly progressive attitudes with a very modern ring. "The old doctrine that a man marries a woman to support her," quipped Walker, "is pretty nearly threadbare to-day."[68] "Every dollar a woman makes," she declared in a 1912 speech to the Federation of Colored Women's Clubs, "some man gets the direct benefit of same. Every woman was by Divine Providence created for some man; not for some man to marry, take home and support, but for the purpose of using her powers, ability, health and strength, to forward the financial . . . success of the partnership into which she may go, if she will. . . ."[69] Being married with three sons and an adopted daughter did not in any way dampen her commitment to gender equality and an expanded role for wives.

Such views were not new. In a pamphlet entitled *The Awakening of the Afro-American Woman*, written in 1897 to celebrate the earlier founding of the National Association of Colored Women, Victoria Earle Matthews referred to black women as "co-breadwinners in their families."[70] Almost twenty years earlier, in 1878, feminist writer and activist Frances Ellen Harper sounded a similar theme of equality when she insisted, "The women as a class are quite equal to the men in energy and executive ability." She went on to recount instances of black women managing small and large farms in the postbellum period.[71]

It is clear that in the process of racial uplift work, black middle-class women also included membership in the labor force as part of their identity. They were well ahead of their time in realizing that their membership in the paid labor force was critical to achieving true equality with men. For this reason, the National Association of Wage Earners insisted that all black women should be able to support themselves.[72] . . .

. . . A number of women began their fight for careers when still very young and continued this battle throughout their lives. Braving the opposition of family and friends, Terrell dared to earn an A.B. degree in mathematics from Oberlin, even though "It was held by most people that women were unfitted to do their work in the home if they studied Latin, Greek and higher mathematics." Upon graduation, she defied her father's furious objection to her employment and took a teaching job at Wilberforce College. For her act of rebellion she was "disinherited" by her irate father, who "refused to write to me for a year."[73] But Terrell enjoyed the full support of her husband, Robert.

In 1963 in *The Feminine Mystique*, Betty Friedan wrote, "I never knew a woman, when I was growing up, who used her mind, played her own part in the world, and also loved, and had children."[74] Her experience, however, was only of white middle-class women. In fact, many black middle-class women did fit this description, and Friedan's lack of acquaintance with these women attests to the deep chasm that has historically separated the worlds of black and white women. As W. E. B. DuBois commented as early as 1924, "Negro women more than the women of any other group in America are the protagonists in the fight for an economically independent womanhood in modern countries. . . . The matter of economic independence is, of course, the central fact in the struggle of women for equality."[75]

Defining Black Womanhood

In the late 1930s when Mary McLeod Bethune, the acknowledged leader of black women at

the time and an adviser to President Franklin Roosevelt on matters affecting the black community, referred to herself as the representative of "Negro womanhood" and asserted that black women had "room in their lives to be wives and mothers as well as to have careers," she was not announcing a new idea.[76] As Terborg-Penn emphasizes:

> . . . most black feminists and leaders had been wives and mothers who worked yet found time not only to struggle for the good of their sex, but for their race. Until the 1970s, however, this threefold commitment—to family and to career and to one or more social movements—was not common among white women. The key to the uniqueness among black feminists of this period appears to be their link with the past. The generation of the woman suffrage era had learned from their late nineteenth-century foremothers in the black women's club movement, just as the generation of the post World War I era had learned and accepted the experiences of the preceding generation. Theirs was a sense of continuity, a sense of group consciousness that transcended class.[77]

This "sense of continuity" with past generations of black women was clearly articulated in 1917 by Mary Talbert, president of the NACW. Launching an NACW campaign to save the home of the late Frederick Douglass, she said, "We realize today is the psychological moment for us women to show our true worth and prove the Negro women of today measure up to those sainted women of our race, who passed through the fire of slavery and its galling remembrances."[78] Talbert certainly lived up to her words, going on to direct the NAACP's antilynching campaign and becoming the first woman to receive the NAACP's Spingarn Medal for her achievements.

What then is the expanded definition of true womanhood found in these black middle-class women's words and embodied in their lives? First, they tended to define womanhood in an inclusive rather than exclusive sense.

Within white society, true womanhood was defined so narrowly that it excluded all but a small minority of white upper- and upper-middle-class women with husbands who were able to support them economically. Immigrant women and poor women—of any color—did not fit this definition. Nor did black women as a whole, regardless of class, because they were all seen as lacking an essential characteristic of true womanhood—virtue. For black women, however, true womanhood transcended class and race boundaries. Anna Julia Cooper called for "reverence for woman as woman regardless of rank, wealth, or culture."[79] Unlike white women, black women refused to isolate gender issues from other forms of oppression such as race and nationality, including the struggles of colonized nations of Africa and other parts of the world. Women's issues, they suggested, were tied to issues of oppression, whatever form that oppression might assume.

As discussed above, black women organized to defend their virtue against the vicious attacks of white society. They pointed out—Fannie Barrier Williams and Ida B. Wells-Barnett forcefully among them—that the real culprits were white males who continued to harass and prey upon them with the tacit support of white women. At times they also chastised black males for failing to protect them. Black women obviously saw themselves as virtuous, both individually and as a group. Yet, apart from defending themselves against these attacks, black women did not dwell upon virtue in defining womanhood. Theirs was not the sexless purity forced on white women by white males who placed their women on pedestals while seeking out black women for their pleasure. . . .

The traditional white ideology of true womanhood separated the active world of men from the passive world of women. As we have seen, women's activities were confined to the home, where their greatest achievement was maintaining their own virtue and decorum and rearing future generations of male leaders. Although elite black women did not reject their domestic roles as such, many expanded permissible public activities beyond charity work to encompass employment and participation in social progress. They founded such organizations as the Atlanta Congress of Colored Women, which historian Erlene Stetson claims was the first grassroots women's movement organized "for social and political good."[80]

The tendency of black women to define womanhood inclusively and to see their roles extending beyond the boundaries of the home led them naturally to include other characteristics in their vision. One of these was intellectual equality. While the "true" woman was portrayed as submissive ("conscious of inferiority, and therefore grateful for support"),[81] according to literary scholar Hazel Carby, black women such as Anna Julia Cooper argued for a "partnership with husbands on a plane of intellectual equality."[82] Such equality could not exist without the pursuit of education, particularly higher education, and participation in the labor force. Cooper, like many other black women, saw men's opposition to higher education for women as an attempt to make them conform to a narrow view of women as "sexual objects for exchange in the marriage market."[83] Education for women at all levels became a preoccupation for many black feminists and activists. Not a few—like Anna Cooper, Mary L. Europe, and Estelle Pinckney Webster—devoted their entire lives to promoting it, especially among young girls. Womanhood, as conceived by black women, was compatible with—indeed, required—intellectual equality. In this they were supported by the black community. While expansion of educational opportunities for women was a preoccupation of white feminists in the nineteenth century, as I noted above, a college education tended to create a dilemma in the lives of white women who found little community support for combining marriage and career. In contrast, as Shirley Carlson emphasizes, "The black community did not regard intelligence and femininity as conflicting values, as the larger society did. That society often expressed the fear that intelligent women would develop masculine characteristics—a thickening waist, a diminution of breasts and hips, and finally, even the growth of facial hair. Blacks seemed to have had no such trepidations, or at least they were willing to have their women take these risks."[84]

In addition, to women's rights to an education, Cooper, Walker, Alexander, Terrell, the leaders of the National Association of Wage Earners, and countless other black feminists and activists insisted on their right to work outside the home. They dared to continue very active lives after marriage. Middle-class black women's insistence on the right to pursue careers paralleled their view that a true woman could move in both the private and the public spheres and that marriage did not require submissiveness or subordination. In fact, as Shirley Carlson has observed in her study of black women in Illinois in the late Victorian period, many activist black women "continued to be identified by their maiden names—usually as their middle names or as part of their hyphenated surnames—indicating that their own identities were not subsumed in their husbands."[85]

While the views of black women on womanhood were all unusual for their time, their insistence on the right of all women—including wives and mothers—to work outside the home was the most revolutionary. In their view the need for paid work was not merely a response to economic circumstances, but the fulfillment of women's right to self-actualization. Middle-class black women like Ida B. Wells-Barnett, Margaret Washington, and Mary Church Terrell, married to men who were well able to support them, continued to pursue careers throughout their lives, and some did so even as they reared children. These women were far ahead of their time, foreshadowing societal changes that would not occur within the white community for several generations. . . .

Rather than accepting white society's views of paid work outside the home as deviant, therefore, black women fashioned a competing ideology of womanhood—one that supported the needs of an oppressed black community and their own desire for gender equality. Middle-class black women, especially, often supported by the black community, developed a consciousness of themselves as persons who were competent and capable of being influential. They believed in higher education as a means of sharpening their talents, and in a sexist world that looked on men as superior, they dared to see themselves as equals both in and out of marriage.

This new ideology of womanhood came to have a profound impact on the conception of black families and gender roles. Black women's insistence on their role as co-breadwinners clearly foreshadows today's dual-career and dual-worker families. Since our conception of the family is inseparably tied to our views of women's and men's roles, the broader definition of womanhood advocated by black women was also an argument against the traditional family. The cult of domesticity was anchored in a patriarchal notion of women as subordinate to men in both the family and the larger society. The broader definition of womanhood championed by black middle-class women struck a blow for an expansion of women's rights in society and a more egalitarian position in the home, making for a far more progressive system among blacks at this time than among whites.

NOTES

1. Quoted in Hazel V. Carby, *Reconstructing Womanhood: The Emergence of the Afro-American Woman Novelist* (New York: Oxford University Press, 1987), p. 26.

2. Ibid.

3. Quoted in Paula Giddings, *When and Where I Enter: The Impact of Black Women and Race and Sex in America* (New York: Bantam Books, 1985), p. 82.

4. Ibid., p. 82.

5. Carby, *Reconstructing Womanhood*, p. 20.

6. Harriet Jacobs, *Incidents in the Life of a Slave Girl*, L. Baria Child, ed. (1861; paperback reprint, New York: Harcourt Brace Jovanovich, 1973), p. 29.

7. Carby, *Reconstructing Womanhood*, pp. 58–59.

8. Ibid., p. 60.

9. Jacobs, *Incidents in the Life of a Slave Girl*, p. 93.

10. Ibid., p. 207.

11. Quoted in Giddings, *When and Where I Enter*, p. 82.

12. Ibid., p. 86.

13. Ibid., p. 87.

14. Ibid., pp. 86–87.

15. Ibid., p. 87.

16. Quoted in Sharon Harley, "Black Women in a Southern City: Washington, D.C., 1890–1920," pp. 59–78 in Joanne V. Hawks and Shiela L. Skemp, eds., *Sex, Race, and the Role of Women in the South* (Jackson, Miss.: University Press of Mississippi, 1983), p. 72.

17. Eleanor Flexner, *Century of Struggle: The Woman's Rights Movement in the United States* (Cambridge: Harvard University Press, 1959), p. 194.

18. Giddings, *When and Where I Enter*, p. 93.

19. Ibid., p. 95. For a discussion of elitism in the "uplift" movement and organizations, see Kevin K. Gains, *Uplifting the Race: Black Leadership, Politics, and Culture in the Twentieth Century* (Chapel Hill, N.C.: University of North Carolina Press, 1996). Black reformers, enlightened as they were, could not entirely escape being influenced by Social Darwinist currents of the times.

20. Deborah Gray White, *Too Heavy a Load: Black Women in Defense of Themselves, 1894–1994* (New York: W. W. Norton & Company, 1999), p. 36.

21. Quoted in Giddings, *When and Where I Enter*, p. 75.

22. Ibid.

23. Ibid.

24. Ibid., p. 59.

25. Ibid.

26. Evelyn Brooks Higginbotham, *Righteous Discontent: The Women's Movement in the Black Baptist Church, 1880–1920* (Cambridge: Harvard University Press, 1993).

27. Ibid., p. 20.

28. Rosalyn Terborg-Penn, "Discontented Black Feminists: Prelude and Postscript to the Passage of the Nineteenth Amendment," pp. 261–278 in Lois Scharf and Joan M. Jensen, eds., *Decades of Discontent: The Woman's Movement, 1920–1940* (Westport, Conn.: Greenwood Press, 1983), p. 264.

29. Ibid., p. 261.

30. Ibid., p. 264.

31. Ibid., p. 266.

32. Ibid., pp. 266–267.

33. Barbara J. Harris, *Beyond Her Sphere: Women and the Professions in American History* (Westport, Conn.: Greenwood Press, 1978), pp. 85–86.

34. Giddings, *When and Where I Enter*, p. 81.

35. John P. Rousmaniere, "Cultural Hybrid in the Slums: The College Woman and the Settlement House, 1889–1984," *American Quarterly* 22 (Spring 1970): p. 56.

36. Ibid., p. 55.

37. Barbara J. Harris, *Beyond Her Sphere*, pp. 101–102.

38. Ibid., pp. 101–102.

39. Rousmaniere, "Cultural Hybrid in the Slums," p. 56.

40. Ibid., p. 61.

41. Quoted in Linda Gordon, "Black and White Visions of Welfare: Women's Welfare Activism, 1890–1945," *Journal of American History* 78 (September 1991): 583.

42. Giddings, *When and Where I Enter*, p. 97.

43. Estelle Freedman, "Separatism as Strategy: Female Institution Building and American Feminism, 1870–1930," pp. 445–462 in Nancy F. Cott, ed., *Women Together: Organizational Life* (New Providence, RI: K. G. Saur, 1994), p. 450; Nancy Forderhase, "'Limited Only by Earth and Sky': The Louisville Woman's Club and Progressive Reform, 1900–1910," pp. 365–381 in Cott, ed. *Women Together: Organizational Life* (New Providence, RI: K. G. Saur, 1994); . . . Mary Dell Brady, "Kansas Federation of Colored Women's Clubs, 1900–1930," pp. 382–408 in Nancy F. Cott, *Women Together*.

44. Higginbotham, *Righteous Discontent*, pp. 206–207.

45. Giddings, *When and Where I Enter*, p. 22.

46. Terborg-Penn, "Discontented Black Feminists," p. 267.

47. Giddings, *When and Where I Enter*, p. 108.

48. Ibid., pp. 108–109.

49. Ibid., p. 113.

50. Linda Gordon, "Black and Whites Visions of Welfare," p. 583.

51. Ibid., p. 582.

52. Ibid., p. 585.

53. Ibid., pp. 568–69.

54. Ibid., p. 109.

55. Quoted in Giddings, ibid., p. 110.

56. Ibid., p. 97.

57. Elsa Barkley Brown, "Womanist Consciousness: Maggie Lena Walker and the Independent Order of Saint Luke," *Signs: Journal of Women in Culture and Society* 14, no. 3 (1989): 188.

58. Shirley J. Carlson, "Black Ideals of Womanhood in the Late Victorian Era," *Journal of Negro History* 77, no. 2 (Spring 1992): 62. Carlson notes that these black women of the late Victorian era also observed the proprieties of Victorian womanhood in their deportment and appearance but combined them with the expectations of the black community for intelligence, education, and active involvement in racial uplift.

59. Giddings, *When and Where I Enter*, pp. 110–111.

60. Brown, "Womanist Consciousness," p. 180.

61. Ibid., p. 178.

62. Quoted in Giddings, *When and Where I Enter*, p. 117.

63. See Rosalyn Terborg-Penn, *African American Women in the Struggle for the Vote, 1850–1920* (Bloomington, Ind.: Indiana University Press, 1998).

64. Rosalyn Terborg-Penn, "Discontented Black Feminists," p. 274.

65. Stephanie J. Shaw, *What a Woman Ought to Be and to Do: Black Professional Women Workers During the Jim Crow Era* (Chicago: University of Chicago Press, 1996), p. 29. Shaw details the efforts of family and community to socialize these women for both personal achievement and community service. The sacrifices some families made included sending them to private schools and sometimes relocating the entire family near a desired school.

66. Ibid., p. 126. Italics added.

67. Giddings, *When and Where I Enter*, p. 108.

68. Brown, "Womanist Consciousness," p. 622.

69. Ibid., p. 623.

70. Carby, *Reconstructing Womanhood*, p. 117.

71. Quoted in Giddings, *When and Where I Enter*, p. 72.

72. Brown, "Womanist Consciousness," p. 182.

73. Quoted in Giddings, *Where and When I Enter*, p. 109.

74. Betty Friedan, *The Feminine Mystique* (New York: Dell, 1963), p. 68.

75. Quoted in Giddings, *Where and When I Enter*, p. 197.

76. Quoted in Terborg-Penn, "Discontented Black Feminists," p. 274.

77. Ibid., p. 274.

78. Quoted in Giddings, *Where and When I Enter*, p. 138.

79. Quoted in Carby, *Reconstructing Womanhood*, p. 98.

80. Erlene Stetson, "Black Feminism in Indiana, 1893–1933," *Phylon* 44 (December 1983): 294.

81. Quoted in Barbara Welter, "The Cult of True Womanhood: 1820–1860," p. 318.

82. Carby, *Reconstructing Womanhood*, p. 100.

83. Ibid., p. 99.

84. Carlson, "Black Ideals of Womanhood in the Late Victorian Era," p. 69. This view is supported by historian Evelyn Brooks Higginbotham's analysis of schools for blacks established by northern Baptists in the postbellum period, schools that encouraged the attendance of both girls and boys. Although, as Higginbotham observes, northern Baptists founded these schools in part to spread white middle-class values among blacks, blacks nevertheless came to see higher education as an instrument of their own liberation (*Righteous Discontent*, p. 20).

85. Ibid., p. 67.

THINKING ABOUT THE READING

How were the needs and goals of black women during the 19th-century movement for gender equality different from those of white women? How did their lives differ with regard to the importance of marriage, motherhood, and employment? What does Landry mean when he says that for these women, "race and gender are inseparable"? What was the significance of the "clubs" for these black women? How does this article change what you previously thought about the contemporary women's movement?

Still a Man's World

Men Who Do "Women's Work"

Christine L. Williams

(1995)

Gendered Jobs and Gendered Workers

A 1959 article in *Library Journal* entitled "The Male Librarian—An Anomaly?" begins this way:

> My friends keep trying to get me out of the library. . . . Library work is fine, they agree, but they smile and shake their heads benevolently and charitably, as if it were unnecessary to add that it is one of the dullest, most poorly paid, unrewarding, off-beat activities any man could be consigned to. If you have a heart condition, if you're physically handicapped in other ways, well, such a job is a blessing. And for women there's no question library work is fine; there are some wonderful women in libraries and we all ought to be thankful to them. But let's face it, no healthy man of normal intelligence should go into it.[1]

Male librarians still face this treatment today, as do other men who work in predominantly female occupations. In 1990, my local newspaper featured a story entitled "Men Still Avoiding Women's Work" that described my research on men in nursing, librarianship, teaching, and social work. Soon afterwards, a humor columnist for the same paper wrote a spoof on the story that he titled, "Most Men Avoid Women's Work Because It Is Usually So Boring."[2] The columnist poked fun at hairdressing, librarianship, nursing, and babysitting—in his view, all "lousy" jobs requiring low

intelligence and a high tolerance for boredom. Evidently people still wonder why any "healthy man of normal intelligence" would willingly work in a "woman's occupation."

In fact, not very many men do work in these fields, although their numbers are growing. In 1990, over 500,000 men were employed in these four occupations, constituting approximately 6 percent of all registered nurses, 15 percent of all elementary school teachers, 17 percent of all librarians, and 32 percent of all social workers. These percentages have fluctuated in recent years: As Table 1 indicates, librarianship and social work have undergone slight declines in the proportions of men since 1975; teaching has remained somewhat stable; while nursing has experienced noticeable gains. The number of men in nursing actually doubled between 1980 and 1990; however, their overall proportional representation remains very low.

Very little is known about these men who "cross over" into these nontraditional occupations. While numerous books have been written about women entering male-dominated occupations, few have asked why men are underrepresented in traditionally female jobs.[3] The underlying assumption in most research on gender and work is that, given a free choice, both men and women would work in predominantly male occupations, as they are generally better paying and more prestigious than predominantly female occupations. The few men who willingly "cross over" must be, as the 1959 article suggests, "anomalies."

Table 1 Men in the "Women's Professions": Number (in thousands) and Distribution of Men Employed in the Occupations, Selected Years

Profession	1975	1980	1990
Registered Nurses			
Number of men	28	46	92
% men	3.0	3.5	5.5
Elementary Teachers[a]			
Number of men	194	225	223
% men	14.6	16.3	14.8
Librarians			
Number of men	34	27	32
% men	18.9	14.8	16.7
Social Workers			
Number of men	116	134	179
% men	39.2	35.0	21.8

Sources: U.S. Department of Labor, Bureau of Labor Statistics, *Employment and Earnings* 38 no. 1 (January 1991), table 22 (employed civilians by detailed occupation), p. 185; vol. 28, no. 1 (January 1981), table 23 (employed persons by detailed occupation), p. 180; vol. 22, no. 7 (January 1976), table 2 (employed persons by detailed occupation), p. 11.

[a] Excludes kindergarten teachers.

Popular culture reinforces the belief that these men are "anomalies." Men are rarely portrayed working in these occupations, and when they are, they are represented in extremely stereotypical ways. For example, in the 1990 movie *Kindergarten Cop*, muscle-man Arnold Schwarzenegger played a detective forced to work undercover as a kindergarten teacher; the otherwise competent Schwarzenegger was completely overwhelmed by the five-year-old children in his class. . . .

[I] challenge these stereotypes about men who do "women's work" through case studies of men in four predominantly female occupations: nursing, elementary school teaching, librarianship, and social work. I show that men maintain their masculinity in these occupations, despite the popular stereotypes. Moreover, male power and privilege is preserved and reproduced in these occupations through a complex interplay between gendered expectations embedded in organizations, and the gendered interests workers bring with them to their jobs. Each of these occupations is "still a man's world" even though mostly women work in them.

I selected these four professions as case studies of men who do "women's work" for a variety of reasons. First, because they are so strongly associated with women and femininity in our popular culture, these professions highlight and perhaps even exaggerate the barriers and advantages men face when entering predominantly female environments. Second, they each require extended periods of educational training and apprenticeship, requiring individuals in these occupations to be at least somewhat committed to their work (unlike those employed in, say, clerical or domestic work). Therefore I thought they would be reflective about their decisions to join these "nontraditional" occupations, making them "acute observers" and, hence, ideal informants about the sort of social and psychological processes I am interested in describing.[4] Third, these occupations vary a great deal in the proportion of men working in them. Although my aim was not to engage in between-group comparisons, I believed that the proportions of men in a work setting would strongly influence the degree to which they felt accepted and satisfied with their jobs.[5]

I traveled across the United States conducting in-depth interviews with seventy-six men and twenty-three women who work in nursing, teaching, librarianship, and social work. Like the people employed in these professions generally, those in my sample were predominantly white (90 percent). Their ages ranged from twenty to sixty-six, and the average age was thirty-eight. I interviewed women as well as men to gauge their feelings and reactions to men's entry into "their" professions. Respondents were intentionally selected to represent a wide range of specialties and levels of education and experience. I interviewed students in professional schools, "front line" practitioners, administrators, and retirees, asking them about their motivations to enter these professions, their on-the-job experiences, and their opinions about men's status and prospects in these fields. . . .

Riding the Glass Escalator

Men earn more money than women in every occupation—even in predominantly female jobs (with the possible exceptions of fashion modeling and prostitution).[6] Table 2 shows that men outearn women in teaching, librarianship, and social work; their salaries in nursing are virtually identical. The ratios between women's and men's earnings in these occupations are higher than those found in the "male" professions, where women earn 74 to 90 percent of men's salaries. That there is a wage gap at all in predominantly female professions, however, attests to asymmetries in the workplace experiences of male and female tokens. These salary figures indicate that the men who do "women's work" fare as well as, and often better than, the women who work in these fields. . . .

Hiring Decisions

Contrary to the experience of many women in the male-dominated professions, many of the men and women I spoke to indicated that there is a *preference* for hiring men in these four occupations. A Texas librarian at a junior high school said that his school district "would hire a male over a female":

[CW: Why do you think that is?]

Because there are so few, and the . . . ones that they do have, the library directors seem to

Table 2 Median Weekly Earnings of Full-Time Professional Workers, by Sex, and Ratio of Female:Male Earnings, 1990

Occupation	Both	Men	Women	Ratio
Registered Nurses	608	616	608	.99
Elementary Teachers	519	575	513	.89
Librarians	489	—*	479	—
Social Workers	445	483	427	.88
Engineers	814	822	736	.90
Physicians	892	978	802	.82
College Teachers	747	808	620	.77
Lawyers	1,045	1,178	875	.74

Source: U.S. Department of Labor, Bureau of Labor Statistics, *Employment and Earnings* 38, no. 1 (January 1991), table 56, p. 223.

*The Labor Department does not report income averages for base sample sizes consisting of fewer than 50,000 individuals.

really . . . think they're doing great jobs. I don't know, maybe they just feel they're being progressive or something, [but] I have had a real sense that they really appreciate having a male, particularly at the junior high. . . . As I said, when seven of us lost our jobs from the high schools and were redistributed, there were only four positions at junior high, and I got one of them. Three of the librarians, some who had been here longer than I had with the school district, were put down in elementary school as librarians. And I definitely think that being male made a difference in my being moved to the junior high rather than an elementary school.

Many of the men perceived their token status as males in predominantly female occupations as an *advantage* in hiring and promotions. When I asked an Arizona teacher whether his specialty (elementary special education) was an unusual area for men compared to other areas within education, he said,

> Much more so. I am extremely marketable in special education. That's not why I got into the field. But I am extremely marketable because I am a man.

. . . Sometimes the preference for men in these occupations is institutionalized. One man landed his first job in teaching before he earned the appropriate credential "because I was a wrestler and they wanted a wrestling coach." A female math teacher similarly told of her inability to find a full-time teaching position because the schools she applied to reserved the math jobs for people (presumably men) who could double as coaches. . . .

. . . Some men described being "tracked" into practice areas within their professions which were considered more legitimate for men. For example, one Texas man described how he was pushed into administration and planning in social work, even though "I'm not interested in writing policy; I'm much more interested in research and clinical stuff." A nurse who is interested in pursuing graduate study in family and child health in Boston said he was dissuaded from entering the program specialty in favor of a concentration in "adult nursing." And a kindergarten teacher described his difficulty finding a job in his specialty after graduation: "I was recruited immediately to start getting into a track to become an administrator. And it was men who recruited me. It was men that ran the system at that time, especially in Los Angeles."

This tracking may bar men from the most female-identified specialties within these professions. But men are effectively being "kicked upstairs" in the process. Those specialties considered more legitimate practice areas for men also tend to be the most prestigious, and better-paying specialties as well. For example, men in nursing are overrepresented in critical care and psychiatric specialties, which tend to be higher paying than the others.[7] The highest paying and most prestigious library types are the academic libraries (where men are 35 percent of librarians) and the special libraries which are typically associated with businesses or other private organizations (where men constitute 20 percent of librarians).[8]

A distinguished kindergarten teacher, who had been voted citywide "Teacher of the Year," described the informal pressures he faced to advance in his field. He told me that even though people were pleased to see him in the classroom, "there's been some encouragement to think about administration, and there's been some encouragement to think about teaching at the university level or something like that, or supervisory-type position."

The effect of this "tracking" is the opposite of that experienced by women in male-dominated occupations. Researchers have reported that many women encounter "glass ceilings" in their efforts to scale organizational and professional hierarchies. That is, they reach invisible barriers to promotion in their careers, caused mainly by the sexist attitudes of men in the highest positions.[9] In contrast to this "glass ceiling," many of the men I interviewed seem to encounter a "glass escalator." Often, despite their intentions, they face invisible pressures to move up in their professions. Like being on a moving escalator, they have to work to stay in place. . . .

Supervisors and Colleagues: The Working Environment

. . . Respondents in this study were asked about their relationships with supervisors and female colleagues to ascertain whether men also experienced "poisoned" work environments when entering nontraditional occupations.

A major difference in the experience of men and women in nontraditional occupations is that men are far more likely to be supervised by a member of their own sex. In each of the four professions I studied, men are overrepresented in administrative and managerial capacities, or, as in the case of nursing, the organizational hierarchy is governed by men. For example, 15 percent of all elementary school teachers are men, but men make up over 80 percent of all elementary school principals and 96 percent of all public school superintendents and assistant superintendents.[10] Likewise, over 40 percent of all male social workers hold administrative or managerial positions, compared to 30 percent of all female social workers.[11] And 50 percent of male librarians hold administrative positions, compared to 30 percent of female librarians, and the majority of deans and directors of major university and public libraries are men.[12] Thus, unlike women who enter "male fields," the men in these professions often work under the direct supervision of other men.

Many of the men interviewed reported that they had good rapport with their male supervisors. It was not uncommon in education, for example, for the male principal to informally socialize with the male staff, as a Texas special education teacher describes:

> Occasionally I've had a principal who would regard me as "the other man on the campus" and "it's us against them," you know? I mean, nothing really that extreme, except that some male principals feel like there's nobody there to talk to except the other man. So I've been in that position.

These personal ties can have important consequences for men's careers. For example, one California nurse, whose performance was judged marginal by his nursing superiors, was transferred to the emergency room staff (a prestigious promotion) due to his personal friendship with the physician in charge. And a Massachusetts teacher acknowledged that his principal's personal interest in him landed him his current job:

[CW: You had mentioned that your principal had sort of spotted you at your previous job and had wanted to bring you here [to this school]. Do you think that has anything to do with the fact that you're a man, aside from your skills as a teacher?]

Yes, I would say in that particular case, that was part of it. . . . We have certain things in common, certain interests that really lined up.

[CW: Vis-à-vis teaching?]

Well, more extraneous things—running specifically, and music. And we just seemed to get along real well right off the bat. It is just kind of a guy thing; we just liked each other. . . .

Interviewees did not report many instances of male supervisors discriminating against them, or refusing to accept them because they were male. Indeed, these men were much more likely to report that their male bosses discriminated against the *females* in their professions. . . .

Of course, not all the men who work in these occupations are supervised by men. Many of the men interviewed who had female bosses also reported high levels of acceptance—although the level of intimacy they achieved with women did not seem as great as with other men. But in some cases, men reported feeling shut-out from decision making when the higher administration was constituted entirely by women. I asked this Arizona librarian whether men in the library profession were discriminated against hiring because of their sex:

> Professionally speaking, people go to considerable lengths to keep that kind of thing out of their [hiring] deliberations. Personally, is another matter. It's pretty common around here to talk about the "old girl network." This is one of the few libraries that I've had any intimate knowledge of which is actually controlled by women. . . . Most of the department heads

and upper level administrators are women. And there's an "old girl network" that works just like the "old boy network," except that the important conferences take place in the women's room rather than on the golf course. But the political mechanism is the same, the exclusion of the other sex from decision making is the same. The reasons are the same. It's somewhat discouraging. . . .

Although I did not interview many supervisors, I did include twenty-three women in my sample to ascertain their perspectives about the presence of men in their professions. All of the women I interviewed claimed to be supportive of their male colleagues, but some conveyed ambivalence. For example, a social work professor said she would like to see more men enter the social work profession, particularly in the clinical specialty (where they are underrepresented). She said she would favor affirmative action hiring guidelines for men in the profession, and yet, she resented the fact that her department hired "another white male" during a recent search. I confronted her about this apparent ambivalence:

[CW: I find it very interesting that, on the one hand, you sort of perceive this preference and perhaps even sexism with regard to how men are evaluated and how they achieve higher positions within the profession, yet, on the other hand, you would be encouraging of more men to enter the field. Is that contradictory to you, or . . . ?]
    Yeah, it's contradictory. . . .

Men's reception by their female colleagues is thus somewhat mixed. It appears that women are generally eager to see men enter "their" occupations, and the women I interviewed claimed they were supportive of their male peers. Indeed, several men agreed with this social worker that their female colleagues had facilitated their careers in various ways (including college mentorship). At the same

time, however, women often resent the apparent ease with which men seem to advance within these professions, sensing that men at the higher levels receive preferential treatment, and thus close off advancement opportunities for women.

But this ambivalence does not seem to translate into the "poisoned" work environment described by many women who work in male-dominated occupations. Among the male interviewees, there were no accounts of sexual harassment (indeed, one man claimed this was a disappointment to him!). However, women do treat their male colleagues differently on occasion. It is not uncommon in nursing, for example, for men to be called upon to help catheterize male patients, or to lift especially heavy patients. Some librarians also said that women asked them to lift and move heavy boxes of books because they were men. . . .

Another stereotype confronting men, in nursing and social work in particular, is the expectation that they are better able than women to handle aggressive individuals and diffuse violent situations. An Arizona social worker who was the first male caseworker in a rural district, described this preference for men:

They welcomed a man, particularly in child welfare. Sometimes you have to go into some tough parts of towns and cities, and they felt it was nice to have a man around to accompany them or be present when they were dealing with a difficult client. Or just doing things that males can do. I always felt very welcomed.

But this special treatment bothered some respondents: Getting assigned all the violent patients or discipline problems can make for difficult and unpleasant working conditions. Nurses, for example, described how they were called upon to subdue violent patients. A traveling psychiatric nurse I interviewed in Texas told how his female colleagues gave him "plenty of opportunities" to use his wrestling skills. . . .

But many men claimed that this differential treatment did not distress them. In fact, several said they liked being appreciated for the special traits and abilities (such as strength) they could contribute to their professions.

Furthermore, women's special treatment of men sometimes enhanced—rather than detracted from—the men's work environments. One Texas librarian said he felt "more comfortable working with women than men" because "I think it has something to do with control. Maybe it's that women will let me take control more than men will." Several men reported that their female colleagues often cast them into leadership roles. . . .

The interviews suggest that the working environment encountered by "nontraditional" male workers is quite unlike that faced by women who work in traditionally male fields. Because it is not uncommon for men in predominantly female professions to be supervised by other men, they tend to have closer rapport and more intimate social relationships with people in management. These ties can facilitate men's careers by smoothing the way for future promotions. Relationships with female supervisors were also described for the most part in positive terms, although in some cases, men perceived an "old girls'" network in place that excluded them from decision making. But in sharp contrast to the reports of women in nontraditional occupations, men in these fields did not complain of feeling discriminated against because they were men. If anything, they felt that being male was an asset that enhanced their career prospects.

Those men interviewed for this study also described congenial workplaces, and a very high level of acceptance from their female colleagues. The sentiment was echoed by women I spoke to who said that they were pleased to see more men enter "their" professions. Some women, however, did express resentment over the "fast-tracking" that their male colleagues seem to experience. But this ambivalence did not translate into a hostile work environment for men:

Women generally included men in their informal social events and, in some ways, even facilitated men's careers. By casting men into leadership roles, presuming they were more knowledgeable and qualified, or relying on them to perform certain critical tasks, women unwittingly contributed to the "glass escalator effect" facing men who do "women's work."

Relationships With Clients

Workers in these service-oriented occupations come into frequent contact with the public during the course of their work day. Nurses treat patients; social workers usually have client case loads; librarians serve patrons; and teachers are in constant contact with children, and often with parents as well. Many of those interviewed claimed that the clients they served had different expectations of men and women in these occupations, and often treated them differently.

People react with surprise and often disbelief when they encounter a man in nursing, elementary school teaching, and, to a lesser extent, librarianship. (Usually people have no clear expectations about the sex of social workers.) The stereotypes men face are often negative. For example, according to this Massachusetts nurse, it is frequently assumed that male nurses are gay:

> Fortunately, I carry one thing with me that protects me from [the stereotype that male nurses are gay], and the one thing I carry with me is a wedding ring, and it makes a big difference. The perfect example was conversations before I was married. . . . [People would ask], "Oh, do you have a girlfriend?" Or you'd hear patients asking questions along that idea, and they were simply implying, "Why is this guy in nursing? Is it because he's gay and he's a pervert?" And I'm not associating the two by any means, but this is the thought process.

. . . It is not uncommon for both gay and straight men in these occupations to encounter people who believe that they are "gay 'til proven otherwise," as one nurse put it. In fact, there are many gay men employed in these occupations. But gender stereotypes are at least as responsible for this general belief as any "empirical" assessment of men's sexual lifestyles. To the degree that men in these professions are perceived as not "measuring up" to the supposedly more challenging occupational roles and standards demanded of "real" men, they are immediately suspected of being effeminate—"like women"—and thus, homosexual.

An equally prevalent sexual stereotype about men in these occupations is that they are potentially dangerous and abusive. Several men described special rules they followed to guard against the widespread presumption of sexual abuse. For example, nurses were sometimes required to have a female "chaperone" present when performing certain procedures or working with specific populations. This psychiatric nurse described a former workplace:

> I worked on a floor for the criminally insane. Pretty threatening work. So you have to have a certain number of females on the floor just to balance out. Because there were female patients on the floor too. And you didn't want to be accused of rape or any sex crimes.

Teachers and librarians described the steps they took to protect themselves from suspicions of sexual impropriety. A kindergarten teacher said:

> I know that I'm careful about how I respond to students. I'm careful in a number of ways—in my physical interaction with students. It's mainly to reassure parents. . . . For example, a little girl was very affectionate, very anxious to give me a hug. She'll just throw herself at me. I need to tell her very carefully: "Sonia, you need to tell me when you want to hug me." That way I can come down, crouch down. Because you don't want a child giving you a hug on your hip. You just don't want to do that. So I'm very careful about body position.

. . . Although negative stereotypes about men who do "women's work" can push men out of specific jobs, their effects can actually benefit men. Instead of being a source of negative discrimination, these prejudices can add to the "glass escalator effect" by pressuring men to move *out* of the most feminine-identified areas and *up* to those regarded as more legitimate for men.

The public's reactions to men working in these occupations, however, are by no means always negative. Several men and women reported that people often assume that men in these occupations are more competent than women, or that they bring special skills and expertise to their professional practice. For example, a female academic librarian told me that patrons usually address their questions to the male reference librarian when there is a choice between asking a male or a female. A male clinical social worker in private practice claimed that both men and women generally preferred male psychotherapists. And several male nurses told me that people often assume that they are physicians and direct their medical inquiries to them instead of to the female nurses.[13]

The presumption that men are more competent than women is another difference in the experience of token men and women. Women who work in nontraditional occupations are often suspected of being incompetent, unable to survive the pressures of "men's work." As a consequence, these women often report feeling compelled to prove themselves and, as the saying goes, "work twice as hard as men to be considered half as good." To the degree that men are assumed to be competent and in control, they may have to be twice as incompetent to be considered half as bad. One man claimed that "if you're a mediocre male teacher, you're considered a better teacher than if you're a female and a mediocre teacher. I think there's that prejudice there." . . .

There are different standards and assumptions about men's competence that follow them into nontraditional occupations. In contrast, women in both traditional and nontraditional occupations must contend with the presumption that they are neither competent nor qualified. . . .

The reasons that clients give for preferring or rejecting men reflect the complexity of our society's stereotypes about masculinity and femininity. Masculinity is often associated with competence and mastery, in contrast to femininity, which is often associated with instrumental incompetence. Because of these stereotypes, men are perceived as being stricter disciplinarians and stronger than women, and thus better able to handle violent or potentially violent situations. . . .

Conclusion

Both men and women who work in nontraditional occupations encounter discrimination, but the forms and the consequences of this discrimination are very different for the two groups. Unlike "nontraditional" women workers, most of the discrimination and prejudice facing men in the "female" professions comes from clients. For the most part, the men and women I interviewed believed that men are given fair—if not preferential—treatment in hiring and promotion decisions, are accepted by their supervisors and colleagues, and are well-integrated into the workplace subculture. Indeed, there seem to be subtle mechanisms in place that enhance men's positions in these professions—a phenomenon I refer to as a "glass escalator effect."

Men encounter their most "mixed" reception in their dealings with clients, who often react negatively to male nurses, teachers, and to a lesser extent, librarians. Many people assume that the men are sexually suspect if they are employed in these "feminine" occupations either because they do or they do not conform to stereotypical masculine characteristics.

Dealing with the stress of these negative stereotypes can be overwhelming, and it probably pushes some men out of these occupations.[14] The challenge facing the men who stay in these fields is to accentuate their positive contribution to what our society defines as essentially "women's work." . . .

NOTES

1. Allan Angoff, "The Male Librarian—An Anomaly?" *Library Journal*, February 15, 1959, p. 553.

2. *Austin-American Statesman*, January 16, 1990; response by John Kelso, January 18, 1990.

3. Some of the most important studies of women in male-dominated occupations are: Rosabeth Moss Kanter, *Men and Women of the Corporation* (New York: Basic Books, 1977); Susan Martin, *Breaking and Entering: Policewomen on Patrol* (Berkeley: University of California Press, 1980); Cynthia Fuchs Epstein, *Women in Law* (New York: Basic Books, 1981); Kay Deaux and Joseph Ullman, *Women of Steel* (New York: Praeger, 1983); Judith Hicks Stiehm, *Arms and the Enlisted Woman* (Philadelphia: Temple University Press, 1989); Jerry Jacobs, *Revolving Doors: Sex Segregation and Women's Careers* (Stanford: Stanford University Press, 1989); Barbara Reskin and Patricia Roos, *Job Queues, Gender Queues: Explaining Women's Inroads into Male Occupations* (Philadelphia: Temple University Press, 1990).

Among the few books that do examine men's status in predominantly female occupations are Carol Tropp Schreiber, *Changing Places: Men and Women in Transitional Occupations* (Cambridge: MIT Press, 1979); Christine L. Williams, *Gender Differences at Work: Women and Men in Nontraditional Occupations* (Berkeley: University of California Press, 1989); and Christine L. Williams, ed., *Doing "Women's Work": Men in Nontraditional Occupations* (Newbury Park, CA: Sage Publications, 1993).

4. In an influential essay on methodological principles, Herbert Blumer counseled sociologists to "sedulously seek participants in the sphere of life who are acute observers and who are well informed. One such person is worth a hundred others who are merely unobservant participants." See "The

Methodological Position of Symbolic Inter-actionism," in *Symbolic Interactionism: Perspective and Method* (Berkeley: University of California Press, 1969), p. 41.

5. The overall proportions in the population do not necessarily represent the experiences of individuals in my sample. Some nurses, for example, worked in groups that were composed almost entirely of men, while some social workers had the experience of being the only man in their group. The overall statistics provide a general guide, but relying on them exclusively can distort the actual experiences of individuals in the workplace. The statistics available for research on occupational sex segregation are not specific enough to measure internal divisions among workers. Research that uses firm-level data finds a far greater degree of segregation than research that uses national data. See William T. Bielby and James N. Baron, "A Woman's Place Is with Other Women: Sex Segregation within Organizations," in *Sex Segregation in the Workplace: Trends, Explanations, Remedies,* ed. Barbara Reskin (Washington, D.C.: National Academy Press, 1984), pp. 27–55.

6. Catharine MacKinnon, *Feminism Unmodified* (Cambridge: Harvard University Press, 1987), pp. 24–25.

7. Howard S. Rowland, *The Nurse's Almanac,* 2d ed. (Rockville, MD: Aspen Systems Corp., 1984), p. 153; Johw W. Wright, *The American Almanac of Jobs and Salaries,* 2d ed. (New York: Avon, 1984), p. 639.

8. King Research, Inc., *Library Human Resources: A Study of Supply and Demand* (Chicago: American Library Association, 1983), p. 41.

9. See, for example, Sue J. M. Freeman, *Managing Lives: Corporate Women and Social Change* (Amherst: University of Massachusetts Press, 1990).

10. Patricia A. Schmuck, "Women School Employees in the United States," in *Women Educators: Employees of Schools in Western Countries* (Albany: State University of New York Press, 1987), p. 85; James W. Grimm and Robert N. Stern, "Sex Roles and Internal Labor Market Structures: The Female Semi-Professions," *Social Problems* 21(1974): 690–705.

11. David A. Hardcastle and Arthur J. Katz, *Employment and Unemployment in Social Work: A Study of NASW Members* (Washington, D.C.: NASW, 1979), p. 41; Reginold O. York, H. Carl Henley and Dorothy N. Gamble, "Sexual Discrimination in Social Work: Is It Salary or Advancement?" *Social Work* 32 (1987): 336–340; Grimm and Stern, "Sex Roles and Internal Labor Market Structures."

12. Leigh Estabrook, "Women's Work in the Library/Information Sector," in *My Troubles Are Going to Have Trouble with Me,* ed. Karen Brodkin Sacks and Dorothy Remy (New Brunswick, NJ: Rutgers University Press, 1984), p. 165.

13. Liliane Floge and D. M. Merrill found a similar phenomenon in their study of male nurses. See "Tokenism Reconsidered: Male Nurses and Female Physicians in a Hospital Setting," *Social Forces* 64 (1986): 931–932.

14. Jim Allan makes this argument in "Male Elementary Teachers: Experiences and Perspectives," in *Doing "Women's Work": Men in Nontraditional Occupations,* ed. Christine L. Williams (Newbury Park, CA: Sage Publications, 1993), pp. 113–127.

THINKING ABOUT THE READING

Compare the discrimination men experience in traditionally female occupations to that experienced by women in traditionally male occupations. What is the "glass escalator effect"? In what ways can the glass escalator actually be harmful to men? What do you suppose might happen to the structure of the American labor force if men did in fact begin to enter predominantly female occupations in the same proportion as women entering predominantly male occupations?

The Global
Dynamics of Population

Demographic Trends

In the past several chapters we have examined the various interrelated sources of social stratification. Race, class, and gender continue to determine access to cultural, economic, and political opportunities. Another source of inequality that we don't think much about, but that has enormous local, national, and global significance is the changing size and shape of the human population and how people are distributed around the planet. Globally, population imbalances between richer and poorer societies underlie most if not all of the other important forces for change that are taking place today. Poor, developing countries are expanding rapidly, while the populations in wealthy, developed countries have either stabilized or, in some cases, declined. When the population of a country grows rapidly, the age structure is increasingly dominated by young people. In slow-growth countries with low birthrates and high life expectancy, the population is much older. Countries with different age structures face different challenges regarding the allocation of important resources.

In our quest to identify the structural factors that shape our everyday experiences, the effects of our *birth cohort* are often overlooked. Birth cohorts are more than just a collection of individuals born within a few years of each other; they are distinctive generations tied together by historical events, national and global population trends, and large-scale societal changes.

The media often play a role in molding each cohort's impression of itself as a group and its relation to other cohorts. These impressions can perpetuate inter-cohort conflict. For instance, younger cohorts, like Generation X, are frequently characterized in the media as apathetic "slackers." Older cohorts, like the "Baby Boomers," are pictured as rich, greedy, and self-righteous. Media coverage of important matters like Social Security reform typically pits these two cohorts against each other in a battle for economic survival. But such broad-brush images are rarely accurate, as Margaret Gullette points out in her article, "'The Xers' versus 'the Boomers.'" She argues that the largely contrived "war" between "Boomers" and "Xers" overshadows some very real potential economic crises that affect everyone: falling wages, shrinking job markets, and overall economic insecurity. According to Gullette, a falsely conceived war between these cohorts makes all of us vulnerable to political manipulation.

Some other large-scale demographic phenomena affect people regardless of their age. Take, for instance, immigration. As social and demographic conditions in poor, developing countries grow worse, pressures to migrate increase. Countries on the receiving end of this migration often experience high levels of cultural, political, and economic fear. Immigration—both legal and illegal—has become one of the most contentious political issues in the United States today. While politicians debate proposed immigration restrictions, people from all corners of the globe continue to come to this country looking for a better life. An informed understanding of this phenomenon requires an awareness of the reasons for migration and the connection between the choices individuals make to immigrate and larger economic conditions that reflect global markets.

Luis Navarro highlights this issue in "To Die a Little: Migration and Coffee in Mexico and Central America." Most North Americans are inclined to see immigration from the perspective of a receiving country. Hence we're likely to concern ourselves with the social, cultural, and economic consequences of large numbers of new (and foreign) people entering the United States, whether legally and illegally. Navarro, however, examines immigration from the perspective of migrants and the consequences for the communities they leave behind in their search for a better life. In linking migration to the global coffee industry, Navarro pushes us to see how the products we enjoy in our everyday lives are intricately connected to the working and living conditions of others.

It is also important to remember that the movement of people between countries like that described by Navarro has set the groundwork for inequality and stratification that extend beyond national borders. Third-world laborers have become a crucial part of the global economic marketplace and an important foreign resource for multinational corporations. Low-skilled jobs are frequently exported to developing countries that have cheaper labor costs. On the surface, it would appear that such an arrangement benefits all involved: The multinational corporations benefit from higher profits, the developing countries benefit from higher rates of employment, the workers themselves benefit from earning a wage that would have otherwise been unavailable to them, and consumers in wealthy countries benefit from less expensive products.

But most of us are unaware of and unconcerned with the harsh conditions under which our most coveted products are made. William Greider, in "These Dark Satanic Mills," discusses the exploitative potential of relying on third-world factories. He uses a particular tragedy, the 1993 industrial fire at the Kader Industrial Toy Company in Thailand, to illustrate how global economics create and sustain international inequality. Greider shows us the complex paradox of the global marketplace: While foreign manufacturing facilities free factory workers from certain poverty, they also ensnare the workers in new and sometimes lethal forms of domination.

Something to Consider as You Read:

A global perspective is a big-picture perspective. As you read these selections, practice thinking about the big factors that may shape individual choices. For example, if you are part of an unusually large growth cohort in your neighborhood, how might that affect classroom size in local schools and, possibly, the quality of your education? Farther down the line, how might this affect job opportunities in your area? If your town has many people employed in a particular manufacturing facility, and the company decides to move the factory, how will that affect you and your family and the choices you make? Continue to think about the ways in which big economic and political changes subsequently change the choices individuals make. Now, add wealth and technology to the equation and consider which countries are going to be in the best position to adjust to these global changes? Who is going to be most affected, possibly even exploited, in this global adjustment?

"The Xers" versus "The Boomers"

A Contrived War

Margaret Morganroth Gullette

(2004)

And the children's teeth shall be set on edge.

—Ezekial 18:2

Soon after our son graduated magna cum laude from Harvard in 1991, he was fired from a new job as a waiter. His employers told him he didn't smile enough. Having taken advantage of the recession to hire more young people than they needed, they had to expel some without cause. Our son was a self-confident adult with wide opportunities, but even so I lost my postmaternal cool.

Sean moved to New York to launch an independent magazine and a writing career, supporting himself through day jobs. His struggles gave us a window—a big, drafty window—on the hand-to-mouth life of the 1990s job market. He worked evenings making cold calls as a telemarketer; he freelanced as a "content provider" (the belittling new Internet word for writer). Simultaneously he joined the growing army of "consultants" and began working for a temp agency, doing computer-assisted design. One such agency, Manpower, was the largest employer in the country. Within six years, he amassed 1099 forms from over a hundred companies bent on outsourcing, none of which paid his Social Security or gave him a health benefit or participation in a

pension plan. Despite the high quality of his work, he was often stonewalled on fees.

Thirty percent of workers have similar—"nonstandard"—new American jobs: contract or other short-term work, with less security, fewer health benefits and pensions, no ladder, less clout. "Permatemps" describes the status of most workers in the computer industry, but at Microsoft they must leave after one year. Isolated and competitive, nonstandard workers must seek employment continually. Unemployment and underemployment are endemic. Whether "Old Economy" or "New Economy," nonstandard conditions are gaining ground. This degradation of work in the First World may turn out to be as profound an economic transformation as the Industrial Revolution.

Meanwhile, how is the postindustrial order being explained to us—not only to parents and adult children, but to the American public? Not, except in progressive circles, as a contestable trend in the treatment of workers, not as "the race to the bottom" or "class war from above," NAFTA at home. Instead, the rhetoric shaping the public record depended heavily on the skillful deployment

371

of two imaginary age categories, "the Xers" and "the Boomers."

Name/Blame

During the recession of the early 1990s, when our son joined the workforce, the media cannily invented the term "slackers," meaning lazy, apathetic, cynical, young adults, apolitical "whiners" who were dependent on their parents and did not have the drive of "our" generation. This was classic victim blaming. Having dissed kids with high school degrees when manufacturing jobs disappeared, now they started dissing college-educated kids when professional and managerial jobs were inadequate to demand. Nevertheless, the term "slacker" spread from coast to coast. The media reported parents berating their kids for not trying harder to find work. (My husband and I were telling our son to get more sleep, take a day off—poor palliatives for our rage at being unable to counter the terminology, let alone the economy. I was also saying, "Watch out for the spin.")

As the recession tailed off, press coverage changed to defend the young, now called "Generation X" or "Xers." (In every future reference to either term, imagine them in quotation marks.) The young writers getting published now were those who resented being called slackers. Slackerdom, they said, was a malicious "myth" or "hoax." Although Xers were still discussed as if they had a single homogeneous character, that character possessed values central to America and was capable of changing and improving through time: sympathetic, *human.* Xers were quoted talking earnestly about growing up, wanting to marry, even—clinching proof that they are human—*investing.* Although they had been called "the Hard-Luck Generation," we began to be told repeatedly how aggressive, competitive, successful, and ruthless they were. A 1997 *Time* magazine cover story gave an order to midlife

workers, "Well, move over," and warned, "So boomers, beware. There's a whole bunch of kids with scores to settle." "Who would have thought the kids would start taking over so soon?" Inciting the economic aggression of "kids" against parents, and warning parents about power loss, was *Time*'s humane mission that week. . . .

But what if young adults are too diverse an assemblage to be sorted together as Xers? When I asked fifty Brandeis students what gender, race, and class Xers are, I found the connotations to be whiteness, maleness, higher education, potential for job success. Women with the same economic characteristics may be members of the club; so too "model Asians," gays, and upwardly mobile African Americans. (Had I asked whether Xers can be fat, I think few would have said yes, so large a role does advertising play in the "youth imaginary" of young people.) "Xer" thus does not seem to include "youth in crisis"—crack sellers, violent offenders—or fast-food servers, teachers, or union organizers. The term is as class narrow as "Yuppie" was but not pejorative. In short, although Xer is the opposite of Boomer in this binary, it is by no means synonymous with "the young." Yet its claim to be scientifically encompassing, to represent *a demographic cohort,* is precisely what authorizes age generalizations.

Now for the other side of the story. Eerily, as "Xers" became sympathetic individuals, journalists turned to maligning a group they identified as "Baby Boomers." When Boomers are present in Xer discourse, they serve as the Other. *They* exist without question. They were said to hold all the good jobs, gobble the perks, and dominate the media, harping on themselves. In the stock market run-up of the 1990s, economic "boom" echoed richly inside "Boomers." They are the plutocratic sellouts with dental plans and pensions. Powerful but undeserving: "deadwood."

"Boomers"—for those who have been living in Siberia—began as a neutral demographic term referring to a birth bulge that between 1946 and 1964 reversed a century-long decline in the birthrate. But it soon became rhetorical, inconsistent. In contexts where power or income or size is the core attribute, the Boomer label bulges out to include war babies of the early 1940s as well as others still active in the workforce. "Boomer" nevertheless quickly became imposed as an identity. . . .

These strategies are hostile. Conservatives use the term "Boomer" to belittle the "generation of '68." (Whether they mean the antiwar protesters, counterculture, or the druggies, these were small subcohorts, not a generation.) The media has been describing them as "the aging Baby Boomers" since 1982, when the youngest were only sixteen. "Aging isn't neutral either: its decline elements are up front. "Now that they're in their 40s, boomers are finally feeling old, and they're blaming you," wrote one woman who identified as an Xer. A "Talk of the Town" piece in the *New Yorker*, ignoring the thirty-some-things in the group, blithely asserted, "Now, in 1998, every baby boomer is middle-aged"; death is "a major item" on their agenda. . . .

Boomers too have a character, but not a perfectible one. Pictured as essentially rich, greedy, self-righteous, unwilling to share their vast economic and cultural power, reckless, undeserving of their luck, and of course *aging*, they possess a not-so-mysterious grudge against photogenic Xers. The jealous elders have acquired a pseudobiography. A *Boston Globe* article described them as "idealistic longhairs" who became "Yuppies" and are now "ready for the glory days of the menopausal and the bald." They are usually depicted as if they were all male, white, and overprivileged: Bill Gates, not women, minorities, or the homeless. They are undeserving because unpleasant: "whiny, sarcastic, narcissistic, self-indulgent, cold, bloodless people." Few writers feel the need to point out that Boomers are too heterogeneous to have a single "character" or opinion. Even

some social scientists ignore their diversity. What exactly are people aged thirty-eight supposed to have in common with people aged fifty-six that they should regularly be polled together?

Such omissions make it appear that all middle-aged people are rich and powerful and wield power uniformly. They can thus be more easily objectified as secure rule-makers and oppressors of the young. . . .

What I noticed—because our son was being shoved into Xerdom and his parents were being made perverse new characters in the social text—is that the media have been creating a war between these two age groups. . . .

Constructing the Enemy

In the guise of defending Xers, the media constructed midlifers as the enemy: the generation "that sucked up too much of the oxygen" that Xers need. . . .

Midlife people with secure Old Economy jobs can be represented as useless. . . . A character in Doug Coupland's *Generation X* says bitterly, "You'd last about ten minutes if you were my age these days, Martin. And I have to endure pinheads like you rusting above me for the rest of my life." Imagined as a class of employers, Boomers can also be represented as the force responsible for "management by the numbers and downsizing" and shipping the jobs overseas, rather than members of a midlife generation made widely vulnerable to having their wages cut at their peak. . . . Name any deterioration of working conditions and it can be blamed on "Boomers" rather than seen as the next wave of global capitalism's power over labor.

Using the term "Boomers" adroitly hides the fact that the people in question are often parents, and that not all of them are doing so well. But a startling 1997 Roz Chast cartoon glances at the meaner reality with three Fathers' Day cards "For Today's Dad" sent by kids-with-jobs to their unemployed fathers.

The first says, "You always thought I was such a slob. Well, guess what, Dad? I got your job." The second boasts, "I'm working full-time, You're still lookin'." The third offers Dad a job "as my personal assistant!" Presumably these are sons, not daughters, who are allowed to voice such nonchalance, resentment, and glee at the overthrow of age hierarchy. It's their fathers who have lost. Younger male-older male competition used to be conceived sexually, as oedipal. The age war relocates it (and sanctions it) within the workforce.

No one could imagine boys jeering at their mothers on Mother's Day, even in jest. (Many young people, girls as well as boys, have watched their single mothers struggling and felt abandoned by their fathers. Even at their midlife peak, women earn only half as much as men.) Mainstream discourse finds it easy to forget that black women raising their grandchildren and last-hired first-fired Latinas are also "Boomers." With women omitted, Mom's precarious work situation and her relentless boss—whatever his age—are muted in the blare of media assertions about Boomer power. . . .

As a menace to the young, Boomers have to be fought. Their superpowers make economic revenge appealing: Calling the Boomers "aging" amounts to revenge. It implies that the enemy are has-beens. To younger workers, it hints that the unjustly rich group may be on the verge of decline, powerful but not omnipotent: a Goliath that David can beat.

Privatizing Social Security is the revenge suggested to the anti-Boomers. The terms "Boomer," "Xer," and "Social Security" constantly appear in combination: in one two-year period I found 282 such articles—an induced panic. Peter G. Peterson, a Wall Street banker who long ago started using the age war as an argument for privatizing Social Security, early predicted "ugly generational conflict" once "[our kids] understand the size of the bad check we are passing them." . . . Metaphors like "bad check" teach the young to be anxious;

group pronouns like "we" and generalizations like "paying for Boomers" focus their anger in an age-graded way. A friend of our son's snapped at me, "I pay 15 percent into FICA, and Social Security won't be there for *me*." I'll wager he had read some of those articles. The ground has been so well prepared that the young can plausibly be represented in the mainstream press as a worried and cohesive group of potential antagonists. . . .

The staging of work scarcity is also serious, especially in any downturn. Age-cohort explanation insidiously preps the young to believe that a young person can have a job only if a person at midlife loses one. . . .

Imagine countercultural anecdotes instead: a company pink-slips fifty midlifers and hires only thirty younger people. That would clearly be seen as exploitation. But how satisfactory would it be if the company fired thirty older workers and hired sixty younger ones at half their wages? From a family perspective, a parent's job loss is devastating, even to adult children who are employed. Does it make sense, if American business is unable to produce enough good jobs for all, for anyone in a family unit to prefer to exchange a parental salary for a starting salary? In a nonfamilial, differently othered labor market, this would be called scabbing. The job-swap myth makes "still" being in the workforce at midlife seem unjust, the way the supposed perks of Boomers—like dental plans—are treated as unjust. It conceals the unwillingness of businesses to offer a dental plan and the powerlessness of young people to ask for it at the hiring interview.

Despite the trumpeting of American prosperity throughout the 1990s, various economic problems have had to be "explained." Female competition, black competition: those binaries put the blame on nondominant workers for failures that are systemic. Now the blame game has been moving into an additional arena, that of age. The Boomer-Xer age binary brings scarcity into the heart of the family, where (when not treated as a joke) it operates openly and sadly—as if midlife unemployment had always been an accepted part of the economy, and younger people had never been able to get jobs unless their parents lost them.

Ignorance and Suffering

Does anyone take this age war seriously? Do real people repeat the stereotypes and scapegoating—the middle-ageism—they've read and heard? If your main goal is to privatize Social Security, you needn't care if Xers repeat it word for word: they got your point. But the rest of us care, and those who notice are saddened by the accusations. The editor of the Simmons College student newspaper wrote, "Older generations look at Generation X as somewhere between a nuisance and a nightmare." Some of my friends' adult children repeat how easy "we" had it when we were young. They're primed to hold an age group responsible for both the rightward trends that have made their lives so tough (declines in scholarship aid, housing starts, and job creation, the growing prevalence of nonstandard work, and 24/7 schedules) and for the changes that no one controls. My friend Linda reports that her twenty-five-year-old daughter told her, accusingly, "You had sex, drugs and rock and roll, and all we have is AIDS." (In fact, according to a 1988 report from the Center for Disease Control, AIDS was growing fastest among people over fifty.)

I am appalled but not surprised that undergraduates have naturalized the Xer category as theirs. In that large Brandeis sociology class, I proposed first off that age divisions are socially constructed, like the gendered and racialized differences they had already studied. They readily agreed. Then I took a written survey, asking, "Are Xers different from Boomers?" Two-thirds answered yes. Only a seventh offered any critique of the binary. All of them thought they were "Xers." Family

resentments get tied to the language provided by the war. . . .

From grade school on, children learn to think of themselves as united by age, but up to a point this cohort identity is modified by looking up to one's parents. The Brandeis students were not resentful of "the Boomers": many regarded them as energetic, successful, or activist. Two students retorted, "The Boomers are our *parents.*" While in college, almost-adult children may use war language, but with compassion. "Oh," gasped an undergraduate remorsefully after I'd given a talk at another college. "When my father lost his job last year, I said, 'Daddy, I don't want to have to compete with *you!*'" Age differences may harden later, in an atomistic and competitive workplace. Cohort-cohesiveness, midlife-othering, and self-absorption can congeal, as in the discomfort of a younger man who thinks that at twenty-three, he suffers from "workplace problems" because "many of the people I work with have children who are my age." If job milieus are conceived as ideally young, it may come to seem odd to have midlife workers around. Younger workers are taught the emotions they are supposed to feel toward midlife people: estrangement, resentment, anger, vengeance. . . .

People in their twenties who might feel this way are involved in two difficult processes simultaneously at the volatile turn of the century: forming new adult relationships with their parents and taking their first steps into the postindustrial global system. Handling both tasks simultaneously may be made more confusing and painful by the age war. . . .

It would be easy (but wrong) to assume that Boomer-bashing comes primarily from our children, who wouldn't knowingly hurt us, rather than from journalism, publishing, advertising, and the business class in general, which have profit stakes in generational otherness. In different ways, the Xer-Boomer war picks off people at all adult ages, separating and disempowering them. . . .

Age War: Managing the Crisis

Our son's hardscrabble mid-twenties had one intellectual benefit: it taught us to see through the contrived war between the Boomers and the Xers, and to see "in the name of the children" as a dangerous weapon that can be twisted flexibly—against the midlife, the workforce, and the future. Why did this form of age warfare occur in the 1990s? My view is that Boomer-bashing explains major historic, economic, and social changes in postindustrial capitalism in a way that reduces resistance to them. Since at least 1973, Americans have seen declines in quality jobs, real wages for men, employment security, and pension vesting; erosion of seniority systems; a rise in economic inequality; the loss of authority in professions such as teaching and medicine. However loudly the bull market roared in the 1990s, and however many billionaires American inequality produced, such losses affect people *at all ages* below the top 10 to 20 percent in income and wealth, and some at the top too. The age war is one spin put on the bad news. . . .

Each new group of the young hitting the job market has become a greater potential crisis. Ordinarily, workers just starting out must be resocialized from their adolescent prework values—the relative indulgence and cooperation of family life, and (for those who go to college) the autonomy of collegiate life—into the steeper hierarchies, greater atomization, self-subordination, and insecurity required by work. Employment compensates for such losses with independent income and anticipation of future augmentations of power. If work appeared futureless, some of the young might resist. . . . In the 1990s the media, treating "the young" as if they were a single economic class, said Xers suffered *disproportionately* from scarcity. Ian William's diatribe against the midlife generation was frequently quoted. "Boomers have the job market in a full nelson, asphyxiating any hope we have of approaching their collective wealth anytime before the year 2050." Hurry up now, it's *my* time. . . .

Age, you could say, manages many crises. Silly as this may seem, the constant noise of blame distracts people from thinking about power, class, or protest. It enables younger people who feel they cannot advance to attribute their woes not to the economic system but to Boomer piggishness. It manipulates history so other unfairnesses seem more equally shared. Boomer-envy deflected the anger of new entrants away from the much-touted members of their own cohort who became millionaires overnight. The age war turns all of us rhetorically toward the "natural" world of generations (seen as cyclical, with a time to start work and a time to bow out) and the little world of the nuclear family (seen as rivalrous). There, the best that adult children can do is to wait with impatience, and the best their midlife parents can do if they can't afford to retire early is to survive with guilt.

By magnifying a youth crisis, the age war disguises a real midlife crisis—the erosion of seniority, meaning not just the economic rewards for aging-into-the-midlife but the psychological and social ones. . . . As Anne Monroe pointed out in *Mother Jones*, discrimination against the middle-aged "is the dark underbelly of downsizing." Even college-educated men between forty-five and fifty-four, a once privileged group, are targeted. Corporations and state and city governments operate as if the only way to raise profits is to cut the wage base, pensions, and perks, not of the bosses but of the next-most-expensive employees. People downsized at midlife have the top cut off their expected age/wage curve. Nothing more needs to be at stake than the bottom line, once cutting "Boomers" also coincides with the young needing these jobs. . . .

If such complex losses can befall people as young as fifty—people who are allegedly so omnipotent—the life course can be poisoned for each cohort as it turns forty-five or forty. Or even younger.

To those under the spell of the age war, whatever their age, middle age may now seem to be an unjust proxy for power and wealth. . . .Thinking that there must be something wrong with the *relative* affluence of the midlife generation is an intellectual and political mistake. Seniority through age hierarchy is not empty veneration; it's a countersystem that brings improved conditions to people as they age into the middle years. Over the past thirty years, more women (white and minority) and men of color have gained this complex seniority than when the American Dream was intended only for some white men. Now that this is a more democratic system, it's more worth defending than in the past. Like any economic distribution it has some problems, but the alternatives are devastating. . . .

If the current midlife generation of workers do not resist middle-ageism for their own sake, they permit a flattened, foreshortened, proletarianized system to pass to their children. *Without seniority, the first wage a young adult earns could be the highest wage she or he ever earns.* Not many of the young ever started at $80,000 a year. They are more likely to begin in the bottom quintile, and 47 percent who begin there stay there. Certainly more young adults need help rising. Without a culturally inscribed seniority system, fewer would get out of their starting quintile. Do even the rich young want an age/wage curve that peaks before they have children or the habit of saving and that declines thereafter? (Would those who are now at midlife have wanted any earlier peak for themselves? If a peak at thirty had been their fate, would any of them have been able to tell a progress narrative as they aged?)

Those currently at midlife hold whatever structural and social advantages they have only temporarily, in trust for the workforce as a whole. The seniority "trust" is turning out to be more fragile than anyone my age ever imagined. A few more shoves like the age war and seniority may disappear forever. The "revenge of the Xers" on the middle aged—if capitalism destroys age hierarchy in their name—will in due course destroy them too. . . .

How Named Age Cohorts Work

The war depends on a supposedly neutral and scientific concept—that of age cohorts based on birth date. Wars take two sides. But a binary based on ages should be harder to manufacture than racial and gender oppositions, if only because the life course is usually seen, subjectively at least, as a continuum. Male-female difference has been fabled in song and story, but Boomers and Xers were never natural objects. The entire infernal machine was jerry-rigged while we watched. . . .

A "generation gap" is not ahistorical and universal, as writers innocent of history like to declare. Long periods can go by—"periods of social equilibrium and stability, when the environment and experience of successive generations remain pretty much the same," historian Al Richmond noted—when no gaps are perceptible. Generation gaps are constructed, rhetorically shaped for their moment. Audre Lorde warned that such constructions are a tool of a repressive society, facilitating historical amnesia. Middle-ageism now functions, for example, to make parents' work experience seem irrelevant and their impotent pain seem like useless nostalgia. It helps to construct younger people nervous about their futures, ignorant about economics and public policy, and selfish about their age class's alleged interests. The young raised in this embattled environment would be unlikely to feel that midlife job loss was an unmitigated evil.

Ethically, the worst evil of the age war may be that it undermines commonalities between parents and children. It pits them against one another as if they were unrelated social groups:

silenced audience versus dominators of discourse, small fraternity against huge horde, poor youths versus rich adults. The setting is a particular stage of the family life course, when two generations are in the workforce together. Middle-ageism and contrived scarcity raise the emotional stakes. For the younger people, the war cruelly depends on a poignant mix, of their youthful desire to be independent and their increasing need for help against market forces. For the midlife parents, it cruelly takes advantage of both their devotion to their children and their anxiety about their own decline. . . .

The age war has been so naturalized that "age" has been invisibly consolidated as a primary explanation of life-chance differences and justifier of contemporary feelings, personnel practices, legal decisions, economic conditions, and understandings of the future. . . . This is the culture war that nobody noticed.

Age Studies and Its Family Values

As members of multigenerational families and as political persons, we can resist age war by refusing to identify ourselves primarily, or at all, as members of named cohorts or (heaven help us) age "subcultures." Each of us gets to choose, after all, how to speak of our multiple identities. In writing as in talking, we can eschew all such terms, even in jest, put them within scare quotes, or, as here subject them to relentless scrutiny. "Boomer" and "Xer" have become almost unusable. . . .

I taught a class of first-year college students in a course called "Culture Matters," where my assignment asked them to find out what the media say "Generation Ys" are. Some came out saying, "I'm supposed to consider myself a 'Y,' but I don't." Others said flatly, "I'm a Y." Ys are being praised in order to disparage the Xers. One subgroup of Xers, the DINKS—double income, no kids—are being set up as the next Goliaths, kitted out to bully the younger Ys. As the mass media move on, Generation Y are the

next victims of its meretricious and deceptive "cult" of younger youth. However thoroughly the theorizing class demolishes cohort naming, this frenzy may well continue. For many people, the dominant media provide the *only* draft of history. Can its writers obtain enough intellectual freedom "somehow not to collaborate with the centralizing powers of our society?" in the words of Edward Said. Can they "make the connections that are otherwise hidden"—and investigate their own age politics?

* * *

The stage of life when two generations are in the workforce together can be a long moment of economic strength and mutual support, in which we stress our proud solidarity—kin united by love and concern over the future. . . .

If we can demonstrate the spuriousness of blaming parents, we can imagine turning that disappointment into politics. Together we may rescue our *mutual* future. . . .

Building a strong multigenerational front starts at the dinner table long before it begins in school and college classrooms. Whether or not they have children, trusted older figures and younger adults can start the conversation at a new place. By sharing age analysis, we can end the state of ignorance in which these cultural combats occur, undo contrived emotions, invent tactics for resisting the assumptions about age that print and visual culture inculcate. We can develop a grand detailed vision of an age politics. Only as the analysis of age comes to be practiced as widely as the analysis of gender and race can we begin to estimate the long-term negative consequences of using age as a wedge issue and having age terms become such peremptory linguistic categories.

From the dinner table and the classroom we can, if need be, step out together into the street, arm in arm. Adding activism to age consciousness, we can try to save the structures and values on which we must all rely: the age/wage curve, seniority, workforce solidarity, life-course continuity. A first step toward mutual rescue is to unmask the war between "the Xers" and "the Boomers" in all its mendacity and malevolence.

THINKING ABOUT THE READING

What is an age cohort? What age cohort do you belong to? Make a list of the various age cohorts that you are aware of and list the characteristics and stereotypes associated with each group. Now list some of the major historical events associated with each group. When do you think of yourself as part of a particular age cohort? What are the greatest challenges you think your age cohort will face in the coming years? Do you think these challenges are accurately portrayed in the media? Gullette argues that the media are creating a false war between age cohorts. Look for examples of this battle in news and other media sources.

To Die a Little

Migration and Coffee in Mexico and Central America

Luis Hernández Navarro

(2004)

Reyno Bartolo Hernández died of heatstroke in the Arizona desert near Yuma on May 22, 2001. He wasn't the only Mexican farmer who lost his life that day trying to cross the border. Thirteen of his countrymen and -women perished along with him in one more of the migratory tragedies of modern history.

Reyno and his companions were small coffee growers from the township of Atzalan, Veracruz. Atzalan is a formerly rich region but in recent years it has been impoverished by senseless policies. Until just a few years ago, few of its residents migrated to the United States. Then the price of coffee fell, and so did the price of citrus fruits and cattle. To make matters worse, bananas were attacked by fruit flies and the coffee crop was overcome by a devastating plant disease.

So little by little, the inhabitants of Atzalan set out along the route blazoned by small farmers from the states of Michoacan, Zacatecas, and Jalisco decades earlier. The coffee farmers began to look for a way to cross the 3,107-kilometer border that separated them from the United States, hoping to get to "the other side." In desperation, they hooked up with the infamous *polleros*, the smugglers who led them to their deaths.

Thomas Navarrete, long-time adviser to the cooperative that many Atzalan growers belong to, notes that the crisis in the region is dramatic and tragic. In many communities, around 70% of the residents have left, most to the United States. Navarrete points out that

before people didn't need to leave their communities, at least not like now. "Even Celso Rodríguez, the president of the cooperative, left to work in Arizona," he says.

The border has become a magnet for these coffee growers. If they get over—and many do—they earn $4–5 an hour, compared to the less than $4 a day they earn at home, if they're lucky. In the coffee communities, the success stories from the other side are impressive. Migrants come back and remodel their houses; they pour a new roof, replace wooden planks with concrete blocks. Everyone can see and envy the changes.

In regions where out-migration was practically unheard of, the flow is now massive. The risks, the bad treatment, the isolation that migrants suffer don't seem to matter much. There's a reward for those who make it.

According to University of Veracruz researcher Mario Pérez Monterosas, Veracruz and Chiapas (Mexico's largest coffee-growing state) form part of the latest migratory region. Between 1995 and 2000, some 800,000 people left Veracruz. Pérez Monterosas reports that Veracruz has been steadily climbing the ladder in the list of the states that contribute to the migrant population in the United States. In 1992 Veracruz was in 30th place, by 1997 it had risen to 27th, in 2000 it held 14th, and by 2002 it had become the fourth-largest sending state in the nation.

Before this wave started, emigration from Veracruz's coffee zones to the United States was so scarce that a 1994 survey registered only one township—Misantla—with cases of migration to the north, and there were only twelve.

The small farmers found dead in Yuma are another figure in the macabre statistics of migration and an indicator of the hardships born of the coffee crisis. Like the 17 bodies that appeared on May 14, 2003 inside and surrounding a trailer truck in Victoria, Texas, and the six drowned trying to swim across the Rio Bravo. Since 1994, when Operation Gatekeeper began, more than 3,000 migrants have died or disappeared, most of them Mexican farmers. That's an average of one a day. Sometimes, relatives of the dead never even find out what happened.

A declaration issued jointly by the Mexican and U.S. governments confirmed the tragedy of Reyno Bartolo and his companions, saying: "Mexico and the United States express their profound sadness and consternation for the death of 14 migrants in the Arizona desert."

A report from the International Coffee Organization on the coffee crisis is a little more explicit about the disaster: "Coffee producers from Mexico have died trying to get into the United States illegally after abandoning their farms . . . In general, the situation stimulates emigration to the cities and to industrialized countries." A motion on the coffee crisis presented in the U.S. House of Representatives on Nov. 13, 2002 mentioned the death of the 14 coffee growers from Veracruz.

But beyond the laments, these declarations say nothing about the reasons that led to their journey, and they avoid pointing the finger at the real culprit: the coffee crisis was caused by the decision of industrialized countries and large companies to end the system of quotas that maintained a balance between supply and demand and kept producer income at a decent level.

The indigenous Chatinos of Oaxaca believe that to migrate is to die a little. The experience of Reyno Bartolo and scores of others shows that frequently they die more

than a little. Their deaths bespeak the tragedy of small coffee growers in Mexico and Central America. Their stories form part of the story of coffee production in the region, and that is a story of government policies that turn farmers into surplus humanity.

Hell and Paradise

Migration and coffee have been associated throughout much of the history of Mexico and Central America. Historically, the coffee harvest has required hiring day laborers from different regions and countries, sometimes far from the coffee plantations themselves.

Between October and March, depending on the altitude and the region of the plants, the crop ripens. Thousands of workers are mobilized for harvest. Large plantations hire pickers. So do small growers. Usually, every member of the farm family works during the coffee harvest to ensure that the crop won't rot on the ground.

Pickers must be experienced. The beans must be selected one by one, to distinguish the ripe ones from the green, without damaging the branches or hurting the new shoots. Coffee plants often grow on steep hillsides where it is difficult to work. The harvested beans, collected in large baskets, must then be carried off on their backs for sorting and drying. Coffee picking is an ability acquired with years of hard work and tradition.

In the mid-1920s some 20,000 indigenous workers from the Chiapas highlands migrated annually to the lower Soconusco region and other coffee-growing lands to work the harvest. Between 1953 and 1960, some 12–18,000 people seasonally migrated each year. Communities in the highlands exported annually about a fifth of the economically active male indigenous population to work in the coffee harvest. To get to the plantations, they had to organize long expeditions, buy food, pay to stay in crowded rooms, and pay tolls to use the roads along the way.

Years later, the Chiapan work force was replaced with Guatemalans. Officially some 90,000 day laborers made the trip from their villages in Guatemala to the Soconusco to work on the plantations.

But the relationship between coffee and migration has undergone a fundamental change since the crisis in international coffee prices in 1989. Today there is a new coffee migration. This time it isn't related to the productive cycle of the plant. The new migration is fleeing the coffee fields and the enforced poverty of low prices. This migration heads north, to the United States, and stays there.

In 1989 the economic clause setting country export quotas of the International Coffee Organization was abandoned with the strong support of the Mexican government. Immediately, the price fell through the floor. Prices have gone up and down since the quota system ended, but since 1997 they have mostly gone down.

The only ones who win in this situation are the large companies and speculators on the commodities markets of New York and London. Coffee-growing communities, already poor, have grown poorer. As a response, thousands of farmers and laborers who cultivate and harvest the crop have decided to leave their homes permanently.

The old migration of laborers to harvest was marked by hardship. They went to the large plantations because they had to, not by choice. There they suffered abuse, hunger, and sickness. The journey was hell.

Indigenous peoples of the highlands remember the suffering: "We'd get an advance from the plantation so when we got there we already had a debt to pay off. Then the debt just gets bigger because the plantation doesn't give you anything, you have to pay for everything, even food . . . In addition to the hard work, we suffered from other things on the plantation. The boss doesn't care about the workers—if they're sick, it's not his concern. So they don't give us good food and we're always hungry . . . Before, the foremen mistreated workers a lot, they whipped them, beat them with branches, with belts, with the flat blade of the machete, kicked them. You got punished for anything. . .we were afraid of the plantation but we put up with it because we were poor."

The new immigration, although subject to many adversities, is a trip to a new world, full of hope. In their dreams, the migrants believe that the hardships and dangers they face as travelers will be compensated by the benefits of a new life in a new country. They leave behind a precarious existence that in recent years has become unendurable. They know the risks of the road, but they still set out. The color of the promised land is dollar-green.

Hugo Cantarero, a small coffee grower from Honduras, was detained and assaulted by Mexican police in Celaya, Guanajuato on his last trip. He is trying again. He explains his dream, as he waits for his chance to cross into Mexico in the Migrant House in Tecun Uman on the Guatemala-Mexico border:

"I have to make an effort to get there. I have a family. You take the risks of what awaits you. It's not safe, you can make it or you can die. Only God knows. In Honduras, you can't make it on a week's wages. A sack of fertilizer that used to cost 150 lempiras costs 380 now. You have to start cutting back on everything. For us, there's no medicine, no clothes, no education, no nothing. In Honduras, nobody has their own house, nobody has their own car. If you're poor you're used to living by God's mercy. But when you get to the United States it's such a beautiful world, so different. With a hundred dollars you can eat 15 days, you can buy a car for a hundred dollars.

"We have a fifty percent chance of making it to the United States and a fifty percent chance of dying along the way. We leave home and maybe never come back. So many Hondurans have died. But in the United States, you have benefits you can't even dream of in Honduras."

The two exoduses differ in many ways but especially in one fundamental aspect: while the migration to harvest forms part of agricultural labor, the march to the United States is not tied to any work identity. When you cross the border, it doesn't matter if you are a coffee-grower or not. You are simply another undocumented laborer in search of a new world.

Small farmers—and coffee growers as part of this group—have been condemned to extinction, declared superfluous and unnecessary. Their communities have been converted into huge warehouses of available work force.

For those who work in coffee, the temporary migration at harvest time can be a hell, but it's reversible. In contrast, those who flee coffee farming seek a modern paradise. As Hans Magnus Enzensberger affirms "nobody emigrates without the hope of promise to be fulfilled." And the United States is still, for them, the land of dreams.

The Emergency

For the past seven years, coffee plants throughout Mexico and Central America are full of beans with no hands to pick them. Red carpets of ripe coffee beans rot on the hillsides.

The small coffee grower has to make an enormous effort to pay hired hands. Many receive payment for the crop only when the harvest is over. They have to obtain credit from their organization, if they are organized, or fall into the hands of usurers. It is very difficult to receive financing. Although there are some laborers who work in exchange for food for the day, others receive almost as much for their work as what the raw coffee receives on the market.

In coffee communities there is widespread hunger, malnutrition, sickness, and death; there is also grief and worry. The price on the international market has fallen below $50 for 100 pounds. For many years, the average price oscillated between $120 and $140. Except for record levels between 1995 and 1996, the coffee price has

been low since 1989 when the economic clauses designed to stabilize prices were abandoned by the International Coffee Organization (ICO).

The coffee-producing countries of the region have been hard hit by the price crisis, especially the families who live off coffee production and harvest. Traditionally a source of income and wealth for the nations that cultivate it, in the past several years coffee has lost the dynamism and importance it once had.

Behind each cup of coffee consumed lies an explosive situation. During the past seven years, thousands of hungry small coffee growers and agricultural workers have blocked the highways and public offices of several Central American countries. In regions that rely on coffee production, out-migration, robbery, violence, and drug cultivation have all increased exponentially. Many growers have succumbed to the temptation to take the machete to the coffee plants and be done with it.

If the trend continues, the economic and social disasters will soon be followed by an environmental disaster. Coffee grows on hillsides and takes four years to begin to produce. Planting corn or converting coffee groves to pasture land to feed cattle results in severe soil erosion and deforested wooded zones.

The situation is urgent and dramatic. Coffee growers have sent out an anguished SOS to their governments, agribusiness companies, and consumers in developed countries. Most seem not to hear.

Coffee in the Region

Coffee came to the shores of the American continent at the end of the eighteenth century. A hundred years later it had become a key crop in Mexico and the countries that now constitute Central America. Fundamental aspects of the economic, social, environmental, and cultural life of these nations turn around the coffee bean.

Contrary to products like bananas, whose production is in the hands of foreigners, coffee cultivation is carried out mostly by national citizens. Not so with large-scale marketing. These links in the productive chain, by far the most lucrative, are controlled mostly and increasingly by transnational companies—either directly or through subsidiaries—that dominate the world market. In Honduras, five exporters control 52% of the market and two are owned by multinationals Newman and Volcafe. Five large foreign companies with subsidiaries in Mexico (AMSA, Jacobs, Expogranos, Becafisa-Volcafe, and Nestle) dominate the marketing chain there.

Coffee cultivation is vital to the economy of the region. Between 1990 and 2000 the region obtained annual income from coffee of around $1.7 billion—11% of the resources obtained from all exports. During the past two decades, coffee cultivation was the most important economic activity in Honduras, above bananas and lumber. It contributed 5–8% of the GDP. In El Salvador, sales of coffee abroad reached 7.7% of GDP in 1985 and had fallen to 1.9% by 2001. In Nicaragua, coffee represented 25% of all exports between 1995 and 2000.

In Mexico, coffee was one of the main agricultural exports and brought in some $600 million a year on average over the past decade. Nearly 6% of the economically active population of that country depended on coffee for their livelihoods.

In exporting nations, the coffee business provides critical income to the rural workforce. Approximately 1.6 million people derive at least part of their income from coffee in Central America—about 28% of the economically active population. In some nations it's much higher—in Nicaragua it rises to 42% and in Guatemala to 31%.

It is estimated that for each producer there are eight farm workers dedicated to coffee. During the past decade in El Salvador, this economic activity generated 155,000 permanent jobs as agricultural workers. These workers earned an average of $7.60 a day in Costa Rica, $3.60 in El Salvador, $3.20 in Guatemala, $3.00 in Honduras, and $2.30 in Nicaragua.

Although in some countries a significant part of the production is concentrated by large growers that form part of the authoritarian oligarchies, there are also many small producers that participate in this economic sector. Agrarian reforms in countries like Mexico, Nicaragua, and El Salvador substantially affected large landholders, in some cases radically changing the social composition of the producers of the sector.

In this region, there are 300,000 direct producers, of which 200,000 are small producers. In Guatemala there are 62,649 producers but they employ 2.25 million workers through the productive chain. In Honduras there are 112,000 producers. In Mexico, the last census showed the figure at 480,000 producers and more than 3 million laborers.

The Disaster

Berta Cáceres is a well-off coffee grower in El Salvador. Or was. "Beginning about five years ago," she recounted to a reporter of *El Diario de Hoy*, "we stopped earning enough to pay costs. I've had to sell thirty head of cattle each year. We've sold our irrigation equipment and suspended the electricity . . . everything nice we had on the property. One of the last head of cattle we had left, this year we had to sell off fifty more. Coffee just doesn't pay."

Although there was a slight increase in price in the last harvest, the international price has fallen to an historic low and there are no expectations that it will improve significantly in the short term. The crisis of overproduction and speculation on the commodities trading floor seems to be permanent.

In Central America, moreover, the economic crisis coincided with an array of natural disasters. In 1998 Hurricane Mitch devastated infrastructure and crops, especially in Honduras. Two earthquakes shook San Salvador in January and

February of 2001. At the end of 2001, tropical storm Michelle damaged Honduras and Nicaragua. Since the spring of 2002 the region has suffered a severe and prolonged drought that led to farm losses of more than 80% in several regions of Guatemala and El Salvador. InterAction, a U.S. nongovernmental organization, calculated in April of 2002 that close to a million people in the region suffered problems of food security.

This situation has worsened in the region due to the implementation of structural adjustment and stabilization programs that have severely affected the agricultural sector. In Guatemala, for example, the office that provided extension services to farmers was closed down. The functions of regulation and redistribution that in some countries were carried out by governmental institutions and state-owned enterprises have been cut.

In Nicaragua a succession of administrations used coffee revenues as a discretionary fund. Resources obtained thanks to the export of the coffee bean have been used as [a] petty cash box to meet the financial needs resulting from earthquakes, eruptions, wars, droughts, and floods. Despite the fact that a price stabilization fund was created in the 1980s through growers' contributions, Nicaraguan coffee farmers did not receive price support in key times.

The crisis in coffee activity has caused severe economic, social, and environmental problems. In economic terms, there has been a clear drop in profits, mainly for small and medium growers and their cooperatives. This has led to a reduction in investment, which in turn leads to a greater drop in employment and income. Agricultural export earnings have plummeted. The increase in unemployment has deepened poverty for rural families and forced emigration. Many growers have destroyed their coffee to plant basic grains and corn, reducing the environmental benefits that coffee production provides.

Export income in Central America fell from $938 million in 2000/2001 to $700 million in 2001/2002. The drop in exports hurt the balance of payments and affected economic activity as a whole, causing financial disaster for some governments.

In addition to the drastic fall in income, the growers of the region suffered from the absence of credit and high interest rates, as well as the high cost of inputs, transportation, and labor. Bankruptcy has led to the loss of plantations and farms, the capacity to obtain new credit, and also the collapse of financial institutions. More and more, this function of providing credit is being taken over by loan sharks.

A survey carried out by the World Bank in Nicaragua and El Salvador in 2001 indicates that small growers have deepening problems keeping their farms. In many cases they have quit caring for the plants. This has meant that plagues have seriously affected productivity. Many growers do not fertilize and do not weed. Yields have dropped by 50%.

Compared to the previous three years, labor demand fell in 2001 by 30% in Guatemala, Honduras, and Nicaragua; 20% in El Salvador; and 12% in Costa Rica. In total, 42 million work days have been lost, or 170,000 fulltime jobs. Income has fallen by $140 million. Day laborers are out of work and out of luck—they don't even benefit from the scarce governmental support that growers previously received in some countries.

Simultaneously, the international coffee market generates hefty profits for the large intermediaries, especially the roasters and branders. Transnational corporations have significantly increased their presence in national markets, as buyers, processors, or retailers.

Gilberto Recinos, a small grower from Huehuetenango, Guatemala, describes the situation: "The small producers depend directly on coffee. If it doesn't pay well, their standard of living goes down; they don't have resources for food, housing or plant cultivation. They lack everything; they have no way to live. The majority is suffering or barely holding on.

"Before many people benefited directly or indirectly from coffee: the workers, the truckers, all had a source of income. Today anyone can see the consequences. Jobs vanished, wages went down, business dried up, and income is no longer generated. It affects education, health, and migration to Mexico or the United States or the capital—for those who have money. And those who don't? We're fried!"

Small Coffins

February 2003. In a hospital located in western El Salvador, Adán Domínguez struggles to stay alive. He suffers from severe malnutrition.

Adán shares a room with another 32 babies who, like him, are on the edge of death. Infants, all of them, sons and daughters of small coffee growers or laborers who work the coffee harvests. Hungry, sick from poverty and want. All are victims of the crisis that brought down the coffee price.

According to reports from El Salvador's Ministry of Health, during 2002 there were 52 children of coffee producers under five who died of malnutrition and 4,000 more became seriously ill.

The doctors in charge of the tending to the tragedy explained: "Many people who depend on coffee are now unemployed. It gets harder and harder for the families to provide for their children."

Divina Belmonte, spokesperson for UNICEF, agrees with this diagnosis. "An increase in infant malnutrition has been reported in various coffee-producing zones of El Salvador," she stated. "Food is scarcer and scarcer, particularly in the provinces of Achuapan, Sonsonete, Santa Ana, and La Libertad, where nearly 30,000 families suffer hunger as a result of the near 50% decline in coffee prices during the last three years. . . ."

Hunger also plagues Guatemala. In 2002, the U.S. Agency for International Development

(USAID) stated that the country was experiencing "an acute crisis in generalized infant malnutrition, caused by the accumulated effects of drought and much reduced employment in the coffee sector. The most recent census information indicates that more than 30,000 children in 91 townships suffer acute malnutrition. Of these, more than 7,000 are in a state of moderate to grave consumption."

The situation was so serious this year that a Guatemalan doctor stated, "What is happening is a catastrophe. There has always been poverty and temporary unemployment, but I have never seen hunger as real as now. People literally have nothing to eat except tortillas."

In Nicaragua conditions are no better. José Manuel Rodríguez, five years old and a resident of Rancho Grande, lost his life to hunger. The same happened to Daniela Díaz and Alexander Díaz, both just two years old. Between June of 2002 and February 2003 21 children died of malnutrition and related sicknesses. The following months were as bad or worse. One after another, their deaths became the cold statistics of the coffee crisis.

"I had four children but one that was 15 months old died on Thursday of malnutrition, lack of food and medicine. I have another three sick but I need help because my house is made of plastic and I don't have anywhere to go when it rains." said Yessenia Martínez, one of the thousands of hungry farm workers in northern Nicaragua, in September of 2002.

In August 2003 coffee workers marched from their mountain homes to the provincial capital of Matagalpa to protest the conditions that caused 14 community members to die of hunger, including two children. Marlyn, a 22-year-old mother and her 16-month old son both participated in the march. She sobbed: "We haven't had anything to eat and we can't stand it any more. This is terrible. There is no work and the children are dying of hunger because now there is nothing in the countryside."

Coffee regions infested with mosquitos, malaria, and dengue are spreading. "The women and children are the most affected," affirmed doctor Juan Carlos Sánchez, director of SILAIS in Matagalpa. . . .

The situation is so terrifying that the report of the mayor of Matagalpa points out that between January and August 2002, there were 120 coffins donated to the rural sector, all of them distributed to families and many of them child-sized. The year before only 50 coffins had been given out.

The Other Border

Guatemalan workers have been migrating to harvest coffee in the Soconusco region of Chiapas for years. Daniela Spencer noted that for many Guatemalan Indians work on the coffee plantations became a form of refuge from mistreatment in their own country. For many years there was a tradition between Mexico and Guatemala of free transit and trade, so much so that it wasn't until 1917 that an immigration office was established in Chiapas. Migratory flows from Central America to Mexico have a long history, although the heaviest traffic began in 1965.

The Soconusco is a natural corridor that connects the Isthmus of Tehuantepec in Mexico with Central America. The region grew wealthy from coffee cultivation during the period when Porfirio Díaz governed pre-revolutionary Mexico. Díaz established a new pattern of settlement based on the agro-export economy. Coffee was exported to Europe through what is now Puerto Madero. In 1908 the first train route was built and in 1965 the Pan-American Highway. Today not only merchandise but also labor moves along these routes on its way to the northern border.

Every year 200,000 Guatemalans come to Mexico to work on the coffee plantations. But they are not the only ones to cross the border. Soconusco has become a transit region—so much so that in the south an undocumented worker is arrested every two minutes. In 2003, 187,000 people without papers were detained.

Nearly 40% of those were in Chiapas. This year, according to data from Mexico's National Institute of Migration, the figure will likely double. Ninety percent come from Guatemala, Honduras, and El Salvador.

The southern border has become a no-man's land for Central American immigrants. In crossing, they are run over by trains, stabbed by bands of delinquents, robbed by police and Army personnel. Many women are raped and killed. Families are split up. Some 100 bands of smugglers operate in the Mexico-Guatemala border zone, charging migrants for getting them a little closer to their destination of the United States.

The Migrant's Story

Even before arriving at the Guatemalan border town of Tecun Uman on their way to Tapachula, Central American migrants are oftentimes victims of extortion. The road to El Salvador already seems long, and you've really just started. You left your family, your property, your coffee farm. You're in debt up to your eyeballs. You know you shouldn't go out on the streets after six. It's too dangerous. This city is a free-for-all of drug-runners and black-market arms dealers. Territory of human smugglers. City of *hortelanos, tricicleteros,* loan sharks, and restaurant owners who live off people like you, people just passing through.

It was already risky getting this far. It's not like it used to be. The U.S. Border Patrol trains the Guatemalan special army forces called *kaibiles.* It provides them with technology. Now you don't have to wait to get to the United States to suffer. The hard line begins in your own country. Then it gets harder in Mexico. Mexico has become Washington's southern gatekeeper, guarding the backyard entrance. The government's Southern Plan sealed the border. Santiago Creel, Mexico's Minister of the Interior said as much: "The Mexican government is prepared to cut off the growing flow of foreigners that use the country as a transit point in their efforts to reach the United States."

The house where you wait to cross is not big enough for everyone who's waiting. You're piled on top of each other. In the night they lock you up with chains and armed guards. They tell you that you'll be part of a crew going to work in the fields of the Soconusco using false papers. You should carry a machete and a gunny sack. You won't cross the Sucihiate River in a tire boat, or swim like others do. But you have to learn to talk like a Mexican, know about that country even if you're just passing through. They sold you a booklet for ten bucks. There you read about Mexico's "Child Heroes," what the president's wife's name is, the colors of the flag. Others even obtain a voter card to given them a new identity.

You wish you could travel in a banana trailer. It has air conditioning so you wouldn't be asphyxiated. But you don't have enough money. Not even for a chicken truck. You have to go by train. You're young and strong. You can stand the days. You won't go by boat. You know what happens to those who take a shark boat to Salina Cruz and then a smaller boat to Acapulco. How they suffer on the rogue seas. What happened on August 16th when two boats sank, one with 20 people on board, the other with 30. Not one person made it to shore. No, this business of "kill or be killed" isn't for you.

You don't know the numbers but it's a lot. Travelers like you who die at sea, in the rivers, on the bridges, on the train tracks, in the trailers. The Center for Central American Resources in El Salvador says that between 1997 and 2000 almost 25,000 Central Americans disappeared seeking the American dream. Ten thousand were Salvadoran. Many of the families still don't know what has happened and may never know.

You're on the Mexican side. You wait for the train, the beast, as it's called here. The train stations stink. You wait hours. There are others like you. Biding their time in graveyards, vacant lots, underneath bridges. As you go on

your way, the vigilance will get worse. Soldiers guard the rails. Your itinerary is not made up by a travel agency. The routes, the operatives of the Migra, your own fatigue, and pure luck will determine your course.

The beast arrives. When the wheels of the convoy begin to move you run as fast as you can, grab hold and hang on. If you get run over, it's the end. How many like you have lost arms and legs? Every month seven or eight train amputees arrive at the regional hospital in Tapachula.

Bad luck. This train doesn't carry grain or sand. But at least it's not raining. Better not to go inside the wagons—if they close you can get asphyxiated. Better to hang on like a monkey, taking care to duck the high tension wires. In the tunnels you move onto the side and tie your arms on with wire. You cannot sleep. If you doze off you fall. You protect yourself from the cold with a windbreaker. You wrap up your hands. In tunnels and on cold days the steel of the train freezes.

This time there aren't any gangs. Often they jump on to steal. To them, 50 pesos can cost your life. The Maras. They chase you, catch you, and beat you up. Hit you in the face and body. Throw you off the train. Abuse the women.

When the immigration agents get on you run to the back and jump. It doesn't matter if the train is moving. They can't catch you. You wait until another train comes by, start to run, then get off in Huamantla. It's near Apizaco, at the end of the longest tunnel, there's a checkpoint. When you see a red antenna that announces the arrival in Lechería and you do it again. That's where most of the cargo trains heading north end up. It's the halfway border, and they'll get you for sure there. If it's not the thieves, it's the police. So you go around the station and wait for the next train. From there the freight trains head out for the north.

You already have a different gaze. Same with everyone else traveling with you. You've become tougher—from the hardships, the fear, the waiting, and the horrors. You smell different. Not just for the sweat and dirt. Little by little, the smell of death gets under your skin. That's what the refuges that help migrants along the route smell like.

You head out to Coahuila, another stop for the freight trains. You cross at Piedras Negras or Ciudad Acuña. You think the vigilance will be less there. But private guards watch the trains. They're even more violent. In less than a year three migrants were assassinated in Coahuila. Elmer Alexander Batrahona was shot. Ismael Jesus Martinez was stoned to death in November 2002. All by the employees of a company called Canine Protection Systems, hired to guard the trains. Its president is Miguel Nassar Daw, son of one of the main men responsible for Mexico's dirty war.

In Saltillo the police stop you. They hit you and take your money. It's like Gabriela Rodriguez Pizarro, Special Rapporteur on the Human Rights of Migrants for the UN says: "In Mexico there is a generalized climate of hostility and many take advantage of the migrant's vulnerability." It doesn't matter that in El Salvador in September of 2000 Vicente Fox offered major efforts to respect the human rights of migrants. Pure rhetoric. Nothing personal.

Your arrive in Laredo. Finally the border. Salvadorans like you work outside the municipal building. They wash the pick-ups of the law enforcement officers. From here you can't get to the other side. Operation Hold the Line, or Rio Grande on the Mexican side, leaves no holes. So you go to Las Antenas, 14 kilometers away. On the edge of the river there are some small beaches. You pay the *patero*—that's what they call *polleros* or smugglers here—to use the rafts and hide in the bushes. They, in turn have to pay a quota for "use rights" to the "Z," the thugs of Osiel Cárdenas, head of the Gulf Cartel.

You shove off into the river and the current takes you. When you reach the other side you start to look for a safe house. There you wait until they put you in a truck with 60 other people. That's how your compatriots died in Victoria, Texas. But it's not your time yet. You're off to Georgia. Your cousin is working the harvest there. It all starts again.

The Exodus

Coffee growers and laborers are the latest link in the historic migration to the United States. They arrive when the border is closed, the cost of the journey, and support networks hardly exist. These new migrants have little or no knowledge of the geography, physical and social, they will face.

To emigrate, coffee growers have to go into debt. They mortgage their land and houses and are charged interest rates of at least 20% a month. Every day that passes is more money they owe. It's urgent that they arrive at their destination quickly. That's why so many die in desperation in the desert.

Often they fall into the hands of abusive smugglers. When the "guides" are from the same region they have a certain responsibility to the family to take care of their "charge." But when they are strangers, they have no commitment to anybody. Ignorance of the journey means that the new migrants frequently fall in with smugglers who sell them or abandon them. They are easy victims of assaults and extortion. All along the way people lie in wait seeking to exploit them.

The coffee farmer sets out for the north ill-prepared. He or she arrives without boots, or water, carrying money. Instead of making a deal in the village or through someone they know in some city in the United States, arrangements are made in bus depots and train stations. It's no wonder that events happen like that of August 2002, when two Chiapan youths were found floating dead in the All-American Canal in California—just yards from U.S. soil.

Alan Bersin, one of the strategists of Operation Gatekeeper, explains the complexity of crossing for new migrants: "Now the ones who cross illegally have to cross extremely difficult terrain, deep rocky canyons, full of thorny bushes, practically without water and with peaks of over 6,000 feet, or over peaks nearly 6,000 feet high, or through desolate and dangerous deserts. Before they crossed in areas with almost immediate access to highways, but today it's a hard walk of two to three days out to the highway. The guides are more necessary than ever and charge accordingly."

Many new migrants do not speak Spanish or it isn't their first language. It's common that in the United States there are no translators in their language. The fact is basic to receive medical attention or legal defense. In the 80s Trique Adolfo Ruiz Álvarez and Mixtec Santiago Ventura Morales were jailed in Oregon for a misunderstanding that derived from not knowing English or Spanish. Álvarez was locked up in a mental institution and sedated for over two years, while Ventura was unjustly held prisoner for four years.

The new migratory flows are directed toward places where migrants didn't go before. The destinations are states located in the east coast such as Georgia, Alabama, Tennessee, or the Carolinas. The conditions there are more difficult. On arrival they must live in bridges, caves, and open fields, where they suffer discrimination—often from their own compatriots established there. . . .

The conditions of the journey, the crossing, and the changes in diet weaken defenses and expose migrants to many illnesses. Several cases of tuberculosis have been reported in cities like San Diego, Los Angeles, and Santa Ana. It is easy to catch something when travelers are locked up together in the trunk of a car for hours. In 2004, 30 cases of Central Americans with malaria were reported in Orizaba, Veracruz and one died. And it's hard to get well. "There are people who come back sick from the north," they say in the Chinantec community of Santiago Yaitepec. "There they don't have *curanderos*, because only young people go, and the old don't leave the village and the young don't know how to cure. Just

kids of 25 or less are the ones who leave for the north, the old people don't want to go."

The United States isn't the only destination. There is heavy migration of Nicaraguan workers to Costa Rica since there they can earn double what they make at home. This situation has become so critical for Nicaraguan plantation owners owing to the lack of labor that President Enrique Bolaños declared in late December of 2003 that the nation could lose up to 200,000 quintals of coffee. . . .

Migration is not limited to the poorest. Even the sons of plantation owners have had to follow the road north to the United States. They are charged with maintaining the family pride; for years they lived a privileged life, wore leather boots, drove big trucks, and looked down on the Indians. Now, those who haven't migrated north wear rubber boots and mended clothes. The men use the dollars from the remittances to hire seasonal workers. And, irony of life, the smugglers treat plantation owners and day laborers the same.

To Die a Little

How does immigration affect the indigenous coffee communities that have conserved their ethnic community identity?

Over 10 years ago, writes researcher Daniel Oliveras de Ita, emigration from San Juan Quiahije in the Chatina region of Oaxaca began when the first tour migrants arrived in the United States. Their main economic activity was coffee growing, working as seasonal laborers or dependent producers for the coffee plantations of the region.

Before going north, the travelers went to the *curanderos*, or healers, of the village. The shamans told them to place candles for the saints, for example to Santiago Yaitepec, or the Virgin of Juquila, or Saint John Quiahije, depending on which saints the *curanderos* said. They instruct them to purify themselves and they have to abstain from having sex for 7–13 days. They also must not swear or fight during this time, they should behave well, and walk straight and narrow so that favors will be granted them.

Those who go north without consulting the *curanderos* have problems, so they communicate with their parents or elders and tell them about the situation. The family represents them and consults with the *curanderos* who tell them what to do to change the luck of their relative on the other side. They are instructed to carry candles to the saints and the dead in the cemetery.

Before going north the youth go with the *curanderos* who eat the sacred mushroom (*hui ya jo*), narrates Narciso García Urbano of Santa María Yolotepec. When they eat the mushroom they see the destiny of the people who will migrate for work. They can see if they will be able to cross the border or if they will have problems along the sway, if they will find work and if it will go well. They see if one will fail in the north. They also go to the graveyard to ask permission and health from the dead, their grandparents. They ask for help from the tomb to care for them along the way, so nothing happens to them and they find work and return well.

In Santiago Yaitepec the people say that to migrate north is to die a little. When a family member is absent, either dead or far way, the rest of the family still performs healing and rituals for them, using photographs and clothing. In the hills the people strike the clothing of the dead and migrants with a staff, and light candles and ask that wherever they are they do not suffer and repent for their sins.

The young people expect to leave. Adolescents begin to migrate at 13. Most work for about three years in the United States and return at 17 to take on their first cargo as topil (a community post that forms part of the traditional cargo system).

Catholic people with strong family ties do not change so drastically in the United States. They continue to carry out community service and perform cargos. These are the ones trained in the Chatina customs.

For others, however, without the preparation and belief in the traditions and customs, they return with new ideas that they often seek to impose. They no longer accept traditional authority and want to be bosses themselves. They refuse to serve in low-level cargos because they come back with money and they feel powerful. They do not obey the political or religious hierarchies. When they return they want to be municipal presidents.

Are the Chatinos of De Ita's study typical of indigenous coffee migrants? We don't know. Migration has transformed the logic of the community, its dreams and its demons. It has had to reinvent itself.

In a recent book, Jonathan Fox and Gaspar Rivera-Salgado note that in spite of the adverse conditions that indigenous migrants face in the United States, many have found ways to build a broad range of political, social, and civic organizations to fight for strategic objectives. In these cases, the migratory mobility of the peoples instead of weakening them has done the opposite. There they have created and recreated identities. Oaxacalifornia, that imaginary community that brings together the many Oaxacan villages where migrants are born and the U.S. cities where they live now is the new space of a transnational society.

The lack of papers and the increased risks in crossing the borders after September 11th make it harder for migrants to return to their home countries. With no real perspective of better coffee prices (the increase in the last harvest is temporary and is still below the costs of production), without possibilities of employment in their places of origin, establishing oneself in the north is becoming progressively more attractive for those who once produced coffee.

Responses to the Crisis

In September 2002, 3,000 Nicaraguan coffee day laborers and their families camped on the Pan-American highway near Las Tunas, about 97 kilometers from the capital. Their presence interrupted traffic. On Wednesday the 11th, they blocked Central America's largest Pacific highway for ten hours.

The majority of the participants have been out of work for months. "We want real jobs, they can't hire us to 'work for food'. We want work with a wage, we want stable jobs." One hundred hours after the protest started, negotiations ended with some important agreements.

But Las Tunas is more the exception than the rule in the coffee-producing world. Instead of leading to open protests, the discontent and despair in the sector have lead to emigration as an escape valve. Protests have broken out in many places, but they do not even begin to reflect the dimensions of the tragedy.

The crisis has struck cooperatives of small producers and their struggles for self-administration. Although the crisis has stimulated conversion to organic coffee, fair trade and gourmet markets, it has also reduced membership in grassroots organizations.

Certainly those market niches have grown with the crisis, to the point where Guatemala has become second-only to Colombia as a global exporter of specialty coffee. The conversion toward these markets has been financed by the World Bank. USAID has funded a $20 million support program for marketing and technical assistance in the area for 2002–2006—just as it did to increase coffee production in Costa Rica to rein in "Sandino-communism" in Nicaragua. But niche marketing benefits a very small percentage of coffee producers and fails to resolve the central issues.

Civil society in Mexico and Latin America has shown a notable lack of interest in the migrants' situation. Migrant services are provided by voluntary organizations with scarce resources, mostly of a religious nature. While in Europe, the global justice movement has made the fight against xenophobia and struggle for universal citizenship central demands and areas of work, for those left in the Americas, support for migrants is nonexistent. The exception has been, as in so many other cases, the Zapatistas. The autonomous governments punish smugglers and assist Central American undocumented migrants, offering them water, housing, and food for free.

Migration in the area has grown so rapidly that no one can deal with it. Governments laud the millions of dollars of remittances that keep their countries afloat and keep quiet about the human rights violations suffered by their countrymen and -women in the United States.

Ironically, coffee is one of the products where Mexican and Central American farmers should be profitable according to the theory of comparative advantages. But instead of a bonanza, coffee cultivation under current conditions has condemned the growers to poverty, exile, death, or charity. Meanwhile, transnational traders and international investment funds accumulate huge fortunes.

THINKING ABOUT THE READING

What is the relationship between coffee production and migration? How do the United States and other developed countries influence this production? Compare this reading with the experiences of the nannies who come from other countries to the United States (Hochschild in Chapter 7). Does this kind of immigration seem more or less desirable and tolerated from the perspective of the receiving country? Discuss some of the distinctions.

The United States and other developed countries are very interested in having "free trade" agreements with developing regions such as Latin American. Is it hypocritical for these nations to want to be able to move their factories and related laws across borders freely, but not want to allow the free movement across borders of immigrants whose lives are affected by these companies and laws?

These Dark Satanic Mills

William Greider

(1997)

. . . If the question were put now to everyone, everywhere—do you wish to become a citizen of the world?—it is safe to assume that most people in most places would answer, no, they wish to remain who they are. With very few exceptions, people think of themselves as belonging to a place, a citizen of France or Malaysia, of Boston or Tokyo or Warsaw, loyally bound to native culture, sovereign nation. The Chinese who aspire to get gloriously rich, as Deng instructed, do not intend to become Japanese or Americans. Americans may like to think of themselves as the world's leader, but not as citizens of "one world."

The deepest social meaning of the global industrial revolution is that people no longer have free choice in this matter of identity. Ready or not, they are already of the world. As producers or consumers, as workers or merchants or investors, they are now bound to distant others through the complex strands of commerce and finance reorganizing the globe as a unified marketplace. The prosperity of South Carolina or Scotland is deeply linked to Stuttgart's or Kuala Lumpur's. The true social values of Californians or Swedes will be determined by what is tolerated in the factories of Thailand or Bangladesh. The energies and brutalities of China will influence community anxieties in Seattle or Toulouse or Nagoya.

. . . Unless one intends to withdraw from modern industrial life, there is no place to hide from the others. Major portions of the earth, to be sure, remain on the periphery of the system, impoverished bystanders still waiting to be included in the action. But the patterns of global interconnectedness are already the dominant reality. Commerce has leapt beyond social consciousness and, in doing so, opened up challenging new vistas for the human potential. Most people, it seems fair to say, are not yet prepared to face the implications. . . .

The process of industrialization has never been pretty in its primitive stages. Americans or Europeans who draw back in horror at the present brutalities in Asia or Latin America should understand that they are glimpsing repetitions of what happened in their own national histories, practices that were forbidden as inhumane in their own countries only after long political struggle. To make that historical point complicates the moral responses, but does not extinguish the social question.

The other realm, of course, is the wealthy nation where the established social structure is under assault, both from market forces depressing wages and employment and from the political initiatives to dismantle the welfare state. The governments' obligations to social equity were erected during the upheavals of the last century to ameliorate the harsher edges of unfettered capitalism; now they are in question again. The economic pressures to shrink or withdraw public benefits are relentless, yet no one has explained how wealthy industrial nations will maintain the social peace by deepening their inequalities.

A standard response to all these social concerns is the reassuring argument that market forces will eventually correct them—if no one interferes. The new wealth of industrialization, it is said, will lead naturally to middle-class democracy in the poorer countries and the barbarisms will eventually be eradicated. In the older societies, it is assumed that technology will create new realms of work that in time replace the lost employment, restore living wages and spread the prosperity widely again. People need only be patient with the future and not interrupt the revolution.

The global system has more or less been proceeding on these assumptions for at least a generation and one may observe that the unfolding reality has so far gravely disappointed these expectations. Nor does the free-market argument conform with the actual history of how democratic development or social equity was advanced over the last two centuries, neither of which emerged anywhere without titanic political struggles. A more pointed contradiction is the hypocrisy of those who make these arguments. If multinational enterprises truly expect greater human freedom and social equity to emerge from the marketplace, then why do they expend so much political energy to prevent these conditions from developing?

In any case, the theoretical arguments about the future do not satisfy the moral question that exists concretely at present. If one benefits tangibly from the exploitation of others who are weak, is one morally implicated in their predicament? Or are basic rights of human existence confined to those civilized societies wealthy enough to afford them? Everyone's values are defined by what they will tolerate when it is done to others. Everyone's sense of virtue is degraded by the present reality. . . .

Two centuries ago, when the English industrial revolution dawned with its fantastic invention and productive energies, the prophetic poet William Blake drew back in moral revulsion. Amid the explosion of new wealth, human destruction was spread over England—peasant families displaced from

their lands, paupers and poorhouses crowded into London slums, children sent to labor at the belching ironworks or textile looms. Blake delivered a thunderous rebuke to the pious Christians of the English aristocracy with these immortal lines:

> And was Jerusalem builded here
> Among these dark Satanic mills?

Blake's "dark Satanic mills" have returned now and are flourishing again, accompanied by the same question.[1]

On May 10, 1993, the worst industrial fire in the history of capitalism occurred at a toy factory on the outskirts of Bangkok and was reported on page 25 of the *Washington Post*. The *Financial Times* of London, which styles itself as the daily newspaper of the global economy, ran a brief item on page 6. The *Wall Street Journal* followed a day late with an account on page 11. The *New York Times* also put the story inside, but printed a dramatic photo on its front page: rows of small shrouded bodies on bamboo pallets—dozens of them—lined along the damp pavement, while dazed rescue workers stood awkwardly among the corpses. In the background, one could see the collapsed, smoldering structure of a mammoth factory where the Kader Industrial Toy Company of Thailand had employed three thousand workers manufacturing stuffed toys and plastic dolls, playthings destined for American children.[2]

The official count was 188 dead, 469 injured, but the actual toll was undoubtedly higher since the four-story buildings had collapsed swiftly in the intense heat and many bodies were incinerated. Some of the missing were never found; others fled home to their villages. All but fourteen of the dead were women, most of them young, some as young as thirteen years old. Hundreds of the workers had been trapped on upper floors of the burning building, forced to jump from third- or fourth-floor windows, since the main exit doors were kept locked by the managers, and the narrow stairways became clotted with trampled bodies or collapsed.

When I visited Bangkok about nine months later, physical evidence of the disaster was gone—the site scraped clean by bulldozers—and Kader was already resuming production at a new toy factory, built far from the city in a rural province of northeastern Thailand. When I talked with Thai labor leaders and civic activists, people who had rallied to the cause of the fire victims, some of them were under the impression that a worldwide boycott of Kader products was under way, organized by conscience-stricken Americans and Europeans. I had to inform them that the civilized world had barely noticed their tragedy.

As news accounts pointed out, the Kader fire surpassed what was previously the worst industrial fire in history—the Triangle Shirtwaist Company fire of 1911—when 146 young immigrant women died in similar circumstances at a garment factory on the Lower East Side of Manhattan. The Triangle Shirtwaist fire became a pivotal event in American politics, a public scandal that provoked citizen reform movements and energized the labor organizing that built the International Ladies Garment Workers Union and other unions. The fire in Thailand did not produce meaningful political responses or even shame among consumers. The indifference of the leading newspapers merely reflected the tastes of their readers, who might be moved by human suffering in their own communities but were inured to news of recurring calamities in distant places. A fire in Bangkok was like a typhoon in Bangladesh, an earthquake in Turkey.

The Kader fire might have been more meaningful for Americans if they could have seen the thousands of soot-stained dolls that spilled from the wreckage, macabre litter scattered among the dead. Bugs Bunny, Bart

Simpson and the Muppets. Big Bird and other *Sesame Street* dolls. Playskool "Water Pets." Santa Claus. What the initial news accounts did not mention was that Kader's Thai factory produced most of its toys for American companies—Toys "R" Us, Fisher-Price, Hasbro, Tyco, Arco, Kenner, Gund and J. C. Penney—as well as stuffed dolls, slippers and souvenirs for Europe.[3]

Globalized civilization has uncovered an odd parochialism in the American character: Americans worried obsessively over the everyday safety of their children, and the U.S. government's regulators diligently policed the design of toys to avoid injury to young innocents. Yet neither citizens nor government took any interest in the brutal and dangerous conditions imposed on the people who manufactured those same toys, many of whom were mere adolescent children themselves. Indeed, the government position, both in Washington and Bangkok, assumed that there was no social obligation connecting consumers with workers, at least none that governments could enforce without disrupting free trade or invading the sovereignty of other nations.

The toy industry, not surprisingly, felt the same. Hasbro Industries, maker of Playskool, subsequently told the *Boston Globe* that it would no longer do business with Kader, but, in general, the U.S. companies shrugged off responsibility. Kader, a major toy manufacturer based in Hong Kong, "is extremely reputable, not sleaze bags," David Miller, president of the Toy Manufacturers of America, assured *USA Today*. "The responsibility for those factories," Miller told ABC News, "is in the hands of those who are there and managing the factory."[4]

The grisly details of what occurred revealed the casual irresponsibility of both companies and governments. The Kader factory compound consisted of four interconnected, four-story industrial barns on a three-acre lot on Buddhamondhol VI Road in the Sampran district west of Bangkok. It was one among Thailand's thriving new industrial zones for garments, textiles, electronics and toys. More than 50,000 people, most of them migrants from the Thai countryside, worked in the district at 7,500 large and small firms. Thailand's economic boom was based on places such as this, and Bangkok was almost choking on its own fantastic growth, dizzily erecting luxury hotels and office towers.

The fire started late on a Monday afternoon on the ground floor in the first building and spread rapidly upward, jumping to two adjoining buildings, all three of which swiftly collapsed. Investigators noted afterwards that the structures had been cheaply built, without concrete reinforcement, so steel girders and stairways crumpled easily in the heat. Thai law required that in such a large factory, fire-escape stairways must be sixteen to thirty-three feet wide, but Kader's were a mere four and a half feet. Main doors were locked and many windows barred to prevent pilfering by the employees. Flammable raw materials—fabric, stuffing, animal fibers—were stacked everywhere, on walkways and next to electrical boxes. Neither safety drills nor fire alarms and sprinkler systems had been provided.

Let some of the survivors describe what happened.

A young woman named Lampan Taptim: "There was the sound of yelling about a fire. I tried to leave the section but my supervisor told me to get back to work. My sister who worked on the fourth floor with me pulled me away and insisted we try to get out. We tried to go down the stairs and got to the second floor; we found that the stairs had already caved in. There was a lot of yelling and confusion. . . . In desperation, I went back up to the windows and went back and forth, looking down below. The smoke was thick and I picked the best place to jump in a pile of boxes. My sister jumped, too. She died."

A young woman named Cheng: "There is no way out [people were shouting], the security guard has locked the main door out! It was horrifying. I thought I would die. I took off my gold ring and kept it in my pocket and put on my name tag so that my body could be identifiable. I had to decide to die in the fire or from jumping down from a three stories' height." As the walls collapsed around her, Cheng clung to a pipe and fell downward with it, landing on a pile of dead bodies, injured but alive.

An older woman named La-iad Nadsnguen: "Four or five pregnant women jumped before me. They died before my eyes." Her own daughter jumped from the top floor and broke both hips.

Chauweewan Mekpan, who was five months pregnant: "I thought that if I jumped, at least my parents would see my remains, but if I stayed, nothing would be left of me." Though her back was severely injured, she and her unborn child miraculously survived.

An older textile worker named Vilaiwa Satieti, who sewed shirts and pants at a neighboring factory, described to me the carnage she encountered: "I got off work about five and passed by Kader and saw many dead bodies lying around, uncovered. Some of them I knew. I tried to help the workers who had jumped from the factory. They had broken legs and broken arms and broken heads. We tried to keep them alive until they got to the hospital, that's all you could do. Oh, they were teenagers, fifteen to twenty years, no more than that, and so many of them, so many."

This was not the first serious fire at Kader's factory, but the third or fourth. "I heard somebody yelling 'fire, fire,'" Tumthong Podhirun testified, " . . . but I did not take it seriously because it has happened before. Soon I smelled smoke and very quickly it billowed inside the place. I headed for the back door but it was locked. . . . Finally, I had no choice but to join the others and jumped out of the window. I saw many of my friends lying dead on the ground beside me."[5]

In the aftermath of the tragedy, some Bangkok activists circulated an old snapshot of two smiling peasant girls standing arm in arm beside a thicket of palm trees. One of them, Praphai Prayonghorm, died in the 1993 fire at Kader. Her friend, Kammoin Konmanee, had died in the 1989 fire. Some of the Kader workers insisted afterwards that their factory had been haunted by ghosts, that it was built on the site of an old graveyard, disturbing the dead. The folklore expressed raw poetic truth: the fire in Bangkok eerily resembled the now-forgotten details of the Triangle Shirtwaist disaster eighty years before. Perhaps the "ghosts" that some workers felt present were young women from New York who had died in 1911.

Similar tragedies, large and small, were now commonplace across developing Asia and elsewhere. Two months after Kader, another fire at a Bangkok shirt factory killed ten women. Three months after Kader, a six-story hotel collapsed and killed 133 people, injuring 351. The embarrassed minister of industry ordered special inspections of 244 large factories in the Bangkok region and found that 60 percent of them had basic violations similar to Kader's. Thai industry was growing explosively—12 to 15 percent a year—but workplace injuries and illnesses were growing even faster, from 37,000 victims in 1987 to more than 150,000 by 1992 and an estimated 200,000 by 1994.

In China, six months after Kader, eighty-four women died and dozens of others were severely burned at another toy factory fire in the burgeoning industrial zone at Shenzhen. At Dongguan, a Hong Kong–owned raincoat factory burned in 1991, killing more than eighty people (Kader Industries also had a factory at Dongguan where two fires have been reported since 1990). In late 1993, some sixty women died at the Taiwanese-owned Gaofu textile plant in Fuzhou Province, many of them smothered in their dormitory beds by toxic fumes from burning textiles. In 1994, a shoe factory fire killed ten persons at Jiangmen; a textile factory fire killed thirty-eight and injured 160 at the Qianshan industrial zone.[6]

"Why must these tragedies repeat themselves again and again?" the *People's Daily* in Beijing asked. The official *Economic Daily* complained: "The way some of these foreign investors ignore international practice, ignore our own national rules, act completely lawlessly and immorally and lust after wealth is enough to make one's hair stand on end."[7]

America was itself no longer insulated from such brutalities. When a chicken-processing factory at Hamlet, North Carolina, caught fire in 1991, the exit doors there were also locked and twenty-five people died. A garment factory discovered by labor investigators in El Monte, California, held seventy-two Thai immigrants in virtual peonage, working eighteen hours a day in "sub-human conditions." One could not lament the deaths, harsh working conditions, child labor and subminimum wages in Thailand or across Asia and Central America without also recognizing that similar conditions have reappeared in the United States for roughly the same reasons.

Sweatshops, mainly in the garment industry, scandalized Los Angeles, New York and Dallas. The grim, foul assembly lines of the poultry-processing industry were spread across the rural South; the *Wall Street Journal's* Tony Horwitz won a Pulitzer Prize for his harrowing description of this low-wage work. "In general," the U.S. Government Accounting Office reported in 1994, "the description of today's sweatshops differs little from that at the turn of the century."[8]

That was the real mystery: Why did global commerce, with all of its supposed modernity and wondrous technologies, restore the old barbarisms that had long ago been forbidden by law? If the information age has enabled multinational corporations to manage production and marketing spread across continents, why were their managers unable—or unwilling—to organize such mundane matters as fire prevention?

The short answer, of course, was profits, but the deeper answer was about power: Firms behaved this way because they could, because nobody would stop them. When law and social values retreated before the power of markets, then capitalism's natural drive to maximize returns had no internal governor to check its social behavior. When one enterprise took the low road to gain advantage, others would follow.

The toy fire in Bangkok provided a dramatic illustration for the much broader, less visible forms of human exploitation that were flourishing in the global system, including the widespread use of children in manufacturing, even forced labor camps in China or Burma. These matters were not a buried secret. Indeed, American television has aggressively exposed the "dark Satanic mills" with dramatic reports. ABC's *20/20* broadcast correspondent Lynn Sherr's devastating account of the Kader fire; CNN ran disturbing footage. Mike Wallace of CBS's *60 Minutes* exposed the prison labor exploited in China. NBC's *Dateline* did a piece on Wal-Mart's grim production in Bangladesh. CBS's *Street Stories* toured the shoe factories of Indonesia.

The baffling quality about modern communications was that its images could take us to people in remote corners of the world vividly and instantly, but these images have not as yet created genuine community with them. In terms of human consciousness, the "global village" was still only a picture on the TV screen.

Public opinion, moreover, absorbed contradictory messages about the global reality that were difficult to sort out. The opening stages of industrialization presented, as always, a great paradox: the process was profoundly liberating for millions, freeing them from material scarcity and limited life choices, while it also ensnared other millions in brutal new forms of domination. Both aspects were true,

but there was no scale on which these opposing consequences could be easily balanced, since the good and ill effects were not usually apportioned among the same people. Some human beings were set free, while other lives were turned into cheap and expendable commodities.

Workers at Kader, for instance, earned about 100 baht a day for sewing and assembling dolls, the official minimum wage of $4, but the constant stream of new entrants meant that many at the factory actually worked for much less—only $2 or $3 a day—during a required "probationary" period of three to six months that was often extended much longer by the managers. Only one hundred of the three thousand workers at Kader were legally designated employees; the rest were "contract workers" without permanent rights and benefits, the same employment system now popularized in the United States.

"Lint, fabric, dust and animal hair filled the air on the production floor," the International Confederation of Free Trade Unions based in Brussels observed in its investigative report. "Noise, heat, congestion and fumes from various sources were reported by many. Dust control was nonexistent; protective equipment inadequate. Inhaling the dust created respiratory problems and contact with it caused skin diseases." A factory clinic dispensed antihistamines or other drugs and referred the more serious symptoms to outside hospitals. Workers paid for the medication themselves and were reimbursed, up to $6, only if they had contributed 10 baht a month to the company's health fund.

A common response to such facts, even from many sensitive people, was: yes, that was terrible, but wouldn't those workers be even worse off if civil standards were imposed on their employers since they might lose their jobs as a result? This was the same economic rationale offered by American manufacturers a century before to explain why American children must work in the coal mines and textile mills. U.S. industry had survived somehow (and, in fact, flourished) when child labor and the other malpractices were eventually prohibited by social reforms. Furthermore, it was not coincidence that industry always assigned the harshest conditions and lowest pay to the weakest members of a society—women, children, uprooted migrants. Whether the factory was in Thailand or the United States or Mexico's *maquiladora* zone, people who were already quite powerless were less likely to resist, less able to demand decency from their employers.

Nor did these enterprises necessarily consist of small, struggling firms that could not afford to treat their workers better. Small sweatshops, it was true, were numerous in Thailand, and I saw some myself in a working-class neighborhood of Bangkok. Behind iron grillwork, children who looked to be ten to twelve years old squatted on the cement floors of the open-air shops, assembling suitcases, sewing raincoats, packing T-shirts. Across the street, a swarm of adolescents in blue smocks ate dinner at long tables outside a two-story building, then trooped back upstairs to the sewing machines.

Kader Holding Company, Ltd., however, was neither small nor struggling. It was a powerhouse of the global toy industry—headquartered in Hong Kong, incorporated in Bermuda, owned by a wealthy Hong Kong Chinese family named Ting that got its start after World War II making plastic goods and flashlights under procurement contracts from the U.S. military. Now Kader controlled a global maze of factories and interlocking subsidiaries in eight countries, from China and Thailand to Britain and the United States, where it owned Bachmann toys.[9]

After the fire Thai union members, intellectuals and middle-class activists from social rights organizations (the groups known in developing countries as nongovernmental organizations, or NGOs) formed the Committee to Support Kader Workers and began demanding justice from the employer. They sent a delegation to Hong Kong to confront Kader officials and investigate the complex corporate linkages of the enterprise. What they discovered was that Kader's partner in the Bangkok toy factory was actually a fabulously wealthy Thai family, the Chearavanonts, ethnic Chinese merchants who own the Charoen Pokphand Group, Thailand's own leading multinational corporation.

The CP Group owns farms, feed mills, real estate, air-conditioning and motorcycle factories, food-franchise chains—two hundred companies worldwide, several of them listed on the New York Stock Exchange. The patriarch and chairman, Dhanin Chearavanont, was said by *Fortune* magazine to be the seventy-fifth richest man in the world, with personal assets of $2.6 billion (or 65 billion baht, as the *Bangkok Post* put it). Like the other emerging "Chinese multinationals," the Pokphand Group operates through the informal networks of kinfolk and ethnic contacts spread around the world by the Chinese diaspora, while it also participates in the more rigorous accounting systems of Western economies.

In the mother country, China, the conglomerate nurtured political-business alliances and has become the largest outside investor in new factories and joint ventures. In the United States, it maintained superb political connections. The Chearavanonts co-sponsored a much-heralded visit to Bangkok by ex-president George Bush, who delivered a speech before Thai business leaders in early 1994, eight months after the Kader fire. The price tag for Bush's appearance, according to the Bangkok press, was $400,000 (equivalent to one month's payroll for all three thousand workers at Kader). The day after Bush's appearance, the Chearavanonts hosted a banquet for a leading entrepreneur from China—Deng Xiaoping's daughter.[10]

The Pokphand Group at first denied any connection to the Kader fire, but reformers and local reporters dug out the facts of the family's involvement. Dhanin Chearavanont himself owned 11 percent of Honbo Investment Company and with relatives and corporate directors held majority control. Honbo, in turn, owned half of KCP Toys (KCP stood for Kader Charoen Pokphand), which, in turn, owned 80 percent of Kader Industrial (Thailand) Company. Armed with these facts, three hundred workers from the destroyed factory marched on the Pokphand Group's corporate tower on Silom Road, where they staged a gentle sit-down demonstration in the lobby, demanding just compensation for the victims.[11]

In the context of Thai society and politics, the workers' demonstration against Pokphand was itself extraordinary, like peasants confronting the nobility. Under continuing pressures from the support group, the company agreed to pay much larger compensation for victims and their families—$12,000 for each death, a trivial amount in American terms but more than double the Thai standard. "When we worked on Kader," said Professor Voravidh Charoenloet, an economist at Chulalongkorn University, "the government and local entrepreneurs and factory owners didn't want us to challenge these people; even the police tried to obstruct us from making an issue. We were accused of trying to destroy the country's reputation."

The settlement, in fact, required the Thai activists to halt their agitation and fall silent. "Once the extra compensation was paid," Voravidh explained, "we were forced to stop. One of the demands by the government was that everything should stop. Our organization had to accept it. We wanted to link with the international organizations and have a great boycott, but we had to cease."

The global boycott, he assumed, was going forward anyway because he knew that international labor groups like the ICFTU and the AFL-CIO had investigated the Kader fire and issued stinging denunciations. I told him that aside from organized labor, the rest of the

world remained indifferent. There was no boycott of Kader toys in America. The professor slumped in his chair and was silent, a twisted expression on his face.

"I feel very bad," Voravidh said at last. "Maybe we should not have accepted it. But when we came away, we felt that was what we could accomplish. The people wanted more. There must be something more."

In the larger context, this tragedy was not explained by the arrogant power of one wealthy family or the elusive complexities of interlocking corporations. The Kader fire was ordained and organized by the free market itself. The toy industry—much like textiles and garments, shoes, electronics assembly and other low-wage sectors—existed (and thrived) by exploiting a crude ladder of desperate competition among the poorest nations. Its factories regularly hopped to new locations where wages were even lower, where the governments would be even more tolerant of abusive practices. The contract work assigned to foreign firms, including thousands of small sweatshops, fitted neatly into the systems of far-flung production of major brand names and distanced the capital owners from personal responsibility. The "virtual corporation" celebrated by some business futurists already existed in these sectors and, indeed, was now being emulated in some ways by advanced manufacturing—cars, aircraft, computers.

Over the last generation, toy manufacturers and others have moved around the Asian rim in search of the bottom-rung conditions: from Hong Kong, Korea and Taiwan to Thailand and Indonesia, from there to China, Vietnam and Bangladesh, perhaps on next to Burma, Nepal or Cambodia. Since the world had a nearly inexhaustible supply of poor people and supplicant governments, the market would keep driving in search of lower rungs; no one could say where the bottom was located. Industrial conditions were not getting better, as conventional theory assured the innocent consumers, but in many sectors were getting much worse. In America, the U.S. diplomatic opening to Vietnam was celebrated as progressive politics. In Southeast Asia, it merely opened another trapdoor beneath wages and working conditions.

A country like Thailand was caught in the middle: if it conscientiously tried to improve, it would pay a huge price. When Thai unions lobbied to win improvements in minimum-wage standards, textile plants began leaving for Vietnam and elsewhere or even importing cheaper "guest workers" from Burma. When China opened its fast-growing industrial zones in Shenzhen, Dongguan and other locations, the new competition had direct consequences on the factory floors of Bangkok.

Kader, according to the ICFTU, opened two new factories in Shekou and Dongguan where young people were working fourteen-hour days, seven days a week, to fill the U.S. Christmas orders for Mickey Mouse and other American dolls. Why should a company worry about sprinkler systems or fire escapes for a dusty factory in Bangkok when it could hire brand-new workers in China for only $20 a month, one fifth of the labor cost in Thailand?

The ICFTU report described the market forces: "The lower cost of production of toys in China changes the investment climate for countries like Thailand. Thailand competes with China to attract investment capital for local toy production. With this development, Thailand has become sadly lax in enforcing its own legislation. It turns a blind eye to health violations, thus allowing factory owners to ignore safety standards. Since China entered the picture, accidents in Thailand have nearly tripled."

The Thai minister of industry, Sanan Kachornprasart, described the market reality more succinctly: "If we punish them, who will want to invest here?" Thai authorities subsequently filed charges against three Kader factory

managers, but none against the company itself nor, of course, the Chearavanont family.[12]

In the aftermath, a deputy managing director of Kader Industrial, Pichet Laokasem, entered a Buddhist monastery "to make merit for the fire victims," *The Nation* of Bangkok reported. Pichet told reporters he would serve as a monk until he felt better emotionally. "Most of the families affected by the fire lost only a loved one," he explained. "I lost nearly two hundred of my workers all at once."

The fire in Bangkok reflected the amorality of the marketplace when it has been freed of social obligations. But the tragedy also mocked the moral claims of three great religions, whose adherents were all implicated. Thais built splendid golden temples exalting Buddha, who taught them to put spiritual being before material wealth. Chinese claimed to have acquired superior social values, reverence for family and community, derived from the teachings of Confucius. Americans bought the toys from Asia to celebrate the birth of Jesus Christ. Their shared complicity was another of the strange convergences made possible by global commerce. . . .

In the modern industrial world, only the ignorant can pretend to self-righteousness since only the primitive are truly innocent. No advanced society has reached that lofty stage without enduring barbaric consequences and despoliation along the way; no one who enjoys the uses of electricity or the internal combustion engine may claim to oppose industrialization for others without indulging in imperious hypocrisy.

Americans, one may recall, built their early national infrastructure and organized large-scale agriculture with slave labor. The developing American nation swept native populations from their ancient lands and drained the swampy prairies to grow grain. It burned forests to make farmland, decimated wildlife, dammed the wild rivers and displaced people who were in the way. It assigned the dirtiest, most dangerous work to immigrants and children. It eventually granted political rights to all, but grudgingly and only after great conflicts, including a terrible civil war.

The actual history of nations is useful to remember when trying to form judgments about the new world. Asian leaders regularly remind Americans and Europeans of exactly how the richest nation-states became wealthy and observe further that, despite their great wealth, those countries have not perfected social relations among rich and poor, weak and powerful. The maldistribution of incomes is worsening in America, too, not yet as extreme as Thailand's, but worse than many less fortunate nations.

Hypocrisies run the other way, too, however. The fashionable pose among some leaders in developing Asia is to lecture the West on its decadent ways and hold up "Asian values" as morally superior, as well as more productive. If their cultural claims sound plausible at a distance, they seem less noble, even duplicitous up close. The Asian societies' supposed reverence for family, for instance, is expressed in the "dark Satanic mills" where the women and children are sent to work. "Family" and "social order" are often mere euphemisms for hierarchy and domination. A system that depends upon rigid control from above or the rank exploitation of weaker groups is not about values, but about power. Nothing distinctive about that. Human societies have struggled to overcome those conditions for centuries.

My point is that any prospect of developing a common global social consciousness will inevitably force people to reexamine themselves first and come to terms with the contradictions and hypocrisies in their own national histories. Americans, in particular, are not especially equipped for that exercise. A distinguished historian, Lawrence Goodwyn of Duke University, once said to me in frustration: You cannot teach American history to American students. You can teach the iconic version, he said, that portrays America as beautiful and unblemished or you can teach a radical version that demonizes the country. But American culture does not equip young people to deal with the "irreconcilable conflicts" embedded in their own history, the past that does not yield to patriotic moralisms. "Race is the most obvious example of what I mean," he said.

Coming to terms with one's own history ought not only to induce a degree of humility toward others and their struggles, but also to clarify what one really believes about human society. No one can undo the past, but that does not relieve people of the burden of making judgments about the living present or facing up to its moral implications. If the global system has truly created a unified marketplace, then every worker, every consumer, every society is already connected to the other. The responsibility exists and invoking history is not an excuse to hide from the new social questions.

Just as Americans cannot claim a higher morality while benefiting from inhumane exploitation, neither can developing countries pretend to become modern "one world" producers and expect exemption from the world's social values. Neither can the global enterprises. The future asks: Can capitalism itself be altered and reformed? Or is the world doomed to keep renewing these inhumanities in the name of economic progress?

The proposition that human dignity is indivisible does not suppose that everyone will become equal or alike or perfectly content in his or her circumstances. It does insist that certain well-understood social principles exist internationally which are enforceable and ought to be the price of admission in the global system. The idea is very simple: every person—man, woman and child—regardless of where he or she exists in time and place or on the chain of economic development, is entitled to respect as an individual being.

For many in the world, life itself is all that they possess; an economic program that deprives them of life's precious possibilities is not only unjust, but also utterly unnecessary. Peasants may not become kings, but they are entitled to be treated with decent regard for their sentient and moral beings, not as cheap commodities. Newly industrialized nations cannot change social patterns overnight, any more than the advanced economies did before them, but they can demonstrate that they are changing.

This proposition is invasive, no question, and will disturb the economic and political arrangements within many societies. But every nation has a sovereign choice in this matter, the sort of choice made in the marketplace every day. If Thailand or China resents the intrusion of global social standards, it does not have to sell its toys to America. And Americans do not have to buy them. If Singapore rejects the idea of basic rights for women, then women in America or Europe may reject Singapore— and multinational firms that profit from the subordination of women. If people do not assert these values in global trade, then their own convictions will be steadily coarsened.

In Bangkok, when I asked Professor Voravidh to step back from Thailand's problems and suggest a broader remedy, he thought for a long time and then said: "We need cooperation among nations because the multinational corporations can shift from one country to another. If they don't like Thailand, they move to Vietnam or China. Right now, we are all competing and the world is getting worse. We need a GATT on labor conditions and on the minimum wage, we need a standard on the minimum conditions for work and a higher standard for children."

The most direct approach, as Voravidh suggested, is an international agreement to incorporate such standards in the terms of trade, with penalties and incentives, even temporary embargoes, that will impose social obligations on the global system, the firms and countries. Most of the leading governments, including the United States, have long claimed to support this idea—a so-called social clause for GATT—but the practical reality is that they do not. Aside from rhetoric, when their negotiators are at the table, they always yield readily to objections from the multinational corporations and developing nations. Both the firms and the governing elites of poor countries have a strong incentive to block the proposition since both profit from a free-running system that exploits the weak. A countering force has to come from concerned citizens. Governments refuse to act, but voters and consumers are not impotent, and, in the meantime, they can begin the political campaign by purposefully targeting the producers— boycotting especially the well-known brand names that depend upon lovable images for their sales. Americans will not stop buying toys at Christmas, but they might single out one or two American toy companies for Yuletide boycotts, based on their scandalous relations with Kader and other manufacturers. Boycotts are difficult to organize and sustain, but every one of the consumer-goods companies is exquisitely vulnerable.

In India, the South Asian Coalition on Child Servitude, led by Kailash Satyarthi, has created a promising model for how to connect the social obligations of consumers and workers. Indian carpet makers are notorious for using small children at their looms— bonded children like Thailand's bonded prostitutes—and have always claimed economic necessity. India is a poor nation and the work gives wage income to extremely poor families, they insist. But these children will never escape poverty if they are deprived of schooling, the compulsory education promised by law.

The reformers created a "no child labor" label that certifies the rugs were made under honorable conditions and they persuaded major importers in Germany to insist upon the label. The exporters in India, in turn, have to allow regular citizen inspections of their workplaces to win the label for their rugs. Since this consumer-led certification system began, the carpet industry's use of children has fallen dramatically. A Textile Ministry official in New Delhi said: "The government is now contemplating the total eradication of child labor in the next few years."[13]

Toys, shoes, electronics, garments—many consumer sectors are vulnerable to similar approaches, though obviously the scope of manufacturing is too diverse and complex for consumers to police it. Governments have to act collectively. If a worldwide agreement is impossible to achieve, then groups of governments can form their own preferential trading systems, introducing social standards that reverse the incentives for developing countries and for capital choosing new locations for production.

The crucial point illustrated by Thailand's predicament is that global social standards will help the poorer countries escape their economic trap. Until a floor is built beneath the market's social behavior, there is no way that a small developing country like Thailand can hope to overcome the downward pull of competition from other, poorer nations. It must debase its citizens to hold on to what it has achieved. The path to improvement is blocked by the economics of an irresponsible marketplace.

Setting standards will undoubtedly slow down the easy movement of capital—and close down the most scandalous operations—but that is not a harmful consequence for people in struggling nations that aspire to industrial prosperity or for a global economy burdened with surpluses and inadequate consumption. When global capital makes a commitment to a developing economy, it ought not to acquire the power to blackmail that nation in perpetuity. Supported by global rules, those nations can begin to improve conditions and stabilize their own social development. At least they would have a chance to avoid the great class conflicts that others have experienced.

In the meantime, the very least that citizens can demand of their own government is

that it no longer use public money to finance the brutal upheavals or environmental despoliation that have flowed from large-scale projects of the World Bank and other lending agencies. The social distress in the cities begins in the countryside, and the wealthy nations have often financed it in the name of aiding development. The World Bank repeatedly proclaims its new commitment to strategies that address the development ideas of indigenous peoples and halt the destruction of natural systems. But social critics and the people I encountered in Thailand and elsewhere have not seen much evidence of real change.

The terms of trade are usually thought of as commercial agreements, but they are also an implicit statement of moral values. In its present terms, the global system values property over human life. When a nation like China steals the property of capital, pirating copyrights, films or technology, other governments will take action to stop it and be willing to impose sanctions and penalty tariffs on the offending nation's trade. When human lives are stolen in the "dark Satanic mills," nothing happens to the offenders since, according to the free market's sense of conscience, there is no crime.

NOTES

1. William Blake's immortal lines are from "Milton," one of his "prophetic books" written between 1804 and 1808. *The Portable Blake*, Alfred Kazin, editor (New York: Penguin Books, 1976).

2. *Washington Post, Financial Times* and *New York Times*, May 12, 1993, and *Wall Street Journal*, May 13, 1993.

3. The U.S. contract clients for Kader's Bangkok factory were cited by the International Confederation of Free Trade Unions headquartered in Brussels in its investigatory report, "From the Ashes: A Toy Factory Fire in Thailand," December 1994. In the aftermath, the ICFTU and some nongovernmental organizations attempted to mount an "international toy campaign" and a few sporadic

demonstrations occurred in Hong Kong and London, but there never was a general boycott of the industry or any of its individual companies. The labor federation met with associations of British and American toy manufacturers and urged them to adopt a "code of conduct" that might discourage the abuses. The proposed codes were inadequate, the ICFTU acknowledged, but it was optimistic about their general adoption by the international industry.

4. Mitchell Zuckoff of the *Boston Globe* produced a powerful series of stories on labor conditions in developing Asia and reported Hasbro's reaction to the Kader fire, July 10, 1994. David Miller was quoted in *USA Today*, May 13, 1993, and on ABC News *20/20*, July 30, 1993.

5. The first-person descriptions of the Kader fire are but a small sampling from survivors' horrifying accounts, collected by investigators and reporters at the scene. My account of the disaster is especially indebted to the investigative report by the International Confederation of Free Trade Unions; Bangkok's English-language newspapers, the *Post* and *The Nation*; the Asia Monitor Resource Center of Hong Kong; and Lynn Sherr's devastating report on ABCs *20/20*, July 30, 1993. Lampan Taptim and Tumthong Podhirun, "From the Ashes," ICFTU, December 1994; Cheng: *Asian Labour Update,* Asia Monitor Resource Center, Hong Kong, July 1993; La-iad Nads-nguen: *The Nation,* Bangkok, May 12, 1993; and Chaweewan Mekpan: *20/20.*

6. Details on Thailand's worker injuries and the litany of fires in China are from the ICFTU report and other labor bulletins, as well as interviews in Bangkok.

7. The *People's Daily* and *Economic Daily* were quoted by Andrew Quinn of Reuters in *The Daily Citizen* of Washington, DC, January 18, 1994.

8. Tony Horwitz described chicken-processing employment as the second fastest growing manufacturing job in America: *Wall Street Journal,* December 1, 1994. U.S. sweatshops were reviewed in "Garment Industry: Efforts to Address the Prevalence and Conditions of Sweatshops," U.S. Government Accounting Office, November 1994.

9. Corporate details on Kader are from the ICFTU and the Asia Monitor Resource Center's *Asian Labour Update,* July 1993.

10. Dhanin Chearavanont's wealth: *Bangkok Post,* June 15, 1993; Pokphand Group ventures in China and elsewhere: *Far Eastern Economic Review,* October 21, 1993; George Bush's appearance in Bangkok: *Bangkok Post,* January 22, 1994. The dinner for Deng's daughter, Deng Nan, was reported in *The Nation,* Bangkok, January 28, 1994.

11. The complex structure of ownership was used to deflect corporate responsibility. Kader's Kenneth Ting protested after the fire that his family's firm owned only a 40 percent stake in the Thai factory, but people blamed them "because we have our name on it. That's the whole problem." The lesson, he said, was to "never lend your name or logo to any company if you don't have managing control in the company." That lesson, of course, contradicted the basic structure of how the global toy industry was organized: *Bangkok Post,* May 17, 1993. The chain of ownership was reported in several places, including *The Nation* of Bangkok, May 28, 1993. Details of the Kader workers' sit-in: *Bangkok Post,* July 13, 1993.

12. Sanan was quoted in the *Bangkok Post,* May 29, 1993.

13. The New Delhi–based campaign against child labor in the carpet industry is admittedly limited to a narrow market and expensive product, but its essential value is demonstrating how retailers and their customers can be connected to a distant factory floor. See, for instance, Hugh Williamson, "Stamp of Approval," *Far Eastern Economic Review,* February 2, 1995, and N. Vasuk Rao in the *Journal of Commerce,* March 1, 1995

THINKING ABOUT THE READING

Greider argues that the tragedy of the Kader industrial fire cannot be explained simply by focusing on greedy families and multinational corporations. Instead, he blames global economics and the organization of the international toy industry. He writes, "The Kader fire was ordained and organized by the free market itself." What do you suppose he means by this? Given the enormous economic pressures that this and other multinational industries operate under, are such tragedies inevitable? Why have attempts to improve the working conditions in Third World factories been so ineffective?

14 Architects of Change

Reconstructing Society

Throughout this book you've seen examples of how society is socially constructed and how these social constructions, in turn, affect the lives of individuals. It's hard not to feel a little helpless when discussing the control that culture, massive bureaucratic organizations, social institutions, systems of social stratification and population trends have over our individual lives. However, social change is as much a part of society as social stability. Whether at the personal, cultural, or institutional level, change is the preeminent feature of modern societies.

Religious institutions are often intertwined with movements for widespread social change. Sometimes the religious ideology that underlies a particular movement is one that emphasizes peace and justice. The civil rights movement of the 1950s and the antiwar movement of the 1960s are two such examples. Other times, however, the supportive religious ideology of a movement can be used to deny civil rights and even incite violence. In his article, "Popular Christianity and Political Extremism in the United States," James Aho describes the relationship between Christianity and violent right-wing extremism. Every American generation, he argues, has experienced movements built on religiously inspired hatred. Today, however, these movements have been able to take advantage of sophisticated weapons and communications technology, making them especially lethal.

In the end, the nature of society, from its large institutions to its small, unspoken rules of everyday life, can be understood only by examining what people do and think. Individuals, acting collectively, can shape institutions, influence government policy, and alter the course of society. It's easy to forget that social movements consist of flesh-and-blood individuals acting together for a cause they believe in. In "Challenging Power," Celene Krauss examines the process by which white, working-class women with very traditional ideas about women's role in the family became community activists in toxic waste protests. She shows how these women became politicized not by the broader ideology of the environmentalist movement but by the direct health threats toxic waste posed to their children.

Something to Consider as You Read:

As you read these selections, consider the connection between people's ideas, beliefs, and goals and the motivation to become involved in social change. Participation in a social movement takes time and resources. What do you care enough about to contribute your time and money? In thinking about the near future, which groups do you think are "worked up" enough about something to give a lot of time and energy in trying to create social change? If these groups prevail, what do you think the future will look like? Do you think there are effective balancing points to counter the effects of extreme social movements?

Popular Christianity and Political Extremism in the United States

James Aho

(1996)

December 8, 1984. In a shootout on Puget Sound, Washington, involving several hundred federal and local law enforcement officials, the leader of a terrorist group comprised of self-proclaimed Christian soldiers is killed, ending a crime spree involving multi-state robberies, armored car heists, arson attacks, three murders, and a teenage suicide.

—Flynn and Gerhardt 1989

Christmas Eve, 1985. A "Christian patriot soldier" in Seattle trying to save America by eliminating the Jewish-Communist leader of the so-called one-world conspiracy, murders an innocent family of four, including two pre-teen children.

—Aho 1994: 35–49

August 1992. In northern Idaho, three persons are killed and two others critically injured in the course of a stand-off between federal marshals, ATF officers, the FBI, and a white separatist Christian family seeking refuge from the "Time of Tribulations" prophesied in the Book of Revelations.

—Aho 1994: 50–65

Three isolated incidents, twelve dead bodies, scores of young men imprisoned, shattered families, millions of dollars in litigation fees and investigation expenses. Why? What can sociology tell us about the causes of these events that they might be averted in the future? In particular, insofar as Christianity figures so prominently in these stories, what role has this religion played in them? Has Christianity been a cause of right-wing extremism in the United States? Or has it been an excuse for extremism occasioned by other factors? Or is the association between right-wing extremism and Christianity merely anecdotal and incidental? Our object is to address these questions.

Extremism Defined

The word "extremism" is used rhetorically in everyday political discourse to disparage and undermine one's opponents. In this sense, it refers essentially to anyone who disagrees with me politically. In this chapter, however, "extremism" will refer exclusively to particular kinds of behaviors, namely, to non-democratic actions, regardless of their ideology—that is, regardless of whether we agree with the ideas behind them or not (Lipset and Raab 1970: 4–17). Thus, extremism includes: (1) efforts to deny civil rights to certain people, including their right to express unpopular views, their right to due process at law, to own property, etc.; (2) thwarting attempts by others to organize in opposition to us, to run for office, or vote; (3) not playing according to legal constitutional rules of political fairness: using personal smears like "Communist Jew-fag" and "nigger lover" in place of rational discussion; and above all, settling differences by vandalizing or destroying the property or life of one's opponents. The test is not the end as such, but the means employed to achieve it.

Cycles of American Right-Wing Extremism

In this [article] we are concerned with the most rabid right-wing extremists, those who have threatened or succeeded in injuring and killing their opponents. We are interested, furthermore, only in such activities as are connected at least indirectly to Christianity. By no means is this limitation of focus intended to suggest that American Christians are characteristically more violent than their non-Christian neighbors. Nor are we arguing that American Christians engage only in right-wing activities. We are focusing on Christianity and on rightist extremism because in America today this connection has become newsworthy and because it is sociologically problematic.

American political history has long been acquainted with Christian-oriented rightist extremism. As early as the 1790s, for example, Federalist Party activists, inspired partly by Presbyterian and Congregationalist preachers, took-up arms against a mythical anti-Christian cabal known as the Illuminati—Illuminati = bringers of light = Lucifer, the devil.

The most notable result of anti-Illuminatism was what became popularly known as the "Reign of Terror": passage of the Alien and Sedition acts (1798). These required federal registration of recent immigrants to America from Ireland and France, reputed to be the homes of Illuminatism, lengthened the time of naturalization to become a citizen from five to fourteen years, restricted "subversive" speech and newspapers—that is, outlets advocating liberal Jeffersonian or what were known then as "republican" sentiments—and permitted the deportation of "alien enemies" without trial.

The alleged designs of the Illuminati were detailed in a three hundred-page book entitled *Proofs of a Conspiracy Against All the Religions and Governments of Europe Carried on in the Secret Meetings of . . . Illuminati* (Robison 1967 [1798]). Over two hundred years later *Proofs of a Conspiracy* continues to serve as a sourcebook for right-wing extremist commentary on American social issues. Its basic themes are: (1) *manichaenism:* that the world is divided into the warring principles of absolute good and evil; (2) *populism:* that the citizenry naturally would be inclined to ally with the powers of good, but have become indolent, immoral, and uninformed of the present danger to themselves; (3) *conspiracy:* that this is because the forces of evil have enacted a scheme using educators, newspapers, music, and intoxicants to weaken the people's will and intelligence; (4) *anti-modernism:* that the results of the conspiracy are the very laws and institutions celebrated by the unthinking masses as "progressive": representative government, the separation of Church and State, the extension of suffrage to the propertyless, free public education, public-health measures, etc.; and (5) *apocalypticism:* that the results of what liberals call social progress are increased crime rates, insubordination to "natural" authorities (such as royal families and property-owning Anglo-Saxon males), loss of faith, and the decline of common decency—in short, the end of the world.

Approximately every thirty years America has experienced decade-long popular resurrections of these five themes. While the titles of the alleged evil-doers in each era have been adjusted to meet changing circumstances, their program is said to have remained the same. They constitute a diabolic *Plot Against Christianity* (Dilling 1952). In the 1830s, the cabal was said to be comprised of the leaders of Masonic lodges: in the 1890s, they were accused of being Papists and Jesuits; in the 1920s, they were the Hidden Hand; in the 1950s, the Insiders or Force X; and today they are known as Rockefellerian "one-world" Trilateralists or Bilderbergers.

Several parallels are observable in these periods of American right-wing resurgence. First, while occasionally they have evolved into democratically-organized political parties holding conventions that nominate slates of candidates to run for office—the American Party, the Anti-Masonic Party, the People's Party, the Prohibition Party—more often, they have become secret societies in their own right, with arcane passwords, handshakes, and vestments, plotting campaigns of counter-resistance behind closed doors. That is, they come to mirror the fantasies against which they have taken up arms. Indeed, it is this ironic fact that typically occasions the public ridicule and undoing of these groups. The most notable examples are the Know Nothings, so-called because under interrogation they were directed to deny knowledge of the organization; the Ku Klux Klan, which during the 1920s had several million members; the Order of the Star Spangled Banner, which flourished during the 1890s; the Black Legion of Michigan, circa 1930; the Minutemen of the late 1960s; and most recently, the *Bruders Schweigen*, Secret Brotherhood, or as it is more widely known, The Order.

Secondly, the thirty-year cycle noted above evidently has no connection with economic booms and busts. While the hysteria of the 1890s took place during a nation-wide depression, McCarthyism exploded on the scene during the most prosperous era in American history. On close view, American right-wing extremism is more often associated with economic good times than with bad, the 1920s, the 1830s, and the 1980s being prime examples. On the contrary, the cycle seems to have more to do with the length of a modern generation than with any other factor.

Third, and most important for our purposes, Christian preachers have played pivotal roles in all American right-wing hysterias. The presence of Dan Gayman, James Ellison, and Bertrand Comparet spear-heading movements to preserve America from decline today continues a tradition going back to Jedidiah Morse nearly two centuries ago, continuing through Samuel D. Burchard, Billy Sunday, G. L. K. Smith, and Fred Schwarz's Christian Anti-Communist Crusade.

In the nineteenth century, the honorary title "Christian patriot" was restricted to white males with Protestant credentials. By the 1930s, however, Catholic ideologues, like the anti-Semitic radio priest Father Coughlin, had come to assume leadership positions in the movement. Today, somewhat uneasily, Mormons are included in the fold. The Ku Klux Klan, once rabidly anti-Catholic and misogynist, now encourages Catholic recruits and even allows females into its regular organization, instead of requiring them to form auxiliary groups.

Christianity: A Cause of Political Extremism?

The upper Rocky Mountain region is the heartland of American right-wing extremism in our time. Montana, Idaho, Oregon, and Washington have the highest per capita rates of extremist groups of any area in the entire country (Aho 1994: 152–153). Research on the members of these groups show that they are virtually identical to the surrounding population in all respects but one (Aho 1991: 135–163)—they are not less formally educated than the surrounding population. Furthermore, as indicated by their rates of geographic mobility, marital stability, occupational choice, and conventional political participation, they are no more estranged from their local communities than those with whom they live. And finally, their social status seems no more threatened than that of their more moderate neighbors. Indeed, there exists anecdotal evidence that American right-wing extremists today are drawn from the more favored, upwardly-mobile sectors of society. They are college-educated, professional suburbanites residing in the rapidly-growing, prosperous Western states (Simpson 1983).

In other words, the standard sociological theories of right-wing extremism—theories holding, respectively, that extremists are typically undereducated, if not stupid, transient and alienated from ordinary channels of belonging, and suffer inordinately from status insecurity—find little empirical support. Additionally, the popular psychological notion that right-wing extremists are more neurotic than the general population, perhaps paranoid to the point of psychosis, can not be confirmed. None of the right-wing political murderers whose psychiatric records this author has accessed have been medically certified as insane (Aho 1991: 68–82; Aho 1994: 46–49). If this is true for right-wing murderers, it probably also holds for extremists who have not taken the lives of others.

The single way in which right-wing extremists *do* differ from their immediate neighbors is seen in their religious biographies. Those with Christian backgrounds generally, and Presbyterians, Baptists and members of independent fundamentalist Protestant groups specifically, all are overrepresented among intermountain radical patriots (Aho 1991: 164–182). Although it concerns a somewhat different population, this finding is consistent with surveys of the religious affiliations of Americans with conservative voting and attitudinal patterns (Lipset and Raab 1970: 229–232, 359–361, 387–392, 433–437, 448–452; Shupe and Stacey 1983; Wilcox 1992).

Correlations do not prove causality. Merely because American extremists are members of certain denominations and sects does not permit the conclusion that these religious groups compel their members to extremism. In the first place, the vast majority of independent fundamentalists, Baptists, and Presbyterians are not political extremists, even if they are inclined generally to support conservative causes. Secondly, it is conceivable that violently-predisposed individuals are attracted to particular religions because of what they hear from the pulpit; and what they hear channels their *already* violent inclinations in political directions.

Today, a man named Gary Yarbrough, gaunt-faced and red-bearded, languishes in federal prison because of his participation in the *Bruders Schweigen*. Although he was recruited into terrorism from the Church of Jesus Christ Christian/Aryan Nations—it was not the church itself that made him violent, at least not in a simplistic way. On the contrary, Yarbrough was the offspring of a notorious Pima, Arizona, family that one reporter (Ring 1985) describes as "very volatile—very anti-police, anti-social, anti-everybody." Charges against its various members have ranged from burglary and robbery to witness-intimidation.

Lloyd, Steve, and Gary Yarbrough are sons of a family of drifters. Red, the father, works as an itinerant builder and miner. Rusty, his wife, tends bar and waitresses. Child rearing, such as it was, is said to have been "severely heavy handed." Nor was much love lost between the parents. Fist fights were common and once Rusty stabbed Red so badly he was hospitalized. Not surprisingly, "the boys did not get very good schooling." Still, mother vehemently defends her boys. One night, she jumped over a bar to attack an overly inquisitive detective concerning their whereabouts.

After a spree of drugs, vandalism, and thievery, Gary, like his brothers, eventually found himself behind bars at the Arizona State Prison. It was there that he was contacted, first by letter and later personally, by the Aryan Nations prison ministry in Idaho. He was the kind of man the church was searching for: malleable, fearless, sentimental, tough. Immediately upon release, Yarbrough moved with his wife and daughter to Idaho to be close to church headquarters. He finally found his calling: working with like-minded souls in the name of Christ to protect God's chosen people, the white race, from mongrelization.

Yarbrough purchased the requisite dark blue twill trousers, postman's shirt, Nazi pins, Sam Browne holster-belt, and 9 mm. semi-automatic pistol. The pastor of the church assigned him to head the security detail. At annual church conventions, he helped conduct rifle training. But Yarbrough was a man of action; he soon became bored with the routine of guarding the compound against aliens who never arrived. He met others in the congregation who shared his impatience. Together in a farm building, deep in the woods, over the napping figure of one of the member's infant children, they founded the *Bruders Schweigen,* swearing together an oath to war against what they called ZOG—Zionist Occupation Government (Flynn and Gerhardt 1989).

The point is not that every extremist is a violent personality searching to legitimize criminality with religion. Instead, the example illustrates the subtle ways in which religious belief, practice, and organization all play upon individual psychology to produce persons prepared to violate others in the name of principle. Let us look at each of these factors separately, understanding that in reality they intermesh in complicated, sometimes contradictory ways that can only be touched upon here.

Belief

American right-wing politics has appropriated from popular Christianity several tenets: the concept of unredeemable human depravity, the idea of America as a specially chosen people, covenant theology and the right to revolt, the belief in a national mission, millennialism, and anti-Semitism. Each of these in its own way has inspired rightist extremism.

The New Israel

The notion of America as the new Israel, for example, is the primary axiom of a fast-growing religiously-based form of radical politics known as Identity Christianity. Idaho's Aryan Nations Church is simply the most well-known Identity congregation. The adjective "identity" refers to its insistence that Anglo-Saxons are in truth the Israelites. They are "Isaac's-sons"—the Saxons—and hence the Bible is *their* historical record, not that of the Jews (Barkun 1994). The idea is that after its exile to what today is northern Iran around seven hundred B.C., the Israelites migrated over the Caucasus mountains—hence their racial type, "caucasian"—and settled in various European countries. Several of these allegedly still contain mementos of their origins: the nation of Denmark is said to be comprised of descendants from the tribe of Dan; the German-speaking Jutland, from the tribe of Judah; Catalonia, Scotland, from the tribe of Gad.

Covenant Theology

Identity Christianity is not orthodox Christianity. Nevertheless, the notion of America as an especially favored people, or as Ronald Reagan once said, quoting Puritan founders, a "city on a hill," the New Jerusalem, is widely shared by Americans. Reagan and most conservatives, of course, consider the linkage between America and Israel largely symbolic.

Many right-wing extremists, however, view the relationship literally as an historical fact and for them, just as the ancient Israelites entered into a covenant with the Lord, America has done the same. According to radical patriots America's covenant is what they call the "organic Constitution." This refers to the original articles of the Constitution plus the first ten amendments, the Bill of Rights. Other amendments, especially the 16th establishing a federal income tax, are considered to have questionable legal status because allegedly they were not passed according to constitutional strictures.

The most extreme patriots deny the constitutionality of the 13th, 14th, and 15th amendments—those outlawing slavery and guaranteeing free men civil and political rights as full American citizens. Their argument is that the organic Constitution was written by white men exclusively for themselves and their blood descendents (Preamble 1986). Non-caucasians residing in America are considered "guest peoples" with no constitutional rights. Their continued residency in this country is entirely contingent upon the pleasure of their hosts, the Anglo-Saxon citizenry. According to some, it is now time for the property of these guests to be confiscated and they themselves exiled to their places of origin (Pace 1985).

All right-wing extremists insist that if America adheres to the edicts of the organic Constitution, she, like Israel before her, shall be favored among the world's nations. Her harvests shall be bountiful, her communities secure, her children obedient to the voices of their parents, and her armies undefeated. But if she falters in her faith, behaving in ways that contravene the sacred compact, then calamities, both natural and human-made, shall follow. This is the explanation for the widespread conviction among extremists today for America's decline in the world. In short, the federal government has established agencies and laws contrary to America's divine compact:

these include the Internal Revenue Service; the Federal Reserve System; the Bureau of Alcohol, Tobacco and Firearms; the Forest Service; the Bureau of Land Management; Social Security; Medicare and Medicaid; the Environmental Protection Agency; Housing and Urban Development; and the official apparatus enforcing civil rights for "so-called" minorities.

Essentially, American right-wing extremists view the entire executive branch of the United States government as little more than "jack-booted Nazi thugs," to borrow a phrase from the National Rifle Association fund-raising letter: a threat to freedom of religion, the right to carry weapons, freedom of speech, and the right to have one's property secure from illegal search and seizure.

Clumsy federal-agency assaults, first on the Weaver family in northern Idaho in 1992, then on the Branch Davidian sect in Waco, Texas, in 1993, followed by passage of the assault weapons ban in 1994, are viewed as indicators that the organic Constitution presently is imperiled. This has been the immediate impetus for the appearance throughout rural and Western America of armed militias since the summer of 1994. The terrorists who bombed a federal building in Oklahoma City in the spring of 1995, killing one hundred sixty-eight, were associated with militias headquartered in Michigan and Arizona. One month after the bombing, the national director of the United States Militia Association warned that after the current government falls, homosexuals, abortionists, rapists, "unfaithful politicians," and any criminal not rehabilitated in seven years will be executed. Tax evaders will no longer be treated as felons; instead they will lose their library privileges (Sherwood 1995).

Millennialism

Leading to both the Waco and Weaver incidents was a belief on the victims' parts that world apocalypse is imminent. The Branch

Davidians split from the Seventh-Day Adventists in 1935 but share with the mother church its own millenarian convictions. The Weavers received their apocalypticism from *The Late Great Planet Earth* by fundamentalist lay preacher Hal Lindsey (1970), a book that has enjoyed a wide reading on the Christian Right.

Both the Davidians and the Weavers were imbued with the idea that the thousand-year-reign of Christ would be preceded by a final battle between the forces of light and darkness. To this end both had deployed elaborate arsenals to protect themselves from the anticipated invasion of "Babylonish troops." These, they feared, would be comprised of agents from the various federal bureaucracies mentioned above, together with UN troops stationed on America's borders awaiting orders from Trilateralists. Ever alert to "signs" of the impending invasion, both fired at federal officers who had come upon their property; and both ended up precipitating their own martyrdom. Far from quelling millenarian fervor, however, the two tragedies were immediately seized upon by extremists as further evidence of the approaching End Times.

Millenarianism is not unique to Christianity, nor to Western religions; furthermore, millenarianism culminating in violence is not new—in part because one psychological effect of end-time prophesying is a devaluation of worldly things, including property, honors, and human life. At the end of the first Christian millennium (A.D. 1000) as itinerant prophets were announcing the Second Coming, their followers were taking-up arms to prepare the way, and uncounted numbers died (Cohn 1967). It should not surprise observers if, as the second millennium draws to a close and promises of Christ's imminent return increase in frequency, more and more armed cults flee to the mountains, there to prepare for the final conflagration.

Anti-Semitism

Many post-Holocaust Christian and Jewish scholars alike recognize that a pervasive anti-Judaism can be read from the pages of the New Testament, especially in focusing on the role attributed to Jews in Jesus' crucifixion. Rosemary Ruether, for example, argues that anti-Judaism constitutes the "left-hand of Christianity," its archetypal negation (Ruether 1979). Although pre-Christian Greece and Rome were also critical of Jews for alleged disloyalty, anti-Semitism reached unparalleled heights in Christian theology, sometimes relegating Jews to the status of Satan's spawn, the human embodiments of Evil itself.

During the Roman Catholic era, this association became embellished with frightening myths and images. Jews—pictured as feces-eating swine and rats—were accused of murdering Christian children on high feast days, using their blood to make unleavened bread, and poisoning wells. Added to these legends were charges during the capitalist era that Jews control international banking and by means of usury have brought simple, kind-hearted Christians into financial ruin (Hay 1981 [1950]). All of this was incorporated into popular Protestant culture through, among other vehicles, Martin Luther's diatribe, *On the Jews and Their Lies,* a pamphlet that still experiences brisk sales from patriotic bookstores. This is one possible reason for a survey finding by Charles Glock and Rodney Stark that created a minor scandal in the late 1960s. Rigidly orthodox American Christians, they found, displayed far higher levels of Jew-hatred than other Christians, regardless of their education, occupation, race, or income (Glock and Stark 1966).

In the last thirty years there has been "a sharp decline" in anti-Semitic prejudice in America, according to Glock (1993: 68). Mainline churches have played some role in this decline by facilitating Christian-Jewish dialogue, de-emphasizing offensive scriptural passages, and ending missions directed at Jews. Nevertheless, ancient anti-Jewish calumnies continue to be raised by leaders of the groups that are the focus of interest in this [article]. Far from being a product of neurotic syndromes like the so-called Authoritarian (or fascist) Personality, the Jew-hatred of many right-wing extremists today is directly traceable to what they have absorbed from these preachments, sometimes as children.

Human Depravity

> There is none righteous, no not one; . . . there is none that doeth the good, no, no one. Their throat is an open sepulchre. With their tongues they have used deceit; the poison of asps in under their lips. In these words of the apostle Paul, John Calvin says God inveighs not against particular individuals, but against all mankind. "Let it be admitted, then, that men . . . are . . . corrupt . . . by a depravity of nature" (Calvin 1966: 34–36; see Romans 3:11–24).

One of the fundamentals of Calvinist theology, appropriated into popular American Christianity, is this: a transcendent and sovereign God resides in the heavens, relative to whom the earth and its human inhabitants are utterly, hopelessly fallen. True, Calvin only developed a line of thought already anticipated in Genesis and amplified repeatedly over the centuries. However, with a lawyer's penetrating logic, Calvin brought this tradition to its most stark, pessimistic articulation. It is this belief that accompanied the Pilgrims in their venture across the Atlantic, eventually rooting itself in the American psyche.

From its beginnings, a particular version of the doctrine of human depravity has figured prominently in American right-wing extremist discourse. It has served as the basis

of its perennial misogyny, shared by both men and women. The female, being supposedly less rational and more passive, is said to be closer to earth's evil. Too, the theology of world devaluation is the likely inspiration for the right-wing's gossipy preoccupation with the body's appetites and the "perilous eroticism of emotion," for its prudish fulminations against music, dance, drink, and dress, and for its homophobia. Here, too, is found legitimation for the right-wing's vitriol against Satanist ouiji boards, "Dungeons and Dragons," and New Age witchcrafters with their horoscopes and aroma-therapies, and most recently, against "pagan-earth-worshippers" and "tree hugging idolaters" (environmentalists). In standing tall to "Satan's Kids" and their cravenness, certain neo-Calvinists in Baptist, Presbyterian, and fundamentalist clothing accomplish their own purity and sanctification.

Conspiratorialism

According to Calvin, earthquakes, pestilence, famine, and plague should pose no challenge to faith in God. We petty, self-absorbed creatures have no right to question sovereign reason. But even in Calvin's time, and more frequently later, many Christians have persisted in asking: if God is truly all-powerful, all-knowing, and all-good, then how is evil possible? Why do innocents suffer? One perennial, quasi-theological response is conspiratorialism. In short, there are AIDS epidemics, murderous holocausts, rampant poverty, and floods because counter-poised to God there exists a second hidden force of nearly equal power and omniscience: the Devil and His human consorters—Jews, Jesuits, Hidden Hands, Insiders, Masons, and Bilderbergers.

By conspiratorialism, we are not referring to documented cases of people secretly scheming to destroy co-workers, steal elections, or run competitors out of business. Conspiracies are a common feature of group life. Instead, we mean the attempt to explain the entirety of human history by means of a cosmic Conspiracy, such as that promulgated in the infamous *Protocols of the Learned Elders of Zion*. This purports to account for all modern institutions by attributing them to the designs of twelve or thirteen—one representing each of the tribes of Israel—Jewish elders (Aho 1994, 68–82). *The Protocols* enjoys immense and endless popularity on the Right; and has generated numerous spin-offs: *The International Jew, None Dare Call It Conspiracy*, and the *Mystery of [Jewish] Iniquity*, to name three.

To posit the existence of an evil divinity is heresy in orthodox Christianity. But, theological objections aside, it is difficult indeed for some believers to resist the temptation of intellectual certitude conspiratorialism affords. This certainty derives from the fact that conspiratorialism in the cosmic sense can not be falsified. Every historical event can, and often is, taken as further verification of conspiracies. If newspapers report a case of government corruption, this is evidence of government conspiracy; if they do not, this is evidence of news media complicity in the conspiracy. If the media deny involvement in a cover-up, this is still further proof of their guilt; if they admit to having sat on the story, this is surely an admission of what is already known.

Practice

Christianity means more than adhering to a particular doctrine. To be Christian is to live righteously. God-fearing righteousness may either be understood as a *sign* of one's salvation, as in orthodox Christianity or, as in Mormonism, a way to *earn* eternal life in the celestial heavens.

Nor is it sufficient for the faithful merely to display righteousness in their personal lives and businesses, by being honest, hard-working, and reliable. Many Christians also are obligated to witness to, or labor toward, salvation in the political arena; to work with others to remake this charnel-house world after the will of God; to help establish God's kingdom on earth. Occasionally this means becoming involved in liberal causes—abolitionism, civil rights, the peace and ecological movements; often it has entailed supporting causes on the Right. In either case it may require that one publicly stand up to evil. For, as Saint Paul said, to love God is to hate what is contrary to God.

Such a mentality may lead to "holy war," the organized effort to eliminate human fetishes of evil (Aho 1994: 23–34). For some, in cleansing the world of putrefaction their identity as Christian is recognized, it is re-known. This is not to argue that holy war is unique to Christianity, or that all Christians participate in holy wars. Most Christians are satisfied to renew their faith through the rites of Christmas, Easter, baptism, marriage, or mass. Furthermore, those who *do* speak of holy war often use it metaphorically to describe a private spiritual battle against temptation, as in "I am a soldier of Christ, therefore I am not permitted to fight" (Sandford 1966). Lastly, even holy war in the political sense does not necessarily imply the use of violence. Although they sometimes have danced tantalizingly close to extremism (in the sense defined earlier), neither Pat Robertson nor Jerry Falwell, for example, have advocated non-democratic means in their "wars" to avert America's decline.

Let us examine the notion of Christian holy war more closely. The sixteenth-century father of Protestant reform, Martin Luther, repudiated the concept of holy war, arguing that there exist two realms: holiness, which is the responsibility of the Church, and warfare, which falls under the State's authority (Luther 1974). Mixing these realms, he says, perverts the former while unnecessarily hamstringing the latter. This does not mean that Christians may forswear warfare, according to Luther. In his infinite wisdom, God has ordained princes to quell civil unrest and protect nations from invasion. Luther's exhortations to German officials that they spare no means in putting down peasant revolts are well known. Indeed, few theologians have "so highly praised the virtues of the State as Luther," says Ernst Troeltsch. Nevertheless, State violence is at best "sinful power to punish sin" for Luther. It is not a sacred instrument (Troeltsch 1960: 539–544, 656–677). To this day, Lutherans generally are less responsive to calls for holy wars than many other Christians.

John Calvin, on the other hand, rejected Luther's proposal to separate church from State. Instead, his goal was to establish a Christocracy in Geneva along Roman Catholic lines, and to attain this goal through force, if need be, as Catholicism had done. Calvin says that not only is violence to establish God's rule on earth permitted, it is commanded. "Good brother, we must bend unto all means that give furtherance to the holy cause" (Walzer 1965: 17, 38, 68–87, 90–91, 100–109; see Troeltsch 1960: 599–601, 651–652, 921–922 n. 399). This notion profoundly influenced Oliver Cromwell and his English revolutionary army known as the Ironsides, so named because of its righteously cold brutality (Solt 1971). And it was the Calvinist ethic, not that of Luther, that was imported to America by the Puritans, informing the politics of Presbyterians and Congregationalists—the immediate heirs of Calvinism—as well as some Methodists and many Baptists. Hence, it is not surprising that those raised in these denominations are often overrepresented in samples of "saints" on armed crusades to save the world for Christ.

Seminal to the so-called pedagogic or educational function of holy war are two requirements. First, the enemy against whom the saint fights must be portrayed in terms appropriate to his status as a fetish of evil. Second, the campaign against him must be equal to his diabolism. It must be terrifying, bloodthirsty, uncompromising.

"Prepare War!" was issued by the now defunct Covenant, Sword and the Arm of the Lord, a fundamentalist Christian paramilitary commune headquartered in Missouri. A raid on the compound in the late 1980s uncovered one of the largest private arms caches ever in American history. Evidently, this arsenal was to be used to combat what the pamphlet calls "Negro-beasts of the field . . . who eat the flesh of men. . . . This cannibalistic fervor shall cause them to eat the dead *and* the living during" the time of Tribulations, prophesied in The Book of Revelation (CSA n.d.: 19). The weapons were also to be directed against "Sodomite homosexuals waiting in their lusts to rape," "Seed-of-Satan Jews, who are today sacrificing people in darkness," and "do-gooders who've fought for the 'rights' of these groups" (CSA n.d.: 19). When the Lord God has delivered these enemies into our hands, warns the pamphlet quoting the Old Testament, "thou shalt save alive nothing that breatheth: but thou shalt utterly destroy them" (CSA n.d.: 20; see Deuteronomy 20: 10–18).

The 1990s saw a series of State-level initiatives seeking to deny homosexuals civil rights. Although most of these failed by narrow margins, one in Colorado was passed (later to be adjudged unconstitutional), due largely to the efforts of a consortium of fundamentalist Christian churches. One of the most influential of these was the Laporte, Colorado, Church of Christ, America's largest Identity congregation (more on Identity Christianity below). Acknowledging that the title of their pamphlet "Death Penalty for Homosexuals" would bring upon them the wrath of liberals, its authors insist that "such slanderous tactics" will not deter the anti-homosexual campaign. "For truth will ultimately prevail, no matter how many truth-bearers are stoned." And what precisely is this truth? It is that the Lord Himself has declared that "if a man also lie with mankind, as he lieth with a woman, both of them have committed an abomination: they shall surely be put to death;

their blood shall be upon them" (Peters 1992: i; see Leviticus 20:13).

Like "Prepare War!," "Death Penalty for Homosexuals" is not satisfied merely to cite biblical references. To justify the extremity of its attack, it must paint the homosexual in luridly terrifying colors. Finding and citing a quote from the most extreme of radical gay activists, their pamphlet warns (CSA n.d.: 19):

> [They] shall sodomize [our] sons. . . . [They] shall seduce them in [our] schools, . . . in [our] locker rooms, . . . in [our] army bunkhouses . . . wherever men are with men together. [Our] sons shall become [their] minions and do [their] bidding. . . . All laws banning homosexual activity will be revoked. Instead, legislation shall be passed which engenders love between men. . . . [They] shall stage plays in which man openly caresses man. . . . The museums of the world will be filled only with paintings of . . . naked lads. . . . Love between men [will become] fashionable and de rigueur. [They] will eliminate heterosexual liaisons. . . . There will be no compromises. . . . Those who oppose [them] will be exiled. [They] shall raise vast private armies . . . to defeat [us]. . . . The family unit . . . will be abolished. . . . All churches who condemn [them] will be closed. . . . The society to emerge will be governed by . . . gay poets. . . . Any heterosexual man will be barred from . . . influence. All males who insist on remaining . . . heterosexual will be tried in homosexual courts of justice.

What should Christians do in the face of this looming specter, asks the pamphlet? "We, today, can and should have God's Law concerning Homosexuality and its judgment of the death penalty." For "they which commit such things," says the apostle Paul, "are worthy of death" (CSA n.d.: 15; see Romans 1:27–32). Extremism fans the flames of extremism.

Organization

Contrary to popular thinking, people rarely join right-wing groups because they have a prior belief in doctrines such as those enumerated above. Rather, they come to believe because they have first joined. That is, people first affiliate with right-wing activists and only then begin altering their intellectual outlooks to sustain and strengthen these ties. The original ties may develop from their jobs, among neighbors, among prison acquaintances, or through romantic relationships.

Take the case of Cindy Cutler, who was last seen teaching music at the Aryan Nations Church academy (Mauer, 1980). Reflecting on the previous decade she could well wonder at how far she had come in such a short time.

Cindy had been raised Baptist. "I was with the Jesus Christ thing, that Jesus was my savior and God was love. We'd go to the beach up to a perfect stranger and say, 'Are you saved?' " Such was the serene existence of an uncommonly pretty thrice born-again teenager then residing in San Diego—until she met Gary Cutler, a Navy man stationed nearby. Gary was fourteen years Cindy's senior and seemed the "good Christian man" she had been looking for when they met one Sunday at Baptist services.

Gary and Cindy were already dating when he discovered Identity Christianity. Brought up as a Mormon, he had left the church when it began granting priesthood powers to Black members during the 1970s. After several years searching for a new religious home, Gary claims to have first heard the Identity message one evening while randomly spinning the radio dial. An Identity preacher was extolling the white race as God's chosen people. Gary says the sermon gave him "new found pride."

In the meantime, Cindy's fondness for Gary was growing. The only problem was his espousal of Identity beliefs. As part of her faith, Cindy had learned that Jews, not Anglo-Saxons, were from Israel, and that Jesus was Jewish. Both of these notions were in conflict with what Gary was now saying. Perhaps, Cindy feared, she and Gary were incompatible after all. How could she ever find intellectual consensus with her fiance?

Gary and Cindy routinely spent time together in Bible study. One evening Cindy saw the light. She had already learned from church that Jews were supposedly "Christ killers." It was this information that enabled her to overcome what she calls her prideful resistance to Identity. The occasion of her conversion was this passage: "My sheep know me and hear my voice, and follow me" (John 10: 27). "That's how I got into Identity," she later said. "I questioned how they [the Jews] could be God's chosen people if they hate my Christ." Having discovered a shared theological ground upon which to stand, Gary and Cindy could now marry.

The point of this story is the sociological truth that the way in which some people become right-wing extremists is indistinguishable from the way others become vegetarians, peace activists, or members of mainline churches (Lofland and Stark 1965; Aho 1991: 185–211). *Their affiliations are mediated by significant others already in the movement.* It is from these others that they first learn of the cause; sometimes it is through the loaning of a pamphlet or videotape; occasionally it takes the form of an invitation to a meeting or workshop. As the relationship with the other tightens, the recruit's viewpoint begins to change. At this stage old friends, family members, and cohorts, observing the recruit spending inordinate time with "those new people," begin their interrogations: "What's up with you, man?" In answer, the new recruit typically voices shocking things: bizarre theologies, conspiracy theories, manichaeistic worldviews. Either because of conscious "disowning" or unconscious avoidance, the recruit finds the old ties loosening, and as they unbind, the "stupidity" and "backwardness" of prior acquaintances becomes increasingly evident.

Pushed away from old relationships and simultaneously pulled into the waiting arms of new friends, lovers, and comrades, the recruit is absorbed into the movement. Announcements of full conversion to extremism follow. To display commitment to the cause, further steps may be deemed necessary: pulling one's children out of public schools where "secular humanism" is taught; working for radical political candidates to stop America's "moral decline"; refusing to support ZOG with taxes; renouncing one's citizenship and throwing away social security card and driver's license; moving to a rugged wilderness to await the End Times. Occasionally it means donning camouflage, taking up high-powered weaponry, and confronting the "forces of satan" themselves.

There are two implications to this sociology of recruitment. First and most obviously, involvement in social networks is crucial to being mobilized into right-wing activism. Hence, contrary to the claims of the estrangement theory of extremism mentioned above, those who are truly isolated from their local communities are the last and least likely to become extremists themselves. My research (Aho 1991, 1994) suggests that among the most important of these community ties is membership in independent fundamentalist, Baptist, or Presbyterian congregations.

Secondly, being situated in particular networks is largely a matter of chance. None of us choose our parents. Few choose their co-workers, fellow congregants, or neighbors, and even friendships and marriages are restricted to those available to us by the happenstance of our geography and times. What this means is that almost any person could find themselves in a Christian patriot communications network that would position them for recruitment into right-wing extremism.

As we have already pointed out, American right-wing extremists are neither educationally nor psychologically different from the general population. Nor are they any more status insecure than other Americans. What makes them different is how they are socially positioned. This positioning includes their religious affiliation. Some people find themselves in churches that expose them to the right-wing world. This increases the likelihood of their becoming right-wingers.

Conclusion

Throughout American history, a particular style of Christianity has nurtured right-wing extremism. Espousing doctrines like human depravity, white America as God's elect people, conspiratorialism, Jews as Christ killers, covenant theology and the right to revolt, and millennialism, this brand of Christianity is partly rooted in orthodox Calvinism and in the theologically questionable fantasies of popular imagination. Whatever its source, repeatedly during the last two centuries, its doctrines have served to prepare believers cognitively to assume hostile attitudes toward "un-Christian"—hence un-American—individuals, groups, and institutional practices.

This style of Christianity has also given impetus to hatred and violence through its advocacy of armed crusades against evil. Most of all, however, the cults, sects, and denominations wherein this style flourishes have served as mobilization centers for recruitment into right-wing causes. From the time of America's inception, right-wing political leaders in search of supporters have successfully enlisted clergymen who preach these principles to bring their congregations into the fold in "wars" to save America for Christ.

It is a mistake to think that modern Americans are more bigoted and racist than their ancestors were. Every American generation has experienced right-wing extremism, even that occasionally erupting into vigilante violence of the sort witnessed daily on the news today. What is different in our time is the sophistication and availability of communications and weapons technology. Today, mobilizations to right-wing causes has been infinitely enhanced by the availability of personal computer systems capable of storing and retrieving information on millions of potential recruits. Mobilization has also been facilitated by cheap shortwave radio and cable-television access, the telephone tree, desktop publishing, and readily available studio-quality recorders. Small coteries of extremists can now activate supporters across immense distances at the touch of a button. Add to this the modern instrumentality for maiming and killing available to the average American citizen: military-style assault weaponry easily convertible into fully automatic machine guns, powerful explosives manufacturable from substances like diesel oil and fertilizer, harmless in themselves, hence purchasable over-the-counter. Anti-tank and aircraft weapons, together with assault vehicles, have also been uncovered recently in private-arms caches in the Western states.

Because of these technological changes, religious and political leaders today have a greater responsibility to speak and write with care regarding those with whom they disagree. Specifically, they must control the temptation to demonize their opponents, lest, in their declarations of war they bring unforeseen destruction not only on their enemies, but on themselves.

REFERENCES

Aho, J. 1991. *The Politics of Righteousness: Idaho Christian Patriotism.* Seattle: University of Washington Press.

———. 1994. *This Thing of Darkness: A Sociology of the Enemy.* Seattle: University of Washington Press.

Barkun, M. 1994. *Religion and the Racist Right: The Origins of the Christian Identity Movement.* Chapel Hill: North Carolina University Press.

Calvin J. 1966. *On God and Man.* F. W. Strothmann (ed.). New York: Ungar.

Cohn, N. 1967. *The Pursuit of the Millennium.* New York: Oxford University Press.

CSA. n.d. "Prepare War!" Pontiac, Missouri: CSA Bookstore.

Dilling, E. 1952. *The Plot Against Christianity.* n.p.

Flynn, K. and G. Gerhardt. 1989. *The Silent Brotherhood: Inside America's Racist Underground.* New York: Free Press.

Glock, C. 1993. "The Churches and Social Change in Twentieth-Century America." *Annals of the American Academy of Political and Social Science, 527:* 67–83.

Glock, C. and R. Stark. 1966. *Christian Beliefs and Anti-Semitism.* New York: Harper & Row.

Hay, M. 1981 (1950). *The Roots of Christian Anti-Semitism.* New York: Anti-Defamation League of B'nai B'rith.

Lindsey, H. 1970. *The Late Great Planet Earth.* Grand Rapids: Zondervan.

Lipset, S. M. and E. Raab. 1970. *The Politics of Unreason: Right-Wing Extremism in America, 1790–1970.* New York: Harper & Row.

Lofland, J. and R. Stark. 1965. "Becoming a World-Saver: A Theory of Conversion to a Deviant Perspective." *American Sociological Review 30:* 862–875.

Luther, M. 1974. *Luther: Selected Political Writings,* J. M. Porter, ed. Philadelphia: Fortress Press.

Mannheim, K. 1952. "The Problem of Generations," in *Essays in the Sociology of Knowledge.* London: Routledge and Kegan Paul.

Mauer, D. 1980. "Couple Finds Answers in Butler's Teachings." *Idaho Statesman.* Sept. 14.

Nisbet, R. 1953. *The Quest for Community.* New York: Harper and Brothers.

Pace, J. O. 1985. *Amendment to the Constitution.* Los Angeles: Johnson, Pace, Simmons and Fennel.

Peters, P. 1992. Death Penalty for Homosexuals. LaPorte, Colorado: Scriptures for America.

Preamble. 1986. "Preamble to the United States Constitution: Who Are the Posterity?" Oregon City, Oregon: Republic vs. Democracy Redress.

Ring, R. H. 1985. "The Yarbrough's." *The Denver Post.* Jan. 6.

Robison, J. 1967 (1798). *Proofs of a Conspiracy. . . .* Los Angeles: Western Islands.

Ruether, R. 1979. *Faith and Fratricide: The Theological Roots of Anti-Semitism.* New York: Seabury.

Sandford, F. W. 1966. *The Art of War for the Christian Soldier.* Amherst, New Hampshire: Kingdom Press.

Schlesinger, A. 1986. *The Cycles of American History.* Boston: Houghton Mifflin.

Sherwood, "Commander" S. 1995. Quoted in *Idaho State Journal.* May 21.

Shupe, A. and W. Stacey. 1983. "The Moral Majority Constituency" in *The New Christian Right,* R. Liebman and R. Wuthnow, eds. New York: Aldine.

Simpson, J. 1983. "Moral Issues and Status Politics" in *The New Christian Right,* R. Liebman and R. Wuthnow, eds. New York: Aldine.

Solt, L. 1971. *Saints in Arms: Puritanism and Democracy in Cromwell's Army.* New York: AMS Press.

Stark, R. and William Bainbridge. 1985. *The Future of Religion: Secularization, Revival and Cult Formation.* Berkeley: University of California Press.

Stouffer, S. A. 1966. *Communism, Conformity and Civil Liberties.* New York: John Wiley.

Troeltsch, E. 1960. *Social Teachings of the Christian Churches.* Trans. by O. Wyon. New York: Harper & Row.

Walzer, M. 1965. *The Revolution of the Saints.* Cambridge, MA: Harvard University Press.

Wilcox, C. 1992. *God's Warriors: The Christian Right in Twentieth Century America.* Baltimore, MD: Johns Hopkins University Press.

THINKING ABOUT THE READING

Describe the religious doctrines that typically characterize right-wing extremist groups in the United States. Compare the groups that Aho describes to the so-called Islamic extremist groups that became the focus of national attention after the attacks of September 11, 2001. How are they alike? How do they differ? After reading Aho's article, do you think that Christianity is a cause of right-wing extremism? If not, how can you account for the religiously inspired rhetoric of such movements? If so, what responsibility do "less extreme" churches have in suppressing extremist groups? In a more general sense, what role do you think religious institutions ought to play in movements for political and social change?

Challenging Power

Toxic Waste Protests and the Politicization of White, Working-Class Women

Celene Krauss

(1998)

Over the past two decades, toxic waste disposal has been a central focus of women's grassroots environmental activism. Women of diverse racial, ethnic, and class backgrounds have assumed the leadership of community environmental struggles around toxic waste issues (Krauss 1993). Out of their experience of protest, these women have constructed ideologies of environmental justice that reveal broader issues of inequality underlying environmental hazards (Bullard 1990, 1994). Environmental justice does not exist as an abstract concept prior to these women's activism. It grows out of the concrete, immediate, everyday experience of struggles around issues of survival. As women become involved in toxic waste issues, they go through a politicizing process that is mediated by their experiences of class, race, and ethnicity (Krauss 1993).

Among the earliest community activists in toxic waste protests were white, working-class women. This [article] examines the process by which these women became politicized through grassroots protest activities in the 1980s, which led to their analyses of environmental justice, and in many instances to their leadership in regional and national toxic waste coalitions. These women would seem unlikely candidates for becoming involved in political protest. They came out of a culture that shares a strong belief in the existing political system, and in which traditional women's roles center around the private arena of family. Although financial necessity may have led them into the workplace, the primary roles from which they derived meaning, identity, and satisfaction are those of mothering and taking care of family. Yet, as we shall see, the threat that toxic wastes posed to family health and community survival disrupted the taken-for-granted fabric of their lives, politicizing women who had never viewed themselves as activists. . . .

This [article] shows how white, working-class women's involvement in toxic waste issues has wider implications for social change. . . . These women . . . fought to close down toxic waste dump sites, to prevent the siting of hazardous waste incinerators, to oppose companies' waste-disposal policies, to push for recycling projects, and so on. Their voices show us . . . that their single-issue community protests led them through a process of politicization and their broader analysis of inequities of class and gender in the public arena and in the family. Propelled into the public arena in defense of their children, they ultimately challenged government, corporations, experts, husbands, and their own insecurities as working-class women. Their analysis of environmental justice and inequality led them to form coalitions with labor and people of color around environmental issues. These women's traditional beliefs about motherhood, family, and democracy served a crucial function in this politicizing process. While they framed their analyses in terms of traditional constructions of gender and the state, they actively reinterpreted these constructions into an oppositional ideology, which became a resource of resistance and a source of power in the public arena.

Subjective Dimensions of Grassroots Activism

In most sociological analysis of social movements, the subjective dimension of protest has often been ignored or viewed as private and individualistic. . . . [Contemporary theories] show us how experience is not merely a personal, individualistic concept: it is social. People's experiences reflect where they fit into the social hierarchy. . . . Thus, white, working-class women interpret their experience of toxic waste problems within the context of their particular cultural history, arriving at a critique that reflects broader issues of class and gender. . . .

. . . This article focuses on the subjective process by which white, working-class women involved in toxic waste protests construct an oppositional consciousness out of their everyday lives, experiences, and identities. As these women became involved in the public arena, they confronted a world of power normally hidden from them. This forced them to re-examine their assumptions about private and public power and to develop a broad reconceptualization of gender, family, and government.

The experience of protest is central to this process and can reshape traditional beliefs and values (see Thompson 1963). My analysis reveals the contradictory ways in which traditional culture mediates white, working-class women's subjective experience and interpretation of structural inequality. Their protests are framed in terms of dominant ideologies of motherhood, family, and a deep faith in the democratic system. Their experience also reveals how dominant ideologies are appropriated and reconstructed as an instrument of their politicization and a legitimating ideology used to justify resistance. For example, as the political economy of growth displaces environmental problems into their communities, threatening the survival of children and family and creating everyday crises, government toxic waste policies are seen to violate their traditional belief that a democratic government will protect their families. Ideologies of motherhood and democracy become political resources which these women use to initiate and justify their resistance, their increasing politicization, and their fight for a genuine democracy.

Methodological Considerations

My analysis is based on the oral and written voices of white, working-class women involved in toxic waste protests. Sources include individual interviews, as well as conference presentations, pamphlets, books, and other written materials that have emerged from this movement. Interviews were conducted with a snowball sample of twenty white, working-class women who were leaders in grassroots protest activities against toxic waste landfills and incinerators during the 1980s. These women ranged in age from twenty-five to forty; all but one had young children at the time of their protest. They were drawn from a cross section of the country, representing urban, suburban, and rural areas. None of them had been politically active before the protest; many of them, however, have continued to be active in subsequent community movements, often becoming leaders in state-wide and national coalitions around environmental and social justice issues. I established contact with these women through networking at activist conferences. Open-ended interviews were conducted between May 1989, and December 1991, and lasted from two to four hours. The interview was designed to generate a history of these women's activist experiences, information about changes in political beliefs, and insights into their perceptions of their roles as women, mothers, and wives.

Interviews were also conducted with Lois Gibbs and four other organizers for the Citizens Clearinghouse for Hazardous Wastes (CCHW). CCHW is a nation-wide organization created by Gibbs, who is best known for her successful campaign to relocate families in Love Canal, New York. Over the past two decades, this organization has functioned as a key resource for community groups fighting around toxic waste issues in the United States. Its leadership and staff are composed primarily of women, and the organization played a key role in shaping the ideology of working-class women's environmental activism in the 1980s.

My scholarly interest in working-class women's community activism grew out of my own involvement as a community activist and organizer in the 1970s. This decade marked the period of my own politicization as a white, middle-class woman working with women from many different racial-ethnic backgrounds as they challenged corporate and governmental policies that were destroying urban, working-class neighborhoods. My subsequent academic research has focused on the community protests of working-class women, who are often forgotten in our understanding of movements for social change. My experiences within the environmental movement helped guide my research and deepen my analysis. Through the issue of toxic waste protests, I have examined different facets of working-class women's community activism, most recently the ways in which consciousness and agency are mediated by different experiences of race and ethnicity (Krauss 1993).

The Process of Politicization

Women identify the toxic waste movement as a women's movement, composed primarily of

mothers. As one woman who fought against an incinerator in Arizona and subsequently worked on other anti-incinerator campaigns throughout the state stressed: "Women are the backbone of the grassroots groups, they are the ones who stick with it, the ones who won't back off." Because mothers are traditionally responsible for the health of their children, they are more likely than others within their communities to begin to make the link between toxic waste and their children's ill health. And in communities around the United States, it was women who began to uncover numerous toxin-related health problems: multiple miscarriages, birth defects, cancer, neurological symptoms, and so on. Given the placement of toxic waste facilities in working-class and low-income communities and communities of color, it is not surprising that women from these groups have played a particularly important role in fighting against environmental hazards.

White, working-class women's involvement in toxic waste issues is complicated by the political reality that they, like most people, are excluded from the policy-making process. For the most part, corporate and governmental disposal policies with far-reaching social and political consequences are made without the knowledge of community residents. People may unknowingly live near (or even on top of) a toxic waste dump, or they may assume that the facility is well regulated by the government. Consequently, residents are often faced with a number of problems of seemingly indeterminate origin, and the information withheld from them may make them unwitting contributors to the ill health of their children.

The discovery of a toxic waste problem and the threat it poses to family sets in motion a process of critical questioning about the relationship between women's private work as mothers and the public arena of politics. The narratives of the women involved in toxic waste protests focus on political transformation, on the process of "becoming" an activist. Prior to their discovery of the link between their family's health and toxic waste, few of these women had been politically active. They saw their primary work in terms of the "private" sphere of motherhood and family. But the realization that toxic waste issues threatened their families thrust them into the public arena in defense of this private sphere. According to Penny Newman:

> We woke up one day to discover that our families were being damaged by toxic contamination, a situation in which we had little, if any, input. It wasn't a situation in which we chose to become involved, rather we did it because we had to . . . it was a matter of our survival. (Newman 1991, 8)

Lois Gibbs offered a similar account of her involvement in Love Canal:

> When my mother asked me what I wanted to do when I grew up, I said I wanted to have six children and be a homemaker. . . . I moved into Love Canal and I bought the American Dream: a house, two children, a husband, and HBO. And then something happened to me and that was Love Canal. I got involved because my son Michael had epilepsy . . . and my daughter Melissa developed a rare blood disease and almost died because of something someone else did. . . . I never thought of myself as an activist or an organizer. I was a housewife, a mother, but all of a sudden it was my family, my children, and my neighbors. . . .

It was through their role as mothers that many of these women began to suspect a connection between the invisible hazard posed by toxic wastes and their children's ill health, and this was their first step toward political activism. At Love Canal, for example, Lois Gibbs's fight to expose toxic waste hazards was triggered by the link she made between her son's seizures and the toxic waste dump site. After reading about toxic hazards in a local newspaper, she thought about her son and then surveyed her neighbors to find that they had similar health problems. In Woburn,

Massachusetts, Ann Anderson found that other neighborhood children were, like her son, being treated for leukemia, and she began to wonder if this was an unusually high incidence of the disease. In Denver, mothers comparing stories at Tupperware parties were led to question the unusually large number of sick and dying children in their community. These women's practical activity as mothers and their extended networks of family and community led them to make the connection between toxic waste and sick children—a discovery process rooted in what Sara Ruddick (1989) has called the everyday practice of mothering, in which, through their informal networks, mothers compare notes and experiences, developing a shared body of personal, empirical knowledge.

Upon making the link between their family's ill health and toxic wastes, the women's first response was to go to the government, a response that reflects a deeply held faith in democracy embedded in their working-class culture. They assumed that the government would protect the health and welfare of their children. Gibbs (1982, 12) reports:

> I grew up in a blue-collar community, I was very patriotic, into democracy . . . I believed in government. . . . I believed that if you had a complaint, you went to the right person in government. If there was a way to solve the problem, they would be glad to do it.

An Alabama activist who fought to prevent the siting of an incinerator describes a similar response:

> We just started educating ourselves and gathering information about the problems of incineration. We didn't think our elected officials knew. Surely, if they knew that there was already a toxic waste dump in our county, they would stop it.

In case after case, however, these women described facing a government that was indifferent, if not antagonistic, to their concerns. At Love Canal, local officials claimed that the toxic waste pollution was insignificant, the equivalent of smoking just three cigarettes a day. In South Brunswick, New Jersey, governmental officials argued that living with pollution was the price of a better way of life. In Jacksonville, Arkansas, women were told that the dangers associated with dioxin emitted from a hazardous waste incinerator were exaggerated, no worse than "eating two or three tablespoons of peanut butter over a thirty-year period." Also in Arkansas, a woman who linked her ill health to a fire at a military site that produced Agent Orange was told by doctors that she was going through a "change of life." In Stringfellow, California, eight hundred thousand gallons of toxic chemical waste pumped into the community [water supply] flowed directly behind the elementary school and into the playground. Children played in contaminated puddles yet officials withheld information from their parents because "they didn't want to panic the public."

Government's dismissal of their concerns about the health of their families and communities challenged these white, working-class women's democratic assumptions and opened a window on a world of power whose working they had not before questioned. Government explanations starkly contradicted the personal, empirical evidence which the women discovered as mothers, the everyday knowledge that their children and their neighbors' children were ill. Indeed, a recurring theme in the narratives of these women is the transformation of their beliefs about government. Their politicization is rooted in a deep sense of violation, hurt, and betrayal from finding out their government will not protect their families. Echoes of this disillusionment are heard from women throughout the country. In the CCHW publication *Empowering Women* (1989, 31) one activist noted:

All our lives we are taught to believe certain things about ourselves as women, about democracy and justice, and about people in positions of authority. Once we become involved with toxic waste problems, we need to confront some our old beliefs and change the way we view things.

Lois Gibbs summed up this feeling when she stated:

There is something about discovering that democracy isn't democracy as we know it. When you lose faith in your government, it's like finding out your mother was fooling around on your father. I was very upset. It almost broke my heart because I really believed in the system. I still believe in the system, only now I believe that democracy is of the people and by the people, that people have to move it, it ain't gonna move by itself.

These women's loss of faith in "democracy" as they had understood it led them to develop a more autonomous and critical stance. Their investigation shifted to a political critique of the undemocratic nature of government itself, making the link between government inaction and corporate power, and discovering that government places corporate interests and profit ahead of the health needs of families and communities. At Love Canal, residents found that local government's refusal to acknowledge the scope of the toxic waste danger was related to plans of Hooker Chemical, the polluting industry, for a multi-million dollar downtown development project. In Woburn, Massachusetts, government officials feared that awareness of the health hazard posed by a dump would limit their plans for real-estate development. In communities throughout the United States, women came to see that government policies supported waste companies' preference of incineration over recycling because incineration was more profitable.

Ultimately, their involvement in toxic waste protests led these women to develop a perspective on environmental justice rooted in issues of class and a critique of the corporate state. They argued that government's claims—to be democratic, to act on behalf of the public interest, to hold the family sacrosanct—are false. One woman who fought an incinerator in Arizona recalled:

> I believed in government. When I heard EPA, I thought, "Ooh, that was so big." Now I wouldn't believe them if they said it was sunny outside. I have a list of the revolving door of the EPA. Most of them come from Browning Ferris or Waste Management, the companies that plan landfills and incinerators.

As one activist in Alabama related:

> I was politically naive. I was real surprised because I live in an area that's like the Bible belt of the South. Now I think the God of the United States is really economic development, and that has got to change.

Another activist emphasized:

> We take on government and polluters. . . . We are up against the largest corporations in the United States. They have lots of money to lobby, pay off, bribe, cajole, and influence. They threaten us. Yet we challenge them with the only things we have—people and the truth. We learn that our government is not out to protect our rights. To protect our families we are now forced to picket, protest and shout. (Zeff. 1989, 31)

In the process of protest, these women were also forced to examine their assumptions about the family as a private haven, separate from the public arena, which would however be protected by the policies and actions of government should the need arise. The issue of toxic waste shows the many ways in which government allows this haven to be invaded by polluted water, hazardous chemicals, and other conditions that threaten the everyday life of the family. Ultimately, these women arrived at a concept of environmental injustice rooted in the inequities of power that displace the costs of toxic waste unequally onto their communities. The result was a critical political stance that contributed to the militancy of their activism. Highly traditional values of democracy and motherhood remained central to their lives: they justified their resistance as mothers protecting their children and working to make the promise of democracy real. Women's politicization around toxic waste protests led them to transform their traditional beliefs into resources of opposition which enabled them to enter the public arena and challenge its legitimacy, breaking down the public/private distinction.

Appropriating Power in the Public Arena

Toxic waste issues and their threat to family and community prompted white, working-class women to redefine their roles as mothers. Their work of mothering came to extend beyond taking care of the children, husband, and housework; they saw the necessity of preserving the family by entering the public arena. In so doing, they discovered and overcame a more subtle process of intimidation, which limited their participation in the public sphere.

As these women became involved in toxic waste issues, they came into conflict with a public world where policy makers are traditionally white, male, and middle class. The Citizen's Clearinghouse for Hazardous Waste, in the summary of its 1989 conference on women and organizing, noted:

> Seventy to eighty percent of local leaders are women. They are women leaders in a

community run by men. Because of this, many of the obstacles that these women face as leaders stem from the conflicts between their traditional female role in the community and their new role as leader: conflicts with male officials and authorities who have not yet adjusted to these persistent, vocal, head-strong women challenging the system. . . . Women are frequently ignored by male politicians, male government officials and male corporate spokesmen.

Entering the public arena meant overcoming internal and external barriers to participation, shaped by gender and class. White, working-class women's reconstructed definition of motherhood became a resource for this process, and their narratives reveal several aspects of this transformation.

For these women, entering the public arena around toxic waste issues was often extremely stressful. Many of them were initially shy and intimidated, as simple actions such as speaking at a meeting opened up wider issues about authority, and experiences of gender and class combined to heighten their sense of inadequacy. Many of these women describe, for example, that their high-school education left them feeling ill-equipped to challenge "experts," whose legitimacy, in which they had traditionally believed, was based on advanced degrees and specialized knowledge.

One woman who fought to stop the siting of an incinerator in her community in Arizona recalled: "I used to cry if I had to speak at a PTA meeting. I was so frightened." An activist in Alabama described her experience in fighting the siting of an incinerator in her community:

I was a woman . . . an assistant Sunday School teacher. . . . In the South, women are taught not to be aggressive, we're supposed to be hospitable and charitable and friendly. We don't protest, we don't challenge authority. So it was kind of difficult for me to get involved. I was afraid to speak. And all of a sudden everything

became controversial. . . . I think a lot of it had to do with not knowing what I was. . . . The more I began to know, the better I was . . . the more empowered.

Male officials further exacerbated this intimidation by ignoring the women, by criticizing them for being overemotional, and by delegitimizing their authority by labeling them "hysterical housewives"—a label used widely, regardless of the professional status of the woman. In so doing, they revealed an antipathy to emotionality, a quality valued in the private sphere of family and motherhood but scorned in the public arena as irrational and inappropriate to "objective" discourse.

On several levels, the debate around toxic waste issues was framed by policy makers in such a way as to exclude women's participation, values, and expression. Women's concerns about their children were trivialized by being placed against a claim that the wider community benefits from growth and progress. Information was withheld from them. Discourse was framed as rational, technical, and scientific, using the testimony of "experts" to discredit the everyday empirical knowledge of the women. Even such details as seating arrangements reflected traditional power relations and reinforced the women's internalization of those relations.

These objective and subjective barriers to participation derived from a traditional definition of women's roles based on the separation of the public and private arenas. Yet it is out of these women's political redefinition of the traditional role of mother that they found the resources to overcome these constraints, ultimately becoming self-confident and assertive. They used the resources of their own experience to alter the power relations they had discovered in the public arena.

The traditional role of mother, of protector of the family and community, served to empower these activists on a number of levels. From the beginning, their view of this role provided the motivation for women to take risks in defense of their families and overcome their fears of participating in the public sphere. A woman who fought the siting of an incinerator in Arkansas described this power:

> I was afraid to hurt anyone's feelings or step on anyone's toes. But I'm protective and aggressive, especially where my children are concerned. That's what brought it out of me. A mother protecting my kids. It appalled me that money could be more important than the health of my children.

A mother in New Jersey described overcoming her fear in dealing with male governmental officials at public hearings, "When I look at a male government official, I remember that he was once a little boy, born of a woman like me, and then I feel more powerful." In talking about Love Canal, Lois Gibbs showed the power of motherhood to carry women into activities alien to their experience:

> When it came to Love Canal, we never thought about ourselves as protestors. We carried signs, we barricaded, we blocked the gates, we were arrested. We thought of it as parents protecting our children. In retrospect, of course, we were protesting. I think if it had occurred to us we wouldn't have done it.

In these ways, they appropriated the power they felt in the private arena as a source of empowerment in the public sphere. "We're insecure challenging the authority of trained experts," notes Gibbs, "but we also have a title of authority, 'mother.'"

Working-class women's experiences as organizers of family life served as a further source of empowerment. Lois Gibbs noted that women organized at Love Canal by constantly analyzing how they would handle a situation in the family, and then translating that analysis into political action. For example, Gibbs explained:

If our child wanted a pair of jeans, who would they go to? Well they would go to their father since their father had the money—that meant we should go to Governor Carey.

Gibbs drew on her own experience to develop organizing conferences that helped working-class women learn to translate their skills as family organizers into the political arena.

> I decided as a housewife and mother much of what I learned to keep the household running smoothly were skills that translated very well into this new thing called organizing. I also decided that this training in running a home was one of the key reasons why so many of the best leaders in the toxic movement—in fact, the overwhelming majority—are women, and specifically women who are housewives and mothers. (Zeff 1989, 177)

Of her work with the CCHW, Gibbs stated:

> In our own organization we're drawing out these experiences for women. So we say, what do you mean you're not an organizer? Are you a homemaker—then God damn it you can organize and you don't know it. So, for example, when we say you need to plan long-term and short-term goals, women may say, I don't know how to do that. . . . We say, what do you mean you don't know how to do that? Let's talk about something in the household—you plan meals for five, seven, fourteen days—you think about what you want for today and what you're going to eat on Sunday—that is short-term and long-term goals.

Movement language like "plug up the toilet," the expression for waste reduction, helped women to reinterpret toxic waste issues in the framework of their everyday experience. "If one does not produce the mess in the first place, one will not have to clean it up later," may sound like a maternal warning, but the expression's use in the toxic waste context implies a radical economic critique, calling for a change in the production processes of industry itself.

As women came to understand that government is not an objective, neutral mediator for the public good, they discovered that "logic" and "objectivity" are tools used by the government to obscure its bias in favor of industry, and motherhood became a strategy to counter public power by framing the terms of the debate. The labels of "hysterical housewives" or "emotional women," used by policy makers to delegitimize the women's authority, became a language of critique and empowerment, one which exposed the limits of the public arena's ability to address the importance of family, health, and community. These labels were appropriated as the women saw that their emotionalism, a valued trait in the private sphere, could be transformed into a powerful weapon in the public arena.

> What's really so bad about showing your feelings? Emotions and intellect are not conflicting traits. In fact, emotions may well be the quality that makes women so effective in the movement. . . . They help us speak the truth.

Finally, through toxic waste protests, women discovered the power they wield as mothers to bring moral issues to the public, exposing the contradictions of a society that purports to value motherhood and family, yet creates social policies that undermine these values:

> We bring the authority of mother—who can condemn mothers? . . . It is a tool we have. Our crying brings the moral issues to the table. And when the public sees our children it brings a concrete, moral dimension to our experience. . . . They are not an abstract statistic.

White, working-class women's stories of their involvement in grassroots toxic waste protests reveal their transformations of initial shyness and intimidation into the self-confidence to challenge the existing system. In reconceptualizing their traditional roles as mothers, these women discovered a new strength. As one activist from Arizona says of herself, "Now I like myself better. I am more assertive and aggressive." These women's role in the private world of family ultimately became a source of personal strength, empirical knowledge, and political strategy in the public sphere. It was a resource of political critique and empowerment which the women appropriated and used as they struggled to protect their families.

Overcoming Obstacles to Participation: Gender Conflicts in the Family

In order to succeed in their fights against toxic wastes in their homes and communities, these women confronted and overcame obstacles not only in the public sphere, but also within the family itself, as their entry into the public arena disrupted both the power relationships and the highly traditional gender roles within the family. Divorce and separation were the manifestations of the crises these disruptions induced. All of the women I interviewed had been married when they first became active in the toxic waste movement. By the time of my interviews with them, more than half were divorced.

A central theme of these women's narratives is the tension created in their marriages by participation in toxic waste protests. This aspect of struggle, so particular to women's lives, is an especially hidden dimension of white, working-class women's activism. Noted one activist from New York:

> People are always talking to us about forming coalitions, but look at all we must deal with beyond the specific issue, the flack that comes with it, the insecurity of your husband that you have outgrown him. Or how do you deal with your children's anger, when they say you love the fight more than me. In a blue-collar community that is very important.

For the most part, white, working-class women's acceptance of a traditional gendered division of labor has also led them to take for granted the power relations within the family. Penny Newman, who was the West Coast Director of CCHW, reflected on the beginnings of her community involvement:

> I had been married just a couple of years. My husband is a fireman. They have very strict ideas of what family life is in which the woman does not work, you stay at home. . . . I was so insecure, so shy, that when I finally got to join an organization, a woman's club, . . . it would take me two weeks to build up the courage to ask my husband to watch the kids that night. I would really plan out my life a month ahead of time just to build in these little hints that there is a meeting coming up in two weeks, will you be available. Now, if he didn't want to do it, or had other plans, I didn't go to the meeting. (Zeff 1989, 183)

Involvement in toxic waste issues created a conflict between these traditional assumptions and women's concerns about protecting their children, and this conflict made visible the power relations within the family. The CCHW publication *Empowering Women* (1989, 33) noted that:

> Women's involvement in grassroots activism may change their views about the world and their relations with their husbands. Some husbands are actively supportive. Some take no stand: "Go ahead and do what you want. Just make sure you have dinner on the table and my shirts washed." Others forbid time away from the family.

Many of these women struggled to develop coping strategies to defuse conflict and accommodate traditional gender-based power relations in the family. The strategies included involving husbands in protest activities and minimizing their own leadership roles. As Lois Gibbs commented: "If you bring a spouse in, if you can make them part of your growth, then the marriage is more likely to survive, but that is real hard to do sometimes." Will Collette, a former director at CCHW, relates the ways in which he has observed women avoiding acknowledged leadership roles. He described this encounter with women involved in a toxic waste protest in New York:

> I was sitting around a kitchen table with several women who were leading a protest. And they were complaining about how Lou and Joe did not do their homework and weren't able to handle reports and so on. I asked them why they were officers and the women were doing all the work. They said, "That's what the guys like, it keeps them in and gives us a little peace at home."

In a similar vein, Collette recalled working with an activist from Texas to plan a large public hearing. Upon arriving at the meeting, he discovered that she was sitting in the back, while he was placed on the dais along with the male leadership, which had had no part in the planning process.

As the women became more active in the public arena, traditional assumptions about gender roles created further conflict in their marriages. Women who became visible community leaders experienced the greatest tension. In some cases, the husbands were held responsible for their wives' activities, since they were supposed to be able to "control" their wives. For example, a woman who fought against an incinerator in Arkansas related:

> When the mayor saw my husband, he wanted to know why he couldn't keep his pretty little wife's mouth shut. As I became more active and more outspoken, our marriage became rockier. My husband asked me to tone it down, which I didn't do.

In other cases, women's morals were often called into question by husbands or other community members. Collette relates the experience of an activist in North Dakota who was rumored to be having an affair. The basis for the rumor, as Collette describes, was that "an uppity woman has got to be promiscuous if she dares to organize. In this case, she was at a late-night meeting in another town, and she slept over, so of course she had to have had sex."

Toxic waste issues thus set the stage for tremendous conflict between these women and their husbands. Men saw their roles as providers threatened: the homes they had bought may have become valueless; their jobs may have been at risk; they were asked by their wives to take on housework and child care. Meanwhile, their wives' public activities increasingly challenged traditional views of gender roles. For the women, their husbands' negative response to their entry into the public sphere contradicted an assumption in the family that both husband and wife were equally concerned with the well-being of the children. In talking about Love Canal, Gibbs explained:

> The husband in a blue-collar community is saying, get your ass home and cook me dinner, it's either me or the issue, make your choice. The woman says: How can I make a choice, you're telling me choose between the health of my children and your fucking dinner, how do I deal with that?

When women were asked to choose between their children and their husbands' needs, they began to see the ways in which the children had to be their primary concern.

At times this conflict resulted in more equal power relations within the marriages, a direction that CCHW tried to encourage by organizing family stress workshops. By and large, however, the families of activist women did not tolerate this stress well. Furthermore, as the women began openly to contest traditional power relations in the family, many

found that their marriages could not withstand the challenges. As one activist from Arkansas described:

> I thought [my husband] didn't care enough about our children to continue to expose them to this danger. I begged him to move. He wouldn't. So I moved my kids out of town to live with my mom.

All twenty women interviewed for this article were active leaders around toxic waste issues in their communities, but only two described the importance of their husband's continuing support. One white woman who formed an interracial coalition in Alabama credited her husband's support in sustaining her resolve:

> I've had death threats. I was scared my husband would lose his job, afraid that somebody's going to kill me. If it weren't for my husband's support, I don't think I could get through all this.

In contrast, most of these activists described the ongoing conflict within their marriages, which often resulted in their abandoning their traditional role in the family, a process filled with inner turmoil. One woman described that turmoil as follows:

> I had doubts about what I was doing, especially when my marriage was getting real rocky. I thought of getting out of [the protest]. I sat down and talked to God many, many times. I asked him to lead me in the right direction because I knew my marriage was failing and I found it hard leaving my kids when I had to go to meetings. I had to struggle to feel that I was doing the right thing. I said a prayer and went on.

Reflecting on the strength she felt as a mother, which empowered her to challenge her government and leave her marriage, she continued:

It's an amazing ordeal. You always know you would protect your children. But it's amazing to find out how far you will go to protect your own kids.

The disruption of the traditional family often reflected positive changes in women's empowerment. Women grew through the protest; they became stronger and more self-confident. In some cases they found new marriages with men who respected them as strong individuals. Children also came to see their mothers as outspoken and confident.

Thus, for these women, the particularistic issue of toxic waste made visible oppression not only in the public sphere, but also in the family itself. As the traditional organization of family life was disrupted, inequities in underlying power relations were revealed. In order to succeed in fighting a toxic waste issue, these women had also to engage in another level of struggle as they reconceptualized their traditional role in family life in order to carry out their responsibilities as mothers.

Conclusion

The narratives of white, working-class women involved in toxic waste protests in the 1980s reveal the ways in which their subjective, particular experiences led them to analyses that extended beyond the particularistic issue to wider questions of power. Their broader environmental critique grew out of the concrete, immediate, everyday experience of struggling around survival issues. In the process of environmental protest, these women became engaged with specific governmental and corporate institutions and they were forced to reflect on the contradictions of their family life. To win a policy issue, they had to go through a process of developing an oppositional or critical consciousness which informed the direction of their actions and challenged the power of traditional policy

makers. The contradiction between a government that claimed to act on behalf of the family and the actual environmental policies and actions of that government were unmasked. The inequities of power between white, working-class women and middle-class, male public officials were made visible. The reproduction within the family of traditional power relationships was also revealed. In the process of protest these women uncovered and confronted a world of political power shaped by gender and class. This enabled them to act politically around environmental issues, and in some measure to challenge the social relationships of power, inside and outside the home.

Ideologies of motherhood played a central role in the politicizing of white, working-class women around toxic waste issues. Their resistance grew out of an acceptance of a sexual division of labor that assigns to women responsibility for "sustaining the lives of their children and, in a broader sense, their families, including husband, relatives, elders and community." . . .

The analysis of white, working-class women's politicization through toxic waste protests reveals the contradictory role played by dominant ideologies about mothering and democracy in the shaping of these women's oppositional consciousness. The analysis these women developed was not a rejection of these ideologies. Rather, it was a reinterpretation, which became a source of power in the public arena. Their beliefs provided the initial impetus for involvement in toxic waste protests, and became a rich source of empowerment as they appropriated and reshaped traditional ideologies and meanings into an ideology of resistance. . . .

REFERENCES

Bullard, Robert D. 1990. *Dumping in Dixie: Race, Class and Environmental Quality.* Boulder, CO: Westview Press.

Bullard, Robert D. 1994. *Communities of Color and Environmental Justice.* San Francisco: Sierra Club Books.

Citizen's Clearing House for Hazardous Wastes. 1989. *Empowering Women.* Washington, DC: Citizen's Clearinghouse for Hazardous Wastes.

Krauss, Celene. 1993. "Women and Toxic Waste Protests: Race, Class and Gender as Resources of Resistance." *Qualitative Sociology* 16(3):247–262.

Newman, Penny. 1991. "Women and the Environment in the United States of America." Paper presented at the Conference of Women and the Environment, Bangladore, India.

Ruddick, Sara. 1989. *Maternal Thinking: Towards a Politics of Peace.* New York: Ballantine Books.

Thompson, E. P. 1963. *The Making of the English Working Class.* New York: Pantheon Books.

Zeff, Robin Lee. 1989. "Not in My Backyard/Not in Anyone's Backyard: A Folklorist Examination of the American Grassroots Movement for Environmental Justice." Ph.D. dissertation, Indiana University.

THINKING ABOUT THE READING

Krauss describes how ordinary women became mobilized to construct a movement for social change when they felt their children's health was being threatened. Did their traditional beliefs about motherhood and family help or hinder their involvement in this protest movement? What effect did their participation have on their own families? Why do the women Krauss interviewed identify the toxic waste movement as a women's movement? Why don't men seem to be equally concerned about these health issues? How did the relative powerlessness of their working-class status shape the women's perspective on environmental justice?

Credits

Chapter 1

From *The Sociological Imagination* by C. Wright Mills. Copyright © 1959 by Oxford University Press, Inc.; renewed 1987 by Yaraslava Mills. Reprinted by permission of the publisher.

"Body Ritual among the Nacirema" by Horace Miner. *American Anthropologist* 58:3, June 1956, pp. 503–507.

Chapter 2

"The My Lai Massacre: A Military Crime of Obedience," by Herbert Kelman and V. Lee Hamilton. In *Crimes of Obedience* (pp.1–20), edited by Herbert Kelman and V. Lee Hamilton. © 1989 by Yale University Press. Reprinted by permission.

Excerpts from "The Mundanity of Excellence: An Ethnographic Report on Stratification and Olympic Swimmers" by Daniel F. Chambliss. *Sociological Theory*, Vol. 7, No. 1, Spring 1989, pp. 70-86. Washington, DC: American Sociological Association. Reprinted by permission.

Chapter 3

Excerpts from "The Crack Attack: Politics and Media in the Crack Scare" from *Crack in America: Demon Drugs and Social Justice* (pp. 18–51), edited by Craig Reinarman and Harry G. Levine. Berkeley: University of California Press. Copyright © 1997 by the Regents of the University of California. Reprinted by permission.

From Babbie, E., *Observing Ourselves: Essays in Social Research,* copyright © 1986. Reprinted with permission of Waveland Press, Inc. All rights reserved.

Chapter 4

Excerpts from *A Geography of Time* (pp. 81-100) by Robert Levine. Copyright ©1997 by Robert Levine. Reprinted by permission of Basic Books, a member of Perseus Books, LLC.

Excerpts from "The Melting Pot," from *The Spirit Catches You and You Fall Down: A Hmong Child, Her American Doctors, and the Collision of Two Cultures* (pp. 181-209), by Anne Fadiman. Copyright 1997 by Anne Fadiman. Reprinted by permission of Farrar, Straus, and Giroux, LLC.

Chapter 5

"Life as the Maid's Daughter: An Exploration of the Everyday Boundaries of Race, Class, and Gender" by Mary Romero, from *Feminisms in the Academy* by Mary Romero, Abigail J. Stewart, and Donna Stanton (eds.) (pp. 157–179). Copyright © 1995. Used by permission of The University of Michigan Press.

Chapter 6

Chapter 7

Chapter 8